core JAVA™ 1.1

Volume 1 - Fundamentals

THE SUNSOFT PRESS

JAVA SERIES

- ***Core Java 1.1,*** ***Volume 1 - Fundamentals***
  Cay S. Horstmann & Gary Cornell
- ***Core Java 1.1,*** ***Volume 2 - Advanced Features***
  Cay S. Horstmann & Gary Cornell
- ***Graphic Java 1.1,*** **Second Edition**
  David M. Geary
- ***Inside Java Workshop***
  Lynn Weaver & Bob Jervis
- ***Instant Java,*** **Second Edition**
  John A. Pew
- ***Java by Example,*** **Second Edition**
  Jerry R. Jackson & Alan L. McClellan
- ***Jumping JavaScript***
  Janice Winsor & Brian Freeman
- ***Just Java 1.1,*** **Third Edition**
  Peter van der Linden
- ***Not Just Java***
  Peter van der Linden

core JAVA™ 1.1

Volume 1 - Fundamentals

CAY S. HORSTMANN • GARY CORNELL

Sun Microsystems Press
A Prentice Hall Title

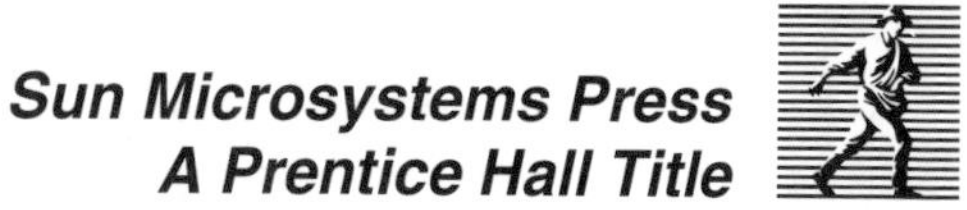

The publisher offers discounts on this book when ordered in bulk quantities.
For more information, contact Corporate Sales Department, Prentice Hall PTR,
One Lake Street, Upper Saddle River, NJ 07458. Phone: 800-382-3419; FAX: 201-236-7141.
E-mail: corpsales@prenhall.com.

Editorial/production supervision: *Navta Associates*
Cover design director: *Jerry Votta*
Cover designer: *Anthony Gemmellaro*
Cover illustration: *Karen Strelecki*
Manufacturing manager: *Alexis R. Heydt*
Marketing manager: *Stephen Solomon*
Acquisitions editor: *Gregory G. Doench*
Sun Microsystems Press publisher: *Rachel Borden*

10 9 8 7 6 5

ISBN 0-13-766957-7

Sun Microsystems Press
A Prentice Hall Title

Contents

vii

Chapter 7
Graphics Programming and Printing, 233

Chapter 8
Event Handling, 291

xi

xiii

xiv

Tables, Examples, and Figures

Tables

Examples

Figures

xvii

xviii

Preface

To the Reader

In late 1995, the Java programming language burst onto the Internet scene and gained instant celebrity status. The promise of Java is that it will become the *universal glue* that connects users with information, whether that information comes from web servers, databases, information providers, and any other imaginable source. Indeed Java is in a unique position to fulfill this promise. It is an extremely solidly engineered language that has gained acceptance by all major vendors. Its built-in security and safety features are reassuring both to programmers and to the users of Java programs. Java even has built-in support that makes advanced programming tasks such as network programming and multithreading straightforward.

In early 1997, JavaSoft released a major upgrade to Java; they called it Java 1.1. Java 1.1 is an amazing achievement for a language that has only been on the market for a little over a year. In our opinion, Java 1.1 is the first version of Java that can be used for something other than "proofs of concepts." (Calling it a 1.1 version shows a becoming modesty on the part of JavaSoft: given all its changes and improvements, Java 2.0 would have been the name that almost any other software vendor would have used.)

The book you have in your hand is the third incarnation of our "Core Java" book. The first edition appeared in early 1996. The second in late 1996. As with the previous editions of this book, we *still target serious programmers who want to put Java to work on real projects.* We still guarantee no nervous text or dancing tooth-shaped characters. We think of you, our reader, as a programmer with a solid background in a programming language. But *you do not need to know C++ or object-oriented programming.* Based on the responses we have received to the earlier editions of this book, we remain confident that experienced Visual Basic, C, COBOL, Delphi or PowerBuilder programmers will have no trouble with this book. (You don't even need any experience in building graphical user interfaces in Windows, UNIX or the Macintosh.)

What we do is assume you want to:

- Write real code to solve real problems

and

- Don't like books filled with toy examples of motorcycle classes or fruit trees.

You will find lots of sample code on the accompanying CD that demonstrates almost every language and library feature that we discuss. We kept the sample programs purposefully simple to focus on the major points, but, for the most part, they aren't fake and they don't cut corners. They should make good starting points for your own code.

We assume you are willing, even eager, to learn about all the advanced features that Java puts at your disposal. For example, we give you a detailed treatment of:

- object-oriented programming;
- the new Java reflection mechanism;
- the new Java 1.1. event model;
- graphical user interface design;
- Exception handling (Java's error handling mechanism).

We *still* don't spend much time on the fun but less serious kind of Java programs whose sole purpose is to liven up your web page. There are quite a few sources for this kind of material already—we recommend John Pew's book *Instant Java,* also published by Sun Microsystems Press/Prentice Hall.

Finally, the first two versions of this book appeared in a single volume: the second edition was already 150 pages larger than the first, which was itself not a thin book. When we sat down to start work on the third edition, it became clear that a one-volume treatment of all the features of Java that serious programmers would need to know was no longer possible. Hence, we decided to break the book up into two volumes. The first volume, which you hold in your hands, concentrates on the underlying Java language along with the basics of using the cross-platform graphics library supplied with the current version of Java. The second volume will go further into the libraries and include detailed discussions of:

- input and output (including object serialization);
- multithreading;
- network programming;
- distributed objects;
- databases;
- native methods;
- JavaBeans.

When writing a book, errors and inaccuracies are inevitable. We'd very much like to know about them. But, of course, we'd prefer to learn about each of them only once. We have put up a list of frequently asked questions, bugs fixes, and workarounds in a web page at `http://www.horstmann.com`. Strategically placed at the end of the FAQ (to encourage you to read through it first) is a Java applet you can use to report bugs and problems.

We hope that you find this book enjoyable and helpful in your Java programming.

About This Book

Chapter 1 gives an overview of the capabilities of Java that set it apart from other programming languages. We explain what the designers of the language set out to do and to what extent they succeeded. Then we give a short history of how Java came into being and how it has evolved.

In Chapter 2, we tell you how to install Java and the companion software for this book from the CD ROM onto your computer. Then we guide you through compiling and running three typical Java programs, a console application, a graphical application, and an applet.

Chapter 3 starts the discussion of the Java language. In this chapter, we cover the basics: variables, loops, and simple functions. If you are a C or C++ programmer, this is smooth sailing because the syntax for these language features is essentially the same as in C. If you come from a non-C background such as Visual Basic or Pascal/Delphi, you will want to read this chapter carefully.

Object-oriented programming (OOP) is now in the mainstream of programming practice, and Java is completely object oriented. Chapter 4 introduces *encapsulation,* the first of two fundamental building blocks of object orientation, and the Java language mechanism to implement it, that is, classes and methods. In addition to the rules of the Java language, we also give advice on sound OOP design. If you are familiar with C++, then you can browse through this chapter quickly. Programmers coming from a non-object-oriented background should expect to spend some time mastering OOP concepts before going further with Java.

Classes and encapsulation are only one part of the OOP story, and Chapter 5 introduces the other, namely *inheritance.* Inheritance lets you take an existing class and modify it according to your needs. This is a fundamental technique for programming in Java. The inheritance mechanism in Java is quite similar to that in C++. Once again, C++ programmers can focus on the differences between the languages.

Chapter 6 shows you how to use Java's notion of an *interface.* Interfaces let you go beyond the simple inheritance model of Chapter 5. Mastering interfaces allows you full access to the power of Java's completely object-oriented approach to programming. We also cover a useful technical feature of Java 1.1 here. These are called *inner classes.* Inner classes help make your code cleaner and more concise.

In Chapter 7, we begin application programming in earnest. We show how you can make windows, how to paint on them, and how to display images. Then we show you how to *really* display images. There are quite a few Java programming tasks that are subtle, and displaying images is one of them. The Java library is optimized to load an image piece by piece, assuming it comes in through a slow network connection. You can ignore the subtlety, but then your image flickers. In this book, we make an effort to dig down into the details and show you how the pros do it. Of course, feel free to skip over this section if you don't care about images now.

Chapter 8 is a detailed discussion of the new event model that was added to Java 1.1. You'll also see how to write the code that responds to basic events like mouse clicks or key presses. Along the way you'll see how to handle basic GUI elements like buttons and text areas.

Chapter 9 discusses the AWT, the *abstract windows toolkit* in great detail. The AWT is how you can use Java to build a cross-platform graphical user interface. On the other hand, if you are used to programming a user interface by dragging controls onto a form and writing a bit of code to glue them together, then you are in for a rude surprise. Right now, the Java Development Kit, as supplied by JavaSoft, has no user interface builder. You need to write code to place every button, text field, menu item, and so on in a window. Even the third-party tools are still quite primitive, and they won't make a lot of sense to you if you don't understand the fundamentals of how to use the AWT. In this chapter, we cover all the techniques needed to place components in a window along with how to handle the events that the GUI components can trigger. We even show you how to use a new feature of Java that lets you build your own components that are truly cross platform. (Because they need not have a counterpart on the user's system.)

After you finish Chapter 9, you finally have all mechanisms in place to write *applets,* those mini-programs that can live inside a web page, and so applets are the topic of Chapter 10. We show you a number of useful and fun applets, but more importantly we show you what goes on behind the scenes.

In Chapter 11, we go back to a more mundane programming issue and show how to use the data structures in the Java library (vectors, hash tables, and so on) and how to write your own (linked lists, queues). This material is important if your Java program needs to store a large amount of data and retrieve it quickly.

Chapter 12 discusses *exception handling*, Java's robust mechanism to deal with the fact that bad things can happen to good programs. For example, a network connection can become unavailable in the middle of a file download, a disk can fill up, and so on. Exceptions give you an efficient way of separating the normal processing code from the error handling. Of course, even after hardening your program by handling all exceptional conditions, it still might fail to work as expected. In the second half of this chapter, we give you some debugging tips. Finally, we guide you through a sample debugging session with the JDB debugger. (That debugger is very primitive, and you would want to use it only if you are really desperate.)

The appendices cover the Java keywords and the automatic Java documentation (javadoc) facility.

Conventions

As is common in many computer books, we use `courier type` to represent computer code.

There are many C++ and Visual Basic (VB) notes that explain the difference between Java and these languages. You can skip over them if you don't have a background in either of those languages.

Notes are tagged with a "notepad" icon that looks like this.

Java comes with a large programming library or Application Programming Interface (API). When using an API call for the first time, we add a short summary description tagged with an API icon at the end of the section. These descriptions are a bit more informal, but we hope also a little more informative than those in the official on-line API documentation.

Programs whose source code is on the CD ROM are listed as examples, for instance Example 2-4: WelcomeApplet.java. (All the example code can be installed on your machine by using the Windows installation program or by untaring the UNIX tar file that is on the CD-ROM.)

CD ROM

The CD ROM on the back of the book contains the latest version of JavaSoft's Java Development Kit. At the time we are writing this, these materials are available only for Windows 95/NT or Solaris 2.

The CD ROM also contains shareware versions of the WinEdit and TextPad text editors customized for use for Java development. It also contains a copy of the very useful WinZip program. (These are all Windows 95/NT programs.) Please read Chapter 2 for detailed installation instructions for the Java Development Kit.

NOTE: People have often asked what the licensing requirements for using our code in a commercial situation are. You can freely use any code from this book for non-commercial use. However, if you do want to use our code as a basis for a commercial product, we simply require that every person on the development team for that project own a copy of Core Java.

Acknowledgements

Cay's love and gratitude go to his wife Hui-Chen and his children Nina and Tommy whose initial enthusiasm for this project turned into patient support as this project dragged on and on and when the second (and now the third) edition came all too quickly. Without their love and support, his workload would have been impossible to bear.

Gary's thanks go to all his friends who endured his stressed-out ways during these trying times—curt phone calls and no social visits were the norm. As in the previous two editions, he wants to again thank Bruce, Caroline, and Kurt. Writing his part of the book would have been impossible without their friendship, support, and gracious hospitality. The encouragement Gary received from Esther Etherington of `javaman.com` was a great help in times of total stress. Finally, as in the first edition, Gary still needs to thank Cay's family—even more so this time around. They were again gracious hosts on his too-frequent visits. They were remarkably patient during the seemingly endless phone calls. They were and are, in a word, extraordinary.

Finally, they would like to thank their editor, Greg Doench of Prentice-Hall, for coordinating the details of the book and CD development process with great determination and resolve under sometimes trying circumstances; Rachel Borden, our publisher at Sun Microsystems, was always there to listen with a patient ear when we complained yet again about another problem—and to do her best to fix it. Nikki Wise and her team at Navta Associates did a superb production job under yet another difficult schedule. Those of you who helped with the first and second edition, we have not forgotten you and we are still very, very grateful. For the third edition, however, we appreciate the careful reviews we received from Aaron M. Mulder.

CHAPTER 1

- Java as a Programming Tool
- Advantages and Disadvantages of Java
- The Java "White Paper" Buzzwords
- Java and the Internet
- A Short History of Java
- Common Misconceptions about Java

An Introduction to Java

To open a computer magazine that does not have a feature article on Java seems impossible. Even mainstream newspapers and magazines like the *New York Times*, the *Washington Post*, and *Business Week* have run numerous articles on Java. It gets better (or worse, depending on your perspective): can you remember the last time National Public Radio ran a 10-minute story on a computer language? Or, a $100,000,000 venture capital fund is set up solely for products produced using a *specific* computer language? CNN, CNBC, you name the mass medium, it seems everyone is talking about how Java will do this or Java will do that.

We decided that you bought this book because you are a serious programmer, so rather than immediately getting caught up in the Internet hype and trying to deal with the limited (if still interesting) truth behind the hype, we will write, in some detail, about Java as a programming language (including, of course, the features added for its use on the Internet). After that, we will try to separate current fact from fancy by explaining what Java can and cannot do on the Internet.

In the end, we should add, a great deal of the hype *will* be justified; it is just not true *yet*. As we write this Java has been out of beta testing for barely a year and is still very much in its infancy. But, just as most babies learn to walk between ages 1 and 2, Java is doing the same. We expect that by the end of 1997 Java will be a full-fledged tool for serious programming. It will, we expect, be fully competitive with languages like Visual Basic and C++. That will be no mean feat—by most accounts, Visual Basic is currently the world's most popular programming language, and C++ is the premier language for systems and applications programming today. In particular, Java 1.1 is, in our opinion, the first version of Java that can realistically be used for anything other than "proofs of concept."(Programs produced with earlier versions of Java required an almost superhuman effort to get them beyond the toy stage.)

Java as a Programming Tool

As a computer language, Java's hype is overdone: Java is certainly a *good* programming language. It could *potentially* have been a great programming language, but it is probably too late for that. Once a language is out in the field, the ugly reality of compatibility with existing code sets in. Moreover, even in cases where changes are possible without breaking existing code, it is hard for the creators of a language as acclaimed as Java to sit back and say "well, maybe we were wrong about X and Y would be better." In sum, while we expect there to be some improvements over time, basically, the structure of the Java language tomorrow will be much the same as it is today.

Having said that, the obvious question is where did the dramatic improvements that we think the 1.1 version of Java has come from? The answer is that they didn't come from major changes in the underlying Java programming language, they came from major changes in the *Java libraries*. JavaSoft changed everything from the names of many of the library functions (to make them more consistent), to changing how graphics worked (by changing the event handling model and rewriting parts from scratch), to adding important features like printing that were not part of Java 1.0. The result is a far more useful programming tool, a tool moreover that, while not yet completely robust, is far less flaky than earlier versions of Java were.

Advantages and Disadvantages of Java

One obvious advantage is a run-time library that provides platform independence: you can use the same code on Windows 95, Solaris, UNIX, Macintosh, and so on. This is necessary for Internet programming. (Although implementations on other platforms usually lag those on Windows and Solaris. For example, as we write this Java 1.1 is not even in beta for the Mac.)

Another programming advantage is that Java has a similar syntax to that of C++ which makes it economical without being absurd. Then again, Visual Basic (VB) programmers will probably find the syntax annoying and miss some of the nicer syntactic VB constructs like `Select Case`.

NOTE: If you are coming from a language other than C++, some of the terms used in this section will be less familiar—just skip those sections. You will be comfortable with all of these terms by the end of Chapter 6.

Java also is fully object oriented—even more so than C++. Everything in Java, except for a few basic types like numbers, is an object. (Object-Oriented design has replaced earlier structured techniques because it has many advantages for

dealing with sophisticated projects. If you are not familiar with Object-Oriented Programming (OOP), Chapters 4 through 6 provide what you need to know.)

However, having yet another, somewhat improved, dialect of C++ would not be enough. The key points are:

- It is far easier to turn out bug-free code using Java than using C++.

  Why? The designers of Java thought hard about what makes C++ code so buggy. They added features to Java that eliminate the *possibility* of creating code with the most common kinds of bugs. (Some estimates say that roughly every 50 lines of C++ code has at least one bug.) Here are some of these new features:

- They eliminated manual memory allocation and deallocation.

  Memory in Java is automatically garbage collected. You *never* have to worry about memory leaks.

- They introduced true arrays and eliminated pointer arithmetic.

  You *never* have to worry about overwriting a key area of memory because of an off-by-one error when working with a pointer.

- They eliminated the possibility of confusing an assignment with a test for equality in a conditional.

  You cannot even compile `if (ntries = 3). . . .` (VB programmers may not see the problem, but, trust us, this is a common source of confusion in C/C++ code.)

- They eliminated multiple inheritance, replacing it with a new notion of *interface* that they derived from Objective C.

  Interfaces give you what you want from multiple inheritance, without the complexity that comes with managing multiple inheritance hierarchies. (If inheritance is a new concept for you, Chapter 5 will explain it.)

NOTE: The Java language specification is public. It can be found on the Web by going to the JavaSoft page and following the links given there. (The JavaSoft home page is at `http://java.sun.com`.)

The Java "White Paper" Buzzwords

The authors of Java have written an influential White Paper that explains their design goals and accomplishments. Their paper is organized along the following eleven buzzwords:

Simple	Portable
Object Oriented	Interpreted
Distributed	High Performance
Robust	Multithreaded
Secure	Dynamic
Architecture Neutral	

We touched on some of these points in the last section. In this section, we will:

- summarize via excerpts from the White Paper what the Java designers say about each buzzword, and
- tell you what we think of that particular buzzword based on our experiences with the current version of Java.

NOTE: As we write this, the White Paper can be found at `http://java.sun.com/doc/language_environment`. (If it has moved, you can find it by marching through the links at the JavaSoft home page.)

Simple

We wanted to build a system that could be programmed easily without a lot of esoteric training and which leveraged today's standard practice. So even though we found that C++ was unsuitable, we designed Java as closely to C++ as possible in order to make the system more comprehensible. Java omits many rarely used, poorly understood, confusing features of C++ that, in our experience, bring more grief than benefit.

The syntax for Java is, indeed, a cleaned-up version of the syntax for C++. There is no need for header files, pointer arithmetic (or even a pointer syntax), structures, unions, operator overloading, virtual base classes, and so on. (See the C++ notes interspersed throughout the text for more on the differences between Java and C++.) The designers did not, however, *improve* on some stupid features in C++, like the `switch` statement. If you know C++, you will find the transition to Java's syntax easy.

If you are a VB programmer, you will not find Java simple. There is much strange syntax (though it does not take long to get the hang of it). More importantly, you must do a lot more programming in Java. The beauty of VB is that its visual design environment provides a lot of the infrastructure for an application almost automatically. The equivalent functionality must be programmed manu-

ally, usually with a fair bit of code, in Java. (See the following description of how JavaSoft is bringing the component-based, "glue" model to Java programming via "Java Beans," a specification for developing plug-and-play components.)

At this point, the Java language is pretty simple, as object-oriented languages go. But there are many subtle points used to solve real-world problems. As time goes by, more and more of these details will be farmed off to libraries and development environments. Products like SunSoft's Java Workshop, Symantec's Visual Café and RogueWave's J Factory, which as we write this exist for only the 1.02 version of Java, have form designers that can make designing the interface of your programs easier. They are far from perfect but are a step forward. (Designing forms with nothing but the JDK is tedious at best and unbearable at worst.) Third-party class libraries are beginning to appear and a lot of code samples (including many libraries) are actually freely available on the Net.

> *Another aspect of being simple is being small. One of the goals of Java is to enable the construction of software that can run stand-alone in small machines. The size of the basic interpreter and class support is about 40K bytes; adding the basic standard libraries and thread support (essentially a self-contained microkernel) adds an additional 175K.*

This is a great achievement.

Object Oriented

> *Simply stated, object-oriented design is a technique that focuses design on the data (= objects) and on the interfaces to it. To make an analogy with carpentry, an "object-oriented" carpenter would be mostly concerned with the chair he was building, and secondarily with the tools used to make it; a "non-object-oriented" carpenter would think primarily of his tools. The object-oriented facilities of Java are essentially those of C++.*

Object orientation has proven its worth in the last 30 years, and it is inconceivable that a modern programming language would not use it. Indeed, the object-oriented features of Java are comparable to C++. The major difference between Java and C++ lies in multiple inheritance, for which Java has found a better solution.

Here, Java 1.1 delivers on the promise made in the White Paper. The metaclass model of Java 1.0 was weak and required a lot of handcoding to do much of anything. The new reflection mechanism (see Chapter 5) and object serialization feature (see Volume 2) make it much easier to implement persistent objects and GUI builders that can integrate off-the-shelf-components.

NOTE: If you do not have any experience with OOP languages you will want to carefully read Chapters 4 through 6. These chapters explain what OOP is and why it is more useful for programming sophisticated projects than traditional, procedure-oriented languages like BASIC or C.

Distributed

> *Java has an extensive library of routines for coping with TCP/IP protocols like HTTP and FTP. Java applications can open and access objects across the Net via URLs with the same ease as when accessing a local file system.*

We have found the networking capabilities of Java to be both strong and easy to use. Anyone who has tried to do Internet programming using another language will revel in how simple Java makes onerous tasks like opening a socket connection. Java even makes common gateway interface (CGI) scripting easier. (We will cover networking in Volume 2 of this book.) The new remote method invocation mechanism enables communication between distributed objects (also covered in Volume 2).

Robust

> *Java is intended for writing programs that must be reliable in a variety of ways. Java puts a lot of emphasis on early checking for possible problems, later dynamic (run-time) checking, and eliminating situations that are error-prone. ... The single biggest difference between Java and C/C++ is that Java has a pointer model that eliminates the possibility of overwriting memory and corrupting data.*

This is also very useful. The Java compiler (in both its original incarnation and in the various improved versions in third-party implementations) detects many problems that, in other languages, would only show up at run time (or, perhaps, not even then). As for the second point, anyone who has spent hours chasing a memory leak caused by a pointer bug will be very happy with this feature of Java.

If you are coming from a language like VB that doesn't use pointers, you are probably wondering why this is so important. C programmers are not so lucky. They need pointers to access strings, arrays, objects, even files. In VB, you do not use pointers for any of these entities, nor do you need to worry about memory allocation for them. On the other hand, if you implement some of the fancier data structures in VB that require pointers using class modules, you need to manage the memory yourself. Java gives you the best of both worlds. You do not need pointers for everyday constructs like strings and arrays. You have the power of pointers if you need it, for example, for linked lists. And you always have complete safety, since you can never access a bad pointer, make memory allocation errors or have to protect against memory leaking away.

Secure

Java is intended to be used in networked/distributed environments. Toward that end, a lot of emphasis has been placed on security. Java enables the construction of virus-free, tamper-free systems.

In the first edition of *Core Java* we said: "Well, one should 'never say never again,'" and we turned out to be right. A group of security experts at Princeton University found the first bugs in the security features of Java 1.0—not long after the JDK 1.0 was shipped. Moreover, they and various other people have continued to find other bugs in the security mechanisms of all subsequent versions of Java. All we can suggest is that you check

1. The URL for the Princeton group:
   `http://www.cs.princeton.edu/sip/`
2. The `comp.risks` newsgroup

for opinions from outside experts on the current status of Java's security mechanisms.

The good side is that the Java team has said that they will have a "zero tolerance" for security bugs and immediately go to work on fixing any bugs found in the applet security mechanism (the browser companies go to work immediately as well). In particular, by making public the internal specifications of how the Java interpreter works, Sun is making it far easier for people to find any bugs in Java's security features—essentially enlisting the outside community in the ever-so-subtle security bug detection process. This makes one more confident that security bugs will be found as soon as possible. In any case, Java makes it extremely difficult to outwit its security mechanisms. The bugs found so far have been very subtle and (relatively) few in number.

NOTE: JavaSoft's URL for security-related issues is currently at:
`http://www.javasoft.com/sfaq`

Here is a sample of what Java's security features are supposed to keep a Java program from doing:

1. Overrunning the run-time stack, like the infamous Internet worm did.
2. Corrupting memory outside its own process space.
3. Reading or writing local files when invoked through a security-conscious class loader, like a Web browser that has been programmed to forbid this kind of access.

All of these features are in place and for the most part seem to work as intended. Java is certainly the most secure programming language to date. But, caution is always in order: though the bugs found in the security mechanism to date were not trivial to find and full details are often kept secret, still it may be impossible to *prove* that Java is secure. So, all we can do is repeat what we said before with even more force attached to it:

"Never say never again"

Regardless of whether Java can ever be proved secure, Java 1.1 now has the notion of signed classes (see the next volume). With a signed class, you can be sure of who wrote it. Once a signing mechanism is in place, any time you trust the author of the class, the class can be allowed more privileges on your machine.

NOTE: A competing code delivery mechanism from Microsoft based on its ActiveX technology relies on digital signatures alone for security. Clearly this is not sufficient—as any user of Microsoft's own products can confirm, programs from well-known vendors do crash and in so doing, create damage. Java has a far stronger security model than ActiveX since it controls the application as it runs and stops it from wreaking havoc. (For example, you can ensure that local file input and output is forbidden even for signed classes.)

Architecture Neutral

The compiler generates an architecture neutral object file format—the compiled code is executable on many processors, given the presence of the Java run time system. The Java compiler does this by generating bytecode instructions which have nothing to do with a particular computer architecture. Rather, they are designed to be both easy to interpret on any machine and easily translated into native machine code on the fly.

This is not a new idea. Twenty years ago, the UCSD Pascal system did the same thing in a commercial product and, even before that, Niklaus Wirth's original implementation of Pascal used the same approach. By using bytecodes, performance takes a major hit (but just-in-time compilers mitigate this, in many cases). The designers of Java did an excellent job developing a bytecode instruction set that works well on today's most common computer architectures. And the codes have been designed to translate easily into actual machine instructions.

Portable

Unlike C and C++, there are no "implementation-dependent" aspects of the specification. The sizes of the primitive data types are specified, as is the behavior of arithmetic on them.

For example, an `int` in Java is always a 32-bit integer. In C/C++, `int` can mean a 16-bit integer, a 32-bit integer, or any other size that the compiler vendor likes. The only restriction is that it must have at least as many bytes as a `short int` and cannot have more bytes than a `long int`. Having a fixed size of number types eliminates a major porting headache. Binary data is stored in a fixed format, eliminating the "big endian/little endian" confusion. Strings are saved in a standard Unicode format.

> *The libraries that are a part of the system define portable interfaces. For example, there is an abstract Window class and implementations of it for UNIX, Windows, and the Macintosh.*

As anyone who has ever tried knows, it is an effort of heroic proportions to write a program that looks good on Windows, the Macintosh, and 10 flavors of UNIX. Despite the claims made by many in the press and by many people involved with Java, the designers of Java have not yet solved this problem. At the present time all we have is a library that, with a lot of work, can give barely acceptable results on different systems. (And there are often *different* bugs on the different platform graphics implementations.) But it is a start. There are many applications in which portability is more important than the nth degree of slickness. In particular, we want to point out that the Java 1.1 graphics libraries are far better than those in earlier versions of Java. It seems quite possible for example to implement standard user interface features such as tabbed dialog boxes that users have come to expect in (pure) Java 1.1 in a robust fashion.

Interpreted

> *The Java interpreter can execute Java bytecodes directly on any machine to which the interpreter has been ported. Since linking is a more incremental and lightweight process, the development process can be much more rapid and exploratory.*

Perhaps this is an advantage while developing an application, but it is clearly overstated. In any case, we have found the compiler in Java 1.1 to be significantly slower than the ones in earlier versions of Java (which themselves were none too fast). If you are used to the speed of VB's or Delphi's development cycle, you will be very disappointed unless you use a faster bytecode compiler. (None exist as we write this: we are waiting eagerly for SunSoft or third parties to come out with the kind of fast compilers that already exist for Java 1.02.)

High Performance

> *While the performance of interpreted bytecodes is usually more than adequate, there are situations where higher performance is required. The bytecodes can be translated on the fly (at run time) into machine code for the particular CPU the application is running on.*

If you use the native Java interpreter to translate the bytecodes, "high performance" is not the term that we would use ("middling to poor" is probably more accurate). While it is certainly true that the speed of the interpreted bytecodes can be acceptable, it isn't fast. (At best Java is only slightly faster than VB4, according to our tests.) On the other hand, you will want to run many Java programs through a true compiler and not restrict yourself to interpreting the bytecodes. For example, you will almost certainly want to do so for any program that is designed to be a stand-alone application on a specific machine. Ultimately, you will want compilers for every platform.

Native code compilers for Java are not yet generally available. (There is one from Asymetrix for Windows platforms, but the version for Java 1.1 version isn't out yet as we write this.) Instead, the first form of compilation that will be available for Java 1.1 are sure to be the *just-in-time* (JIT) compilers. These work by compiling the bytecodes into native code once, caching the results, and then calling them again, if needed. This speeds up loops tremendously since one has to do the interpretation only once. Although still slightly slower than a true native code compiler, a just-in-time compiler can give you a 10- or even 20-fold speedup for some programs and will almost always be significantly faster than the Java interpreter.

For example, Symantec had JITs for Java 1.02 in its versions of Café for Windows and Café for the Macintosh. Microsoft has one in its J++ product, and Borland has one in development for Windows as well. Sun has one in development for Solaris, and IBM has one in development for AIX and OS/2.

Multithreaded

(Multithreading is the ability for one program to do more than one thing at once, for example, printing while getting a fax.)

> *[The] benefits of multithreading are better interactive responsiveness and real-time behavior.*

If you have ever tried to do multithreading in another language, you will be pleasantly surprised at how easy it is in Java. Threads in Java also have the capacity to take advantage of multiprocessor systems if the base operating system does so. On the downside, thread implementations on the major platforms differ widely, and Java makes no effort to be platform independent in this regard. Only the code for calling multithreading remains the same across machines; Java offloads the implementation of multithreading to the underlying operating system. (Threading will be covered in Volume 2.)

Dynamic

> *In a number of ways, Java is a more dynamic language than C or C++. It was designed to adapt to an evolving environment. Libraries can freely add new methods and instance variables without any effect on their clients. In Java, finding out run time type information is straightforward.*

This is an important feature in those situations where code needs to be added to a running program. A prime example is code that is downloaded from the Internet to run in a browser. Also, in Java 1.0, finding out run-time type information was anything but straightforward, Java 1.1 gives the programmer full insight into both the structure and behavior of its objects. This gives hope that there will soon be Java GUI builders that will rival Visual Basic in flexibility and ease-of-use.

Java and the Internet

The idea here is simple: users will download Java bytecodes from the Internet and run them on their own machines. Java programs that work on Web pages are called *applets*. (Actually it is the bytecodes, rather than the source file, that you download and then run.) To use an applet, you need a Java-enabled Web browser, which will interpret the bytecodes for you. Because Sun is licensing the Java source code and insisting that there be no changes in the language and basic library structure, you can be sure that a Java applet will run on any browser that is advertised as Java enabled. Note that Netscape 2.x and Netscape 3.x are only *Java 1.02 enabled* as is Internet Explorer 3.0. Most companies have announced Java 1.1 support in their browsers. *However, until most users have upgraded their browsers to ones that support Java 1.1, applets will need to be written using Java 1.02.* (For a full treatment of Java 1.02, we suggest that you look at the second edition of our Core Java book.)

We suspect that, ultimately, most of the initial hype around Java stems from the lure of making money from special-purpose software. You have a nifty "Will Writer" program. Convert it to an applet, and charge people per use—presumably, most people would be using this kind of program infrequently. Once commerce on the Net is widespread, this seems to be inevitable—and desirable. (Some people are taking this too far. They predict a time when everyone downloads software from the Net on a per-use basis. This might be great for software companies, but we think it is absurd, for example, to expect people to download and pay for a spell-checker applet each time they send an e-mail message.)

Here are some of the advantages of applets for users of the World Wide Web that we see as realistic now and in the immediate future:

1. Since Java is a true programming language, it can do far more than scripting languages like JavaScript or VBScript can ever hope to do. It can, for example, draw sophisticated images on the fly, or process large amounts of user input easily.
2. Applets can use a modern graphical user interface (GUI). This includes text boxes, buttons, list boxes, and so on. In Java 1.1 you can even add your own custom interface components. Java applets can also trap user events like keystrokes, mouse movements, and the like.
3. Processing is offloaded to the user's system, which, presumably, is going to do it much faster than some host that is dealing with a few thousand hits at that moment. Moreover, if a great deal of data needs to be computed, you do not have to worry about the speed of transmission from the host machine since the data is computed locally. By the way, this relates to one area in which Java is way overhyped: adding animation to Web pages. Sure, this is easy to do (see the chapter on multithreading in Volume 2), but if the animation involves the user downloading 1 megabyte of GIF files with a 28.8K modem, you will not have a happy user. What people should do instead (if possible), is think of fast ways to compute the special effects. This lets the applet generate the data using the local processor instead of downloading it.
4. Special-purpose Java applets (usually called content and protocol handlers) allow a Java-enabled Web browser to deal with new types of information dynamically. Suppose you invent a nifty fractal compression algorithm for dealing with humongous graphics files and want to let someone sample your technology before you charge them big bucks for it. Write a Java content handler that does the decompression and send it along with the compressed files. The HotJava browser by Sun Microsystems supports this feature. Netscape 2.0 and 3.0 do not, nor did Internet Explorer 3.

Applets at Work

This book includes a few sample applets; ultimately, the best source for applets is the Web itself. Some applets on the Web can only be seen at work; many others include the source code. When you become more familiar with Java, these applets can be a great way to learn more about Java. A good Web site to check for Java applets is Gamelan—`http://www.gamelan.com`. (By the way, *gamelan* also stands for a special type of Javanese musical orchestra. Attend a gamelan performance if you have a chance—it is gorgeous music.)

To place an applet onto a Web page, you need to know or work with someone who knows hypertext markup language (HTML). The number of HTML tags needed for a Java applet are few and easy to master (see Chapter 10). Using general HTML tags to design a Web page is a design issue—it is not a programming problem.

As you can see in Figure 1-1, when the user downloads an applet, it works much like embedding an image in a Web page. (For those who know HTML, we mean one set with an IMG tag.) The applet becomes a part of the page, and the text flows around the space used for the applet. The point is, the image is *alive.* It reacts to user commands, changes its appearance, and sends data between the computer viewing the applet and the computer serving it.

Figure 1-1 shows a good example of a dynamic Web page. This is a part of the virtual laboratory at the physics department of the University of Oregon. You can see some HTML text on top and the running applet on the bottom. (The lightbulb breaks if you add power without sufficient resistors. It glows if you add the right number of resistors, thus teaching students about Ohm's law.)

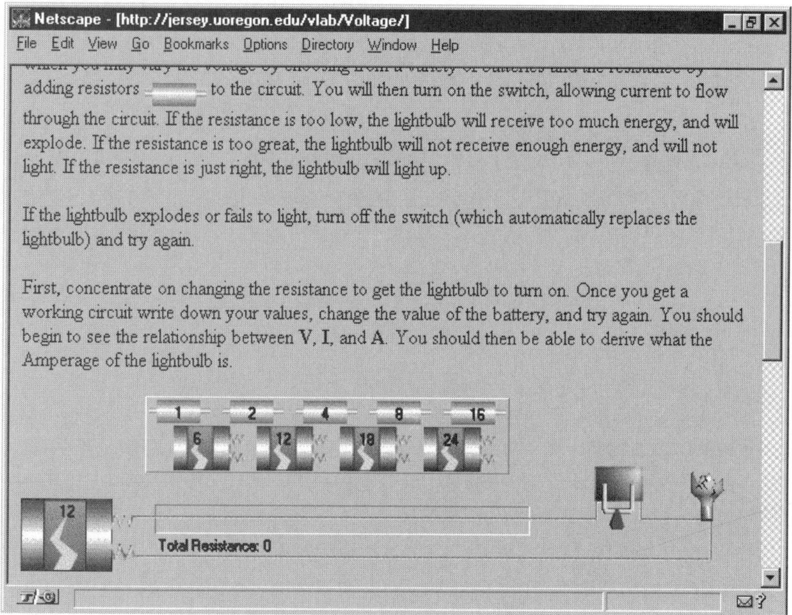

Figure 1-1: Applet for Ohm's law *Courtesy of Sean Russell*

A Short History of Java

This section gives a short history of Java's evolution. It is based on various published sources (most importantly, on an interview with Java's creators in the July 1995 issue of *SunWorld's* on-line magazine).

Java goes back to 1991, when a group of Sun engineers, led by Patrick Naughton and Sun Fellow (and all-around computer wizard) James Gosling, wanted to design a small computer language that could be used for consumer devices like cable TV switchboxes. Since these devices do not have a lot of power or memory, the language had to be small and generate very tight code. Also, because different manufacturers may choose different central processing units (CPUs), it was important not to be tied down to any single architecture. The project got the code name "Green."

The requirements for small, tight code led them to resurrect the model that a language called UCSD Pascal tried in the early days of PCs and Niklaus Wirth had pioneered before that. What Wirth pioneered and UCSD Pascal did commercially, and the Green project engineers did as well, was to design a portable language that generated intermediate code for a hypothetical machine. (These are often called *virtual machines*—hence, the Java Virtual Machine or JVM.) This intermediate code could then be used on any machine that had the correct interpreter. Intermediate code generated with this model is always small, and the interpreters for intermediate code can also be quite small, so this solved their main problem.

The Sun people, however, come from a UNIX background so they based their language on C++, rather than Pascal. In particular, they made the language object oriented rather than procedure oriented. But, as Gosling says in the interview, "All along, the language was a tool, not the end." Gosling decided to call his language "Oak." (Presumably because he liked the look of an oak tree that was right outside his window at Sun.) The people at Sun later realized that Oak was the name of an existing computer language, so they changed the name to Java.

In 1992, the Green project delivered its first product, called "*7." It was an extremely intelligent remote control. (It had the power of a SPARCStation in a box that was 6" by 4" by 4". Unfortunately, no one was interested in producing this at Sun, and the Green people had to find other ways to market their technology. However, none of the standard consumer electronics companies were interested. The group then bid on a project to design a cable TV box that could deal with new cable services such as video on demand. They did not get the contract. (Amusingly, the company that did was led by the same Jim Clark who started Netscape—a company that did much to make Java successful.)

The Green Project (with a new name of "First Person Inc.") spent all of 1993 and half of 1994 looking for people to buy its technology—no one was found. (Patrick Naughton, one of the founders of the group and the person who ended up doing most of the marketing, claims to have accumulated 300,000 air miles in trying to sell the technology.) First Person was dissolved in 1994.

While all of this was going on at Sun, the World Wide Web part of the Internet was growing bigger and bigger. The key to the Web is the browser that takes the hypertext page and translates it to the screen. In 1994, most people were using Mosaic, a noncommercial Web browser that came out of the supercomputing center at the University of Illinois in 1993. (Mosaic was partially written by Marc Andreessen for $6.85 an hour as an undergraduate student on a work-study project. He moved on to fame and fortune as one of the cofounders and the chief of technology at Netscape.)

In the *SunWorld* interview, Gosling says that in mid-1994, the language developers realized that "We could build a real cool browser. It was one of the few things in the client/server mainstream that needed some of the weird things we'd done: architecture neutral, real-time, reliable, secure—issues that weren't terribly important in the workstation world. So we built a browser."

The actual browser was built by Patrick Naughton and Jonathan Payne and evolved into the HotJava browser that we have today. The HotJava browser was written in Java to show off the power of Java. But the builders also had in mind the power of what are now called applets, so they made the browser capable of interpreting the intermediate bytecodes. This "proof of technology" was shown at SunWorld '95 on May 23, 1995, and inspired the Java craze that continues unabated today.

The big breakthrough for widespread Java use came in the fall of 1995, when Netscape decided to make the next release of Netscape (Netscape 2.0) Java enabled. Netscape 2.0 came out in January of 1996, and it has been (as have all subsequent releases) Java enabled. Other licensees include IBM, Symantec, Borland, and many others. Even Microsoft has licensed and supports Java. Internet Explorer 3 is Java enabled and the next version of Windows will be Java enabled. (Note that both Internet Explorer 3.0 and their Java environment J++ —even in its 1.1 version—use the older 1.02 version of Java however.)

Sun released the first version of Java in early 1996. It was followed by Java 1.02 a couple of months later. People quickly realized that Java 1.02 was not going to cut it for serious application development. Sure, you could use Java 1.02 to make a nervous text applet. (The source code for one of the most popular applets is called `NervousText.Java;` it moves text randomly around in a canvas. It is still supplied as one of the samples with the JDK 1.1 although it has not been updated to use the new features of Java 1.1.) But you couldn't even *print* in Java 1.02. To be blunt, Java 1.02 was not ready for prime time.

The big announcements about Java's future features trickled out over the first few months of 1996. Only at the JavaOne conference held in San Francisco in May of 1996 did the bigger picture of where Java was going become clearer. At JavaOne the people at JavaSoft outlined their vision of the future of Java with a seemingly endless stream of improvements and new libraries. We were, to say the least, suspicious that all this would take *years* to come to pass. We are happy to report that while not everything they have outlined has come to pass, surprisingly much was incorporated in an equally surprisingly short amount of time into Java 1.1.

Common Misconceptions about Java

In summary, what follows is a list of some common misconceptions about Java, along with commentary.

Java is an extension of HTML.

Java is a programming language; HTML is a way to describe the structure of a Web page. They have nothing in common except that there are HTML extensions for placing Java applets on a Web page.

Java is an easy programming language to learn.

No programming language as powerful as Java is easy. You always have to distinguish how easy it is to write toy programs and how hard it is to do serious work. Also, consider that only four chapters in this book discuss the Java language. The remaining chapters of both volumes show how to put the language to work, using the Java *library.* The Java library contains over 150 classes and interfaces. Just listing every possible function and constant in the library along with a one- or two-sentence description of them takes more than 250 pages. (The annotated listing of all the Java 1.02 library, which is quite a bit smaller than the Java 1.1 library, included a reasonable number of code snippets, but it took more than 1500 printed pages!) Luckily, you do not need to know every function and constant listed in the 250 pages of the (hypertext-based) Java Application Programming User's Guide, but you do need to know surprisingly many of them in order to use Java for anything realistic.

Java is an easy environment in which to program.

The native Java development environment is not an easy environment to use—except for people who swear by 1970s command-line tools. The main selling point of products like SunSoft's Java Workshop is that they begin to bring Java development into the modern era of VB-style drag-and-drop form designers combined with an integrated development platform including decent debugging facilities. We are eagerly awaiting integrated environments for Java 1.1 development.

Java will become a universal programming language for all platforms.

This is possible, in theory, and it is certainly the case that every vendor but Microsoft seems to want this to happen. But we wonder if you would then get a lowest-common-denominator approach to the design. Java applications do not yet look (and, perhaps, can never look) as good as, say, Windows applications developed with Visual Basic, Delphi, or MFC. In any case, the graphics toolkit, though much improved in Java 1.1, is still too primitive to make the design task pleasant. Of course, we expect the libraries to get better and there is no reason why one couldn't use the Java language to access more powerful class libraries as is done in Visix's Vibe product or even to access a Windows class library like Microsoft's MFC. (Also, there are already many 1.02 based GUI libraries that are "100% pure Java" since they extend the Java libraries without using any native code. There are sure to be even better libraries soon that extend greatly the libraries in Java 1.1, for example, the Java Foundation Classes that were announced by an alliance of JavaSoft, Netscape, and IBM. Gamelan is a good starting place to search for these libraries.)

Java is interpreted, so it is too slow for serious applications on a specific platform.

Many programs spend most of their time on things like user-interface interactions. All programs, no matter what language they are written in, will detect a mouse click in adequate time. It is true that we would not do CPU-intensive tasks with the interpreter supplied with the Java development kit. However, on platforms where a just-in-time compiler is available, all you need to do is run the bytecodes through it and most performance issues simply go away. Finally, Java is great for network-bound programs. Experience has shown that Java can comfortably keep up with the data rate of a network connection, even when doing computationally intensive work such as encryption. As long as Java is faster than the data that it processes, it does not matter that C++ might be faster still. Java is easier to program, and it is portable. This makes Java a great language for implementing network services.

All Java programs run inside a Web page.

All Java *applets* run inside a Web browser. That is the definition of an applet—a Java program running inside a browser. But it is entirely possible, and quite useful, to write stand-alone Java programs that run independently of a Web browser. These programs (usually called *applications*) are completely portable. Just take the code and run them on another machine! And because Java is more convenient and less error-prone than raw C++, it is a good choice for writing programs. It will be an even more compelling choice once it is combined with database access tools like Sun's JDBC (see Volume 2). It is certainly the obvious choice for a first language in which to learn programming.

Most of the programs in this book are stand-alone programs. Sure, applets are interesting, and right now most useful Java programs are applets. But we believe that stand-alone Java programs will become extremely important, very quickly.

Java eliminates the need for CGI scripting.

Not yet. With today's technology, CGI is still the easiest communication path between applet and server. The server will still need a CGI script to deal with the information sent by the applet. (Of course, we feel you can *write* the CGI scripts in Java much more easily than in Perl or C, but that is a separate issue.) In particular, there are technologies on the horizon that greatly reduce the need for CGI scripts. Servlets give you the same execution environment on the server that applets have on the client. JDBC (see Volume 2) permits direct database manipulations by the client of information lying on the server.

Java will revolutionize client-server computing.

This is possible. The JDBC discussed in Volume 2 certainly makes using Java for client-server development easier. As third-party tools continue to be developed, we expect database development with Java to be as easy as the Net library makes network programming.

With Java, I can replace my computer with a $500 "Internet appliance."

Some people are betting big that this is going to happen. We believe it is pretty absurd to think that people are going to give up a powerful and convenient desktop for a limited machine with no local storage. However, if your Java-powered computer has enough local storage for the inevitable situation when your local intranet goes down, a Java-powered network computer is a viable option for a "zero administration initiative" to cut the costs of computer ownership in a business. (We should note that companies like Corel are porting their office productivity suites to Java. For a beta version of Corel's Word Perfect Suite for Java, go to their Web site at `www.corel.com`.)

We also see an Internet appliance as a portable *adjunct* to a desktop. Provided the price is right, wouldn't you rather have an Internet-enabled *telephone* with a small screen to read your e-mail or see the news? Because the Java kernel is so small, Java is the obvious choice for such a telephone or other Internet "appliance."

Java will allow the component-based model of computing to take off.

No two people mean the same thing when they talk about components. Regarding visual controls, like ActiveX components that can be dropped into a graphical user interface (GUI) program, Java 1.1 includes the Java Beans initiative (see Volume 2). Java Beans can potentially do the same sorts of things as ActiveX components *except* they are *automatically* cross-platform and

automatically come with a security manager. All this shows that the success of the Java Beans initiative will go far towards making Java successful.

The trouble is, that as we write this, there are no GUI builders like Visual Basic that take advantage of Java Beans. Until these kinds of environments exist, the Java Bean, component-based model for Java development will stay on hold. It is worth noting that Microsoft has given a way to use ActiveX controls directly from Java in their Internet Explorer browser and that JavaSoft has a direct Java Beans to ActiveX bridge that is in beta as we write this. As for working with distributed computing models that use common object request broker (CORBA) compatible interfaces and OpenDoc, this is already happening through the Java IDL (interface definition language—see Volume 2).

CHAPTER 2

- Installing the Java Compiler and Tools
- Navigating the Java Directories
- Windows 95/NT as a Programming Environment
- Compiling and Running Java Programs
- Using TextPad and WinEdit
- Graphical Applications
- Applets
- Troubleshooting

The Java Programming Environment

This chapter is about getting Java to work in various environments, concentrating on Windows 95 since that seems to be the most common platform. It is somewhat unusual for a book at this level to provide so many tips for various platforms; experienced programmers do not usually need to be told how to work with most software. However, at this point, the setup of Java is somewhat complex, and "gotchas" abound.

NOTE: A good, general source of information on Java can be found via the links on the Java frequently asked questions (FAQ) page: `www.www-net.com/java/faq/`.

Installing the Java Compiler and Tools

The most complete versions of Java 1.1 are available for Sun's Solaris 2.x, Windows NT, or Windows 95 (Java 1.1 is identical for both versions of Windows). Versions of Java 1.1 in various states of development exist for Linux, OS/2, Macintosh, Windows 3.1, and a few other platforms. In particular, if you use a PC and you want to use the Java features described in this book, you must have Windows 95 or NT to run Java. Realistically, you also need either a Pentium or a very fast 486, a minimum of 16 MB of memory, and at least 50 MB of free hard disk space.

NOTE: JavaSoft has released a 1.1.1 version of the JDK. This is strictly a bug fix. Since they may well be up to a JDK 1.1.9 by the time you read this, we will simply say 1.1 in this chapter and elsewhere in this book.

TIP: For one of the big three—Solaris, Windows, or the Mac—you will want to periodically visit the Java home page to see if a more recent release is available for your platform. Point your browser to `java.sun.com`. For other platforms, you will need to cruise the Web or contact the vendor. A good place to turn to is the `comp.lang.java.programmer` newsgroup.

The CD that accompanies this book contains a version of the 1.1 Java Development Kit (JDK) for Windows NT/Windows 95 and Solaris. The installation instructions in this chapter assume that you have Windows 95 or NT 4.0. The CD-ROM packaged with this book comes with a standard Windows installation program that unpacks the files needed to install the Windows version and runs JavaSoft's installation program. The Solaris files are in tar format. You will need to unpack these archives manually and follow the installation instructions on the CD-ROM. The CD-ROM does *not* contain support for the Macintosh. Once a Macintosh version of Java 1.1 is available, you can download it from `java.sun.com` and install it by following the directions given there.

NOTE: Only the installation instructions for Java are system dependent. If a full version of Java exists for your operating system, then, once you get Java up and running, everything else in this book should apply to you. System independence is a major benefit of Java. (Occasionally there are minor problems in practice, especially on Macs where command-line tools don't fit the Mac model very well.)

Development Environments for Windows Users

If your programming experience comes from VB, Delphi, or a modern PC or Macintosh version of C or C++, you are used to a development environment with a built-in text editor and menus to compile and launch a program along with an integrated debugger. The basic JDK contains nothing even remotely similar. *Everything* is done from the command line. We will tell you how to install and use the basic JDK, because at the time of this writing, the integrated design environments (IDEs) for Java do not yet support Java 1.1.

The CD-ROM also contains two excellent shareware programming editors for Windows: TextPad and WinEdit. Both make developing Java programs easier, and we used them both for developing and testing most of the programs in this book. We asked the authors of these programs to create the necessary configuration and batch files for Java programming, and we have included these files on the CD. Since you can compile and execute source code from within these editors, they can become your de facto IDE as you work through this book. (We hope, of course, if you choose to use one of them beyond the trial period, you will pay the small fee asked to the vendors.)

However, if you have a Java IDE such as Java Workshop, Microsoft J++, or Symantec Café that has been updated to Java 1.1, then you can continue using it and manually add the special files and packages that are used in this book. We will give you general instructions, but of course the details depend on the particular environment that you are using. Fair warning: If you add a package to a commercial environment but the environment doesn't seem to find it, please contact the vendor, not us, for technical assistance.

In sum, you have at this time three choices for a development environment under Windows:

1. Install the JDK and the Java-enhanced version of TextPad or WinEdit from the CD-ROM.
2. Install the JDK from the CD-ROM and use your favorite ASCII editor (it must support long file names).
3. Install just the Core Java code, not the JDK, and use it with the Java 1.1 development environment that you already own.

If you hate choices, just pick the first option. It will work fine. You simply write the source code for your program in the editor. When you are happy with it, you can use various TextPad or WinEdit menu items to compile, execute, or see the frequent syntax error message you will encounter for the first few weeks of working with Java.

Commercial development environments such as Java Workshop tend to be more cumbersome to use for a simple program, since you have to set up a separate project for each program you write. These environments have the edge if you write larger Java programs, consisting of many source files. (And usually their bytecode compilers are so much faster than the one in the JDK as to often make the extra work, even for a small program, worthwhile!)

Installation Tips

If you are working with Windows 95 or NT and choose to use one of the text editors on the CD-ROM, install the following components:

- The JDK
- Core Java files
- TextPad or WinEdit

If you choose to use your own ASCII text editor, such as EDIT or vi, install the following components:

- The JDK
- Core Java files

If you have an integrated Java 1.1 environment, install the Core Java files and nothing else.

CD-ROM Installation

Here are more detailed instructions.

When you insert the CD-ROM, it should automatically offer to install the software. If it does not, go to the `\WINDOWS` directory. Run the Install.exe program. If you don't have your own Java 1.1 compiler, select the "Install JDK1.1.2 & Documentation" box, as shown in Figure 2-1. This runs the JavaSoft setup program that installs the JDK. It is the usual, InstallShield-based installation routine whose look and feel should be familiar to any user of any version of Microsoft Windows.

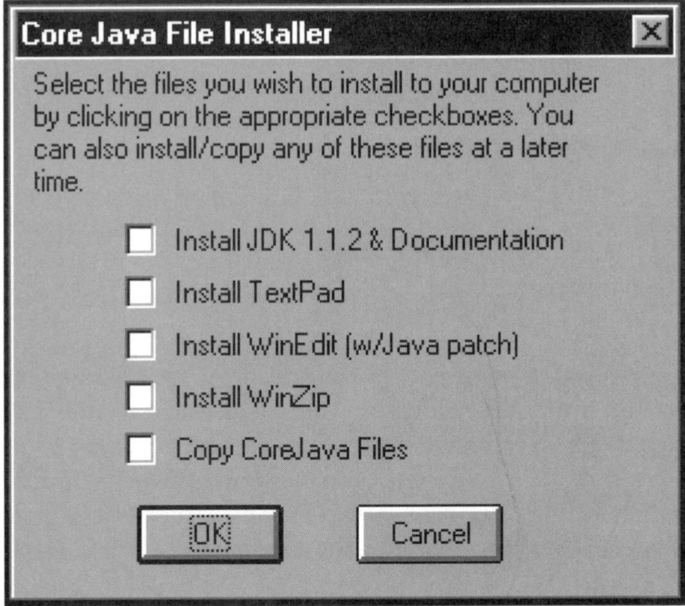

Figure 2-1: The CD-ROM installation program

When the setup program prompts you for the installation directories, the default for the version on the CD is `c:\jdk1.1.2`. (You can change the disk drive letter if you do not have enough room on drive C. If you make any change at all to the installation directory, you *must* manually edit the `AUTOEXEC.BAT` file and update the `PATH` and `CLASSPATH`—the installer does not pay any attention to where you put the files and always uses the default location.) Whether or not you install the JDK, you should select the "Copy CoreJava Files" box, since you will need the Core Java files when you run the examples in this book. When the setup program prompts you for the installation directory, you should accept the default `\CoreJavaBook`.

Finally, you can choose to have any of the following three shareware programs to install:

- TextPad
- WinEdit
- WinZip

By now, you may be feeling like the person who buys a gas grill, only to find that it is actually a gas grill assembly kit, not a ready-to-use grill. There is a reason, after all, why this is called the Java Development *Kit*. Undoubtedly, all this confusion will end once integrated development environments support the most up-to-date versions of Java.

Checking Your Configuration

When the installation is complete, check your AUTOEXEC.BAT file. There should be two modifications:

The PATH should contain the Java compiler directory (such as \jdk1.1.2\bin). For example,

```
SET PATH=. . .;C:\jdk1.1.2\bin; . . .
```

There must also be an environment variable called CLASSPATH that looks like this for the default installation:

```
SET CLASSPATH=C:\jdk1.1.2\lib;.;C:\CoreJavaBook
```

The exact order of the directories in the path and class path does not matter, nor does the case. If you already have a class path, the installer should add the \jdk1.1.2\lib, the "." (for the current directory) and the \CoreJavaBook directories to the end. (If you installed the JDK to a different location than the default C:\jdk1.1.2, then you must manually update the PATH and CLASSPATH.)

Finally, as always, you need to reboot your computer in order to make the changes to the path and class path effective.

TIP: On UNIX, the directories of the class path are separated by colons. You must use an absolute path for each directory in the class path, for example,

```
setenv CLASSPATH /jdk1.1.2/lib:.:$(HOME)/CoreJavaBook
```

A relative path ~/CoreJavaBook does not work.

Adding Core Java Files to an Integrated Development Environment

If you already have another development environment such as Java Workshop, Microsoft J++, or Symantec Café, and your version supports Java 1.1, then installing the JDK may interfere with your existing installation. You will want to contact your vendor to see exactly what they suggest doing. (Some vendors' IDE coexist nicely with Sun's JDK; others get *very* confused.) In any case you should install the Core Java files.

Note that you still may not be able to use the Core Java files easily. The reason is that once the Core Java files are installed into the `\CoreJavaBook` directory, you need to add that directory to the class path of your development environment. This may be as simple as locating the CLASSPATH environment variable in your `AUTOEXEC.BAT` file. Or you may need to set an option in your development environment, or edit another file such as `SC.INI` for Symantec's Café. Be careful—in some environments a new setting *overrides* all others, whereas in others the additional setting gets *appended* to the regular settings. Consult the documentation of your environment and contact the vendor for assistance if necessary.

Navigating the Java Directories

In your explorations of Java, you will occasionally want to peek inside the Java system files. And, of course, you will need to work extensively with our *Core Java* files. Table 2-1 shows the Java directory tree. (The layout will be different if you have an integrated development environment and the root will be different if you are using a JDK 1.1.X.)

Table 2-1: Java directory tree

`\jdk`		
	`docs`	*library documentation in HTML format is here*
		`guide`
		`images`
	`bin`	*the compiler and tools are here*
	`demo`	`(lots of subdirectories)` *look here for demos*
	`include`	*files for native methods (see Volume 2)*
		`win32`
	`.hotjava`	*created after you use the applet viewer for the first time*
	`lib`	`(lots of subdirectories)` *library files*
	`src`	`(lots of subdirectories)` *look in the various subdirectories for the library source*

The two most important subdirectories in this tree are `\docs` and `\src`. The `\docs` directory contains the Java library documentation in HTML format. You can view it with any Web browser, such as Netscape.

TIP: Set a bookmark in your browser to the local version of `tree.html` as shown in Figure 2-2. You will be referring to this page a lot as you go further with Java!

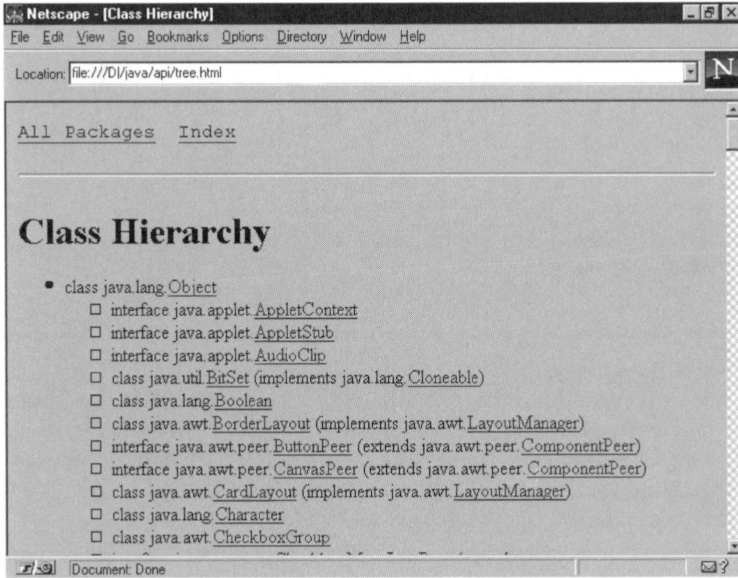

Figure 2-2: A starting point for the library documentation

The `src` directory contains the source code for the public part of the Java libraries. As you become more comfortable with Java, you may find yourself in situations for which this book and the on-line information do not provide what you need to know. At this point, the source code for Java is a good place to begin digging. It is occasionally reassuring to know that you can always dig into the source to find out what a library function really does. For example, if you are curious about the inner workings of the `Hashtable` class, you can look inside `src\java\util\Hashtable.java`.

Here is the beginning of how the program files in this book are organized:

```
\CoreJavaBook
    corejava
    ch2
        Welcome.java
        WelcomeApplet.java
        ImageViewer.java
    ch3
        FirstSample.java
        LotteryOdds.java
        LotteryDrawing.java
        Mortgage.java
        MortgageLoop.java
        Retirement.java
        SquareRoot.java
    . . .
```

NOTE: The `corejava` directory is very important. It contains a number of useful Java routines that we wrote to supplement missing features in the standard Java library. These files are needed for a number of examples in the book. It is crucial that your CLASSPATH environment variable is set to include the `\CoreJavaBook` directory so that the programs can find our files, such as our console input class `\CoreJavaBook\corejava\Console.class`.

There is a separate directory for each chapter of this book. Each of these directories has separate subdirectories for sample files. For example, `\CoreJavaBook\ch2\ImageViewer` contains the source code and compiled code for the ImageViewer application that you will encounter later in this chapter. (There is no source code for Chapter 1.)

Windows 95/NT as a Programming Environment

If you have done all your programming in Windows, using a comfortable programming environment such as VB, Delphi, or one of the C++-integrated environments, you may find the JDK primitive. ("Quaint" may be a more charitable word for it.) In this section, we give a few tips for working with Windows 95/NT. If you are a seasoned veteran or if you do not use Windows 95/NT, just skip this section.

Long File Names

Even if you are an experienced programmer under previous versions of DOS or Windows 3.1, Windows 95 has one major new feature—*long file names.* If you are coming from DOS or Windows 3.1, you know that a DOS file can have, at most, eight characters in the name and three characters in the extension, such as `WLCMAPPL.HTM`. These are the so-called 8.3 file names. With Windows 95 or NT, you can use as many characters as you like. For example, you can call a file `WelcomeApplet.html`. This is welcome news, indeed. In fact, you *do not* have a choice when dealing with Java; all Java source files use long file names. They *must* have the four-letter extension *java*. Luckily, most of the new versions of the traditional DOS utility functions included in Windows NT or Windows 95 understand long file names. For example, you can type

```
del WelcomeApplet.html
```

or

```
copy *.java a:
```

Of course, if you prefer, you can delete and copy the files through the Explorer, but many programmers type faster than they mouse, and, therefore, prefer the command line.

To let you use programs that were written before long file names were invented, Microsoft gives each long file name an 8.3 file name *alias.* These aliases contain a ~ character, for example, `WELCOM~1.HTM`. If there are two files in the same directory whose names start with `WELCOM` and have `HTM` in the extension, then their aliases are `WELCOM~1.HTM` and `WELCOM~2.HTM`. In the event that there are 8.3 aliases for some files in the directory (which will always be the case when you use long file names) be careful when deleting files, especially when you use wild cards. For example, the command

```
del *.HTM
```

will delete all files with the extension `HTM` and all files whose extension *starts with* `HTM`. In particular, all `*.html` files will also be deleted.

Windows Explorer gives you access to the long file names. But if you are working with a DOS shell, how do you find the long file name?

- The DIR command shows the 8.3 alias on the left and the long file name on the right.

```
MS-DOS Prompt

D:\CoreJavaBook\ch2>dir

 Volume in drive D is DISK2_VOL1
 Volume Serial Number is 15DD-1D24
 Directory of D:\CoreJavaBook\ch2

.              <DIR>        02-18-96  2:45p .
..             <DIR>        02-18-96  2:45p ..
WELCOME        <DIR>        02-18-96  2:45p Welcome
WELCOM~1       <DIR>        02-18-96  2:45p WelcomeApplet
IMAGEV~1       <DIR>        02-18-96  2:45p ImageViewer
         0 file(s)              0 bytes
         5 dir(s)     264,044,544 bytes free

D:\CoreJavaBook\ch2>_
```

Figure 2-3: The DIR command with long file names

After a few weeks, you will get into the habit of looking at the right-hand side and ignoring the left-hand side.

One of the programs that has not yet been adapted to long file names is the command-line version of PKZIP. If you use the venerable PKZIP 2.04g to bundle and compress files, you will find that it only packs and unpacks the 8.3 file names.

You can make a real hash out of a collection of Java files by using the DOS version of PKZIP. Instead, you should use a modern zipping tool like WinZip. We include a shareware copy of WinZip on the CD-ROM. For example, you can use WinZip to peek inside the `CLASSES.ZIP` file in the `\lib` directory.

Long file names can even contain spaces. You may have noticed that some programs are installed in a directory with the name `Program Files`. As you can imagine, this can be confusing for some DOS commands that traditionally expect spaces to separate the file names and command options. You need to enclose any file or directory name that contains spaces in quotation marks, for example,

```
del "The first applet in the Core Java book.java"
```

Don't worry. We will not use file names like that in our examples.

Long file names are not case sensitive *for DOS commands.* For example,

```
del WelcomeApplet.java
```

and

```
del welcomeapplet.JAVA
```

both have the same effect. But Windows 95 *retains the case* that you used when you first created the file. For example, if you named the file `WelcomeApplet.java`, then Windows will use the uppercase `W` and `A` in the directory display and all directory dialog boxes.

NOTE: Java, on the other hand, *is* case sensitive. As you will soon see, a file like `WelcomeApplet.java` contains a class with the same name, `WelcomeApplet`. If you compile this file with the command

```
javac welcomeapplet.java
```

then the compiler will ask DOS to open the file. DOS has no problem opening the `welcomeApplet.java` file, but the compiler will insist that it cannot find a `welcomeapplet` class. You will get some strange error message that relates to the file not being found. The moral is that anytime you cannot compile a file that you know is there, check the case of the file name with the DIR command or with Explorer. If you notice the problem and regret your decision, you can use the `ren` command to change the look of the file name.

```
ren welcomeapplet.java WelcomeApplet.java
```

Multiple Windows

When using the JDK, multiple DOS windows are a way of life. You run the editor in one DOS window and the compiler in another. Graphical applications, applets, and the browser run in other windows. Windows 95 has a nifty *task bar* at the bottom of the screen that lets you easily switch between windows.

Figure 2-4: The task bar

If you use a computer with a small screen (such as a laptop computer), you may find that the task bar takes up valuable screen real estate. You can *hide* the task bar. (Click on an empty area of the task bar with the right mouse button, then select Properties and Auto Hide.) This tells Windows to display the task bar only when you move the mouse toward the bottom of the screen. (You can also drag the task bar to another corner of your screen if you like.)

Keyboard Shortcuts

The mouse was originally designed by researchers in the prestigious SRI International lab. One of their unstated goals seems to have been to slow you down so the computer can keep up with you. Programmers do not like to be slowed down, and their programmer comrades at Microsoft have fought the mouse maniacs and kept a number of *keyboard shortcuts* in the operating system. Here are a few of these keystroke combinations that we have found helpful.

ALT+TAB: This key combination displays a small window with icons, one for each running task.

Figure 2-5: The ALT+TAB task switcher

Keep your thumb on the ALT key and hold down TAB. Different icons will be selected. Let go of both keys, and you switch to the selected window.

CTRL+ESC: This key combination pops up the Start menu in the task bar. If you arrange your most-used program icons into the first level of the Start menu, then you can run them with a couple of keystrokes.

TIP: Put the MS-DOS prompt, TextPad/WinEdit, and Netscape into the first level of the Start menu. (To edit the Start menu, right-click on an empty area of the task bar, then select Properties and Start Menu Programs.)

SHIFT+F10: This key combination pops up a *context menu,* just as if you had clicked the right mouse button.

Under Windows 95, the CTRL+ALT+DEL key combination does not reboot the computer. Instead, it pops up a window of all active applications, like this:

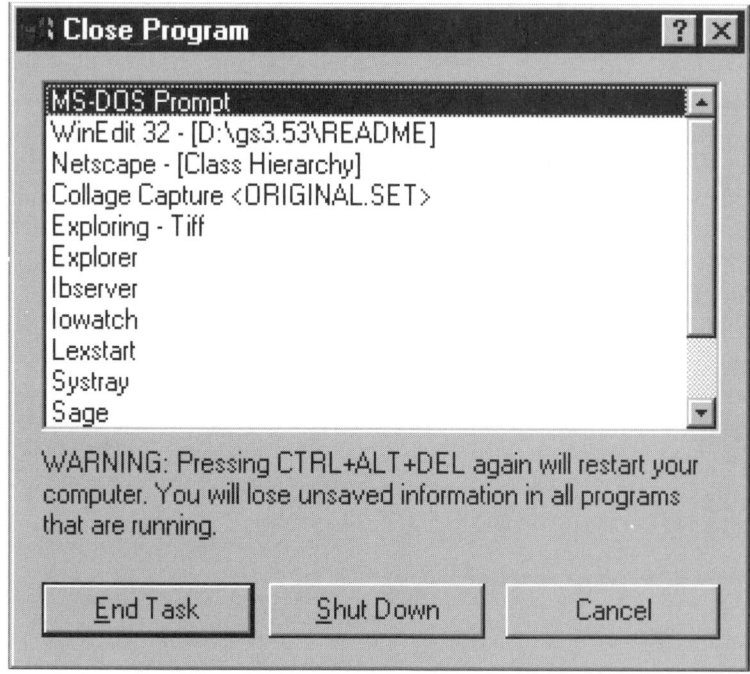

Figure 2-6: The CTRL+ALT+DEL Close Program dialog

If you have a nonresponsive program:

1. Pop up this box.
2. Select the program from the given list.
3. Click on the End Task button. (You may need to wait a few seconds before this has any effect.)

Hitting CTRL+ALT+DEL *twice* does reboot the computer, so you want to have a steady hand when using this key combination.

More on DOS Shells

The humble MS-DOS shell has come a long way from that in earlier versions of Windows. In fact, the DOS shell in Windows 95 is, in many ways, a better DOS than DOS. For starters, as you have seen, you can run multiple DOS shells and toggle between them. You can also launch Windows applications directly from the DOS shell. For example, if you type

```
notepad
```

into a DOS prompt and hit ENTER, the Notepad program starts up. This is certainly faster than clicking on Start Menu | Programs | Accessories | Notepad.

TIP: If you use the DOS shell, you should use the DOSKEY program. The DOSKEY utility keeps a *command history*. Type the up and down arrow keys to cycle through the previously typed commands. Use the left and right arrow keys to edit the current command. Type the beginning of a command and hit F8 to complete it. For example, if you have typed

```
appletviewer WelcomeApplet.html
```

once, then you just type

```
apF8
```

to instantly retype the command. You get a chance to edit it, in case you want to issue a slightly different command.

To install DOSKEY automatically, simply add the line

```
DOSKEY /INSERT
```

into your `AUTOEXEC.BAT` file and reboot.

The EDIT Program

If you need to do a quick edit and you do not want to wait for your regular editor to start, try the EDIT program that comes with Windows 95. You will be pleasantly surprised. This is not the QuickBasic editor that came with DOS 5 and 6, but a completely different program. In particular, this editor handles long file names, *and* it can edit up to 10 files at a time. You switch between the files by hitting ALT+1, ALT+2, and so on. You can even launch the editor with a wild card:

```
edit *.java
```

Unfortunately, EDIT is still a DOS program, which means that it is difficult to cut and paste between it and other Windows programs. (It can be done, but you need to use the Mark, Copy, and Paste icons on the top of the DOS shell, not the usual editor commands.) Of course, you can cut and paste between different files that are loaded into the editor. (You can use TextPad or WinEdit if you want a more efficient way to cut and paste text between Windows programs.)

Compiling and Running Java Programs

There are two methods for compiling and launching a Java program: from the command line and from an editor. Let us do it the hard way first: from the command line. Go to the `\CoreJavaBook\ch2\Welcome` directory. Then enter the following commands:

```
javac Welcome.java
java Welcome
```

You should see the message shown in Figure 2-7 on the screen:

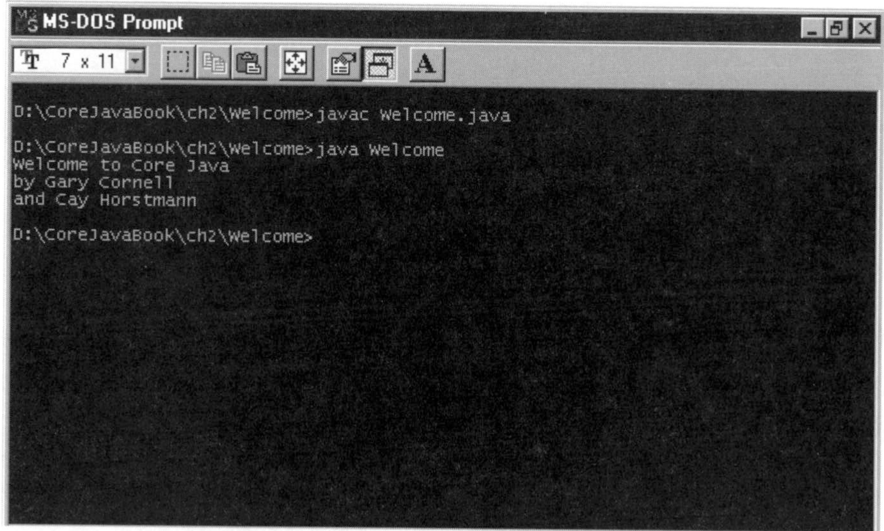

Figure 2-7: Compiling the first Java program

Congratulations! You have just compiled and run your first Java program.

What happened? The `javac` program is the Java compiler. It compiles the file `Welcome.java` into the file `Welcome.class`. The `java` program is the Java interpreter. It interprets the bytecodes that the compiler placed in the class file.

The `Welcome` program is extremely simple. It simply prints a message to the console. You may enjoy looking inside the program shown in Example 2-1—we will explain how it works in the next chapter.

Example 2-1: Welcome.java

```
public class Welcome
{  public static void main(String[] args)
   {  String greeting[] = new String[3];
      greeting[0] = "Welcome to Core Java";
      greeting[1] = "by Cay Horstmann";
      greeting[2] = "and Gary Cornell";

      int i;
      for (i = 0; i < greeting.length; i++)
         System.out.println(greeting[i]);
   }
}
```

NOTE: Every integrated environment has commands for compiling and running programs. If you do not use TextPad or WinEdit, read your documentation to find out how to compile and run programs. If you want to use TextPad or WinEdit, read the next section.

Using TextPad and WinEdit

Compiling and Running Programs

We grew quite comfortable with the customized versions of TextPad and WinEdit in the course of writing this book. Both editors use the normal editing commands that most Windows programs expect. (The keystrokes for most tasks are customizable as well.) They both come with a complete help system, so we will not go into the details of using them as an editor. (It should take an experienced programmer maybe 15 minutes to master either product.)

In this section, we will show you the steps needed to run the Welcome program from inside the editing environment. Then, we will explain the advantages of using one of the shareware editors we supply for the situations when you make a typo or three.

To compile and run the `Welcome` program from the customized version of WinEdit:

1. Start up WinEdit.
2. Choose File | Open and work with the dialog box to find and then load the `Welcome.java` source code.
3. Select Project | Compile from the menu. This runs the Java compiler and captures any error messages. (We hope there are none.) While Java is compiling the file, you see a screen like this:

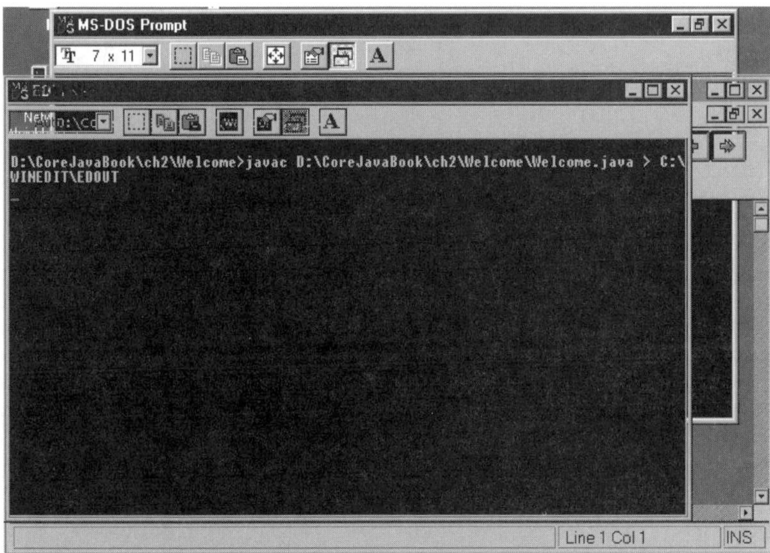

Figure 2-8: The compiler window in WinEdit

WinEdit has automatically opened a temporary DOS shell to run the Java compiler. When the compiler has finished, you will see a dialog box that looks like this:

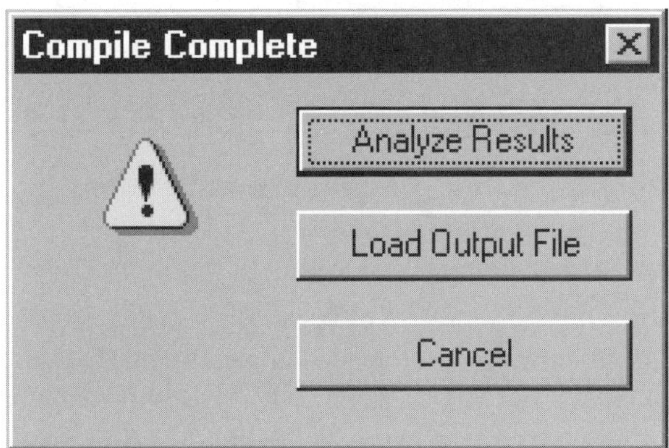

Figure 2-9: The Compile Complete notification in WinEdit

Hit the Analyze Results button. There should be a message `"No errors or warnings"` in the status bar. Then select Project | Execute to see the compiled code at work. This pops up another DOS window for the output.

When you use TextPad, the procedure is similar.

1. Start up TextPad.
2. Choose File | Open and work with the dialog box to find and then load the `Welcome.java` source code.
3. Select Tools | Java Compiler (or the keyboard shortcut ALT+0) to run the Java compiler.
4. Select Tools | Run Java (or the keyboard shortcut ALT+1) to execute the compiled program.

Figure 2-10 shows a Java program launched from TextPad.

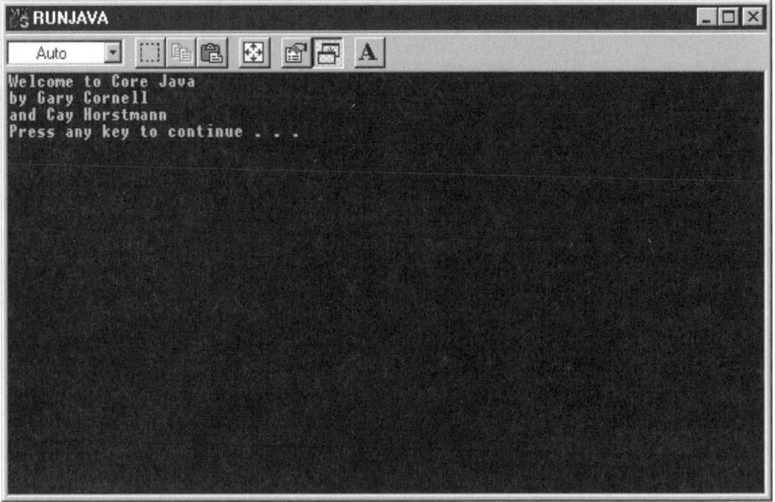

Figure 2-10: Running a Java program from TextPad

Locating Compilation Errors

Presumably, our program did not have typos or bugs. (It was only a few lines of code, after all.) Let us suppose, for the sake of argument, that you occasionally have a typo (perhaps even a bug) in your code. Try it out—ruin our file, for example, by changing the capitalization in the first few lines like this:

```
Public class Welcome
{  Public Static void main(String[] args)
   {  String Greeting[] = new String[3];
      greeting[0] = "Welcome to Core Java";
      greeting[1] = "by Gary Cornell";
      greeting[2] = "and Cay Horstmann";
```

```
        int i;
        for (i = 0; i < greeting.length; i++)
            System.out.println(greeting[i]);
    }
}
```

Now run the Java compiler again. Now WinEdit will put the cursor onto the offending line

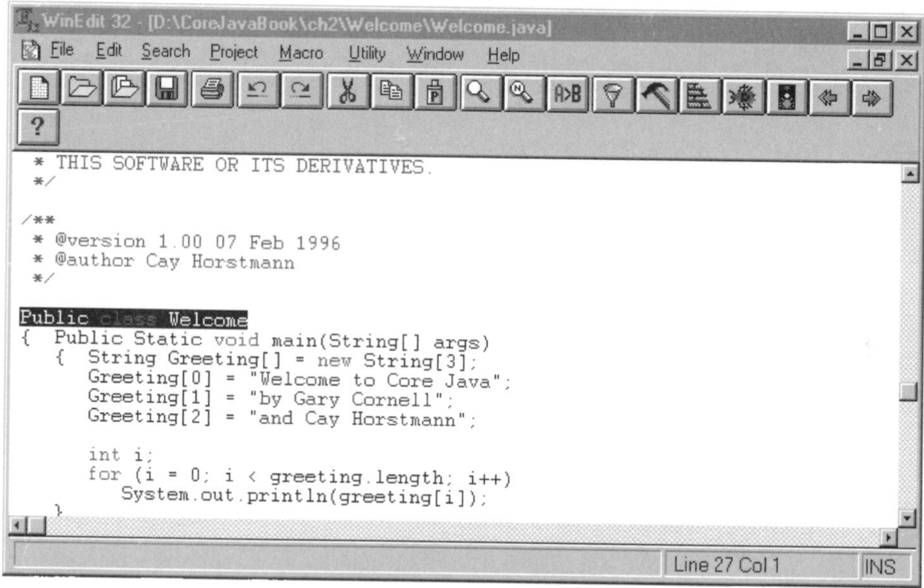

Figure 2-11: Locating compiler errors in WinEdit

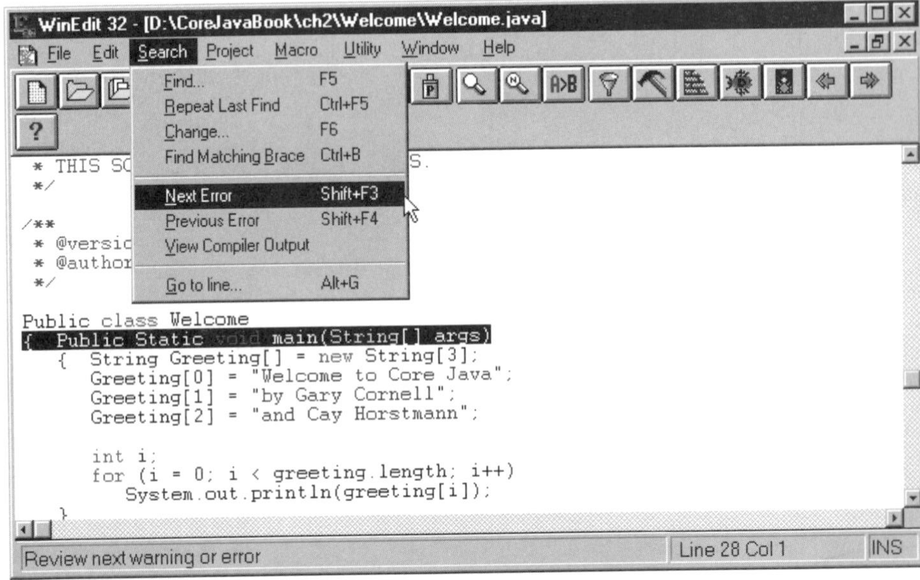

Figure 2-12: Moving to the next error in WinEdit

TextPad shows the error messages in a separate window. Double-click on the first line of an error message to move to the matching location in the file. Use the Search | Next error command (or Search | Jump Next in TextPad) to walk through the remaining error messages.

Graphical Applications

The `Welcome` program was not terribly exciting. Next, let us run a graphical application. This program is a very simple GIF file-viewer. It simply loads and displays a GIF file. Again, let us first compile and run it from the command line.

1. Open a DOS shell window.
2. Change to the directory `\CoreJavaBook\ch2\ImageViewer`.
3. Enter

```
javac ImageViewer.java
java ImageViewer
```

A new program window pops up with our ImageViewer application.

Now select File | Open and look for a GIF file to open. (We supplied a couple of sample files in the directory.)

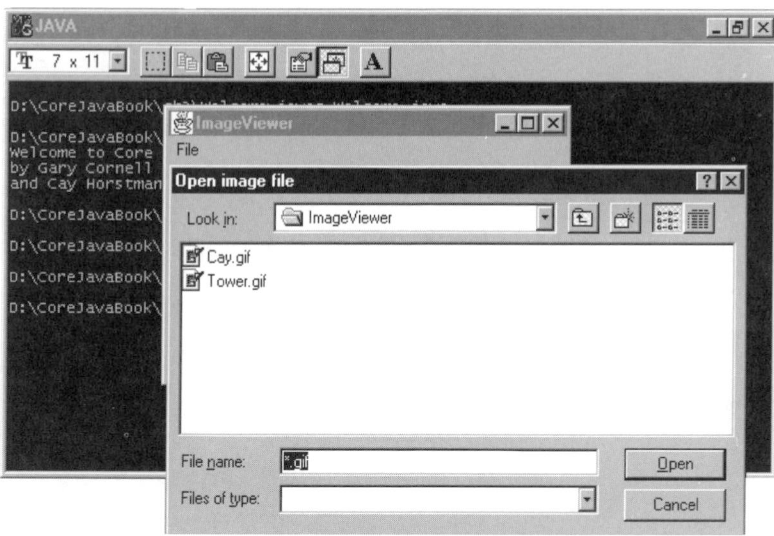

Figure 2-13: Running the ImageViewer application

To close the program, click on the Close box in the title bar or pull down the system menu and close the program. (To compile and run this program inside WinEdit or a development environment, do the same as before. For example, for WinEdit, choose Project | Compile, then choose Project | Run.)

We hope that you find this program interesting and useful. Have a quick look at the source code. The program is substantially longer than the first program, but it is not terribly complex if you consider how much code it would take in C or C++ to write a similar application. In VB, of course, it is easy to write or, rather, drag and drop, such a program—you need only add about two lines of code to make it functional. At this time, Java does not have a visual interface builder, so you need to write code for everything, as shown in Example 2-2. You will learn how to write graphical programs like this in Chapters 7–9.

Example 2-2: ImageViewer.java

```
import java.awt.*;
import java.awt.event.*;
import java.awt.image.*;
import java.net.*;
import java.io.*;

public class ImageViewer extends Frame
   implements ActionListener
{  public ImageViewer()
   {  setTitle("ImageViewer");
```

```
      MenuBar mbar = new MenuBar();
      Menu m = new Menu("File");
      MenuItem m1 = new MenuItem("Open");
      m1.addActionListener(this);
      m.add(m1);
      MenuItem m2 = new MenuItem("Exit");
      m2.addActionListener(this);
      m.add(m2);
      mbar.add(m);
      addWindowListener(new WindowAdapter()
      {  public void windowClosing(WindowEvent e)
            { System.exit(0); }
      } );
      setMenuBar(mbar);
      setSize(300, 400);
      show();
   }

   public void actionPerformed(ActionEvent evt)
   {  String arg = evt.getActionCommand();
      if (arg.equals("Open"))
      {  FileDialog d = new FileDialog(this,
            "Open image file", FileDialog.LOAD);
         d.setFile("*.gif");
         d.setDirectory(lastDir);
         d.show();
         String f = d.getFile();
         lastDir = d.getDirectory();
         if (f != null)
            image = Toolkit.getDefaultToolkit().getImage(lastDir
+ f);
         repaint();
      }
      else if(arg.equals("Exit")) System.exit(0);
   }

   public void paint(Graphics g)
   {  g.translate(getInsets().left, getInsets().top);
      if (image != null)
         g.drawImage(image, 0, 0, this);
   }

   public static void main(String args[])
   {  new ImageViewer();
   }

   private Image image = null;
   private String lastDir = "";
}
```

Applets

The first two programs presented in this book are Java *applications*, stand-alone programs like any native programs. On the other hand, as we mentioned in the last chapter, most of the hype about Java comes from its ability to run *applets* inside a Web browser. We want to show you how to build and run an applet from the command line. Finally, we will load the applet into the applet viewer that comes with the JDK.

First, go to the directory `\CoreJavaBook\ch2\WelcomeApplet`, then enter the following commands:

```
javac WelcomeApplet.java
appletviewer WelcomeApplet.html
```

Here is what you see in the applet viewer window.

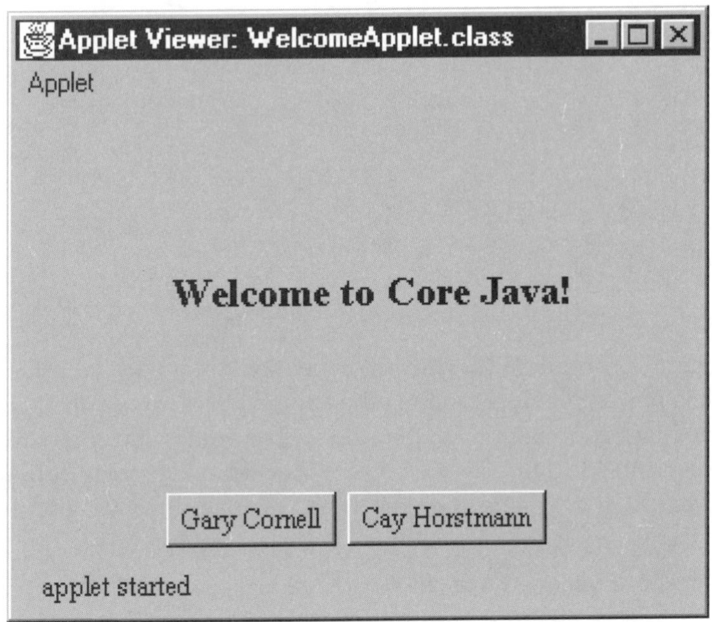

Figure 2-14: The WelcomeApplet applet as viewed by the applet viewer

The first command is the now-familiar command to invoke the Java compiler. This compiles the `WelcomeApplet.java` source into the bytecode file `WelcomeApplet.class`. This time, however, we do not run the Java interpreter; we use the `appletviewer` program instead. This program is a special tool included with the JDK that lets you quickly test an applet. You need to give it an HTML file, rather than the name of a `Java.class` file. The contents of the `WelcomeApplet.html` file are shown below in Example 2-3.

Example 2-3: WelcomeApplet.html

```
<HTML>
<TITLE>WelcomeApplet</TITLE>
<BODY>
<HR>
This applet is from the book
<A HREF="http://www.sun.com/smi/ssoftpress/catalog/java_series.html">
Core Java</A> by
<A HREF="http://www.horstmann.com">
Cay Horstmann</A>
and
<A HREF="mailto:gcornell@ix.netcom.com">
Gary Cornell</A>,
published by Sun Microsystems Press/Prentice-Hall

<APPLET CODE=WelcomeApplet.class WIDTH=200 HEIGHT=200>
<PARAM NAME=greeting VALUE="Welcome to Core Java!">
</APPLET>

<HR>
<A href="WelcomeApplet.java">The source.</A>
</BODY>
</HTML>
```

If you are familiar with HTML, you will notice some standard HTML instructions and the new APPLET tag, telling the appletviewer to load the applet whose code is stored in `WelcomeApplet.class`. The appletviewer ignores all other codes in this file. But a Java 1.1-aware browser will display both the traditional HTML text and the applet on the same Web page. (See Chapter 9 for more on these tags.)

Try it out. You need a Java 1.1-enabled browser.

1. Start your Java 1.1-enabled browser.
2. Select File | Open File (or the equivalent).
3. Go to the `\CoreJavaBook\ch2\WelcomeApplet` directory.

You should see the `WelcomeApplet.html` file in the file dialog. Load that file. Your browser now loads the applet, including the surrounding text. It will look something like Figure 2-15. (Note this used an older version of Netscape which was not Java 1.1-enabled.)

Figure 2-15: Running the WelcomeApplet applet in HotJava

If you have a Java 1.1-enabled browser you can see that this application is actually alive and willing to interact with the Internet. Click on the Gary Cornell button. The applet directs the browser to pop up a mail window, with Gary's address already filled in. Click on the Cay Horstmann button. The applet directs the browser to display Cay's Web page.

Notice that neither of these two buttons works in the applet viewer. The applet viewer has no capabilities to send mail or display a Web page, so it ignores your requests. The applet viewer is good for testing applets in isolation, but you need to put it inside a Java 1.1-enabled browser to see how applets interact with the browser and the Internet.

TIP: You can also compile and run applets from inside TextPad or WinEdit. As always, select "compile," then "run." This time, the run command launches a batch file that realizes you are running an applet, not an application. It builds an HTML file on the fly and launches the applet-viewer. If you use an integrated environment such as Workshop it will have its own commands to launch an applet.

Finally, the code for the Welcome applet is shown in Example 2-4. At this point, do not give it more than a glance. We will come back to writing applets in Chapter 10.

Example 2-4: WelcomeApplet.java

```
import java.applet.*;
import java.awt.*;
import java.awt.event.*;
import java.net.*;

public class WelcomeApplet extends Applet
   implements ActionListener
{  public void start()
   {  setLayout(new BorderLayout());
      Label l = new Label(getParameter("greeting"),
         Label.CENTER);
      l.setFont(new Font("Times", Font.BOLD, 18));
      add(l, "Center");
      Panel p = new Panel();
      Button b1 = new Button("Cay Horstmann");
      b1.addActionListener(this);
      p.add(b1);
      Button b2 = new Button("Gary Cornell");
      b2.addActionListener(this);
      p.add(b2);
      add(p, "South");
   }

   public void actionPerformed(ActionEvent evt)
   {  String arg = evt.getActionCommand();
      String uName;
      URL u;
      if (arg.equals("Cay Horstmann"))
         uName = "http://www.horstmann.com";
      else if (arg.equals("Gary Cornell"))
         uName = "mailto:gcornell@ix.netcom.com";
      else return;
      try
      {  u = new URL(uName);
         getAppletContext().showDocument(u);
      }
      catch(Exception e)
      {  showStatus("Error " + e);
      }
   }
}
```

Troubleshooting

We want to end this section with a few tips whose discovery caused us some grief; we hope you can learn from our pain.

PATH, CLASSPATH, and Other Environment Variables

The single most common problem we encountered with Java is an incorrect PATH or CLASSPATH environment variable. Assuming you used the directory of `jdk`, then you need to make sure that:

1. The `\jdk\bin` directory (or the directory containing your integrated environment's executables or the directory where you placed the JDK) must be on the *PATH*.
2. The `\jdk\lib` and the current directory (that is, the . directory) must be on the *CLASSPATH*.
3. The `CoreJavaBook` directory must also be on the *CLASSPATH*.

(Some environments use a JAVA_HOME environment variable, an `ini` file or a registry entry; please consult the documentation for your environment for more information.).

Double-check these settings and reboot your computer if you run into trouble. (If you did not follow our recommendation to install the JDK in the `jdk` directory, remember to replace `jdk` by `jdk1.1.1` or `jdk1.1.2` or whatever is the location of the Java directory used by your version of the JDK.)

Memory Problems

If you have only 16 MB of memory, you may get "insufficient memory" errors from the Java compiler. In that case, close memory hogs like Netscape and Microsoft Exchange. If you have less than 16 MB of memory, you will probably be unable to compile large programs.

NOTE: Only the compiler and applet viewer pig out on memory. Once you compile an application, you should have no trouble running it with the Java interpreter or Netscape, even with less than 16 MB of memory.

Case Sensitivity

Java is case sensitive. HTML is sometimes case sensitive. DOS is not case sensitive. This caused us no end of grief, especially since Java can give very bizarre error messages when it messes up because of a spelling error. Always check file names, parameter names, class names, keywords, and so on for capitalization.

About Other Platforms

Watch the Web for information on other platforms. For starters, keep track of the discussions on the groups `comp.lang.java.*` such as `comp.lang.java.programmer`. They will often report information first on updates or on versions for new platforms. This also seems to be the place where (after you filter out some noise) you will see reports on problems with current versions.

IBM has a site for their Java work on OS/2 and Win 3.1 (`ncc.hursley.ibm.com/`).

The latest information about Linux can usually be found on the Linux news groups, and one site that will usually have the current version is `ftp://java.blackdown.org/pub/Java/`.

Updates and Bug Fixes

The CD-ROM contains several hundred files, and some of them are bound to have minor glitches and inconsistencies. We will keep a list of frequently asked questions, bug reports, and bug fixes on the Web page `http://www.horstmann.com/corejava.html`. *Please* read the FAQ before sending in a complaint or bug report. We also welcome any suggestions for improvements.

CHAPTER 3

- A Very Simple Java Program
- Comments
- Data Types
- Variables
- Assignments and Initializations
- Operators
- Strings
- Control Flow
- Class Methods (User-Defined Functions)
- Arrays

Fundamental Programming Structures in Java

At this point, we are assuming that you successfully installed Java and were able to run the sample programs in Chapter 2. It is time to show how to program in Java. This chapter shows you how the basic programming concepts such as data types, loops, and user-defined functions (actually, they are usually called *methods* in Java) are implemented. If you are an experienced C++ programmer, you can get away with just skimming this chapter: concentrate on the C/C++ notes that are interspersed throughout the text. Programmers coming from another background, such as Visual Basic (VB), will find most of the concepts familiar and all of the syntax maddening—you will want to read this chapter very carefully.

Unfortunately, getting output from Java is cumbersome. For this reason, almost all the sample programs in this chapter will be "toy" programs, designed to illustrate a concept. In all cases they will simply send or receive information to or from the console. (For example, if you are using Windows 95, the console is an MS-DOS window.) In particular, we will be writing *applications* rather than *applets* in this chapter.

If output in Java is cumbersome, input is even worse. Since it is hard to write even toy programs without a decent method of getting input from the user, the CD contains sufficient code for doing simple (prompted) input. We suggest not worrying too much about how input works at first. We will explain some of the details later in this chapter and finish it off in the next chapter.

A Very Simple Java Program

Let's look more closely at about the simplest Java program you can have:

```
public class FirstSample
{  public static void main(String[] args)
   {  System.out.println("We will not use 'Hello world!'");
   }
}
```

After you compile this *source code*, you obtain a bytecode file. When you run the bytecode file through the Java interpreter, this example simply displays the quoted string on the console (an MS-DOS window for users of Windows 95).

It is worth spending all the time you need in order to understand the framework of this sample; the pieces will reoccur in all applications. First and foremost, *Java is case sensitive*. If you made any mistakes in capitalization (such as typing `Main` instead of `main`), the program will not compile.

Having said this, let's look at this source code from the top. The keyword `public` is called an *access modifier;* these control what other parts of a program can use this code. We will have more to say about access modifiers in Chapter 5. The keyword `class` is there because everything in a Java program lives inside a class. Although we will spend a lot more time on classes in the next chapter, for now think of a class as a container for the data and methods (functions) that make up part or all of an application. As mentioned in Chapter 1, classes are the building blocks with which all Java applications and applets are built. *Everything* in a Java program must be inside a class.

Following the keyword `class` is the name of the class. You need to make the file name for the source code the same as the name of the class with the extension *.java* appended. Thus, we would store this code in a file called `FirstSample.java` (notice that long file names are needed). The compiled bytecode file is then automatically called `FirstSample.class` and stored in the same directory. The Java compiler looks at the name of the class and not at the name of the file where the source code was stored to determine the file name for the compiled bytecode file.

(The CD stores the code for each sample in its own directory. For example, the first sample program is stored in the `\CoreJavaBook\ch3\FirstSample` directory.)

NOTE: Applets have a different structure—see Chapter 10 for information on applets.

When you use

```
java NameOfClass
```

to run a compiled program, the Java interpreter always starts execution with the code in the `main` method in the class you indicate. Thus, you *must* have a `main`

method for your code to execute. You can, of course, add your own methods to a class and call them from the `main` method. (We cover writing your own methods later in this chapter.)

Next, notice the braces in the source code. In Java, as in C/C++ (but not in Pascal or VB), braces are used to delineate the parts (usually called *blocks*) in your program. A VB programmer can think of the outermost pair of braces as corresponding to a Sub/End Sub pair; a Pascal programmer can relate them to the first begin/end pair. In Java, the code for any method must be started by an open brace and so ended by a close brace. (We will have more to say about braces later in this chapter.)

Brace styles have inspired an inordinate amount of useless controversy. We use a style that lines up the braces that delineate each block. Since white space is irrelevant to the Java compiler, you can use whatever brace style you like. We will have more to say about the use of braces when we talk about the various kinds of loops.

If you are not a C++ programmer, don't worry about the keywords `static void`. For now, just think of them as part of what you need to get a Java program to compile. By the end of Chapter 4, you will understand this incantation completely. The point to remember for now is that every Java application must have a `main` method whose header is identical to the one shown here.

C++ NOTE: You know what a class is. Java classes are similar to C++ classes, but there are a few differences that can trap you. For example, in Java *all* functions are member functions of some class, and the standard terminology refers to them as *methods* rather than member functions. Thus, in Java you must have a shell class for the `main` method. You may also be familiar with the idea of *static member functions*. These are functions defined inside a class that do not operate on objects. The `main` method (function) in Java is always static. Finally, as in C/C++, the `void` keyword indicates that this method (function) does not return a value.

VB NOTE: The closest analogy in VB would be a program that uses a Sub Main rather than a startup form. Recall that if you choose to have a Sub Main, *everything* has to be explicitly called from Sub Main.

Next, turn your attention to this fragment.

```
{   System.out.println("We will not use 'Hello world!'");
}
```

Braces mark the beginning and end of the *body* of the method. This method has only one statement in it. As in most programming languages, you can think of Java statements as being the sentences of the language. In Java *every statement must end with a semicolon.* (For those coming from a Pascal background, the semicolon in Java is not the statement separator, but rather the statement terminator.)

In particular, neither white space nor carriage returns mark the end of a statement, so statements can span lines if need be. There are essentially no limits on the length of a statement. Here we are using a statement that outputs a single line of text to the console.

Here we are using the `System.out` object and asking it to use its `println` method. The `println` method works with a string and displays it on the standard console. It then adds a line feed. Note that Java, like C/C++ and VB (but not Pascal), use double quotes for strings. (See the section on strings later in this chapter for more information.)

Methods in Java, like functions in any programming languages, can use zero, one, or more *arguments* (some languages call them *parameters*). Even the `main` method in Java accepts what the user types on the command line as its argument. You will see how to use this information later in this chapter. (Even if a method takes zero arguments, you must still use empty parentheses.)

NOTE: You also have a `print` method in `System.out` that doesn't add a carriage return/line feed combination to the string.

C++ NOTE: Although in Java, as in C/C++, the `main` method receives an array of command-line arguments, the array syntax in Java is different. A `String[]` is an array of strings and so `args` denotes an array of strings. The name of the program is not stored in the `args` array, however. For example, when you start up the program `Bjarne.java` as

```
java Bjarne Stroustrup
```

from the command line, then `args[0]` will be `Stroustrup` and not `Bjarne` or `java`.

Comments

Comments in Java, like comments in most programming languages, do not show up in the executable program. Thus, you can add as many comments as needed without fear of bloating the code. Java has three ways of showing comments. The most common method is a `//`, to be used for a comment that will run from the `//` to the end of the line.

```
System.out.println("We will not use 'Hello world!'");
// is this too cute?
```

In the case of `//` comments, the end of a line is marked by a carriage return, a line feed, or both.

When larger comments are needed, you can mark each line with a `//`, but it is more common to use the `/*` and `*/` that let you block off a larger comment. This is shown in Example 3-1.

Example 3-1: FirstSample.java

```
/*
This is the first sample program in Core Java Chapter 3
Copyright (C) 1997 Cay Horstmann and Gary Cornell
*/

public class FirstSample
{  public static void main(String[] args)
   {  System.out.println("We will not use 'Hello, World!'");
   }
}
```

The // comment style is painful to modify when you need to extend comments over multiple lines, so we suggest using it only when you are sure the comment will never grow. (Comments do not nest in Java.)

Finally, there is a third kind of comment that can be used to generate documentation automatically. This comment uses a `/**` to start and a `*/` to end. For more on this type of comment and on automatic documentation generation, please see Appendix II.

Data Types

Java is an example of a *strongly typed language*. This means that every variable must have a declared type. There are eight *primitive types* in Java. Six of them are number types (four integer and two floating-point types); one is the character type `char`, used for characters in Unicode encoding (see the section on the `char` type), and one is a `boolean` type for truth values.

NOTE: Java 1.1 has an arbitrary precison arithmetic package built into it. "Big numbers" as they are called, however, are Java *objects* and not a new Java type. You will see an example of a computation with big numbers in Chapter 5.

VB NOTE: Java hasn't any type analogous to the Variant data type, in which you can store all possible types. It does have a way of converting all types to strings for display purposes that you will see later in this chapter.

Integers

The integer types are for numbers without fractional parts. Negative values are allowed. Java provides the four integer types shown in Table 3-1.

Table 3-1: Java integer types

Type	Storage Requirement	Range (inclusive)
`int`	4 bytes	–2,147,483,648 to 2,147,483,647 (just over 2 billion)
`short`	2 bytes	–32,768 to 32,767
`long`	8 bytes	–9,223,372,036,854,775,808L to 9,223,372,036,854,775,807L
`byte`	1 byte	–128 to 127

In most situations, the `int` type is the most practical. If you want to represent the national debt in pennies, you'll need to resort to a `long`. The `byte` and `short` types are mainly intended for specialized applications such as low-level file handling, or for large arrays when storage space is at a premium. The point is that, under Java, the integer types do not depend on the machine on which you will be running the Java code. This alleviates a major pain for the programmer who wants to move software from one platform to another, or even between operating systems on the same platform. A C program that runs well on a SPARC may exhibit integer overflow under Windows 3.1. Since Java programs must run with the same results on all machines by its design, the ranges for the various types are fixed. Of course, having platform-independent integer types brings a small performance penalty, but in the case of Java, this is not a particular problem. (There are worse bottlenecks....)

Long integer literals have a suffix `L` (for example, `4000000000L`). Hexadecimal numbers have a prefix `0x`, for example, `0xCAFE`.

C++ NOTE: In C and C++, `int` denotes the integer type that depends on the target machine. On a 16-bit processor, like the 8086, integers are 2 bytes. On a 32-bit processor like the Sun SPARC, they are 4-byte quantities. On an Intel Pentium, the integer type depends on the operating system: for DOS and Windows 3.1, integers are 2 bytes. When using 32-bit mode for Windows 95 or Windows NT programs, integers are 4 bytes. In Java, the sizes of all numeric types are platform independent.

VB NOTE: The ranges for the integer types are quite different in Java. An integer in VB corresponds to a `short` in Java. The `int` type in Java corresponds to the `Longint` type in VB, and so on.

Floating-Point Types

The floating-point types denote numbers with fractional parts. There are two floating-point types, as shown in Table 3-2.

Table 3-2: Floating-point types

Type	Storage Requirement	Range
`float`	4 bytes	range, roughly ±3.40282347E+38F (6–7 significant decimal digits)
`double`	8 bytes	range, roughly ±1.79769313486231570E+308 (15 significant digits)

The name `double` refers to the fact that these numbers have twice the precision of the `float` type. (Some people call these *double-precision* variables.) Here, the type of choice in most applications is `double`. The limited precision of `float` is simply not sufficient for many situations. Seven significant (decimal) digits may be enough to precisely express your annual salary in dollars and cents, but it won't be enough for your company president's salary. The only reason to use `float` is in the rare situations in which the slightly faster processing of single-precision numbers is important or when you need to store a large number of them.

Literals of type `float` have a suffix `F`, for example, `3.402F`. Floating-point literals without a suffix (such as 3.402) are of type `double`. All the floating-point types follow the IEEE 754 specification. They will overflow on range errors and underflow on operations like a divide-by-zero.

The Character Type (`char`)

First, the `char` type, unlike the string literals, uses single quotes to denote a `char`. Second, the `char` type denotes characters in the Unicode encoding scheme. You may not be familiar with Unicode, and, fortunately, you don't need to worry much about it if you don't program international applications. (Even if you do, you still won't have to worry about it too much because Unicode was designed to make the use of non-Roman characters easy to handle.) Because Unicode was designed to handle essentially all characters in all written languages in the world, it is a 2-byte code. This allows 65,536 characters, unlike ASCII/ANSI, which is a 1-byte code allowing only 255 characters. The familiar ASCII/ANSI code that you use in Windows programming is a subset of Unicode. More precisely, it is the first 255 characters in the Unicode coding scheme. Thus, character codes like `'a'`, `'1'`, and `'['` are valid Unicode characters. Unicode characters are most often expressed in terms of a hexadecimal encoding scheme that runs from `'\u0000'` to `'\uFFFF'` (with `'\u0000'` to `'\u00FF'` being the ordinary ASCII/ANSI characters). The `\u` prefix indicates a Unicode value and the four hexadecimal digits tell you what unicode character. For example, `\u2122` is the trademark symbol (™). (For more on Unicode, you might want to check out their Web site at `www.unicode.org`.)

Besides the `\u` escape character that indicated the encoding of a Unicode character, Java allows you to use the following escape sequences for special characters.

`\b`	backspace	`\u0008`
`\t`	tab	`\u0009`
`\n`	linefeed	`\u000a`
`\r`	carriage return	`\u000d`
`\"`	double quote	`\u0022`
`\'`	single quote	`\u0027`
`\\`	backslash	`\u005c`

NOTE: Although you can theoretically use any Unicode character in a Java program, whether you can actually see it displayed depends on your browser and (ultimately) on your operating system. For example, we could not use Java to output Kanji on a machine running the U.S. version of Windows 95. For more on internationalization issues, please see Volume 2.

C++ NOTE: In C and C++, `char` denotes an *integral* type, namely, 1-byte integers. The standard is coy about the exact range. It can be either 0…255 or –128…127. In Java, `char` data are not numbers. Converting from numbers to characters requires an explicit cast in Java. (Chars can be considered as integers if need be without an explicit cast.)

Boolean

The `boolean` type has two values, `false` and `true`. It is used for logical testing using the relational operators that Java, like any programming language, supports.

C++ NOTE: In C, there is no Boolean type. Instead, the convention is that any non-zero value denotes true, and zero denotes false. In C++, a Boolean type (called `bool`, not `boolean`) has recently been added to the language standard. It, too, has values `false` and `true`, but for historical reasons conversions between Boolean values and integers are allowed, and you can still use numbers or pointers in test conditions. In Java, you cannot convert between numbers and Boolean values—not even with a cast.

VB NOTE: In VB any non-zero value is regarded as true and zero is regarded as false. This simply will not work in Java—you cannot use a number where a Boolean value is needed.

Variables

Java, like C++ and Pascal-based languages, requires you to declare the type of a variable. (Of course, good programming practice in VB would require this as well.) You declare a variable by placing the type first, followed by the name of the variable. Here are some examples:

```
byte b; // for space sensitive considerations
int anIntegerVariable;
long aLongVariable; // for the national debt in pennies
char ch;
```

Notice the semicolon at the end of each declaration (and the positioning of the comments in the first and third line). The semicolon is necessary because a declaration is a complete Java statement.

You cannot use a Java reserved word for a variable name. (See Appendix I for a list of reserved words.) The rules for a variable name are as follows:

A name must begin with a letter and be a sequence of letters or digits. A letter is defined as `'A'-'Z'`, `'a'-'z'`, `'_'`, `'$'`, or any Unicode character that denotes a letter in a language. For example, German users can use umlauts such as `'ä'` in variable names, Greek speakers could use a µ. Digits are `'0'-'9'` and any Unicode characters that denote a digit in a language. Symbols like `'+'` or `'©'` cannot be used inside variable names. *All* characters in the name of a variable are significant and *case is also significant*. The length of a variable name is essentially unlimited.

TIP: If you are really curious as to what Unicode characters are "letters" as far as Java is concerned, you can use the `isJavaIdentifierStart` and `isJavaIdentifierPart` methods in the `Character` class to check.

You can include multiple declarations on a single line

```
int i, j; //both are integers unlike in VB!
```

but we generally comment and initialize each variable separately and so prefer declarations on separate lines.

Assignments and Initializations

After you declare a variable, you should explicitly initialize it by means of an assignment statement—you should never have uninitialized variables. (And the compiler will usually prevent you from having them anyway.) You assign to a previously declared variable using the variable name on the left, an equal sign (=), and then some Java expression that has an appropriate value on the right.

```
int foo; // this is a declaration
foo = 37; // this is an assignment
```

Here's an example of an assignment to a character variable:

```
char yesChar;
yesChar = 'Y';
```

Notice that chars (unlike string literals) use single quotes to identify the character. It is also possible to use a direct hexadecimal representation of a Unicode char. To do this, you must translate the Unicode character number into a four digit hexadecimal code—and you must use the two leading zeros if needed. For example, a capital `'A'` has Unicode (and ASCII/ANSI, of course) code decimal 65 = hex 41. If you wanted to use the code for the character, you could use:

```
char capitalA;
capitalA = '\u0041'; // decimal 65
```

Finally, in Java you can put declarations anywhere in your code, but you can only declare a variable once in any block in a method. (See the section on Control Flow in this chapter for more on blocks.)

NOTE: One nice feature of Java that it inherited from C/C++ is the ability to both declare and initialize a variable on the same line. (This is usually called a definition of a variable and is not technically an assignment.) This is also done with an = sign. For example:

```
int i = 10; // we will countdown with this
```

Conversions between Numeric Types

Java does not have any trouble multiplying, say, an integer by a double—it will treat the result as a double. More generally, any binary operations on numeric variables of different types will be acceptable and be treated in the following fashion:

- If any of the operands is of type `double`, the other one will be treated as a `double` for the scope of the operation.
- Otherwise, if any of the operands is of type `float`, the other one will be treated as a `float`.

- Otherwise, if any of the operands is of type `long`, the other one will be treated as a `long`.

This works similarly down the line of the integer types: `int`, `short`, and `byte`.

On the other hand, there are obviously times when you want to consider a `double` as an integer. All numeric conversions are possible in Java, but, of course, information may be lost. These conversions are usually done by means of *casts*. The syntax for casting is to give the target type in parentheses, followed by the variable name. For example:

```
double x = 9.997;
int nx = (int)x;
```

Then the variable `nx` has the value 9, as casting a floating-point value to an integer discards the fractional part.

If you want to *round* a floating-point number to the *nearest* integer (which is the more useful operation in most cases), use the `Math.round` method:

```
double x = 9.997;
int nx = (int)Math.round(x);
```

Now the variable `nx` has the value 10. You still need to use the cast (`int`) when you call `round`. The return value of the `round` function is a `long`, and a `long` can only be assigned to an `int` with an explicit cast since there is the possibility of information loss.

NOTE: Java does not complain ("throw an exception" in Java-speak—see Chapter 12) if you try to cast a number of one type to another that is out of the range for the target type. The result will be a truncated number that has a different value. It is, therefore, a good idea to explicitly test that the value is in the correct range before you perform the cast.

C++ NOTE: You cannot cast between Boolean values and any numeric type.

Finally, Java allows you to make certain assignment conversions by assigning the value of a variable of one type to another without an explicit cast. Those that are permitted are

```
byte →short →int →long →float →double
```

where you can always assign a variable of a type that is to the left to the type on its right in the list above.

Constants

Java has only very limited ways for defining constants. In particular, you cannot define local constants for an individual method like `main`. Instead, you can only have constants that are available to all the methods in the class. These are usually called *class constants*. The keywords used in this example will be explained in Chapter 4, but here is an example of using a class constant:

```
class UsesConstants
{  public static final double G = 32;
   // gravitation in feet/second squared;
   public static void main(String[] args)
   {  System.out.println(G + " feet per second squared");
   }
}
```

Note that the definition appears before the function header that defines the `main` method and must use the keywords `static final`.

C++ NOTE: `const` is a reserved Java keyword, but it is not currently used for anything. You must use `public static final` for a global constant. For a local constant, just pretend it is a variable.

Operators

The usual arithmetic operators `+ - * /` are used in Java for addition, subtraction, multiplication, and division. The `/` operator denotes integer division if both arguments are integers, and floating-point division otherwise. Integer remainder (i.e., the mod function) is denoted by `%`. For example, `15 / 4` is 3, `15 % 2` is 1, and `11.0 / 4` is 2.75. You can use the arithmetic operators in your variable initializations:

```
int n = 5;
int a = 2 * n; // a is 10
```

There is actually a shortcut for using binary arithmetic operators in an assignment. For example,

```
x += 4;
```

is equivalent to

```
x = x + 4;
```

(In general, place the operator to the left of the = sign.)

Exponentiation

Unlike languages like VB, Java has no operator for raising a quantity to a power: you must use the `pow` function. The `pow` function is part of the `Math` class in `Java.lang`. The usual way of doing exponentiation is via the statement:

```
double y = Math.pow(x, a);
```

which sets `y` to be `x` raised to the power a (x^a). The `pow` function takes arguments that are both of type `double` and returns a `double` as well.

NOTE: The `Math` class in Java has the full complement of functions a scientist or engineer would need. For example, there are constants for π and e (as doubles so they are very accurate). You also have the square root, natural log, exponential and trig functions. However, even people who would never use any of these scientific functions will occasionaly need the `Math` class because it also contains methods for rounding off floats and longs, taking the maximum and minimum of two numbers of the same type, the absolute value function, and the greatest integer function.

Increment and Decrement Operators

Programmers, of course, know that one of the most common operations with a numeric variable is to add or subtract one. Java, following in the footsteps of C and C++, has both increment and decrement operators: `x++` adds one to the current value of the variable `x`, and `x--` subtracts one from it. For example, the code

```
int n = 12;
n++;
```

changes `n` to 13. Because these operators change the value of a variable, they cannot be applied to numbers themselves. For example, `4++` is not a legal statement.

There are actually two forms of these operators; you have seen the "postfix," i.e., after the variable form. There is also a prefix form, `++n`. Both change the value of the variable by one. The difference between the two only appears when they are used inside expressions. The prefix form does the addition first; the postfix form evaluates to the old value of the variable.

```
int m = 7;
int n = 7;
int a = 2 * ++m; // now a is 16, m is 8
int b = 2 * n++; // now b is 14, n is 8
```

We recommend against using `++` inside other expressions as this often leads to annoying bugs that are hard to track down. (Of course, while it is the `++` operator that gives the C++ language its name, it also led to the first joke made by anti-C++ programmers who have long complained about the bug-ridden code that is too often produced by sloppy C++ coding. This joke points out that even the name of the language contains a bug: "After all, it should really be called ++C, since we only want to use a language after it has been improved." Java programmers, on the other hand, really are dealing with a ++C. This is because Java really does make it easier to produce bug-free code. It does this by eliminating many of C++ more bug-prone features such as pointer arithmetic, memory allocation, and null-terminated arrays of chars. Of course, it does retain the murky side effects of prefix and postfix `++`.)

Relational and Boolean Operators

The value of a variable or expression is compared with a double equal sign, `==`. For example, the value of

```
(3 == 7)
```

is `false`.

VB NOTE: It is important to remember that Java uses different symbols for assignment and equality testing.

C++ NOTE: Java eliminates the possibility of bugs resulting from the use of the = sign when you meant the ==. A line that begins `if (k=0)` won't even compile since this evaluates to the integer 0, which doesn't convert to a Boolean value in Java.

Use a `!=` for inequality. For example, the value of

```
(3 != 7)
```

is `true`.

Finally, you have the usual `<` (less than), `>` (greater than), `<=` (less than or equal), and `>=` (greater than or equal) operators.

Java, following C++, uses `&&` for the logical *and* operator and `||` for the logical *or* operator. As you can easily remember from the `!=` operator, the exclamation point is the negation operator. The `&&` and `||` operators are evaluated in "short circuit" fashion. This means that when you have something like:

```
A && B
```

once the truth value of the expression `A` has been determined to be false, the value for the expression `B` is *not* calculated. (See the sections on conditionals for an example of where this is useful.)

Bitwise Operators

When working with any of the integer types, you have operators that can work directly with the bits that make up the integers. This means that you can use masking techniques to get at individual bits. The bitwise operators are:

`&` ("and") `|` ("or") `^` ("xor") `~` ("not")

VB NOTE: Remember that ^ is the xor operator and not the power operator.

These operators work on bit patterns. For example, if `foo` is an integer variable, then

```
int fourthBit = (foo&8)/8;
```

gives you a one if the fourth bit from the right in the binary representation of foo is one, and a zero if not. This technique lets you mask out all but a single bit when need be.

There are also >> and << operators, which shift a bit pattern to the right or left. There is no need to use these operators to divide and multiply by powers of two, though. Compilers are almost certainly smart enough to change multiplication by powers of two into the appropriate shift operators. There is even a >>> operator that fills the top bits with zero, whereas >> extends the sign bit into the top bits. There is no <<< operator.

C++ NOTE: In C/C++, there is no guarantee as to whether >> performs an arithmetic shift (extending the sign bit) or a logical shift (filling in with zeroes). Implementors are free to choose whatever is more efficient. That means the C/C++ >> operator is really only defined for non-negative numbers. Java removes that ambiguity.

Parentheses and Operator Hierarchy

As in all programming languages, you are best off using parentheses to indicate the order in which you want operations to be carried out. However, in Java the hierarchy of operations is as follows:

`[] . ()` (method call)	left to right
`! ~ ++ --` + (unary) – (unary) `()` (cast) `new`	right to left
`* / %`	left to right
`+ -`	left to right
`<< >> >>>`	left to right
`< <= > >= instanceof`	left to right
`== !=`	left to right
`&`	left to right
`^`	left to right
`|`	left to right
`&&`	left to right
`||`	left to right
`?:`	left to right
`= += -= *= /= %= &= |= ^= <<= >>= >>>=`	right to left

If no parentheses are used, operations are performed in the hierarchical order indicated. Operators on the same level are processed from left to right, except for those that are right associative, as indicated in the preceding table.

C++ NOTE: Unlike C or C++, Java does not have a comma operator. However, you can use a *comma-separated list of expressions* in the first and third slot of a `for` statement.

Strings

Strings are sequences of characters, such as `"hello"`. Java does not have a built-in string type. Instead, the standard Java library contains a predefined class called, naturally enough, `String` that contains most of what you want.

```
String e = ""; // an empty string
String greeting = "Hello";
```

Concatenation

Java, like most programming languages, allows you to use the + sign to join (concatenate) two strings together.

```
String expletive = "Expletive";
String PG13 = "deleted";
String message = expletive + PG13;
```

The above code makes the value of the string variable message `"Expletivedeleted"`. (Note the lack of a space between the words: the + sign joins two strings together in the order received, *exactly* as they are given.)

When you concatenate a string with a value that is not a string, the latter is converted to a string. (As we will see in Chapter 5, every Java object can be converted to a string.) For example:

```
String rating = "PG" + 13;
```

sets `rating` to the string `"PG13"`.

This feature is commonly used in output statements; for example,

```
System.out.println("The answer is " + answer);
```

is perfectly acceptable and will print what one would want (and with the correct spacing because of the space after `is`).

VB NOTE: Although Java will convert a number to a string when concatenating with another string, it does not add a space in front of a positive value.

Substrings

You extract a substring from a larger string with the `substring` method of the `String` class. For example,

```
String greeting = "Hello";
String s = greeting.substring(0, 4);
```

creates a string consisting of the characters `"Hell"`. Java counts strings in a peculiar fashion: the first character in a string has position 0, just like in C and C++. (In C, there was a technical reason for counting positions starting at 0, but that reason has long gone away, and only the nuisance remains.)

For example, the character `'H'` has position 0 in the string `"Hello"`, and the character `'o'` has position 4. The second argument of `substring` is the first position that you *do not* want to copy. In our case, we want to copy the characters in positions 0, 1, 2, and 3 (from position 0 to position 3 inclusive). As `substring` counts it, this means from position 0 inclusive to position 4 *exclusive.*

There is one advantage to the way `substring` works: it is easy to compute the length of the substring. The string `s.substring(a, b)` always has `b - a` characters. For example, the substring `"Hell"` has length 4 – 0 = 4.

String Editing

To find out the length of a string, use the `length` method. For example:

```
String greeting = "Hello";
int n = greeting.length(); // is 5.
```

Just as `char` denotes a Unicode character, `String` denotes a sequence of Unicode characters. It is possible to get at individual characters of a string. For example, `s.charAt(n)` returns the Unicode character at position `n`, where `n` is between 0 and `s.length()` – 1.

However, you can't *change* a character in the string. If you want to turn `greeting` into `"Help!"`, you cannot change the third position of `greeting` into a `'p'` and the fourth position into a `'!'`. If you are a C programmer, this will make you feel pretty helpless. How are you going to modify the string? In Java, it is quite easy: take the substring that you want to keep and concatenate it with the characters that you want to replace.

```
greeting = greeting.substring(0, 3) + "p!";
```

This changes the current value of the `greeting` variable to `"Help!"`.

Since you cannot change the individual characters in a Java string, the documentation refers to the objects of the `String` class as being *immutable.* You should think of them as first-class objects just like the number 3 is always 3, and the string `"Hello"` will always contain the character sequence

'H', 'e', 'l', 'l', 'o'. You cannot change these values. You can, however, change the contents of the string *variable* greeting and make it refer to a different string. (Just as you can make a numeric variable currently holding the value 3 hold the value 4.)

Isn't that a lot less efficient? It would seem simpler to change the characters than to build up a whole new string from scratch. Well, yes and no. Indeed, it isn't efficient to generate a new string that holds the concatenation of "Hel" and "p!". But immutable strings have one great advantage: The compiler can arrange that strings are *shared*.

To understand how this works, think of the various strings as sitting on the heap. (For non C/C++ programmers, think of them as just being located in memory somewhere.) String variables then point to locations on the heap. For example, the substring greeting.substring(0, 3) is just a pointer to the existing "Hello" string, together with the range of characters that are used in the substring. Overall, the designers of Java decided that the efficiency of string-sharing outweighs the inefficiency of immutability.

Look at your own programs; we suspect that most of the time, you don't change strings—you just compare them. Of course, there are some cases in which direct manipulation of strings is more efficient. (One example is when assembling strings from individual characters that come from a file or the keyboard.) For these situations, Java provides a separate StringBuffer class that we describe in Volume 2. If you are not concerned with the efficiency of string handling (which is not a bottleneck in many Java applications anyway), you can ignore StringBuffer and just use String.

C++ NOTE: C programmers generally are bewildered when they see Java strings for the first time, because they think of strings as arrays of characters:

```
char greeting[] = "Hello";
```

That is the wrong analogy: a Java string is roughly analogous to a char* pointer,

```
char* greeting = "Hello";
```

When you replace greeting with another string, the Java code does roughly the following:

```
char* temp = malloc(6);
strncpy(temp, greeting, 3);
strcpy(temp + 3, "p!");
greeting = temp;
```

Sure, now greeting points to the string "Help!". And even the most hardened C programmer must admit that the Java syntax is more pleasant than a sequence of strncpy calls. But what if we make another assignment to greeting?

```
greeting = "Howdy";
```

Don't we have a memory leak? After all, the `"Help!"` string was allocated on the heap. C and C++ programmers *must* change their way of thinking because Java does automatic garbage collection. Java automatically reclaims any unused memory. If the string `"Help!"` is no longer needed, its memory will eventually be recycled.

If you are a C++ programmer and use the `string` class defined by ANSI C++, you will be much more comfortable with the Java `String` type. C++ `string` objects also perform automatic allocation and deallocation of memory. The memory management is performed explicitly by constructors, assignment operators, and destructors. However, C++ strings are mutable—you can modify individual characters in a string.

Testing Strings for Equality

To test whether or not two strings are equal, use the `equals` method;

```
s.equals(t)
```

returns `true` if the strings `s` and `t` are equal, `false` otherwise. For the `equals` method, `s` and `t` can be string variables or string constants. For example,

```
"Hello".equals(command)
```

is perfectly legal.

Do *not* use the == operator to find out if two strings are equal! It only determines whether or not the strings are stored in the same location.

Sure, if the strings are in the same location, they must be equal. But it is entirely possible to store multiple copies of identical strings in different places.

```
String greeting = "Hello"; //initialize greeting to a string
if (greeting == "Hello") . . . // probably true
if (greeting.substring(0, 4) == "Hell") . . . // probably false
```

If the compiler would always arrange for equal strings to be shared, then you could use == for testing equality, but it doesn't and you can't. (The trouble is that string storage is implementation dependent. The standard implementation only shares string constants, not strings that are the result of operations like + or `substring`.) Therefore, *never* use == to compare strings.

C++ NOTE: If you are used to the C++ `string` class, you have to be particularly careful about equality testing. That class does overload the == operator to test for equality of the string contents. It is pretty silly that Java goes out of its way to give strings the same "look and feel" as numeric values, but then makes strings behave like pointers for equality testing. The language designers could have redefined == for strings, just as they made a special arrangement for +. Oh well, every language has its share of inconsistencies.

C programmers never use == to compare strings, but use `strcmp` instead. The Java function `compareTo` is the exact analog to `strcmp`. You can use

```
if (greeting.compareTo("Help") == 0) . . .
```

but it seems clearer to use `equals` instead.

To test if two strings are identical except for the upper/lowercase letter distinction, use the `equalsIgnoreCase` method.

Useful String Functions

The `String` class in Java contains more than 50 methods. A surprisingly large number of them are sufficiently useful so that we can imagine using them on a day-to-day basis. The following table summarizes the ones we found most useful.

Signature	Description
`char charAt(int index)`	Returns the character at the specified location.
`int compareTo(String anotherString)`	Compares this string to another specified string in Unicode order (this is alphabetical for English with upper case letters coming before lower case letters.) It returns a positive integer if the other string comes after the original string, 0 if they are equal, and negative if it comes before.
`boolean endsWith(String suffix)`	Determines whether the string ends with some suffix (useful for URLs for example).
`boolean equals(Object anObject)`	Compares this string to the specified object (because they didn't want to overload the == operator).
`boolean equalsIgnoreCase(String anotherString)`	Compares this string to another object regardless of case. (Although we couldn't test it completely, it is supposed to work for all alphabets.)
`int indexOf(String str)`	Returns the location of the first occurrence of the specified substring or –1 if the string parameter is not a substring.
`int indexOf(String str, int fromIndex)`	Starting the search at the position indicated by the integer parameter, returns the location of the first occurrence of the specified substring or –1 if the string parameter is not a substring.

Signature	Description
`int lastIndexOf(String str)`	Returns the location of the last occurrence of the string parameter as a substring or –1 if it is not a substring.
`int lastIndexOf(String str, int fromIndex)`	Starting at the location given by the index parameter, returns the location of the last occurrence of the specified substring if one exists or –1 if it is not a substring.
`int length()`	Returns the length of the string.
`String replace(char oldChar, char newChar)`	Makes a new string that replaces all occurrences of `oldChar` with `newChar`.
`boolean startsWith(String prefix)`	Determines whether this string starts with a certain string.
`String substring(int beginIndex)`	Returns a string which is made up of the part of the original string that starts at the given location.
`String substring(int beginIndex, int endIndex)`	Returns the piece of the string between the two endpoints specified (inclusive).
`String toLowerCase()`	Converts all of the characters in the string to lower case.
`String toUpperCase()`	Converts all of the characters in this String to upper case.
`String trim()`	Returns a new string by eliminating all leading and trailing spaces in the original string.

Reading Input

Reading input from the terminal is unbelievably difficult in plain Java. Naturally, that is not a problem for graphical programs that collect user input from a dialog box. But it is a problem for anyone who wants to write simple programs to learn the language. Consider a common task—reading a floating-point number. This turns out to be a nightmare of epic proportions. Before you look at the code, relax—the code library for this book gives you a simpler method for achieving this task. Example 3-2 shows what you have to do in plain Java:

Example 3-2: ReadDoubleTest.java

```
import java.io.*;
import java.text.*;

public class ReadDoubleTest
   // shows how to read a double the hard way
{  public static void main(String[] args)
   {  System.out.println
           ("Enter a number, I'll add two to it.");
      double x; // the number we wish to read
      try
```

```
        {   InputStreamReader isr
                = new InputStreamReader(System.in);
            BufferedReader br
                = new BufferedReader(isr);
            String s = br.readLine();
            DecimalFormat df = new DecimalFormat();
            Number n = df.parse(s);
            x = n.doubleValue();
        }
        catch(IOException e)
        {   x = 0;
        }
        catch(ParseException e)
        {   x = 0;
        }
        System.out.println(x + 2);
    }
}
```

That is great if you get paid by the lines of code that you write. For the rest of us, this book provides a simpler way. If you use the `Console` class in the `corejava` package, then you can read a floating-point number as follows:

```
import corejava.*; // important--imports corejava package

public class ConsoleTest
{  public static void main(String[] args)
   {  double x = Console.readDouble("Enter a number, I'll add
      two to it.");
      System.out.println(x + 2);
   }
}
```

Directions for Using the `Console` Class

Before we go on (so that we can give you some examples that are at least somewhat nontrivial!), this sidebar shows you what is needed in order to use the `Console` class to get various kinds of prompted input from the keyboard. The `Console` class has three methods. These methods let you:

- Capture an integer by a prompted input
- Capture a floating-point number with a prompted input
- Capture a string or word by a prompted input

The `Console` class may be found in the `corejava` subdirectory of the CoreJavaBook code that you can install from the CD. To use the `Console` class, it is important that you set up your CLASSPATH environment variable as described in Chapter 2.

Directions for Using the `Console` Class (continued)

Be sure to add the line: `import corejava.*;` to each program that uses the `Console` class. Then you can use this class as in the following example:

```
import corejava.*;
public class StringPromptSample
{   public static void main(String[] args)
    {   String yourName;
        yourName = Console.readString
           ("Please enter your name.");
        System.out.println("Hello " + yourName);
    }
}
```

If you compile and run this program, you will see that the `readString` method displays the string prompt and grabs the text the user enters before he or she hits the ENTER key.

More generally, you will have the following methods available to you (all use a string prompt):

`readWord(String prompt)` reads the string until the first space is entered.

`readInt(String prompt)` reads an integer. If you do not enter an integer, it reprompts you to enter the integer correctly.

`readDouble(String prompt)` reads a floating-point number in the double range. If you do not enter a floating point number, it reprompts you to do so.

All these functions can be "broken out of" by hitting the CTRL+C combination, which kills any Java application under Windows or Unix.

Formatting Output

You can print a number to the console (a DOS window, for example) by the statement `System.out.print(x)`.That command will print `x` with the maximum number of non-zero digits for that type. For example,

```
x = 10000.0 / 3.0;
System.out.print(x);
```

prints

```
3333.3333333333335
```

That is a problem if you want to display, for example, dollars and cents.

In Java 1.1, you can now *format* a number in order to make it look more appealing. The `NumberFormat` class in the `java.text` package has three methods that yield standard *formatters* for

- numbers
- currency values
- percentage values

Suppose that the United States locale is your default locale. (A *locale* is a set of specifications for country-specific properties of strings and numbers, such as collation order, currency symbol, and so on. Locales are an important concept for writing *internationalized* applications—programs that are acceptable to users from countries around the world. We will discuss internationalization in Volume 2.) Then, the value `10000.0 / 3.0` will print as

```
3,333.333
$3,333.33
333,333%
```

in these three formats. As you can see, the formatter adds the commas that separate the thousands, currency symbols ($), and percent signs.

To obtain a formatter for the default locale, use one of the three functions

```
NumberFormat.getNumberInstance()
NumberFormat.getCurrencyInstance()
NumberFormat.getPercentInstance()
```

Each of these functions returns an object of type `NumberFormat`. You can use that object to format one or more numbers. The `format` method then returns a string that contains the formatted number. Usually, you will simply display the newly formated number by printing the string:

```
double x = 10000.0 / 3.0;
NumberFormat nf = NumberFormat.getNumberInstance();
String fx = nf.format(x); // the string "3,333.33"
System.out.println(fx);
```

You can also obtain number formats that are appropriate for different locales. For example, let us look up the number formats that are used by German locale and use them to print our test output. There is a predefined object named `Locale.GERMAN` of a new type called `Locale` that knows about German number formatting rules. When we pass that `Locale` object to the `getNumberInstance` method, we obtain a formatter that follows those German rules.

```
double x = 10000.0 / 3.0;
NumberFormat nf = NumberFormat.getNumberInstance(Locale.GERMAN);
System.out.println(nf.format(x));
NumberFormat nf = NumberFormat.getCurrencyInstance(Locale.GERMAN);
System.out.println(nf.format(x));
```

This code prints the numbers

```
3.333,333
3.333,33 DM
```

Note that the German convention for periods and commas in numbers is the exact opposite from the U.S. convention: a comma is used as the decimal separator, and a period is used to separate thousands. Also, the formatter knows that the currency symbol (DM) is placed *after* the number.

Finally, you can create your own format. For example, you may want to show the number with six digits after the decimal point, but no thousands separator. To do this, you must define a `DecimalFormat`.

Indicate your formatting requirements in a format string that indicates what the number should look like.

```
DecimalFormat df = new DecimalFormat("0.######");
System.out.println(df.format(x));
```

This code prints the number in the following form:

```
3333.333333
```

As you can see, there is no longer a thousands separator, and there are six digits after the decimal point.

You can use the following characters in the format string:

Symbol	Meaning
`0`	A digit
`#`	A digit; don't show if it is a leading or trailing zero
`.`	Location of decimal separator
`,`	Location of grouping separator
`;`	Separates formats for positive and negative numbers
`-`	Negative prefix
`%`	Divide by 100 and show as percentage
any other symbol	Include symbol in output string

Here are a few examples.

Format String	Sample Number	Explanation
`,##0.00`	1,234.50	Two digits after the decimal point; show trailing zeroes Separate groups of thousands with commas If number is < 1, print leading zero (e.g., 0.123)
`$,##0.00;($,##0.00)`	($1,234.50)	Enclose negative numbers in parentheses instead of using a minus sign also prepends the $ symbol
`0.######`	1234.5	If number is between –1 and 1, print leading zero (e.g., 0.123) Don't show trailing zeroes

The `DecimalFormat` mechanism works well for formatting numbers such as currency values. However, it is not suitable for scientific notation, tables with fixed column widths, or numbers in octal or hexadecimal format. For those applications, you can use the `Format` class that we provide as part of the `corejava` package.

Directions for Using the `Format` Class

Not only did we give you a `Console` class to read characters from the screen, we also supply you with a class that can format output nicely. Rather than reinvent the wheel, we simply reimplemented the C `printf` function that has a good set of formatting options and is, for the most part, easy to use. For example, to format a floating-point number with a field width of 10 and two digits after the decimal point, you use

```
Format.print(System.out,"Your monthly payment is %10.2f\n",
   payment);
```

That sends a string like

```
"Your monthly payment is     1141.30\n"
```

to `System.out`. If you'd rather capture that string in a string variable, use

```
String s = new Format("Your monthly payment is %10.2f\n")
   .form(payment);
```

Directions for Using the `Format` Class (continued)

The output string contains all characters of the format string, except that the format specification (starting with a `%`) is replaced by the formatted value. However, a `%%` denotes a percent sign.

Unlike the `printf` statement in C, you can have only one formatted value at a time. If you need to print two values, use two calls.

```
Format.print(System.out, "With rate %6.3f", 100 * y);
Format.print(System.out, "%%, your monthly payment is
   %10.2f\n", payment);
```

Apart from the `%m.nf` format, the most common format is `%nd`, to print an integer in a field with width *n*. Those two will get you a long way, and you may never need to learn more about the formatting codes.

Here are the rules for the formatting specifiers. The code starts with % and ends with one of the letters `c`, `d`, `e`, `E`, `f`, `g`, `G`, `i`, `o`, `s`, `x`, `X`. They have the following meanings:

`f`	Floating-point number in fixed format
`e, E`	Floating-point number in exponential notation (scientific format). The `E` format results in an uppercase `E` for the exponent (`1.14130E+003`), the `e` format in a lowercase `e`.
`g, G`	Floating-point number in general format (fixed format for small numbers, exponential format for large numbers). Trailing zeroes are suppressed. The `G` format results in an uppercase `E` for the exponent (if any), the `g` format in a lowercase `e`.
`d, i`	Integer in decimal
`x`	Integer in hexadecimal
`o`	Integer in octal
`s`	String
`c`	Character

In between the % and the format code are the following fields. They are all optional.

+	Force display of + for positive numbers
0	Show leading zeroes
–	Align left in the field
space	Prepend a space in front of positive numbers
#	Use "alternate" format. Add `0` or `0x` for octal or hexadecimal numbers. Don't suppress trailing zeroes in general floating-point format.

Finally, to use our `Format` class, you must also add the `import corejava.*` before any class that will use it.

A Mortgage Calculator

As our first semi-serious application for Java, let's write a program that calculates the cost of a mortgage. We will use our `Console` class to prompt the user to enter the principal amount, the term in years, and the interest rate. The program will then output the mortgage amount per month.

NOTE: We use the following standard formula to calculate the mortgage payment.

$$\frac{\text{principal} \times \text{monthlyInterest}}{(1 - (1/(1 + \text{monthlyInterest})^{\text{Years} \times 12}))}$$

Example 3-3 shows the code.

Example 3-3: Mortgage.java

```
import corejava.*;
import java.text.*;

public class Mortgage
{  public static void main(String[] args)
   {  double principal;
      double yearlyInterest;
      int years;

      principal = Console.readDouble
         ("Loan amount (no commas):");
      yearlyInterest = Console.readDouble
         ("Interest rate in % (ex: use 7.5 for 7.5%):")/100;
      years = Console.readInt("The number of years:");

      double monthlyInterest = yearlyInterest / 12;
      double payment = principal * monthlyInterest
         / (1 - (Math.pow(1/(1 + monthlyInterest),
            years * 12)));
      System.out.println("Your payment is ");
      NumberFormat nf = NumberFormat.getCurrencyInstance();
      System.out.println(nf.format(payment));
   }
}
```

Control Flow

Java, like any programming language, supports both conditional statements and loops to determine control flow. We start with the conditional statements and then move on to loops. We end with the somewhat cumbersome `switch` statement that can be used when you have many values of a single expression to test for. Before we get into the actual control structures, you need to know more about *blocks*.

A block is any number of simple Java statements that are surrounded by a pair of braces. Blocks define the scope of your variables. However, it is not possible to declare identically named variables in two different blocks in the same method that exist at the same time.

NOTE: Since the scope of a variable starts at the place it was declared and goes to the end of the block in which it was declared, if you want to have a variable accessible to all the code in a method, you must declare it at the beginning of the method before you start any blocks.

C++ NOTE: The Java control flow constructs are identical to those in C and C++, with one exception. There is no `goto`, but there is a "labelled" version of `break` that you can use to break out of a nested loop (where you perhaps would have used a `goto` in C).

Conditional Statements

The simplest conditional statement in Java has the form

```
if (condition) statement;
```

but in Java, as in most programming languages, you will often want to execute multiple statements when a single condition is true. In this case, the conditional takes the form:

```
if (condition) { block }
```

The condition must be surrounded by parentheses, and here the "block" is, as indicated before, any number of statements that are surrounded by a pair of braces. (See Figure 3-1). For example:

```
if (yourSales >= target)
{   performance = "Satisfactory";
    bonus = 100;
}
```

Figure 3-1: Flowchart for the `if` statement

Here, all the statements surrounded by the braces will be executed when `yourSales` is greater than or equal to `target`.

NOTE: A block (sometimes called a *compound statement*) allows you to have more than one (simple) statement in any Java programming structure that might otherwise have a single (simple) statement.

The more general conditional in Java looks like this (see Figure 3-2):

`if (`*condition*`)` *statement*$_1$ `else` *statement*$_2$`;`

or, more likely,

`if (`*condition*`) {`*block*$_1$`} else {`*block*$_2$`}`

For example:

```
if (yourSales >= target)
{  performance = "Satisfactory";
   bonus = 100 + 0.01 * (yourSales - target);
}
else
{  performance = "Unsatisfactory";
   bonus = 0;
}
```

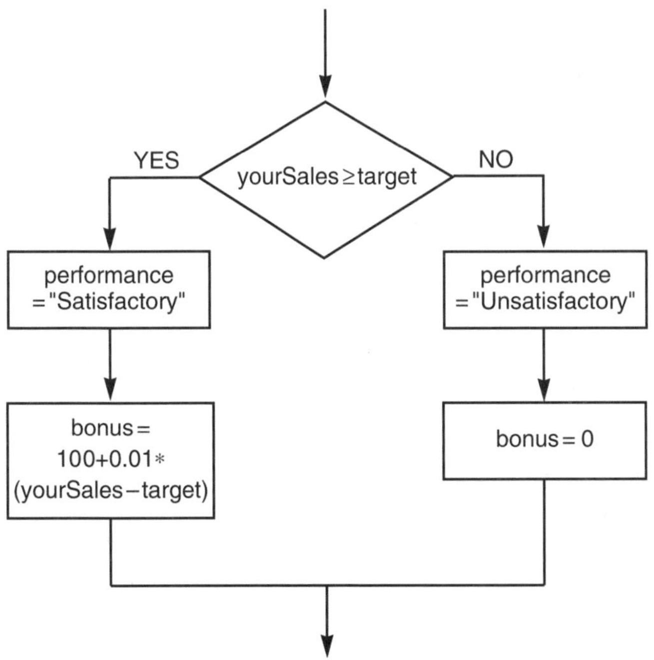

Figure 3-2: Flowchart for the `if/else` statement

The `else` part is always optional (see Figure 3-3). An `else` groups with the closest `if`. For example:

```
if {yourSales >= 2 * target)
{  performance = "Excellent";
   bonus = 1000;
}
else if {yourSales >= 1.5 * target)
{  performance = "Fine";
   bonus = 500;
}
else if (yourSales >= target)
{  performance = "Satisfactory";
   bonus = 100;
}
else
{  System.out.println("You're fired");
}
```

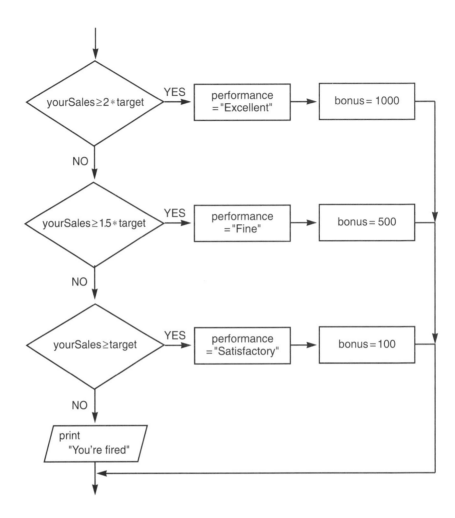

Figure 3-3: Flowchart for `if/else if` (multiple branches)

Finally, Java supports the ternary `?` operator that is occasionally useful. The expression condition `? e1 : e2` evaluates to `e1` if the `condition` is `true`, to `e2` otherwise. For example, `(x < = y) ? x : y` gives the smaller of x and y (or x if x = y).

NOTE: Because of the short circuit evaluation built into Java,

```
if (x != 0 && 1 / x > 0) // no problems ever
```

does not evaluate `1 / x` if x is zero, and so cannot lead to a divide-by-zero error.

Indeterminate Loops

In Java, as in all programming languages, there are control structures that let you repeat statements. There are two forms for repeating loops that are best when you do not know how many times a loop should be processed (these are "indeterminate loops").

First, there is the `while` loop that only executes the body of the loop while a condition is `true`. The general form is:

```
while (condition) { block }
```

The `while` loop will never execute if the condition is `false` at the outset (see Figure 3-4). In Example 3-4, let's use our `Console` class to determine how long it will take to save a specific amount of money, assuming you get a specified interest rate per year and deposit the same amount of money per year.

Example 3-4: Retirement.java

```
import corejava.*;

public class Retirement
{  public static void main(String[] args)
   {  double goal;
      double interest;
      double payment;
      int years = 0;
      double balance = 0;

      goal = Console.readDouble
         ("How much money do you need to retire?");
      payment = Console.readDouble
         ("How much money will you contribute every year?");
      interest = Console.readDouble
         ("Interest rate in % (ex: use 7.5 for 7.5%):") / 100;

      while (balance < goal)
      {  balance = (balance + payment) * (1 + interest);
         years++;
      }

      System.out.println
         ("Your can retire in " + years + " years.");
   }
}
```

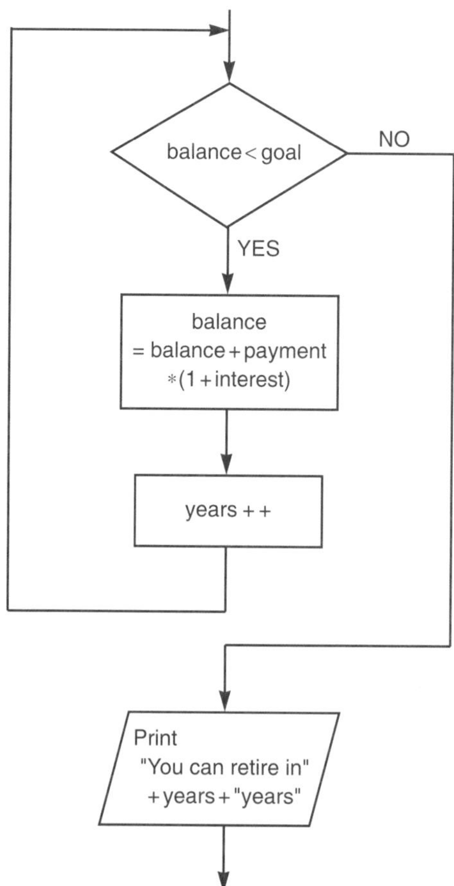

Figure 3-4: Flowchart for `while` statement

In this case, we are incrementing a counter and updating the amount currently accumulated in the body of the loop until the total exceeds the targeted amount. (Don't rely on this program to plan for your retirement. We left out a few niceties such as inflation and your life expectancy.)

A `while` loop tests at the top. Therefore, the code in the block may never be executed. If you want to make sure a block is executed at least once, you will need to move the test to the bottom. This is done with the `do` version of a `while` loop. Its syntax looks like this:

```
do { block } while (condition);
```

This executes the block and only then tests the condition. It then repeats the block and retests the condition, and so on. For instance, the code in Example 3-5 computes an approximation to the square root of any positive number, using an iterative process. Figure 3-5 illustrates this.

Example 3-5: SquareRoot.java

```
import corejava.*;

public class SquareRoot
{  public static void main(String[] args)
   {  double a = Console.readDouble("Please enter a number:");

      double xnew = a / 2;
      double xold;

      do
      {  xold = xnew;
         xnew = (xold + a / xold) / 2;
         System.out.println(xnew);
      }
      while (Math.abs(xnew - xold) > 1E-4);
   }
}
```

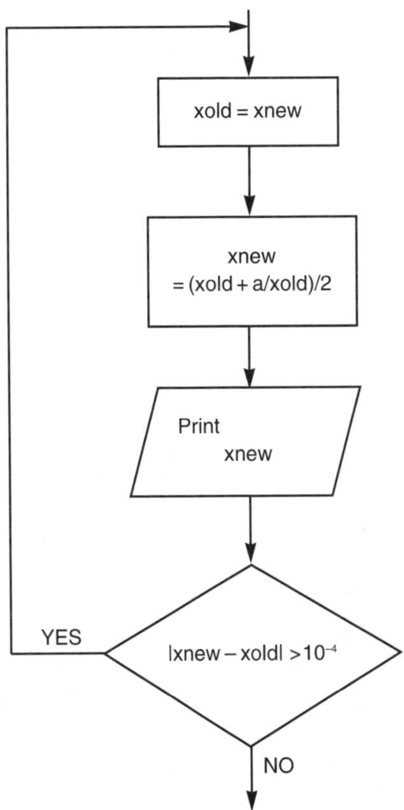

Figure 3-5: Flowchart for `do/while` statement

Finally, since a block may contain *any* Java statements, you can nest loops as deeply as you want.

Determinate Loops

Java, like C++, has a very general construct to support iteration. As Figure 3-6 shows, the following prints the numbers from 1 to 10 on the screen.

```
for (int i = 1; i <= 10; i++)
    System.out.println(i);
```

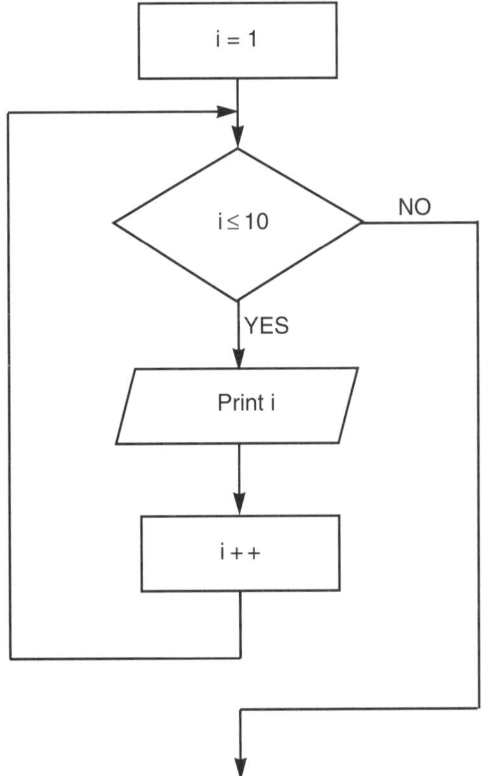

Figure 3-6: Flowchart for `for` statement

The idea is that the first slot of the `for` statement will (usually) hold the counter initialization. (The first slot is occasionally declared and initialized there, as in this example). The second slot gives the condition which will be tested before each new pass through the loop, and the third slot explains how to change the state of the counter. What follows the initialization can be a simple Java statement or a block. (Thus, nested `for` loops are possible in Java.)

Although Java, like C++, allows almost any expression in the various slots of a `for` loop, it is an unwritten rule of good taste that the three slots of a `for` statement should only initialize, test, and update a counter variable. One can write very obscure loops by disregarding this rule.

Even within the bounds of good taste, much is possible. This is because you can have variables of any type and use any method of updating them, so you can have loops that count down:

```
for (int i = 10; i > 0; i--)
    System.out.println("Counting down " + i);
System.out.println("Blastoff!");
```

Or, you can have loops in which the variables and increments are of one of the floating-point types.

NOTE: Again, be careful about testing for equality of floating-point numbers. A `for` loop that looks like this:

```
for (x = 0; x != 10; x += 0.01)
```

may never end.

Example 3-6 shows a reasonable use of floating-point numbers in a loop by extending the mortgage program to print out the monthly payments for a range of interest rates around the entered value that go up and down by .125%.

Example 3-6: MortgageLoop.java

```
import corejava.*;

public class MortgageLoop
{  public static void main(String[] args)
   {  double principal;
      double yearlyInterest;
      int years;

      principal = Console.readDouble
         ("Loan amount (no commas):");
      yearlyInterest = Console.readDouble
         ("Interest rate in % (ex: use 7.5 for 7.5%):") / 100;
      years = Console.readInt
         ("The number of years:");

      double y;
      for (y = yearlyInterest - 0.01;
         y <= yearlyInterest + 0.01; y += 0.00125)
      {  double monthlyInterest = y / 12;
         double payment = principal * monthlyInterest
            / (1 - (Math.pow(1/(1 + monthlyInterest),
```

```
                years * 12)));
            Format.print(System.out,
                "With rate %6.3f", 100 * y);
            Format.print(System.out,
               "%%, your monthly payment is $%10.2f\n", payment);
        }
    }
}
```

When you declare a variable in the first slot of the `for` statement, the scope of such a variable extends until the end of the body of the `for` loop. In particular, if you do this, you cannot use that value of this variable outside the loop. Therefore, if you wish to use the end value of a loop counter outside the `for` loop, be sure to declare it outside the header for the loop!

Of course, a `for` loop is equivalent to a `while` loop; choose the one that fits your picture of the situation. More precisely,

```
for (statement1; expression1; expression2) { block };
```

is completely equivalent to:

```
{  statement1;
   while (expression1)
   {  block;
      expression2;
   }
}
```

Multiple Selections—the `switch` Statement

The `if/else` construct can be cumbersome when you have to deal with multiple selections with many alternatives. Unfortunately, the only alternative available in Java is almost as cumbersome—it is not nearly as neat as VB's Select Case statement, which allows you to test for ranges or for values in any type. Java, following the lead of C/C++, calls the device for multiple selection a `switch` statement. Unfortunately, the designers didn't improve on C/C++'s `switch` statement. You still can select only against a `char` or against all the integer types but `long`. You still cannot use a range of values.

For example, if you set up a menuing system with four alternatives like that in Figure 3-7, you could use code that looks like this:

```
int choice = Console.readInt("Select an option (1 to 4)");
// reads one keypress
switch(choice)
{  case 1:
      . . .
      break;
   case 2:
      . . .
      break;
```

```
    case 3:
       . . .
       break;
    case 4:
       . . .
       break;
    default:
       // bad input
       break;
 }
```

Figure 3-7: Flowchart for `switch` statement

Unlike in languages like VB, it is possible for multiple switches to be triggered because execution falls through to another case unless a `break` keyword gets you out of the whole `switch` statement. (It is extremely unusual to use a `switch` statement without a `break` keyword in every case. In the extremely rare situation where you want the "fall through" behavior, you ought to clearly comment it.)

In general, execution starts at the `case` label, matching the value on which the selection is performed, and continues until the next `break` or the end of the switch. The `default` clause is optional.

Labeled Breaks

Although the designers of Java kept the `goto` as a reserved word, they decided not to include it in the language. In general, `goto` statements are considered poor style. Some programmers feel the anti-goto forces have gone too far (see, for example, the famous article of Donald Knuth called "Structured Programming with goto's"). They argue that unrestricted use of `goto` is error-prone, but that an occasional jump *out of a loop* is beneficial. The Java designers agreed and even added a new statement to support this programming style, the labeled break.

Let us first look at the unlabeled `break` statement. The same `break` statement that you use to exit a `switch` can also be used to break out of a loop. For example,

```
while (years <= 100)
{  balance = (balance + payment) * (1 + interest);
   if (balance > goal) break;
   years++;
}
```

Now the loop is exited if either `years > 100` occurs on the top of the loop or `balance > goal` occurs in the middle of the loop. Of course, you could have achieved the same effect without a break. You would need an `if/else` inside the loop and another termination condition in the loop header.

Unlike C/C++, Java also offers a *labeled break* statement that lets you break out of multiple nested loops. The reason for this is simple: occasionally something weird happens inside a deeply nested loop. In that case, you may want to break completely out of all the nested loops. It is inconvenient to program that simply by adding extra conditions.

Here's an example that shows this at work. Notice that the label must precede the outermost loop out of which you want to break. It also must be followed by a colon (:).

```
int n;
read_data:
while(. . .)
{  . . .
   for (. . .)
   {  n = Console.readInt(. . .);
      if (n < 0) // should never happen—can't continue
         break read_data;
      // break out of read_data loop
      . . .
   }
}
// check for sucess or failure here
if (n < 0)
{  // deal with bad situation
}
else
{  // got here normally
}
```

If there was a bad input, the labeled break moves past the end of the labeled block. As with any use of the `break` statement, you then need to test if the loop exited normally or as a result of a break.

Class Methods (User-Defined Functions)

Like any programming language, Java has a way of breaking down complex tasks into simpler tasks via user-defined gadgets (traditionally called *functions*). Every modern programming language takes pride in introducing a new terminology for these gadgets. As mentioned previously, in Java the terminology *method* is used instead of functions. (Well, it is used most of the time; the designers and documenters are somewhat inconsistent. They occasionally slip and use the C/C++ function terminology.) We will follow in the footsteps of the designers of Java and use the term *method* with an occasional slip when it seems appropriate. (In the next chapter, we will try to survey the ideas behind Object-Oriented Programming that led to the multitude of possible terminologies.)

A method definition must occur inside a class. It can occur anywhere inside the class, although custom places all the other methods of a class before the `main` method. There are many types of methods, but in this chapter we will use only those that, like `main`, are `public static`. For now, don't worry about what this means—it has to do with which other methods can use a method—we will explain the terminology in the next chapter.

C++ NOTE: Java does not have "global" functions. All functions must be defined inside a class. The functions we study in this chapter don't yet operate on objects and are, therefore, defined as `static`. Except for visibility issues, there is no difference between a C function and a static Java method.

For example, suppose we want to write a program that computes the odds on winning any lottery that requires bettors to choose a certain number of numbers from the range 1 to n. For example, if you must match six numbers from the numbers 1 to 50, then there are $(50 \cdot 49 \cdot 48 \cdot 47 \cdot 46 \cdot 45)/(1 \cdot 2 \cdot 3 \cdot 4 \cdot 5 \cdot 6)$ possible outcomes, so your chance is 1 in 15,890,700. Good luck!

Just in case someone asks you to participate in a "pick 7 out of 38" lottery, you will want a method that computes the odds. Later we'll put it together with a `main` function that asks you for how many numbers you need to choose and then asks for the highest number from which to draw.

Here's the method:

```
public static long lotteryOdds(int high, int number)
{   long r = 1;
    int i;
    for (i = 1; i <= number; i++)
    {   r = r * high / i;
        high--;
    }
    return r;
}
```

Notice the header for the `lotteryOdds`:

```
public static long lotteryOdds(int high, int number)
```

In general, the header for a method starts with keywords—in our case, `public static`—that explain the scope of the method. Next, the method header lists the type of the returned value. In our case, a `long`. Next comes the name of the method, and finally the types and names of its arguments.

After the header comes the code that implements the method. Notice the brace structure in the example above: the outermost braces (that start after the function header) mark off what is traditionally called the *body*. Variables declared inside a method (like the `int i` for the loop counter in our `lotteryOdds)` are *local* to the method. They can neither be accessed nor contaminate any similarly named variables in the other methods of the class. More precisely, when a method is called, the local variables for all function arguments are initialized as indicated in the body of the method (local variables in a class are not given default values), and the memory for them will automatically be reclaimed. Within a method, of course, the scope of a variable is determined by the block in which it is declared.

The `return` statement causes an immediate exit from the method. The expression following the `return` keyword is the method result. Methods in Java can return values of any Java type. On the other hand, methods need not return any value. In this case, the return type is `void`. (Functions that do this are commonly referred to as *procedures* in VB.)

Example 3-7 is an application that actually calls the `lotteryOdds` method as needed from the `main` method.

Example 3-7: LotteryOdds.java

```
import corejava.*;

public class LotteryOdds
{  public static long lotteryOdds(int high, int number)
   {  long r = 1;
      int i;
      for (i = 1; i <= number; i++)
      {  r = r * high / i;
         high--;
      }
      return r;
   }

   public static void main(String[] args)
   {  int numbers = Console.readInt
         ("How many numbers do you need to draw?");
      int topNumber = Console.readInt
         ("What is the highest number you can draw?");
      long oddsAre = lotteryOdds(topNumber, numbers);

      System.out.println
         ("Your odds are 1 in " + oddsAre + ". Good luck!");
   }
}
```

Notice how the `lotteryOdds` method is called from the `main` method in our application:

```
long oddsAre = lotteryOdds(topNumber, numbers);
```

As you can see, method calls for user-defined methods occur (return types permitting) in any expression for which a value is required. In our case, since the method belongs to the `lotteryOdds` class, we can call the method simply by giving its name followed by the argument. (As opposed to something like `System.out.println`, for which we need to give the object `System.out` on which the method operates.)

When this line of code is processed, Java uses the current values of the `topNumber` and `numbers` variables and passes this information to the `lotteryOdds` method. *All arguments to methods in Java are passed by value and not by reference.* It is, therefore, *impossible* to change variables by means of method calls. In particular, you cannot write a "swap" method in Java. See Chapter 4. (On the other hand, if you are familiar with pointers, since arrays and objects in Java are actually pointers, methods can modify the contents of arrays and objects. They just can't modify numbers.)

C++ NOTE: Methods in Java are similar but not identical to functions in C++. For example, there is no analog to function prototypes in Java. They are not required because functions can be defined after they are used—the compiler makes multiple passes through the code. More significantly, pointer and reference arguments do not exist in Java: you cannot pass the location of a variable. Overloading function names is always possible, just like in C++.

In general, `public` methods can be called from other classes. (An example of this is our use of the `println` method, which is a `public` method in `PrintStream`.)

Arguments and return values in methods can be of any type. In particular, they can be arrays (see the next section) or classes (see the next chapter).

Class Variables

Occasionally, you need to declare a variable that will be accessible by all the methods in the class. (It is possible but not recommended to declare a variable that can be seen outside its class—i.e., a true global variable.) Usually these are called *class variables* because the scope of such a variable is potentially the whole class. The syntax is similar to the *class constants* that you saw earlier, and class variables are declared above the `main` method, using the following syntax.

```
class Employee
{
   private static double socialSecurityRate = 7.62;
   public static void main(String[] args)
   { . . .}
}
```

Class variables can be shadowed by variables of the same name declared in a block inside a method of the class (although this is a rather strange way to program). Note that class variables, unlike local variables, are given default values automatically. (Objects get Null, booleans get false, numeric types are 0, and so on.)

It is also possible to call a method that has a `void` return type simply for its side effects—for example, to change the state of the class variables. This is done

simply by giving the method's name with the appropriate arguments as a stand-alone statement.

Finally, although it completely defeats the premises behind Object-Oriented Programming, by replacing the keyword `private` with the keyword `public`, one can have true global variables accessible by all methods in an application.

C++ NOTE: Except for visibility issues, there is no difference between a global variable in C/C++ and a static variable in Java.

Recursion

Recursion is a general method of solving problems by reducing them to simpler problems of a similar type. The general framework for a recursive solution to a problem looks like this:

Solve recursively (problem)

  If the problem is trivial, do the obvious

  Simplify the problem

  Solve recursively (simpler problem)

  Turn (if possible) the solution to the simpler problem(s) into a solution to the original problem

A recursive subprogram constantly calls itself, each time in a simpler situation, until it gets to the trivial case, at which point it stops. For the experienced programmer, thinking recursively presents a unique perspective on certain problems, often leading to particularly elegant solutions and, therefore, equally elegant programs. (For example, most of the very fast sorts, such as QuickSort, are recursive.)

For a Web-oriented example of recursion, consider the problem of designing a "Web crawler" that will search *every* hyperlink that is accessible from the page that you are currently on. The pseudo-code for this kind of application is:

Recursive URL search(link)

Do

  find next link

  Recursive URL search(next link)

Until no more links

There are actually two types of recursion possible. The first is where the subprogram calls only itself. This is called *direct recursion*. The second type is called, naturally enough, *indirect recursion*. This occurs, for example, when a method calls another method that, in turn, calls the first one. Both types of recursion are possible in Java and (unlike Pascal, say) no special incantations are needed for the indirect situation.

Let's look at a recursive way to compute the lottery odds. If you draw 1 number out of 50, your chances are plainly 1 in 50. In general, we can write

```
public static long lotteryOdds(int high, int number)
{   if (number == 1) return high;
    . . .
}
```

That wasn't too bad. Now let's look at the number of possible ways of drawing 6 numbers out of 50. Let's just grab one number. There are 50 chances. That leaves us with 5 numbers out of 49. Aha! A simpler problem. There are `lotteryOdds(49, 5)` ways to pick those five numbers. That gives a total of `50 * lotteryOdds(49, 5)` possibilities to pick the six numbers. Actually, we have to fudge a little and divide that result by six because our process counts each combination six times, depending which number we choose first.

Replacing the 50 and 6 with the general parameters `high` and `number`, we get the recursive solution

```
public static long lotteryOdds(int high, int number)
{   if (number <= 0) return 0; // just in case
    else if (number == 1) return high;
    else return high * lotteryOdds
       (high - 1, number - 1) / number;
}
```

Note that the `number` argument gets decremented in each recursive call and, therefore, must eventually reach 1 and end. This is very important when implementing recursion, you must be sure your recursion ends!

In this case, the recursive solution is actually somewhat less efficient than the loop that we used previously, but it clearly shows the syntax (or rather the absence of any special syntax) of the recursive call.

Arrays

In Java, arrays are first-class objects. You are better off not thinking about how arrays are implemented in Java—accept them as objects that exist in and of themselves. For example, you can assign one array of integers to another, just as you can assign one integer variable to another.

Once you create an array, you cannot change its size (although you can, of course, change an individual array element). If you need to expand the size of an array while a program is running, you need to use a different Java object called a *vector*. (See Chapter 12 for more on vectors and how to handle multi-dimensional arrays.)

You have already seen some examples of Java arrays. The `String[] args` argument in the `main` method says the only parameter in the `main` method is an array of strings. In this case, the first ("zeroth" = `args[0]`) entry is the first command-line argument; `args[1]` is the second command-line argument, and so on.

Arrays are the first example of objects whose creation the programmer must explicitly handle. This is done through the `new` operator. For example:

```
int[] arrayOfInt = new int[100];
```

sets up an array that can hold 100 integers. The array entries are *numbered from 0 to 99* (and not 1 to 100). Once created, the entries in an array can be filled, for example, by using a loop:

```
int[] arrayOfInt = new int[100];
for (int i = 0; i < 100; i++)
   arrayOfInt[i] = i;  // fills the array with 0 to 99
```

Entries from an array can be used anywhere a value of that type can be used. If you try to access, say, the 101st element of an array declared as having 100 elements, Java will compile and you will be able to run your program. It will, however, stop the program when this statement is encountered. If you assign one array to another, then both refer to the same set of values. Any change to one will affect the other.

Java has a shorthand to create an array object and initialize it at the same time. Here's an example of the syntax at work:

```
int[] smallPrimes = {2,3,5,7,11,13};
```

Notice that you do not use a call to `new` when you use this syntax.

Finally, Java has an extremely useful method in its `System` class for copying all or part of an array to another array. The syntax for this is:

```
System.arraycopy(sourceArray, sourcePosition,
    destinationArray, destinationPosition,
    numberOfEntriesToCopy);
```

For example, the following program sets up two arrays and then copies the last four entries of the first array to the second array. The copy starts at position 2 in the source array and copies starting at position 3 of the target. It copies 4 entries.

```
public class ArrayExample
{  public static void main(String args[])
   {   int[] smallPrimes = {2,3,5,7,11,13};
       int[] bigInts = {1001,1002,1003,1004,1005,1006,1007};
       System.arraycopy(smallPrimes, 2, bigInts, 3, 4);
       for (int i = 0; i < bigInts.length; i++)
       { System.out.println(i +
            " entry after copy is " + bigInts[ i]);
       }
   }
}
```

The output of this program is:

```
0 entry after copy is 1001
1 entry after copy is 1002
2 entry after copy is 1003
3 entry after copy is 5
4 entry after copy is 7
5 entry after copy is 11
6 entry after copy is 13
```

C++ NOTE: You can define an array variable either as `int[] arrayOfInt` or as `int arrayOfInt[]`. Most Java programmers prefer the former style because it neatly separates the type `int[]` (integer array) from the variable name.

A Java array is quite different from a C/C++ array on the stack. It is, however, essentially the same as a pointer to an array allocated on the *heap*. The `[]` operator is predefined to perform *bounds checking*. There is no pointer arithmetic—you can't increment `arrayOfInt` to point to the second element in the array.

You can tell that arrays are pointers because their contents can be modified when you pass an array to a function and because arrays can be assigned.

VB NOTE: There is no way to use index ranges in a Java array.

Arrays can be used in a user-defined method exactly as any other type. However, since arrays in Java are actually hidden references, the method can change the elements. Example 3-8 is a Shell sort that sorts whatever integer array is passed to it.

Example 3-8: ShellSort.java

```
ppublic class ShellSort
{  public static void sort(int[] a)
   {  int n = a.length;
      int incr = n / 2;
      while (incr >= 1)
      {  for (int i = incr; i < n; i++)
         {  int temp = a[i];
            int j = i;
            while (j >= incr && temp < a[j - incr])
            {  a[j] = a[j - incr];
               j -= incr;
            }
            a[j] = temp;
         }
         incr /= 2;
      }
   }

   public static void main(String[] args)
   {  // make an array of ten integers
      int[] a = new int[10];
      int i;
      // fill the array with random values
      for (i = 0; i < a.length; i++)
         a[i] = (int)(Math.random() * 100);
      // sort the array
      sort(a);
      // print the sorted array
      for (i = 0; i < a.length; i++)
         System.out.println(a[i]);
   }
}
```

NOTE: We used the simplest possible increments for the Shell sort (powers of 2). Much better sequences of increments are possible such as 1, 4, 13, 40,...

The return type of a method can also be an array. This is really useful when a method computes a sequence of values. For example, let us write a method that draws a sequence of numbers in a simulated lottery and then returns the sequence. The header of the function is

```
public static int[] drawing(int high, int number)
```

In Example 3-9, the method makes two arrays, one that holds the numbers 1, 2, 3, ..., `high` from which the lucky combination is drawn, and one to hold the numbers that are drawn. The first array is abandoned when the method exits and will eventually be garbage collected. The second array is returned as the computed result.

Example 3-9: LotteryDrawing.java

```
import corejava.*;

public class LotteryDrawing
{  public static int[] drawing(int high, int number)
   {  int i;
      int numbers[] = new int[high];
      int result[] = new int[number];
      // fill an arrays with numbers 1 2 3 . . . high
      for (i = 0; i < high; i++) numbers[i] = i + 1;
      for (i = 0; i < number; i++)
      {  int j = (int)(Math.random() * (high - i));
         result[i] = numbers[j];
         numbers[j] = numbers[high - 1 - i];
      }
      return result;
   }

   public static void main(String[] args)
   {  int numbers = Console.readInt
         ("How many numbers do you need to draw?");
      int topNumber = Console.readInt
         ("What is the highest number you can draw?");

      int[] a = drawing(topNumber, numbers);
      ShellSort.sort(a);
      System.out.println
("Bet the following combination. It'll make you rich!");
      int i;
      for (i = 0; i < a.length; i++)
         System.out.println(a[i]);
   }
}
```

CHAPTER 4

- Introduction to Object Oriented Programming
- Using Existing Classes
- Starting to Build Your Own Classes
- Packages
- Class Design Hints

Objects and Classes

This chapter will:

- Introduce you to Object-Oriented Programming (OOP)
- Show you how Java implements OOP by going further into its notion of a *class* and how you can use existing classes supplied by Java or by third parties
- Show you how to write your own *reusable* classes that can perform nontrivial tasks

If you are coming from an object based language like early versions of VB or a procedural oriented language like BASIC, COBOL, or C, you will want to read this chapter carefully. You may also need to spend a fair amount of time on the introductory sections. OOP requires a different way of thinking than procedure oriented languages (or even object based languages like VB). The transition is not always easy, but you do need some familiarity with OOP to go further with Java. (We are, however, assuming you are comfortable with a procedure oriented language or VB.)

For experienced C++ programmers, this chapter, like the previous chapter, will present familiar information; however, there are enough differences between how OOP is implemented in Java and how it is done in C++ to warrant your reading the later sections of this chapter (concentrating on the C++ notes).

Because you need to understand a fair amount of terminology in order to make sense of OOP, we'll start with some concepts and definitions. Then, we'll show you the basics of how Java implements OOP. We should note, however, that it is possible to write endlessly about the ideas behind OOP. A quick survey of *Books in Print* shows that there are more than 150 books with "Object Oriented Programming" in the title, and more seem to appear each week. (We do make references to the literature, if you need more information on the ideas behind OOP and object oriented design.)

Introduction to Object Oriented Programming

OOP is the dominant programming paradigm these days, having replaced the "structured," procedure-based programming techniques that were developed in the early '70s. Java is totally object oriented, and it is not possible to program it in the procedural style that you may be most comfortable with. We hope this section—especially when combined with the example code supplied in the text and on the CD—will give you enough information about OOP to become productive with Java.

Let's begin with a question that, on the surface, seems to have nothing to do with programming: How did companies like Compaq, Dell, Gateway, Micron Technologies, and the other major personal computer manufacturers get so big, so fast? Most people would probably say they made generally good computers and sold them at rock-bottom prices in an era when computer demand was skyrocketing. But go further—how were they able to manufacture so many models so fast and respond to the changes that were happening so quickly?

Well, a big part of the answer is that these companies farmed out a lot of the work. They bought components from reputable vendors and then assembled them. They often didn't invest time and money in designing and building power supplies, disk drives, motherboards, and other components. This made it possible for the companies to produce a product and make changes quickly for less money than if they had done the engineering themselves.

What the personal computer manufacturers were buying was "prepackaged functionality." For example, when they bought a power supply, they were buying something with certain properties (size, shape, and so on) and a certain functionality (smooth power output, amount of power available, and so on). Compaq provides a good example of how effective this operating procedure is. When Compaq moved from engineering all of the parts in their machines to buying many of the parts, they dramatically improved their bottom line.

OOP springs from the same idea. Your program is made of objects, with certain properties and operations that the objects can perform. The current state may change over time, but you always depend on objects not interacting with each other in undocumented ways. Whether you build an object or buy it might depend on your budget or on time. But, basically, as long as objects satisfy your specifications, you don't care how the functionality was implemented. In OOP, you only care about what the objects *expose*. So, just as clone manufacturers don't care about the internals of a power supply as long as it does what they want, most Java programmers don't care how the audio clip component in Figure 4-1 is implemented as long as it does what *they* want.

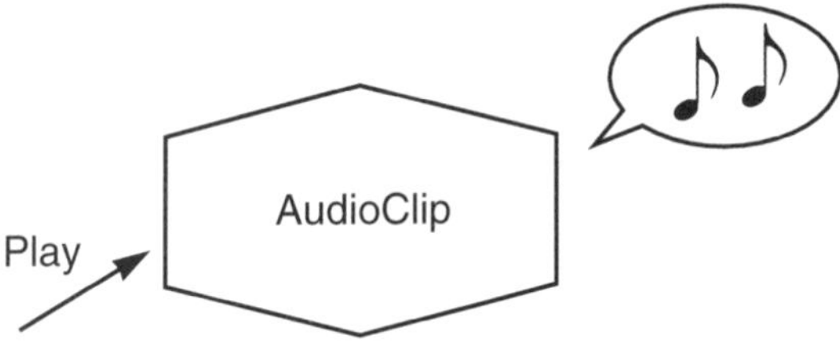

Figure 4-1: An audio clip object

Traditional structured programming consists of designing the data structures and then manipulating them with functions in specific ways that are theoretically sure to terminate. (These functions are usually called *algorithms.*) This is why the designer of the original Pascal, Niklaus Wirth, called his famous book on programming *Algorithms + Data Structures = Programs* (Prentice Hall, 1975). Notice that in Wirth's title, algorithms come first, and data structures come second. This mimics the way programmers worked at that time. First, you decided how to manipulate the data; then, you decided what structure to impose on the data in order to make the manipulations easier. OOP reverses the order and puts data structures first, then looks at the algorithms that operate on the data.

The key to being most productive in OOP is to make each object responsible for carrying out a set of related tasks. If an object relies on a task that isn't its responsibility, it needs to have access to an object whose responsibilities include that task. The first object then asks the second object to carry out the task by means of a more generalized version of the function call that you are familiar with in procedural programming. (Recall that in Java these function calls are usually called *method calls.*) In OOP jargon, you *have clients send messages to server objects.*

In particular, an object should never directly manipulate the internal data of another object. All communication should be via messages, that is, method calls. By designing your objects to handle all appropriate messages and manipulate their data internally, you maximize reusability and minimize debugging time.

Of course, just as with modules in a procedure-oriented language, you will not want an individual object to do *too* much. Both design and debugging are simplified when you build small objects that perform a few tasks, rather than humongous objects with internal data that are extremely complex, with hundreds of functions to manipulate the data.

The Vocabulary of OOP

You need to understand some of the terminology of OOP to go further. The most important term is *class,* which you have already seen in the code in Chapter 3. A class is usually described as the template or blueprint from which the object is actually made. This leads to the standard way of thinking about classes: as cookie cutters. Objects are the cookies themselves. The "dough," in the form of memory, will need to be allocated as well. Java is pretty good about hiding this "dough preparation" step from you. You simply use the `new` keyword to obtain memory, and the built-in garbage collector will eat the cookies when nobody uses them any more. (Oh well, no analogy is perfect.) When you create an object from a class, you are said to have *created an instance* of the class. When you have a line like

```
AudioClip meow = new AudioClip();
```

you are using the `new` operator to create a *new instance* of the `AudioClip` class as shown in Figure 4-2. (Actually, it turns out that you must work harder in Java to create real audio clips. We just want to show the syntax here.)

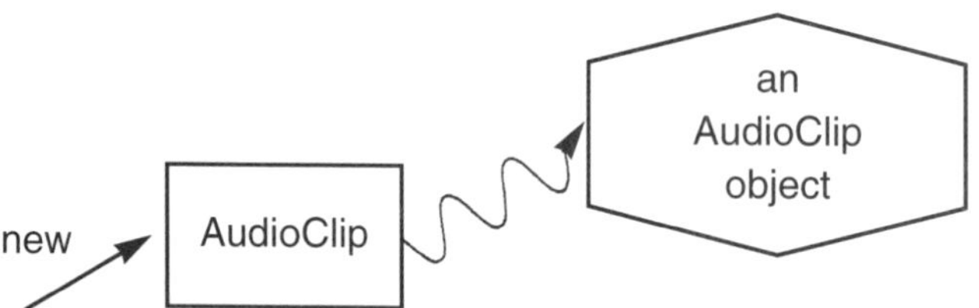

Figure 4-2: Creating a new object

As you have seen, everything you write in Java is inside a class, and Java is composed of many classes. Unfortunately, as you will see in this and the following chapters, the built-in classes in Java do not supply as rich a toolkit as languages like VB, Delphi, or Microsoft Foundation *Classes* (MFC) do. Thus, you must create your own classes for many basic tasks that, in other languages, are taken for granted.

However, when you do write your own classes, another tenet of OOP makes this easier: classes can be (and in Java always are) built on other classes. Java, in fact, comes with a "cosmic base class," that is, a class from which all other classes are built. We say that a class that builds on another class *extends* it. In Java, all classes extend the cosmic base class called, naturally enough, `Object`. You will see more about the `Object` base class in the next chapter.

When you extend a base class, the new class initially has all the properties and methods of its parent. You can choose whether you want to modify or simply keep any method of the parent, and you can also supply new methods that

apply to the child class only. The general concept of extending a base class is called *inheritance*. (See the next chapter for more on inheritance.)

Encapsulation (sometimes called data hiding) is another key concept in working with objects. Formally, encapsulation is nothing more than combining data and behavior in one package and hiding the implementation of the data from the user of the object. The data in an object are usually called its *instance variables* or *fields*, and the functions and procedures in a Java class are called its *methods* (see Figure 4-3). A specific object that is an instance of a class will have specific values for its fields that define its current *state*.

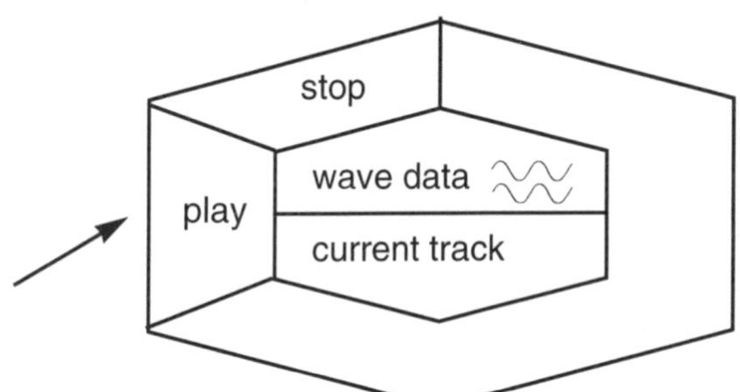

Figure 4-3: Encapsulation of data in an object

It cannot be stressed enough that the key to making encapsulation work is to have programs that *never* access instance variables (fields) in a class. Programs should interact with this data *only* through the object's methods. Encapsulation is the way to give the object its "black box" behavior, which is the key to reuse and reliability. Since this means an object may totally change how it stores its data but, as long as it continues to use the same methods to manipulate the data, no other object will know or care.

Objects

To work with OOP, you should be able to identify three key characteristics of objects. (For those who can remember back to high school, think of them as analogous to the "Who, What, and Where" that teachers told you characterize an event.) The three key questions are:

- What is the object's behavior?
- What is the object's state?
- What is the object's identity?

All objects that are instances of the same class share a family resemblance by supporting similar *behavior*. The behavior of an object is defined by the messages it accepts.

Next, each object stores information about what it currently looks like and how it got to be the way it currently is. This is what is usually called the object's *state*. An object's state may change over time, but not spontaneously. A change in the state of an object must be a consequence of messages sent to the object (otherwise you break encapsulation). However, the state of an object does not completely describe it. Since, each object has a distinct *identity*. For example, in an order-processing system, two orders are distinct even if they request identical items. Notice that the individual objects that are instances of a class *always* differ in their identity and *usually* differ in their state.

These key characteristics can influence each other. For example, the state of an object can influence its behavior. (If an order is "shipped" or "paid," it may reject a message that asks it to add or remove items. Conversely, if an order is "empty," that is, no items have yet been ordered, it should not allow itself to be shipped.)

In a traditional procedure-oriented program, you start the process at the top, with the `main` function. When designing an object-oriented system, there is no "top," and newcomers to OOP often wonder where to begin. The answer is: You first find classes and then you add methods to each class.

TIP: A simple rule of thumb in identifying classes is to look for nouns in the problem analysis. Methods, on the other hand, correspond to verbs.

For example, in an order-processing system, some of these nouns are:

- item
- order
- shipping address
- payment
- account

These nouns may lead to the classes `Item`, `Order`, and so on.

Next, one looks for verbs. Items are *added* to orders. Orders are *shipped* or *canceled*. Payments are *applied* to orders. With each verb, such as "add," "ship," "cancel," and "apply," you have to identify the one object that has the major responsibility for carrying it out. For example, when a new item is added to an order, the order object should be the one in charge since it knows how it stores and sorts items. That is, `add` should be a method of the `Order` class that takes an `Item` object as a parameter.

Of course, the "noun and verb" rule is only a rule of thumb, and only experience can help you decide which nouns and verbs are the important ones when building your classes.

Relationships between Classes

The most common relationships between classes are:

- *use*
- *containment* ("has–a")
- *inheritance* ("is–a")

The *use* relationship is the most obvious and also the most general. For example, the `Order` class uses the `Account` class, since `Order` objects need to access `account` objects to check for credit status. But the `Item` class does not use the `Account` class, since `Item` objects never need to worry about customer accounts. Thus, a class uses another class if it manipulates objects of that class.

In general, a class `A` uses a class `B` if:

- a method of `A` sends a message to an object of class `B`, or
- a method of `A` creates, receives, or returns objects of class `B`.

TIP: Try to minimize the number of classes that use each other. The point is, if a class `A` is unaware of the existence of a class `B`, it is also unconcerned about any changes to `B`! (And this means that changes to `B` do not introduce bugs into `A`.)

The *containment* relationship is easy to understand because it is concrete; for example, an `Order` object contains `Item` objects. Containment means that objects of class `A` contain objects of class `B`. Of course, containment is a special case of use; if an `A` object contains a `B` object, then at least one method of the class `A` will make use of that object of class `B`.

The *inheritance* relationship denotes specialization. For example, a `RushOrder` class inherits from an `Order` class, as shown in Figure 4-4. The specialized `RushOrder` class has special methods for priority handling and a different method for computing shipping charges, but its other methods, such as adding items and billing, are inherited from the `Order` class. In general, if class `A` extends class `B`, class `A` inherits methods from (or extends) class `B` but has more capabilities. (Inheritance will be more fully described in the next chapter, in which we discuss this important notion at some length.)

NOTE: These three essential relationships between classes form the foundation of object-oriented design. *Class diagrams* show the classes (usually denoted with boxes or clouds) and their relationships (denoted with lines with various decorations that are maddeningly different from one methodologist to the next). Figure 4- 4 shows an example, using the "unified Booch/Rumbaugh notation."

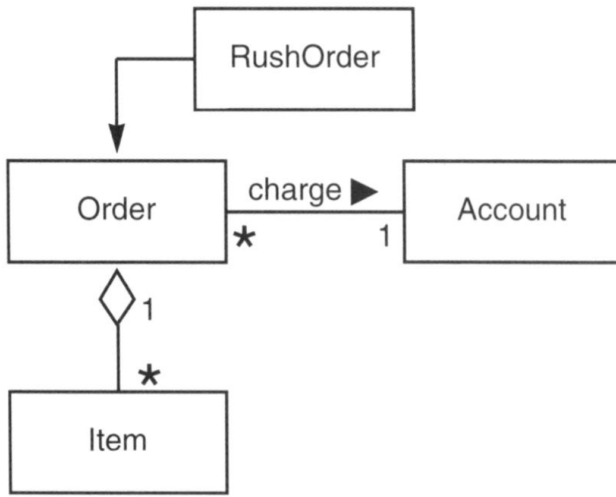

Figure 4-4: A class diagram

Contrasting OOP with Traditional Procedural Programming Techniques

We want to end this short introduction to OOP by contrasting OOP with the procedural model that you may be more familiar with. In procedure-oriented programming, you identify the tasks to be performed and then:

- By a stepwise refinement process, break the task to be performed into subtasks, and these into smaller subtasks, until the subtasks are simple enough to be implemented directly (this is the top-down approach).
- Write procedures to solve simple tasks and combine them into more sophisticated procedures, until you have the functionality you want (this is the bottom-up approach).

Most programmers, of course, use a mixture of the top-down and bottom-up strategies to solve a programming problem. The rule of thumb for discovering procedures is the same as the rule for finding methods in OOP: look for verbs, or actions, in the problem description. The important difference is that in OOP, you *first* isolate the classes in the project. Only then do you look for the methods of the class. And there is another important difference between traditional procedures and OOP methods: each method is associated with the class that is responsible for carrying out the operation.

For small problems, the breakdown into procedures works very well. But for larger problems, classes and methods have two advantages. Classes provide a convenient clustering mechanism for methods. A simple Web browser may require 2,000 functions for its implementation, or it may require 100 classes with an average of 20 methods per class. The latter structure is much easier to grasp by the programmer or to handle by teams of programmers. The encapsulation built into classes helps you here as well: classes hide their data representations

from all code except their own methods. As Figure 4–5 shows, this means that if a programming bug messes up data, it is easier to search for the culprit among the 20 methods that had access to that data item than among 2,000 procedures.

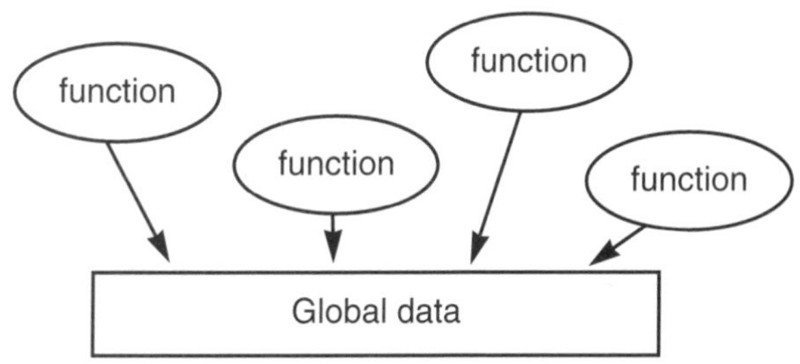

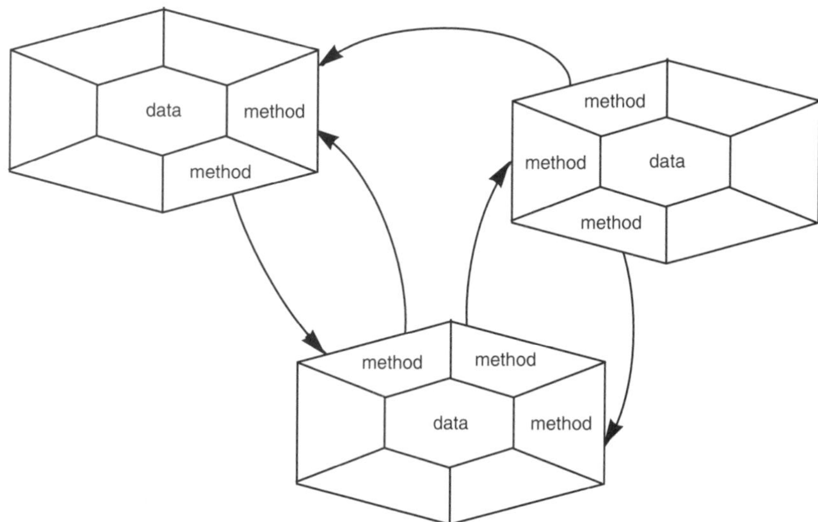

Figure 4-5: Procedural vs. OO programming

You may say that this doesn't sound much different than *modularization*. You have certainly written programs by breaking the program up into modules that communicate with each other through procedure calls only, not by sharing data. This (if well done) goes far in accomplishing encapsulation. However, in many programming languages (such as C and VB), the slightest sloppiness in programming allows you to get at the data in another module—encapsulation is easy to defeat.

There is a more serious problem: while classes are factories for multiple objects with the same behavior, you cannot get multiple copies of a useful module. Suppose you have a module encapsulating a collection of orders, together with a spiffy balanced binary tree module to access them quickly. Now it turns out that you actually need *two* such collections, one for the pending orders and one for the completed orders. You cannot simply link the order tree module twice. And you don't really want to make a copy and rename all procedures in order for the linker to work!

Classes do not have this limitation. Once a class has been defined, it is easy to construct any number of instances of that class type (whereas a module can have only one instance).

We have only scratched a very large surface. The end of this chapter has a short section on "Class Design Hints," but for more information on understanding the OOP design process, here are some book recommendations.

NOTE: The definitive book on object-oriented design with the Booch methodology is

> *Object-Oriented Analysis and Design,* 2nd Edition, by Grady Booch, (Benjamin Cummings, 1994).

You can find a lighter version of the methodology adapted to both C++ and Java in

> *Practical Object-Oriented Development in C++ and Java,* by Cay S. Horstmann, (John Wiley & Sons, 1997).

VB NOTE: If you are used to VB, the best book to read to get a sense of object-oriented design is *Doing Objects in Microsoft Visual Basic 5.0,* by Deborah Kurota (Ziff-Davis Press, 1997).

Using Existing Classes

Since you can't do anything in Java without classes, we have shown you many classes at work. Unfortunately, many of these are quite anomalous in the Java scheme of things. A good example of this is our `Console` class. You have seen that you can use our `Console` class without needing to know how it is implemented—all you need to know is the syntax for its methods. That is the point of encapsulation and will certainly be true of all classes. Unfortunately, the `Console` class *only* encapsulates functionality; it neither needs nor hides data. Since there is no data, you do not need to worry about making objects and initializing their instance fields—there aren't any!

Object Variables

For most classes in Java, you create objects, specify their initial state, and then work with the objects.

To access objects, you define object variables. For example, the statement

```
AudioClip meow; // meow doesn't refer to any object
```

defines an object variable, `meow`, that can refer to objects of type `AudioClip`. It is important to realize that the variable `meow` *is not an object* and, in fact, does not yet even refer to an object . You cannot use any methods on the variable at this time.

```
meow.play(); // not yet.
```

Use the `new` operator to create an object.

```
meow = new AudioClip();
    // does create an instance of AudioClip
```

Now you can start applying `AudioClip` methods to `meow`. (Actually, it is a little harder in Java to obtain a real audio clip. Here we just use audio clips to introduce the typical object notation.)

Most of the time, you will need to create multiple instances of a single class.

```
AudioClip chirp = new AudioClip();
```

Now there are two objects of type `AudioClip`, one attached to the object variable `meow` and one to the object variable `chirp`.

If you assign one variable to another variable using the equal sign,

```
AudioClip wakeUp = meow;
```

then both variables refer to the *same* object. This can lead to surprising behavior in your programs if you are not careful. For example, if you call

```
meow.play();
wakeUp.stop();
```

the audio clip object will play and then stop, since the *same* audio clip is referred to by the `wakeUp` and `meow` variables.

But suppose you want `meow` and `wakeUp` to refer to different objects, so you can change one of them without changing the other. As it turns out, there is no method available to change audio clips, and there isn't a method available to make a copy of one.

NOTE: Many classes do have a method called `clone` that makes a true copy. When you `clone` an existing object, you get a copy that reflects the current state of the object. Now, however (unlike when you use the equal sign), the two objects exist independently, so they can diverge over time. We will discuss the `clone` method further in the next chapter.

You can explicitly set an object variable to `null` to indicate that it currently refers to no objects.

```
wakeUp = null;
. . .
if (wakeUp != null) wakeUp.play();
```

If you call a method through a `null` variable like that of Figure 4-6, then a run-time error occurs. Local object variables are not automatically initialized to `null`. You must initialize them, either by calling `new` or by setting them to `null`.

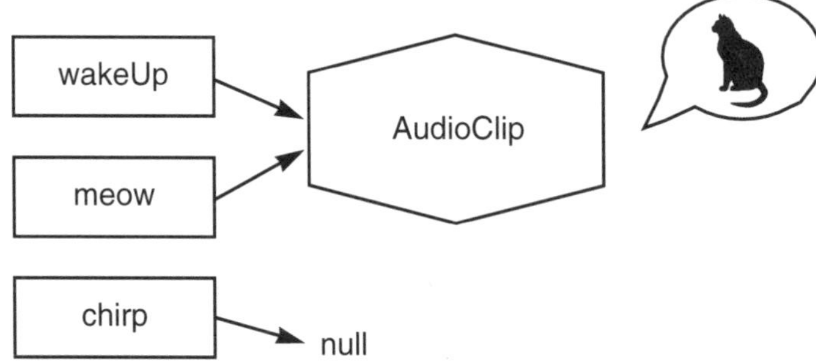

Figure 4-6: Object variables

C++ NOTE: Many people mistakenly believe that Java object variables behave like C++ references. But in C++ there are no null references, and references cannot be assigned. You should think of Java object variables as analogous to *object pointers* in C++. For example,

```
AudioClip meow; // Java
```

is really the same as

```
AudioClip* meow; // C++
```

Once you make this association, everything falls into place. Of course, an `AudioClip*` pointer isn't initialized until you initialize it with a call to `new`. The syntax is almost the same in C++ and Java.

```
AudioClip* meow = new AudioClip(); // C++
```

If you copy one variable to another, then both variables refer to the same audio clip—they are pointers to the same object. The equivalent of the Java `null` object is the C++ `NULL` pointer.

All Java objects live on the heap. When an object contains another object variable, that variable still contains just a pointer to yet another heap object.

In C++, pointers make you nervous because they are so error-prone. It is easy to create bad pointers or to mess up memory management. In Java, these problems simply go away. If you use an uninitialized pointer, the run-time system will reliably generate a run-time error, instead of producing random results. You don't worry about memory management because the garbage collector takes care of it.

C++ makes quite an effort, with its support for copy constructors and assignment operators, to allow the implementation of objects that copy themselves automatically. For example, a copy of a linked list is a new linked list with the same contents but with an independent set of links. This makes it possible to design classes with the same copy behavior as the built-in types. In Java, you must use the `clone` method to get a complete copy of an object.

VB NOTE: Object variables in VB are actually quite close to object variables in Java—both have the capacity to point to objects; you even have an analogous use of `new`. The difference, of course, is that, in VB you use `set` rather than the equal sign to make one object variable point to another object and you must reclaim the memory yourself!

The `GregorianCalendar` *Class of the Java library*

It is time to go further into the ways of working with Java and third-party classes that are more typical than our `Console` class. Let's start with a class to represent dates, such as December 31, 1999. There is a class called `Date` that comes with Java. An instance of the `Date` class has a state, namely *a particular point in time,* counted in milliseconds from a fixed point, the so-called *epoch,* which is January 1, 1970 (Perhaps `Time` would have been a better name for this class.) But as it turns out, the `Date` class is not very useful for manipulating dates. Java 1.1 takes the point of view that a description of a point in time such as "December 31, 1999, 23:59:59" is an arbitrary convention, governed by a *calendar,* in this case the Gregorian calendar, which is the 365 day (with occasional leap year) calendar used in most places of the world. The same point in time would be described quite differently in the Chinese or Hebrew Lunar calendars, not to mention the calendar used by your customers from Mars.

To manipulate dates in the Gregorian calendar, you can use the `GregorianCalendar` class in Java. For example,

```
GregorianCalendar todaysDate = new GregorianCalendar();
```

does the following:

1. It creates a new instance of the `GregorianCalendar` class called `todaysDate`.
2. At the same time, it initializes the state of the `todaysDate` object to be the current date (as maintained by the host operating system).

You can also create an instance of the `GregorianCalendar` class with a specific date:

```
GregorianCalendar preMillenium = new GregorianCalendar(1999,11,31);
```

This creates a `GregorianCalendar` instance called `preMillenium`, with the initial state of December 31, 1999. (Somewhat curiously, the months are counted from 0. Therefore, 11 is December. There are constants like `Calendar.DECEMBER` if you need them.)

Note that the `GregorianCalendar` class is actually a `Date/Time` class, so you can also set the time. (If you don't set it, it defaults to midnight at the beginning of the new day.) For example:

```
GregorianCalendar preMillenium
   = new GregorianCalendar(1999,11,31,23,59,59);
```

would give you a `GregorianCalendar` object whose instance fields are set at one second to midnight on December 31, 1999. (When you use `GregorianCalendar()`, you get a date instance with the time set at the time maintained in the operating system.)

Now you may be wondering: Why use classes to represent dates rather than (as in some languages) a built-in type? The reason is simple: language developers are reluctant to add too many basic types. For example, suppose Java had a notation like #6/1/95#, which is used in VB to denote an example of `Date` type. Since the ordering for year, month, and day is different in different locales, the *language designers* would need to foresee all the issues of internationalization. If they do a poor job, the language becomes an unpleasant muddle, but unhappy programmers are powerless to do anything about it. By making `GregorianCalendar` into a class, the design task is offloaded to a library designer. If the class is not perfect, other programmers can easily write their own class. (In fact, we will do just this in the next section.)

Unlike our `Console` class, the `GregorianCalendar` class must have encapsulated data (instance fields) to maintain the date to which it is set. Without looking at the source code, *it is impossible to know the representation used internally by these classes.* But, of course, the whole point is that this doesn't matter, and this is what makes it possible to use the `GregorianCalendar` class in a system-independent way.

What *matters* are the methods that a class exposes. If you look at the documentation for the `GregorianCalendar` class, you will find that it has 28 public methods, most of which are not of general interest.

In this book, we present a method in the following format, which is essentially the same as the on-line documentation.

`java.util.GregorianCalendar`←name of class

- `void add(int field, int amount)`←name of method

  Date Arithmetic function. Adds the specified amount of time to the given time field. For example, to add 7 days to the current calendar date, call `c.add(Calendar.DATE, 7)`.

  Parameters: (omitting those that are self-explanatory):

`field`	the field to modify (using one of the constants documented in the `get` method)
`amount`	the amount by which the field should be changed (can be negative)

Here are the most useful methods of the `GregorianCalendar` class, together with a couple of not so useful ones.

`java.util.GregorianCalendar`

- `GregorianCalendar()`

  Constructs a calendar object that represents the current time in the default time zone with the default locale.

- `GregorianCalendar(int year, int month, int date)`

  Constructs a Gregorian calendar with the given date.

  Parameters:

`year`	the year of the date
`month`	the month of the date. This value is 0-based. e.g., 0 for January.
`date`	the day of the month

- `GregorianCalendar(int year, int month, int date, int hour, int minutes, int seconds)`

  Constructs a Gregorian calendar with the given date and time.

  Parameters:

`year`	the year of the date
`month`	the month of the date. This value is 0-based. e.g., 0 for January.
`date`	the day of the month
`hour`	the hour (between 0 and 23)
`minutes`	the minutes (between 0 and 59)
`seconds`	the seconds (between 0 and 59)

- `boolean equals(Object when)`

  Compares this calendar object with `when` and returns `true` if the objects represent the same point in time.

- `boolean before(Object when)`

  Compares this calendar object with `when` and returns `true` if it comes before `when`.

- `boolean after(Object when)`

  Compares this calendar object with `when` and returns `true` if it comes after `when`.

- `int get(int field)`

  Gets the value of a particular field.

Parameters:	`field`	one of
	`Calendar.ERA`	
	`Calendar.YEAR`	
	`Calendar.MONTH`	
	`Calendar.WEEK_OF_YEAR`	
	`Calendar.WEEK_OF_MONTH`	
	`Calendar.DATE`	
	`Calendar.DAY_OF_MONTH`	
	`Calendar.DAY_OF_YEAR`	
	`Calendar.DAY_OF_WEEK`	
	`Calendar.DAY_OF_WEEK_IN_MONTH`	
	`Calendar.AM_PM`	
	`Calendar.HOUR`	
	`Calendar.HOUR_OF_DAY`	
	`Calendar.MINUTE`	
	`Calendar.SECOND`	
	`Calendar.MILLISECOND`	
	`Calendar.ZONE_OFFSET`	
	`Calendar.DST_OFFSET`	

- `void set(int field, int value)`

  Sets the value of a particular field. Use this method with caution—you can create impossible dates.

Parameters:	`field`	one of the constants accepted by `get`
	`value`	the new value

- `void set(int year, int month, int date)`

  Sets the date fields to a new date.

Parameters:	`year`	the year of the date
	`month`	the month of the date. This value is 0-based. e.g., 0 for January.
	`date`	the day of the month

- `void set(int year, int month, int date, int hour, int minutes, int seconds)`

  Sets the date and time fields to new values.

Parameters:	`year`	the year of the date
	`month`	the month of the date. This value is 0-based. e.g., 0 for January.
	`date`	the day of the month
	`hour`	the hour (between 0 and 23)
	`minutes`	the minutes (between 0 and 59)
	`seconds`	the seconds (between 0 and 59)

- `void add(int field, int amount)`

  Date arithmetic function. Adds the specified amount of time to the given time field. For example, to add 7 days to the current calendar date, call `c.add(Calendar.DATE, 7)`.

Parameters:	`field`	the field to modify (using one of the constants documented in the `get` method)
	`amount`	the amount by which the field should be changed (can be negative)

- `void setGregorianChange(Date date)`

  Sets the date at which the Julian calendar ends and the Gregorian calendar (with a more precise leap year correction) starts. The default is 00:00:00 local time, October 15, 1582.

Parameters:	`date`	the desired Gregorian cutover date.

- `Date getGregorianChange()`

  Gets the date at which the calendar switches from Julian to Gregorian.

Mutator and Accessor Methods

At this point, you are probably asking yourself: How do I get at the current day or month or year for the date encapsulated in a specific `GregorianCalendar` object? And how do I change the values if I am unhappy with them? You can find out how to carry out these tasks by looking at the API reference of the preceding section.

The `GregorianCalendar` class has a rather atypical way of accessing the information stored in a calendar object. Most classes would have methods such as `getYear`, `getMonth`, and so on, to access the object state. However, the `GregorianCalendar` class has a single catch-all `get` method that can be used to query the state of a large number of settings, not just the year, month, and so on, but also information such as the weekday. To select the item that you want to get, you pass a constant defined in the `Calendar` class, such as `Calendar.MONTH` or `Calendar.DAY_OF_WEEK`:

```
GregorianCalendar todaysDate = new GregorianCalendar();
System.out.println(todaysDate.get(Calendar.MONTH));
System.out.println(todaysDate.get(Calendar.DAY_OF_WEEK));
```

You can change a date with one of the `set` methods or with the `add` method. For example,

```
dueDate.set(1999,12,31);
```

There is a conceptual difference between the `get` method on the one hand and the `set` and `add` methods on the other hand. The `get` method only looks up the state of the object and reports on it. The `set` and `add` methods modify the state of the object. Methods that change instance fields are called *mutator methods* and those that only access instance fields without modifying them are called *accessor methods.* The convention in Java is to use the lowercase prefix `get` for accessor methods and `set` for mutator methods. For example, the `GregorianCalendar` class has methods `getGregorianChange` and `setGregorianChange`. Actually, the `GregorianCalendar` class is a little strange—to access year, month, day, hour, minute, and second fields, you don't use separate `get` accessors but a single `get` method. The `getGregorianChange` and `setGregorianChange` methods,

even though they are of no practical interest except for calendar enthusiasts, are more characteristic of typical Java methods. In the next section, we will introduce a `Day` class that is easier to understand than the `GregorianCalendar` and whose methods are similar to those of typical Java classes.

C++ NOTE: In C++, it is important to make a formal distinction between mutator operations that change an object and accessor operations that merely read its data fields. The latter need to be declared as `const` operations. This is not needed in Java.

VB NOTE: The analogous situation (in VB4 or VB5) is that mutator methods correspond to a Property Let or Property Set procedure, and accessor methods correspond to a Property Get procedure.

Using Our `Day` Class

Unfortunately, even if you look at *all* the methods in the `GregorianCalendar` class to see if your idea of what is important corresponds to ours, you will quickly discover that this class is not only unintuitive to use but is also missing certain types of functionality. There are instances in which you want to find the difference between two dates. For example, a retirement calculator certainly needs to compute the difference between today's date and the user's retirement date. The question then arises, What is the best way to add this functionality to the `GregorianCalendar` class? Could we build on the `GregorianCalendar` class (i.e., use *inheritance*—to be described in the next chapter)?

When we tried this, we discovered that the `GregorianCalendar` class did not let us easily access the information we needed to do date calculations. There is a method for finding out if the current date comes before the retirement date, but that doesn't do us a lot of good—we know we aren't retired yet. The method won't tell us how many days will elapse until our well-deserved retirement. Just out of curiosity, we examined the source code for the `GregorianCalendar` class and discovered that in principle we could use the `getTimeinMillis` method to obtain the time in milliseconds that have elapsed since January 1, 1970. We could then divide the difference by 1000*60*60*24 = 86,400,000 to get the number of days since January 1, 1970 but this is hardly convenient.

NOTE: The CD includes the source code for all of the publicly available parts of Java. As you become more experienced with Java, you will find the source code extremely useful for getting ideas about and (occasional) insights into Java programming.

We, therefore, decided to write our own `Day` class to give you a better example of a class with cleanly designed accessor and mutator functions. The source code (it's around 150 lines of code) has been installed in the `corejava` package inside the `\CoreJavaBook` directory of your hard disk during the installation described in Chapter 2. (When you finish this chapter, you may want to glance through the source code to see the basic ideas. Fair warning: some of the code is fairly obscure because of the algorithms needed to work with a year that is, in reality, slightly more than 365 days long.)

We allow two ways to create an instance of our `Day` class that are similar to the two methods for Java's `Date` class:

```
Day todaysDate = new Day();
Day preMillenium = new Day(1999, 12, 31);
```

Unlike Java's `GregorianCalendar` class, our class does not do anything with the time of day and will also prevent you from creating an illegal date. Furthermore, we specify the month in a more natural way, starting at 1 = January and going up to 12 = December.

To create an object of our `Day` class, you need to make sure that Java knows where the `Day` class is. (This can be done by setting the CLASSPATH variable appropriately to include the CoreJava directory and using `import corejava.*` or copying the `Day` class to the directory in which you are working.) What we want to stress here is that once you know how to create an instance of the `Day` class, then all you need to use our class is the following list that tells you how our methods affect the current state of an instance of the `Day` class:

`corejava.Day`

- `void advance(int n)`

  Advances the date currently set by a specified number of days. For example, `d.advance(100)` changes `d` to a date 100 days later.

- `int getDay(), int getMonth(), int getYear()`

  Returns the day, month, or year of this day object. Days are between 1 and 31, months between 1 and 12, and years can be any year (such as 1996 or –333). The class knows about the switch from the Julian to the Gregorian calendar in 1582.

- `int weekday()`

  Returns an integer between 0 and 6, corresponding to the day of the week (0 = Sunday).

- `int daysBetween(Day b)`

  This method is one of the main reasons we created the `Day` class. It calculates the number of days between the current instance of the `Day` class and instance `b` of the `Day` class.

Notice that our `Day` class has no method for changing the date other than to use the `advance` method.

The following code combines the `Console` class with our `Day` class in order to calculate how many days you have been alive.

```
import corejava.*;
  public class DaysAlive
  {  public static void main(String[] args)
     {  int year;
        int month;
        int day;

        month = Console.readInt
           ("Please enter the month, 1 for January and so on");
        day = Console.readInt
           ("Please enter the day you were born.");

        year = Console.readInt
                ("Please enter the year you were born
                (starting with 19..)");

        Day birthday = new Day(year, month, day);
        Day today = new Day();
        System.out.println("You have been alive "
           + today.daysBetween(birthday) + " days.");
     }
  }
```

NOTE: If you try to enter invalid data, the program will terminate with an exception. See Chapter 12 for more on exceptions.

A Calendar Program

As a more serious example of putting it all together, here is the code for an application that prints out a calendar for the month and year specified in the command-line argument. For example, if you compile this class (make sure our `Day` class is available, of course) and then run

```
java Calendar 12 1999
```

you will see the calendar for December 1999. (December 31 is rather conveniently on a Friday that year, by the way.)

```
12    1999
Sun   Mon   Tue   Wed   Thu   Fri   Sat
                    1     2     3     4
 5     6     7      8     9    10    11
12    13    14     15    16    17    18
19    20    21     22    23    24    25
26    27    28     29    30    31
```

There are two issues in writing a calendar program like this: you have to know the weekday of the first day of the month, and you have to know how many days the month has. We sidestep the latter problem with the following trick: we make a `Day` object that starts out with the first of the month.

```
Day d = new Day(y, m, 1); // start date of the month
```

After printing each day, we advance `d` by one day:

```
d.advance(1);
```

In Example 4-1 we check the month (`d.getMonth()`) and see if it is still the same as `m`. If not, we are done.

Example 4-1: Calendar.java

```
import corejava.*;

public class Calendar
{  public static void main(String[] args)
   {  int m;
      int y;
      if (args.length == 2)
      {  m = Format.atoi(args[0]);
         y = Format.atoi(args[1]);
      }
      else
      {  Day today = new Day(); // today's date
         m = today.getMonth();
         y = today.getYear();
      }

      Day d = new Day(y, m, 1); // start date of the month

      System.out.println(m + " " + y);
      System.out.println("Sun Mon Tue Wed Thu Fri Sat");
      for( int i = 0; i < d.weekday(); i++ )
         System.out.print("    ");
      while (d.getMonth() == m)
```

```
        {   if (d.getDay() < 10) System.out.print(" ");
            System.out.print(d.getDay());
            if (d.weekday() == 6)
               System.out.println("");
            else
               System.out.print("   ");
            d.advance(1);
        }
        if (d.weekday() != 0) System.out.println("");
    }
}
```

PITFALL: There is a tendency for programmers coming from languages that have the by value, by reference distinction for function parameters to assume that since objects are references, they are passed by reference. Unfortunately, that is wrong!

First off, consider trying to write a swap method for days. Because you got tired of writing the three lines of code that are needed, you decide to write once and for all:

```
static void swap_days(Day a, Day b)
{   Day temp = b;
    b = a;
    a = temp;
}
```

Unfortunately the call `swap_days(foo, bar)` (as opposed to writing the three lines of code) still does nothing, `foo` and `bar` still refer to whatever they did before the call—*because* they were passed by value to the `swap_days` method.

As another example of this phenomenon, consider the following method that *tries* to change the delivery date for a software product:

```
static void changeDeliveryDay(Day d, int yearsDelayed)
// won't work
{   int month = d.getMonth();
    int day = d.getDay();
    int year = d.getYear();
    d = new Day(year + yearsDelayed, month, day);
}
```

Suppose you call this function as follows:

```
target = new Day(1996, 10, 15);
changeDeliveryDay(target, 2);
```

in order to change the delivery date to be two years later. Does target now have the correct state?

What we are doing seems natural at first glance. It *looks* like the target object is changed inside the method so that it refers to a new `Day` object since the parameter certainly is being changed to a new day object. However *this code will also not work*. The point is that Java never passes method parameters by reference. The variable d in the changeDeliveryDay method is a *copy* of the target variable. Now it is true that both of these variables are references and they do both point to the same Day object right after the method is called. It is also true that the assignment

```
d = new Day(year + yearsDelayed, month, day);
```

changes the value of the d object variable inside the method. It now refers (points) to a new Day object. The original target variable, however, has not changed; it *still* refers to the original Day object. Thus, the method call does not change what the target refers to at all. (The d object variable is abandoned when Java finishes executing the method, and the memory allocated for it will eventually be garbage collected.)

To sum up: *In Java, methods can never change the values of their parameters.*

On the other hand, as you have seen repeatedly, methods can change the *state* of an object used as a parameter. They can do this since they have access to the mutator methods and data of the object the parameter points to. Here's a version of a method to change the delivery day that will do the job.

```
static void changeDeliveryDay(Day d, int yearsDelayed)
// works
{     int ndays = 365 * yearsDelayed;
      d.advance(ndays);
}
```

This method changes the state of d by using the advance method of the Day class. It doesn't try to attach a different object to d; it simply uses the fact that it can access and change the data of d via its mutator methods. When you call this method with a parameter equal to target, the advance method updates target when it is called by the line d.advance(ndays). This changes the state of the target object as we wanted to do.

Starting to Build Your Own Classes

You saw how to write simple classes in Chapter 3. In that chapter, the classes were all designed to run as stand-alone programs and depended only on the classes built into Java and our little Console class. When you said

```
java Mortgage
```

for example, the Java interpreter looked for the main method in the Mortgage class and ran it. The main method, in turn, called other methods of the class as needed. Although you will see more about methods like main later in this chapter, this kind of class is not what we are concerned with in this chapter. In more sophisticated Java programs, the class you choose to run from the interpreter will usually have very little functionality other than starting up the various objects that do the actual work of your program.

What we want to do in the rest of this chapter (and in the next chapter) is show you how to write the kind of "workhorse classes" that are needed for more sophisticated applications. These classes do not (and often cannot) stand alone: they are the building blocks for *constructing* stand-alone programs.

The simplest syntax for a class in Java is:

```
class NameOfClass
{  // definitions of the class's features
   // includes methods and instance fields
}
```

The outermost pair of braces (block) defines the code that will make up the class. Our convention is to use initial caps for class names. Just as with the classes from Chapter 3, individual method definitions define the operations of the class. The difference is that we want to allow other classes to use our classes while still maintaining encapsulation of the data. This means that we now want to allow for (encapsulated) instance fields that will hold the private data for these classes.

NOTE: We adopt the policy that the methods for the class come first and the instance fields come at the end. (Perhaps this, in a small way, encourages the notion of leaving instance fields alone.)

An `Employee` *Class*

Consider the following, very simplified version of an `Employee` class that might be used by a business in writing a payroll system.

```
class Employee
{  public Employee(String n, double s, Day d)
   {  name = n;
      salary = s;
      hireDay = d;
   }
   public void raiseSalary(double byPercent)
   {  salary *= 1 + byPercent / 100;
   }
   public int hireYear()
   {  return hireDay.getYear();
   }
   public void print()
   {  System.out.println(name + " " + salary + " " + hireYear());
   }
   public String getName()
   {  return name;
   }
   private String name;
   private double salary;
   private Day hireDay;
}
```

We will break down the code in this class in some detail in the sections that follow. First, though, example 4-2 shows some code that lets you see how to use the `Employee` class.

Example 4-2: EmployeeTest.java

```
import java.util.*;
import corejava.*;

public class EmployeeTest
{  public static void main(String[] args)
   {  Employee[] staff = new Employee[3];

      staff[0] = new Employee("Harry Hacker", 35000,
         new Day(1989,10,1));
      staff[1] = new Employee("Carl Cracker", 75000,
         new Day(1987,12,15));
      staff[2] = new Employee("Tony Tester", 38000,
         new Day(1990,3,15));
      int i;
      for (i = 0; i < 3; i++) staff[i].raiseSalary(5);
      for (i = 0; i < 3; i++) staff[i].print();
   }
}

class Employee
{  public Employee(String n, double s, Day d)
   {  name = n;
      salary = s;
      hireDay = d;
   }
   public void print()
   {  System.out.println(name + " " + salary + " "
         + hireYear());
   }
   public void raiseSalary(double byPercent)
   {  salary *= 1 + byPercent / 100;
   }
   public int hireYear()
   {  return hireDay.getYear();
   }

   private String name;
   private double salary;
   private Day hireDay;
}
```

To run the sample code, compile this EmployeeTest class and run it with the Java interpreter. This will create three instances of the Employee class with some sample data and then print out the state of the objects in order for us to see whether or not our class appears well constructed.

C++ NOTE: In Java, all functions are defined inside the class itself. This does not automatically make them inline functions. There is no analog to the C++ syntax:

```
class Employee
{  //...
};
void Employee::raiseSalary(double byPercent) // C++, not Java
{  salary *= 1 + byPercent / 100;
}
```

Analyzing the Employee Class

In the sections that follow, we want to dissect the Employee class. Let's start with the methods in this class. As you can see by examining the source code, this class has five methods, whose headers look like this:

```
public Employee(String n, double s, Day d)
public String getName()
public void raiseSalary(double byPercent)
public int hireYear()
public void print()
```

The keyword public is called an *access modifier*. In Java, these access modifiers describe who can use the method or who can use the class if a modifier is used in the name of the class. The keyword public means that any method in any class that has access to an instance of the Employee class can call the method. (There are four possible access levels; they are covered in this and the next chapter.)

Next, notice that there are three *instance fields* that will hold the data we will manipulate inside an instance of the Employee class.

```
private String name;
private double salary;
private Day hireDay;
```

The private keyword makes sure that no outside agency can access the instance fields *except* through the methods of our class. In this book, instance fields will almost always be private. (Exceptions occur only when we have to implement very closely collaborating classes, for example, a List and a Link class in a linked list data structure.)

NOTE: It is possible to use the `public` keyword with your instance variables, but it would be a very bad idea. Having `public` data fields would allow any part of the program to read and modify the instance variables. That completely ruins encapsulation and, at the risk of repeating ourselves too often, we strongly urge against using public instance fields.

Finally, notice that we use an instance field that is itself an instance of our `Day` class. This is quite usual: classes will often contain instance fields that are themselves class instances.

For the `Employee` class to compile, either the `Day` class must be in the same directory as the `Employee` class, or your CLASSPATH environment variable must point to the `CoreJavaBook` directory.

NOTE: Please see the section *Packages* later in this chapter if you want to use all of our classes in the simplest fashion without worrying about the location of the source files, and for more information on access modifiers for classes.

First Steps with Constructors

Let's look at the first method listed in our `Employee` class.

```
public Employee(String n, double s, Day d)
{  name = n;
   salary = s;
   hireDay = d;
}
```

This is an example of a *constructor method*. It is used to initialize objects of a class—giving the instance variables the initial state you want them to have. You didn't see any methods like this in Chapter 3 because we didn't initialize any objects in that chapter.

For example, when you create an instance of the `Employee` class with code like this:

```
hireDate = new Day(1950, 1, 1);
Employee number007 = new Employee
   ("James Bond", 100000, hireDate);
```

you have set the instance fields as follows:

```
name = "James Bond";
salary = 100000;
hireDay = January 1, 1950 //actually a Day class with this
                          //data encapsulated
```

The `new` method is always used together with a constructor to create the class. This forces you to set the initial state of your objects. In Java, you cannot create an instance of a class without initializing the instance variables (either explicitly

or implicitly). The reason for this design decision is simple: an object created without a correct initialization is always useless and occasionally dangerous. In many languages, like Delphi, you can create uninitialized objects; the result is almost always the platform equivalent of a general protection fault (GPF) or segmentation fault, which means memory is being corrupted.

While we will have more to say about constructor methods later in this chapter, for now, always keep the following in mind:

1. A constructor has the same name as the class.
2. A constructor may (as in this example) take one or more (or even no) parameters.
3. A constructor is always called with the `new` keyword.
4. A constructor has no return value.

Remember, too, the following important difference between constructors and other methods:

- A constructor can only be called with `new`. You can't apply a constructor to an existing object to reset the instance fields. For example, `d.Day(1950, 1, 1)` is an error.

Of course, if resetting all fields of a class is an important and recurring operation, the designers of the class can provide a mutator method such as `empty` or `reset` for that purpose. We want to stress that only the supplied mutator methods will let you revise the state of the instance variables in an already constructed class (assuming, of course, that all data are private).

It is possible to have more than one constructor in a class. You have already seen this in both Java's `GregorianCalendar` class and our `Day` class. (You saw two of the three constructors available in the `GregorianCalendar` class and both of the constructors available in our `Day` class.)

C++ NOTE: Constructors work the same way in Java as they do in C++. But keep in mind that all Java objects are constructed on the heap and that a constructor must be combined with `new`. It is a common C++ programmer error to forget the `new` operator:

```
Employee number007("James Bond", 100000, hireDate);
    // C++, not Java
```

That works in C++ but does not work in Java.

CAUTION: Be careful not to introduce local variables with the same names as the instance fields. For example, the following constructor will not set the salary.

```
public Employee(String n, double s, Day d)
{  name - n;
   hireDay = d;
   float salary = s;
}
```

The local variable `salary` *shadows* the instance field `salary`. This is a nasty error that can be hard to track down. You just have to be careful in all of your methods that you don't use variable names that equal the names of instance fields.

The Methods of the `Employee` Class

The first three methods in our `Employee` class should not pose many problems. They are much like the methods you saw in the previous chapter. Notice, however, that all of these methods can access the private instance fields by name. This is a key point: instance fields are always accessible by the methods of their own class.

For example,

```
public void raiseSalary(double byPercent)
{  salary *= 1 + byPercent / 100;
}
```

sets a new value for the `salary` instance field in the object that executes this method. (This particular method does not return a value.) For example, the call

```
number007.raiseSalary(5);
```

raises `number007`'s salary by increasing the `number007.salary` variable by 5%.

Of the remaining methods in this class, the most interesting is the one that returns the year hired. Recall that it looks like this:

```
public int hireYear()
{  return hireDay.getYear();
}
```

Notice that this method returns an integer value, and it does this by applying a method to the `hireDay` instance variable. This makes perfect sense because `hireDay` is an instance of our `Day` class, which indeed has a `getYear` method.

Finally, let's look more closely at the rather simple `getName` method.

```
public String getName()
{  return name;
}
```

This is an obvious example of an accessor method. Because it works directly with a field in the class, it is sometimes called a *field accessor method*. It simply returns the current state of the `name` field.

For the class implementor, it is obviously more trouble to write both a private field and a public accessor method than to simply write a public data field. But programmers using the class are not inconvenienced—if `number007` is the name of the instance of the `Employee` class, they simply write `number007.getName()`, rather than `number007.name`.

The point is that the `name` field has become "read-only" to the outside world. Only operations of the class can modify it. In particular, should the value ever be wrong, only the class operations need to be debugged.

By the way, the function is called `getName()` because it would be confusing to call it `name()`—that is already taken by the instance variable itself and it would be confusing to have a variable and a method with the same name. (In any case, the convention in Java is that accessor methods begin with a lowercase `get`.)

Now, because secret agents come and go, one might want to modify the class at some later point to allow for a field mutator that resets the name of the current "007." But this would be done by the maintainers of the class as the need arises.

The point to keep in mind is that, in most classes, private data fields are of a technical nature and of no interest to anyone but the implementor of the operations. When the user of a class has a legitimate interest in both reading and setting a field, the class implementors need to supply *three* items:

- a private data field
- a public field accessor method
- a public field mutator method

This is a lot more tedious than supplying a single public data field, but there are considerable benefits:

1. The internal implementation can be changed without affecting any code other than the operations of the class.

Of course, the accessor and mutator methods may need to do a lot of work—especially when the data representation of the instance fields is changed. But that leads us to our second benefit.

2. Mutator methods can perform error-checking, whereas code that simply assigns to a field cannot.

Our `Day` class is a good example of a class that should *not* have mutators for each field. Suppose we had methods called `setDay`, `setMonth`, and `setYear` that do the obvious things. Suppose `d` was an instance of our `Day` class. Now consider the code:

```
d.setDay(31);
d.setMonth(3);
d.setYear(1996);
```

If the date encapsulated in `d` was currently at February 1, then the `setDay` operation described above would set it to an invalid date of February 31. What do you think `setDay` should do in this case? At first glance, this appears to be only a nuisance, but if you think this through carefully, you will find that there is no good answer.

Should an invalid `setDay` abort the program? Well, how *would* you then safely set the date from February 1 to March 31? Of course, you could set the month first:

```
d.setMonth(3);
d.setDay(31);
```

That will work. Now, how do you change it back to February 1? This time, you can't set the month first. These functions would be a real hassle to use.

So perhaps `setDay` should just quietly adjust the date? If you set the date to February 31, then maybe the date should be adjusted to March 2 or 3, depending on whether the year is a leap year or not. The Java `GregorianCalendar` class does exactly that when the "lenient" flag is turned on. We think this is a lousy idea. Consider again our effort to set the date from February 1 to March 31.

```
d.setDay(31); // now it is March 2 or 3
d.setMonth(3); // still March 2 or 3
```

Or perhaps `setDay` should temporarily make an invalid date and count on the fact that the programmer won't forget to adjust the month. Then we lose a major benefit of encapsulation: the guarantee that the object state is never corrupted.

We hope we have convinced you that a mutator that sets only the `day` field is not worth the trouble. It is obviously better to supply a single `setDate(int, int, int)` function that does the error-checking needed. (This also fits one's mental model better—after all, one sets a date and not a day, month, and year.)

PITFALL: Be careful not to write accessor methods that return references to mutable objects. Consider the following example.

```
class Employee
{  . . .
   public String getName() { return name; }
   public Day getHireDay() { return hireDay; }
   private String name;
   private double salary;
   private Day hireDay;
}
```

This breaks the encapsulation! Consider the following rogue code:

```
Employee harry = . . .;
Day d = harry.getHireDay();
d.advance(-3650);
// let's give Harry ten years added seniority
```

The reason is subtle. Both `d` and `harry.hireDay` refer to the same object.

Changing `d` automatically changes the private state of the employee object!
Why didn't the `getName` method suffer from the same problem? Couldn't someone get the name and change it? No. The name is a string, and strings are *immutable*. There is no method that can change a string. In contrast, `Day` objects are mutable. There is exactly one mutator, namely `advance`.

The remedy is to *clone* the `hireDay` field before returning it in the accessor method. A clone is an exact copy of an object that is stored in a new location. We will discuss cloning in detail in Chapter 5. Here is the corrected code:

```
class Employee
{  . . .
   public Day getHireDay() { return (Day)hireDay.clone(); }
}
```

As a rule of thumb, always use `clone` whenever you need to return a copy of a mutable data field.

Method Access to Private Data

You know that a method can access the private data of the object on which it is invoked. What many people find surprising is that a method can access the private data of *all objects of its class*. For example, consider a method `compare` that compares two dates.

```
class Day
{  . . .
   boolean equals(Day b)
   {  return year == b.year && month == b.month
         && day == b.day;
   }
}
```

A typical call is

```
if (hireday.equals(d)) . . .
```

This method accesses the private fields of `hireday`, which is not surprising. It also accesses the private fields of `d`. This is legal because `d` is an object of type `Day`, and a method of the `Day` class is permitted to access the private fields of *any* object of type `Day`.

C++ NOTE: C++ has the same rule. A member function can access the private features of any object of its class, not just the implicit argument.

Private Methods

When implementing a class, we make all data fields private, but what about the methods? While `public` data are dangerous, `private` methods occur quite frequently. These methods can be called only from other operations of the class. The reason is simple: to implement operations, you may wish to break up the code into many separate methods. Many of these methods are not particularly useful to the public. (For example, they may be too close to the current implementation or require a special protocol or calling order.) Such methods are best implemented as `private` operations.

- To implement a `private` method in Java, simply change the `public` keyword to `private`.

As an example, consider how our `Day` class might require a method to test whether or not a year is a leap year. By making the method private, we are under no obligation to keep it available if we change to another implementation. The method may well be *harder* to implement or *unnecessary* if the data representation changes: this is irrelevant. The point is that as long as the operation is private, the designers of the class can be assured that it is never used outside the other class operations and can simply drop it. Had the method been public, we would be forced to reimplement it if we changed the representation, because other code might have relied on it. In sum, choose private methods:

- For those methods that are of no concern to the class user
- For those methods that could not easily be supported if the class implementation were to change

Static Methods

The last method modifier we want to talk about in this chapter is the `static` modifier. You saw the `static` modifier used to create class constants in Chapter 3. Classes can have both static fields and static methods. Static fields do not change from one instance of a class to another, so you should think of them as belonging to a class. Similarly, static methods belong to a class and do not operate on any instance of a class. This means that you can use them without creating an instance of a class. For example, all of the methods in the `Console` class are static methods as are all the methods in the `Math` class built into Java. This is why a syntax like

```
double x = Console.readDouble();
double x = Math.pow(3, 0.1);
```

makes perfect sense.

The general syntax for using a static method from a class is:

```
ClassName.staticMethod(parameters);
```

and the general syntax for using a static field is:

```
ClassName.staticFieldName;
```

NOTE: Because static methods do not work with an instance of the class they can only access static fields. In particular, if a method needs to access a nonstatic instance field of an object, it cannot be a static method.

C++ NOTE: Static variables and methods in Java are the same as static data members and member functions in C++. As in C++, the term "static" makes no sense. The original purpose of `static` in C/C++ was to denote local variables that don't go away when the local scope is exited. In that context, the term "static" indicates that the variable stays around and is still there when the block is entered again. Then `static` got a second meaning in C/C++, to denote, with file scope, functions and global variables that could not be accessed from other files. Finally, C++ reused the keyword for a third, unrelated interpretation, to denote variables and functions that belong to a class but not to any particular object of the class. That is the same meaning that the keyword has in Java.

As another example, consider the header for the `main` method:

```
public static void main(String[] args)
```

Since `main` is `static`, you don't need to create an instance of the class in order to call it—and the Java interpreter doesn't either. For example, if your `main` method is contained in the class `Mortgage` and you start the Java interpreter with

```
java Mortgage
```

then the interpreter simply starts the `main` method without creating an object of the `Mortgage` class. Because of this, `main` can only access static instance fields in the class. It is actually not uncommon for `main` to create an object of its own class!

```
class Application
{  . . .
   public static void main(String[] args)
   {  Application a = new Application();
      . . .
   }
}
```

This allows you to refer to instance variables of the class via the `a` object variable.

As a more serious example of a class that combines both static and public methods, the following class provides a random-number generator that is a significant improvement over the one supplied with Java. (Java uses a simple "linear congruential generator" that can be nonrandom in certain situations by displaying undesirable regularities. This is especially true when it is used to plot random points in space or for certain kinds of simulations.) The idea for the improvement is simple (we found it in Donald E. Knuth's *Semi-Numerical Algorithms,* which is Volume 2 of his *Art of Computer Programming* [Addison-Wesley, 1981]). Instead of using the random number supplied by a call to

```
java.lang.Math.random();
```

we created a class that:

1. adds the convenience of generating random integers in a specific range and
2. is more "random" than the one supplied with Java (but takes about twice as long).

The class works in the following way:

1. It fills up a small array with random numbers, using the built-in random number generator. The size of the array and the array itself are made class constants (i.e., declared with `private static final`). This way, all instances of the `randomInteger` class can share this information. (This is obviously more efficient than regenerating this information in each instance.)
2. It has a public method, called `draw`, for drawing a random integer in the specified range. (You will need to create an instance of our `RandomIntGenerator` class in order to use this method.)
3. The `draw` method, in turn, uses a static method called `nextRandom` that actually implements the algorithm described in Knuth's *Semi-Numerical Algorithms,* p. 32. The way this works is the method calls the built-in random number generator twice: the first time tells us which random array element to take, and the second time, we use the resulting random number to replace the "used-up" element in the array. (It is conceptually clearer to have these operations done in a static method, since all instances of our `RandomIntGenerator` class will share these operations.)
4. We use one Java feature in this example that you haven't yet seen. It's called a *static initialization block.* Use these blocks whenever simple initialization statements for static members are either not possible or simply too clumsy. For example, the `RandomIntGenerator` class needs to initialize the buffer entries before you can call the `nextRandom` method for the first time. You need a loop to initialize the buffer array, and a loop cannot be coded with a simple initializer.

As you can see in the `RandomIntGenerator` class, the syntax for a static initialization block is simply the keyword `static` followed by the braces that mark any Java code block. Java then executes the statements in the block once, before any method of that class is called. In particular, as with all static methods, you can only refer to the static data of the class in a static initialization block. You can't refer to object instance fields. Finally, you can have as many static initialization blocks as you want in a Java class. They are executed top to bottom.

5. The class constructor defines the range of integers.

The code is shown below.

```
public class RandomIntGenerator
{  public RandomIntGenerator(int l, int h)
   {  low = l;
      high = h;
   }

   public int draw()
   {  int r = low
         + (int)((high - low + 1) * nextRandom());
      if (r > high) r = high;
      return r;
   }

   public static void main(String[] args)
   {  RandomIntGenerator r1
         = new RandomIntGenerator(1, 10);
      RandomIntGenerator r2
         = new RandomIntGenerator(0, 1);
      int i;
      for (i = 1; i <= 100; i++)
         System.out.println(r1.draw() + " " + r2.draw());
   }

   private static double nextRandom()
   {  int pos =
         (int)(java.lang.Math.random() * BUFFER_SIZE);
      if (pos == BUFFER_SIZE) pos = BUFFER_SIZE - 1;
      double r = buffer[pos];
      buffer[pos] = java.lang.Math.random();
      return r;
   }

   private static final int BUFFER_SIZE = 101;
   private static double[] buffer
      = new double[BUFFER_SIZE];
   static //initialization of static data
```

```
    {  int i;
       for (i = 0; i < BUFFER_SIZE; i++)
          buffer[i] = java.lang.Math.random();
    }

    private int low;
    private int high;
}
```

Following is an example using our random integer generator. Note that the test program is simply included in the RandomIntGenerator class.

```
class RandomIntGenerator
{  . . .
   public static void main(String[] args)
   {  RandomIntGenerator r1
         = new RandomIntGenerator(1, 10);
      RandomIntGenerator r2
         = new RandomIntGenerator(0, 1);
      int i;
      for (i = 1; i <= 100; i++)
         System.out.println(r1.draw() + "  " + r2.draw());
   }
}
```

More on Object Construction and Destruction

Overloading

Recall that both Java's GregorianCalendar class and our Day class had more than one constructor. We could use:

```
Day today = new Day();
```

or

```
Day preMillenium =  new Day(1999,12,31);
```

This capability is called *overloading*. Overloading occurs if several methods have the same name (in this case, the Day constructor method) but different arguments. The Java interpreter must sort out which method to call. (This is usually called *overloading resolution*.) It picks the correct method by matching the argument types in the headers of the various methods with the types of the values used in the specific method call. (Even if there are no arguments, you must use the empty parentheses.) A compile-time error occurs if the compiler cannot match the arguments or if more than one match is possible.

NOTE: Java allows you to overload any method—not just constructor methods.

Overloading is something we will return to in the next chapter. For those familiar with OOP method overloading (sometimes called *adhoc polymorphism*) must be distinguished from true polymorphism, which Java also does support.

Instance Field Initialization

Since you can overload the constructor methods in a class, you can obviously build in many ways to set the instance fields of your classes. It is always a good idea to make sure that, regardless of the constructor call, every instance field is set to something meaningful. Actually, Java does set all instance fields to a default value (numbers to zero, objects to `null`, booleans to `false`), if you don't set them explicitly. But it is considered poor programming practice to rely on this. Certainly, it makes it harder for someone to use your code if variables are being initialized invisibly.

NOTE: In this regard, instance variables differ from local variables in a method. Local variables must be initialized explicitly.

For example, if our `Day` class did not have any constructors, then the day, month, and year fields would be initialized with zero whenever you made a new `Day` object. (That wouldn't be a good idea. In the Julian/Gregorian calendar, there is no year 0—the year 1 B.C. is immediately followed by 1 A.D. For that reason, we supply explicit constructors.)

If all constructors of a class need to set a particular instance variable to the same value, then there is a convenient syntax for doing the initialization. You simply assign to the field in the class definition. For example, when you initialize a `Customer` object, you would want to set the `nextOrder` instance variable to 1 all the time. This can be done as in the following code:

```
class Customer
{  public Customer(String n)
   {  name = n;
      accountNumber = Account.getNewNumber();
   }
   public Customer(String n, int a)
   {  name = n;
      accountNumber = a;
   }
   . . .
   private String name;
   private int accountNumber;
   private int nextOrder = 1;
}
```

Now the `nextOrder` field is set to 1 in all `Customer` objects.

We recommend that you use this convenient syntax whenever a field is set to the same constant value by all constructors.

A *default constructor* is a constructor with no parameters. If your class has no constructors whatsoever, Java provides a default constructor for you. It sets *all* the instance variables to their default values. So, all numeric data contained in the instance fields would be zeroed out, and all object variables would point to `null` and all booleans would be false.

This only applies when your class has no constructors. If you design your class with a constructor, then Java insists that you provide a default constructor if you want the users of your class to have the ability to create an instance via a call to

```
new ClassName()
```

For example, the `Customer` class defines no constructors that use no parameters, so it is illegal for the users of the class to call

```
c = new Customer(); // ERROR--no default constructor
```

C++ NOTE: In C++, you cannot directly initialize data members of a class. All data must be set in a constructor.

Java has no analog for the C++ initializer list syntax, such as:

```
Customer::Customer(String n)
:   name(n),
    accountNumber(Account.getNewNumber())
{}
```

C++ uses this special syntax to call the constructor for member objects. In Java, there is no need for it because objects have no member objects, only pointers to other objects.

The `this` Object Reference

Occasionally, you want to access the current object in its entirety and not a particular instance variable. Java has a convenient shortcut for this—the `this` keyword. In a method, the keyword `this` refers to the object on which the method operates.

For example, many Java classes have a method called `toString()` that prints out the object. (For example, Java's `Date` class has this method.) You can print out the current date stored in a date variable by saying `this.toString()`.

More generally, provided your class implements a `toString()` method, you can print it out simply by calling:

```
System.out.println("Customer.computeOverdue: " + this)
```

This is a useful strategy for debugging. We will later see other uses for the `this` object.

There is a second meaning for the `this` keyword. If *the first line of a constructor* has the form `this(. . .)`, then the constructor calls another constructor of the same class. Here is a typical example:

```
class Customer
{   public Customer(String n)
    {   this(n, Account.getNewNumber());
    }
    public Customer(String n, int a)
    {   name = n;
        accountNumber = a;
    }
    . . .
}
```

When you call `new Customer("James Bond")`, then the `Customer(String)` constructor calls the `Customer(String, int)` constructor.

This is a useful device to factor out (combine) common code between constructors.

In sum, as you have seen, constructors are somewhat complex in Java. Before a constructor is called, all instance fields are initialized to the value you specified in the class or to their default values (zero for numbers, `null` for objects, `false` for booleans). The first line of your constructor may call another constructor.

C++ NOTE: The `this` object in Java is identical to the `this` pointer in C++. However, in C++ it is not possible for one constructor to call another. If you want to factor out common initialization code in C++, you must write a separate member function.

Object Destruction and the `finalize()` Method

Many languages, such as C++ and Delphi, have explicit destructor methods for the cleanup code that may be needed. The most common activity in a destructor is reclaiming the memory set aside for objects. Since Java does automatic garbage collection, manual memory reclamation is not needed, and Java does not support destructors.

Of course, some objects utilize a resource other than memory, such as a file or a handle to another object that uses system resources. In this case, it is important that the resource be reclaimed and recycled when it is no longer needed.

Java does allow you to add a `finalize()` method to any class. The `finalize()` method will be called before the garbage collector sweeps away the object. In practice, *do not rely on the* `finalize` *method* for recycling any resources that are in short supply—you simply cannot know when this method will be called.

NOTE: Java 1.1 had added a static method called `runFinalizersOnExit` in the `System` class that will guarantee that finalizer methods are called before Java shuts down.

If a resource needs to be closed as soon as you have finished using it, you need to manage it manually. Add a `dispose` method that *you* call to clean up what needs cleaning. Just as importantly, if a class you use has a `dispose` method, you will want to call it to reclaim what the designers of the class thought was important to reclaim. In particular, if your class has an instance field that has a `dispose` method, provide a `dispose` method that invokes that field's `dispose`.

A `CardDeck` *Class*

To put together the information in this chapter, we want to show you the code needed for the simplest card game of all. The program chooses two cards at random, one for you and one for the computer. The highest card wins.

The underlying object structure in this example is this: a class called `Card` is used to build up a class called `CardDeck`. A card stores its value (a number between 1 and 13 to denote ace, 2, . . . 10, jack, queen, or king) and its suit (a number between 1 and 4 to denote clubs, diamonds, hearts, or spades). Don't worry about the `final` for the class and for some of the methods in this example. We will explain the significance of this use of the `final` keyword as applied to classes and methods in the next chapter.

```
final class Card // don't worry about the final for now
{  public static final int ACE = 1;
   public static final int JACK = 11;
   public static final int QUEEN = 12;
   public static final int KING  = 13;
   public static final int CLUBS = 1;
   public static final int DIAMONDS = 2;
   public static final int HEARTS = 3;
   public static final int SPADES = 4;

   . . .

   private int value;
   private int suit;
}
```

Here's the constructor for the `Card` object. As you might expect, it takes two integers, one for the value and one for the suit.

```
public Card(int v, int s)
{  value = v;
   suit = s;
}
```

The card deck stores an array of cards.

```
class CardDeck
{  . . .
   private Card[] deck;
   private int cards;
}
```

The `cards` field counts how many cards are still in the deck. At the beginning, there are 52 cards, and the count will go down as we draw cards from the deck.

Here's the constructor for the `CardDeck` class:

```
public CardDeck()
{  deck = new Card[52];
   fill();
   shuffle();
}
```

Notice that this constructor initializes the array of `Card` objects. After the array of cards is allocated, it will automatically be filled with cards and shuffled. The `fill` method fills the card deck with 52 cards.

The idea of the `shuffle` method is to choose randomly which of the cards becomes the last one. We then swap the last card with the chosen card and repeat the process with the remainder of the pile.

The full code for the `CardDeck` class is shown here in Example 4-3. Note the code for the game in the `main` method.

Example 4-3: CardDeck.java

```
import corejava.*;

public class CardDeck
{  public CardDeck()
   {  deck = new Card[52];
      fill();
      shuffle();
   }

   public void fill()
   {  int i;
      int j;

      for (i = 1; i <= 13; i++)
         for (j = 1; j <= 4; j++)
            deck[4 * (i - 1) + j - 1] = new Card(i, j);
      cards = 52;
   }

   public void shuffle()
   {  int next;
```

```
        for (next = 0; next < cards - 1; next++)
        {   int r = new
                RandomIntGenerator(next, cards - 1).draw();
            Card temp = deck[next];
            deck[next] = deck[r];
            deck[r] = temp;
        }
    }

    public final Card draw()
    {   if (cards == 0) return null;
        cards--;
        return deck[cards];
    }

    public static void main(String[] args)
    {   CardDeck d = new CardDeck();
        int i;
        int wins = 0;
        int rounds = 10;

        for (i = 1; i <= rounds; i++)
        {   Card yours = d.draw();
            System.out.print("Your draw: " + yours + " ");
            Card mine = d.draw();
            System.out.print("My draw: " + mine + " ");
            if (yours.rank() > mine.rank())
            {   System.out.println("You win");
                wins++;
            }
            else
                System.out.println("I win");
        }
        System.out.println
    ("Your wins: " + wins + " My wins: " + (rounds - wins));

    }

    private Card[] deck;
    private int cards;
}
```

Example 4-4 is the complete code for the `Card` class. Note how we encapsulate the integers that represent the card's suit and value and only return information about them. Also note that once a `Card` object is constructed, its contents can never change.

Example 4-4: Card.java

```
public final class Card
{
   public static final int ACE = 1;
   public static final int JACK = 11;
   public static final int QUEEN = 12;
   public static final int KING  = 13;
   public static final int CLUBS = 1;
   public static final int DIAMONDS = 2;
   public static final int HEARTS = 3;
   public static final int SPADES = 4;

   public Card(int v, int s)
   {  value = v;
      suit = s;
   }

   public int getValue()
   {  return value;
   }

   public int getSuit()
   {  return suit;
   }

   public int rank()
   {  if (value == 1)
         return 4 * 13 + suit;
      else
         return 4 * (value - 1) + suit;
   }

   public String toString()
   {  String v;
      String s;
      if (value == ACE) v = "Ace";
      else if (value == JACK) v = "Jack";
      else if (value == QUEEN) v = "Queen";
      else if (value == KING) v = "King";
      else v = String.valueOf(value);
      if (suit == DIAMONDS) s = "Diamonds";
      else if (suit == HEARTS) s = "Hearts";
      else if (suit == SPADES) s = "Spades";
      else /* suit == CLUBS */ s = "Clubs";
      return v + " of " + s;
   }

   private int value;
   private int suit;
}
```

Packages

Java allows you to group classes in a collection called a *package*. Packages are convenient for organizing your work and for separating your work from code libraries provided by others.

For example, we give you a number of useful classes in a package called `corejava`. The standard Java library is distributed over a number of packages, including `java.lang`, `java.util`, `java.net`, and so on. The standard Java packages are examples of a hierarchical package. Just as you have nested subdirectories on your hard disk, you can organize packages using levels of nesting. All standard Java packages are inside the `java` package hierarchy.

One reason for nesting packages is to guarantee the uniqueness of package names. Suppose someone else has the bright idea of calling their package `corejava`. By nesting it inside a package hierarchy, such as `horstmann-cornell.corejava`, we could have kept our package distinct from any other `corejava` package. You can have as many levels of nesting as you like. In fact, to absolutely guarantee a unique package name, Sun recommends that you use your company's Internet domain name (which presumably is unique) written in reverse order as a package prefix. For example, CoreBooks is a domain that we registered, so we might have called the `corejava` package

```
COM.corebooks.corejava
```

When you write a package, you must put the name of the package on top of your source file, *before* the code that defines the classes in the package. For example, the files in our `corejava` package start like this:

```
package corejava;
```

If you look into the `GregorianCalendar.java` file of the Java library, you will see the line:

```
package java.util;
```

This means that the `GregorianCalendar.java` file is part of the `java.util` package. The `package` statement must be the first statement in the file after any comments.

If your source file has no package declaration, Java adds the classes in it to its default package.

Using Packages

You can use the public classes in a package in two ways. The first is simply to give the full name of the package. For example:

```
int i = corejava.Console.readInteger();
java.util.GregorianCalendar today
   = new java.util.GregorianCalendar();
```

That is obviously tedious. The simpler, and more common, approach is to use the `import` keyword. You can then refer to the classes in the package without giving their full names. You can import a specific class or the whole package. You place the `import` statement before the source code of the class that will use it. For example:

```
import corejava.*; // imports all the classes in the
                   // corejava package
import java.util.*;
```

then you can use:

```
int i = Console.readInteger();
GregorianCalendar today = new java.util.GregorianCalendar();
```

You can also import a specific class inside a package. In this case, you adjust the `import` statement as in the following:

```
import corejava.Console; // imports only the Console class
```

Normally, importing all classes in a package is simpler. It has no negative effect on compile time or code size, so there is generally no reason not to do it. However, if two packages each have classes with the same name, then you can't import them both.

Finally, you can only use the `*` to import a single package. You cannot use `import java.*` to import all packages with the `java` prefix.

How the Compiler Locates Packages

All files of a package must be located in a subdirectory that matches the full package name. For example, all files in our `corejava` package must be in the subdirectory `corejava`. All files in the `java.util` package are in a subdirectory `java\util` (`java/util` on UNIX).

These subdirectories need not branch off directly from the root directory; they can branch off from any directory named in the CLASSPATH environment variable. Suppose your CLASSPATH is as follows:

```
CLASSPATH=c:\jdk\lib;c:\CoreJavaBook;.
```

Suppose your code contains the lines:

```
import java.util.*;
import corejava.*;
```

If you use the class `Console`, the compiler looks for the following files:

```
c:\jdk\lib\Console.class

c:\jdk\lib\corejava\Console.class

c:\jdk\lib\java\util\Console.class

c:\CoreJavaBook\Console.class

c:\CoreJavaBook\java\util\Console.class
```

```
c:\CoreJavaBook\corejava\Console.class
.\Console.class
.\jdk\util\Console.class
.\corejava\Console.class
```

When it finds a matching file, it checks that the package name matches the path and that the file contains a public class named `Console` inside the package.

Actually, if you look inside `c:\jdk\lib`, you may not find the subdirectory `java\util`. Instead, there often is just a single ZIP file, `classes.zip`. If you look inside that ZIP file with a ZIP viewer like WinZip, you will see the paths and the class files. If you like, you can also zip up your own packages in a file named `classes.zip` that is located on the class path.

In addition, the compiler always searches the `java.lang` package. You never need to specify it, nor do you need to import it.

When you make a package, it is your responsibility to place the object files in the correct subdirectory. For example, if you compile a file that starts with the line

```
package acme.util;
```

then you must put the resulting class file into the subdirectory `acme\util`. The compiler won't do it for you.

C++ NOTE: C++ programmers usually confuse `import` with `#include`. The two have nothing in common. In C++, you must use `#include` to include the declarations of external features, because the C++ compiler does not look inside any files except the one that it is compiling and explicitly included header files. The Java compiler will happily look inside other files provided you tell it where to look.

In Java, you can entirely avoid the `import` mechanism by explicitly naming all packages, such as `java.util.GregorianCalendar`. In C++, you cannot avoid the `#include` directives.

The only benefit of the `import` statement is convenience. You can refer to a class by a name shorter than the full package name. For example, after an `import java.util.*` (or `import java.util.GregorianCalendar`) statement, you can refer to the `java.util.GregorianCalendar` class simply as `GregorianCalendar`.

The analogous construction in C++ is the *namespace* feature. Think of the `package` and `import` keywords in Java as the analogs of `namespace` and `using` in C++.

Package Scope

We have already encountered the access modifiers `public` and `private`. Features tagged as `public` can be used by any class. Private features can only be

used by the class that defines them. If you don't specify either `public` or `private`, then the feature (that is, the class, method or variable) can be accessed by all methods in the same *package*.

For example, if the class `Card` is not defined as a public class, then only other classes in the same package (such as `CardDeck`) can access it. For classes, that is a very reasonable default. However, methods should generally be either explicitly public or private, and instance and static variables should be private.

NOTE: Every source file can contain, at most, one public class, which must have the same name as the file.

Class Design Hints

Without trying to be comprehensive or tedious, we want to end this chapter with some hints that may make your classes more acceptable in well-mannered OOP circles.

1. *Always keep data private.*

   This is first and foremost: doing anything else violates encapsulation. You may need to write an accessor or mutator method occasionally, but you are still better off keeping the instance fields private. Bitter experience has shown that how the data are represented may change, but how they are used will change much less frequently. When data are kept private, changes in their representation do not affect the user of the class, and bugs are easier to detect.

2. *Always initialize data.*

   Java won't initialize local variables for you, but it will initialize instance variables of objects. Don't rely on the defaults, but initialize the variables explicitly, either by supplying a default or by setting defaults in all constructors.

3. *Don't use too many basic types in a class.*

   The idea is to replace multiple *related* uses of basic types with other classes. This keeps your classes easier to understand and to change. For example, replace the following instance fields in a `Customer` class

   ```
   private String street;
   private String city;
   private String state;
   private int zip;
   ```

   with a new class called `Address`. This way, you can easily cope with changes to addresses, such as the need to deal with international addresses.

4. *Not all fields need individual field accessors and mutators.*

   You may need to get and set a person's salary. You certainly won't need to change his or her hiring date once the object is constructed. And, quite often, objects have instance variables that you don't want others to get or set, for example, the array of cards in the card deck.

5. *Use a standard form for class definitions.*

   We always list the contents of classes in the following order:

   public features

   package scope features

   private features

   Within each section, we list:

   constants

   constructors

   methods

   static methods

   instance variables

   static variables

   After all, the users of your class are more interested in the public interface than in the details of the private implementation. And they are more interested in methods than in data.

6. *Break up classes with too many responsibilities.*

   This hint is, of course, vague: "too many" is obviously in the eye of the beholder. However, if there is an obvious way to make one complicated class into two classes that are conceptually simpler, seize the opportunity. (On the other hand, don't go overboard; 10 classes, each with only one method, is usually overkill.)

   Here is an example of a bad design. In our card game, we could do without the `Card` class by having the deck store two arrays: one for the suits and one for the values. That would make it hard to draw and return a card, so we would need to fake it with functions that can look up the properties of the top card on the deck.

```
class CardDeck // bad design
{  public void CardDeck() { . . . }
   public void shuffle() { . . . }
   public int getTopValue() { . . . }
   public int getTopSuit() { . . . }
```

```
    public int topRank() { . . . }
    public void draw() { . . . }

    private int[] value;
    private int[] suit;
    private int cards;
}
```

As you can see, this is implementable, but it is clumsy. It makes sense to introduce the `Card` class because the cards are meaningful objects in this context.

7. *Make the names of your classes and methods reflect their responsibilities.*

   Just as variables should have meaningful names that reflect what they do, so should classes. (The standard library certainly contains some dubious examples, such as the `Date` class that describes time.)

   A good convention is that a class name should be a noun (`Order`) or a noun preceded by an adjective (`RushOrder`) or a gerund (an "ing" word—`BillingAddress`). As for methods, follow the standard convention that accessor methods begin with a lowercase `get` (`getDay`), and mutator methods use a lowercase `set` (`setSalary`). The implementors of Java 1.1 actually made a concerted effort to improve the method names from Java 1.0, so that now most of the accessor methods begin with `get` and most of the mutator methods begin with `set`.

CHAPTER 5

- First Steps with Inheritance
- Casting
- Abstract Classes
- `Object`: The Cosmic Superclass
- The `Class` Class (Run-TIme Type Identification)
- Reflection
- Protected Access
- Design Hints for Inheritance

Inheritance

The last chapter introduced OOP. This chapter explains most of the remaining concepts you need to know, particularly those that deal with deriving new classes from existing classes. This concept is usually called *inheritance* and was briefly touched upon in the last chapter. Recall that the idea behind inheritance is that you can reuse or change the methods of existing classes, as well as add new instance fields and new methods in order to adapt them to new situations. This technique is essential in Java programming. (For example, as you will see in Chapter 7, you cannot even show text or graphics in a window in Java without using inheritance!)

As with the previous chapter, if you are coming from a procedure-oriented language like C or COBOL, you will want to read this chapter carefully. The same holds true for *all* users of VB (even VB4 or VB5 users—the more limited object model used in VB does not have inheritance).

For experienced C++ programmers or those coming from another object-oriented language like Smalltalk, this chapter will seem largely familiar, but there are *many* differences between how inheritance is implemented in Java and how it is done in C++ or in other object-oriented languages. You will probably want to read the later sections of this chapter carefully.

First Steps with Inheritance

Let's return to the `Employee` class that we discussed in the previous chapter. Suppose (alas) you work for a company at which managers are treated substantially differently than other employees. Their raises are computed differently; they have access to a secretary; and so on. This is the kind of situation that in OOP cries out for inheritance. Why? Well, you need to define a new class,

Manager, and add functionality, but you can retain some of what you have already programmed in the Employee class, and *all* the instance fields of the original class can be preserved. More abstractly, there is an obvious "is–a" relationship between Manager and Employee. Every manager *is an* employee: this "is a" relationship is the hallmark of inheritance.

Here is some code for extending the Employee class to be a Manager class.

```
class Manager extends Employee
{  public Manager(String n, double s, Day d)
   {  super(n, s, d);
      secretaryName = "";
   }

   public void raiseSalary(double byPercent)
   {  // add 1/2% bonus for every year of service
      Day today = new Day();
      double bonus = 0.5 * (today.getYear() - hireYear());
      super.raiseSalary(byPercent + bonus);
   }

   public String getSecretaryName()
   {  return secretaryName;
   }

   public void setSecretaryName(String name)
   {  secretaryName = name;
   }

   private String secretaryName;
}
```

Let's go over the new features of this class, line by line. First, notice that the header for this class is a little different:

```
class Manager extends Employee
```

The keyword extends indicates that you are making a new class that derives from an existing class. The existing class is called the *superclass, base class,* or *parent class*. The new class is called the *subclass, derived class,* or *child class.* The terms superclass and subclass are those most commonly used by Java programmers, although we prefer the parent/child analogy, which also ties in nicely with the "inheritance" theme.

The Employee class is a superclass, but not because it is superior to its subclass or contains more functionality. *In fact, the opposite is true:* subclasses have *more* functionality than their superclasses. For example, as you will see when we go over the rest of the Manager class code, it encapsulates more data and has more functionality than its superclass `Employee`. As another example, you will see in the next chapter Java has a superclass `Window`, which is extended to many useful subclasses, such as `FileDialog`.

NOTE: The prefixes *super* and *sub* come from the language of sets used in theoretical computer science and mathematics. The set of all employees *contains* the set of all managers, and this is described by saying it is a *superset* of the set of managers. Similarly, the set of all file dialog windows is *contained* by the set of all windows, so it is a *subset* of the set of all windows.

Next, notice the constructor for the `Manager` class:

```
public Manager(String n, double s, Day d)
{   super(n, s, d);
    secretaryName = "";
}
```

The keyword `super` always refers to the superclass (in this case, `Employee`). So the line

```
super(n, s, d);
```

is shorthand for "call the constructor of the `Employee` class with `n`, `s`, and `d` as parameters." The reason for this line is that every constructor of a subclass is responsible for constructing the data fields of the superclass; for example, by calling the superclass constructor to initialize the data fields of the superclass. Unless the subclass constructor is happy with the default constructor of the superclass, it must explicitly use `super` with the appropriate parameters. The call to `super` must be the first line in the constructor for the subclass.

Next, as this example shows, subclasses can have more instance fields than the parent class. Following good programming practices, we set the `secretaryName` instance field to the empty string in order to initialize it. (By default, it would have been initialized to `null`.)

If you compare the `Manager` class with the `Employee` class, you will see that many of the methods are not repeated. This is because, unless otherwise specified, a subclass uses the methods of the superclass. In particular, when inheriting from a superclass, you need to indicate only the *differences* between the subclass and superclass. The ability to reuse methods in the superclass is automatic. Therefore, we do not need to give a new definition of, for example, a `getName` method, since the one in the superclass does what we need. The *factoring* out of common functionality by moving it to a parent class is essential to the proper use of inheritance in object-oriented programming.

However, do note that we are giving a new definition of the `raiseSalary` method:

```
public void raiseSalary(double byPercent)
{  // add 1/2% bonus for every year of service
   Day today = new Day();
   double bonus = 0.5 * (today.getYear() - hireYear());
   super.raiseSalary(byPercent + bonus);
}
```

because, as mentioned previously, this method must work differently for managers and (ordinary) employees.

The need to redefine methods is one of the main reasons to use inheritance; this is a good example. Life being the way it is, raises for managers are calculated differently than those for nonmanagers. In this case, suppose you give a company-wide raise of five percent. For managers, the `raiseSalary` method however does the following:

1. It calculates a bonus percentage increase based on time employed.
2. Then, because of the use of `super` in the line

   ```
   super.raiseSalary(byPercent + bonus);
   ```

   the method looks to the `raiseSalary` method of the superclass and passes it a parameter that adds the original parameter and a bonus of half a percent for each year the managers have been employed since they were hired.

The result is that when you give all employees a raise of five percent, the managers will *automatically* be given a larger raise. Here's an example of this at work: we make a new manager and set the manager's secretary's name:

```
Manager boss = new Manager("Carl Cracker", 75000,
   new Day(1987,12,15));
boss.setSecretaryName("Harry Hacker");
```

We make an array of three employees:

```
Employee[] staff = new Employee[3];
```

We populate the array with a mix of employees and managers:

```
staff[0] = boss;
staff[1] = new Employee("Harry Hacker", 35000,
   new Day(1989,10,1));
staff[2] = new Employee("Tony Tester", 38000,
   new Day(1990,3,15));
```

We raise everyone's salary by five percent:

```
for (i = 0; i < 3; i++) staff[i].raiseSalary(5);
```

Now `staff[1]` and `staff[2]` each get a raise of three percent because they are `Employee` objects. However, `staff[0]` is a `Manager` object and gets a higher raise. Finally, let's print out all employee records and the name of the secretary.

```
for (i = 0; i < 3; i++) staff[i].print();
System.out.println(boss.getName() + "'s current secretary is "
   + boss.getSecretaryName());
```

Because we didn't define a special `print` method for managers, all three objects are printed with the `Employee` print method. (We could have changed the `print` method in the `Manager` class in order to print out the current name of a manager's secretary.) Example 5-1 is the full sample code that shows you the `Manager` class at work.

Example 5-1: ManagerTest.java

```
import java.util.*;
import corejava.*;

public class ManagerTest
{  public static void main(String[] args)
   {  Employee[] staff = new Employee[3];

      staff[0] = new Employee("Harry Hacker", 35000,
         new Day(1989,10,1));
      staff[1] = new Manager("Carl Cracker", 75000,
         new Day(1987,12,15));
      staff[2] = new Employee("Tony Tester", 38000,
         new Day(1990,3,15));
      int i;
      for (i = 0; i < 3; i++) staff[i].raiseSalary(5);
      for (i = 0; i < 3; i++) staff[i].print();
   }
}

class Employee
{  public Employee(String n, double s, Day d)
   {  name = n;
      salary = s;
      hireDay = d;
   }
   public void print()
   {  System.out.println(name + " " + salary + " "
         + hireYear());
   }
   public void raiseSalary(double byPercent)
   {  salary *= 1 + byPercent / 100;
   }
   public int hireYear()
```

```
    {  return hireDay.getYear();
    }

    private String name;
    private double salary;
    private Day hireDay;
}

class Manager extends Employee
{   public Manager(String n, double s, Day d)
    {  super(n, s, d);
       secretaryName = "";
    }

    public void raiseSalary(double byPercent)
    {  // add 1/2% bonus for every year of service
       Day today = new Day();
       double bonus = 0.5 * (today.getYear() - hireYear());
       super.raiseSalary(byPercent + bonus);
    }

    public void setSecretaryName(String n)
    {  secretaryName = n;
    }

    public String getSecretaryName()
    {  return secretaryName;
    }

    private String secretaryName;
}
```

C++ NOTE: Inheritance is similar in Java and C++. Java uses the `extends` keyword instead of the `":"` token. Java uses the keyword `super` to refer to the base class. In C++, you would use the name of the base class with the `::` operator instead. For example, the `raiseSalary` function of the `Manager` class would call `Employee::raiseSalary` instead of `super.raiseSalary`. In a C++ constructor, you do not call `super`, but you use the initializer list syntax to construct the base class. The `Manager` constructor looks like this in C++:

```
Manager::Manager(String n, double s, Day d) // C++
: Employee(n, s, d)
{
}
```

Inheritance need not stop at deriving one layer of classes. We could have an `Executive` class that derives from `Manager`, for example. The collection of all

classes extending from a common parent is called an *inheritance hierarchy*. As shown in Figure 5-1, the path from a particular class to its ancestors in the inheritance hierarchy is its *inheritance chain.*

There is usually more than one chain of descent from a distant ancestor class. You could derive a `Programmer` class from `Employee` class or a `Secretary` class from `Employee`, and they would have nothing to do with the `Manager` class (or with each other). This process can continue as long as is necessary.

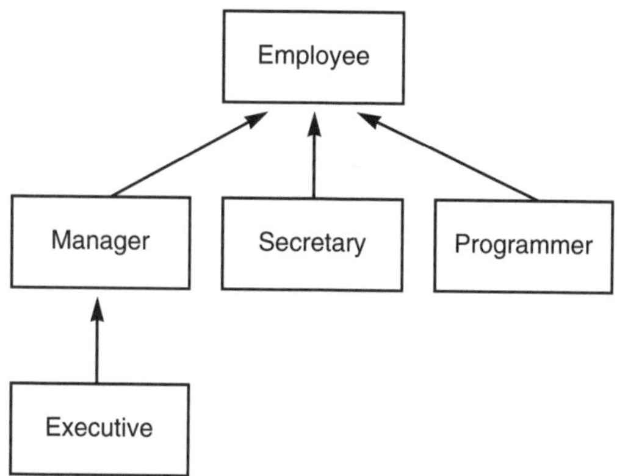

Figure 5-1: Employee inheritance hierarchy

Working with Subclasses

One way to know whether or not inheritance is right for your program is to keep in mind that any object of the subclass must be useable in place of the superclass object. If this is not true, do not use inheritance. (This is a more concrete way of thinking of the "is–a" relationship that is the hallmark of inheritance.) In particular, subclass objects are useable in any code that uses the superclass.

For example, you can assign a subclass object to a superclass variable. We did that in the sample code of the preceding section.

```
Employee[] staff = new Employee[3];
Manager boss = new Manager("Carl Cracker", 75000,
   new Day(1987,12,15));
staff[0] = boss;
```

In this case, the variables `staff[0]` and `boss` refer to the same area of memory. However, `staff[0]` is considered to be only an `Employee` object by the compiler.

Similarly, a subclass object can be passed as an argument to any method that expects a superclass parameter.

The converse is false in general: a superclass object cannot usually be assigned to a subclass object. For example, it is not legal to make the assignment:

```
boss = staff[i]; // ERROR
```

The reason is clear: the subclass object may have more fields than the superclass object (as it does in this case), and the subclass methods have to be able to access those fields. If the fields are not accessible, run-time errors will result. Always keep in mind that subclass objects have at least as many data items as objects from the superclass because fields can only be added, not taken away, in inheritance.

C++ NOTE: Java does not support multiple inheritance. (For ways to recover much of the functionality of multiple inheritance, see the section on Interfaces in the next chapter.)

Objects Know How to Do Their Work: Polymorphism

It is important to understand what happens when a method call is applied to objects of various types in an inheritance hierarchy. Remember that in OOP, you are sending messages to objects, asking them to perform actions. When you send a message that asks a subclass to apply a method using certain parameters, here is what happens:

- The subclass checks whether or not it has a method with that name and with *exactly* the same parameters. If so, it uses it.

If not,

- Java moves to the parent class and looks there for a method with that name and those parameters. If so, it calls that method.

Since Java can continue moving up the inheritance chain, parent classes are checked until the chain of inheritance stops or until Java finds a matching method. (If Java cannot find a matching method anywhere in the inheritance chain, you get a compile-time error.) Notice that methods with the same name can exist on many levels of the chain. This leads to one of the fundamental rules of inheritance:

- A method defined in a subclass with the same name and parameter list as a method in one of its ancestor classes hides the method of the ancestor class from the subclass.

For example, the `raiseSalary` method of the `Manager` class is called instead of the `raiseSalary` method of the `Employee` class when you send a `raiseSalary` message to a `Manager` object.

NOTE: The name and parameter list for a method is usually called the method's *signature*. For example, `raiseSalary(double)` and `raiseSalary(boolean)` are two methods with different signatures. In Java, having methods in a class or in a superclass and a subclass with the same signature but differing return types will give you a compile-time error. For instance, you cannot have a method `void raiseSalary(double)` in the `Employee` class and a method `int raiseSalary(double)` in the `Manager` class.

An object's ability to decide what method to apply to itself, depending on where it is in the inheritance hierarchy, is usually called *polymorphism*. The idea behind polymorphism is that while the message may be the same, objects may respond differently. Polymorphism can apply to any method that is inherited from a superclass.

The key to making polymorphism work is called *late binding*. This means that the compiler does not generate the code to call a method at compile time. Instead, every time you apply a method to an object, the compiler generates code to calculate which method to call, using type information from the object. (This process is also called *dynamic binding* or *dynamic dispatch*.) The traditional method call mechanism is called *static binding*, since the operation to be executed is completely determined at compile time. Static binding depends on the method alone; dynamic binding depends on the type of the object variable *and* the position of the actual object in the inheritance hierarchy.

NOTE: Many Java users follow C++ terminology and refer to *virtual functions* for functions that are dynamically bound.

C++ NOTE: In Java, you do not need to declare a method as virtual. This is the default behavior. If you do *not* want a function to be virtual, you tag it as `final`. (We discuss this in the next section.)

To sum up, inheritance and polymorphism let the application spell out the general way to proceed. The individual classes in the inheritance hierarchy are responsible for carrying out the details—using polymorphism to determine which methods to call. Polymorphism in an inheritance hierarchy is sometimes called *true polymorphism*. The idea is to distinguish it from the more limited kind of name overloading that is not resolved dynamically but is resolved statically at compile time.

Preventing Inheritance: Final Classes and Methods

Occasionally, you want to prevent someone from deriving a class from one of your classes. Classes that cannot be parent classes are called `final` classes, and you use the `final` modifier in the definition of the class to indicate this. For example, the `Card` class from the last chapter was `final`, so its header began:

```
final class Card
```

You can also make a specific method in a class `final`. If you do this, then no subclass can override that method. (All methods in a `final` class are automatically `final`.) A class or method is made `final` for one of two reasons:

1. Efficiency

   Dynamic binding has more overhead than static binding—thus, virtual methods run slower. The dynamic dispatching mechanism is slightly less efficient than a straight procedure call. More importantly, the compiler cannot replace a trivial method with inline code because it is possible that a derived class would override that trivial code. The compiler can put `final` methods in line. For example, if `e.getName()` is `final`, the compiler can replace it with `e.name`. (So you get all the benefits of direct access to instance fields *without violating encapsulation*.)

   Microprocessors hate procedure calls because procedure calls interfere with their strategy of getting and decoding the next instructions while processing the current one. Replacing calls to trivial procedures with inline code is a big win. This is more important for a true compiler than for an interpreter like the one supplied with the current JDK, but JITs can take advantage of this, and true Java compilers for all platforms are in the works.

2. Safety

   The flexibility of the dynamic dispatch mechanism means that you have no control over what happens when you call a method. When you send a message, such as `e.getName()`, it is possible that `e` is an object of a derived class that redefined the `getName` method to return an entirely different string. By making the method `final`, you avoid this possible ambiguity.

We used `final` methods and `final` classes in the `Card` class of the preceding chapter. We knew that nobody would derive a new class from the `Card` class, so we made it `final` for efficiency reasons. The `String` class in the Java library is `final` for probably the same reasons.

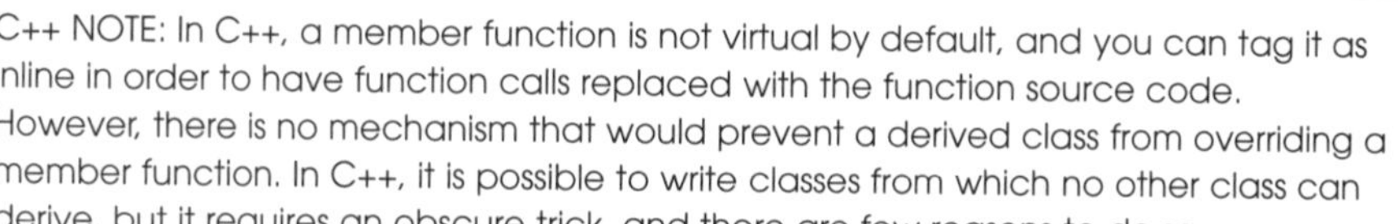

C++ NOTE: In C++, a member function is not virtual by default, and you can tag it as inline in order to have function calls replaced with the function source code. However, there is no mechanism that would prevent a derived class from overriding a member function. In C++, it is possible to write classes from which no other class can derive, but it requires an obscure trick, and there are few reasons to do so.

Casting

Recall from Chapter 3 that the process of converting from one basic type to another was called casting and Java has a special notation for casts. For example:

```
double x = 3.405;
int nx = (int)x
```

converts the variable `x` into an integer, discarding the fractional part.

Just as you occasionally need to convert a floating-point number to an integer, you also need to convert an object from one class to another. As with converting basic types, this process is also called *casting*. To actually make a cast, you use a syntax similar to what you used for casting between variables of the basic types. Surround the target type with parentheses and place it before the object you want to cast. For example:

```
Manager boss = (Manager)staff[0];
```

There is only one reason why you would want to make a cast—to use an object in its full capacity after its actual type has been downplayed. For example, in the `Manager` class, the `staff` array had to be an array of `Employee` objects since *some* of its entries were regular employees. We would need to cast the managerial elements of the array back to `Manager` in order to access any of its new fields. (Note that in the sample code for the first section, we made a special effort to avoid the cast. We initialized the `boss` variable with a `Manager` object before storing it in the array. We needed the correct type in order to set the secretary of the manager.) Similarly, we needed to make a cast when we used the `Math.round` method on a `double` (since `round` returned a `long`).

As you know, in Java, every object variable has a type. The type describes the kind of object the variable refers to and what it can do. For example, `staff[i]` refers to an `Employee` object (so it can also refer to a `Manager` object).

You rely on these descriptions in your code, and the compiler checks that you do not promise too much when you describe a variable. If you assign a subclass object to a superclass variable, you are promising less, and the compiler will simply let you do it. If you assign a superclass object to a subclass variable, you are promising more, and you must confirm that you mean what you say to the compiler with the `(Subclass)` cast notation.

What happens if you try to cast down an inheritance chain and you are "lying" about what an object contains?

```
Manager boss = (Manager)staff[1]; // Error
```

When the program runs, Java notices the broken promise, generates an exception (see the sidebar later on in this chapter and Chapter 12), and the program will usually die. It is good programming practice to find out whether or not your object is an instance of another object before doing a cast. This is accomplished with the `instanceof` operator. For example:

```
if (staff[1] instanceof Manager)
{  boss = (Manager)staff[1];
     . . .
}
```

Finally, the compiler will not let you make a cast if there is no chance for the cast to succeed. For example, the cast

```
Window w = (Window)staff[1];
```

will not succeed because `Window` is not a subclass of `Employee`.

To sum up:

- You can cast only within an inheritance hierarchy.
- Use `instanceof` to check a hierarchy before casting from a parent to a child class.

Actually, converting the type of an object by performing a cast is not usually a good idea. In our example, you do not need to cast an `Employee` object to a `Manager` object for most purposes. The `print` and `raiseSalary` methods will work correctly on both types because the dynamic binding that makes polymorphism work locates the correct method automatically. The only reason to make the cast is to use a method that is unique to managers, such as `getSecretaryName`. If it is important to get the name of a secretary for an object of type `Employee`, you should redesign that class and add a `getSecretaryName` method, which simply returns an empty string. This makes more sense than trying to remember which array locations stored which type, or making tedious type inquiries. Remember, it takes only one bad cast to terminate your program.

C++ NOTE: Java uses the cast syntax from the "bad old days" of C, but it works like the safe `dynamic_cast` operation of C++. For example,

```
Manager boss = (Manager)staff[1]; // Java
```

is the same as

```
Manager* boss = dynamic_cast<Manager*>(staff[1]); // C++
```

with one important difference. If the cast fails, it does not yield a `null` object, but throws an exception. In this sense, it is like a C++ cast of *references*. This is a pain in

the neck. In C++, you can take care of the type test and type conversion in one operation.

```
Manager* boss = dynamic_cast<Manager*>(staff[1]); // C++
if (boss != NULL) . . .
```

In Java, you use a combination of the `instanceof` operator and a cast.

```
if (staff[1] instanceof Manager)
{  Manager boss = (Manager)staff[1];
   . . .
}
```

Abstract Classes

As you move up the inheritance hierarchy, classes become more general and probably more abstract. At some point, the ancestor class becomes *so* general that you think of it more as a framework for other classes than as a class with specific instances you want to use. Consider, for example, an electronic messaging system that integrates your e-mail, faxes, and voice mail. It must be able to handle text messages, fax messages, and voice messages.

Following the principles of OOP, the program will need classes called `TextMessage`, `VoiceMessage`, and `FaxMessage`. Of course, a mailbox needs to store a mixture of these messages types, so it will access them through references to the common parent class `Message`. The inheritance hierarchy is shown in Figure 5-2.

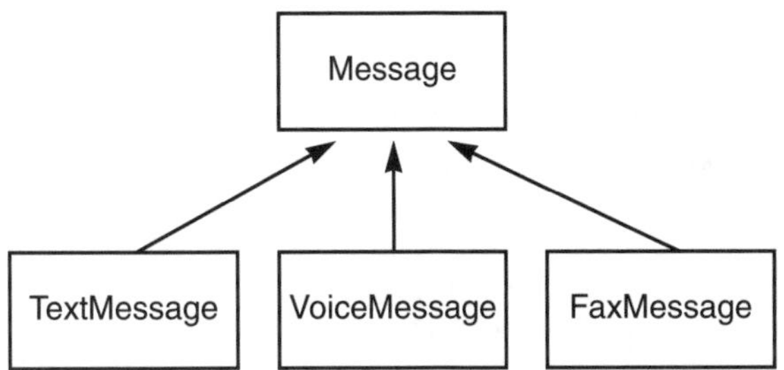

Figure 5-2: Inheritance diagram for message classes

Why bother with so high a level of abstraction? The answer is that it makes the design of your classes cleaner. (Well, it does once you are familiar with OOP.) Ultimately, one of the keys to OOP is to understand how to factor out common operations to a higher level in the inheritance hierarchy. In our case, all messages have a common method, namely `play()`. It is easy to figure out how to play a voice message—you send it to the loudspeaker. You play a text message by showing it in a text window and a fax message by showing it in a graphics window. But how do you implement `play()` in the parent class `Message`?

The answer is that you can't. In Java, you use the `abstract` keyword to indicate that a method cannot yet be specified in class. For added clarity, a class with one or more abstract methods must itself be declared abstract.

```
public abstract class Message
{  . . .
   public abstract void play();
}
```

Abstract classes can have (some) concrete data and methods. For example, the `Message` class can store the sender of the mail message and have a concrete method that returns the sender's name.

```
abstract class Message
{  public Message(String from) { sender = from; }

   public abstract void play();
   public String getSender() { return sender; }

   private String sender;
}
```

The key point is that, in addition to the ordinary methods you have seen, an abstract class has at least one *abstract method.* An abstract method promises that all nonabstract descendants of this abstract class will implement that abstract method. Abstract methods act as placeholder methods that are implemented in the subclasses.

TIP: It is common to think that abstract classes should have only abstract methods. This is not true: it always makes sense to move as much functionality as possible into a superclass, whether or not it is abstract. In particular, move common instance fields and *nonabstract* operations to the abstract superclass. Only those operations that cannot be implemented in the superclass should be given to the subclasses.

C++ NOTE: In C++, an abstract method is called a *pure virtual function* and is tagged with a trailing = 0 , such as in

```
class Message // C++
{  public:virtual void play() = 0;
   . . .
}
```

As in Java, a C++ class is abstract if it has at least one pure virtual function, but there is no special syntax to denote abstract classes.

To see a realization of this abstract class and also of the `play` method, try this code for the `TextMessage` class:

```
class TextMessage extends Message
{  public TextMessage(String from, String t)
   { super(from); text = t; }

   public void play() { System.out.println(text); }

   private String text;
}
```

Notice that we need only to give a concrete definition of the abstract `play` method in the `TextMessage` class.

Here's the code for the sample messaging program. Don't worry too much about the code for playing the wave file in this example; it uses a few language features, such as exceptions and streams, that we will discuss in Chapter 12 and Volume 2. It also uses an undocumented feature of Java that lets you play audio clips from within an application as opposed to an applet. This is a teaching example, so we kept the user interface simple and ugly to allow you to focus on the OOP aspects instead of being distracted by GUI code. When you run the program, you can leave a text message by typing it in or leave a voice message by typing in the name of an audio file. We supply you with two sample audio files on the CD, or you can use your own. They must be in `.au` format. Example 5-2 shows the code.

Example 5-2: MailboxTest.java

```
iimport java.io.*;
import sun.audio.*;
import corejava.*;

public class MailboxTest
{  public static void main(String[] args)
   {  Mailbox mbox = new Mailbox();
      while (true)
      {  System.out.println(mbox.status());
         String cmd = Console.readString
               ("play, text, voice, quit> ");
         if (cmd.equals("play"))
         {  Message m = mbox.remove();
            if (m != null)
            {  System.out.println("From: " + m.getSender());
               m.play();
            }
         }
```

```
            else if (cmd.equals("text"))
            {  String from = Console.readString("Your name: ");
               boolean more = true;
               String msg = "";
               System.out.println
                  ("Enter message, 'exit' when done");

               while (more)
               {  String line = Console.readString();
                  if (line.equals("exit"))
                     more = false;
                  else msg = msg + line + "\n";
               }
               mbox.insert(new TextMessage(from, msg));
            }
            else if (cmd.equals("voice"))
            {  String from = Console.readString("Your name: ");
               String msg
                  = Console.readString("Audio file name: ");
               mbox.insert(new VoiceMessage(from, msg));
            }
            else if (cmd.equals("quit"))
               System.exit(0);
         }
      }
   }

abstract class Message
{  public Message(String from) { sender = from; }

   public abstract void play();
   public String getSender() { return sender; }

   private String sender;
}

class TextMessage extends Message
{  public TextMessage(String from, String t)
   { super(from); text = t; }

   public void play() { System.out.println(text); }

   private String text;
}

class VoiceMessage extends Message
{  public VoiceMessage(String from, String f)
```

```
    { super(from); filename = f; }

    public void play()
    {  AudioPlayer ap = AudioPlayer.player;
       try
       {  AudioStream as
                = new AudioStream(new FileInputStream(filename));
          ap.start(as);
       }
       catch(IOException e) {}
    }

    private String filename;
}


class Mailbox
{  public Message remove()
   {  if (nmsg == 0) return null;
      Message r = messages[out];
      nmsg--;
      out = (out + 1) % MAXMSG;
      return r;
   }

   public void insert(Message m)
   {  if (nmsg == MAXMSG) return;
      messages[in] = m;
      nmsg++;
      in = (in + 1) % MAXMSG;
   }

   public String status()
   {  if (nmsg == 0) return "Mailbox empty";
      else if (nmsg == 1) return "1 message";
      else if (nmsg < MAXMSG) return nmsg + " messages";
      else return "Mailbox full";
   }

   private final int MAXMSG = 10;
   private int in = 0;
   private int out = 0;
   private int nmsg = 0;
   private Message[] messages = new Message[MAXMSG];
}
```

Catching Exceptions

We will cover exception handling fully in Chapter 12, but once in a while you will encounter code that involves exceptions. Here is a quick introduction on what the exceptions are and how to handle them.

When an error occurs at run time, a Java program can "throw an exception." For example, code that attempts to open a file can throw an exception if the file unexpectedly cannot be opened. Throwing an exception is less violent and less fatal than terminating the program because it provides the option of "catching" the exception and dealing with it.

If an exception is not caught anywhere, the program will terminate and a message will be printed to the console giving the type of the exception.

Without going into too much detail, here is the basic syntax. To run code that might throw an exception, you have to place it inside a "try" block. Then you have to provide an emergency action to deal with the exception, in the unlikely case that one actually occurs.

```
try
{   code that might
    throw exceptions
}   catch(ExceptionType e)
{   emergency action
}
```

We used that mechanism in the code that plays an audio clip.

```
try
{   AudioStream as
    = new AudioStream(new FileInputStream(filename));
    ap.start(as);
}
catch(IOException e) {}
```

The above says, in effect, "Do not end the program if you have an I/O (input/output) error—just ignore the error and do not play the clip."

The compiler is somewhat selective as to which exceptions *must* be handled. For example, when you access an array or perform a cast, you need not supply an exception handler, even though the array index or the cast might be invalid, causing the code to throw an exception. However, for other operations, such as input and output, you must specify what you want to happen when there is a problem.

Exceptions are a complex topic, and it is not generally a good idea to ignore them when they happen. But a full discussion will have to wait until Chapter 12.

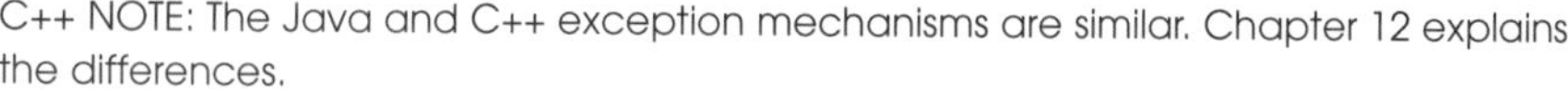

C++ NOTE: The Java and C++ exception mechanisms are similar. Chapter 12 explains the differences.

`Object`: The Cosmic Superclass

The `Object` class is the ultimate ancestor—every class in Java extends `Object`. However, you don't have to say:

```
class Employee extends Object
```

since the ultimate parent class `Object` is taken for granted if no parent is explicitly mentioned. Because *every* class in Java extends `Object`, it is important to be familiar with the services provided by the `Object` class. We will go over the basic ones in this chapter and refer you to later chapters or to the on-line documentation for what is not covered here. (Several methods of `Object` come up only when dealing with threads—see Volume 2 for more on threads.)

The `equals` method in `Object` tests whether or not one object is equal to another. The `equals` method in the `Object` parent class determines whether or not two objects point to the same area of memory. Other classes in the Java hierarchy are free to override `equals` for a more meaningful comparison. You will often find yourself overriding `equals` in your classes.

C++ NOTE: In C++, there is no cosmic root class. One is not needed, because templates do a better job for generic programming. But Java has no templates, so you have to make do with a common ancestor class.

C++ programmers may be surprised that the cast from `Employee[]` to `Object[]` is legal. Even if `Object` was a base class of `Employee` in C++, the equivalent cast from `Employee**` to `Object**` would not be legal. (Of course, the cast from `Employee*` to `Object*` is legal in C++.)

There is a security reason behind this restriction. If the cast `"Derived** → Base**"` were permitted, you could corrupt the contents of an array. Consider this code:

```
Employee** a; // C++
Object** p = a; // not legal, but suppose it was
p[0] = new AudioClip();
    // legal, AudioClip also inherits from Object
for (i = 0; i < n; i++) a[i].raiseSalary(3);
    // ouch, now the audio clip gets a raise!
```

If you try the equivalent Java code, you will notice that the `Object[]` array still remembers its original type (`Employee[]` in our example). It will throw an exception if you try to insert any nonemployee object into it. This ensures that a generic array cannot be corrupted.

Here are versions of the API descriptions of the basic parts of the `Object` class:

`java.lang.Object`

- `Class getClass()`

  Returns a `Class` object that contains information about the object. As you will see in the next section, Java has a run-time representation for classes that is encapsulated in the `Class` class that you can often use to your advantage.

- `boolean equals(Object obj)`

  Compares two objects for equality; returns `true` if the objects point to the same area of memory, and `false` otherwise.

- `Object clone()`

  Creates a clone of the object. Java allocates memory for the new instance and copies the memory allocated for the current object.

Note: Cloning an object is important but it also turns out to be a fairly subtle process filled with potential pitfalls for the unwary. We will have a lot more to say about the `clone` method at the end of this chapter.

- `String toString()`

  Returns a string that represents the value of this object. Almost all classes override this method in order to give you a printed representation of the object's current state. For example, you have seen the `toString` method used with the `Day` class in order to give a string representation of the date.

TIP: Instead of writing `x.toString()`, you can write `"" + x`. This concatenates the empty string with the string representation of `x` that is exactly `x.toString()`.

Object Wrappers

Occasionally, you need to convert a basic type like `int` to an object. All basic types have class counterparts. For example, there is a class `Integer` corresponding to the basic type `int`. These kinds of classes are usually called *object wrappers*. The wrapper classes have obvious names: `Integer`, `Long`, `Float`, `Double`, `Byte`, `Character`, `Void`, and `Boolean`. (The first five inherit from the common parent wrapper `Number`.) The wrapper classes are `final`. (So you can't override the `toString` method in `Integer` in order to display numbers using

Roman numerals, sorry.) You also cannot change the values you store in the object wrapper.

The major reason why wrappers were invented is *generic programming*. The container classes that we describe in Chapter 11 can store arbitrary objects. But they cannot store numbers unless they are turned into objects of a class. Here is a simple example that illustrates the concept of generic programming. Suppose you want to find the index of an element in an array. This is a generic situation, and by writing the code for objects, you can reuse it for employees, dates, or whatever.

```
static int find(Object[] a, Object key)
{  int i;
   for (i = 0; i < a.length; i++)
      if (a[i].equals(key)) return i;
   return -1; // not found
}
```

For example,

```
Employee[] staff;
Employee harry;
. . .
int n = find(staff, harry);
```

But what if you want to find a number in an array of floating-point numbers? Here is where wrappers come in handy. By using `Double` objects instead of `double` variables, you can take advantage of the generic code.

```
Double[] values;
. . .
int n = find(values, new Double(3.14));
```

PITFALL: Some people think that the wrapper classes can be used to implement methods that can modify numeric arguments. However, that is not correct. Recall from Chapter 4 that it is not possible to write a Java function that increments an integer.

```
static void increment(int x) // won't work
{  x++; // increments local copy
}
static void main(String[] args)
{  int a = 3;
   increment(a);
   . . .
}
```

Changing `x` has no effect on `a`. Could this be overcome by using an `Integer` instead of an `int`?

```
static void increment(Integer x) // won't work
{   . . .
}
static void main(String[] args)
{   Integer a = new Integer(3);
    increment(a);
    . . .
}
```

After all, now a and x are references to the same object. If we managed to update x, then a would also be updated. The problem is that `Integer` objects are *immutable:* the information contained inside the wrapper can't change. In particular, there is no analog to the statement x++ for `Integer` objects. Thus, you cannot use these wrapper classes to create a method that modifies numeric arguments.

You will often see the number wrappers for another reason. The designers of Java found the wrappers a convenient place to put certain basic methods, like the ones for converting strings of digits to numbers. The place is convenient, but the functionality, unfortunately, isn't.

To convert a string to an integer, you need to use the following statement:

```
int x = Integer.parseInt(s);
```

This has nothing to do with `Integer` objects—`parseInt` is a static method. But the `Integer` class was a good place to put it. Unfortunately, there is no corresponding `parseDouble` in the `Double` class. Instead, you must use the cumbersome

```
double x = new Double(s).doubleValue();
```

What this does is:

1. Use a constructor in the `Double` class that accepts a string of digits in the form of a double and gives you a `Double` object,
2. Use the `doubleValue` method in the `Double` class that returns an actual double.

(VB users are probably longing for a simple Val function.)

Actually, in real life it is even worse: you have to contend with the possibility that the string has leading or trailing spaces or that it may contain nondigits. So, a correct version would be as follows:

```
try
{   x = new Double(s.trim()).doubleValue();
}
catch(NumberFormatException e)
{   x = 0;
}
```

You will need this kind of long-winded code everywhere in Java.

In Java 1.1, there is another method for parsing numbers, although it isn't any simpler. You can use the `parse` method of the `DecimalFormat` class. When `s` is a string and `df` is an object of type `DecimalFormat`, then the method call `df.parse(s)` returns an object of type `Number`.

```
DecimalFormat df = new DecimalFormat(); // uses default locale
Number n = df.parse(s);
```

Actually, `Number` is an abstract class, and the returned object is an object of either type `Long` or `Double`, depending on the contents of the string `s`. You can use the `instanceof` operator to find out the return type of the object:

```
if (n instanceof Double) Double d = (Double)n;
```

But in practice, you don't usually care about the return type. The `doubleValue` method is defined for the `Number` class, and it returns the floating-point equivalent of the `number` object, whether it is a `Long` or a `Double`. That is, you can use the following code:

```
try
{  x = new DecimalFormat().parse(s.trim()).doubleValue();
}
catch(ParseException e)
{  x = 0;
}
```

Using the `DecimalFormat` has one advantage: the string can contain group separators for thousands such as `"12,301.4"`. But, as so often, the library designer giveth, and the library designer taketh away—this method cannot handle scientific notation such as `"1.23014E4"`.

We found this so cumbersome that we wrote our own string-to-number conversions in the `corejava` package. You simply use a statement like this:

```
x = Format.atof(s);
```

The API notes show some of the more important methods of the `Integer` class. The other number classes implement some (but not all) of the corresponding methods.

java.lang.Integer

- `int intValue()`

  Returns the value of this `Integer` object as an `int` (overrides the `intValue` method in the `Number` class).

- `static String toString(int i)`

  Returns a new `String` object representing the specified integer in base 10.

- `static String toString(int i, int radix)`

  Lets you return a representation of the number `i` in the base specified by the `radix` parameter.

- `static int parseInt(String s)`

  Returns the integer's value, assuming the specified `String` represents an integer in base 10.

- `static int parseInt(String s, int radix)`

  Returns the integer's value, assuming the specified `String` represents an integer in the base specified by the `radix` parameter.

- `static Integer valueOf(String s)`

  Returns a new `Integer` object initialized to the integer's value, assuming the specified `String` represents an integer in base 10.

- `static Integer valueOf(String s, int radix)`

  Returns a new `Integer` object initialized to the integer's value, assuming the specified `String` represents an integer in the base specified by the `radix` parameter.

Big Numbers

Java 1.1 introduces a couple of handy subclasses of the `Math` class called `BigInteger` and `BigDecimal`. These are classes for manipulating numbers with an arbitrarily long sequence of digits. The `BigInteger` class implements arbitrary precision integer arithmetic, and `BigDecimal` does the same for floating-point numbers. You usually construct big numbers out of strings by using one of the `BigInteger` or `BigDecimal` constructors that takes a string.

```
BigInteger b =
   new BigInteger("1234567890123456789012345678901234567890");
```

There are no constructors that take ordinary numbers, but you can use the static `valueOf` method:

```
BigInteger a = BigInteger.valueOf(100);
```

Unfortunately, you cannot use the familiar mathematical operators such as `+` and `*` to combine big numbers. Instead, you must use the appropriate methods in the correct big number class.

```
BigInteger c = a.add(b); // c = a + b
BigInteger d = c.multiply(b.add(BigInteger.valueOf(2)));
   // d = c * (b + 2)
```

C++ NOTE: Unlike C++, Java has no programmable operator overloading. There was no way for the programmer of the `BigInteger` class to redefine the + and * operators to give the `add` and `multiply` operations of the `BigInteger` classes. The language designers did overload the + operator to denote concatenation of strings. They chose not to overload other operators, and they did not give Java programmers the opportunity to overload operators themselves.

Example 5-3 shows a version of the lottery odds program that we introduced in Chapter 3, modified to work with big numbers. For example, if you are invited to participate in a lottery in which you need to pick 60 numbers out of a possible 490 numbers, then this program will tell you that your odds are 1 in 716395843461995557415116222540092933411717612789263493493351013459481104668848. Good luck!

Example 5-3: BigIntegerTest.java

```
import corejava.*;
import java.math.*;

public class BigIntegerTest
{  public static BigInteger lotteryOdds(int high, int number)
   {  BigInteger r = new BigInteger("1");
      int i;
      for (i = 1; i <= number; i++)
      {  r = r.multiply(BigInteger.valueOf(high))
            .divide(BigInteger.valueOf(i));
         high--;
      }
      return r;
   }

   public static void main(String[] args)
   {  int numbers = Console.readInt
      ("How many numbers do you need to draw?");
      int topNumber = Console.readInt
         ("What is the highest number you can draw?");
      BigInteger oddsAre = lotteryOdds(topNumber, numbers);

      System.out.println("Your odds are 1 in " + oddsAre +
        ". Good luck!");
   }
}
```

Reading a Page in the HTML Documents

At this point, you have seen all the basic terms that Java uses to describe its methods, classes, and interfaces. Once you are comfortable with this information, you will often consult the API documentation. Figures 5-3 through 5-5 show the pages of API documentation for the `Double` class. As you can see, the API documentation pages are always organized in the same way:

1. The name of the class (or interface).
2. The inheritance chain for this class (starting from `java.lang.Object`).
3. The name of the class along with the access modifiers such as `public` or `final`, the classes it extends, and the interfaces it implements. (For example, as you can see in Figure 5-3, `Double` extends `Number`, which extends `Object`).
4. A (more or less useful) discussion of the class (occasionally, this includes some sample code).
5. A list of all the methods in the class, with the constructors given first.
6. A more detailed discussion of the methods.

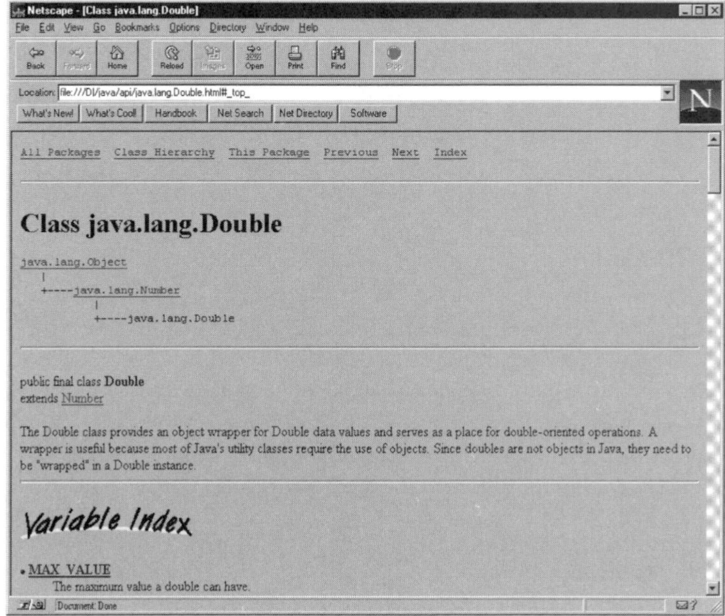

Figure 5-3: tree.html

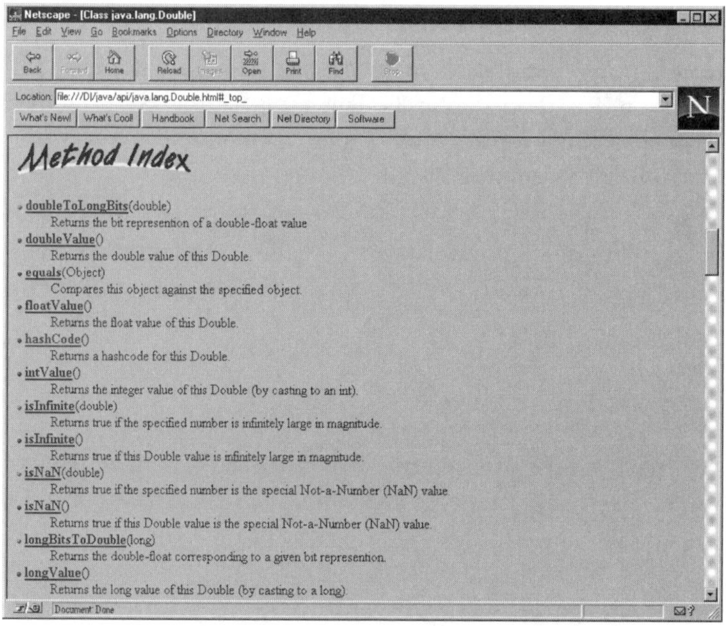

Figure 5-4: API Pages for `Double` class (Part 1)

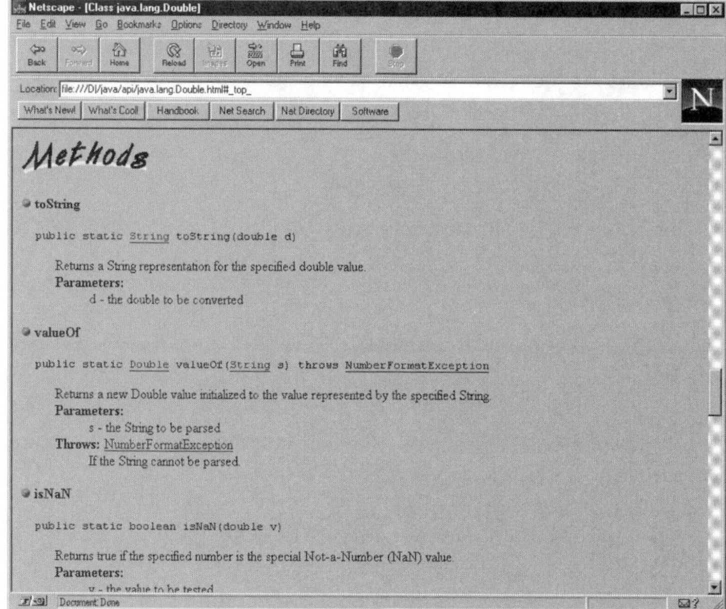

Figure 5-5: API Pages for `Double` class (Part 2)

The `Class` Class (Run-Time Type Identification)

While your program is running, Java always maintains what is called run-time type identification (RTTI) on all objects. This information keeps track of the class to which each object belongs. Run-time type information is used by Java to select the correct methods to execute at run time.

However, you can also access this information by working with a special Java class. The class that holds this information is called, somewhat confusingly, `Class`. The `getClass()` method in the `Object` class returns an instance of `Class` type.

```
Employee e ;
. . .
Class cl = e.getClass();
```

Probably the most commonly used method of `Class` is `getName`. This returns the name of the class. You can use it in a simple `println`; for example, the code

```
System.out.println(e.getClass().getName() + " " + e.getName());
```

prints

```
Employee Harry Hacker
```

if `e` is an employee; the code prints

```
Manager Harry Hacker
```

if `e` is a manager.

Aside from asking an object for the name of its corresponding class object, you can ask for the class object corresponding to a string by using the static `forName` method.

```
String className = "Manager";
Class cl = Class.forName(className);
```

You would use this method if the class name is stored in a string that varies at run time. This works if `className` is the name of a class or interface. Otherwise, it throws an exception.

TIP: An occasionally handy shortcut is to use string concatenation when creating the string to use in the `forName` method. For example, suppose you had `MarketingManager` and `ProgrammerManager` classes. Then, you could use:

```
String division = "Marketing";
String jobTitle = "Manager";
typeOfManager = division + jobTitle;
Class cl = Class.forName(typeOfManager);
```

There is a third method for obtaining an object of type `Class`. If `T` is any Java type, then `T.class` is the matching class object. For example:

```
Class cl1 = Manager.class;
Class cl2 = int.class;
```

Note that `Class` really describes a *type*, which may or may not be a class.

Another example of a useful method is one that lets you create an instance of a new class on the fly. This method is called, naturally enough, `newInstance()`. For example:

```
e.getClass().newInstance();
```

would create a new instance of the same class type as `e`. The `newInstance` method calls the default constructor (the one that takes no arguments) to initialize the newly created object.

Using a combination of `forName` and `newInstance` lets you create an object from a class name stored in a string.

```
String s = "Manager";
Object m = Class.forName(s).newInstance();
```

NOTE: If you need to provide parameters for the constructor of a class created this way, then you can't use statements like the above, instead you must use the `newInstance` method in the `Constructor` class. (This is one of several classes in the `java.lang.reflect` package. We will discuss reflection later in this chapter.)

C++ NOTE: The `newInstance` method corresponds to the idiom of a *virtual constructor* in C++. However, virtual constructors in C++ are not a language feature but just an idiom that needs to be supported by a specialized library. The `Class` class is similar to the `type_info` class in C++, and the `getClass` method is equivalent to the `typeid` operator. The Java `Class` is quite a bit more versatile than `type_info`, though. The C++ `type_info` can only reveal a string with its name, not create new objects of that type.

java.lang.Class

- `String getName()`

  Returns the name of this class.

- `Class getSuperclass()`

  Returns the superclass of this class as a `Class` object.

- `Class[] getInterfaces()`

  Returns an array of `Class` objects that give the interfaces implemented by this class; returns an array of length 0 if this class implements no interfaces. Somewhat confusingly, interface descriptions are also stored in `Class` objects.

- `boolean isInterface()`

  Returns `true` if this class is an interface and `false` if not.

- `String toString()`

  Returns the name of this class or this interface. The word *class* precedes the name if it is a class; the word *interface* precedes the name if it is an interface. (See the next chapter for more on interfaces.) This method overrides the `toString` method in `Object`.

- `static Class forName(String className)`

  Returns the `Class` object representing the class with name `className`.

- `Object newInstance()`

  Returns a new instance of this class.

`java.lang.reflect.Constructor`

- `Object newInstance(Object[] args)`

  Constructs a new instance of the constructor's declaring class.

Parameters:	`args`	The parameters supplied to the constructor

Reflection

In Java 1.0, the class `Class` was fairly limited. In Java 1.1, it has been greatly enhanced to give a very rich and elaborate toolset to the Java programmer. You can now use the methods of the class `Class` to write programs that manipulate Java code dynamically. The major reason for this enhancement is *Java Beans,* the component architecture for Java (see Volume 2 for more on Beans). Java must now support tools like the ones users of Visual Basic or Delphi have grown accustomed to. In particular, when new classes are added at design or run time, rapid application development tools that are Java Beans enabled need to be able to inquire about the capabilities of the classes (beans) that were added. (This is equivalent to the process that occurs when you add controls in Visual Basic to the toolbox.)

A program that can analyze the capabilities of classes is called *reflective.* The package that brings this functionality to Java is called `java.lang.reflect`. The new reflection mechanism is extremely powerful. As the next four sections show, you can use it to:

- Analyze the capabilities of classes at run time
- Inspect objects at runtime, for example, to write a single `toString` method that works for *all* classes
- Implement generic array manipulation code
- Take advantage of `Method` objects that work just like function pointers in languages such as C++

(Please note that the section on JavaBeans in Volume 2 will have a discussion of the parts of the reflection mechanism relevant to Java Beans.)

Using Reflection to Analyze the Capabilities of Classes

Here is a brief overview of the most important parts of the reflection mechanism in Java 1.1 for letting you examine the structure of a class. There are three classes in `java.lang.reflect` called `Field`, `Method`, and `Constructor`. These describe the data fields, the operations, and the constructors of a class, respectively. All three classes have a method called `getName` that returns the name of the item. The `Field` class has a method `getType` that returns an object, again of type `Class`, that describes the field type. The `Method` and `Constructor` classes have methods to report the return type and the types of the parameters used for these functions. All three of these classes also have a method called `getModifiers` that returns an integer, with various bits turned on and off that describe the modifiers used, such as `public` and `static`. You can then use the static methods in the `Modifier` class in `java.lang.reflect` in order to analyze the integer that `getModifiers` returns. For example, there are methods like `isPublic`, `isPrivate`, or `isFinal` in the `Modifier` class that you could use to tell you whether a method or constructor was `public`, `private`, or `final`. All you have to do is have the appropriate method in the `Modifier` class work on the integer that `getModifiers` returns. You can also use the `Modifier.toString` method to print the modifiers.

The `getFields()`, `getMethods()`, and `getConstructors()` methods of the `Class` class return arrays of the *public* fields, operations, and constructors that the class supports as arrays of objects of the appropriate class from `java.lang.reflect`. The `getDeclaredFields()`, `getDeclaredMethods()`, and `getDeclaredConstructors()` methods of the `Class` class return arrays consisting of all fields, operations, and constructors in the class.

Example 5-4 shows you how to print out all information about a class. The program prompts you for the name of a class and then writes out the signatures of all public methods and constructors as well as the names of all public data fields of a class. For example, if you enter

```
java.lang.Double
```

then Example 5.4 prints

```
class java.lang.Double extends java.lang.Number
{
public java.lang.Double(double);
public java.lang.Double(java.lang.String);

public static java.lang.String toString(double);
public static java.lang.Double valueOf(java.lang.String);
public static boolean isNaN(double);
public static boolean isInfinite(double);
public boolean isNaN();
public boolean isInfinite();
public java.lang.String toString();
public byte byteValue();
public short shortValue();
public int intValue();
public long longValue();
public float floatValue();
public double doubleValue();
public int hashCode();
public boolean equals(java.lang.Object);
public static native long doubleToLongBits(double);
public static native double longBitsToDouble(long);
static native double valueOf0(java.lang.String);

public static final double POSITIVE_INFINITY;
public static final double NEGATIVE_INFINITY;
public static final double NaN;
public static final double MAX_VALUE;
public static final double MIN_VALUE;
public static final java.lang.Class TYPE;
private double value;
private static final long serialVersionUID;
}
```

Example 5-4: ReflectionTest.java

```
import java.lang.reflect.*;
import corejava.*;

public class ReflectionTest
{  public static void main(String[] args)
   {  String name = Console.readString
         ("Please enter a class name (e.g. java.util.Date): ");
      try
      {  Class cl = Class.forName(name);
         Class supercl = cl.getSuperclass();
         System.out.print("class " + name);
         if (supercl != null && !supercl.equals(Object.class))
            System.out.print(" extends " + supercl.getName());
         System.out.print("\n{\n");
         printConstructors(cl);
         System.out.println();
         printMethods(cl);
         System.out.println();
         printFields(cl);
         System.out.println("}");
      }
      catch(ClassNotFoundException e)
      {  System.out.println("Class not found.");
      }
   }


   public static void printConstructors(Class cl)
   {  Constructor[] constructors = cl.getDeclaredConstructors();

      for (int i = 0; i < constructors.length; i++)
      {  Constructor c = constructors[i];
         Class[] paramTypes = c.getParameterTypes();
         String name = cl.getName();
         System.out.print(Modifier.toString(c.getModifiers()));
         System.out.print(" " + name + "(");
         for (int j = 0; j < paramTypes.length; j++)
         {  if (j > 0) System.out.print(", ");
            System.out.print(paramTypes[j].getName());
         }
         System.out.println(");");
      }
   }

   public static void printMethods(Class cl)
   {  Method[] methods = cl.getDeclaredMethods();
```

```
        for (int i = 0; i < methods.length; i++)
        {  Method m = methods[i];
           Class retType = m.getReturnType();
           Class[] paramTypes = m.getParameterTypes();
           String name = m.getName();
           System.out.print(Modifier.toString(m.getModifiers()));
           System.out.print(" " + retType.getName() + " " + name
              + "(");
           for (int j = 0; j < paramTypes.length; j++)
           {  if (j > 0) System.out.print(", ");
              System.out.print(paramTypes[j].getName());
           }
           System.out.println(");");
        }
     }

     public static void printFields(Class cl)
     {  Field[] fields = cl.getDeclaredFields();

        for (int i = 0; i < fields.length; i++)
        {  Field f = fields[i];
           Class type = f.getType();
           String name = f.getName();
           System.out.print(Modifier.toString(f.getModifiers()));
           System.out.println(" " + type.getName() + " " + name
              + ";");
        }
     }
}
```

What is remarkable about this program is that it can analyze any class that the Java interpreter can load, not just the classes that were available when the program was compiled. We will use this program in the next chapter to peek inside the new inner classes that were added to Java 1.1.

`java.lang.Class`

- `Field[] getFields()`
- `Field[] getDeclaredFields()`

  The `getFields` method returns an array containing `Field` objects for the public fields. The `getDeclaredField` method returns an array of `Field` objects for all fields. The methods return an array of length 0 if there are no such fields or the `Class` object represents a primitive or array type.

- `Method[] getMethods()`
- `Method[] getDeclaredMethods()`

  Return an array containing `Method` objects that give you all the public methods (for `getMethods`) or all methods (for `getDeclaredMethods`) of the class or interface. This includes those inherited from classes or interfaces above it in the inheritance chain.

- `Constructor[] getConstructors()`
- `Constructor[] getDeclaredConstructors()`

  Return an array containing `Constructor` objects that give you all the public constructors (for `getConstructors`) or all constructors (for `getDeclaredConstructors`) of the class represented by this `Class` object.

`java.lang.reflect.Field`

`java.lang.reflect.Method`

`java.lang.reflect.Constructor`

- `Class getDeclaringClass()`

  Return the `Class` object for the class that defines this constructor, method, or field.

- `Class[] getExceptionTypes()`

  (In `Constructor` and `Method` classes.) Returns an array of `Class` objects that represent the types of the exceptions thrown by the method.

- `int getModifiers()`

  Returns an integer that describes the modifiers of this constructor, method, or field. Uses the methods in the `Modifier` class to analyze the return value.

- `String getName()`

  Returns a string that is the name of the constructor, method, or field.

- `Class[] getParameterTypes()`

  (In `Constructor` and `Method` classes.) Returns an array of `Class` objects that represent the types of the parameters.

Using Reflection to Analyze Objects at Runtime

In the preceding section, we saw how we can find out the *names* and *types* of the data fields of any object:

- Get the corresponding `Class` object
- Call `getDeclaredFields` on the `Class` object.

In this section, we go one step further and actually look at the *contents* of the data fields. Of course, it is easy to look at the contents of a specific field of an object whose name and type is known when you write a program. But reflection lets us look at fields of objects that were not known at compile time.

The key method to achieve this is the `get` method in the `Field` class. If `f` is an object of type `Field` (for example, one obtained from `getDeclaredFields`) and `obj` is an object of the class of which `f` is a field, then `f.get(obj)` returns an object whose value is the current value of the field of `obj`. This is all a bit abstract, so let's run through an example.

```
Employee harry = new Employee("Harry Hacker", 35000,
   new Day(10, 1, 1989));
Class cl = harry.getClass();
   // the class object representing Employee
Field f = cl.getField("name");
   // the name field of the Employee class
Object v = f.get(harry);
   // the value of the name field of the harry object
```

Actually, there is a problem with this code. Since the `name` field is a private field, the `get` method will throw an `IllegalAccessException`. You can only use the `get` method to get the values of accessible fields. We either must make the field public or move the code inside the `Employee` class. Note that the security mechanism of Java lets you find out what fields any object has, but it won't let you read the values of those fields unless you have access permission. When we put this kind of code to work in our next example program, we will move it inside the `Employee` class.

There is another issue with the `get` method that we need to deal with. The `name` field is a `String`, and so it is not a problem to return the value as an `Object`. But suppose we want to look at the `salary` field. That is a `double`, and in Java, number types are not objects. To handle this, you can either use the `getDouble` method of the `Field` class, or, if you call `get`, then Java's reflection mechanism automatically wraps the field value into the appropriate wrapper class, in this case, `Double`.

Of course, you can also set the values that you can get. The call `f.set(obj, value)` sets the field represented by `f` of the object `obj` to the new value.

Example 5-5 shows how to write a generic `toString` method that works for *any* class. It uses `getDeclaredFields` to obtain all data fields. For each field, it obtains the name and the value. Each value is turned into a string by invoking *its* `toString` method.

```
Field f = fields[i];
   r += f.getName() + "=";
Object val = f.get(obj);
r += val.toString();
```

In example 5-5, the generic `toString` method is added to the `Employee` class.

Example 5-5: ToStringTest.java

```
import java.lang.reflect.*;
import corejava.*;

public class ToStringTest
{  public static void main(String[] args)
   {  Employee e  = new Employee("Harry Hacker", 35000,
         new Day(1996,12, 1));
      System.out.println(e);
   }
}

class Employee
{  public Employee(String n, double s, Day d)
   {  name = n;
      salary = s;
      hireDay = d;
   }

   public void print()
   {  System.out.println(name + "  " + salary + "  "
         + hireYear());
   }

   public void raiseSalary(double byPercent)
   {  salary *= 1 + byPercent / 100;
   }

   public int hireYear()
   {  return hireDay.getYear();
   }

   public String toString()
   {  Class cl = getClass();
      String r = cl.getName() + "[";
      Class sc = cl.getSuperclass();
```

```
      if (!sc.equals(Object.class)) r += sc + ",";
      Field[] fields = cl.getDeclaredFields();
      for (int i = 0; i < fields.length; i++)
      {  Field f = fields[i];
         r += f.getName() + "=";
         try
         {  r += f.get(this);
         } catch (IllegalAccessException e)
         {  r += "???";
         }
         if (i < fields.length - 1)
            r += ",";
         else
            r += "]";
      }
      return r;
   }

   private String name;
   private double salary;
   private Day hireDay;
}
```

Unfortunately, you must manually paste the `toString` code into every class. You cannot simply put it in some base class and have other classes derive from it. The reason why you can't is worth stressing: *the base class would not have access rights for the derived class fields.*

Using Reflection to Write Generic Array Code

The `Array` class in `java.lang.reflect` allows you to create arrays dynamically. For example, when you use this feature with the `arrayCopy` method from Chapter 3 you can dynamically expand an existing array while preserving the current contents.

VB NOTE: Although not as convenient as Redim Preserve, this technique is sure to be welcome to VB programmers who have long since grown accustomed to the convenience the Redim Preserve command provides.

The problem we want to solve is pretty typical: suppose you have an array of some type that is full and you want to grow it. And suppose you are sick of writing the grow-and-copy code by hand. You want to write a generic method to grow an array.

```
Employee[] a = new Employee[100];
. . .
// array is full
a = (Employee[])growArray(a);
```

How can we write such a generic method? It helps that an `Employee[]` array can be converted to an `Object[]` array. That sounds promising. Here is a first attempt to write a generic method. We simply grow the array by 10% + 10 elements (since the 10% growth is not substantial enough for small arrays).

```
static Object[] arrayGrow(Object[] a) // not useful
{  int newLength = a.length * 11 / 10 + 10;
   Object[] newArray = new Object[newLength];
   System.arraycopy(a, 0, newArray, 0, a.length);
   return newArray;
}
```

However, there is a problem with actually *using* the resulting array. The type of the array that this code returns is an array of *objects* (`Object[]`) because we created the array using the line of code:

```
new Object[newLength]
```

An array of objects *cannot* be cast to an array of employees (`Employee[]`). Java would generate a `ClassCast` exception at run time. The point, as we mentioned earlier, is that a Java array remembers the type of its entries, that iss the element type used in the `new` expression that created it. It is legal to cast an `Employee[]` temporarily to an `Object[]` array and then cast it back, but an array that started its life as an `Object[]` array can never be cast into an `Employee[]` array. To make this kind of generic array codes we need to be able to make a new array of the *same* type as the original array. For this, we need the methods of the `Array` class in the `java.lang.reflect` package. The key is the static `newInstance` method of the `Array` class that constructs a new array. You must supply the type for the entries and the desired length as parameters to this method.

```
Object newArray = Array.newInstance(componentType, newLength);
```

To actually carry this outs we need to get the length and component type of the original array.

The length is obtained by calling `Array.getLength(a)`. The static `getLength` method of the `Array` class gets the length of any array. To get the component type of the new array, we have to go a slightly different route.

- First, get the class object of `a`.
- Confirm that it is indeed an array.
- Then, use the `getComponentType` method of the `Class` class (which is defined for only class objects that represent arrays) in order to find the right type for the array.

Why is `getLength` a method of `Array` but `getComponentType` a method of `Class`? We don't know—the distribution of the reflection methods seems a bit adhoc at times.

Here's the code:

```
static Object arrayGrow(Object a) // useful
{  Class cl = a.getClass();
   if (!cl.isArray()) return null;
   int length = Array.getLength(a);
   int newLength = length * 11 / 10 + 10;
   Class componentType = a.getClass().getComponentType();
   Object newArray = Array.newInstance(componentType,
      newLength);
   System.arraycopy(a, 0, newArray, 0, length);
   return newArray;
}
```

Note that this `arrayGrow` method can be used to grow arrays of any type, not just arrays of objects.

```
int[] ia = { 1, 2, 3, 4 };
ia = (int[])arrayGrow(a);
```

Note that the parameter of `arrayGrow` is declared to be of type `Object`, *not an array of objects* (`Object[]`). The integer array type `int[]` can be converted to an `Object`, but not to an array of objects!

Example 5-6 shows both array grow methods in action. Note that the cast of the return value of `badArrayGrow` will throw an exception.

Example 5-6: ArrayGrowTest.java

```
import java.lang.reflect.*;
import corejava.*;

public class ArrayGrowTest
{  public static void main(String[] args)
   {  int[] a = { 1, 2, 3 };
      Day[] b = { new Day(1996, 1, 1), new Day(1997, 3, 26) };
      a = (int[])goodArrayGrow(a);
      arrayPrint(a);
      b = (Day[])goodArrayGrow(b);
      arrayPrint(b);
      System.out.println
         ("The following call will generate an exception.");
      b = (Day[])badArrayGrow(b);
   }

   static Object[] badArrayGrow(Object[] a)
   {  int newLength = a.length * 11 / 10 + 10;
      Object[] newArray = new Object[newLength];
      System.arraycopy(a, 0, newArray, 0, a.length);
      return newArray;
   }
```

```
   static Object goodArrayGrow(Object a)
   {  Class cl = a.getClass();
      if (!cl.isArray()) return null;
      Class componentType = a.getClass().getComponentType();
      int length = Array.getLength(a);
      int newLength = length + 10;

      Object newArray = Array.newInstance(componentType,
         newLength);
      System.arraycopy(a, 0, newArray, 0, length);
      return newArray;
   }

   static void arrayPrint(Object a)
   {  Class cl = a.getClass();
      if (!cl.isArray()) return;
      Class componentType = a.getClass().getComponentType();
      int length = Array.getLength(a);
      System.out.println(componentType.getName()
         + "[" + length + "]");
      for (int i = 0; i < Array.getLength(a); i++)
         System.out.println(Array.get(a, i));
   }
}
```

Method Pointers!

On the surface, Java does not have method pointers—ways of giving the location of a method to another method in order that the second method can invoke it later. In fact, the designers of Java have said that method pointers are dangerous and error-prone and that Java *interfaces* (discussed in the next chapter) are a superior solution. However, it turns out that Java now does have method pointers, as a (perhaps accidental) byproduct of the reflection package.

To see method pointers at work, recall that you can inspect or set a field of an object with the `get` method of the `Field` class. Similarly, the `Method` class has an `invoke` method which lets you call the method that is wrapped in the current `Method` object. The signature for the `invoke` method is:

```
Object invoke(Object obj, Object args[])
```

The first parameter is the implicit parameter, and the array of objects provides the explicit parameters. For a static method, the first parameter is ignored—you can set it to `null`. If the method has no explicit parameters, you pass `null` for the `args` parameter. For example, if `m1` represents the `getName` method of the `Employee` class, the following code shows how you can call it:

```
String n = (String)m1.invoke(harry, null);
```

As with the `get` and `set` methods of the `Field` type, there's a problem if the parameter or return type is not a class but a basic type. You must wrap any of the basic types into their corresponding wrappers before inserting them into the `args` array. Conversely, the `invoke` method will return the wrapped type and not the basic type. For example, suppose that `m2` represents the `raiseSalary` method of the `Employee` class. Then, you need to wrap the `double` parameter into a `Double` object.

```
Object[] args = { new Double(5.5); }
m2.invoke(harry, args);
```

How do you obtain a `Method` object? You can, of course, call `getDeclaredMethods` and search through the returned array of `Method` objects until you find the method that you want. Or you can call the `getMethod` method of the `Class` class. This is similar to the `getField(String)` method that takes a string with the field name and returns a `Field` object. However, there may be several methods with the same name, so you need to be careful that you get the right one. For that reason, you must also supply an array that gives the correct parameter types. For example, here is how you can get method pointers to the `getName` and `raiseSalary` methods of the `Employee` class.

```
Method m1 = Employee.class.getMethod("getName", null);
Method m2 = Employee.class.getMethod("raiseSalary",
   new Class[] { double.class } );
```

The second parameter of the `getMethod` method is an array of `Class` objects. It is usually easiest to make that array on the fly, as we did in the example above.

```
new Class[] { double.class }
```

is an array of `Class` objects of length 1, filled with one element, namely, the class object `double.class`.

Now that we have seen the syntax of `Method` objects, let's put them to work. Example 5-7 is a program that prints a table of values for a function such as `Math.sqrt` or `Math.sin`. The printout looks like this:

```
public static native double java.lang.Math.sqrt(double)
      1.0000 |       1.0000
      2.0000 |       1.4142
      3.0000 |       1.7321
      4.0000 |       2.0000
      5.0000 |       2.2361
      6.0000 |       2.4495
      7.0000 |       2.6458
      8.0000 |       2.8284
      9.0000 |       3.0000
     10.0000 |       3.1623
```

The code for printing a table is, of course, independent of the actual function that is being tabulated.

```
double dx = (to - from) / (n - 1);
for (double x = from; x <= to; x += dx)
{  double y = f(x); // where f is the function to be tabulated
   Format.print(System.out, "%12.4f |", x);
   Format.print(System.out, "%12.4f\n", y);
}
```

We want to write a generic `printTable` method that can tabulate any function. We will pass the function as a parameter of type `Method`.

```
static void printTable(double from, double to, int n, Method f)
```

Of course, `f` is not actually a function, so we cannot simply write `f(x)` to evaluate it. Instead, we must supply x in the parameter array (suitably wrapped as a `Double`), use the `invoke` method and unwrap the return value.

```
Object[] args = { new Double(x) };
Double d = (Double)f.invoke(null, args);
double y = d.doubleValue();
```

The first parameter of `invoke` is `null` because we are calling a static function.

Here is a sample call to `printTable` that tabulates the `Math.sqrt` function.

```
printTable(1, 10, 10,
   java.lang.Math.class.getMethod("sqrt",
   new Class[] { double.class }));
```

The hardest part is to get the method object. Here, we get the method of the `java.lang.Math` class that has the name `sqrt` and whose parameter list contains just one type, `double`.

Example 5-7 shows the complete code of the `printTable` method and a couple of test runs.

Example 5-7: MethodPointerTest

```
import java.lang.reflect.*;
import corejava.*;

public class MethodPointerTest
{  public static void main(String[] args) throws Exception
   {  printTable(1, 10, 10,
         MethodPointerTest.class.getMethod("square",
            new Class[] { double.class }));
      printTable(1, 10, 10,
java.lang.Math.class.getMethod("sqrt",
         new Class[] { double.class }));
   }
```

```
    public static double square(double x) { return x * x; }

    public static void printTable(double from, double to,
        int n, Method f)
    {   System.out.println(f);
        double dx = (to - from) / (n - 1);
        for (double x = from; x <= to; x += dx)
        {   Format.print(System.out, "%12.4f |", x);
            try
            {   Object[] args = { new Double(x) };
                Double d = (Double)f.invoke(null, args);
                double y = d.doubleValue();
                Format.print(System.out, "%12.4f\n", y);
            }   catch (Exception e)
            {   System.out.println("???");
            }
        }
    }
}
```

As this example shows clearly, you can do anything with `Method` objects that you can do with function pointers in C. Just as in C, this style of programming is usually quite inconvenient and always error-prone. What happens if you invoke a method with the wrong parameters? The `invoke` method throws an exception.

Also, the parameters and return values of `invoke` are necessarily of type `Object`. That means you must cast back and forth a lot. As a result, the compiler is deprived of the chance to check your code. That means that errors surface only during testing, when they are more tedious to find and fix.

For that reason, we suggest that you use `Method` objects in your own programs only when absolutely necessary. Using interfaces and inner classes (the subject of the next chapter) is almost always a better idea. In particular we echo the developers of Java and suggest not using `Method` objects for callback functions. Using interfaces for the callbacks (see the next chapter as well) leads to code that runs faster and is a lot more maintainable.

Protected Access

As you know, instance fields in a class are usually tagged as `private` and methods are tagged as `public`. Any features declared `private` are not visible to other classes. This is also true for subclasses. A subclass cannot access the private data members of its superclass.

For example, the `raise` method of the `Manager` class cannot access the `hireDay` field directly when computing the bonuses. It has to use the public interface like all other methods.

```
class Manager extends Employee
{  . . .
   public void raiseSalary(double byPercent)
   {  // add 1/2% bonus for every year of service
      Day today = new Day();
      double bonus = 0.5 * (today.getYear() -
         hireYear()); // can't use hireDay.year
      super.raiseSalary(byPercent + bonus);
   }
}
```

There are, however, times when you want a subclass to have access to a method or to data from a parent class. In that case, you declare the feature as `protected`. For example, if the base class `Employee` declares the `hireDay` object as `protected` instead of `private`, then the `Manager` methods can access it directly.

In practice, you should use the `protected` attribute with caution. Suppose your class is used by other programmers and it contains protected data. Unbeknownst to you, other programmers may derive classes from your class and start accessing the protected instance fields. In this case, you can no longer change the implementation of your class without upsetting the other programmers. That is against the spirit of OOP, which encourages data encapsulation.

Protected methods make more sense. A class may declare a method as `protected` if it is tricky to use. This indicates that the subclasses (which, presumably, know their ancestors well) can be trusted to use the method correctly, but other classes cannot.

Protected Access and Cloning

A good example of where protected access is necessary is the `clone` method in the class `Object`. Recall why you will often want to clone an object rather than copy it in a variable. When you make a copy of a variable, the original and the copy are references to the same object. (See Figure 5-6). This means a change to either variable also affects the other. Also, as we mentioned in the previous chapter, you never want to return a mutable object as the value of a method because this violates encapsulation; you always want to return a *clone* of the object.

```
Day bday = new Day(1959, 6, 16);
Day d = bday;
d.advance(100); // oops--also changed bday
```

If you would like that `d` to be a new object that begins as identical to `bday` but may later change to a different state, then you use the `clone()` method.

```
Day bday = new Day(1959, 6, 16);
Day d = (Day)bday.clone();
   // must cast--clone returns an object
d.advance(100); // ok--bday unchanged
```

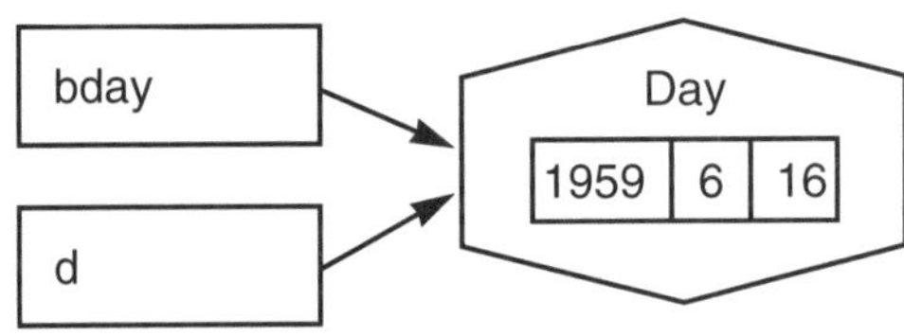

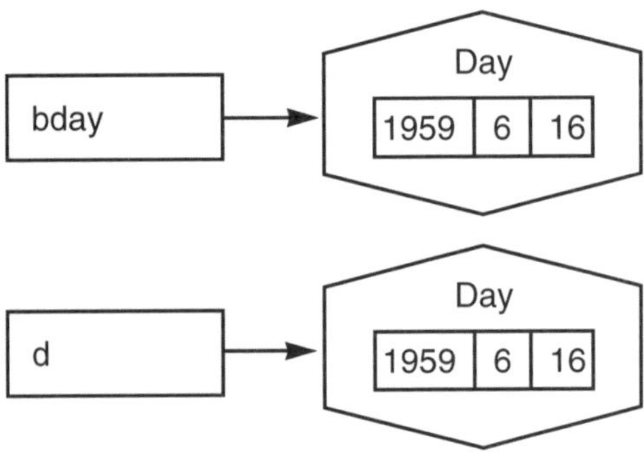

Figure 5-6: Copying and cloning

But it isn't quite so simple. The `clone` method is a protected method of `Object`, which means that your code cannot simply call it. Only the `Day` class can clone `Day` objects. There is a reason for this. Think about the way in which the `Object` class can implement `clone`. It knows nothing about the object at all, so it can make only a bit-by-bit copy. If all data fields in the object are numbers or other basic types, a bitwise copy is just fine. It is simply another object with the same base types and fields. But if the object contains pointers (that is, other objects), then the bitwise copy contains exact copies of the pointer fields, so the original and the cloned objects still share some information. This is shown in Figure 5-7.

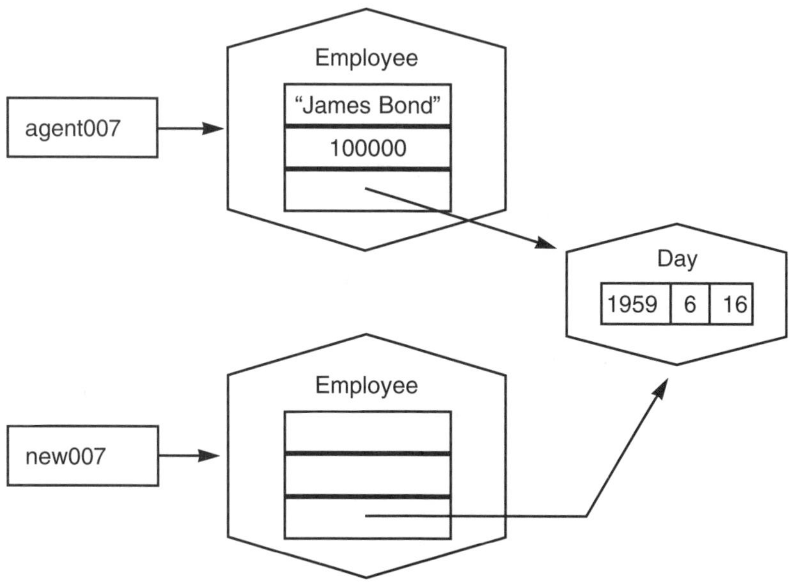

Figure 5-7: Original and cloned objects sharing information

It is up to the derived class to make a judgment whether or not

1. the default `clone` method is good enough,
2. the default `clone` method can be patched up by calling `clone` on the object instance variables,
3. the situation is hopeless and `clone` should not be attempted.

The third option is actually the default. To choose either the first or the second option, a class must

1. implement the `Cloneable` *interface* and
2. redefine the `clone` method with the public access privilege.

We will discuss interfaces in Chapter 6. Actually, in this case, the appearance of the `Cloneable` interface is very different from the normal use of interfaces. In this case, the interfaces merely serve as a tag, indicating that the class designer understands the cloning process. Objects are so paranoid about cloning that they generate a run-time exception if an object requests cloning but does not implement that interface.

Here is the drudgery that the `Day` class has to do to redefine `clone`.

```
public class Day implements Cloneable
{  . . .
   public Object clone()
   {  try
      {  return super.clone();
      }  catch (CloneNotSupportedException e)
      {  // this shouldn't happen, since we are Cloneable
         return null;
      }
   }
}
```

And that is the easy case. If we want to clone `Employee`, we have to call the `Object` clone method to make a bitwise copy, then clone the `Day` object.

```
public class Employee implements Cloneable
{  . . .
   public Object clone()
   {  try
      {  Employee e = (Employee)super.clone();
         e.hireDay = hireDay.clone();
         return e;
      }  catch (CloneNotSupportedException e)
      {  // this shouldn't happen, since we are Cloneable
         return null;
      }
   }
}
```

As you can see, cloning is a subtle business, and it makes sense that it is defined as `protected` in the `Object` class. (See Volume 2 for an elegant method for cloning objects, using the new object serialization features of Java.)

C++ NOTE: As it happens, `protected` features in Java are visible to all subclasses as well as all other classes in the same package. This is slightly different from the C++ meaning of `protected`.

Here is a summary of the four access modifiers in Java that control visibility.

1. visible to the class only (`private`)
2. visible to the world (`public`)
3. visible to the package and all subclasses (`protected`)
4. visible to the package (the default—no modifier needed)

Design Hints for Inheritance

We want to end this chapter with some hints for using interitance that we have found useful.

1. *Common operations and fields belong in the superclass.*

   This is why we put the `sender` field into the `Message` class, rather than replicating it in `TextMessage` and `VoiceMessage`.

2. *Use inheritance to model the "is–a" relationship.*

   Inheritance is a handy code-saver, and sometimes people overuse it. For example, suppose we need a `Contractor` class. Contractors have names and hire dates, but they do not have salaries. Instead, they are paid by the hour, and they do not stay around long enough to get a raise. There is the temptation to derive `Contractor` from `Employee` and add an `hourlyWage` field.

```
class Contractor extends Employee
{  public Contractor(String name, double wage, Day hireDay)
   {  super(name, 0, hireDay);
      hourlyWage = wage;
   }
   private double hourlyWage;
}
```

   This is *not* a good idea, however, and it will cause you no end of grief when you implement methods for printing paychecks or tax forms. You will end up writing more code than you would have by not inheriting in the first place.

   The contractor/employee relationship fails the "is–a" test. A contractor is not a special case of an employee (although the IRS is pushing to make this true).

3. *Don't use inheritance unless* all *inherited methods make sense.*

   Suppose we want to write a `Holiday` class . Surely every holiday is a day, so we can use inheritance.

```
class Holiday extends Day { . . . }
```

   Unfortunately, this is somewhat subtle. When we say that `Holiday` extends `Day`, we have to consider that we are talking about the *class* `Day`, as specified by its public methods. One of the public methods of `Day` is `advance`. And `advance` can turn holidays into nonholidays, so it is not an appropriate operation for holidays.

```
Holiday xmas;
xmas.advance(10);
```

In that sense, a holiday is a day *but* not a `Day`.

4. Use polymorphism, not type information.

   Whenever you find code of the form

```
if (x is of type 1)
   action1(x);
else if (x is of type 2)
   action2(x);
```

   think polymorphism.

   Do `action1` and `action2` represent a common concept? If so, make the concept a method of a common parent class or interface of both types. Then you can simply call

```
x.action();
```

   and have the dynamic dispatch mechanism inherent in polymorphism launch the correct action.

   The point is that code using polymorphic methods or interface implementations is much easier to maintain and extend than code that uses multiple type tests.

CHAPTER 6

- Interfaces
- Inner Classes

Interfaces and Inner Classes

You have now seen all the basic tools for doing object-oriented programming in Java. This chapter shows you two advanced techniques that are quite a bit more complex. Despite their less obvious nature, you will need to master them in order to complete your Java tool chest.

The first, called an *interface,* is Java's way of dealing with the common situation of wanting a class to reflect the behavior of two (or even more) parents. (This is often called multiple inheritance.) After we cover interfaces—which were part of Java 1.0—we move on to the new mechanism of *inner classes* that was added in Java 1.1. Inner classes are more of a convenience than a necessity; there will often be workarounds if you decide that using them is not to your taste. However, as we will show you in this chapter, there are a few situations where there are no convenient workarounds, and so inner classes are necessary in these specialized circumstances. In particular, inner classes are important to write concise code for the handling of graphical user interface events.

Interfaces

Suppose you wanted to write a general sorting routine that would work on many different kinds of Java objects. You now know how to organize this in an object-oriented fashion. You have the class `Sortable` with the method `compare` that determines whether or not one sortable object is less than, equal to, or greater than another.

Now you can implement a generic sorting algorithm. Here is an implementation of a shell sort, for sorting an array of `Sortable` objects.

```
abstract class Sortable
{  public abstract int compare(Sortable b);

   public static void shell_sort(Sortable[] a)
   {  int n = a.length;
      int incr = n / 2;
      while (incr >= 1)
      {  for (int i = incr; i < n; i++)
         {  Sortable temp = a[i];
            int j = i;
            while (j >= incr
               && temp.compare(a[j - incr]) < 0)
            {  a[j] = a[j - incr];
               j -= incr;
            }
            a[j] = temp;
         }
         incr /= 2;
      }
   }
}
```

This seems quite elegant. You would then use polymorphism to get the sorting routine in all the subclasses of the `Sortable` abstract class (by overriding the `compare` method in the subclass).

For example, to sort an array of employees (ordering them by—what else—their salary), we

1. derive `Employee` from `Sortable`,
2. implement the `compare` method for employees,
3. call `shell_sort` on the employee array.

Here's an example of the extra code needed to do this in our `Employee` class:

```
class Employee extends Sortable
{  . . .
   public int compare(Sortable b)
   {  Employee eb = (Employee)b;
      if (salary < eb.salary) return -1;
      if (salary > eb.salary) return 1;
      return 0;
   }

   public static void main(String[] args)
   {  Employee[] staff = new Employee[3];
      . . .
      Sortable.shell_sort(staff);
      . . .
   }
}
```

There is, unfortunately, a major problem with implementing this strategy in Java. For example, we wrote a `Tile` class that models tiled windows on a screen desktop. Tiled windows are rectangles plus a "z-order." Windows with a larger z-order are displayed in front of those with a smaller z-order. To reuse code, we inherit `Tile` from `Rectangle`, a class that is already defined in the `java.awt` package.

```
class Tile extends Rectangle
{  public Tile(int x, int y, int w, int h, int zz)
   {  super(x, y, w, h);
      z = zz;
   }

   private int z;
}
```

Now we would like to sort an array of tiles by comparing z-orders. If we try to apply the procedure for making tiles sortable, we get stuck at step (1). We cannot derive `Tile` from `Sortable`—it already derives from `Rectangle`!

The point is that, in Java, a class can have only one superclass. Other programming languages, in particular C++, allow a class to have more than one superclass. This is called *multiple inheritance.*

Instead, Java introduces the notion of *interfaces* to recover much of the functionality that multiple inheritance gives you. The designers of Java chose this road because multiple inheritance makes compilers either very complex (as in C++) or very inefficient (as in Eiffel). (Interfaces are the preferred method of implementing "callback functions" in Java—see the section on callbacks later in this chapter for more on this important topic.)

So what is an interface? Essentially, it is a promise that your class will implement certain methods with certain signatures. You even use the keyword `implements` to indicate that your class will keep these promises. The way in which these methods are implemented is up to the class, of course. The important point, as far as the compiler is concerned, is that the methods have the right signature.

For example, suppose you wanted to create an interface called `Sortable` that could be used by any class that will sort. The code for the `Sortable` interface might look like this:

```
public interface Sortable
{  public int compare(Sortable b);
}
```

This code promises that any class that implements the `Sortable` interface will have a `compare` method that will take a `Sortable` object. A `Sortable` object, in turn, is any instance of a class that implements `Sortable` (therefore, any class that has a `compare` method). Of course, the way in which the `compare` method works (or even whether or not it works as one would expect) in a specific class depends on the class that is implementing the `Sortable` interface. The key point is that any class can promise to implement `Sortable`—regardless of whether or not its superclass promises the same. All descendants of such a class would implement `Sortable`, since they all would have access to a `compare` method with the right signature.

To tell Java that your class implements `Sortable`, you have the class header read something like this:

```
class Tile extends Rectangle implements Sortable
```

Then, all you need to do is implement a `compare` method inside the class.

```
class Tile extends Rectangle implements Sortable
{  public int compare(Sortable b)
   {  Tile tb = (Tile)b;
      return z - tb.z;
   }
   . . .

   private int z;
}
```

Example 6-1 is the complete code for the tile example. Note that we needed to put the static `shell_sort` method in a separate class, `Sort`. You cannot put static methods into interfaces. (There is no reason for this restriction—it is merely an oversight in the language design.)

Example 6-1: TileTest.java

```
import java.awt.*;

public class TileTest
{  public static void main(String[] args)
   {  Tile[] a = new Tile[20];

      int i;
      for (i = 0; i < a.length; i++)
         a[i] = new Tile(i, i, 10, 20,
            (int)(100 * Math.random()));

      Sort.shell_sort(a);

      for (i = 0; i < a.length; i++)
         System.out.println(a[i]);
   }
}
```

```
interface Sortable
{  public int compare(Sortable b);
}

class Sort
{  public static void shell_sort(Sortable[] a)
   {  int n = a.length;
      int incr = n / 2;
      while (incr >= 1)
      {  for (int i = incr; i < n; i++)
         {  Sortable temp = a[i];
            int j = i;
            while (j >= incr
               && temp.compare(a[j - incr]) < 0)
            {  a[j] = a[j - incr];
               j -= incr;
            }
            a[j] = temp;
         }
         incr /= 2;
      }
   }
}

class Tile extends Rectangle implements Sortable
{  public Tile(int x, int y, int w, int h, int zz)
   {  super(x, y, w, h);
      z = zz;
   }

   public int compare(Sortable b)
   {  Tile tb = (Tile)b;
      return z - tb.z;
   }

   public String toString()
   {  return super.toString() + "[z=" + z + "]";
   }

   private int z;
}
```

C++ NOTE: C++ has multiple inheritance and all the complications that come with it, such as virtual base classes, dominance rules, and transverse pointer casts. Few C++ programmers use multiple inheritance, and some say it should never be used. Other programmers recommend using multiple inheritance only for "mix-in" style inheritance, in which a class is derived from base classes with no data and only virtual functions. These are the same as Java interfaces!

NOTE: Microsoft has long been a proponent of using interfaces instead of using multiple inheritance. Somewhat ironically as a result of this, the Java notion of an interface is essentially equivalent to how Microsoft used interfaces in the definition of their COM/OLE specification. As a result of this unlikely convergence of minds, it is relatively easy to use Java to build COM/OLE objects like ActiveX controls. This is done (pretty much transparently to the coder) in, for example, Microsoft's J++ product and is also the basis for JavaSoft's Beans-to-ActiveX bridge.

Properties of Interfaces

Although interfaces are not instantiated with `new`, they have certain properties similar to ordinary classes. For example, once you set up an interface, you can declare that an object variable will be of that interface type with the same notation used to declare a variable to be of a specific class type:

```
Sortable x = new Tile(. . .);
Tile y = new Tile(. . .);

if (x.compare(y) < 0) . . .
```

Also, nothing prevents you from extending one interface in order to create another. This allows for multiple chains of interfaces that go from a greater degree of generality to a greater degree of specialization. For example, suppose you had an interface called `Moveable`.

```
public interface Moveable
{  public void move(double x, double y);
}
```

Then, you could imagine an interface called `Powered` that extends it:

```
public interface Powered extends Moveable
{  public String powerSource();
}
```

NOTE: Unfortunately, the Java documentation often refers to *classes* when it means *classes* or *interfaces*. You have to use contextual clues to decide whether the public reference is only to classes or to both classes and interfaces.

Although you cannot put instance fields or static methods in an interface, you can supply constants in them. For example:

```
public interface Powered extends Moveable
{   public String powerSource(PoweredVehicle);
    public final int speedLimit = 95;
}
```

Classes can implement multiple interfaces. This gives you the maximum amount of flexibility in defining a class's behavior. For example, Java has an important interface built into it, called `Cloneable`; if your class implements `Cloneable`, the `clone` method in the `Object` class will make a bitwise copy of your class's objects. If your class doesn't implement `Cloneable`, then the `clone` method causes a run-time error when any code attempts to make a clone of your object. Suppose, therefore, you want cloneability and sortability. Then you simply implement both interfaces.

```
class Tile extends Rectangle implements Cloneable, Sortable
```

Interfaces and Callbacks

Suppose you want to implement a `Timer` class in Java. You want to be able to program your class to:

- start the timer,
- have the timer measure some time interval,
- then carry out some action when the correct time has elapsed.

For this to be practical, the `Timer` class needs a way of communicating with the calling class. This is usually called a *callback function.* Interfaces are the preferred way to implement callback functions in Java. To see why, let's peek inside the `Timer` class.

```
class Timer extends Thread
{  . . .
   public void run()
   {  while (true)
      {  sleep(interval);
         // now what?
      }
   }
}
```

(Don't worry about the fact that this class has to extend Java's built-in `Thread` class. Threads have many uses—one of the simplest is to sleep until some time has elapsed. You will read more about threads in Chapter 12.)

The object constructing a `Timer` object must somehow tell the timer what to do when the time is up. In C++, the code creating the timer gives it a pointer to a function, and the timer calls that function at the end of every interval. Java has no function pointers. It uses interfaces instead. So the `//now what` comment in the preceding code is replaced by a method call that was declared inside an interface.

Thus, in addition to the `Timer` class, we need the interface `Timed`. It has a single method called `tick`.

```
interface Timed
{  public void tick(Timer t);
}
```

Any class wanting to be called from a timer must implement that interface.

```
class AlarmClock implements Timed
{  AlarmClock()
   {  Timer t = new Timer(this);
      t.setInterval(1000); // 1000 milliseconds
   }

   public void tick(Timer t)
   {  if(t.time() >= wakeUpTime)
         wakeUp.play();
   }
}
```

Here's the code for the `Timer` class. Notice how the constructor of the `Timer` class receives the pointer to the object that needs to be notified. It is notified through the `tick()` method, which passes the `this` reserved variable that identifies it to the `tick` method in the `Timed` interface.

```
class Timer extends Thread
{  Timer(Timed t) { owner = t; }
   . . .
   public void run()
   {  while (true)
      {  sleep(interval);
         owner.tick(this);
      }
   }
   Timed owner;
}
```

This code explains only how an interface can be used to supply a notification mechanism and, hence, callback functions. For the full details of threads and the rest of the timer implementation, see Volume 2.

C++ NOTE: As we saw in Chapter 5, Java does have the equivalent of function pointers, namely, `Method` objects. However, they are difficult to use and cannot be checked at compile time. Whenever you would use a function pointer in C++, you should use polymorphism in Java, either by deriving from a base class or by implementing an interface. You can derive from only one base class, but you can implement any number of interfaces. It is quite common in Java to have trivial interfaces for callback protocols.

Inner Classes

Inner classes are a new feature added to Java 1.1. An *inner class* is a class that is defined inside another class. Why would you want to do that? There are four reasons:

- An object of an inner class can access the implementation of the object that created it—including data that would otherwise be private.
- *Anonymous* inner classes are handy when you want to define callbacks on the fly.
- Inner classes can be hidden from other classes in the same package.
- Inner classes are very convenient when writing programs that use the new event model of Java 1.1.

You will soon see examples that demonstrate the first three benefits. (For the new event model, please turn to Chapter 8.)

C++ NOTE: C++ has *nested classes.* A nested class is contained inside the scope of the enclosing class. Here is a typical example: a linked list class defines a class to hold the links, and a class to define an iterator position.

```
class LinkedList
{
public:
    class Iterator
    {
    public:
        void insert(int x);
        int erase();
        . . .
    };
    . . .
private:
    class Link
```

```
        {
        public:
            Link* next;
            int data;
        };
        . . .
    };
```

The nesting is a relationship between *classes,* not *objects.* A `LinkedList` object does *not* have subobjects of type `Iterator` or `Link`.

There are two benefits: *name control* and *access control.* Because the name `Iterator` is nested inside the `LinkedList` class, it is externally known as `LinkedList::Iterator` and cannot conflict with another class called `Iterator`. In Java, this benefit is not as important since Java *packages* give the same kind of name control. Note that the `Link` class is in the *private* part of the `LinkedList` class. It is completely hidden from all other code. For that reason, it is safe to make its data fields public. They can be accessed by the methods of the `LinkedList` class (which has a legitimate need to access them), and they are not visible elsewhere. In Java, this kind of control was not possible until inner classes were introduced. (See Chapter 11 for an example of a Java implementation of linked lists that uses inner classes.)

However, the Java inner classes have an additional feature that makes them richer and therefore potentially more useful than nested classes in C++. An object that comes from an inner class has an implicit reference to the outer class object that instantiated it. Through this pointer, it gains access to the total state of the outer object. You will see the details of the Java mechanism for doing this in this section.

The `Property` Interface

Let us now develop a more realistic example to show where inner classes are useful. We build a *property editor.* This is a sheet that shows properties of various objects and lets you modify them. What is a property? It is something that has a name, a value, and that can be set to a new value. At the beginning of this chapter, you have learned that such a collection of methods can be expressed as an *interface:*

```
interface Property
{   public String get();
    public void set(String s);
    public String name();
}
```

Since we do not yet know how to write a graphical program, we will implement our property editor in a way that is much more mundane. Our editor simply displays the properties on the screen, numbers them, and asks the user which one should be modified. Then it asks for the new value of the property. Here is a sample interaction:

```
1:Harry Hacker's salary=35000.0
2:Carl Cracker's salary=75000.0
3:Carl Cracker's years on the job=9
Change which property? (0 to quit) 2
New value: 94000
```

Here is the code for the `PropertyEditor` class. Note that the property editor does not need to know anything about properties, except that it can get and set them.

```
class PropertyEditor
{  public PropertyEditor(Property[] p)
   {  properties = p;
   }

   public void editProperties()
   {  while (true)
      {  for (int i = 0; i < properties.length; i++)
            System.out.println((i + 1) + ":"
               + properties[i].name()
               + "=" + properties[i].get());
         int n = Console.readInt
            ("Change which property? (0 to quit)");
         if (n == 0) return;
         if (0 < n && n <= properties.length)
         {  String value
               = Console.readString("New value:");
            properties[n - 1].set(value);
         }
      }
   }

   Property[] properties;
}
```

Using an Inner Class to Implement the `Property` Interface

Now let us add a property to the `Employee` class in order to put the class in a position to work with our property editor. An employee object will now expose a `SalaryProperty` object that can be given to a property editor.

```
Employee carl = new Employee("Carl Cracker",
   75000, new Day(1987, 12, 15));

Property carlsSalary = carl.getSalaryProperty();
```

Of course, `Property` is just an interface. The object returned by the `getSalaryProperty` method must be an object of a class implementing that interface. In fact, in our example, it will be an instance of the class

`SalaryProperty`—which will be an *inner class* implementing the `Property` interface.

```
class Employee
{  . . .

   private class SalaryProperty implements Property
   {  public String get() { . . . }
      public void set(String s) { . . . }
      public String name() { . . . }
   }

   public Property getSalaryProperty()
   {  return new SalaryProperty();
   }
}
```

The `SalaryProperty` class is a *private* class inside `Employee`. This is a safety mechanism—since only `Employee` methods can generate `SalaryProperty` objects. Note that only inner classes can be private. Regular classes always have either package or public visibility.

Let us implement the `get` method. For this, the `SalaryProperty` object must report the salary *of the employee that instantiated it.* For example, in the code

```
Property carlsSalary = carl.getSalaryProperty();
double s = carlsSalary.get();
```

the `get` method must return Carl's salary.

In Java, an object created by an inner class can automatically access *all* data fields of the object that created it. This allows the code for the `get` method to be extremely simple:

```
private class SalaryProperty implements Property
{  public String get()
   {  return "" + salary;
   }
   . . .
}
```

The name `salary` in the code above refers to the `salary` field of the outer class object that created this `SalaryProperty`. This is quite innovative. Traditionally, a method could refer to the data fields of the object invoking the method. An inner class method gets to access both its own data fields *and* those of the outer object creating it.

This means, of course, that an object of an inner class always gets an implicit reference to the object that created it. (See Figure 6-1.)

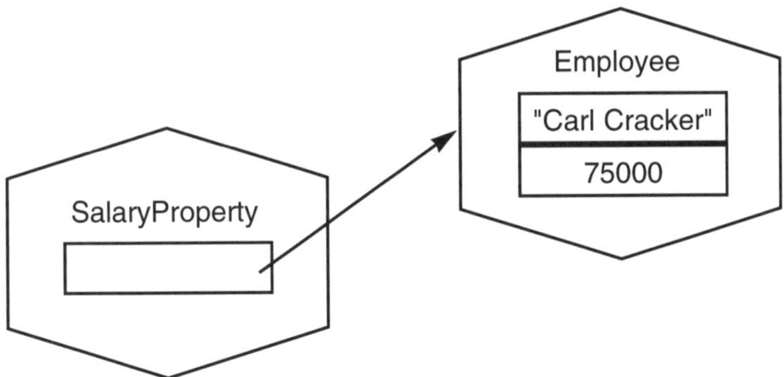

Figure 6-1: An object of an inner class

This reference is invisible in the Java code—it is a detail of the implementation of the inner class.

Next, let us see an example of an inner class method that accesses both its own data fields and that of the outer object. We will define the `set` method in the `SalaryProperty` object so that it can change the employee's salary, but it can do so only *once*. If you want to change the salary twice, then you must obtain two `SalaryProperty` objects. Here is the code for the method:

```
private class SalaryProperty implements Property
{  . . .
   public void set(String s)
   {  if (isSet) return; // can set once
      double sal = Format.atof(s);
      if (sal > 0)
      {  salary = sal;
         isSet = true;
      }
   }
   private boolean isSet = false;
}
```

The name `isSet` refers to the field of the inner object; the name `salary` refers to the outer object.

Let us assume that the reference to the outer object is called `outer`. (It actually is called something different internally.) Then, the code of the `set` method can be visualized as follows:

```
public void set(String s)
{  if (this.isSet) return; // can set once
   double sal = Format.atof(s);
   if (sal > 0)
   {  outer.salary = sal;
      this.isSet = true;
   }
}
```

The `outer` reference is set in the constructor.

```
private class SalaryProperty implements Property
{  SalaryProperty(Employee o) { outer = o; }

   private Employee outer; // this is what happens internally
}
```

Again, `outer` is not a Java keyword. We just use it to indicate the mechanism involved in an inner class.

Note that while you can refer to the outer object as `Employee.this`, the version of inner clases added to Java 1.1 and supported in the current version of the JDK 1.1 does not fully support member access through such a reference.

Example 6-2 shows the complete program that tests inner classes implementing the `Property` interface. There are two instances of the `SalaryProperty` for the same employee object, allowing us to change the salary twice. We also added a second property, called the `SeniorityProperty`, that reports how many years an employee has been with the company. The `set` method of this property does nothing—you can update a salary but you can't change history. The `PropertyEditor` just treats this class as yet another property.

Example 6-2: PropertyTest.java

```
import corejava.*;

public class PropertyTest
{  public static void main(String[] args)
   {  Employee harry = new Employee("Harry Hacker",
         35000, new Day(1989, 10, 1));
      Employee carl = new Employee("Carl Cracker",
         75000, new Day(1987, 12, 15));

      PropertyEditor editor = new PropertyEditor(
            new Property[]
            {  harry.getSalaryProperty(),
```

```
                harry.getSalaryProperty(),
                carl.getSalaryProperty(),
                carl.getSeniorityProperty()
             });

      System.out.println("Before:");
      harry.print();
      carl.print();
      System.out.println("Edit properties:");
      editor.editProperties();
      System.out.println("After:");
      harry.print();
      carl.print();
   }
}

interface Property
{  public String get();
   public void set(String s);
   public String name();
}

class PropertyEditor
{  public PropertyEditor(Property[] p)
   {  properties = p;
   }

   public void editProperties()
   {  while (true)
      {  for (int i = 0; i < properties.length; i++)
            System.out.println((i + 1) + ":"
               + properties[i].name()
               + "=" + properties[i].get());
         int n = Console.readInt
            ("Change which property? (0 to quit)");
         if (n == 0) return;
         if (0 < n && n <= properties.length)
         {  String value
               = Console.readString("New value:");
            properties[n - 1].set(value);
         }
      }
   }

   Property[] properties;
}
```

```
class Employee
{  public Employee(String n, double s, Day d)
   {  name = n;
      salary = s;
      hireDay = d;
   }
   public void print()
   {  System.out.println(name + " " + salary + " "
         + hireYear());
   }
   public void raiseSalary(double byPercent)
   {  salary *= 1 + byPercent / 100;
   }
   public int hireYear()
   {  return hireDay.getYear();
   }

   private class SalaryProperty implements Property
   {  public String name()
      {  return name + "'s salary";
      }
      public String get()
      {  return "" + salary;
      }

      public void set(String s)
      {  if (isSet) return; // can set once
         double sal = Format.atof(s);
         if (sal > 0)
         {  salary = sal;
            isSet = true;
         }
      }
      private boolean isSet = false;
   }

   public Property getSalaryProperty()
   {  return new SalaryProperty();
   }

   private class SeniorityProperty implements Property
   {  public String name()
      {  return name + "'s years on the job";
      }
      public String get()
      {  Day today = new Day();
         int years = today.daysBetween(hireDay) / 365;
         return "" + years;
      }
```

```
        public void set(String s)
        {} // can't set seniority
    }

    public Property getSeniorityProperty()
    {   return new SeniorityProperty();
    }

    private String name;
    private double salary;
    private Day hireDay;
}
```

Are Inner Classes Useful? Are They Actually Necessary?

Inner classes are a major addition to the language. Java started out with the goal of being simpler than C++. But inner classes are anything but simple. The syntax is complex. (It will get more complex as we study anonymous inner classes later in this chapter.) It is not obvious how inner classes interact with other features of the language, such as access control and security.

Has Java started down the road to ruin that has afflicted so many other languages, by adding a feature that was elegant and interesting rather than needed?

While we won't try to answer this question completely, it is worth noting that inner classes are a phenomenon of the *compiler,* not the virtual machine. Inner classes are translated into regular class files (with `$` signs delimiting outer and inner class names), and the virtual machine does not have any special knowledge about them.

For example, the `SalaryProperty` class inside the `Employee` class is translated to a class file `Employee$SalaryProperty.class`. To see this at work, try out the following experiment: run the `ReflectionTest` program of Chapter 5, and give it the class `Employee$SalaryProperty` to reflect upon. You will get the following printout:

```
class Employee$SalaryProperty
{
Employee$SalaryProperty(Employee);

public java.lang.String name();
public java.lang.String get();
public void set(java.lang.String);

private final Employee this$Employee;
private boolean isSet;
}
```

You can plainly see that the compiler has generated an additional data field `this$Employee` for the reference to the outer class. (The name `this$Employee` is synthesized by the compiler—you cannot refer to it in your code.)

If the compiler can do this transformation, couldn't you simply program the same mechanism by hand? Let's try it. We would make `SalaryProperty` a regular class, outside the `Employee` class. When constructing a `SalaryProperty` object, we pass it the `this` pointer of the object that is creating it.

```
class Employee
{  . . .

   public Property getSalaryProperty()
   {  return new SalaryProperty(this);
   }
}

class SalaryProperty implements Property
{  String get() { . . . }
   public void set(String s) { . . . }
   public String name() { . . . }
   SalaryProperty(Employee o) { outer = o; }

   private Employee outer;
}
```

Now let us look at the `get` method. It needs to return `outer.salary`.

```
class SalaryProperty implements Property
{  public String get()
   { return "" + outer.salary; // ERROR
   }
   . . .
}
```

Here we run into a problem. The inner class can access the private data of the outer class, but our external `SalaryProperty` class cannot. We can use a public accessor `getSalary()` in this case. But look at the `set` method. We need to set the salary, and the `Employee` class has no `setSalary` mutator. Maybe we don't want to add one. After all, the `SalaryProperty` object had a built-in protection: the salary can be set only by the recipient of the property object, and it can be set only *once.* A public `setSalary` mutator would have no such restriction.

Thus, inner classes are genuinely more powerful than regular classes, since they have more access privileges.

Could we have done away with the inner class entirely and simply have `Employee` implement the `Property` interface? But that would not work, either. There are two separate properties that the `Employee` class spawns: the

SalaryProperty and the SeniorityProperty. Had Employee simply implemented the get and set methods itself, rather than delegating them to other classes, it could have implemented only one or the other behavior. And even if there was only a single behavior to implement, the property objects need to have their own independent *state*. Each SalaryProperty object has a separate flag to indicate whether it has already used up its opportunity to set the salary. If Employee had implemented the get and set methods itself, there would not be a separate state.

Let us summarize. Inner classes are useful in all of the following circumstances:

- A helper object needs to control the private implementation of a class, but you don't want to grant that access to others.
- A class needs to spawn helper objects with the same protocol but different implementations of the protocol.
- A class needs to spawn helper objects that have their own state.

Local and Anonymous Inner Classes

If you look carefully at the code of the PropertyTest example, you will find that you need the name of the types SalaryProperty and SeniorityProperty only once: when you create an object of those types in the getSalaryProperty and getSeniorityProperty methods.

When you have a situation like this, Java lets you define the classes *locally in a single method*. Let us look at the getSeniorityProperty method in order to illustrate this concept.

```
public Property getSeniorityProperty()
{  class SeniorityProperty implements Property
   {  public String name()
      {  return name + "'s years on the job";
      }
      public String get()
      {  Day today = new Day();
         int years = today.daysBetween(hireDay) / 365;
         return "" + years;
      }
      public void set(String s)
      {} // can't set seniority
   }

   return new SeniorityProperty();
}
```

Local classes have a great advantage—they are completely hidden from the outside world. No method except getSeniorityProperty has any knowledge of the getSeniorityProperty class.

You can go even a step further. Since you want to make only a single object of this class, you don't even need to give it a name. You can return an object of an *anonymous class.*

```
public Property getSeniorityProperty()
{     return new Property ()
   {  public String name()
      {  return name + "'s years on the job";
      }
      public String get()
      {  Day today = new Day();
         int years = today.daysBetween(hireDay) / 365;
         return "" + years;
      }
      public void set(String s)
      {} // can't set seniority
   }
}
```

This is a very cryptic syntax indeed. It means:

Create a new object of a class that implements the `Property` interface, where the required three methods `name`, `get`, and `set` are the ones defined inside the braces `{ }`. The parameters used to construct the object are given inside the parentheses `( )` following the supertype name. In general, the syntax is

```
new SuperType (construction parameters)
{ inner class methods and data
}
```

Here *`SuperType`* can be an interface, such as `Property`. Then the inner class *implements* that interface. Or `SuperType` can be a class. Then, the inner class *extends* that class.

An anonymous inner class cannot have constructors because the name of a constructor must be the same as the name of a class, and the class has no name. Instead, the construction parameters are given to the *superclass* constructor. In particular, whenever an inner class implements an interface, it cannot have any construction parameters.

You have to look very carefully to see the difference between the construction of a new object of a class and the construction of an object of an anonymous inner class extending that class. If the closing parenthesis of the construction parameter list is followed by an opening brace, then an anonymous inner class is being defined.

```
Button b = new Button("Ok");
   // a Button object
Button b = new Button("Help") { ... };
   // an object of an inner class extending Button
```

Are anonymous inner classes a great idea or are they a great way of writing obfuscated code? Probably a bit of both. When the code for an inner class is short, just a few lines of simple code, then they are a great timesaver, but it is exactly timesaving features that lead you down the slippery slope to an "Obfuscated Java Code contest."

It is a shame that the designers of Java did not try to improve the syntax of anonymous classes, since, generally, Java syntax is a great improvement over C++. The designers of the inner class feature could have helped the human reader with syntax such as

```
Button b = new class extends Button("Help") { ... };
    // not the actual Java syntax
```

But they didn't. We recommend using anonymous inner classes with great restraint.

Local Classes That Access Local Variables

Local classes have a few other peculiarities. For example, they cannot just access the fields of their outer classes; they can even access local variables! Here is a rather dramatic illustration of this capability. Rather than allowing the `SalaryProperty` a single chance to change the salary, we give it a counter `setCount` that is incremented whenever the salary is set. Once it has reached a value `maxSetCount`, then the salary cannot be set further. However, `maxSetCount` is a *local* variable of the `getSalaryProperty` method; in fact, it is a parameter variable.

```
public Property getSalaryProperty(final int maxSetCount)
    {  class SalaryProperty implements Property
       {  public String name()
          {  return name + "'s salary";
          }
          public String get()
          {  return "" + salary;
          }
          public void set(String s)
          {  if (setCount >= maxSetCount) return;
             double sal = Format.atof(s);
             if (sal > 0)
             {  salary = sal;
                setCount++;
             }
          }

          int setCount = 0;
       }
       Property p = new SalaryProperty();
       return p;
    }
```

Maybe this should not be so surprising. The line

```
if (setCount >= maxSetCount) return;
```

is inside the `getSalaryProperty` method, so why shouldn't it have access to the `maxSetCount` value?

To see why there actually is a subtle issue, let us consider the flow of control more closely.

- The `getSalaryProperty` method is called.
- The object `p` is generated, and the method returns it.
- At this point the method exits, and the `maxSetCount` variable no longer exists.
- Much later, some other code calls `p.set(value)`.

For the code of the `set` method to work, the `SalaryProperty` class must have made a copy of the `maxSetCount` field before it went away as a local variable of the `getSalaryProperty` method. That is indeed exactly what happened. If you use the `ReflectionTest` program again to spy on the `Employee$1$SalaryProperty` class, you get the following output:

```
class Employee$1$SalaryProperty
{
Employee$1$SalaryProperty(int, Employee);

public java.lang.String name();
public java.lang.String get();
public void set(java.lang.String);

private final int val$maxSetCount;
private final Employee this$Employee;
int setCount;
}
```

Note the extra `int` parameter to the constructor and the `val$maxSetCount` data field. When an object is created, the value `maxSetCount` is passed into the constructor and stored in the `val$maxSetCount` field. This sounds like an extraordinary amount of trouble for the implementors of the compiler. The compiler must detect access of local variables, make matching data fields for each one of them, and copy the local variables into the constructor so that the data fields can be initialized as copies of them.

The methods of a local class can refer only to local variables that are declared `final`. For that reason, the `maxSetCount` parameter was declared `final` in our example. A local variable that is declared `final` cannot be modified. Thus, it is guaranteed that the local variable and copy that is made inside the local class always have the same value.

Have the language designers finally gone off the deep end here? Frankly, we think so. This feature seems to offer marginal added value, at a great cost in complexity.

Anonymous Adapters

Let us finish this chapter with an application of anonymous inner classes that is often used when programming with the new event model of Java 1.1. You need to have objects that implement certain interfaces when using the new Java 1.1 mechanism for communicating events. These are called *listener interfaces.* Objects that implement these listener interfaces need to be added to the source of the events they will track. For example, the `WindowListener` interface defines *seven* methods

```
void windowActivated(WindowEvent)
void windowClosed(WindowEvent)
void windowClosing(WindowEvent)
void windowDeactivated(WindowEvent)
void windowDeiconified(WindowEvent)
void windowIconified(WindowEvent)
void windowOpened(WindowEvent)
```

that need to be implemented in order to have a window respond to the usual events like closing itself.

A method call

```
void addWindowListener(WindowListener)
```

is then used to add an object of a class that implements `WindowListener` to the list of objects that get notified when a window event occurs.

We want to define a class that exits the system when the window is closing, but does nothing in the remaining six cases. Of course, we can implement a class in which all seven functions that are advertised in the interface are actually defined, six of them as do-nothing functions.

```
class WindowCloser implements WindowListener
{  void windowActivated(WindowEvent e) {}
   void windowClosed(WindowEvent e) {}
   void windowClosing(WindowEvent e) { System.exit(0); }
   void windowDeactivated(WindowEvent e) {}
   void windowDeiconified(WindowEvent e) {}
   void windowIconified(WindowEvent e) {}
   void windowOpened(WindowEvent e) {}
}
```

Then, we can pass an object of that class to the `addWindowListener` method:

```
addWindowListener(new WindowCloser());
```

But this can seem like a lot of trouble just to define the reaction to one window event. The designers of the windowing toolkit thought so, too. They therefore added a base class called `WindowAdapter` that has all seven methods of the interface already defined as do-nothing methods. Using this adapter class, it is easy to install a handler that exits the system when the window is closing:

```
addWindowListener(new WindowAdapter()
{  public void windowClosing(WindowEvent e)
   {  System.exit(0);
   }
} );
```

Since the anonymous inner class inherits from `WindowAdapter`, all of its methods are there so that it does implement the `WindowListener` interface—they just do nothing. However, we override one of them, `windowClosing`, in order to exit the program when the user closes the window. This use of anonymous inner classes is very common when programming user-interface event handling. You will see many more examples in Chapter 8. The syntax is somewhat cryptic at first, but you will get used to it very soon.

CHAPTER 7

- Introduction
- Frames and Windows
- Displaying Information in a Window
- Events and the `Update` and `Paint` Functions
- Text and Fonts
- Colors
- Drawing Shapes
- Filling Shapes
- Paint Mode
- Images
- Buffering
- Image Acquisition
- Printing

Graphics Programming and Printing

To this point, you have only seen how to write programs that take input from the keyboard, fuss with it, and then display the results on the console screen. This type of program is old-fashioned and not what users want. Modern programs don't work this way and neither do Web pages. This chapter starts you on the road to writing Java programs that use a graphical user interface (GUI). In particular, you will learn how to write programs that size and locate windows on the screen, display text with multiple fonts in a window, display images, and so on. You will also see the basic methods for using the new printings features of Java 1.1. (The next two chapters show you how to process events such as keystrokes and mouse clicks, and how to add interface elements such as menus and buttons to your applications.) When you finish these three chapters, you will know what is needed to write *stand-alone* graphical applications. Chapter 10 shows how to program applets embedded in Web pages that use these features.

Introduction

Java gives you a class library for basic GUI programming called the Abstract Window Toolkit or AWT. The greatest strength of the AWT is that it is supposed to be platform independent. This means that Sun Microsystems has programmed the AWT so code *should* work with no change on various operating systems. (They usually concentrate on Solaris and Windows 95/NT first, support for the Mac comes only down the road. Solaris and Windows are also usually the first platforms where improvements show up or where bugs get squashed.) People from outside Sun have ported the AWT to other platforms such as SGI's, OS/2 or Linux.

The drawback to platform independence is that it must necessarily be a "lowest common denominator approach." Applications built with the AWT simply do not look as nice as native Windows or Macintosh applications. Also, there are occasionally *different* bugs on the various platforms. Hence:

If you need to be sure that an AWT-based program will run on multiple platforms, you need to test the code on those platforms. JavaSoft's motto of "write once, run anywhere" may be the eventual goal, but it is not yet what is happening in practice. The current practice is usually described as "write once, debug everywhere."

By the way, at one point, the AWT was called the Alternative Window Toolkit, but there are still only a few alternatives to the AWT available at this time. (And if you choose to use one of them, you run the risk of losing platform independence.)

NOTE: What are fast becoming available are not *replacements* for the AWT but *extensions* of it. It is worth checking out some of these libraries. For example, a companion book in the SunSoft Java series, "Graphic Java 1.1" contains some quite useful classes that extend the AWT. Also, JavaSoft, Netscape, and IBM have announced an alliance to build a quite powerful library of graphical components called the Java Foundation Classes. Even Microsoft has announced a set of classes that will extend the AWT.

The first version of AWT was somewhat primitive, not very well documented, and not particularly powerful. (This prompted many programmers to call it the "Awkward Window Toolkit" in casual conversation.) The current version of the AWT, while not much better documented is much more useful than the version of the AWT that was in Java 1.0. For example:

- Windows can be sized and positioned as one would want.
- There are many more (and better) tools for image manipulation.
- The event model is far more flexible.

(We will discuss event handling in the next chapter and image manipulation in Volume 2.)

Finally, we do have to warn you that if you have programmed Microsoft Windows applications using VB, Delphi, or Visual C++, you know about the ease of use that comes with the graphical layout tools these products provide. These tools let you design the visual appearance of your application and then they generate much (often all) of the GUI code for you. While some GUI builders are now available for Java 1.0 programming, as we write this book, no

released products work with Java 1.1. Moreover, even when released, these products are unlikely to be as mature as the corresponding tools for Windows. In any case, to fully understand graphical user interface programming (or even, we feel, to use these tools effectively), you need to know how to build a user interface manually. Naturally, this often requires writing *a lot of code.*

Frames and Windows

In the AWT, a top-level window (that is, a window that is not contained inside another window) is called a *frame.* Frames are example of what are called *containers* in the AWT. This means, as you will see in Chapters 8 and 9, a frame can contain other user interface components such as buttons and text fields. In this section, we want to go over the most common methods for working with a frame.

Although the first version of the AWT lacked many of the methods you needed to make frames look and feel the way most users would expect, the 1.1 version of the AWT has pretty much everything you need. You can set the size and location of a frame or move a frame to the top in the "Z-order," for example. However, while the functionality is now more or less what you would expect, creating a useable frame in the AWT still isn't quite as simple as you might expect. To make a frame class that is useable, you must:

- Resize and (possibly) reposition the frame. (By default, frames are sized at 0 pixels by 0 pixels and are always in the top left corner of the screen.)
- Extend the Java `Frame` class by adding event handling code so that the user can *close* it in the way that the user expects, for example, by clicking on the Close button in Windows.

Since the code for making a frame closeable has nothing to do with graphics programming and everything to do with event handling , we will postpone dealing with this problem until the next chapter. Still, we want the windows for the example programs in this chapter to be closeable in the way that you expect. To do this we will use a class called `CloseableFrame` in our `corejava` package. Our `CloseableFrame` class extends the usual AWT `Frame` class by including the necessary event handling code so that it will close itself down in response to a user's request. In addition, any class that extends our `CloseableFrame` class starts out:

- At the default location for a frame (the top left corner)
- With a size of 300 by 200 pixels
- Displaying a title bar that contains the name of the class.

(You'll soon see the methods needed to change all these defaults.)

The following code gives about the simplest example of using our `CloseableFrame` class:

Example 7-1: Using our `CloseableFrame` class

```
import corejava;
import java.awt.*;

public FirstFrame extends CloseableFrame
{  public static void main(String[]args)
   {  FirstFrame f = new FirstFrame();
      f.show();
   }
}
```

Figure 7-1 shows you what you will see:

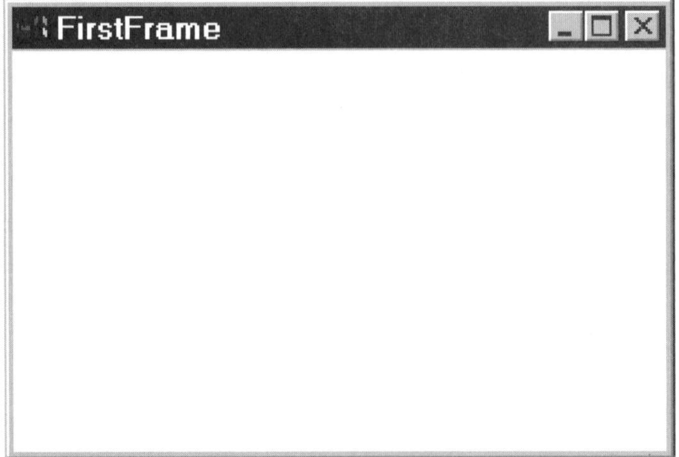

Figure 7-1: Using our `CloseableFrame` class

Let's go over the code, line by line. First, we have imported the AWT package and our `corejava` package. Next is the standard header for a new class. In this case, the class is called `FirstFrame`. The key line

```
FirstFrame f = new FirstFrame();
```

declares and makes a new `FirstFrame` object. Once this line is processed, Java will build the data structure that contains all the necessary information so that the underlying windowing system can display a window. Since our class extends our `CloseableFrame` class, it starts out by using the information con-

tained in our `CloseableFrame` class, such as having a default size of 300 × 200 pixels and the name of the class in the title bar. Finally, you still need to use the `show` method in order to make Java display the frame. This is a method of the class `Window` which is a superclass of `Frame`. Unfortunately, we can't call `show` for you in the `CloseableFrame` constructor; you need to call it only after Java has processed the code in the subclass constructor. In this simple example, the subclass `FirstFrame` has no constructor, so you can't see this rule at work. But in most realistic examples, the constructor for the subclass of a frame class contains the code that lays out the user interface of the application. That layout must happen before the call to `show`.

The `Frame` class itself has only a few methods for changing how frames look and feel: probably the most important are the `setTitle` method for changing the title bar and the `setResizable` method, which takes a `boolean` to determine if a frame is resizeable by the user (see the API notes). Of course, through the magic of inheritance most of the methods for working with the size and position of a frame come from the various superclasses of `Frame`. Figure 7-2 illustrates the inheritance chain for the `Frame` class.

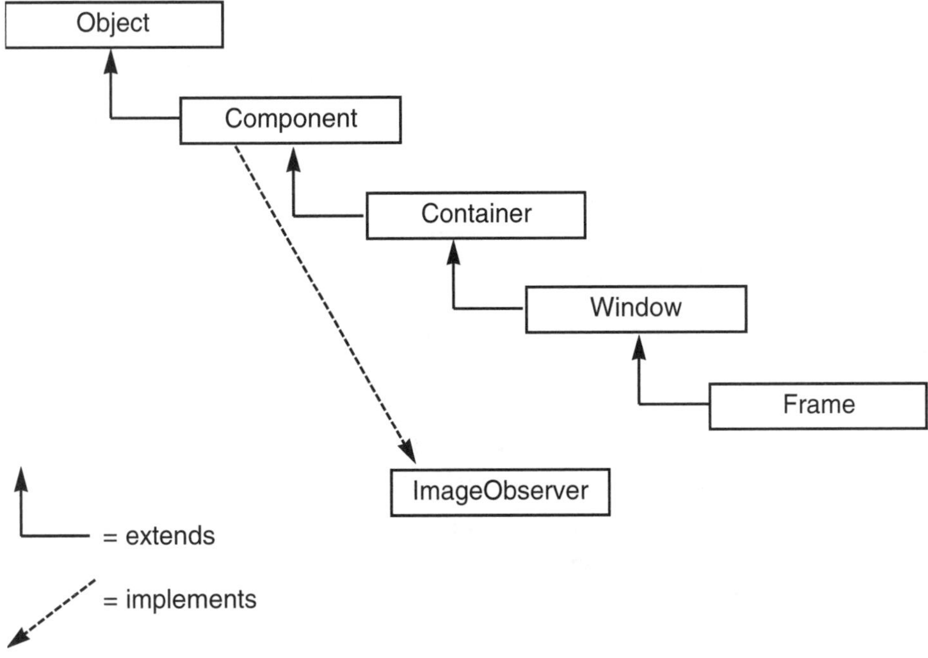

Figure 7-2: Inheritance hierarchy for the `Frame` class

As the API notes indicate, the `Component` class (which is the ancestor of all non-menu GUI objects) and the `Window` class, which is the frame's class parent, are where you usually need to look in order to find the methods to resize and reshape frames. For example, the `Window` class is where the `show` method lives that you use to display the component.

Similarly, the `setLocation` method in the `Component` class lets you reposition a component. If you make the call

```
setLocation(int x, int y)
```

the top left corner is x pixels across and y pixels down (where (0,0) is the top left corner). Note that for a frame, the coordinates are taken relative to the whole screen. (As you will see in the next chapter for other components, the measurements are taken relative to the container.)

TIP: The API notes for this section give what we think are the most important methods for giving frames the proper look and feel. Some of these methods are defined in the `Frame` class. Others come from the parent classes of `Frame`. At some point, you may need to search the API docs to see if the AWT has methods for some special purpose. Unfortunately, that is a bit tedious to do with the JDK documentation. For subclasses, the API docs only list *overridden* methods. For example, `show` is applicable to objects of type `Frame`, but because it is simply inherited from the `Window` class, the `Frame` documentation doesn't show it. If you feel that Java should have a method to do something and it isn't listed in the documentation for the class you are working with, try looking at the API docs for the methods of the *superclasses* of that class. The top of each API page has hyperlinks to the superclasses.

To give you an idea of what you can do with the AWT, we end this section by showing you a sample program that positions one of our closeable frames so that:

- Its area is ¼ that of the whole screen
- It is centered in the middle of the screen.

For example, if the screen was 800 × 600 pixels, we need a frame that is 400 × 300 pixels and we need to move it so the top left-hand corner is at (200,150).

To do this, we need a method to find out the screen resolution. This obviously requires interacting with the underlying operating system since this is the only place where this information is likely to be stored. In Java, you usually get at system-dependent information via what is called a *toolkit*. The `Toolkit` class has a method called `getScreenSize` that returns the screen size as a `Dimension` object. (A `Dimension` object encapsulates a height and a width.) Here's a fragment you use to get the screen size:

```
Toolkit tk = Toolkit.getDefaultToolkit();
Dimension d = tk.getScreenSize();
int screenHeight = d.height;
int screenWidth = d.width;
```

Example 7-2 is the complete program.

Example 7-2: CenteredFrame.java

```
import java.awt.*;
import corejava.*;

public class CenteredFrame extends CloseableFrame
{  public CenteredFrame()
   {  Toolkit tk = Toolkit.getDefaultToolkit();
      Dimension d = tk.getScreenSize();
      int screenHeight = d.height;
      int screenWidth = d.width;
      setSize(screenWidth / 2, screenHeight / 2);
      setLocation(screenWidth / 4, screenHeight / 4);
   }

   public static void main(String[] args)
   {  Frame f = new CenteredFrame();
      f.show();
   }
}
```

`java.awt.Component`

- `boolean isVisble()`

  checks if this component is set to be visible. Components are initially visible, with the exception of top-level components such as `Frame`.

- `void setVisible(boolean b)`

  shows or hides the component depending on whether `b` is true or false.

- `boolean isShowing()`

  checks if this component is showing on the screen. For this, it must be visible and be inside a container that is showing.

- `boolean isEnabled()`

  checks if this component is enabled. An enabled component can receive keyboard input.

  Components are initially enabled.

- `void setEnabled(boolean b)`

  enables or disables a component.

- `Point getLocation()`

  returns the location of the top left corner of this component, relative to the top left corner of the surrounding container.

- `Point getLocationOnScreen()`

  returns the location of the top left corner of this component, using the screen's coordinates.

- `void setLocation(int x, int y)`
- `void setLocation(Point p)`

  move the component to a new location. The x and y coordinates (or `p.x` and `p.y`) are using the coordinates of the container if the component is not a top-level component, or the coordinates of the screen if the component is top level (for example, a `Frame`).

- `Dimension getSize()`

  gets the current size of this component (useful if you have allowed the user to resize the frame.)

- `void setSize(int width, int height)`
- `setSize(Dimension d)`

  resize the component to the specified width and height.

`java.awt.Window`

- `void toFront()`

  shows this window on top of any other windows.

- `void toBack()`

  moves this window to the back of the stack of windows on the desktops and rearranges all other visible windows accordingly.

`java.awt.Frame`

- `void setResizable(boolean b)`

  determines whether the user can resize the frame.

- `void setTitle(String s)`

  sets the text in the title bar for the frame to the string `s`.

Displaying Information in a Window

In this section, we show you how to display information in a frame. For example, rather than displaying "Not a Hello, World program" in text mode in a console window as we did in Chapter 3, we will display the message in a window, as shown in Figure 7-3.

Figure 7-3: A simple graphical program

Every time you need a user interface component that is similar to one of the basic AWT components, you use inheritance to create the class with the additional functionality. For example, our `CloseableFrame` class inherits from the AWT `Frame` class, and all of the classes in this chapter are derived from `CloseableFrame`.

To draw on a frame, you use inheritance and override the `paint` method. The `paint` method takes one parameter of type `Graphics`. The `Graphics` parameter is similar to a device context in Windows or a graphics context in X11 programming.. Here's what the framework looks like:

```
class NotHelloWorld1 extends CloseableFrame
{  public static void main(String[] args)
   {  Frame f = new CloseableFrame();
      f.show();
   }
   public void paint(Graphics g)
   {  . . . //code for drawing the message will go here
   }
}
```

In general, anytime you want to put text messages or graphics into a window, you need to override the `paint` method whose skeleton was shown in the above code. As this code also shows, you need to write a new class for this.

VB NOTE: VB programmers rarely need a device context, but it is there just the same. For now, think of a `Graphics` object as being like a Picture box that fills the Form (which actually encapsulates a graphics context). On a `Graphics` object, like a Picture box, you have certain methods for drawing, changing colors, fonts, and pen styles.

A `Graphics` object remembers a collection of settings for drawing images and text, such as what font you set or the current color. All drawing in Java must go through a `Graphics` object as does all communication with a printer. Measurement on a `Graphics` object for screen display is done in pixels. The (0,0) coordinate denotes the top left corner of the component on whose surface you are drawing.

Displaying text (usually called *rendering text*) is considered a special kind of drawing. For example, a `Graphics` object has a `drawString` method that has the following syntax:

```
drawString(String s, int xCoord, int yCoord)
```

In our case, we want to draw the string "Not a Hello, World Program" in our original window, roughly one quarter of the way across and halfway down. Although we don't yet know how to measure the size of the string, we'll start the string at coordinates (75, 100). This means the first character in the string will start at a position 75 pixels to the left and 100 pixels down. (Actually, it is the baseline for the text that is 100 pixels down—see below for more on how text is measured.) Example 7-3 shows the complete code:

Example 7-3: NotHelloWorld1.java

```
import java.awt.*;
import corejava.*;

public class NotHelloWorld1 extends CloseableFrame
{  public void paint(Graphics g)
   {  g.drawString("Not a Hello, World program", 75, 100);
   }

   public static void main(String[] args)
   {  Frame f = new NotHelloWorld1();
      f.show();
   }
}
```

Events and the `Update` and `Paint` Functions

Just like Microsoft Windows or X Window programming, and unlike most DOS programs, a graphical Java program is event driven. The programmer describes what needs to occur when a particular event happens. However, as with all event driven programs, the sequence of events is beyond the control of the programmer since users may perform operations in any order.

For example, parts of an application may need to be redrawn in response to a user action or some other external circumstance. Perhaps the user increased the size of the window or minimized and then restored the application. If the user popped up another window and it covered an existing window and then made it disappear, the application window that was covered is now corrupted and will need to be redrawn. (The graphics system in Java does not save the pixels underneath.) And, of course, when you want Java to display a window, it needs to process the code that specifies how (and where) it should draw the initial elements.

VB NOTE: There is no way to make graphics persistent in Java by setting a property analogous to `AutoRedraw`; you will always need to write the code in, for example, the `paint` method to do the redrawing.

Each time Java needs to redraw a window, no matter what the reason, the Java event handler notifies the window. This triggers a call to the `update` method. The default implementation for `update` (in the base class for all AWT classes, `Component`) is to erase the background of the window and then to call `paint`. In most cases, we can leave `update` alone and just redefine `paint`. For example, in the preceding section, we defined the `paint` method so it will always draw the same message on the screen. This means that even if the frame is covered and then uncovered, the user will always see the same message on the frame since the `paint` method will be called automatically then. (On very slow systems, there may be a momentary delay while Java redraws the text.)

The `update` method, like the `paint` method, takes a single parameter of type `Graphics`. As with the `paint` method, you use the `Graphics` object in the `update` method to:

- Render graphics on the window
- Check the current state of the `Graphics` object
- Modify the current `Graphics` state.

Text and Fonts

To display text, you must first select a font. You specify a font by its name, such as "SansSerif," the style (plain, **bold**, *italic*, or ***bold italic***), and the point size. The following fonts are available on all systems:

SansSerif

Serif

`Monospaced`

Dialog

`DialogInput`

These font names are always mapped by Java to fonts that actually exist on the client machine. For example, on a Windows system, SansSerif is mapped to Arial.

NOTE: Prior versions of Java used font names Helvetica, TimesRoman, Symbol, and ZapfDingbats. These font names are now deprecated.

The Java fonts contain the usual ASCII characters as well as symbols. For example, if you print the character `'\u2297'` in the Dialog font, then you get a ⊗ character. Only those symbols that are defined in the Unicode character set are available. (See the sidebar at the end of this section for more information about available symbols and adding more fonts.)

As you might expect, `Font` is an object in Java, so we need to create a font via a call to `new` before you can use it. In this case, `Font` requires parameters that define its properties in its constructor. The syntax is

```
Font(String name, int style, int size)
```

where one uses something like `Font.BOLD` in the `style` parameter in order to get bold.

Here's the code in a `paint` method that would let you display at the same location as before: "Not a Hello, World program" in the standard SansSerif font on your system using 14-point bold type

```
public void paint(Graphics g)
{  Font f = new Font("SansSerif", Font.BOLD, 14);
   g.setFont(f);
   g.drawString("Not a Hello, World program", 75, 100);
}
```

Actually, since we now have the freedom to choose fonts and font styles, let's display the text with a mixture of Roman and italic letters:

Not a *Hello, World* program

We need two fonts, the base font, `f`, and its italicized version:

```
Font f = new Font("SansSerif", Font.BOLD, 14);
Font fi = new Font("SansSerif", Font.BOLD + Font.ITALIC, 14);
```

Now we have a problem. We need to know how long the string `Not a` in `SansSerif` Bold 14-point is in *pixels* so that we can tack the `Hello, World` string right after i.

To measure a string, you use the `FontMetrics` class. This class encapsulates a lot of information about a font, such as global size properties of the font. It also lets you measure the sizes of strings rendered in the font. For example, the `stringWidth` method of `FontMetrics` takes a string and returns its current width in pixels.

VB NOTE: You cannot mix fonts in Java without carefully positioning the strings yourself. There is no notion of a last point referenced.

To use the `FontMetrics` class in Java, you should become familiar with terminology taken from typesetting in order to handle fonts properly (see Figure 7-4). Many of the properties used in typesetting correspond to methods of the `FontMetrics` class.

Figure 7-4: Typesetting terms illustrated

The *baseline* is the imaginary line where, for example, characters like a basic "e" would rest. The *ascent* is the distance from the baseline to the top of an *ascender,* which is the upper part of a letter like "b" or "k," or an uppercase character. The *descent* is the distance from the baseline to a *descender,* which is the lower portion of a letter like "p" or "g." These correspond to the `getAscent` and `getDescent` methods of the `FontMetrics` class.

You also need the getLeading and getHeight methods of the FontMetrics class, which correspond to what typesetters call *leading* and *height.* Leading is the space between the descent of one line and the ascent of the next line. The height of a font is the distance between successive baselines, which is the same as descent + leading + ascent.

Some characters, typically those with diacritics such as "Í," extend above the normal ascent. (There is, in fact, a slight chance that such characters may overlap with descenders from the preceding line.) The *maximum ascent* is the largest height of such a character. Similarly, the *maximum descent* is the largest depth of a descender. You would use the ascent and descent measurements for line spacing and the maximum ascent and descent if you need to determine the maximum screen area occupied by a font.

These vertical measurements are properties of the font. In contrast, horizontal measurements are properties of the individual characters. In a proportionally spaced font such as Serif or Sans Serif, different characters have different sizes. For example, a "w" is much wider than an "l." In fact, the size of a word may not even equal the sum of the sizes of its characters because some fonts move certain character pairs closer together. (This process is called *kerning.*) For example, the pair "Av" is often kerned. The stringWidth method of the FontMetrics object of a font computes the width of any string and thus takes into account any kerning that may have occurred.

The following code displays the mixed font text "Not a *Hello, World* program" using the FontMetric class to position the various pieces of the text correctly:

```
public void paint(Graphics g)
{  Font f = new Font("SansSerif", Font.BOLD, 14);
   Font fi = new Font("SansSerif", Font.BOLD + Font.ITALIC, 14);
   FontMetrics fm = g.getFontMetrics(f);
   FontMetrics fim = g.getFontMetrics(fi);
   String s1 = "Not a ";
   String s2 = "Hello, World";
   String s3 = " Program";
   int cx = 75;
   int cy = 100;
   g.setFont(f);
   g.drawString(s1, cx, cy);
   cx += fm.stringWidth(s1);
   g.setFont(fi);
   g.drawString(s2, cx, cy);
   cx += fim.stringWidth(s2);
   g.setFont(f);
   g.drawString(s3, cx, cy);
}
```

Actually, this code is unrealistic. Allocating fonts and font metrics is time consuming; it is usually best to allocate them only once. We'll do that in the code for Example 7-4 by:

- Making the fonts and font metrics into variables of our extended `Frame` class
- Setting them once in a `setFonts` method.

We then call the `setFonts` method in the `paint` method. (Note that it would have been more logical to set the fonts in the constructor for the frame, but this is not possible since the graphics context does not yet exist when we first construct the frame.)

While we are at it, we want to make one final improvement: we want to center the string in the window. The `getSize` method of `Component`, a parent class of `Frame`, returns the size of the frame. Unless the user resizes the window, it will be the size that was set by the constructor for the frame (or the last call to `setSize` if there was one). However, `getSize` returns the size of the whole window, *including* the borders and the title bar. The `getInsets` method returns a structure that gives the measurements of the borders around the four sides, so by using it you can get the useable, or client, area easily. For example:

```
getSize().height - getInsets().top - getInsets().bottom
```

is the useable height.

Figure 7-5: Insets

We can use this information to properly center the string. Note that this program repositions the text so that the string stays centered no matter how the user resizes the window.

VB NOTE: Think of `getSize` as corresponding to Height and Width and `getInsets.top`, for example, as corresponding to the height of the menu bar and title bar (usually this is Height-ScaleHeight).

Example 7-4 is the program listing. Figure 7-6 shows the screen display.

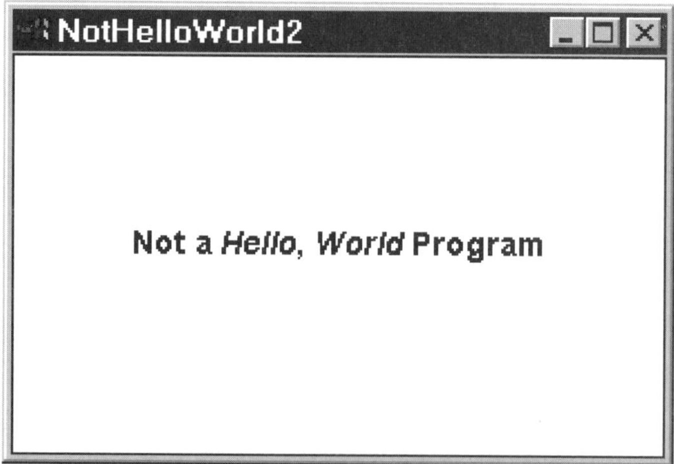

Figure 7-6: Using multiple fonts

Example 7-4: NotHelloWorld2.java

```
import java.awt.*;
import corejava.*;

public class NotHelloWorld2 extends CloseableFrame
{  public void setFonts(Graphics g)
   {  if (fontsSet) return;
      f = new Font("SansSerif", Font.BOLD, 14);
      fi = new Font("SansSerif",
         Font.BOLD + Font.ITALIC, 14);
      fm = g.getFontMetrics(f);
      fim = g.getFontMetrics(fi);
      fontsSet = true;
   }
```

```
   public void paint(Graphics g)
   {  setFonts(g);
      String s1 = "Not a ";
      String s2 = "Hello, World";
      String s3 = " Program";
      int w1 = fm.stringWidth(s1);
      int w2 = fim.stringWidth(s2);
      int w3 = fm.stringWidth(s3);

      Dimension d = getSize();
      Insets in = getInsets();
      int clientWidth = d.width - in.right - in.left;
      int clientHeight = d.height - in.bottom - in.top;
      int cx = (clientWidth - w1 - w2 - w3) / 2 + in.left;
      int cy = clientHeight / 2 + in.top;
      g.drawRect(in.left, in.top,
         clientWidth - 1, clientHeight - 1);

      g.setFont(f);
      g.drawString(s1, cx, cy);
      cx += w1;
      g.setFont(fi);
      g.drawString(s2, cx, cy);
      cx += w2;
      g.setFont(f);
      g.drawString(s3, cx, cy);
   }

   public static void main(String args[])
   {  Frame f = new NotHelloWorld2();
      f.show();
   }

   private Font f;
   private Font fi;
   private FontMetrics fm;
   private FontMetrics fim;
   private boolean fontsSet = false;
}
```

You may wonder how your Java programs can use the dozens of other fonts that are installed on your computer. The sidebar at the end of this section explains how the AWT gets font information and how you can add new fonts to the collection of fonts that Java knows about.

Unfortunately, it is not easy to find out what additional fonts are available on your system. There is a `getFontList` method in the `Toolkit` class. It returns an array of strings with the font names that are known to be available. But that list is just the list of standard fonts, SansSerif, Serif, Monospaced, and so on. User installed fonts are not reported.

The sample program in Example 7-5 *should* run through the list of fonts that are available, displaying the font name and a sample. But in the current version of Java, it runs through only the standard "factory-installed" fonts.

Example 7-5. FontsAvailable.java

```
import java.awt.*;
import corejava.*;

public class FontsAvailable extends CloseableFrame
{  public void paint(Graphics g)
   {  String [] fontList = getToolkit().getFontList();
      Font defaultFont = g.getFont();
      for (int i = 0; i < fontList.length; i++)
      {  g.setFont(defaultFont);
         g.drawString(fontList[i], 20, i * 20 + 40);
         Font f = new Font(fontList[i], Font.PLAIN, 14);
         g.setFont(f);
         g.drawString("ABCabc123\u00C6\u00C7\u2297",
            120, i * 20 + 40);
      }
   }

   public static void main(String[] args)
   {  Frame f = new FontsAvailable();
      f.show();
   }
}
```

`java.awt.Font`

- `Font(String name, int style, int size)`

  creates a new font object.

Parameters:	`name`	the font name (e.g., "Serif")
	`style`	the style (`Font.PLAIN`, `Font.BOLD`, `Font.ITALIC` or `Font.BOLD + Font.ITALIC`)
	`size`	the point size (e.g., 12)

`java.awt.FontMetrics`

- `int getAscent()`

  gets the font ascent—the distance from the baseline to the tops of uppercase characters.

- `int getDescent()`

  gets the font descent—the distance from the baseline to the bottoms of descenders.

- `int getLeading()`

  gets the font leading—the space between the bottom of one line of text and the top of the next line.

- `int getHeight()`

  gets the total height of the font—the distance between the two baselines of text (descent + leading + ascent).

- `int getMaxAscent()`

  gets the maximum height of all characters in this font.

- `int getMaxDescent()`

  gets the maximum descent of all characters in this font.

- `int stringWidth(String str)`

  computes the width of a string.

Parameters:	`str`	the string to be measured

`java.awt.Graphics`

- `void setFont(Font font)`

  selects a font for the graphics context. That font will be used for subsequent text-drawing operations.

Parameters:	`font`	a font

- `FontMetrics getFontMetrics()`

  gets the metrics of the current font.

- `void drawString(String str, int x, int y)`

  draws a string in the current font and color.

Parameters:	`str`	the string to be drawn
	`x`	the *x*-coordinate of the start of the string
	`y`	the *y*-coordinate of the baseline of the string

`java.awt.Container`

- `Insets getInsets()`

  Returns an `Insets` object that describes the internal area of the container. Inset objects encapsulate four integers: top, bottom, left, and right. The return value of `getInsets` indicates the size of the border of the container. A frame, for example, will have a top inset that corresponds to the combined height of the frame's title and menu bar.

Fonts and the `font.properties` file

The AWT looks at the `font.properties` file in the `\lib` directory to find out which fonts are available and which symbol sets are contained in a specific font. To be able to use more fonts in Java than the default ones, you need to modify this file. Let us look at a typical entry in this file:

```
serif.0=Times New Roman,ANSI_CHARSET
serif.1=WingDings,SYMBOL_CHARSET,NEED_CONVERTED
serif.2=Symbol,SYMBOL_CHARSET,NEED_CONVERTED
exclusion.serif.0=0100-ffff
fontcharset.serif.1=sun.awt.windows.CharToByteWingDings
fontcharset.serif.2=sun.awt.CharToByteSymbol
```

This means: To render a character in the Serif font, first check if it is in the "0" range, that is, it is not in the excluded area `0100-ffff`. If it is not excluded, use the Times New Roman font to render it. Next, check if the class `sun.awt.windows.CharToByteWingDings` will accept the character. This (undocumented) class extends the (equally undocumented) class `sun.io.CharToByteConverter`. There are two key methods in these classes that you work with: The method call:

```
boolean canConvert(char)
```

tests whether Java can convert a character. To actually perform the conversion, you need to supply two arrays: one for source characters and one for the target bytes. Then you call:

```
int convert(char[] input, int inStart, int inPastEnd,
   byte[] output, int outStart, int outPastEnd)
```

This method converts the `inPastEnd-inStart` characters in the array `input`, starting from `inStart`, and places them into the byte array `output`, starting at `outStart`. It also fills out at most `outPastEnd - outStart` bytes. (You may wonder why the `convert` method uses arrays instead of simply converting one character into a byte. The reason is that in some encoding schemes, such as the Japanese Shift-JIS code, some characters are encoded as single bytes, others as multiple bytes, with "shift" characters switching between character sets.)

Fonts and the `font.properties` file (continued)

If the `canConvert` method returns `true`, then Java will render the character in the `WingDings` font. Otherwise, Java tries the `Symbol` font. If this fails as well, Java renders the character as a `'?'`.

Note that font descriptions are dependent on the operating system. The lines in these examples describe fonts for Windows. In other operating systems, the font descriptions will be different. For example, the description of the Times font in Solaris looks like this:

```
serif.plain.0=
    -linotype-times-medium-r-normal—*-%d-*-*-p-*-iso8859-1
```

You can add your own fonts to the `font.properties` file. For example, if you run Java under Windows, add the following lines:

```
bookman.0=Bookman,ANSI_CHARSET
exclusion.bookman.0=0100-ffff
```

You can then make a font:

```
new Font("Bookman", Font.PLAIN, 12).
```

You can even add your own font maps. Let us consider the most common case, that is, when characters in your font are described by single bytes. To add your own font map:

- Extend the (undocumented and poorly named) class `sun.io.CharToByte8859_1`. (ISO 8859-1 is the Latin-1 8-bit character set, one of ten 8-bit character sets in the ISO 8859 standard. This Java class can be used as the base class for *any* Unicode to 8-bit code conversion, not just Latin-1.)
- Override two methods: `canConvert`, which returns `true` for those Unicode characters that are part of your font, and `convert`, which converts a character array into the equivalent byte arrays.

Here is a practical example. Suppose that you have a Russian font in ISO 8859-5 format. Omitting a couple of technical exceptions, the mapping from Unicode to ISO 8859-5 is simple:

```
'\u0021'...'\u007E': ch -> ch
'\u0401'...'\u045F': ch -> ch - 0x0360
```

Here is a converter class that does the conversion.

```
public class CharToByteRussian extends sun.io.CharToByte8859_1
{  public boolean canConvert(char ch)
   {  return 0x0021 <= ch && ch <= 0x007E
         || 0x0401 <= ch && ch <= 0x45F;
}

public int convert(char[] input, int inStart, int inPastEnd,
   byte[] output, int outStart, int outPastEnd)
```

Fonts and the `font.properties` file (continued)

```
throws ConversionBufferFullException;
{   int outIndex = outStart;
    for (int i = inStart; i < inPastEnd; i++)
    {   char ch = input[i];
        byte b = 0;
        if (0x0021 <= ch && ch <= 0x007E)
            b = (byte)ch;
        if (0x0401 <= ch && ch <= 0x45F)
            b = (byte)(ch - 0x0360);
        if (b != 0)
        {   if (outIndex >= outPastEnd)
            throw new ConversionBufferFullException();
            output[outIndex] = b;
            outIndex++;
        }
    }
    return outIndex - outStart;
}
}
```

To add the Russian font to Java, you need to place the class `CharToByteRussian` somewhere on your class path. Then add the following lines to `font.properties`:

```
russian.0=RUSSIAN,SYMBOL_CHARSET,NEED_CONVERTED
fontcharset.russian.0=CharToByteRussian
```

Colors

The `setColor` method call selects a color that is used for all subsequent drawing operations on the graphics context or component. To draw in multiple colors, you select a color, draw, then select another color and draw again.

The `setColor` method takes a parameter of type `Color`. You can either pick one of the 13 standard colors listed in Table 7-1 or specify a color by its red, green, and blue components. Using a scale of 0–255 (that is, one byte). for the redness, blueness and greeness, the most general `Color` constructor is:

```
Color(byte redness, byte  greeness, byte blueness)
```

Here are some examples of setting colors:

```
f.setColor(Color.pink);
f.drawString("Hello", 75, 100);
f.setColor(new Color(0, 128, 128)); // a dull blue-green
f.drawString("World", 75, 125);
```

Table 7-1: Standard Colors

black	green	red
blue	lightGray	white
cyan	magenta	yellow
darkGray	orange	
gray	pink	

To set the *background color,* you use the `setBackground` method of the `Component` class, an ancestor of `Frame`. In fact, you should set the background before displaying the frame for the first time.

```
Frame f = new MyFrame();
f.setBackground(Color.white);
f.show();
```

Similarly, if you want to change the color Java uses to display information such as text on a frame, use the `setForeground` method on the frame.

TIP: Occasionally useful and often amusing special effects can be obtained by using the `brighter()` and `darker()` methods of the `Color` class, which, as their names suggest, return either brighter or darker versions of the current color. Using the `brighter` method is also a good way to highlight an item. Actually, `brighter()` is just a little bit brighter. To make a color really stand out, apply it three times: `c.brighter().brighter().brighter()`.

Java gives you predefined names for many more colors in the `SystemColor` class. The constants in this class encapsulate the colors used for various elements of the user's system. For example,

```
f.setBackground(SystemColor.window)
```

sets the background color of the frame `f` to the default used by all windows on the user's desktop. Using the colors in the `SystemColor` class is particularly useful when you want to draw user interface elements so that the colors match those already found on the user's desktop. Table 7-2 lists the system color names and their meanings.

Table 7-2: System Colors

`desktop`	Background color of desktop
`activeCaption`	Background color for captions
`activeCaptionText`	Text color for captions
`activeCaptionBorder`	Border color for caption text
`inactiveCaption`	Background color for inactive captions
`inactiveCaptionText`	Text color for inactive captions
`inactiveCaptionBorder`	Border color for inactive captions
`window`	Background for windows
`windowBorder`	Color of window border frame
`windowText`	Text color inside windows
`menu`	Background for menus
`menuText`	Text color for menus
`text`	Background color for text
`textText`	Text color for text
`textHighlight`	Background color for highlighted text
`textHighlightText`	Text color for highlighted text
`control`	Background color for controls
`controlText`	Text color for controls
`controlLtHighlight`	Light highlight color for controls
`controlHighlight`	Highlight color for controls
`controlShadow`	Shadow color for controls
`controlDkShadow`	Dark shadow color for controls
`inactiveControlText`	Text color for inactive controls
`scrollbar`	Background color for scrollbars
`info`	Background color for spot-help text
`infoText`	Text color for spot-help text

`java.awt.Color`

- `Color(int r, int g, int b)`

  creates a color object.

Parameters:	`r`	the red value (0–255)
	`g`	the green value (0–255)
	`b`	the blue value (0–255)

`java.awt.Graphics`

- `void setColor(Color c)`

  changes the current color. All subsequent graphics operations will use the new color.

  Parameters: `c` the new color

`java.awt.Component`

- `void setBackground(Color c)`

  sets the background color.

  Parameters: `c` the new background color

- `void setForeground(Color c)`

  sets the foreground color.

  Parameters: `c` the new foreground color

Drawing Shapes

You use the `drawLine`, `drawArc`, `drawPolyLine`, and `drawPolygon` methods in `java.awt.Graphics` to draw straight and curved lines on a graphics object. For example, in Java, a *polygon* is a closed sequence of line segments. The easiest way to draw a polygon in Java is to:

- create a polygon object,
- add points to the object,
- use the `drawPolygon(Polygon p)` method described here to draw the polygon.

(There is another `drawPolygon` method that takes two arrays, one for each of the *x*- and *y*-coordinates of the end points of the line segments, but it is less convenient to use.)

If you want a sequence of line segments that is not closed (that is, the first and the last point are not automatically joined), then use the `drawPolyline` method instead.

TIP: Polygons with very closely spaced points are useful to render curved shapes. (In Example 7-6, we draw a spiral made up of many vertices.)

Now let's draw these figures. In Figure 7-7 we have drawn a Pac Man shape (by using an arc and two line segments), a pentagon (with one side missing because the `drawPolygon` function does not close polygons), and a spiral (actually, a polygon with many closely spaced points).

Note again the use of the `getInsets` method in the `paint` method. For no good reason, the (0,0) origin of the coordinate system is the top left corner of the frame, on the frame's border, and not the top left corner of the drawable area. Of course, we cannot draw on the border, so this is always inconvenient. Therefore, *every* `paint` procedure that draws inside a frame should first move the origin. This can be done by passing the right information to the `translate` method of the `Graphics` class, as in the following code.

```
g.translate(getInsets().left, getInsets().top);
```

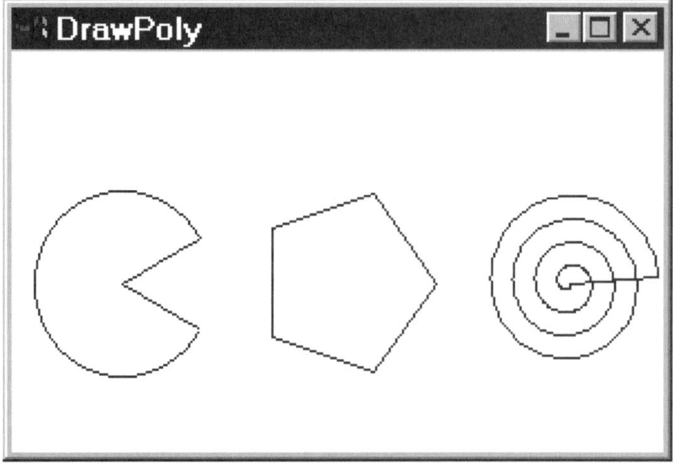

Figure 7-7: Drawing arcs and polygons in Java

Example 7-6: DrawPoly.java

```
import java.awt.*;
import corejava.*;

public class DrawPoly extends CloseableFrame
{  public void paint(Graphics g)
   {  g.translate(getInsets().left, getInsets().top);
      int r = 40; // radius of circle bounding Pac Man(R)
      int cx = 50; // center of that circle
      int cy = 100;
      int angle = 30; // opening angle of mouth
```

```
      int dx = (int)(r * Math.cos(angle * Math.PI / 180));
      int dy = (int)(r * Math.sin(angle * Math.PI / 180));

      g.drawLine(cx, cy, cx + dx, cy + dy); // lower jaw
      g.drawLine(cx, cy, cx + dx, cy - dy); // upper jaw
      g.drawArc(cx - r, cy - r, 2 * r, 2 * r, angle,
         360 - 2 * angle);

      Polygon p = new Polygon();
      cx = 150;
      int i;
      for (i = 0; i < 5; i++)
         p.addPoint(
            (int)(cx + r * Math.cos(i * 2 * Math.PI / 5)),
            (int)(cy + r * Math.sin(i * 2 * Math.PI / 5)));

      g.drawPolygon(p);

      Polygon s = new Polygon();
      cx = 250;
      for (i = 0; i < 360; i++)
      {  double t = i / 360.0;
         s.addPoint(
            (int)(cx + r * t * Math.cos(8 * t * Math.PI)),
            (int)(cy + r * t * Math.sin(8 * t * Math.PI)));
      }
      g.drawPolygon(s);
   }

   public static void main(String args[])
   {  Frame f = new DrawPoly();
      f.show();
   }
}
```

`java.awt.Graphics`

- `void drawLine(int x1, int y1, int x2, int y2)`

  draws a line between the points with coordinates (`x1`,`y1`) and (`x2`,`y2`).

Parameters:	`x1`	the first point's *x*-coordinate
	`y1`	the first point's *y*-coordinate
	`x2`	the second point's *x*-coordinate
	`y2`	the second point's *y*-coordinate

- `void drawArc(int x, int y, int width, int height, int startAngle, int arcAngle)`

  draws an arc bounded by the rectangle with the upper left corner (*x*, *y*) and the given width and height. The arc starts at `startAngle` and spans the `arcAngle`. (That is, the end angle is `startAngle` + `arcAngle`.) Angles are measured in degrees and follow the usual mathematical conventions: 0 degrees is at the three-o'clock position, and positive angles indicate counter-clockwise rotation. The Pac Man figure in Figure 7-7 illustrates how to use these parameters

Parameters:	`x`	the *x*-coordinate
	`y`	the *y*-coordinate
	`width`	the width of the rectangle
	`height`	the height of the rectangle
	`startAngle`	the beginning angle
	`arcAngle`	the angle of the arc (relative to *startAngle*)

- `void drawPolygon(Polygon p)`

  draws a path joining the points in the `Polygon` object.

Parameters:	`p`	a polygon

- `void drawPolygon(int[] xPoints, int[] yPoints, int nPoints)`

  draws a polygon joining a sequence of points.

Parameters:	`xPoints`	an array of *x*-coordinates of the corner points
	`yPoints`	an array of *y*-coordinates of the corner points
	`nPoints`	the number of corner points

- `void drawPolyline(int[] xPoints, int[] yPoints, int nPoints)`

  draws a path joining a sequence of points. The path is not closed unless the first and last point are identical.

Parameters:	`xPoints`	an array of *x*-coordinates of the corner points
	`yPoints`	an array of *y*-coordinates of the corner points
	`nPoints`	the number of corner points

- `void translate(int x, int y)`

  Sets the point with coordinates *x, y* in the usual coordinates (i.e., the one with 0,0 at the top left) to be the new origin.

Drawing Rectangles

The `drawRect`, `drawRoundRect`, `draw3DRect`, and `drawOval` functions render the outlines of rectangles and ellipses (called ovals in the AWT). Figure 7-8 shows the various rectangle styles and the oval. Example 7-7 is the code that drew Figure 7-8.

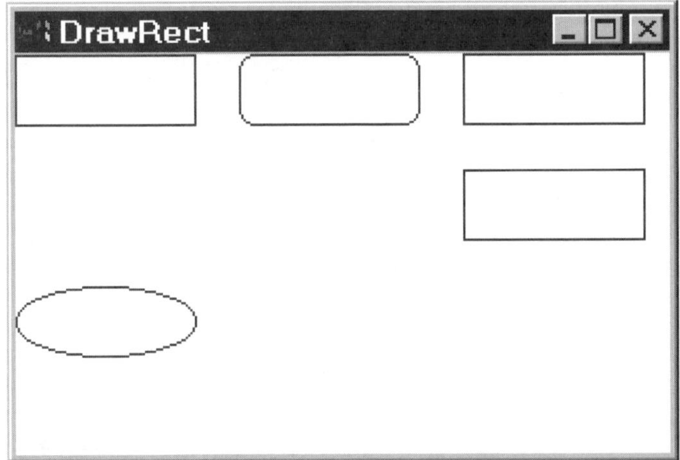

Figure 7-8: Rectangles and ovals

Example 7-7: DrawRect.java

```
import java.awt.*;
import corejava.*;

public class DrawRect extends CloseableFrame
{  public void paint(Graphics g)
   {  g.translate(getInsets().left, getInsets().top);
      g.setColor(Color.blue);
      g.drawRect(0, 0, 80, 30);
      g.drawRoundRect(100, 0, 80, 30, 15, 15);
      g.draw3DRect(200, 0, 80, 30, true);
      g.draw3DRect(200, 50, 80, 30, false);
      g.drawOval(0, 100, 80, 30);
   }
```

```
    public static void main(String args[])
    {  Frame f = new DrawRect();
       f.show();
    }
}
```

java.awt.Graphics

- `void drawRect(int x, int y, int width, int height)`

  draws the outline of the rectangle. Note that the third and fourth parameters are *not* the opposite corner points.

Parameters:	`x`	the *x*-coordinate of the top left corner
	`y`	the *y*-coordinate of the top left corner
	`width`	the width of the rectangle
	`height`	the height of the rectangle

- `void drawRoundRect(int x, int y, int width, int height, int arcWidth, int arcHeight)`

  draws the outline of the rectangle, using curved arcs for the corners.

Parameters:	`x`	the *x*-coordinate of the top left corner
	`y`	the *y*-coordinate of the top left corner
	`width`	the width of the rectangle
	`height`	the height of the rectangle
	`arcWidth`	the horizontal diameter of the arcs at the corners
	`arcHeight`	the vertical diameter of the arcs at the corners

- `void draw3DRect(int x, int y, int width, int height, boolean raised)`

  draws the outline of a raised (3-D) rectangle. Note that the third and fourth parameters are *not* the opposite corner points.

Parameters:	`x`	the *x*-coordinate of the top left corner
	`y`	the *y*-coordinate of the top left corner
	`width`	the width of the rectangle
	`height`	the height of the rectangle
	`raised`	`true` to have the rectangle appear above the window; `false` to have it appear "pushed in"

- `void drawOval(int x, int y, int width, int height)`

  draws the outline of an ellipse. The parameters specify the bounding rectangle.

Parameters:	`x`	the x-coordinate of the top left corner of the bounding rectangle
	`y`	the y-coordinate of the top left corner of the bounding rectangle
	`width`	the width of the bounding rectangle
	`height`	the height of the bounding rectangle

Filling Shapes

You can tell the AWT to fill the interiors of closed shapes (rectangles, ellipses, polygons, and pie chart segments) with a color. The method calls are similar to the ones used for the `draw` calls of the preceding section, except that `draw` is replaced by `fill`.

- `void fillRect(int x, int y, int width, int height)`
- `void fillRoundRect(int x, int y, int width, int height, int arcWidth, int arcHeight)`
- `void fill3DRect(int x, int y, int width, int height, boolean raised)`
- `void fillOval(int x, int y, int width, int height)`
- `void fillArc(int x, int y, int width, int height, int startAngle, int arcAngle)`
- `void fillPolygon(Polygon p)`
- `void fillPolygon(int[] xPoints, int[] yPoints, int nPoints)`

To *fill* rectangles and ovals simply means to color the inside of the shape with the current color. However, there is one minor point to be aware of, as Figure 7-9 illustrates: When you *fill* a rectangle, you get one pixel less on the right and on the bottom of the rectangle than when you *draw* it. When you look closely at the output of the test program (Example 7-8), you can see that the top and left line segments of the drawn rectangles are covered by the subsequent fills, but the right and bottom line segments are not. This is different from the Windows API, where the end points of lines and rectangles are neither drawn nor filled.

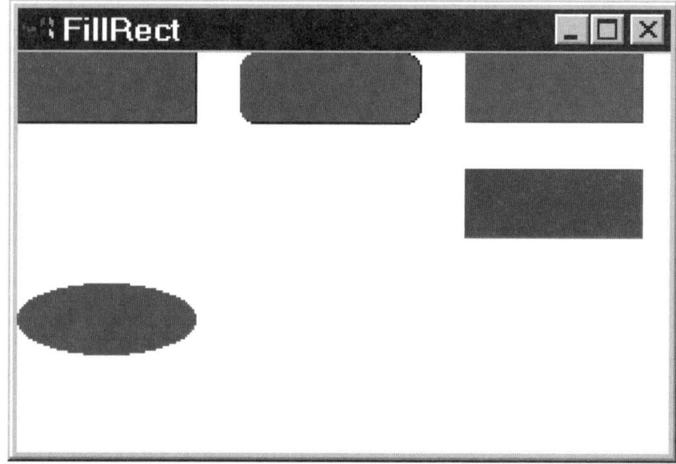

Figure 7-9: Filled rectangles and ovals

Example 7-8: FillRect.java

```
import java.awt.*;
import corejava.*;

public class FillRect extends CloseableFrame
{  public void paint(Graphics g)
   {  g.translate(getInsets().left, getInsets().top);
      g.drawRect(0, 0, 80, 30);
      g.drawRoundRect(100, 0, 80, 30, 15, 15);
      g.drawOval(0, 100, 80, 30);
      g.setColor(Color.red);
      g.fillRect(0, 0, 80, 30);
      g.fillRoundRect(100, 0, 80, 30, 15, 15);
      g.fill3DRect(200, 0, 80, 30, true);
      g.fill3DRect(200, 50, 80, 30, false);
      g.fillOval(0, 100, 80, 30);
   }

   public static void main(String args[])
   {  Frame f = new FillRect();
      f.show();
   }
}
```

Note that filling arcs and polygons is quite different from drawing them. Arcs are filled as pie segments by joining the center of the enclosing rectangle with the two end points of the arc and filling the interior. To see this, look at the filled Pac Man in the screen picture in Figure 7-10.

Polygons, on the other hand, are filled according to the "alternating" rule. For the alternating rule, a point is inside if an infinite ray with the point as origin crosses the path an odd number of times. The effect shows up nicely in the filled spiral in Example 7-9.

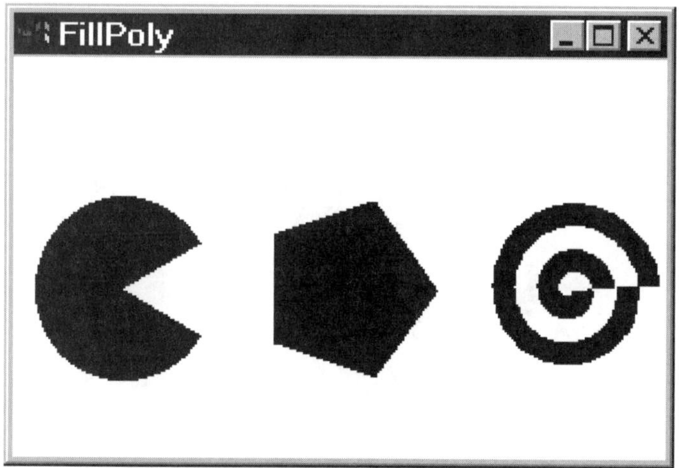

Figure 7-10: Filled shapes

Example 7-9: FillPoly.java

```
import java.awt.*;
import corejava.*;

public class FillPoly extends CloseableFrame
{  public void paint(Graphics g)
   {  g.translate(getInsets().left, getInsets().top);
      int r = 40; // radius of circle bounding Pac Man(R)
      int cx = 50; // center of that circle
      int cy = 100;
      int angle = 30; // opening angle of mouth

      int dx = (int)(r * Math.cos(angle * Math.PI / 180));
      int dy = (int)(r * Math.sin(angle * Math.PI / 180));

      g.fillArc(cx - r, cy - r, 2 * r, 2 * r, angle,
         360 - 2 * angle);

      Polygon p = new Polygon();
      cx = 150;
      int i;
```

```
        for (i = 0; i < 5; i++)
            p.addPoint(
                (int)(cx + r * Math.cos(i * 2 * Math.PI / 5)),
                (int)(cy + r * Math.sin(i * 2 * Math.PI / 5)));

        g.fillPolygon(p);

        Polygon s = new Polygon();
        cx = 250;
        for (i = 0; i < 360; i++)
        {   double t = i / 360.0;
            s.addPoint(
                (int)(cx + r * t * Math.cos(8 * t * Math.PI)),
                (int)(cy + r * t * Math.sin(8 * t * Math.PI)));
        }
        g.fillPolygon(s);
    }

    public static void main(String args[])
    {   Frame f = new FillPoly();
        f.show();
    }
}
```

Paint Mode

When you paint shapes on top of one another, the AWT draws the last drawn shape on top of everything under it. In addition to this *overwrite* paint mode, the AWT also has a second method of combining new shapes with the old window contents; this is usually called *XOR* paint mode.

XOR paint mode is used for highlighting a portion of the screen. Suppose you draw a filled rectangle over a part of the screen. If you draw on top of pixels that are already in the current color, then the AWT changes them to the color specified in the `setXORMode` call. If you draw on top of pixels in the color of the `setXORMode` parameter, the AWT changes them to the current color. Any other colors under the highlighted area are also changed by the AWT in some way. The key point is that XOR is a *toggle*. If you draw the same shape twice in XOR mode, the second drawing erases the first, and the screen looks just as it did at the outset. Example 7-10 provides some sample code.

Usually, you use the background (like Figure 7-11) color as the argument to `setXORMode`.

Example 7-10: XOR.java

```
import java.awt.*;
import corejava.*;

public class XOR extends CloseableFrame
{  public void paint(Graphics g)
   {  g.translate(getInsets().left, getInsets().top);
      setBackground(Color.black);
      g.setColor(Color.red);
      g.fillRect(10, 10, 80, 30);
      g.setColor(Color.green);
      g.fillRect(50, 20, 80, 30);
      g.setColor(Color.blue);
      g.fillRect(130, 40, 80, 30);
      g.setXORMode(Color.green);
      g.fillRect(90, 30, 80, 30);
   }

   public static void main(String[] args)
   {  Frame f = new XOR();
      f.show();
   }
}
```

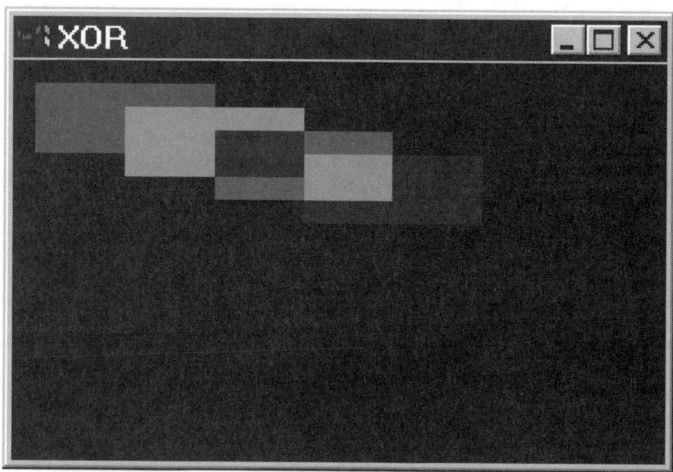

Figure 7-11: Combining colors in XOR mode

`java.awt.Graphics`

- `void setPaintMode()`

  sets the graphics context to use "paint mode," in which new pixels replace old ones.

- `void setXORMode(Color xor_color)`

  sets the graphics context to use "XOR mode." The color of a pixel is determined as `old_color ^ new_color ^ xor_color`. If you draw the same shape twice, then it is erased and the screen is restored to its original appearance.

Parameters:	`xor_color`	the color to which the current color should change during drawing

Images

You have already seen how to build up simple images by drawing lines and shapes. Complex images, such as photographs, are usually generated externally, for example, with a scanner or special image-manipulation software. (As you will see in Volume 2, it is also possible to produce an image, pixel by pixel, and store the result in a Java array. This is common for fractal images, for example.)

Once images are stored in local files or someplace on the net, you can then read them into a Java application and display them on `Graphics` objects. To read a graphics file into an application, you use a `Toolkit` object. A `Toolkit` object can read in GIF and JPEG files. (Many programs are available to convert another image format (such as Windows bitmap) to one that Java can use.)

As you saw before, to get a `Toolkit` object, use the static `getDefaultToolkit` method of the `Toolkit` class. Here is the code to get a local image file:

```
String name = "blue-ball.gif";
Image image = Toolkit.getDefaultToolkit().getImage(name);
```

To get an image file off the net, you must supply the URL. For example,

```
URL u = new URL("http://www.someplace.com/anImage.gif");
Image image = Toolkit.getDefaultToolkit().getImage(u);
```

(See Volume 2 for more on URLs and networking.)

Now the variable image contains the GIF file image so you can display it on the `Graphics` object.

```
  public void paint(Graphics g)
  {  g.drawImage(image, 0, 0, this);
  }
```

The `drawImage` command renders the image in the window. Example 7-11 takes this a little bit further and *tiles* the window with the graphics image. The result looks like Figure 7-12.

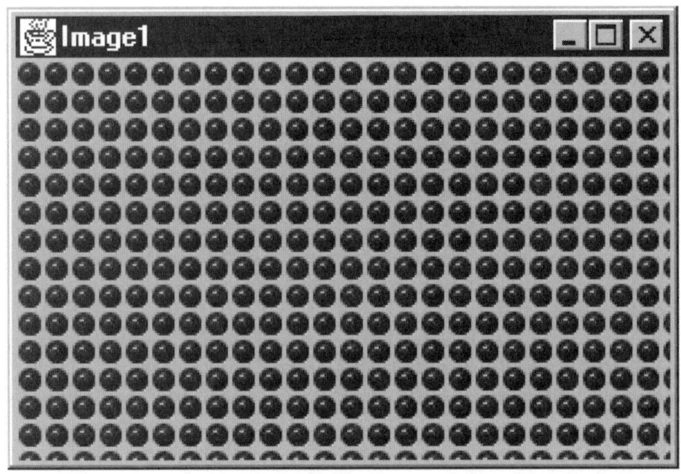

Figure 7-12: Window with tiled graphics image

Example 7-11: Image1.java

```
import java.awt.*;
import java.awt.image.*;
import java.net.*;
import corejava.*;

public class Image1 extends CloseableFrame
{  public Image1()
   {  image = Toolkit.getDefaultToolkit().getImage
         ("blue-ball.gif");
   }

   public void paint(Graphics g)
   {  Dimension d = getSize();
      Insets in = getInsets();
      g.translate(in.left, in.top);
      int clientWidth = d.width - in.right - in.left;
      int clientHeight = d.height - in.bottom - in.top;
```

```
            int imageWidth = image.getWidth(this);
            int imageHeight = image.getHeight(this);

            g.drawImage(image, 0, 0, this);
            for (int i = 0; i <= clientWidth / imageWidth; i++)
               for (int j = 0;
                        j <= clientHeight / imageHeight; j++)
                     if (i + j > 0)
                        g.copyArea(0, 0, imageWidth, imageHeight,
                           i * imageWidth, j * imageHeight);
      }

      public static void main(String args[])
      {  Frame f = new Image1();
         f.show();
      }

      private Image image;
}
```

We do the tiling in the `paint` method. We compute the sizes of the client area of the window and of the image, using the `insets` method. Then we draw one copy of the image in the top left corner and use the `copyArea` call to copy it into the entire window.

`java.awt.Toolkit`

- `Toolkit getDefaultToolkit()`

  returns the default toolkit.

- `Image getImage(String` *`filename`*`)`

  returns an image that will read its pixel data from a file.

Parameters:	`filename`	the file containing the image (e.g., a GIF or JPEG file)

`java.awt.Graphics`

- `boolean drawImage(Image img, int x, int y, ImageObserver observer)`

  draws a scaled image. Note: This call may return before the image is drawn.

Parameters:	`img`	the image to be drawn
	`x`	the *x*-coordinate of the upper left corner

	`y`	the *y*-coordinate of the upper left corner
	`observer`	the object to notify of the progress of the rendering process (may be null)

- `boolean drawImage(Image img, int x, int y, int width, int height, ImageObserver observer)`

  draws a scaled image. The system scales the image to fit in a region width*height pixels. Note: This call may return before the image is drawn.

Parameters:	`img`	the image to be drawn
	`x`	the *x*-coordinate of the upper left corner
	`y`	the *y*-coordinate of the upper left corner
	`width`	the desired width of image
	`height`	the desired height of image
	`observer`	the object to notify of the progress of the rendering process (may be `null`)

Buffering

If you run the `Image1` program on a moderately slow computer, you can watch how it slowly fills the window. When something the user does requires that Java repaint the window (i.e., causes a call to the `paint` method), the window again *slowly* fills with the images.

This naive image handling does not work well if you are concerned about performance or if the image arrives slowly over a network connection. In the next few sections of this chapter, we explain how the professionals deal with images. If the discussion gets too technical, just skip this section and come back when you actually have to deal with images.

First, you may have noticed that the preceding program sometimes flickers when it redraws the screen. That is because it is the `update` method, not the `paint` method, that the AWT calls when it notifies the window that it has to redraw itself. The default action of `update` is to:

1. Erase the screen.
2. Then, repaint it.

In our case, erasing the screen is not necessary because we completely cover it with the image. This problem is simple to solve: we just override `update` by calling `paint` directly.

```
void update(Graphics g)
{  paint(g);
}
```

To speed up the screen refresh, we first build the entire screen image in its own image buffer. We can then paint the screen by drawing just that one buffer into it. That makes the drawing much smoother and faster. The cost is the time and memory needed to fill the buffer. As an added benefit, we only need to recompute the buffer when the user makes the screen area larger.

NOTE: Windows users should think of what is occurring after the buffer is filled as corresponding to using the `BitBlt` API call.

VB NOTE: If you are using VB, think of this as corresponding to a call to `PaintPicture`.

You create a buffer with the `createImage` command. To draw into that buffer rather than directly into the window, you need to work with the graphics context that is attached *to the buffer.* (The graphics context parameter of the `update` and `paint` functions is attached to the screen window.) This is done with the `getGraphics` method call of the `Image` class, which returns a `Graphics` object (i.e., a graphics context).

Here is the code for this:

```
Image buffered_image = createImage(client_width,
client_height);
Graphics bg = buffered_image.getGraphics();
// all drawing commands that use bg fill the buffered_image
bg.drawImage(image, 0, 0, this);
for (int i = 0; i <= client_width / image_width; i++)
   for (int j = 0; j <= client_height / image_height; j++)
      if (i + j > 0) // skip the first tile
         bg.copyArea(0, 0, image_width, image_height,
            i * image_width, j * image_height);
bg.dispose();
```

All drawing commands that use `bg` fill the buffered image.

NOTE: Notice the last line.

```
bg.dispose();
```

Don't forget to dispose of a graphics context when you are done with it. Graphics contexts occupy more than just memory. They attach to finite resources in the operating systems, so you can't just rely on the garbage collection mechanism to release and then recycle them.

Finally, when Java has finished building the image, display it in the window.

```
void paint(Graphics g)
{  // if the window size has increased, recompute
   // bufferedImage
   . . .
   g.drawImage(bufferedImage, 0, 0, null);
}
```

java.awt.Component

- `void update(Graphics g)`

  updates the component; unless overridden, it erases the screen area and calls the `paint` method.

Parameters:	`g`	the graphics context to use for the drawing

- `Image createImage(int width, int height)`

  creates an off-screen image buffer to be used for double buffering.

Parameters:	`width`	the width of the image
	`height`	the height of the image

java.awt.Graphics

- `void copyArea(int x, int y, int width, int height, int dx, int dy)`

  copies an area of the screen.

Parameters:	`x`	the *x*-coordinate of the upper left corner of the source area
	`y`	the *y*-coordinate of the upper left corner of the source area
	`width`	the width of the source area
	`height`	the height of the source area
	`dx`	the horizontal distance from the source area to the target area

`dy`	the vertical distance from the source area to the target area

- `void dispose()`

  disposes of this graphics context and releases operating system resources. You should always dispose of the graphics contexts that you allocate, but not the ones handed to you by `paint` or `update`.

`java.awt.Image`

- `Graphics getGraphics()`

  gets a graphics context to draw into this image buffer.

Image Acquisition

The buffering technique you saw works well if you draw lines or text into the buffer. However, *it does not work for images*. If you try out the code that we have described so far, the paint procedure will probably paint a blank rectangle! The reason for that is subtle but important.

The AWT was written with the assumption that an image may arrive slowly over a network connection. The *first* call to the `drawImage` function recognizes that the GIF file has not yet been loaded. Instead of loading the file and returning to the caller when the image is actually loaded, Java spawns a new thread of execution to load the image *and then returns to the caller without actually having completed that task.* (See Volume 2 for more on threads.)

This is—to say the least—surprising to anyone who expects that a function won't return until it has done its job. But here the multithreaded aspect of Java works against your assumptions. What will happen is that Java will run the code in your program in parallel with the code to load the image. Eventually, the image will be loaded and available. Of course, in the meantime, our code has tiled the entire buffer with copies of a blank array.

The solution, of course, is to find out when the GIF image is completely loaded and *then* tile the buffer. When we were trying to figure out how this is accomplished (and this is a technique you should be prepared to use yourself), we needed to look at the Java on-line documentation and then study the ancestors of the `Frame` class as shown in Figure 7-2 on page 237. As Figure 7-2 showed, `Frame` extends `Window`, which extends `Container`, which extends `Component`, which extends `Object` *and implements* `ImageObserver`.

`ImageObserver` is an interface with a single method, `imageUpdate`. This is a *callback* function. That is, the thread that loads the image periodically calls the `imageUpdate` function of the object that was passed as the last argument of the `drawImage` call

```
bg.drawImage(image, 0, 0, this);
```

That parameter must be of type `ImageObserver`. Now you know why we passed `this` as the last parameter. The `this` object is our application object derived from `Frame`. Since `Frame` (indirectly) implements `ImageObserver`, `this` is a legal argument. (By the way, you pass `null` if you don't want to be notified of the image acquisition process.)

The default implementation of `imageUpdate` simply calls `update`. Now you know why the first program worked and why it flickered more than it should have. During the first call to `paint`, the first call to `drawImage` returned immediately, and the first attempt at tiling didn't actually work. But as soon as the image was acquired, the `paint` procedure was called again and the screen was rendered correctly.

However, this mechanism fails if we use buffering. The sole reason for using buffering was not to render the screen again with every call to `paint`. Instead, we must let the initial image acquisition take its course and build up the buffer only when it is finished.

If you want to track the image acquisition process, you can override the `imageUpdate` function in `ImageObserver`. The `imageUpdate` function has six parameters (see the API notes). The second parameter, `infoflags`, indicates the kind of notification that should be used in a particular call. The image acquisition mechanism notifies the observer many times during the acquisition process. The `imageUpdate` function is called when the image size is known, each time that a chunk of the image is ready, and, finally, when the entire image is complete. When you use an Internet browser and look at a Web page that contains an image, you know how these notifications are translated into actions. An Internet browser lays out a Web page as soon as it knows the sizes of the images in the page. Then it gradually fills in the images, as more detailed information becomes available.

However, we are not interested in incremental rendering. Our code just needs to wait for the image to be complete before it starts filling the buffer with tiled copies of the image. A special class, `MediaTracker`, makes it easy to program this delay. A media tracker can track the acquisition of one or more images. (The name "media" suggests that the class should also be able to track audio files or other media. While such an extension may be available in the future, the current implementation tracks images only.)

You add an image to a tracker object with the following command

```
MediaTracker tracker = new MediaTracker();
Image img = Toolkit.getDefaultToolkit().getImage(name);
int id = 1; // the ID used to track the image loading process
tracker.addImage(img, id);
```

You can add as many images as you like. Each of them should have a different ID number, but you can choose any numbering that is convenient. To wait for an image to be loaded completely, you execute the following code:

```
try { tracker.waitForID(id); }
catch (InterruptedException e) {}
```

The `try/catch` statements are necessary for a technical reason; we will discuss the general topic of exception handling in Chapter 12 and the `InterruptedException` in the multithreading chapter of Volume 2. In our sample program, we just insert this code into the constructor. It has the effect of waiting until the image is loaded completely.

If you want to acquire multiple images, then you can add them all to the media tracker object and wait until they are all loaded. This is achieved with the following code:

```
try { tracker.waitForAll(); }
catch (InterruptedException e) {}
```

Example 7-12 shows the improved image rendering program. The constructor waits until the blue ball graphic is completely loaded. The `paint` method assembles the tiled image in a background buffer and draws that buffer. The `update` method calls `paint` without erasing the image.

Example 7-12: Image2.java

```
import java.awt.*;
import java.awt.image.*;
import java.net.*;
import java.io.*;
import corejava.*;

public class Image2 extends CloseableFrame
{  public Image2()
   {  image = Toolkit.getDefaultToolkit().getImage
         ("blue-ball.gif");
      MediaTracker tracker = new MediaTracker(this);
      tracker.addImage(image, 0);
      try { tracker.waitForID(0); }
      catch (InterruptedException e) {}
      imageWidth = image.getWidth(null);
      imageHeight = image.getHeight(null);
   }

   public void update(Graphics g)
   {  paint(g);
   }
```

```
   public void paint(Graphics g)
   {  Insets in = getInsets();
      g.translate(in.left, in.top);
      Dimension d = getSize();
      int clientWidth = d.width - in.right - in.left;
      int clientHeight = d.height - in.bottom - in.top;

      if (clientWidth > bufferWidth
         || clientHeight > bufferHeight)
      // size has increased
      {  bufferWidth = clientWidth;
         bufferHeight = clientHeight;

         bufferedImage = createImage(bufferWidth,
            bufferHeight);
         Graphics bg = bufferedImage.getGraphics();
         bg.drawImage(image, 0, 0, null);
         for (int i = 0; i <= bufferWidth / imageWidth;
             i++)
            for (int j = 0;
               j <= bufferHeight / imageHeight; j++)
               if (i + j > 0) bg.copyArea(0, 0, imageWidth,
                  imageHeight, i * imageWidth,
                     j * imageHeight);
         bg.dispose();
      }
      g.drawImage(bufferedImage, 0, 0, null);
   }

   public static void main(String args[])
   {  Frame f = new Image2();
      f.show();
   }

   private int bufferWidth = 0;
   private int bufferHeight = 0;
   private int imageWidth = 0;
   private int imageHeight = 0;
   private Image image;
   private Image bufferedImage;
}
```

java.awt.image.ImageObserver

- `boolean imageUpdate(Image img, int infoflags, int x, int y, int width, int height)`

  notifes the observer of progress in the rendering process.

Parameters:		
	`img`	the image that is being acquired
	`infoflags`	a combination of the following flags:
	• `ABORT`	the image acquisition was aborted
	• `ALLBITS`	all bits of the image are now available
	• `ERROR`	an error was encountered in the acquisition process
	• `FRAMEBITS`	a complete frame of a multi-frame image is now available for drawing
	• `HEIGHT`	the height of the image is now known (and passed in the height argument of this call)
	• `PROPERTIES`	the properties of the image are now available
	• `SOMEBITS`	some (but not all) bits of the image are available. The x, y, width, and height arguments of this call give the bounding box of the new pixels
	• `WIDTH`	the width of the image is now known (and passed in the width argument of this call)
	`x, y, width, height`	further information about the image, dependent on `infoflags`

java.awt.Component

- `void repaint()`

  causes a repaint of the component by calling `update` "as soon as possible."

- `public void repaint(int x, int y, int width, int height)`

  causes a repaint of a part of the component by calling `update` "as soon as possible."

Parameters:	`x`	the *x*-coordinate of the top left corner of the area to be repainted
	`y`	the *y*-coordinate of the top left corner of the area to be repainted
	`width`	the width of the area to be repainted
	`height`	the height of the area to be repainted

`java.awt.MediaTracker`

API

- `void addImage(Image image, int id)`

  adds an image to the list of images being tracked. When the image is added, the image loading process is started.

Parameters:	`image`	the image to be tracked
	`id`	the identifier used to later refer to this image

- `boolean waitForID(int id)`

  waits until all images with the specified ID are loaded.

- `void waitForAll()`

  waits until all images that are being tracked are loaded.

Printing

The 1.1 version of the AWT supports printing. Making a simple printout is easy in Java. Just as you use a `Graphics` object to render text and graphics in a window, you put text and graphics on the printed page by using a special graphics context. Essentially the same code for displaying information on the screen works on a printer.

Since printing contexts and graphics contexts are supposed to work similarly, it shouldn't come as a surprise that in Java 1.1 a "printing context" is also an instance of a subclass of the `Graphics` class. The difference is that a printing context must support an additional interface called, naturally enough, `PrintGraphics`. This means you can use the `instanceof` operator in your code to determine if you are printing on a usual graphics context or a printer context:

```
if (g instanceof PrintGraphics)
    // printing
else
    // drawing on screen
```

The `PrintGraphics` interface is simple: it contains a single method to get a `PrintJob` object. `PrintJob` objects encapsulate printing information such as the size of the paper in the printer. (Caution: these features do not work on all platforms as we write this.)

Here is what you need to do to print:

1. Get a `PrintJob` object.
2. Get a `Graphics` object that implements the `PrintGraphics` interface.
3. Use that graphics context to draw all text and graphics for the first page.
4. Call `dispose` on the graphics object to eject the page from the printer.
5. Repeat steps 2 through 4 for the other pages.
6. Call `end` on the print job object to terminate the print job.

Let us look at these steps in detail.

You get a `PrintJob` object by using the `getPrintJob` method in the `Toolkit` class. (You have seen toolkits earlier in this chapter. Recall that the toolkit object returned by the `getToolkit` acts as the interface between Java and platform-specific information.)

A typical call to get a `PrintJob` object looks like this:

```
Frame f = this;
String jobtitle = "Test Page";
Properties props = new Properties();
PrintJob pjob = getToolKit().getPrintJob(f, jobtitle, props);
```

The third parameter, of type `Properties`, is intended to pass system-dependent print parameters to the printer. `Properties` objects store key/value pairs. (For more information on them, please consult Chapter 11). For example, the `Properties` parameter might contain information like

```
numCopies = 2
```

which is set with the command

```
props.put("numCopies", "2");
```

This particular property works on Solaris but not on Windows. Since print properties are platform dependent, you usually pass `null` as the third parameter of the call to `getPrintJob`.

When Java executes the `getPrintJob` call, it tells the operating system to show a print dialog (see Figure 7-13 for a sample of the Windows version).

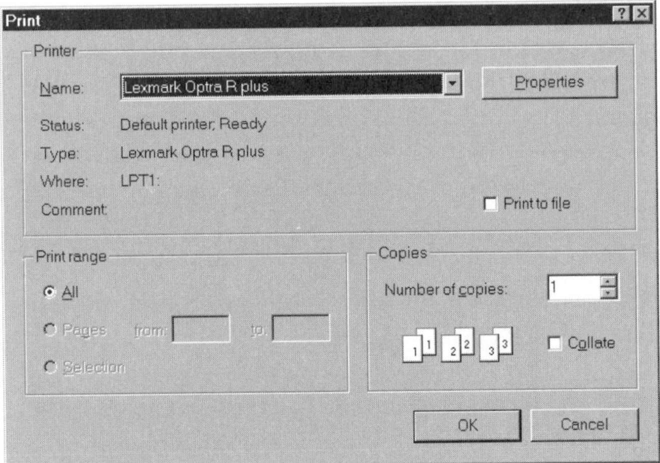

Figure 7-13. A print dialog

If the user clicks Cancel in the Print dialog box, the call to `getPrintJob` returns `null`, not a print job object. The typical code for printing, therefore, starts like this:

```
PrintJob pjob = getToolKit().getPrintJob(this, jobtitle, null);
if (pjob != null)
{  . . .
}
```

TIP: Currently, there is no published information about what properties can be legally passed to `getPrintJob`. Under Solaris, a handful of print properties are available, but under Windows, you cannot yet set any print properties from within Java 1.1. If you want to check whether print properties are supported on your platform, pass a non-null `Properties` object to the `getPrintJob` call. Then, Java adds the various default and user-specified settings to the `Properties` object. You can see what properties have been added with the command

```
props.list(System.out);
```

Once you have a `PrintJob` object, you get the printing context, which is an object of a subclass of `Graphics`. You obtain that object by making a call to the `getGraphics()` method in the `PrintJob` class.

```
Graphics pg = pjob.getGraphics();
```

This call returns the printing context that will represent the page on which you want to print. Printing in Java is always page oriented. You need to get a new printing context for each page.

Next, you start printing on the graphics context. If you just want to print the contents of a frame, without worrying about page numbers and other adornments that are specific to the printed page, then you can simply call the `paint` method but give it the printing context instead of the graphics context of the frame. When you are done with the page, call `dispose`. This call acts as a form feed and so ejects the page from the printer. Each page you print in Java requires a call to `dispose` to tell the AWT that the page is over. You should also, as we did, call `pjpb.end()` when you have finished printing. This tells the print spooler that the job is over.

Let us put all the pieces together:

```
PrintJob pjob = getToolkit().getPrintJob(this,
   "Printing Test", null);
if (pjob != null)
{  Graphics pg = pjob.getGraphics();
   if (pg != null)
   {  paint(pg);
      pg.dispose(); // flush page
   }
   pjob.end();
}
```

Example 7-13 is a complete program that displays and prints the same image, consisting of text and graphics. When the user selects the File | Print menu option, the code in the `print` method is executed. The constructor of the `PrintingTest` class sets up the menu and the event handler for the menu selection—you can skip past this code for now. We will discuss menus and event handlers in detail in Chapter 8.

The `paint` method is called automatically by AWT when the inside of the frame is being painted. The same method is called explicitly in the `print` method, when you select File | Print from the menu.

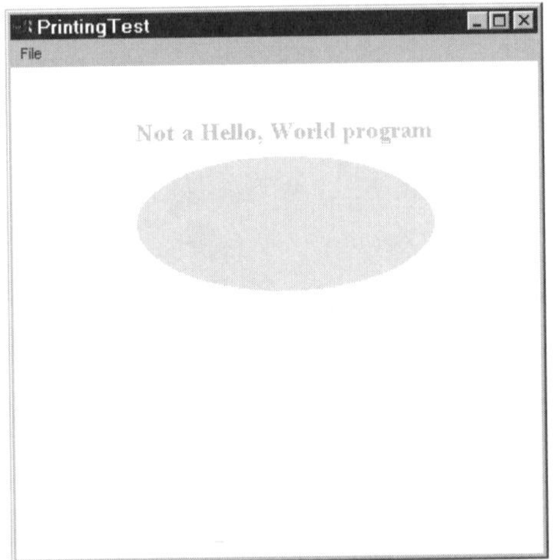

Figure 7-14: The display of the PrintingTest program

Example 7-13: PrintingTest.java

```
import java.awt.*;
import java.awt.event.*;
import java.util.*;
import corejava.*;

public class PrintingTest extends CloseableFrame
{  public PrintingTest()
   {  MenuBar mb = new MenuBar();
      Menu m = new Menu("File");
      MenuItem mi = new MenuItem("Print");
      mi.addActionListener(new ActionListener()
         {  public void actionPerformed(ActionEvent evt)
            { print(); }
         });
      m.add(mi);
      mb.add(m);
      setMenuBar(mb);

      setForeground(Color.pink);
   }

   public void print()
   {  PrintJob pjob = getToolkit().getPrintJob(this,
         "Printing Test", null);

      if (pjob != null)
      {  Graphics pg = pjob.getGraphics();
```

```
            if (pg != null)
            {  paint(pg);
               pg.dispose(); // flush page
             }
           pjob.end();
        }
    }

    public void paint(Graphics g)
    {  g.setFont(new Font("Serif", Font.BOLD, 18));
       int xleft = 96;
       int ybase = 96;
       String message = "Not a Hello, World program";
       g.drawString(message, xleft, ybase);
       int yheight = 96;
       int xwidth = g.getFontMetrics().stringWidth(message);
       g.setColor(Color.yellow);
       g.fillOval(xleft, ybase + 12, xwidth, yheight);
    }

    public static void main(String args[])
    {  Frame f = new PrintingTest();
       f.setSize(400, 400);
       f.show();
    }
}
```

If you have a color printer, you may be surprised when you see the printout of this program. The oval shows up in yellow, as it does on the screen. But the message is printed in black, although it is displayed in pink.

It is clear why the oval prints in yellow. We set the color of the graphics context to yellow in the statement

```
g.setColor(Color.yellow);
```

But why was the message displayed in pink? It used the *foreground color* of the frame. When AWT calls the `paint` method to repaint the frame, it obtains a graphics context object, sets the color of the graphics context to the color of the component that needs repainting, and then passes the graphics context to the `paint` procedure. Thus, `paint` is called with a graphics context that has its current color set to pink.

However, when the graphics context was called from the `print` procedure, it was obtained from the `getPrintJob` command. That command does not set the current color of the graphics context.

> Not only do printing contexts not inherit the color of the parent frame, they also do not have a default font. If you neglect to set a font for the printing context, the Windows version of Java 1.1.1 crashes!

There is another remarkable fact about the printout. Recall that AWT measures screen coordinates in *pixels*. For example, the yellow oval is 96 pixels high. But this does not make sense for printers. Different printers have different resolutions. If a printer has a resolution of 300 dots per inch, 96 pixels is almost ⅓ inch. On a printer with a resolution of 600 dots per inch, the same pixels cover a distance of only ⅙ inch. This would be a problem. Not only would images come out tiny on a high-resolution printer, but the images and the text would not match up. An 18-point font is printed in the same size regardless of the resolution of the printer, namely, at a height of 18 point or ¼ inch. (Recall that one point is 1/72 of an inch.)

Indeed, printing context coordinates are not measured in pixels. Instead, AWT takes into account the screen resolution and the printing resolution and selects a coordinate system so that the printout matches the screen picture. Let us run through an example. You can get the screen resolution with the `getScreenResolution` method of the `Toolkit` class. Of course, Java can't sense what monitor you have attached—a 17-inch monitor uses fewer dots per inch than a 14-inch monitor for the same resolution. Instead, Java chooses a reasonable approximation. Under Windows, Java assumes a *nominal screen resolution* of 96 dots per inch. This is the value returned by `getScreenResolution`. Then, the printing context has a coordinate system in which 96 pixels denote one inch on the printed page. When actually drawing graphics, Java will query the printer driver about the printer resolution. Suppose you have a 600 dpi (dots per inch) printer. Then, the AWT internally multiplies all coordinates with 600 / 96. It is nice that this is automatic and that you don't have to worry about keeping graphics aligned on the printer.

However, there is a major drawback. Since 96 does not divide 600 evenly, roundoff errors are inevitable. These roundoff errors show up as tiny notches of mismatched lines. For example, if you run the `PrintGrid` program of Example 7-14 and print the "graph paper," you may see that the horizontal line ends extend slightly beyond the rightmost vertical line. Also, the lines on the printout are quite thick—since the thinnest line on the screen is 1/96 of an inch, you can't print lines that are thinner than that.

The AWT method of forcing the printer resolution to match the screen resolution can be considered only a temporary fix. In the long run, application developers will demand support for programming perfect printouts. We anticipate that the 2-D imaging model in the next generation of the AWT will provide this support.

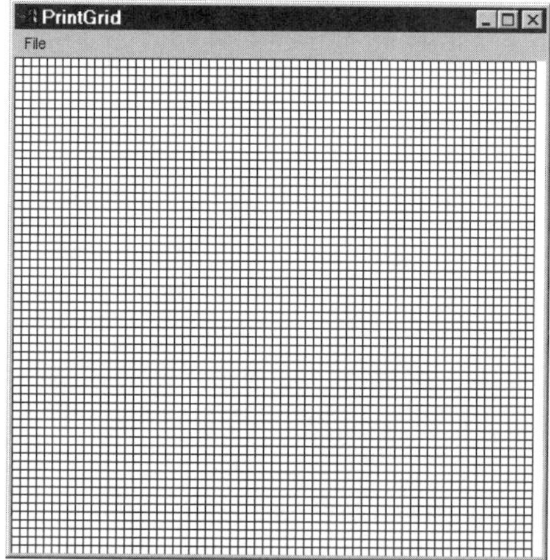

Figure 7-15: The display of the PrintGrid program

Example 7-14: PrintGrid.java

```
import java.awt.*;
import java.awt.event.*;
import java.util.*;
import corejava.*;

public class PrintGrid extends CloseableFrame
{  public PrintGrid()
   {  MenuBar mb = new MenuBar();
      Menu m = new Menu("File");
      MenuItem mi = new MenuItem("Print");
      mi.addActionListener(new ActionListener()
         {  public void actionPerformed(ActionEvent evt)
            { print(); }
         });
      m.add(mi);
      mb.add(m);
      setMenuBar(mb);
   }

   public void print()
   {  PrintJob pjob = getToolkit().getPrintJob(this,
         "Printing Test", null);
```

```
      if (pjob != null)
      {  Graphics pg = pjob.getGraphics();
         if (pg != null)
         {  paint(pg);
            pg.dispose(); // flush page
          }
          pjob.end();
      }
   }

   public void paint(Graphics g)
   {  g.translate(getInsets().left, getInsets().top);
      int resolution = getToolkit().getScreenResolution();
      int width = 4 * resolution; // 4 inches
      int distance = resolution / 16; // 1/16 inch

      for (int i = 0; i <= width; i += distance)
      {  g.drawLine(i, 0, i, width);
         g.drawLine(0, i, width, i);
      }
   }

   public static void main(String args[])
   {  Frame f = new PrintGrid();
      f.setSize(400, 400);
      f.show();
   }
}
```

Although you don't need to know the resolution of the printer to render graphics on a printing context, you can still query it with the `getPageResolution` method of the `PrintJob` class. That method returns the numbers of dots per inch for your printer. (It is not clear what it does for printers with different horizontal and vertical resolutions). A more important method of the `PrintJob` class is `getDimension`. It gives the paper size in points. For example, for an 8.5" × 11" sheet of paper, it returns 612 × 792 points. However, it does not take into account the nonprinting area (typically ¼ inch at all four sides). And Java 1.1.1 for Windows does not even take landscape mode into account. If you switch the orientation of the printer from portrait to landscape, the `getDimension` method still returns 612 × 792 for a sheet that is obviously now 11" × 8.5"!

`java.awt.PrintGraphics`

- `PrintJob getPrintJob()`

  returns the `PrintJob` associated with the `PrintGraphics` object.

`java.awt.PrintJob`

- `Graphics getGraphics()`

  returns a graphics object that implements the `PrintGraphics` interface. This object represents a single page to be printed.

- `void end()`

  ends printing. Performs cleanup and ends spooling of print job.

- `Dimension getPageDimension()`

  returns the dimension of the page, measured in points.

- `int getPageResolution()`

  returns the resolution of your printer in dots per inch. (Currently assumes vertical resolution always equals horizontal resolution).

CHAPTER 8

- Creating a Closeable Frame
- Basics of Event Handling
- The JDK 1.1 Event Hierarchy
- Semantic and Low-Level Events
- Event Handling Summary
- Individual Events
- Focus Events
- Window Events
- Keyboard Events
- Mouse Events
- Menus
- Advanced Menu Topics
- Separating GUI and Application Code
- Multicasting
- Advanced Event Handling
- Survival Tip for Java 1.0 Programmers

Event Handling

Event handling is of fundamental importance to programs with a graphical user interface. To go beyond the toy, console-based programs that you have seen so far, you must master how Java handles events. This chapter explains how the event model in Java 1.1 works. This chapter also shows how to use some simple GUI elements like buttons and menus. In particular, this chapter discusses how to work with the basic events generated by these GUI components. (The next chapter explains in great detail how to put together all the components that the AWT offers along with a full coverage of the events they generate.)

The Java 1.1 event model is different than the one used in earlier versions of Java. If you are already familiar with Java 1.0, you will need to learn a new way of coding: one that bears little, if any, relation to the way you used to do things. Note, however, that while JavaSoft has said that code written following the older event model should still work in Java 1.1, moving to the new event model promises both performance improvements and a greater degree of flexibility. The older event model is summarized at the end of this chapter. You can tell the compiler to issue a warning whenever you use one of the older event handling methods by compiling your source code with the `-deprecation` switch. (There is some potential for incompatibility down the road. JavaSoft has not said they will be supporting the older event model indefinitely.)

NOTE: If you need to write applets that can run under old browsers that are still using Java 1.0, such as Netscape Navigator 2.0 or 3.0 or Internet Explorer 3.0, then you must use the Java 1.0 event model.

Creating a Closeable Frame

In Chapter 7, rather than using the basic `Frame` class supplied by the AWT, we used the `CloseableFrame` class from our `corejava` package as the basis for all of our programs. There was a good reason for this. It is easy to show a blank window (frame); it requires work in order to make a window that is closeable by the user. The problem is that in Java, a window is not closeable in the ways a user expects (such as by clicking on the Close button) without extra code being written.

To create our `CloseableFrame` class, we had to add the necessary code to allow the window to be closed when the user wants to close it. The `CloseableFrame` class in our `corejava` package is only about 10 lines of code, but we think the brevity of the code that we used actually makes it harder to focus on how the event model works. So, in the beginning of this chapter we will show you *three* different closeable frame classes. The first is coded in the most direct manner possible. The direct approach requires the most code but has the advantage of illustrating how to use the new event model in the most straightforward fashion. The second version of our closeable frame is somewhat less verbose but requires use of an auxiliary class. The third version is the code for the `CloseableFrame` class in the `corejava` package. It uses an inner class (see Chapter 6) in order to have the shortest and most concise code possible. We want to stress, however, that all three versions work equally well—which model you choose to follow is ultimately a matter of taste.

First, as you also saw in the last chapter, a program that creates a frame from scratch must do the following:

- Create the frame by a call to `new`.
- Set the size of the frame by using the `setSize` method. (By default, it has width and height zero.)
- Position it on the user's screen, if need be, using the `setLocation` method. (By default, the frame will be in the top left corner)
- Call the `show` method to make the frame *visible* and to bring it to the front. (By default, it is not visible.)

Here is a program that follows these steps but leaves the frame in the default position at the top left corner. But, *please* don't run this program yet: there is one very important rule when developing programs that use the AWT:

Save all of your work-in-progress before running the program.

The problem is that it is sometimes hard to kill a program that uses the AWT, as you will see if you run the code given in Example 8-1. You may, in fact, seem to

have locked up your machine. (In particular, while developing a Java program, even after you know how to write the code that allows windows to close normally, windows sometimes still won't close unless you resort to the method we describe next.)

Example 8-1: VisibleFrameTest.java

```
import java.awt.*;

public class VisibleFrameTest
{  public static void main(String[] args)
   {  VisibleFrame f = new VisibleFrame();
      f.show();
   }
}

class VisibleFrame extends Frame
{  VisibleFrame()
   {  setSize(300, 200);
   }
}
```

Let's go over the code, line by line. First, we have imported all the classes in AWT package (`java.awt.*`). We use inheritance to specify that the class `VisibleFrame` that we define is just like a basic `Frame`, except that its size is not 0×0.

The key line

```
VisibleFrame f = new VisibleFrame();
```

in the `main` method makes a new `VisibleFrame` object. At this point, Java will build the data structure that contains all the necessary information for the underlying windowing system to display a window. The call to `new` does not display the frame; instead, the next line contains the call to the `show` method, which will actually display the frame. However, as we mentioned in the last chapter, before you can see a frame, you need to resize it. Here, we make the window 300 pixels wide by 200 pixels high by using the `setSize` method in the constructors of the `VisibleFrame` class. The window will appear in the top left corner since we didn't use the `setLocation` method in order to reposition it. It will also have no title bar since there is no call to `setTitle`. The running program is shown in Figure 8-1—it is a truly boring top-level window.

Figure 8-1: The simplest visible frame

Remember: if you don't explicitly size a frame, all frames will be 0 by 0 pixels. This means that frames are not visible until you resize them.

In general, you should check the resolution of the user's screen and have code that resizes the frames accordingly: a window that looks nice on a laptop screen will look like a postage stamp on a high-resolution screen. (As mentioned in the last chapter, you can obtain the screen dimensions in pixels on the user's system by using the `getScreenSize` method of the `Toolkit` class. You can then use information to compute at run time the window size you think best for your project directly from the screen size.) For this and many other of the examples in this chapter, we will just use values that we hope work acceptably on most displays. Feel free to change the window dimensions if you have a higher-resolution screen.

OK, suppose you do run this program. How do you (try to) close the window? If you look carefully at the window shown in Figure 8-1, you will find it has a close box in its upper, right-hand corner. Unfortunately, clicking on this close box doesn't close the window. Clicking on the upper, left-hand corner reveals a menu (see Figure 8-2), but selecting Close from the menu doesn't work either.

Nothing obvious will get this application to close. You will soon see how to write programs that can be closed properly, but right now you need a way to kill a wayward, windowed Java application.

- Under Windows 95 or NT, carefully press CTRL+ALT+DEL.

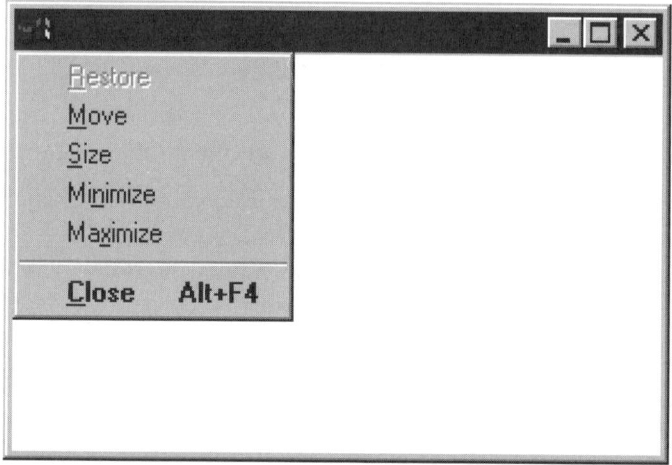

Figure 8-2: The system menu of a Java program under Windows

You have to be careful when pressing CTRL+ALT+DEL. If you press the key combination twice, your computer reboots immediately, and you lose all work in all open applications. If you do it right (that is, hit the key combination only once), you get a dialog box similar to the one shown in Figure 8-3. This dialog box lists all running programs. Select the Java program you want to shut down and click on the End Task button. If a dialog box comes up that alerts you that the program isn't responding, confirm that you do want to end it.

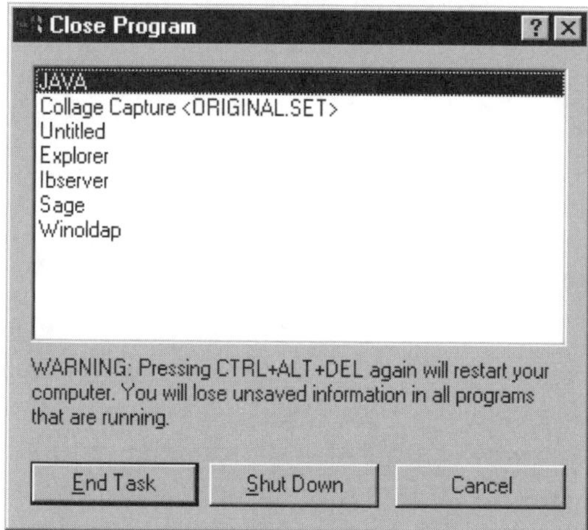

Figure 8-3: The Windows Close Program dialog

Under Solaris you have two choices:

- Select Destroy from the program menu

or

- Terminate the program with extreme prejudice with the `kill -9` command.

Obviously, you can't very well tell a user of your program that the natural way to end your program is via something like a CTRL+ALT+DEL "three-finger salute" or using `kill -9`. Unfortunately, in Java the default behavior for a frame is to ignore all requests to close itself—this necessitates writing a fair amount of code in order to allow the user to terminate a graphically based program.

To have a closeable frame, we need a frame that is like a standard frame in most respects, except that it closes itself when the user asks it to. As you saw in Chapter 5, Java has a powerful language construct to deal with just this situation: inheritance. We need to derive a new window class from the standard `Frame` class that will respond to a request to close itself. To add the needed code to derive this new kind of frame class, you need to know how events are handled in Java 1.1—that's what we take up next.

Basics of Event Handling

Any operating system that supports graphical user interfaces must constantly be monitoring the environment for events such as keystrokes or mouse clicks. The operating system then reports these events to the programs that are running. Each program then decides what, if anything, to do in response to these events. In languages like Visual Basic, the correspondence between events and code is obvious. One writes code for each specific event of interest and places the code in what is usually called an *event procedure.* For example, a Visual Basic button named `HelpButton` would have a `HelpButton_Click` event procedure associated with it, and VB would activate the code in this procedure in response to that button being clicked. Each Visual Basic component (i.e., graphical user interface element) responds to a fixed set of events, and it impossible to change the events a Visual Basic component responds to.

On the other hand, if you use a language like raw C to do event driven programming, you need to write the code that checks the event queue constantly for what the operating system is reporting. (This is usually done by encasing your code in a giant loop with a massive switch statement!) This is obviously rather ugly, and, in any case, it is much more difficult to code. The advantage is that the events you can respond to are not as limited as in languages like Visual Basic that go to great lengths to hide the event queue from the programmer.

Java 1.1 takes an approach somewhat between the Visual Basic approach and the raw C approach in terms of power and, therefore, in resulting complexity. Within the limits of the events that the AWT knows about, you completely control how events are transmitted from the *event sources* (such as buttons or scrollbars) to *event listeners*. You can designate any object to be an event listener—in practice,you pick an object that can conveniently carry out the response you want to the event. This *event delegation model* gives you much more flexibility than is possible with Visual Basic, where the listener is predetermined, but it requires more code and is more difficult to untangle (at least until you get used to it).

Event sources have methods that allow you to register event listeners with them. When an event happens to the source, Java sends a notification of that event to all the listener objects that were registered for that event. Which events sources can report to listeners is determined by the nature of the source and by the knowledge that the AWT has about system events related to the source. (As usual, this is a lowest common denominator approach: you have no guarantee that the AWT can respond to all the events that a program written directly for a specific platform could respond to.)

To sum up, here's an overview of how event handling in the JDK 1.1 works:

- A listener object is an instance of a class that implements a special interface called (naturally enough) a *listener interface.*
- An event source is an object that can register listener objects and send them notifications when events occur. These notifications are methods of the listener interface.

You register the listener object with the source object with lines of code that follow the model:

```
eventSourceObject.addEventListener(eventListenerObject);
```

For example,

```
Button b = new Button("Clear");
b.addActionListener(canvas);
```

Now the `canvas` object is notified whenever an "action event" occurs in the button. (For buttons, as you might expect, an action event is a button click.)

Code like the above implies that the class to which the `canvas` listener object belongs must implement the appropriate interface (which in this case is called `ActionListener`). As with all interfaces in Java, implementing an interface means supplying methods with the right signatures. To implement the `ActionListener` interface, the listener class must have a method (called `actionPerformed`) that receives an `ActionEvent` object as a parameter.

There are eleven listener interfaces altogether in the `java.awt.Event` package:

```
ActionListener                KeyListener
AdjustmentListener            MouseListener
ComponentListener             MouseMotionListener
ContainerListener             TextListener
FocusListener                 WindowListener
ItemListener
```

Obviously, a lot of classes and interfaces to keep track of can be a bit overwhelming. Fortunately, the principle is simple. A class that is interested in receiving events registers itself with the event source. It then gets the events that it asked for (see Figure 8-4).

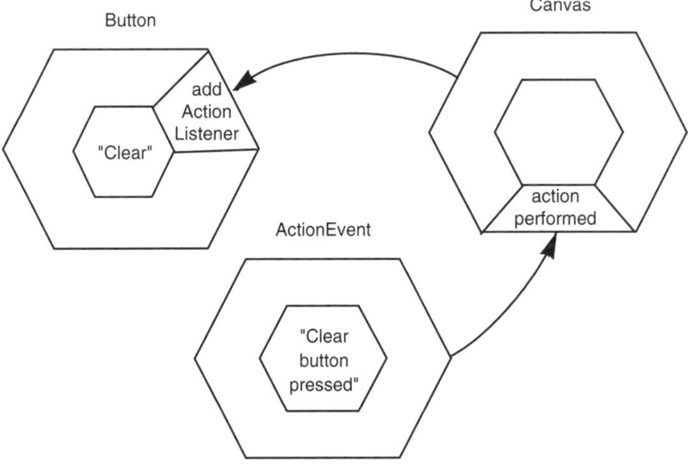

Figure 8-4: Event delivery

NOTE: People coming from a C/C++ background may be wondering: why the proliferation of objects, methods, and interfaces that are needed for event handling? You are used to doing graphical user interface programming environments by writing callbacks with generic pointers or handles. This won't work in Java. The Java event model is *strongly typed:* the compiler watches out that events are sent only to objects that are capable of handling them.

Capturing Window Events

Let us return to our original problem: to listen to a user's attempt to close a window. We will turn the `VisibleFrame` class into a `FirstCloseableFrame` class. When the program user tries to close the window, a `WindowEvent` is generated

by the class that represents the window. In our case, that is the FirstCloseableFrame class. We must now have an appropriate listener object and add it to the list of listeners.

```
f.addWindowListener(x); // what is x?
```

There are then always two questions you need to ask:

- Who *can* listen to this event?
- Who *is* going to listen to this event?

The answer to the first question is always: an object of a class that implements the WindowListener interface.

The simplest way (if not necessarily the most flexible—see below) to answer the second question of who to register to listen to the event is not to make a new class but rather to have the FirstCloseableFrame class itself listen to its own window events. To do this, we must implement the WindowListener interface inside the FirstCloseableFrame class.

```
class FirstCloseableFrame implements WindowListener
{   . . .
}
```

Now the FirstCloseableFrame class can listen to window events. Next, we must make sure that it does listen. Since it happens that the event source and the listener are the same object, we can register the listener with a line like the following:

```
f.addWindowListener(f);
```

Actually, this kind of code is more likely to be found in the constructor for the object, not the main method of the program. In this case, the listener object is this as in the following code:

```
class FirstCloseableFrame implements WindowListener
{  public FirstCloseableFrame()
   {  addWindowListener(this);
      show();
   }
}
```

Well, we are almost ready to give the full code for a closeable frame. Before we do that, though, let's look at one more stage in the code-building process for our FirstCloseableFrame class. This code gives you the framework for the simplest kind of event driven code, using the Java 1.1 event model. Note that the code is not only not complete, it won't even compile—for important reasons that we will soon describe.

```
//won't compile for important reasons
import java.awt.*;
import java.awt.event.*;
//this is the new event package in the JDK 1.1

class FirstCloseableFrame extends Frame implements
   WindowListener
{  public FirstCloseableFrame()
   {  addWindowListener(this);
   }
}
```

What we have done is add the necessary `import` statements to the fragment, made our `FirstCloseableFrame` class extend `Frame`, and *said that* our class will implement the necessary `WindowListener` interface. As above, the line (set in bold above):

```
addWindowListener(this);
```

then sets the closeable frame to be both the source and the listener for window events that happen inside itself.

Of course, the reason why this code won't even compile is that saying we will implement an interface isn't enough. We still need to *implement* the methods required for the `WindowListener` interface in the `FirstCloseableFrame` class. Our class, which has said that it will be a `WindowListener`, *must therefore implement all the methods defined in the* `WindowListener` *interface.*

There are actually seven methods in the `WindowListener` interface. Java calls them as the responses to seven distinct events that could happen to a window. The names are self-explanatory; their signatures are as follows.

```
void windowClosed(WindowEvent e)
void windowIconified(WindowEvent e)
void windowOpened(WindowEvent e)
void windowClosing(WindowEvent e)
void windowDeiconified(WindowEvent e)
void windowActivated(WindowEvent e)
void windowDeactivated(WindowEvent e)
```

As is always the case in Java, any class that implements this interface must implement all seven methods. The class shown in Example 8-2 does this:

Example 8-2: FirstCloseableFrame.java

```
import java.awt.*;
import java.awt.event.*;

public class FirstCloseableFrame extends Frame implements
   WindowListener
```

```
{   public FirstCloseableFrame()
    {   setTitle("First Closeable Frame");
        setSize(300,300);
        addWindowListener(this);
    }

    public void windowClosing(WindowEvent e){System.exit(0);}
    public void windowClosed(WindowEvent e){}
    public void windowIconified(WindowEvent e){}
    public void windowOpened(WindowEvent e){}
    public void windowDeiconified(WindowEvent e){}
    public void windowActivated(WindowEvent e){}
    public void windowDeactivated(WindowEvent e){}

    public static void main(String[] args)
    {   FirstCloseableFrame f = new FirstCloseableFrame();
        f.show();
    }
}
```

Note that six of the window event methods in our example don't do anything. All we do is overload the `windowClosing` method to call the `System.exit` method that shuts down the program.

`Java.awt.event.WindowEvent`

- `Public Window getWindow()`

  returns a reference to the window that generated the event.

Adapter Classes

Implementing six methods that don't do anything is the kind of tedious busywork that nobody likes. To simplify this task, each of the listener interfaces comes with a companion *adapter* class that implements all the methods in the interface but does nothing with them. For example, the `WindowAdapter` class has seven do-nothing methods. This means the adapter class automatically satisfies the technical requirements that Java imposes for implementing the associated listener interface.

The AWT has an adapter class for each of the seven listener interfaces that has more than one method. (The remaining four interfaces have only a single method each, so there is no benefit in having adapter class for these interfaces.)

A list of the adapter classes follows.

```
ComponentAdapter          MouseAdapter
ContainerAdapter          MouseMotionAdapter
FocusAdapter              WindowAdapter
KeyAdapter
```

In the case of the closeable frame, we want to override just one of the seven methods:

```
class WindowCloser extends WindowAdapter
{  void windowClosing(WindowEvent e)
   {  System.exit(0);
   }
}
```

Now we can register an object of type `WindowCloser` as the event listener, and the frame class no longer needs to implement the listener interface.

```
class SecondCloseableFrame extends Frame
{  public SecondCloseableFrame()
   {  WindowCloser wc = new WindowCloser();
      addWindowListener(wc);
      . . .
   }
}
```

Could we have avoided adding the `WindowCloser` class? That is, could we have added the `windowClosing` method directly into the `SecondCloseableFrame` class and have *it* extend the adapter? No—the `SecondCloseableFrame` class *already* extends another class, namely, `Frame`, and in Java, a class can extend only one other class.

However, there is an alternative that is almost as good. We can make the listener class into an *anonymous inner class* of the frame, using the technique described in Chapter 6. As Example 8-3 shows, this is what we did in the actual `CloseableFrame` class of the `corejava` package.

Example 8-3: CloseableFrame.java

```
package corejava;

import java.awt.*;
import java.awt.event.*;

public class CloseableFrame extends Frame
{  public CloseableFrame()
   {  addWindowListener(new WindowAdapter() { public void
         windowClosing(WindowEvent e) { System.exit(0); } } );
      resize(300, 200);
      setTitle(getClass().getName());
```

```
    }
}
```

The key piece of code in this example is:

```
addWindowListener(new WindowAdapter()
   {  public void windowClosing(WindowEvent e)
      {  System.exit(0);
      }
   } );
```

This code does the following:

- Defines a class without a name that extends the `WindowAdapter` class.
- Adds a `windowClosing` method to that anonymous class. (As before, this method closes the window and exits the program.)
- Inherits the remaining six do-nothing methods from `WindowAdapter`.
- Creates an object of this class. That object does not have a name, either.
- Passes that object to the `addWindowListener` method.

Naturally, the syntax for using anonymous inner classes for event listeners takes some getting used to. The payoff is that the resulting code is as short as possible.

NOTE: We want to stress that our using an anonymous inner adapter class is purely technical. You can always rewrite Java code that uses an anonymous inner class for event handling to use explicit outer classes.

The JDK 1.1 Event Hierarchy

Having given you a taste of how event handling works, we want to turn to a more general discussion of event handling in Java 1.1. As you might expect, event handling in Java is object oriented, with all events descending from a common superclass. The superclass for all events is `EventObject` in the `java.util` package. (The common superclass is not called `Event` since that is the name of the event class in the old event model. Although the old model is now deprecated, it is still a part of the current AWT.)

The `EventObject` class has a subclass `AWTEvent`, which is the parent of all AWT event classes. Figure 8-5 shows the inheritance diagram of the AWT events. You can even add your own custom events by subclassing `EventObject` or one of the other event classes, as you will see at the end of this chapter.

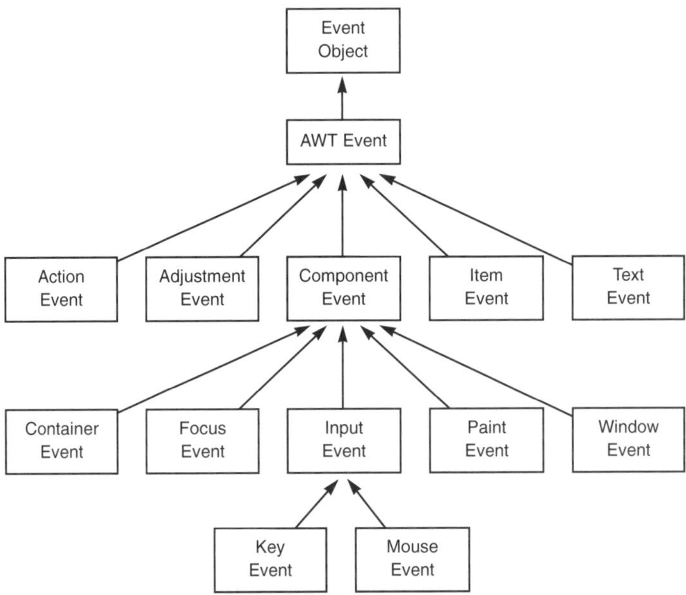

Figure 8-5: Inheritance diagram of the AWT event classes

When a source object needs to tell a listener object that an event happened, the AWT:

- Calls the appropriate method of the listener interface
- Passes it an object that descends from `EventObject`.

This event object encapsulates the event. All this happens automatically once you register the listener with the source. When necessary, you can then use accessor (`get`) methods to analyze the objects of type `EventObject` that were passed to the listener object. (See below for an example of this.)

Some of the AWT event classes are of no practical use for the Java programmer. For example, the AWT inserts `PaintEvent` objects into the event queue, but these objects are not delivered to listeners. Java programmers should override the `paint` and `update` methods to control repainting. Here is a list of those AWT event types that are actually passed to listeners.

`ActionEvent`	`FocusEvent`	`MouseEvent`
`AdjustmentEvent`	`ItemEvent`	`TextEvent`
`ComponentEvent`	`KeyEvent`	`WindowEvent`
`ContainerEvent`		

You will see examples of all of these event types in this chapter and the next chapter.

An Example: Which Button Was Clicked?

Here is a simple but typical example of why you need to be able to analyze an event object. A listener object registers itself to multiple buttons so that it can listen to them. Each time any of the buttons is clicked, the listener object then receives an `ActionEvent` that indicates a button click. That's nice but, of course, you want to know *which* button was clicked.

Before we can give you the program that shows you how to identify which button was clicked, we need to explain how to add a button to a frame. (For more on GUI elements, please see Chapter 9.) Adding buttons to a frame occurs through a call to a method named (quite mnemonically) `add`. For example,

```
public class ButtonTest extends CloseableFrame
{  public ButtonTest()
   {  add(new Button("Yellow"));
      add(new Button("Blue"));
      add(new Button("Red"));
   }
}
```

The `add` method takes as a parameter the specific component to be added to the frame. Here we create three components of type `Button`. When constructing the button, you specify the string that you want to appear on the face of the button.

TIP: If you need to refer to the button later (or, more generally, to a component you add to your interface), you will want to maintain a reference to it. For example:

```
public class ButtonTest extends CloseableFrame
{  public ButtonTest()
   {  yellowButton = new Button("Yellow")
      add(yellowButton);
      . . .
   }
   . . .
   private yellowButton;
}
```

Laying Out Buttons

If you add the appropriate `main` method to create the `SampleButtonTest` frame given by the little code snippet above, you will see that the result looks like Figure 8-6, which is not quite what you would expect since we tried to add three distinct buttons.

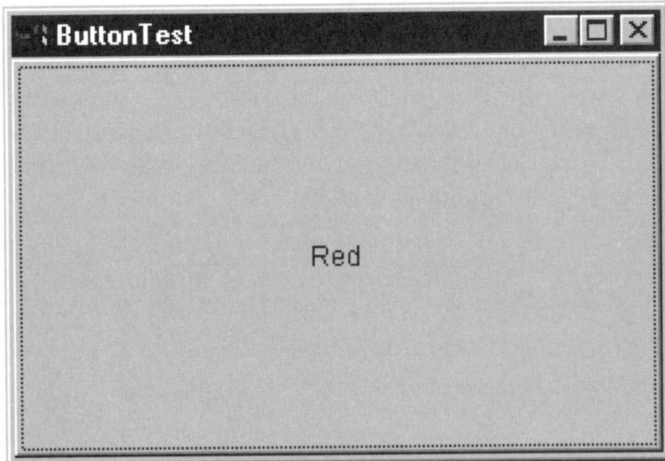

Figure 8-6: Badly laid out buttons

How do we cure the strangeness shown in Figure 8-6? The problem is that we did not tell the frame how to *lay out* the buttons. It laid them out on top of each other, and made each of them essentially fill the entire frame—that's why you see only the "Red" button in Figure 8-6. This is not a great way of laying out a bunch of buttons, but it is easy to tell the frame to do much better than this.

The AWT has a very general and very elegant mechanism for laying out components in a container: these are called *layout managers.* In our program, the one line that was missing in the fragment above was for the statement that added a *layout manager* to the frame. We will use one of the most common layout managers in our example; it's called a *flow layout.* The JDK then lays out the components automatically following the rules determined by which layout manager you are using, *regardless of the size of the window.*

A *flow layout manager* like the one we will use in the code that follows simply adds components (buttons, in our case) until the current row is full; then it starts a new row of components (buttons). Moreover, the flow layout manager keeps each set of components centered in an individual row. (For more on layout managers, please see Chapter 9.)

Here is a modification of the program you just saw that adds a flow layout manager and a few more buttons. You can see the flow layout manager in action when you resize the test application given below (see Figure 8-7). If you make the window narrower, the layout manager rearranges the buttons automatically. Regardless of how the user resizes the window, you can be sure the buttons always stay neatly centered. Layout managers are a neat feature of Java and a great savings in programming time.

```
public class ButtonTest extends CloseableFrame
{  public ButtonTest()
   {  setLayout(new FlowLayout());
      add(new Button("Yellow"));
      add(new Button("Blue"));
      add(new Button("Red"));
      add(new Button("Orange"));
      add(new Button("Black"));
      add(new Button("White"));
   }
}
```

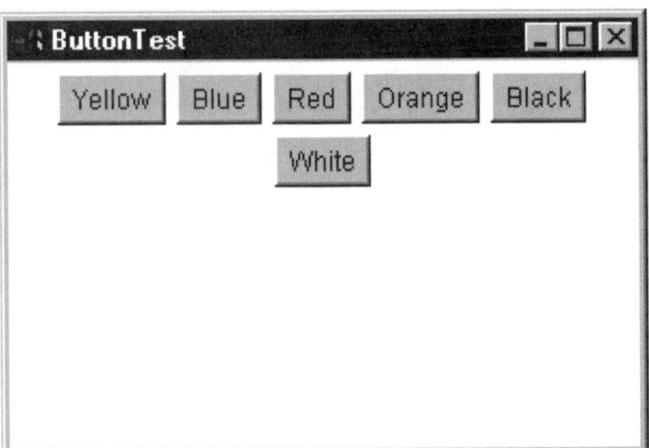

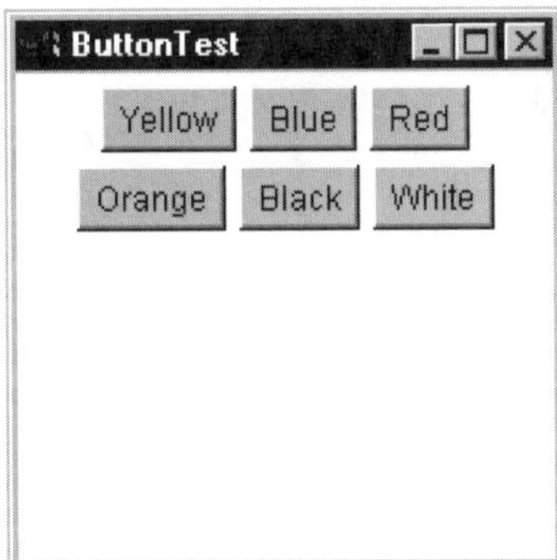

Figure 8-7: Changing the window size rearranges the buttons automatically

Getting Buttons to Respond

Now that we can add the buttons to a frame, we want to add the code that makes them change the background color when the user clicks on one of them. This task requires implementing the `ActionListener` interface, which has one method: `actionPerformed()`.

The flowing simple program extends the code above by letting a click on a button change the background color. This requires a call to the `setBackground` method, followed by a call to `repaint` in order to make the color actually change. Note the key lines inside the loop inside the constructor for the `ButtonTest` class look like this for a button named `b`

```
b.addActionListener(this);
```

which adds the frame as a listener to action events for all the buttons. Example 8-4 is the full code for this example.

Example 8-4: ButtonTest.java

```
import java.awt.*;
import java.awt.event.*;
import corejava.*;

public class ButtonTest extends CloseableFrame
   implements ActionListener
{  public ButtonTest()
   {  setLayout(new FlowLayout());

      Button yellowButton = new Button("Yellow");
      add(yellowButton);
      yellowButton.addActionListener(this);
         // who is gonna listen? this frame

      Button blueButton = new Button("Blue");
      add(blueButton);
      blueButton.addActionListener(this);

      Button redButton = new Button("Red");
      add(redButton);
      redButton.addActionListener(this);

      Button orangeButton = new Button("Orange");
      add(orangeButton);
      orangeButton.addActionListener(this);

      Button blackButton = new Button("Black");
      add(blackButton);
      blackButton.addActionListener(this);

      Button whiteButton = new Button("White");
      add(whiteButton);
      whiteButton.addActionListener(this);
   }
   public void actionPerformed(ActionEvent evt)
   {  String arg = evt.getActionCommand();
      Color color = Color.black;
      if (arg.equals("Yellow")) color = Color.yellow;
      else if (arg.equals("Blue")) color = Color.blue;
      else if (arg.equals("Red")) color = Color.red;
      else if (arg.equals("Orange")) color = Color.orange;
      else if (arg.equals("Black")) color = Color.black;
      else if (arg.equals("White")) color = Color.white;
      setBackground(color);
      repaint();
   }
```

```
    public static void main(String[] args)
    {  Frame f = new ButtonTest();
       f.show();
    }
}
```

The `ActionListener` interface we used in this example is a general-purpose event handler. It is used in four separate scenarios:

1. When a button is clicked
2. When an item is selected from a list box with a double click
3. When a menu item is selected
4. When the [Enter] key is clicked in a text field

The way to use the `ActionListener` interface is the same in all situations: the `actionPerformed` method (which is the only method in `ActionListener`) takes an object of type `ActionEvent` as a parameter. This object gives you information about the event that happened via its accessor methods.

You can use the `getSource` method in the `EventObject` class to find out the component (that is, the button, list box, menu, or text field) that produced the action event. In the code above, we used the `getActionCommand` accessor method in the `ActionEvent` class. This method returns the command string associated with this action. For buttons, it turns out that the method returns the button label.

java.awt.Button

- `Button(String label)`

  constructs a button.

  Parameters: `label` the label you want on the face of the button

java.awt.Container

- `setLayout(LayoutManager m)`

  sets the layout manager for this container.

- `add(Component c)`

  adds a component to this container.

java.awt.event.ActionEvent

- `String getActionCommand()`

  returns a string that identifies the action. This string is one of the following:

  - a button label (when the user clicks a button)
  - a menu option (when the user selects a menu item)
  - a list item (when the user selects a list item by double-clicking)
  - the contents of a text field (when the user clicks [ENTER] in the text field)

Semantic and Low-Level Events

The AWT makes a useful distinction between *low-level* and *semantic* events. A semantic event is one that expresses what the user is doing, such as "clicking that button." Low-level events are those events that make this possible. In the case of a button click, this is a series of mouse moves and a mouse click. Or it might be a keystroke; this happens if the user selects the button with the Tab key and then he or she activates it with the space bar. Similarly, adjusting a scroll bar is a semantic event, but dragging the mouse is a low-level event.

There are four semantic event classes in the `java.awt.event` package.

- `ActionEvent` (button click, menu selection, double click on list box item, clicking [ENTER] in a text field)
- `AdjustmentEvent` (the user adjusted a scroll bar)
- `ItemEvent` (the user made a selection from a set of checkbox or list items)
- `TextEvent` (the contents of a text box or text area were changed)

There are six low-level event classes.

- `ComponentEvent` (the component was resized, moved, shown, or hidden); also is the base class for all low-level events
- `KeyEvent` (a key was pressed or released)
- `MouseEvent` (the mouse button was depressed, released, moved, or dragged)
- `FocusEvent` (a component got focus, lost focus)
- `WindowEvent` (the window was activated, deactivated, iconified, deiconified, or closed)
- `ContainerEvent` (notifies you that a component has been added or removed)

Figure 8-5 on page 304 showed you the event hierarchy.

Event Handling Summary

Table 8-1 shows all AWT listener interfaces, events, and event sources. Notice that this table gives a number of events that track the *focus* of components and the *activation* of windows—these concepts are explained in the sections that follow.

Table 8-1: Event Handling Summary

Interface	Methods	Parameter	Events generated by

`ActionListener`	`actionPerformed`	`ActionEvent`
		`getActionCommand`
		`getModifiers`
			`Button`
			`List`
			`MenuItem`
			`TextField`

`AdjustmentListener`	`adjustmentValueChanged`	`AdjustmentEvent`
		`getAdjustable`
		`getAdjustmentType`
		`getValue`
			`Scrollbar`

`ItemListener`	`itemStateChanged`	`ItemEvent`
		`getItem`
		`getItemSelectable`
		`getStateChange`
			`Checkbox`
			`CheckboxMenuItem`
			`Choice`
			`List`

`TextListener`	`textValueChanged`	`TextEvent`	`TextComponent`

`ComponentListener`	`componentMoved`
	`componentHidden`
	`componentResized`
		`ComponentEvent`
		`getComponent`
			`Component`

`ContainerListener`	`componentAdded`
	`componentRemoved`
		`ContainerEvent`
		`getChild`
		`getContainer`
			`Container`

`FocusListener`	`focusGained` `focusLost`	`FocusEvent` `IsTemporary`	`Component`

`KeyListener`	`keyPressed`
	`keyReleased`
	`keyTyped`
		`KeyEvent`
		`getKeyChar`
		`getKeyCode`
		`getKeyModifiersText`
		`getKeyText`
		`IsActionKey`
			`Component`

MouseListener	mousePressed mouseReleased mouseEntered mouseExited mouseClicked	MouseEvent getClickCount getX getY getPoint TranslatePoint IsPopupTrigger	Component
MouseMotionListener	mouseDragged mouseMoved		Component
WindowListener	windowClosing windowOpened windowIconified windowDeiconified windowClosed windowActivated windowDeactivated	WindowEvent getWindow	Window

Let's go over the event delegation mechanism one more time in order to make sure that you understand the relationship between event classes, listener interfaces, and adapter classes.

Event *sources* are user interface components, windows, and menus. The operating system notifies an event source about interesting activities, such as mouse moves and keystrokes. The event source describes the nature of the event in an *event object*. It also keeps a list of *listeners*, objects that want to be called when the event happens. The event source then calls the appropriate method of the *listener interface* to deliver information about the event to the various listeners. The source does this by passing the appropriate event object to the method in the listener class. The listener analyzes the event object to find out more about the event. For example, the `getX` and `getY` methods of the `MouseEvent` class tell the listener the current location of the mouse.

With one exception, each event type corresponds to a listener interface. The one exception is that both `MouseListener` and `MouseMotionListener` receive `MouseEvent` objects. This is done for efficiency—there are a lot of mouse events as the user moves the mouse around, and a listener that just cares about mouse *clicks* will not be bothered with unwanted mouse *moves*.

Furthermore, Java supplies a corresponding *adapter* class to all listener interfaces with more than one method. The adapter class defines all the methods of the interface to do nothing. You use adapter classes as a time-saving tool: use them when you want to override just a few of the listener interface methods.

The high-level semantic events are quite natural for GUI programming—they correspond to user input. To better understand the low-level events in Table 8-1, let us briefly review some terminology.

- A *component* is a user interface element such as a button, text field, or scroll bar.
- A *container* is a screen area or component that can contain components, such as a window or an applet.

(Recall that you had a brief encounter with the flow layout manager earlier in this chapter. Its job, like that of all layout managers, is to arrange components inside a container. You will see a lot more about components and containers in the next chapter.)

All low-level events inherit from `ComponentEvent`. This class has a method called `getComponent` which reports the component that originated the event. For example, if a key event was fired because of an input into a text field, then `getComponent` returns a reference to that text field.

As we discussed before, the `PaintEvent` is not intended for programming—it is simply for the convenience of the AWT implementors. A `ContainerEvent` is generated whenever a component is added or removed. This is quite different from the other events that we saw. Button clicks and keystrokes come from the user in a random fashion, but adding or removing components is a consequence of your programming. Therefore, you don't need an event notification mechanism—you could have programmed the notification yourself. This event was provided to make user interface generators simpler to program. Unless you have a dynamically changing user interface, you will not need to worry about it.

`Java.awt.event.ComponentEvent`

- `Component getComponent()`

  returns a reference to the component that is the source for the event. This is the same as `(Component)getSource()`.

Individual Events

In the sections that follow we will discuss in more detail the focus, component, and window events that we have already briefly discussed. After that, we take up the events that are not linked to specific user interface components, in particular, events related to keystrokes, mouse activity, and menu selections. You can find a detailed discussion of events generated by user interface components, such as button clicks, list selections, and scroll bar adjustments, in the next chapter.

Focus Events

In Java, a component has the *focus* if it can receive keystrokes. For example, in Java, a text field has the focus when the cursor (caret) mark becomes visible. At that point you can enter text into the text field. When a button has the focus, you can "click" it by pressing the space bar. Only one component can have the focus at a time. A component can *lose focus* if the user selects another component, which then *gains focus.* A component gains focus if the user clicks the mouse inside it. With the mouseless navigation features added to Java 1.1, the user can also use the TAB key to give focus to each component in turn. (The tab order is determined by the order you used to add the component; see the next chapter for more on this.)

In most GUI environments, there is a visual clue to which component currently has the focus. A text field has a blinking caret, buttons have a dotted rectangle around the label, and so on.

VB NOTE: In VB, the concepts of "focus" and "being able to receive keystrokes" are not identical. A control can have focus, but if you set the `KeyPreview` property of the form to `true`, then the keystrokes go to the form.

A focus listener must implement two methods, `focusGained` and `focusLost`. These methods are triggered when the event *source* gains or loses the focus. Each of these methods has a `FocusEvent` parameter. There are two useful methods for this class. The `getComponent` method reports the component that gained or lost the focus, and the `isTemporary` method returns `true` if the focus change was *temporary.* (A temporary focus change occurs when a component gave up control temporarily but will automatically get it back. This happens, for example, when the user selects a different active window. As soon as user selects the current window again, the same control regains the focus.)

One use for trapping focus events is error checking. Suppose you have a text field that contains a credit card number. When the user is done editing the field and moves to another field, you trap the lost focus event. If the credit card format was not formatted properly, you call `requestFocus()` to give the focus back to the credit card field.

```
void lostFocus(FocusEvent evt)
{  if (evt.getComponent() == ccField)
   {  if (!checkFormat(ccField.getText()))
         ccField.requestFocus();
   }
}
```

NOTE: If you provide your own "lightweight" components, you want to trap the focus events to redraw the component with an "active" or "inactive" look. You will see an example of a lightweight component at the end of the next chapter.

Window Events

A (top-level) window is *active* if it can currently receive keystrokes from the operating system. The active window is usually indicated by a highlighted title bar. Only one window can be active at one time. As you saw earlier, you can be notified whenever one of the following events occurs in a window:

- The window has opened
- The window has closed
- The window becomes active
- The window becomes inactive
- The window becomes iconified (minimized)
- The window becomes deiconified (restored to its original size)
- The user wants to close the window

For example, as you saw earlier, our `CloseableFrame` class has an event handler that closes the application when the user wants to close the frame. This closure required trapping the `WindowClosing` event.

Here is one obvious scenario where you will want to trap some of the other window events. Suppose your application displays an animation. You can stop the animation when the window is not active or when it is minimized (iconified). You would restart it only when the window becomes active or visible again.

Keyboard Events

When the user pushes a key, a `keyPressed KeyEvent` is generated. When the user releases the key, a `keyRelease KeyEvent` is triggered. You trap these events in the `keyPressed` and `keyReleased` methods of any class that implements the `KeyListener` interface. Use these methods to trap raw keystrokes. A third method, `keyTyped`, combines the two: it reports on the *characters* that were generated by the user's keystrokes.

The best way to see what happens is with an example. But before we can do that, we have to add a little more terminology. Java makes a distinction between characters and *virtual key codes*. Virtual key codes are indicated with a prefix of `VK_`, such as `VK_A` or `VK_SHIFT`. Virtual key codes correspond to keys on the keyboard. For example, `VK_A` denotes the key marked A. There is no separate lowercase virtual key code—the keyboard does not have separate lowercase keys.

NOTE: Virtual key codes are similar (and related to) the *scan codes* of a PC keyboard.

So, suppose that the user types an uppercase "A" in the usual way, by depressing the SHIFT key and then the A key. Java reports *five* events in response to this user action. Here are the actions and the associated events:

Pressed the SHIFT key (`keyPressed` called for `VK_SHIFT`)

Pressed the A key (`keyPressed` called for `VK_A`)

Typed "A" (`keyTyped` called for an "A")

Released the A key (`keyReleased` called for `VK_A`)

Released the SHIFT key (`keyReleased` called for `VK_SHIFT`)

On the other hand, if the user typed a lowercase `"a"` by simply depressing the A key, then there are only three events:

Pressed the A key (`keyPressed` called for `VK_A`)

Typed `"a"` (`keyTyped` called for an "a")

Released the A key (`keyReleased` called for `VK_A`)

Thus, the `keyTyped` procedure reports the *character* that was typed ("A" or "a", whereas the `keyPressed` and `keyReleased` methods report on the actual *keys* that the user pressed.

To work with the `keyPressed` and `keyReleased` methods, you want to first check the *key code.*

```
public void keyPressed(KeyEvent evt)
{  int keyCode = evt.getKeyCode();
   . . .
}
```

The key code will equal one of the following (reasonably mnemonic) constants. They are defined in the `KeyEvent` class.

```
VK_A . . . VK_Z
VK_0 . . . VK_9
VK_COMMA, VK_PERIOD, VK_SLASH, VK_SEMICOLON, VK_EQUALS,
VK_OPEN_BRACKET, VK_BACK_SLASH, VK_CLOSE_BRACKET,
VK_BACK_QUOTE, VK_QUOTE
VK_SPACE, VK_ENTER, VK_BACK_SPACE, VK_TAB, VK_ESCAPE
VK_SHIFT, VK_CONTROL, VK_ALT, VK_META
VK_NUM_LOCK, VK_SCROLL_LOCK, VK_CAPS_LOCK
VK_PAUSE, VK_PRINTSCREEN
VK_PAGE_UP, VK_PAGE_DOWN, VK_END, VK_HOME, VK_LEFT, VK_UP,
VK_RIGHT, VK_DOWN
VK_F1 . . .VK_F12
VK_NUMPAD0 . . . VK_NUMPAD9
VK_MULTIPLY, VK_ADD, VK_SEPARATER [sic], VK_SUBTRACT,
VK_DECIMAL, VK_DIVIDE
VK_DELETE, VK_INSERT
VK_HELP, VK_CANCEL, VK_CLEAR, VK_FINAL
VK_CONVERT, VK_NONCONVERT, VK_ACCEPT, VK_MODECHANGE, VK_KANA,
VK_KANJI
VK_UNDEFINED
```

To find the current state of the SHIFT, CONTROL, ALT and META keys, you can of course track the `VK_SHIFT`, `VK_CONTROL`, `VK_ALT` and `VK_META` key presses, but that is tedious. Instead, simply use the `isShiftDown`, `isControlDown`, `isAltDown` and `isMetaDown` methods.

For example, the following code tests whether the user presses SHIFT + RIGHT ARROW:

```
public void keyPressed(KeyEvent evt)
{  int keyCode = evt.getKeyCode();
   if (keyCode == VK_RIGHT && evt.isShiftDown())
   { . . .
   }
}
```

In the `keyTyped` method, you call the `getChar` method to obtain the actual character that was typed.

Example 8-5 shows how to handle keystrokes. The program is a simple implementation of the Etch-A-Sketch™ toy shown in Figure 8-8. You move a pen up, down, left, and right with the cursor keys. If you hold down the SHIFT key, the pen moves by a larger increment. Or, if you are used to the vi editor, you can bypass the cursor keys and use the i, j, k, m keys to move the pen. The uppercase I, J, K, M move the pen by a larger increment. We trap the cursor keys in the `keyPressed` method and the characters in the `keyTyped` method.

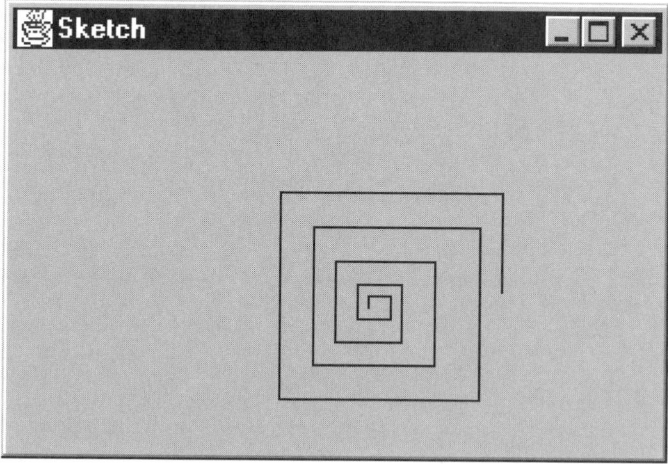

Figure 8-8: A sketch program

Example 8-5: Sketch.java

```
import java.awt.*;
import java.awt.event.*;
import corejava.*;

public class Sketch extends CloseableFrame
   implements KeyListener
{  Sketch()
   {  addKeyListener(this);
   }

   public void keyPressed(KeyEvent evt)
   {  int keyCode = evt.getKeyCode();
      int modifiers = evt.getModifiers();
      int d;
      if ((modifiers & InputEvent.SHIFT_MASK) != 0)
         d = 5;
      else
         d = 1;
      if (keyCode == KeyEvent.VK_LEFT) add(-d, 0);
      else if (keyCode == KeyEvent.VK_RIGHT) add(d, 0);
      else if (keyCode == KeyEvent.VK_UP) add(0, -d);
      else if (keyCode == KeyEvent.VK_DOWN) add(0, d);
   }

   public void keyReleased(KeyEvent evt)
   {}
```

```
   public void keyTyped(KeyEvent evt)
   {  char keyChar = evt.getKeyChar();
      int d;
      if (Character.isUpperCase(keyChar))
      {  d = 5;
         keyChar = Character.toLowerCase(keyChar);
      }
      else
         d = 1;
      if (keyChar == 'j') add(-d, 0);
      else if (keyChar == 'k') add(d, 0);
      else if (keyChar == 'i') add(0, -d);
      else if (keyChar == 'm') add(0, d);
   }

   public void update(Graphics g)
   {  paint(g);
      requestFocus();
   }

   public void paint(Graphics g)
   {  g.translate(getInsets().left, getInsets().top);
      g.drawLine(start.x, start.y, end.x, end.y);
      start.x = end.x;
      start.y = end.y;
   }

   public void add(int dx, int dy)
   {  end.x += dx;
      end.y += dy;
      repaint();
   }

   public static void main(String[] args)
   {  Frame f = new Sketch();
      f.show();
   }

   private Point start = new Point(0, 0);
   private Point end = new Point(0, 0);
}
```

`java.awt.event.KeyEvent`

- `char getKeyChar()`

  returns the character that the user typed.

- `int getKeyCode()`

  returns the virtual key code of this key event.

- `boolean isActionKey()`

  returns `true` if the key in this event is an "action" key. The following keys are action keys: HOME, END, PAGE UP, PAGE DOWN, UP, DOWN, LEFT, RIGHT, F1 ... F12, PRINT SCREEN, SCROLL LOCK, CAPS LOCK, NUM LOCK, PAUSE, INSERT, DELETE, ENTER, BACKSPACE, DELETE and TAB.

- `static String getKeyText(int keyCode)`

  returns a string describing the key code. For example, `getKeyText(KeyEvent.VK_END)` is the string "End".

- `static String getKeyModifiersText(int modifiers)`

  returns a String describing the modifier keys, such as SHIFT or CTRL + SHIFT.

Parameters:	`modifiers`	the modifier state, as reported by `getModifiers`

`java.awt.event.InputEvent`

- int `getModifiers()`

  returns an integer whose bits describe the state of the modifiers Shift, Control, Alt, and Meta. This method applies to both keyboard and mouse events. To see if a bit is set, test the return value against one of the bit masks `SHIFT_MASK`, `CONTROL_MASK`, `ALT_MASK`, `META_MASK`, or use one of the following methods.

- `boolean isAltDown()`
- `boolean isControlDown()`
- `boolean isMetaDown()`
- `boolean isShiftDown()`

  which return `true` if the modifier key was held down when this event was generated.

Mouse Events

You do not need to handle mouse events explicitly if you just want the user to be able to click on a button or menu. These mouse operations are handled internally by the various components in the graphical user interface and then translated into the appropriate semantic event. You can react to that event in an `actionPerformed` or `itemStateChanged` method. However, if you want to enable the user to draw with the mouse, you will need to trap mouse move, click, and drag events.

In this section, we will show you a simple graphics editor application that allows the user to place, move, and erase squares on a canvas (see Figure 8-9).

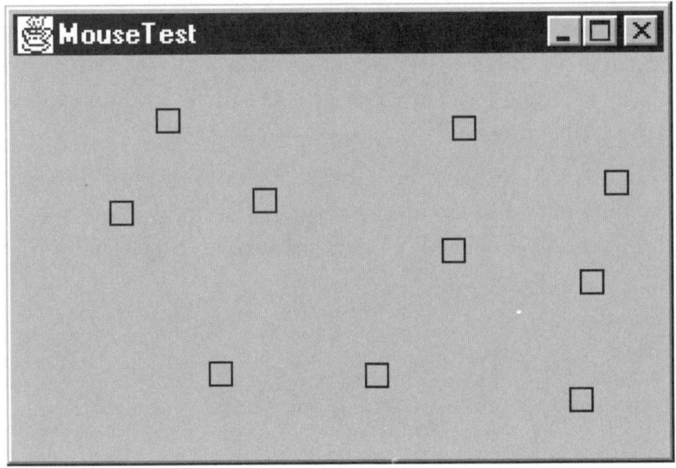

Figure 8-9: A mouse test program

When the user clicks a mouse button, Java calls the `mouseClicked` method of the listener object. By using the `getX` and `getY` methods on the `MouseEvent` argument, you can obtain the *x*- and *y*-coordinates of the mouse pointer when the mouse was clicked. If you want to distinguish between single and double clicks, use the `getClickCount` method.

You can even get triple clicks, but your users will hate you if you force them to exercise their fingers too much. Unless they come from an Emacs background, they will also hate you if you inflict keystroke + mouse click combinations, such as CONTROL + SHIFT + CLICK, on them. If you do want to check the state of the SHIFT, CONTROL, ALT, and META keys, you do it in the same way as you just saw for key events: use the `isShiftDown`, `isControlDown`, `isAltDown`, and `isMetaDown` methods.

For example, here is a handler for the CONTROL + SHIFT + triple click command.

```
public void mouseClicked(MouseEvent evt)
{  int x = evt.getX();
   int y = evt.getY();

   int modifiers = evt.getModifiers();
   int clickCount = evt.getClickCount();
   if ( evt.isShiftDown() && evt.isControlDown()
      && clickCount >= 3)
   {  Graphics g = getGraphics();
      g.translate(getInsets().left, getInsets().top);
      g.drawString("Yikes", x, y);
   }
}
```

You are also supposed to be able to distinguish between the mouse buttons by testing the return value of `getModifiers` against the values `BUTTON1_MASK`, `BUTTON2.MASK`, `BUTTON3_MASK`. However, this feature is not working correctly in the release of Java 1.1 with which we are working.

Here is the `mouseClicked` function for our sample program. When you click onto a pixel that is not inside any of the squares that have been drawn, a new square is added. When you double-click inside an existing square, it is erased.

```
public void mouseClicked(MouseEvent evt)
{  int x = evt.getX();
   int y = evt.getY();
   {  current = find(x, y);
      if (current < 0) // no square under the cursor
         add(x, y);
      else if (evt.clickCount >= 2)
         remove(current);
   }
}
```

As the mouse moves over a window, the window receives a steady stream of mouse movement events. These are ignored by most applications. However, our test application traps the events in order to change the cursor to a different shape (a cross hair) when it is under a square. This is done with the `getPredefinedCursor` method of the `Cursor` class. Table 8-2 lists the constants to use with this method along with what the cursors look like under Windows. (Note that many of these cursors look the same under Windows, but you should check how they look on your platform.)

```
public void mouseMoved(MouseEvent evt)
{  int x = evt.getX();
   int y = evt.getY();

   if (find(x, y) >= 0)
      setCursor(Cursor.getPredefinedCursor(CROSSHAIR_CURSOR));
   else
      setCursor(Cursor.getDefaultCursor());
}
```

NOTE: Custom cursors are not currently possible in Java.

Table 8-2: Cursor Shapes in Java Under Windows

Icon	Constant
	DEFAULT_CURSOR
	CROSSHAIR_CURSOR
	HAND_CURSOR
	MOVE_CURSOR
	TEXT_CURSOR
	WAIT_CURSOR
	N_RESIZE_CURSOR
	NE_RESIZE_CURSOR
	E_RESIZE_CURSOR
	SE_RESIZE_CURSOR
	S_RESIZE_CURSOR
	SW_RESIZE_CURSOR
	W_RESIZE_CURSOR
	NW_RESIZE_CURSOR

If the user presses a mouse button while the mouse is in motion, `mouseDragged` calls are generated instead of `mouseClicked` calls. Our test application lets you drag the square under the cursor. Before the square is moved, we erase the old location by drawing it over itself in XOR mode. (A bug under Windows 95 seems to leave the four pixels at the corners of the square intact.) Then we set the new location for the square and draw it again.

```
public void mouseDragged(MouseEvent evt)
{   int x = evt.getX();
    int y = evt.getY();
    current = find(x, y);
    if (current >= 0)
    {   Graphics g = getGraphics();
        g.translate(getInsets().left, getInsets().top);
        g.setXORMode(getBackground());
        draw(g, current);
        squares[current].x = x;
        squares[current].y = y;
        draw(g, current);
        g.dispose();
    }
}
```

Finally, we need to explain how to listen to mouse events. Mouse clicks are reported through the `mouseClicked` procedure, which is part of the `MouseListener` interface. Because many applications are interested only in mouse clicks and not in mouse moves and because mouse move events occur so frequently, the mouse move and drag events are in a separate interface called `MouseMotionListener`. We capture mouse motion events simply, by having the frame class implement the `MouseMotionListener` interface and by registering itself as a listener to its own mouse motion events.

```
public class MouseTest extends CloseableFrame
    implements MouseMotionListener
{   MouseTest()
    {   addMouseMotionListener(this);
        . . .
    }
    public void mouseMoved(MouseEvent evt)
    {   . . .
    }
    public void mouseDragged(MouseEvent evt)
    {    . . .
    }
    . . .
}
```

For the `mouseClicked` method, the situation is not as simple. The `MouseEvent` interface has five methods, `mouseClicked`, `mousePressed`, `mouseReleased`, `mouseEntered`, and `mouseExited`. We have no interest in four of them. Therefore, we use the `MouseAdapter` class that defines all these methods to do nothing, and we build an inner class that redefines `mouseClicked` to call the `mouseClicked` method of the outer class. Note that the outer class does *not* implement the `MouseListener` interface.

```
public class MouseTest extends CloseableFrame
   implements MouseMotionListener
{  MouseTest()
   {  addMouseListener(new MouseAdapter()
         {  public void mouseClicked(MouseEvent evt)
            {  MouseTest.this.mouseClicked(evt);
            }
         });
      . . .
   }
   public void mouseClicked(MouseEvent evt) {...}
   . . .
}
```

Example 8-6 is the program listing.

Example 8-6: MouseTest.java

```
import java.awt.*;
import java.awt.event.*;
import corejava.*;

public class MouseTest extends CloseableFrame
   implements MouseMotionListener
{  MouseTest()
   {  addMouseListener(new MouseAdapter()
         {  public void mouseClicked(MouseEvent evt)
            {  MouseTest.this.mouseClicked(evt);
            }
         });
      addMouseMotionListener(this);
   }

   public void paint(Graphics g)
   {  g.translate(getInsets().left, getInsets().top);
      for (int i = 0; i < nsquares; i++)
         draw(g, i);
   }
```

```
public int find(int x, int y)
{  for (int i = 0; i < nsquares; i++)
      if (squares[i].x - SQUARELENGTH / 2 <= x &&
            x <= squares[i].x + SQUARELENGTH / 2
            && squares[i].y - SQUARELENGTH / 2 <= y
            && y <= squares[i].y + SQUARELENGTH / 2)
         return i;
   return -1;
}

public void draw(Graphics g, int i)
{  g.drawRect(squares[i].x - SQUARELENGTH / 2,
      squares[i].y - SQUARELENGTH / 2,
      SQUARELENGTH,
      SQUARELENGTH);
}

public void add(int x, int y)
{  if (nsquares < MAXNSQUARES)
   {  squares[nsquares] = new Point(x, y);
      nsquares++;
      repaint();
   }
}

public void remove(int n)
{  nsquares—;
   squares[n] = squares[nsquares];
   if (current == n) current = -1;
   repaint();
}

public void mouseClicked(MouseEvent evt)
{  int x = evt.getX();
   int y = evt.getY();

   int modifiers = evt.getModifiers();
   int clickCount = evt.getClickCount();
   if ((modifiers & InputEvent.CTRL_MASK) != 0
      && (modifiers & InputEvent.SHIFT_MASK) != 0
      && clickCount >= 3)
   {  Graphics g = getGraphics();
      g.translate(getInsets().left, getInsets().top);
      g.drawString("Yikes", x, y);
      return;
   }
```

```
      current = find(x, y);
      if (current < 0) // not inside a square
      {  add(x, y);
      }
      else if (evt.getClickCount() >= 2)
      {  remove(current);
      }
   }

   public void mouseMoved(MouseEvent evt)
   {  int x = evt.getX();
      int y = evt.getY();

      if (find(x, y) >= 0)
         setCursor(Cursor.getPredefinedCursor(CROSSHAIR_CURSOR));
      else
         setCursor(Cursor.getDefaultCursor());
   }

   public void mouseDragged(MouseEvent evt)
   {  int x = evt.getX();
      int y = evt.getY();
      current = find(x, y);
      if (current >= 0)
      {  Graphics g = getGraphics();
         g.translate(getInsets().left, getInsets().top);
         g.setXORMode(getBackground());
         draw(g, current);
         squares[current].x = x;
         squares[current].y = y;
         draw(g, current);
         g.dispose();
      }
   }

   public static void main(String args[])
   {  Frame f = new MouseTest();
      f.show();
   }

   private static final int SQUARELENGTH = 10;
   private static final int MAXNSQUARES = 100;
   private Point[] squares = new Point[MAXNSQUARES];
   private int nsquares = 0;
   private int current = -1;
}
```

`java.awt.event.MouseEvent`

- `int getX()`
- `int getY()`
- `Point getPoint()`

  return the x (horizontal), y (vertical) coordinate, or point where the event happened, using the coordinate system of the source.

- `void translatePoint(int x, int y)`

  translates the coordinates of the event by moving x units horizontally and y units vertically.

- `int getClickCount()`

  returns the number of consecutive mouse clicks associated with this event. (The time interval for what constitutes "consecutive" is system dependent.)

Menus

AWT supports the kind of pull-down menus that are familiar from Windows and Motif applications. A *menu bar* on top of the window contains the names of the pull-down menus. Clicking on a name opens the menu containing *menu items* and *submenus.* When the user clicks on a menu item, Java closes all menus and sends a message to the program. Figure 8-10 shows a typical menu with a submenu.

Adding menus is straightforward. You create a menu bar.

```
MenuBar mb = new MenuBar();
```

For each menu, you create a menu object.

```
Menu editMenu = new Menu("Edit");
```

You add menu items, separators, and submenus to the menu object.

```
MenuItem pasteItem = new MenuItem("Paste");
editMenu.add(pasteItem);
editMenu.addSeparator();
editMenu.add(optionsMenu);
...
```

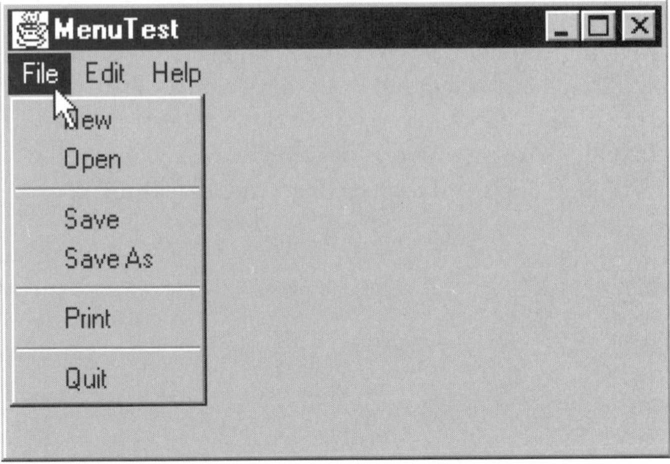

Figure 8-10: A menu

When the user selects a menu, Java triggers an action event. You need to install an action event listener for each menu item.

```
pasteItem.addActionListener(this);
```

Unfortunately, adding menu items and listeners by hand is incredibly tedious. Here is some code to build up a typical menu.

```
Menu m = new Menu("Edit");
MenuItem mi = new MenuItem("Undo");
mi.addActionListener(this);
m.add(mi);
mi = new MenuItem("Redo");
mi.addActionListener(this);
m.add(mi);
m.addSeparator();
mi = new MenuItem("Cut");
mi.addActionListener(this);
m.add(mi);
mi = new MenuItem("Copy");
mi.addActionListener(this);
m.add(mi);
mi = new MenuItem("Paste");
mi.addActionListener(this);
m.add(mi);
menuBar.add(m);
```

This is tedious for long menus, so we wrote a procedure called `makeMenu` that takes the drudgery out of making menus. This procedure takes three parameters. The first parameter is either a string or a menu. If it is a string, `makeMenu` makes a menu with that title. The second parameter is an array of items, each of which is a string, a menu item, or `null`. The `makeMenu` procedure makes a menu item out of each string and a separator out of each `null`, then adds all items and separators to the menu. The third parameter is the listener for the menu items. (We assume that all menu items have the same listener.) Here is the call to `makeMenu` that is equivalent to the preceding menu construction code.

```
mbar.add(makeMenu("Edit",
   new Object[]
   {  "Undo",
      "Redo",
      null,
      "Cut",
      "Copy",
      "Paste",
   },
   this));
```

Here's the source code for the `makeMenu` procedure which can easily be added to any program that requires a sophisticated menuing system.

```
private static Menu makeMenu(Object parent,
    Object[] items, Object target)
 {  Menu m = null;
    if (parent instanceof Menu)
       m = (Menu)parent;
    else if (parent instanceof String)
       m = new Menu((String)parent);
    else
       return null;

    for (int i = 0; i < items.length; i++)
    {  if (items[i] instanceof String)
       {  MenuItem mi = new MenuItem((String)items[i]);
          if (target instanceof ActionListener)
             mi.addActionListener((ActionListener)target);
          m.add(mi);
       }
       else if (items[i] instanceof CheckboxMenuItem
          && target instanceof ItemListener)
       {  CheckboxMenuItem cmi
             = (CheckboxMenuItem)items[i];
          cmi.addItemListener((ItemListener)target);
          m.add(cmi);
       }
       else if (items[i] instanceof MenuItem)
       {  MenuItem mi = (MenuItem)items[i];
          if (target instanceof ActionListener)
             mi.addActionListener((ActionListener)target);
```

```
            m.add(mi);
         }
         else if (items[i] == null)
            m.addSeparator();
      }

      return m;
   }
```

NOTE: In Windows programs, menus are generally defined in an external resource file and tied to the application with resource identifiers. It is possible to build menus programmatically, but it is not commonly done except in VB. In Java, menus are still usually built inside the program because, even in Java 1.1, the mechanism for dealing with external resources is far more limited than it is in Windows.

As with buttons, you catch menu selection events in the `actionPerformed` method. You can tell that an action originated from a menu by verifying, with the `instanceof` operator, that the type of the event source is a menu item using the `instanceof` operator. To find which menu item was selected, get the source of the action command with the `getSource` method, then get the menu label with the `getLabel` method:. Here is some sample code that does this:

```
public void actionPerformed(Event evt)
{  if (evt.getSource() instanceof MenuItem)
   {  MenuItem mi = (MenuItem)evt.getSource();
      String arg = mi.getLabel();
      if (arg.equals("Open")) . . .
      else if (arg.equals("Save")) . . .
      . . .
   }
}
```

TIP: Some programmers use the `getActionCommand` method to get the menu label. However, if you use keyboard shortcuts for menu items, the `getActionCommand` returns `null`. The method used in the preceding example works for both menu selections and keyboard shortcuts.

`java.awt.Menu`

- `Menu(String label)`

  Parameters: `label` the label for the menu in the menu bar or parent menu

- `void add(MenuItem item)`

  adds a menu item (or a menu).

  Parameters: `item` the item or menu to add

- `void addSeparator()`

  adds a separator line to the menu.

- `void insert(String label, int index)`

  adds a new item to the menu at a specific index.

  Parameters: `label` the label for the menu item
  `index` where to add the item

- `void insert(MenuItem menu, int index)`

  adds a new submenu to the menu at a specific index.

  Parameters: `menu` the menu to be added
  `index` where to add the item

- `void insertSeparator(int index)`

  adds a separator to the menu.

  Parameters: `index` where to add the separator

- `void remove(int index)`

  removes a specific item from the menu.

  Parameters: `index` the position of the item to remove

`java.awt.MenuItem`

- `MenuItem(String label)`

  Parameters: `label` the label for this menu item; (the label "-" is reserved for a separator between menu items)

Advanced Menu Topics

Now that you have seen how to build basic menus, let us look at three advanced topics.

- Check box menu items
- Pop-up menus
- Keyboard shortcuts for menus

Check Box Menu Items

A *check box* menu item is one that can display a check box next to the name (see Figure 8-11). When the user selects the menu item, the item automatically toggles between checked and unchecked. A `CheckboxMenuItem` does *not* call `actionPerformed` when it is selected. If you want to be notified at the moment of selection, you must install an `ItemListener` object. The `itemStateChanged` method in this interface is triggered when the check box changes state. If you don't need to be notified at the exact moment the user selected the item, you can simply use the `getState` method of the `CheckboxMenuItem` class to test the current state of the menu item. Use the `setState` method to set the state.

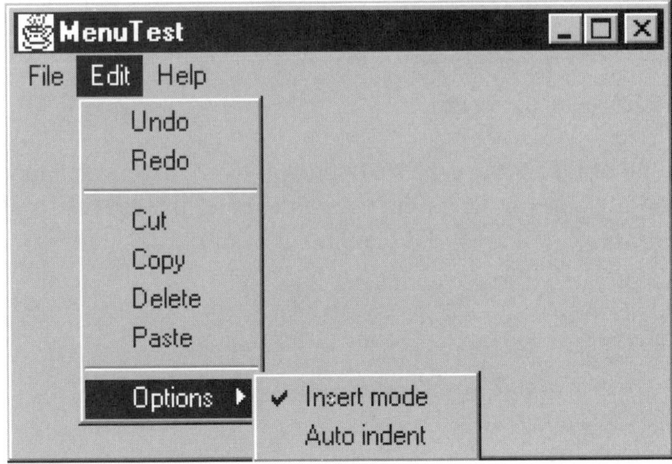

Figure 8-11: A checked menu item

Pop-up Menus

A *pop-up menu* is a menu that is not attached to a menu bar but that floats somewhere (see Figure 8-12).

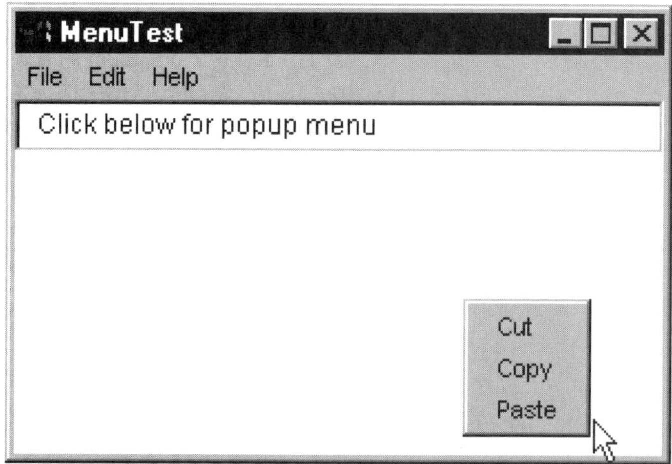

Figure 8-12: A pop-up menu

When an action of the user means that you will want to pop up a menu, use the `show` method. You specify the parent component and the location of the pop-up, using the coordinate system of the parent. For example:

```
PopupMenu popup = new PopupMenu();
makeMenu(popup,
   new Object[] { "Cut", "Copy", "Paste" },
   this);
. . .
popup.show(this, x, y);
```

Usually you write code to pop up a menu when the user clicks a particular mouse button, the so-called *pop-up trigger*. In Windows, the pop-up trigger is the nonprimary (usually, the right) mouse button. To pop up a menu when the user clicks the pop-up trigger:

- Install a mouse listener.
- Add code like the following to the mouse event handler:

```
public void mouseClicked(MouseEvent evt)
{  if (evt.isPopupTrigger())
      popup.show(evt.getComponent(),
         evt.getX(), evt.getY());
}
```

This code will show the pop-up menu at the mouse location where the user clicked the pop-up trigger. (Actually, at the time of this writing, this code does not work. The `isPopupTrigger` method never returns `true`. Presumably, this defect will be fixed in a later version. For that reason, the code in the `MenuTest`

program (Example 8-7) that is in the next section pops up the menu no matter which mouse button you use.)

`java.awt.event.MouseEvent`

- boolean isPopupTrigger()

  should return `true` if this mouse event is the pop-up-menu trigger.

`java.awt.CheckBoxMenuItem`

- `CheckboxMenuItem(String label)`

  constructs the checkbox menu item with the given label.

- `CheckboxMenuItem(String label, boolean state)`

  constructs the checkbox menu item with the given label and the given initial state (`true` is checked).

- `boolean getState()`

  returns the check state of this item (`true` is checked).

- `void setState(boolean state)`

  sets the check state of this item.

Keyboard Shortcuts

It is a real convenience for the experienced user to select menu items by *keyboard shortcuts.* For example, many users are familiar with the shortcuts CTRL + C, CTRL + X and CTRL +V for the Edit | Copy, Edit | Cut, and Edit | Paste menu items under Windows. In Java, you can specify keyboard shortcuts for menus, *provided* you restrict yourself to CTRL key combinations such as CTRL + C or CTRL + LEFT.

To make a menu item with a keyboard shortcut, pass an object of type `MenuShortcut` to the `MenuItem` constructor. Supply the shortcut key (without CTRL) to the `MenuShortcut` constructor, using the virtual key codes you saw earlier in the chapter:

```
MenuItem mi1 = new MenuItem("Copy",
   new MenuShortcut(KeyEvent.VK_C));
MenuItem mi2 = new MenuItem("Copy",
   new MenuShortcut(KeyEvent.VK_LEFT));
```

Java automatically displays the keyboard shortcuts in the menu (see Figure 8-13).

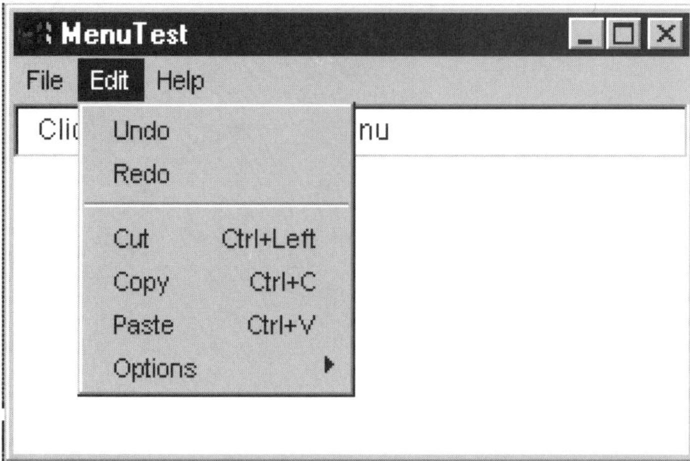

Figure 8-13: Keyboard shortcuts

When the user presses the shortcut key combination, then this automatically selects the menu option.

NOTE: Under Windows, ALT+F4 closes a window. But this is not a shortcut that was, or could be, programmed in Java. It is a shortcut defined by an operating system. This key combination will always trigger the `WindowClosing` event for the active window regardless of whether there is a Close item on the menu.

Example 8-7 is a sample program that generates a set of menus. It shows all the features that we saw in this section: nested menus, checkbox menu items, a pop-up menu and keyboard shortcuts.

Example 8-7: MenuTest.java

```
import java.awt.*;
import java.awt.event.*;
import corejava.*;

public class MenuTest extends CloseableFrame
   implements ActionListener, ItemListener
{  public MenuTest()
   {  MenuBar mbar = new MenuBar();

      mbar.add(makeMenu("File",
         new Object[]
         {  "New",
            "Open",
```

```
            null,
            "Save",
            "Save As",
            null,
            "Print",
            "Quit"
        },
        this));

    mbar.add(makeMenu("Edit",
        new Object[]
        {   "Undo",
            "Redo",
            null,
            new MenuItem("Cut",
                new MenuShortcut(KeyEvent.VK_LEFT)),
            new MenuItem("Copy",
                new MenuShortcut(KeyEvent.VK_C)),
            new MenuItem("Paste",
                new MenuShortcut(KeyEvent.VK_V)),
            makeMenu("Options",
                new Object[]
                {   new CheckboxMenuItem("Insert mode"),
                    new CheckboxMenuItem("Auto indent"),
                },
                this)
        },
        this));

    mbar.add(makeMenu("Help",
        new Object[]
        {   "Index",
            "About",
        },
        this));

    setMenuBar(mbar);

    popup = new PopupMenu();
    makeMenu(popup,
        new Object[]
        {   "Cut",
            "Copy",
            "Paste"
        },
        this);
```

```
      /* pop-up menus and keyboard shortcuts don't work in
         an empty frame, so we add some components
      */
      Panel p = new Panel();
      p.add(popup); // add pop-up menu to frame
      p.addMouseListener(new MouseAdapter()
         {  public void mouseClicked(MouseEvent evt)
            {  popup.show(evt.getComponent(),
                  evt.getX(), evt.getY());
            }
         });
      add(p, "Center");
      add(new TextField("Click below for popup menu"),
         "North");
   }

   private static Menu makeMenu(Object parent,
      Object[] items, Object target)
   {  Menu m = null;
      if (parent instanceof Menu)
         m = (Menu)parent;
      else if (parent instanceof String)
         m = new Menu((String)parent);
      else
         return null;

      for (int i = 0; i < items.length; i++)
      {  if (items[i] instanceof String)
         {  MenuItem mi = new MenuItem((String)items[i]);
            if (target instanceof ActionListener)
               mi.addActionListener((ActionListener)target);
            m.add(mi);
         }
         else if (items[i] instanceof CheckboxMenuItem
            && target instanceof ItemListener)
         {  CheckboxMenuItem cmi
               = (CheckboxMenuItem)items[i];
            cmi.addItemListener((ItemListener)target);
            m.add(cmi);
         }
         else if (items[i] instanceof MenuItem)
         {  MenuItem mi = (MenuItem)items[i];
            if (target instanceof ActionListener)
               mi.addActionListener((ActionListener)target);
            m.add(mi);
         }
         else if (items[i] == null)
            m.addSeparator();
      }
```

```
        return m;
    }

    public void actionPerformed(ActionEvent evt)
    {   MenuItem c = (MenuItem)evt.getSource();
        String arg = c.getLabel();
        if(arg.equals("Quit"))
            System.exit(0);
        else if (arg.equals("About"))
            popup.show(this, 100, 100);
        else System.out.println(arg);
    }

    public void itemStateChanged(ItemEvent evt)
    {   CheckboxMenuItem c
            = (CheckboxMenuItem)evt.getSource();
        System.out.print(c.getLabel() + " ");
        if (!c.getState()) System.out.print("de");
        System.out.println("selected");
    }

    public static void main(String args[])
    {   Frame f = new MenuTest();
        f.show();
    }

    PopupMenu popup;
}
```

`java.awt.MenuShortcut`

- `MenuShortcut(int key)`

  constructs a menu shortcut with the given virtual key.

Parameters	`key`	the virtual keycode for the key to use as shortcuts

`java.awt.MenuItem`

- `MenuItem(String label, MenuShortcut s)`

  constructs a `MenuItem` object with the given label and shortcut.

Separating GUI and Application Code

Up to now, we have not really used the feature that the Java 1.1 event model lets us choose an arbitrary listener for events—we always chose `this`, the current frame, to be the listener. For simple programs, such as the demonstration programs in this chapter, this choice is certainly appropriate. However as programs get larger, it makes a lot of sense to *separate* the responsibilities of getting user input and executing commands because it is common to have multiple ways to activate the same command. The user can choose a certain function through a menu, a keystroke, or a button on a toolbar. (On a more naive level it also often make sense to separate out the code for building the user interface and the code for how it responds.)

The following strategy is the one we use to separate the user interface code and the application code.

1. Make an object for every command.
2. Make each command object a listener for the events that trigger it.
3. Handle events that don't directly map to commands in the window that generates them.

For example, suppose we want to add multiple interfaces to the color change application. To change the background color, you can

- Click on one of the buttons
- Select a color from a menu
- Press a key (B = blue, Y = yellow, R = red)

We make a class `ColorCommand` that is responsible for changing colors. We make three objects—`blueCommand`, `yellowCommand`, and `redCommand`—of this class. We make these objects the listeners for the user interface events from the buttons and the menu items. For example, the `blueCommand` object is a listener for both the button labeled "Blue" and the menu item labeled "Blue." However, the keystroke events cannot be directly routed to a command until we figure out what key was typed. Therefore, the frame is the listener for key events.

Example 8-8 shows the code.

Example 8-8: SeparateGUITest.java

```
import java.awt.*;
import java.awt.event.*;
import corejava.*;

public class SeparateGUITest extends CloseableFrame
   implements KeyListener
{  SeparateGUITest()
   {  blueCommand = new ColorCommand(Color.blue, this);
      yellowCommand = new ColorCommand(Color.yellow, this);
      redCommand = new ColorCommand(Color.red, this);

      MenuBar mbar = new MenuBar();
      Menu m = new Menu("Color");
      MenuItem mi;
      mi = new MenuItem("Yellow");
      mi.addActionListener(yellowCommand);
      m.add(mi);
      mi = new MenuItem("Blue");
      mi.addActionListener(blueCommand);
      m.add(mi);
      mi = new MenuItem("Red");
      mi.addActionListener(redCommand);
      m.add(mi);
      mbar.add(m);
      setMenuBar(mbar);

      setLayout(new FlowLayout());
      Button b;
      b = new Button("Yellow");
      b.addActionListener(yellowCommand);
      add(b);
      b = new Button("Blue");
      b.addActionListener(blueCommand);
      add(b);
      b = new Button("Red");
      b.addActionListener(redCommand);
      add(b);

      addKeyListener(this);
   }

   public void keyPressed(KeyEvent evt)
   {}

   public void keyReleased(KeyEvent evt)
   {}
```

```
    public void keyTyped(KeyEvent evt)
    {  char keyChar
          = Character.toLowerCase(evt.getKeyChar());
       if (keyChar == 'b') blueCommand.execute();
       else if (keyChar == 'y') yellowCommand.execute();
       else if (keyChar == 'r') redCommand.execute();
    }

    public static void main(String args[])
    {  Frame f = new SeparateGUITest();
       f.show();
    }

    private ColorCommand blueCommand;
    private ColorCommand yellowCommand;
    private ColorCommand redCommand;
}

class ColorCommand implements ActionListener
{  public ColorCommand(Color c, Component comp)
   {  color = c;
      target = comp;
   }

   public void actionPerformed(ActionEvent evt)
   {  execute();
   }

   public void execute()
   {  target.setBackground(color);
   }

   private Color color;
   private Component target;
}
```

Multicasting

All AWT event sources support a *multicast* model for listeners. This means that the same event can be sent to more than one listener object. Multicasting is useful if an event is *potentially* of interest to many parties. Rather than trying to decide at the outset who needs to receive the event, multicasting allows all registered listeners a chance to react to the event. For example, we could have used multicasting in the program of the preceding section to simplify the event handling. Rather than having the frame window analyze the keystrokes, we could have sent the keystrokes to each command object, each of which could have

looked at the key event and handled it if it was interested. (Of course, multicasting events too widely might make your application feel less "peppy.")

CAUTION: According to JavaSoft, "The API makes no guarantees about the order in which the events are delivered to a set of registered listeners for a given event on a given source." In particular, a listener should not consume the event—consumption is meaningless when the delivery order is random.

Here we will show a different application of multicasting. We will have a simple application that can spawn multiple windows with the File | New command. And it can close all windows with the File | Close all command—see Figure 8-14.

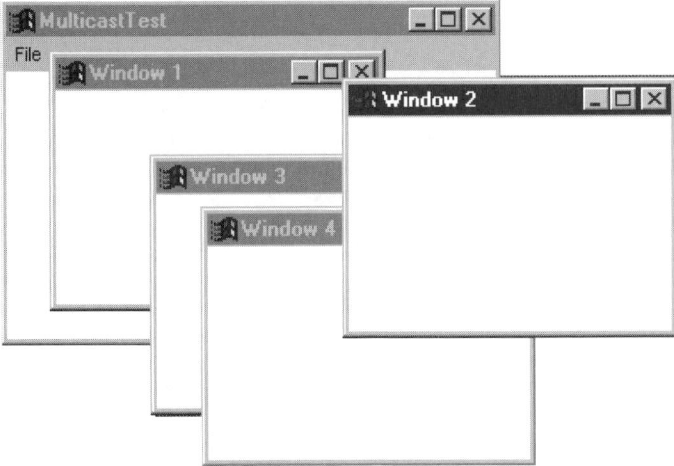

Figure 8-14: All windows listen to the Close all command

The listener to the File | New menu item is the application frame window—it makes the new child windows. But the File | Close all menu item has multiple listeners—each child window is added to the set of listeners. When that menu option is selected, all windows receive it and close themselves. Example 8-9 shows the source code.

Example 8-9: MulticastTest.java

```
import java.awt.*;
import java.awt.event.*;
import corejava.*;

class MulticastTest extends CloseableFrame
   implements ActionListener
{  public MulticastTest()
   {  MenuBar mbar = new MenuBar();
      Menu m = new Menu("File");
      newItem = new MenuItem("New");
      newItem.addActionListener(this);
      m.add(newItem);
      closeAllItem = new MenuItem("Close all");
      m.add(closeAllItem);
      mbar.add(m);
      setMenuBar(mbar);
   }

   public void actionPerformed(ActionEvent evt)
   {  if (evt.getSource() == newItem)
      {  SimpleFrame f = new SimpleFrame();
         counter++;
         f.setTitle("Window " + counter);
         f.setSize(200, 150);
         f.setLocation(30 * counter, 30 * counter);
         f.show();
         closeAllItem.addActionListener(f);
      }
   }

   public static void main(String args[])
   {  new MulticastTest();
   }

   int counter = 0;
   private MenuItem newItem;
   private MenuItem closeAllItem;
}

class SimpleFrame extends Frame
   implements ActionListener
{  public void actionPerformed(ActionEvent evt)
   {  if (evt.getSource() instanceof MenuItem)
      {  MenuItem mi = (MenuItem)evt.getSource();
         if (mi.getLabel().equals("Close all"))
            dispose();
      }
   }
}
```

Advanced Event Handling

In this section, we show you various advanced event handling techniques that bypass or augment the regular event handling mechanism. You'll see:

- Consuming events
- Using secondary event loops
- Adding custom events

Consuming Events

Occasionally, you will want to capture an event so that it is not passed on to a user interface component. For example, suppose that we want to prevent a button from being clicked. The program in Example 8-10 does this for a silly reason—if you try to click on the button labeled "Red," the button jumps away to a random location. A more serious application would be a user interface builder where, depending on a switch, buttons need to be able to be dragged without being activated.

To stop a button from being activated:

- We trap the `mousePressed` event that comes before Java synthesizes the `mouseClicked` and `action` events.
- Then, we *consume* that event.

The result is that as far as any registered listeners are concerned, the `mouseClicked` and `action` events never happened. In fact, if you look closely at the red button as you click on it, you will notice that it does not "flash" like other buttons do when they are clicked. That shows that Java has trapped the mouse click before the native button control had a chance to react to it.

Example 8-10. ConsumeTest.java

```
import corejava.*;
import java.awt.*;
import java.awt.event.*;

public class ConsumeTest extends CloseableFrame
   implements ActionListener
{  public ConsumeTest()
   {  setLayout(new FlowLayout());

      yellowButton = new Button("Yellow");
      add(yellowButton);
      yellowButton.addActionListener(this);
         // who is gonna listen? this frame
```

```
        blueButton = new Button("Blue");
        add(blueButton);
        blueButton.addActionListener(this);

        redButton = new Button("Red");
        add(redButton);
        redButton.addActionListener(this);

        redButton.addMouseListener(new MouseAdapter()
            {  public void mousePressed(MouseEvent evt)
                {  redButton.setLocation(rand.draw(),
                      rand.draw());
                   evt.consume();
                }
            });
    }

    public void actionPerformed(ActionEvent evt)
    {  String arg = evt.getActionCommand();
       Color color = Color.black;
       if (arg.equals("Yellow")) color = Color.yellow;
       else if (arg.equals("Blue")) color = Color.blue;
       else if (arg.equals("Red")) color = Color.red;
       setBackground(color);
       repaint();
    }

    public static void main(String[] args)
    {  Frame f = new ConsumeTest();
       f.show();
    }

    Button yellowButton;
    Button blueButton;
    Button redButton;
    RandomIntGenerator rand
       = new RandomIntGenerator(50, 200);
}
```

`java.awt.AWTEvent`

- `void consume()`

  consumes a low-level event and thereby prevents it from being sent to a user interface component.

- `boolean isConsumed()`

  returns `true` if the event was consumed.

Manipulating the Event Queue

When the operating system generates an event in response to a user action such as a mouse click, the part of the AWT that communicates with the operating system receives the operating-system-level event and turns it into an AWT event. Java then deposits the event into an *event queue*. The part of the AWT that dispatches events to listeners:

- Fetches events from the event queue
- Locates the listener object for that event
- Invokes the appropriate listener procedure for that event

An event queue is important for performance reasons. Events that occur frequently (such as mouse moves) or that are slow to carry out (such as painting) can be *combined* in the queue. If the program has not managed to extract mouse move or paint events and Java inserts a new event, then Java can combine it with the existing event to make a single new event. For example, we can have the new mouse position update the old one, or a new paint event can contain a request to repaint the combined areas of the old paint events.

Occasionally, it is useful to manipulate the event queue directly. For example, you can remove events from the queue, thereby bypassing how events would normally be delivered. Or, you can add new events into the queue, allowing a richer event handling than is possible in the basic Java event model. The example programs in this section show you how to remove events from the queue in order to bypass the normal event flow. In the section on custom events that follows, we show you how to insert custom event objects into the queue; these events will then be delivered in the usual way without you needing to do any more work.

NOTE: Inserting or removing events is an advanced technique. If performed improperly or maliciously, it can wreak havoc with an application. For that reason, applets—the Java applications that are downloaded from foreign computers and run inside your browser—do not allow access to the system event queue.

You obtain an object representing the event queue by using the method call

```
EventQueue evtq
    = Toolkit.getDefaultToolkit().getSystemEventQueue();
```

You insert a new event into the event queue with the `postEvent` method:

```
evtq.postEvent(new ActionEvent(this,
    ActionEvent.ACTION_PERFORMED, "Blue"));
```

You remove an event with the `getNextEvent` method. (The `peekEvent` method returns the next event in the queue, but it does not remove it.)

Let us put manipulating the event queue to work by implementing a *secondary event loop.* In a secondary event loop, you are only interested in a particular event and you need to manually remove all the events until you find the one you need.

Using a secondary event loop allows you to force the user to do certain actions sequentially. For example, suppose you want to have a drawing program where the user clicks on two points sequentially in order to draw a line. If you use a secondary event loop when you prompt the user to click the mouse, the user cannot wander off and use scroll bars or menus, since you can throw away all mouse activity that are not mouse clicks.

This turns out to be a major pain to implement in an event driven style. In a purely event driven program, we would have one method that prompts the user to click on the first point. A separate method, namely, the mouse listener, would be activated with every mouse click. The listener would need to keep track of whether the event that it is processing is a part of the line drawing sequence or not. Then, if it decides that it is part of the line drawing operation, it needs to decide if it is the first or the second click. This is tedious. Instead, we want to write a method called `getClick` that waits until it has a mouse click from the user and returns the point that was clicked. Once we have such a method, it is straightforward to prompt the user to specify a line:

```
displayPrompt("Please click on a point");
Point p = getClick();
displayPrompt("Please click on another point");
Point q = getClick();
g.drawLine(p.x, p.y, q.x, q.y);
```

The `getClick` method requires the use of a secondary event loop. That loop grabs events until it finds a mouse click.

```
while (true)
{  AWTEvent evt = eq.getNextEvent();
   if (evt.getID() == MouseEvent.MOUSE_CLICKED)
   {  MouseEvent mevt = (MouseEvent)evt;
      Point p = mevt.getPoint();
      Graphics g = getGraphics();
      g.translate(getInsets().left, getInsets().top);
      g.drawOval(p.x - 2, p.y - 2, 4, 4);
      return p;
   }
}
```

Example 8-11 shows the source code for this application.

Example 8-11: EventQueueTest.java

```
import java.awt.*;
import java.awt.event.*;
import corejava.*;

public class EventQueueTest extends CloseableFrame
{  public void run()
   {  displayPrompt("Please click on a point");
      Point p = getClick();
      displayPrompt("Please click on another point");
      Point q = getClick();
      Graphics g = getGraphics();
      g.translate(getInsets().left, getInsets().top);
      g.drawLine(p.x, p.y, q.x, q.y);
      displayPrompt("Done!");
   }

   public void displayPrompt(String s)
   {  Graphics g = getGraphics();
      g.translate(getInsets().left, getInsets().top);
      g.clearRect(0, 0, getSize().width, 50);
      g.drawString(s, 0, 30);
   }

   public Point getClick()
   {  EventQueue eq
         = Toolkit.getDefaultToolkit()
            .getSystemEventQueue();
      while (true)
      {  try
         {  AWTEvent evt = eq.getNextEvent();
            if (evt.getID() == MouseEvent.MOUSE_CLICKED)
            {  MouseEvent mevt = (MouseEvent)evt;
               Point p = mevt.getPoint();
               Graphics g = getGraphics();
               g.translate(getInsets().left,
                  getInsets().top);
               g.drawOval(p.x - 2, p.y - 2, 4, 4);
               return p;
            }
         }
         catch(InterruptedException e)
         {}
      }
   }

   public static void main(String[] args)
   {  EventQueueTest f = new EventQueueTest();
      f.show();
      f.run();
   }
}
```

CAUTION: Using secondary event loops in this way does go against the event driven programming paradigm which insists that the user, and not the program, should be in control.

`java.awt.EventQueue`

- `AWTEvent peekEvent()`

  returns a reference to the `AWTEvent` object that describes the next event.

- `AWTEvent getNextEvent()`

  returns a reference to the `AWTEvent` object that describes the next event and removes it from the queue.

- `void postEvent(AWTEvent anEvent)`

  places the event on the event queue.

  Parameters: `anEvent` the event you want to post

Adding Custom Events

In the last section of this chapter, we will do some fairly sophisticated programming. We want to show you how to build a *custom event type* that you can insert into the AWT event queue and then have it dispatched to a listener, just like regular AWT events. For the example in this section, we will make a new event type that we call `TimerEvent`. The associated listener will have one method called `timeElapsed`.

If you like, you can just use our timer class in your code without worrying about how it is implemented because using it is simple: after you make a timer object and add a listener for it, the listener will be notified whenever a specific (settable) time interval has elapsed. Here is how you can put the timer to work:

```
public class CustomEventTest extends CloseableFrame
   implements TimerListener
{  public CustomEventTest()
   {  Timer t = new Timer(1000);
         // deliver timer clicks every 1000 milliseconds
      t.addTimerListener(this);
         // notify the timeElapsed method of this class
   }
```

```
      public void timeElapsed(TimerEvent evt)
      {   . . .
            // this code is executed every 1000 milliseconds
      }
      . . .
}
```

As you can see, this timer has a very similar "look and feel" to the other AWT events. In particular, C/C++ Windows programmers will be very comfortable with this approach since Windows uses the event queue to deliver timer notifications.

Now let us see how to implement such a custom event. We start with the needed listener interface.

```
interface TimerListener
{   public void timeElapsed(TimerEvent evt);
}
```

Any class that wants timer notifications using our timer events must implement this interface. The `TimerEvent` class is pretty simple:

- It extends the `AWTEvent` superclass since all events in the AWT event queue must have type `AWTEvent`.
- The constructor for the timer event receives the object that is the source of the event (that is, the timer object).

We also need to give an *event ID number* to the superclass. It does not matter what positive integer we choose, as long as we stay outside the range that the AWT uses for its own events.

How to find an unused ID? To quote JavaSoft: "Programs should choose event ID values which are greater than the integer constant: `java.awt.AWTEvent.RESERVED_ID_MAX`."

```
class TimerEvent extends AWTEvent
{   public TimerEvent(Timer t) { super(t, TIMER_EVENT); }
    public static final int TIMER_EVENT =
        AWTEvent.RESERVED_ID_MAX  + 5555;
}
```

Finally, we need to implement the `Timer` class itself. The AWT event mechanism requires that event sources extend the class `Component`. Normally, components are user interface elements that are placed inside a window. We will simply take the attitude that a timer is an invisible component as it is, for example, in Visual Basic.

To write the code that constructs the interval that the timer "ticks," we need to use threads. (Threads are discussed in the second volume of this book, so you will need to take the thread handling code on faith for now.) Whenever the specified time interval has elapsed, we make a new timer event and insert it into the event queue. Here's the code for this with the pieces that are needed to post the event in bold:

```
class Timer extends Component implements Runnable
{  public Timer(int i)
   {  interval = i;
      Thread t = new Thread(this);
      t.start();
   }

   public void run()
   {  while (true)
      {  try { Thread.sleep(interval); }
         catch(InterruptedException e) {}

         EventQueue evtq
            = Toolkit.getDefaultToolkit().getSystemEventQueue();
         TimerEvent te = new TimerEvent(this);
         evtq.postEvent(te);
      }
   }
   . . .
   private int interval;
}
```

After this code is processed, we know that Java has inserted our custom timer events into the queue. Event delivery is not automatic however, so our custom timer event will not be sent to anyone without additional code.

How do we make sure our custom event is sent to interested parties? The answer is that is the responsibility of the *component* to:

- Manage the listeners for the events that it generates
- Dispatch the events in to the listeners that are registered for them

For the purpose of this sample we implement only a single listener. The `addTimerListener` method remembers the object that wants to listen to the timer events. Java calls the `processEvent` method whenever the AWT removes an event from the queue whose source was the timer. If the event is a timer event and we added a listener for it, then Java invokes its `timeElapsed` method.

```
class Timer extends Component implements Runnable
{  . . .
   public void addTimerListener(TimerListener l)
   {  listener = l;
   }

   public void processEvent(AWTEvent evt)
   {  if (evt instanceof TimerEvent)
      {  if (listener != null)
            listener.timeElapsed((TimerEvent)evt);
      }
      else super.processEvent(evt);
   }

   private TimerListener listener;
}
```

NOTE: For an industrial-strength timer component, one would need to support multi-casting and listener removal as well.

As it turns out, there is one more (undocumented) problem. The AWT code that removes events from the queue and dispatches them to the event source will deliver them only if it is convinced that the container supports the new event model. One way to convince it is to call the `enableEvents` method in the `Component` class. This method takes a parameter that gives a mask for the AWT events we want to enable for this component. We don't care about AWT events at all since we are only interested in our custom timer event, so we pass a mask of 0. This happens in the constructor of the `Timer` object.

Example 8-12 shows the complete source code. As you can see, it is possible to add custom events to the AWT mechanism using relatively little code.

Example 8-12: CustomEventTest.java

```
import java.awt.*;
import java.awt.event.*;
import corejava.*;

public class CustomEventTest extends CloseableFrame
   implements TimerListener
{  public CustomEventTest()
   {  Timer t = new Timer(1000);
      t.addTimerListener(this);
   }
```

```
    public void timeElapsed(TimerEvent evt)
    {  Graphics g = getGraphics();
       g.translate(getInsets().left, getInsets().top);
       g.drawRect(0, 0, ticks, 10);
       ticks++;
    }

    public static void main(String[] args)
    {  CustomEventTest f = new CustomEventTest();
       f.show();
    }

    int ticks = 0;
}

interface TimerListener
{  public void timeElapsed(TimerEvent evt);
}

class Timer extends Component implements Runnable
{  public Timer(int i)
   {  interval = i;
      Thread t = new Thread(this);
      t.start();
      evtq = Toolkit.getDefaultToolkit()
         .getSystemEventQueue();
      enableEvents(0);
   }

   public void addTimerListener(TimerListener l)
   {  listener = l;
   }

   public void run()
   {  while (true)
      {  try { Thread.sleep(interval); }
         catch(InterruptedException e) {}
         TimerEvent te = new TimerEvent(this);
         evtq.postEvent(te);
      }
   }

   public void processEvent(AWTEvent evt)
   {  if (evt instanceof TimerEvent)
      {  if (listener != null)
            listener.timeElapsed((TimerEvent)evt);
      }
      else super.processEvent(evt);
   }
```

```
    private int interval;
    private TimerListener listener;
    private static EventQueue evtq;
}

class TimerEvent extends AWTEvent
{   public TimerEvent(Timer t) { super(t, TIMER_EVENT); }
    public static final int TIMER_EVENT
       = AWTEvent.RESERVED_ID_MAX  + 5555;
}
```

`Java.awt.Component`

- `void enableEvents(long maskForEvents)`

  enables the component to insert events into the event queue even when there is no listener for a particular event type.

Parameter:	`maskForEvents`	a mask of event types to enable, made up of constants such as `ACTION_EVENT_MASK` that are defined in the `AWTEvent` class.

Survival Tip for Java 1.0 Programmers

(If you have never programmed graphical user interfaces in Java before or aren't going to be building applets (see Chapter 10) that run on an older browser, then this section will only be of historical interest to you.)

If you have programmed graphical user interfaces in Java 1.0, then you may well be horribly confused after reading this chapter. In Java 1.0, life was simple: you didn't need to worry about listeners. Instead, you added code in methods like `action` and `handleEvent` to the classes that contained the user interface elements. For example, the button test program would look like this:

```
public class ButtonTest extends CloseableFrame
{   public ButtonTest()
    {   setLayout(new FlowLayout());

        Button yellowButton = new Button("Yellow");
        add(yellowButton);

        Button blueButton = new Button("Blue");
        add(blueButton);

        Button redButton = new Button("Red");
        add(redButton);
    }
```

```
    public boolean action(Event evt, Object arg)
    {  Color color = Color.black;
       if (arg.equals("Yellow")) color = Color.yellow;
       else if (arg.equals("Blue")) color = Color.blue;
       else if (arg.equals("Red")) color = Color.red;
       setBackground(color);
       repaint();
       return true;
    }

    public static void main(String[] args)
    {  Frame f = new ButtonTest();
       f.show();
    }
}
```

There are two important differences between the new event model and the older one:

In Java 1.0, a button click is *always* received by the object that contained the button. In Java 1.1, information about the button click is sent only to objects that were added as an `actionListener` for the button.

In Java 1.0, all events are caught in the `action` and `handleEvent` methods. In Java 1.1, there are 29 separate methods (such as `actionPerformed` and `windowClosing`) that can react to events.

For simple programs (such as this button test program), the old event model is easier to program (although whether it is conceptually as simple is another question). But for complex programs, the old event model has severe limitations. The new model, while initially more involved, is far more flexible and will be potentially faster since events are sent far more selectively. And at any rate, Java IDEs will increasingly come with tools that automatically produce the needed event handling code for you.

There is an easy and a hard part in what you need to do to transform your 1.0 program to a 1.1 program. The easy part is tracking the changes in method names in order to get rid of the deprecated methods. For example, `resize` is now called `setSize`. The hard part is to replace all the `action` and `handleEvent` methods with the equivalent functionality in 1.1.

JavaSoft has prepared a script to help you with the easy part. The script automatically replaces all calls to deprecated methods such as `resize` with calls to the newly named methods such as `setSize`. (Actually, the script is not very selective—it replaces *all* uses of `resize`, not just those that are applied to `Frame` objects. So you should save your files before launching that script!)

The harder part, changing the `action` and `handleEvent` code, is going to require hand coding. As far as we are aware, no tools are available to help you with this. Here is a fairly straightforward, if tedious, method of changing your code to work with the new event model.

1. Look at your `action` and `handleEvent` methods and make a list of the events that you handled.
2. Find out, for example from Table 8-1, which listener methods you need.
3. Move the code from the `action` and `handleEvent` methods to the listener methods.
4. Find out which interfaces are used to declare those listener methods. Have your frame or applet class implement all these interfaces. Implement all remaining methods of those interfaces as "do nothing" methods.
5. Find out which components generate the events, again from Table 8-1.
6. Add the `this` object as a listener to those components.

CHAPTER 9

- Introduction to Buiding a User Interface
- Canvases
- Text Input
- Text Areas
- Making Choices
- Scroll Bars
- Sophisticated Layout Management
- Flow Layouts Revisited
- Border Layout
- Card Layout
- Grid Layout
- Grid Bag Layout
- Using No Layout Manager
- Custom Layout Managers
- Printing Components
- Dialog Boxes
- Data Exchange
- Lightweight User Interface Elements

User Interface Components

Although the last chapter was primarily designed to show you how to use the new event model in Java 1.1, you did take the first steps toward building a graphical user interface in Java. This chapter shows you the remaining tools you need to master in order to build a full-featured graphical user interface with Java. We'll show you all the remaining user interface components along with a detailed look at all the layout managers that the AWT has to offer.

At the present time, the components that come with the AWT, such as buttons and text fields, use the look and feel of the equivalent component on the native platform. For example, a Java button on Windows looks just like the usual Windows button. A button on Motif looks just like a Motif button. (This is because these AWT interface elements ultimately create and use the native equivalent.) There are two advantages to this strategy. The user interface of Java applications looks familiar. And it was initially easier to reuse existing elements than to reimplement them all. But there is a downside—only those user interface elements that are available on *all* platforms, such as buttons and scroll bars, are supported by the AWT. The AWT does not provide fancy controls such as tabbed dialogs and tool bars.

At the end of the chapter, we will show you a way to build user interface components that do not subclass an existing AWT interface element. These *lightweight components* (as they are usually called) do not use native interface elements coming from the underlying windowing system. This means that they are potentially far less limiting than the standard AWT components. By using lightweight components, you could potentially give your application a uniform look and feel across platforms. We are not sure how successful this approach will ultimately be since the framework is still being formed. But it is worth noting that JavaSoft, IBM, and Netscape have announced a vast collection of lightweight components as part of their Java Foundation Classes. These will include components like tabbed dialog boxes that many users have long wanted in the AWT. Of course, regardless of the ultimate success of using lightweight components to give a uniform cross-platform look and feel, the techniques are useful when you need a special-purpose control. We show you an example of this at the end of this chapter—a command button that holds an image.

Introduction to Building a User Interface

To build a user interface, you obviously need to decide how your interface should look. In particular, what components are needed and how should they appear? This is often easiest with old-fashioned paper and pencil since the JDK has no form designer like those in VB or Delphi. When you are satisfied with the design, you need to convert the design to Java code. Unfortunately, because of the lack of a form designer in the JDK to generate code templates, you need to write code for *everything*. In particular, code (often lots of it) is needed to:

1. Make the components in the user interface look the way you want them to,
2. Position (lay out) the user interface components where you want them to be inside a window,
3. Handle user input; in particular, program the components to recognize the events to which you want them to respond.

Of course, if you have a Java 1.1-enabled development environment, it will probably have a layout tool that automates some or all of these tasks. Nevertheless, it is important to know exactly what goes on "under the hood" since even the best of these tools will usually require hand-tweaking in order to get a professional look and feel.

Let's start by reviewing the program from the last chapter that used buttons to change the background color of a frame (see Figure 9-1).

Let us quickly recall how we built this program:

1. We defined the look of each button by setting the label string in the constructor, for example:

   ```
   Button yellowButton = new Button("Yellow")
   ```

2. We added a flow layout manager to the frame. The flow layout manager controlled how Java will lay out the buttons:

   ```
   setLayout(new FlowLayout());
   ```

3. We then added the individual buttons, for example, with:

   ```
   add(yellowButton);
   ```

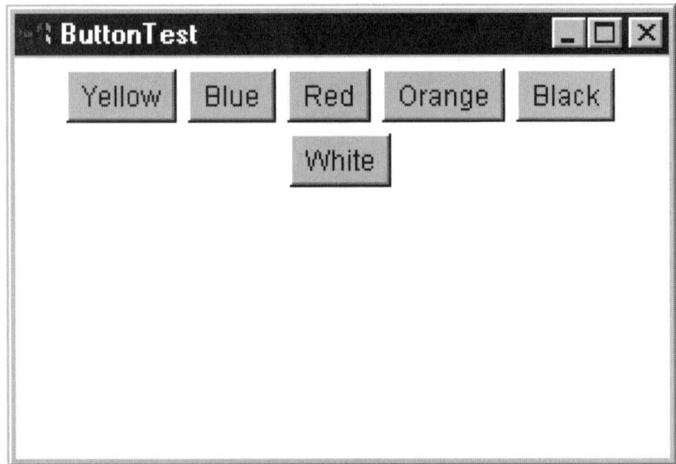

Figure 9-1: A frame with buttons managed by a flow layout

4. Then we added the needed event handlers, for example:

```
yellowButton.addActionListener(this);
```

Then, as you saw in the last chapter, the flow layout manager took responsibility for arranging the buttons in the frame. Moreover, it keeps the buttons centered in the frame, even when the user resizes the frame.

Java comes with five layout managers as well as enabling you to make your own layout managers: we will cover all of them later on in this chapter. However, to whet your appetite, we want to briefly describe a popular layout manager called the *border layout manager,* which is actually the default layout manager for a frame. Unlike the flow layout manager, which completely controls the position of each component, the border layout manager lets you choose where you want to place each component. You can choose to place the component in the center, north, south, east, or west of the frame. For example:

```
class MyFrame extends Frame
{  . . .
   add(yellowButton, "North");
}
```

Note that the default layout manager for frames *is* a border layout, so we didn't actually need to explicitly set it.

A `BorderLayout` is not very useful by itself. Figure 9-2 shows what happens when you use the code snippet above. The button has grown to fill the entire northern region of the frame. And, if you were to add multiple buttons to the northern region, they would also just be superimposed on the first button. This is a problem similar to what you saw in the last chapter, when we added buttons into a frame without specifying a layout. We will see in the next section how to solve this problem by using a *panel* to hold the buttons.

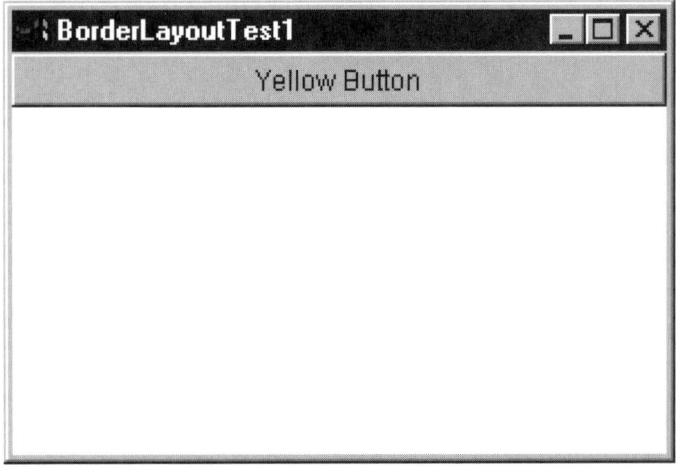

Figure 9-2: A frame with a single button managed by a border layout

`java.awt.Container`

- `setLayout(LayoutManager m)`

  sets the layout manager for this container.

- `void add(Component c)`

  adds a component to this container under the control of the current layout manager.

- `void add(Component c, Object constraints)`

Parameters	`c`	the component to add
	`constraints`	an identifier understood by the layout manager

As you can see by looking at Figure 9-2, it is not enough to dump all the buttons into a frame and let the layout manager worry about arranging them. You obviously need a more precise method of locating components. One common method used in Java is to divide a top-level window into *panels.* Panels act as (smaller) containers for interface elements and can themselves be arranged

inside a window under the control of a layout manager. For example, you can have one panel in the northern area for the buttons and another in the center for text. Panels can also be nested inside of each other so they can let you do fairly precise positioning of components. This approach to layout is certainly enough for prototyping and is often enough for a polished application. (See the section on the `GridBagLayout` on page 424 for the most precise way to position components.)

VB NOTE: Think of a panel as corresponding to a picture box without a boundary—it is invisible to the user but still functions as a container.

For example, look at Figure 9-3. The three buttons at the top of the screen are all contained in a panel. The panel is put into the "south" end of the frame.

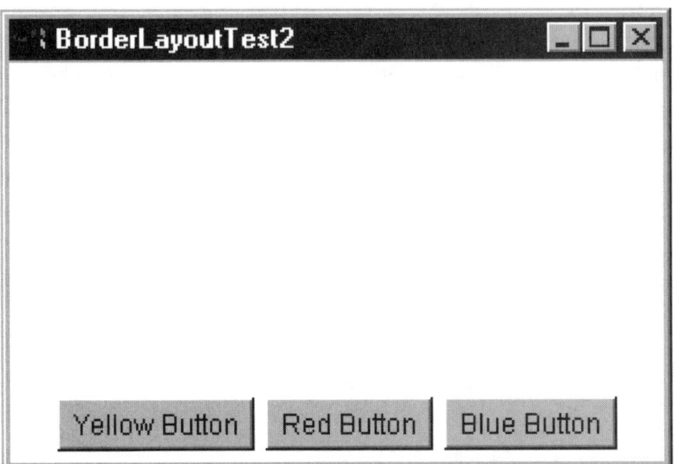

Figure 9-3: A panel placed at the south end of the frame

So, suppose you want to add a panel with three buttons as in Figure 9-3. As you might expect, you first create a new instance of a `Panel` object before you add the individual buttons to it. The default layout manager for a panel is a `FlowLayout`, which is a good choice for this situation. Finally, you add the individual buttons, using the `add` method you have seen before. Since you are adding buttons to a panel and haven't changed the default layout manager, the position of the buttons is under the control of the `FlowLayout` manager. This means the buttons stay centered within the panel and they do not expand to fill the entire area of the panel. Here's a code fragment that adds a panel containing three buttons in the south end of a container.

```
public PanelTest()
{  . . .
   Panel p = new Panel();
   p.add(yellowButton);
   p.add(blueButton);
   p.add(redButton);
   add(p, "South");
}
```

NOTE: When Java displays a window, the panel boundaries are not visible to the user. Panels are just an organizing mechanism for the user interface designer.

Each container type has its own default layout manager. As you just saw, the `Panel` class and its subclass `Applet` (see the next chapter for more on applets) use a `FlowLayout` as the default layout manager; `Window` (and the subclasses `Dialog` and `Frame`) uses a `BorderLayout`. In this example, we used the default `FlowLayout` manager for the panel and the default `BorderLayout` for the containing frame. However, there are obviously times when you want to set the layout manager to something other than the default for the container. You do this with the `setLayout` method that you have already seen. For a `Panel` (but not for other containers), you can also supply the layout manager object in the constructor.

`java.awt.Panel`

- `Panel(LayoutManager m)`

  sets the layout manager for the panel.

Canvases

Once you start filling up a window with lots of interface elements and multiple panels, it is best not to draw directly onto the window surface any more because your drawing may interfere with the components you placed on the window. Instead, you should add a *canvas* to the window. A canvas is simply a rectangular area in which you can draw by subclassing the `paint` method appropriately. (In contrast, a panel is a rectangular area into which you can place user interface components.) Note that the `Component` class is the parent class of the `Canvas` class, so `Canvas` inherits the methods of the `Component` class. Making a canvas is a bit more complex than using a panel because you must specify how to draw on the canvas. This means:

- You must derive a new class from `Canvas`.
- Then, override the `paint` procedure in your derived class to do the drawing.

For example, we will use a canvas in the sample program for this section to draw the face of a clock. Just as we derived classes from `Frame` in the previous chapter to draw on the entire frame, we now derive a new class from `Canvas` to draw on a specific area of the window. Here is the beginning of the `ClockCanvas` class, although all the functionality is not yet implemented:

```
class ClockCanvas extends Canvas
{  public void paint(Graphics g)
   {  g.drawOval(0, 0, 100, 100);
      // draw hour and minute hand
      . . .
   }
   public void tick() { minutes++; repaint(); }
   public void reset() { minutes = 0; }
   private int minutes = 0;
}
```

We also added methods `tick` and `reset` to communicate with the canvas.

Our sample program which is given in Example 9-1 is a bit complicated since it has both a class derived from `Frame` and a class derived form `Canvas`.

- The class derived from `Frame` describes how the main window is different from the default window. (In our case, the difference is simply that it has buttons and a canvas.)
- The class derived from `Canvas` describes how our canvas is different from the default. (It draws a clock face!)

Notice that we didn't need to extend the `Panel` class because the standard class already does everything needed to manage the buttons that we want to place on the window. Example 9-1 is the complete program.

Example 9-1: CanvasTest.java

```
import java.awt.*;
import java.awt.event.*;
import corejava.*;

public class CanvasTest extends CloseableFrame
   implements ActionListener
{  public CanvasTest()
   {  Panel p = new Panel();
      Button tickButton = new Button("Tick");
      p.add(tickButton);
      tickButton.addActionListener(this);
      Button resetButton = new Button("Reset");
      p.add(resetButton);
      resetButton.addActionListener(this);
```

```
      Button closeButton = new Button("Close");
      p.add(closeButton);
      closeButton.addActionListener(this);
      add(p, "South");
      clock = new ClockCanvas();
      add(clock, "Center");
   }

   public void actionPerformed(ActionEvent evt)
   {  String arg = evt.getActionCommand();
      if (arg.equals("Tick")) clock.tick();
      else if (arg.equals("Reset")) clock.reset();
      else if (arg.equals("Close")) System.exit(0);
   }

   public static void main(String[] args)
   {  Frame f = new CanvasTest();
      f.show();
   }

   private ClockCanvas clock;
}

class ClockCanvas extends Canvas
{  public void paint(Graphics g)
   {  g.drawOval(0, 0, 100, 100);
      double hourAngle = 2 * Math.PI * (minutes - 3 * 60)
           / (12 * 60);
      double minuteAngle = 2 * Math.PI * (minutes - 15)
          / 60;
      g.drawLine(50, 50,
         50 + (int)(30 * Math.cos(hourAngle)),
         50 + (int)(30 * Math.sin(hourAngle)));
      g.drawLine(50, 50,
         50 + (int)(45 * Math.cos(minuteAngle)),
         50 + (int)(45 * Math.sin(minuteAngle)));
   }

   public void reset()
   {  minutes = 0;
      repaint();
   }

   public void tick()
   {  minutes++;
      repaint();
   }

   private int minutes = 0;
}
```

Text Input

Obviously, Java programs would have little use if they could only draw pretty pictures. You need to have a way to accept input from a user. In Java, there are two components used to get text input: *text fields* and *text areas*. The difference between them is that a text field can accept only one line of text and a text area can accept multiple lines of text. The classes are called `TextField` for single-line input and `TextArea` for multiple lines of text.

Both these classes inherit from a class called `TextComponent`. You will not be able to construct a `TextComponent` yourself since its constructor is not public. On the other hand, as is so often the case in Java, when you go searching through the API documentation, you may find that the methods you are looking for are actually in the parent class `TextComponent` rather than in the derived class. For example, as the API notes that follow indicate, the methods that get or set the text in a text field or text area or the methods used to determine if (or to set whether) a text component can be edited by the user are actually methods in `TextComponent`.

`java.awt.TextComponent`

- `void setText(String t)`

  changes the text of a text component.

  Parameters: `t` the new text

- `String getText()`

  returns the text contained in this text component.

- `void setEditable(boolean b)`

  determines whether the user can edit the contents of the `TextComponent`.

Text Fields

The usual way to add a text field to a window is to actually add it to a panel or other container— just as you would a button:

```
Panel p = new Panel();
TextField tf = new TextField("Default input", 20);
p.add(tf);
```

This code adds a text field and initializes the text field by placing the string `"Default input"` inside it. The second parameter of this constructor sets the width. In this case the width is 20 "columns." Unfortunately, a column is a rather imprecise measurement. One column is the expected width of one character in the font you are using for the text. The idea is that if you expect the inputs to be n characters or less, you are supposed to specify n as the column width. In practice, this measurement doesn't work out too well, and you should add 1 or 2 to the maximum input length to be on the safe side. Also, keep in mind that the number of columns is only a hint to the AWT that gives the *preferred* size. If the layout manager needs to grow or shrink the text field, it can adjust its size. The column width that you set in the `TextField` constructor is not an upper limit on the number of characters the user can enter. The user can still type in longer strings, but the input scrolls when the text exceeds the length of the field, which is irritating. If you need to reset the column at run time, you can do that with the `setColumns` method.

TIP: After changing the size of a text box with the `setColumns` method, you need to call the `validate` method of the surrounding container.

```
hourField.setColumns(10);
validate();
```

The `validate` method recomputes the size and layout of all components in a container. After you use the `validate` method, Java repaints the container and the changed size of the text field will be visible.

In general, you want to let the user add text (or edit the existing text) in a text field. For this, quite often text fields start out blank. To make a blank text field, just leave the string out as a parameter for the `TextField` constructor:

```
TextField tf = new TextField(20);
```

(You can also use the empty string in the previous version of the constructor.)

You can change the contents of the text field at any time with the `setText` method from the `TextComponent` parent class mentioned in the previous section. For example:

```
hourField.setText("12");
```

And, as was also mentioned in the previous section, you can find out what the user typed by calling the `getText` method. This method returns the exact text that the user typed. To trim any extraneous spaces from the data in a text field, apply the `trim` method to the return value of `getText`:

```
String hour = hourField.getText().trim();
```

To change the font in which the user text appears, use the `setFont` method in `java.awt.Component` (see Chapter 7 for more on this method).

Let us put a few text fields to work in our clock program. Figure 9-4 shows the running application. Instead of a reset button, there are now two text fields for entering the hours and minutes. Whenever the contents of the text fields change, the clock is updated.

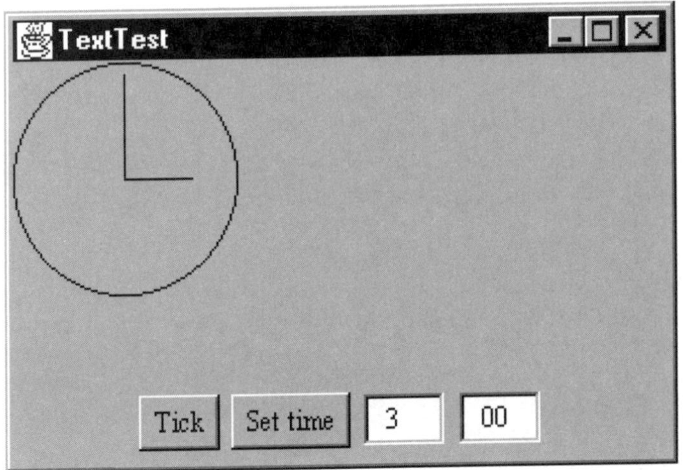

Figure 9-4: Text box example

To track every change in the text field, we install a *text listener.* Each text box calls the `textValueChanged` method whenever the content of the field changes. In that method, we use the `getText` method to obtain the current user input string from the text fields. Unfortunately, that is what we get: a string. We need to convert the string to an integer. Java would like us to use the unbelievably complex incantation

```
int hours = Integer.parseInt(hourField.getText().trim());
```

But this code won't work right when the user types a noninteger string, such as `"two"`, into the text field, or even leaves the field blank. Try it out: the terminal window will display an ugly error message complaining about a `java.lang.NumberFormatException`.

We could use our `atoi` helper function in the `corejava` package in Example 9-2, but it does no error checking at all, which isn't good for user interface design. We will tackle the issue of validating input in the next section.

Example 9-2: TextTest.java

```
import java.awt.*;
import java.awt.event.*;
import corejava.*;

public class TextTest extends CloseableFrame
   implements TextListener
{  public TextTest()
   {  Panel p = new Panel();
```

```
        hourField = new TextField("12", 3);
        p.add(hourField);
        hourField.addTextListener(this);

        minuteField = new TextField("00", 3);
        p.add(minuteField);
        minuteField.addTextListener(this);

        Button b = new Button("Pack");
        p.add(b);
        b.addActionListener(new ActionListener()
           {  public void
              actionPerformed(ActionEvent evt)
              {  hourField.setColumns(10);
                 validate();
              }
           });

        add(p, "South");
        clock = new ClockCanvas();
        add(clock, "Center");
     }

     public void textValueChanged(TextEvent evt)
     {  {  int hours
              = Integer.parseInt(hourField.getText().trim());
           int minutes
              = Integer.parseInt(minuteField.getText().trim());
           clock.setTime(hours, minutes);
        }
     }

     public static void main(String[] args)
     {  Frame f = new TextTest();
        f.show();
     }

     private TextField hourField;
     private TextField minuteField;
     private ClockCanvas clock;
  }

  class ClockCanvas extends Canvas
  {  public void paint(Graphics g)
     {  g.drawOval(0, 0, 100, 100);
        double hourAngle
           = 2 * Math.PI * (minutes - 3 * 60) / (12 * 60);
        double minuteAngle = 2 * Math.PI * (minutes - 15) / 60;
```

```
        g.drawLine(50, 50,
            50 + (int)(30 * Math.cos(hourAngle)),
            50 + (int)(30 * Math.sin(hourAngle)));
        g.drawLine(50, 50,
            50 + (int)(45 * Math.cos(minuteAngle)),
            50 + (int)(45 * Math.sin(minuteAngle)));
    }

    public void setTime(int h, int m)
    {   minutes = h * 60 + m;
        repaint();
    }

    public void tick()
    {   minutes++;
        repaint();
    }

    private int minutes = 0;
}
```

`java.awt.Component`

- `void validate()`

  recomputes the size of a component or the size and layout of the components in a container.

`java.awt.TextField`

- `TextField(int cols)`

  constructs an empty `TextField` with a specified number of columns.

  Parameters: `cols` the number of columns in the field

- `TextField(String text, int cols)`

  constructs a new `TextField` with an initial string and the specified number of columns.

  Parameters: `text` the text to display

  `cols` the number of columns

- `setColumns(int cols)`

  tells the text field the number of columns it should use.

  Parameters: `cols` the number of columns

Input Validation

The problems mentioned in the last section are commonplace—if you have a place to enter information, you will need to check that the input makes sense before you work with it. In our example, we need to make sure that the user types in a number. That is, the user is allowed to enter only digits "0" ... "9" and a minus sign "–". The minus sign, if present at all, must be the *first* symbol of the input string. In this section, we will develop a class `IntTextBox` that extends the `TextBox` class and enforces these rules. (As soon as you see more about text areas, you can modify the code we give for text fields to apply to them quite easily.)

First, let us reject all keystrokes that cannot occur in a number; we want to accept only 0...9 and –. To do this:

- We make the `IntTextBox` listen to key events.
- When the key the user entered is not one of the legal keystrokes, we *consume* the key event.

Since our code will consume illegal keystrokes, they are never passed on to the underlying native widget that underpins the text field. This means that they will not appear in the text box, so the user will never see them.

Here is some code that can consume unwanted keystrokes.

```
public IntTextField(int defval, int size)
{  super("" + defval, size);
   addKeyListener(new KeyAdapter()
      {  public void keyTyped(KeyEvent evt)
         {  char ch = evt.getKeyChar();
            if (!('0' <= ch && ch <= '9'
               || ch == '-'
               || Character.isISOControl(ch)))
                 evt.consume();
         }
      });
}
```

This code does the following:

1. It installs a key listener.
2. The key listener implements only one method, `keyTyped`. The other methods use the defaults inherited from `KeyAdapter`. (Note that we implement the `keyAdaptor` class as an anonymous inner class.)
3. In the `keyTyped` method, we check if the character is a digit or minus sign.

4. We also allow control characters such as backspace or tab. We test this with the `Character.isISOControl` method.
5. We then consume the event.

VB NOTE: Although quite a bit more complicated than the equivalent of setting `KeyAscii` to 0 in a key event procedure, the preceding code *is* the equivalent in Java to this common task. This means you will need to use similar code when porting your VB code over to Java.

Now that we have filtered out all unwanted keystrokes, there is a second class of errors that we need to worry about—illegal combinations of legal keystrokes. In our situation, there is no restriction on the digits, but there is a restriction on the minus sign. There can be at most one, and it must be the first character of the input string. For example, the input string `-34` is legal, but `3-4` is not. (To make the code simpler, we also do not allow `--3`.) We cannot eliminate these faulty inputs by character filtering. Instead:

- We wait for the input to occur.
- Then, we analyze the changed text to see if it is acceptable.
- If it is not a legal input, then we restore the previous input.

We are almost done, but the obvious cure of simply restoring the previous input has one subtle problem associated with it: Restoring the prior input also resets the position of the caret (the vertical bar that denotes the insertion position). To fix this:

- We also save the caret position before each keystroke and restore it to its original position.

See Example 9-3 for the code of the `IntTextField` class. Don't worry about the exception and the `try` block—we will get to that in Chapter 12. Example 9-4 shows how to put the `IntTextField` class to use. This program runs much better than the one in the preceding example. Since no illegal strings can be entered, there never are any exceptions.

Example 9-3: ValidationTest.java

```
import java.awt.*;
import java.awt.event.*;
import corejava.*;

public class ValidationTest extends CloseableFrame
   implements TextListener
{  public ValidationTest()
   {  Panel p = new Panel();
      hourField = new IntTextField(12, 3);
      p.add(hourField);
      hourField.addTextListener(this);

      minuteField = new IntTextField(0, 3);
      p.add(minuteField);
      minuteField.addTextListener(this);

      add(p, "South");
      clock = new ClockCanvas();
      add(clock, "Center");
   }

   public void textValueChanged(TextEvent evt)
   {  clock.setTime(hourField.getValue(),
         minuteField.getValue());
   }

   public static void main(String[] args)
   {  Frame f = new ValidationTest();
      f.show();
   }

   private IntTextField hourField;
   private IntTextField minuteField;
   private ClockCanvas clock;
}

class ClockCanvas extends Canvas
{  public void paint(Graphics g)
   {  g.drawOval(0, 0, 100, 100);
      double hourAngle
         = 2 * Math.PI * (minutes - 3 * 60) / (12 * 60);
      double minuteAngle = 2 * Math.PI * (minutes - 15) / 60;
      g.drawLine(50, 50,
         50 + (int)(30 * Math.cos(hourAngle)),
         50 + (int)(30 * Math.sin(hourAngle)));
      g.drawLine(50, 50,
```

```
        50 + (int)(45 * Math.cos(minuteAngle)),
        50 + (int)(45 * Math.sin(minuteAngle)));
   }

   public void setTime(int h, int m)
   {  minutes = h * 60 + m;
      repaint();
   }

   public void tick()
   {  minutes++;
      repaint();
   }

   private int minutes = 0;
}
```

Example 9-4: IntTextField.java

```
package corejava;

import java.awt.*;
import java.awt.event.*;

public class IntTextField extends TextField
   implements TextListener
{  /**
    * Creates the text field
    * @param defval an integer default,
    * @param size the size of the text field
    */
   public IntTextField(int defval, int size)
   {  super("" + defval, size);
      addTextListener(this);
      addKeyListener(new KeyAdapter()
         {  public void keyTyped(KeyEvent evt)
            {  char ch = evt.getKeyChar();
               if (!('0' <= ch && ch <= '9'
                     || ch == '-'
                     || Character.isISOControl(ch)))
                  evt.consume();
               else
                  lastCaretPosition = getCaretPosition();
            }
         });
      lastValue = "" + defval;
   }
```

```
    public void textValueChanged(TextEvent evt)
    {  checkValue();
    }

    private void checkValue()
    {  try
       {  Integer.parseInt(getText().trim() + "0");
          lastValue = getText();
       }
       catch(NumberFormatException e)
       {  setText(lastValue);
          setCaretPosition(lastCaretPosition);
       }
    }

    /**
    * Get the integer data value
    * @return the integer data value
    * @remark if invalid, returns the valid prefix (or 0 if none)
    * This only happens when the field is blank or contains just

    * a single -
    */

    public int getValue()
    {  checkValue();
       try
       {  return Integer.parseInt(getText().trim());
       }
       catch(NumberFormatException e)
       {  return 0;
       }
    }

    private String lastValue;
    private int lastCaretPosition;
}
```

NOTE: If the character the user enters is not one of the allowable ones, some user interface designs insist that the computer beep at the user in response to an illegal keypress. This is certainly not something that we would recommend, but you can do this in Java with the beep method of the `Toolkit` class:

```
Toolkit.getDefaultToolkit().beep();
```

`java.awt.TextComponent`

- `int getCaretPosition()`

  returns the position of the current insertion point (which is indicated by the insertion caret).

- `void setCaretPosition(int pos)`

  sets the insertion point (which is the position of the insertion caret).

Text Areas

Sometimes you need to collect user input that is more than one line long. As mentioned earlier, you use the `TextArea` component for this. When you place a text area component in your program, a user can enter any number of lines of text, using the ENTER key to separate them. Each line ends with a `\n` as far as Java is concerned. If you need to break up what the user enters into separate lines, you can use the `StringTokenizer` class (see Volume 2). Figure 9-5 shows a text area at work.

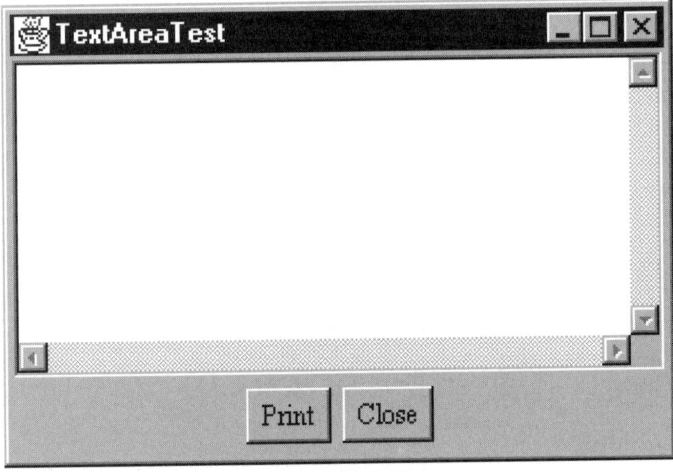

Figure 9-5: A text area

In the constructor for the `TextArea` component, you specify the number of rows and columns for the text area. For example:

```
Comments = new TextArea(8, 40); // 8 lines of 40 columns each
```

where the columns parameter works as before—and you still need to add a few more columns for safety's sake. Also, as before, the user is not restricted to the number of rows and columns; the text simply scrolls when the user inputs too much. You can also use the `setColumns` method to change the number of columns and the `setRows` method to change the number of rows. These numbers only indicate the preferred size—the layout manager can still grow or shrink the text area.

By default, the text area has both horizontal and vertical scroll bars. There is a constructor that lets you choose whether you want vertical or horizontal scroll bars. However, once you set them in the constructor, you cannot change your mind later. The scrolling is handled internally in the text area—your program does not receive scroll events.

Example 9-5 is the complete code for the text area demo. This program simply lets you edit text into a text area. Click on Print to print the contents of the frame. This program uses the `PrintGraphics` class that was introduced in Chapter 7. Only the text that is visible in the text area will be printed. (We also use the `printAll` method to print the frame contents. You'll see more on this method when we discuss printing of components in greater detail later in this chapter.)

Example 9-5: TextAreaText.java

```
import java.awt.*;
import java.awt.event.*;
import corejava.*;

public class TextAreaTest extends CloseableFrame
   implements ActionListener
{  public TextAreaTest()
   {  Panel p = new Panel();

      printButton = new Button("Print");
      p.add(printButton);
      printButton.addActionListener(this);

      add(p, "South");
      ta = new TextArea(8, 40);
      add(ta, "Center");
   }

   public void actionPerformed(ActionEvent evt)
   {  PrintJob pjob = getToolkit().getPrintJob(this,
         getTitle(), null);

      if (pjob != null)
      {  Graphics pg = pjob.getGraphics();
         if (pg != null)
```

```
        {  printAll(pg);
           pg.dispose(); // flush page
         }
         pjob.end();
      }
   }

   public static void main(String[] args)
   {  Frame f = new TextAreaTest();
      f.show();
   }

   private TextArea ta;
   private Button printButton;
}
```

java.awt.TextArea

- `TextArea(int rows, int cols)`

  constructs a new text area.

Parameters:	`rows`	the number of rows
	`cols`	the number of columns

- `TextArea(int rows, int cols, int scrollBarLook)`

  constructs a new text area with the specified kind of scrollbars.

Parameters:	`rows`	the number of rows
	`cols`	the number of columns

	`scrollBarLook`	one of the constants:
		`SCROLLBARS_BOTH`
		`SCROLLBARS_HORIZONTAL_ONLY`
		`SCROLLBARS_NONE`
		`SCROLLBARS_VERTICAL_ONLY`

- `TextArea(String text, int rows, int cols)`

  constructs a new text area with an initial text.

Parameters:	`text`	the initial text
	`rows`	the number of rows
	`cols`	the number of columns

- `void setColumns(int cols)`

  tells the text area the preferred number of columns it should use.

Parameters:	`cols`	the number of columns

- `void setRows(int rows)`

  tells the text area the preferred number of columns it should use.

  Parameters: `rows` the number of rows

Labels and Labeling Components

Labels are components that hold one line of plain text. They have no decorations (for example, no boundaries). They also do not react to user input. You can use a label to identify components. For example, unlike buttons, text components have no label to identify them. To label a component that does not itself come with an identifier:

- Construct a `Label` component with the correct text.
- Place it close enough to the component you want to identify so that the user can see that the label identifies the correct component.

The constructor for a `Label` lets you specify the initial text (and also the alignment of the text.) The `setText` method lets you set the text of the label at run time. Labels can be positioned inside a container like any other component. This means you can use the techniques you have seen before to place labels where you need them. For example, if you look at the Figure 9-6, which comes from the search and replace program from the next section, you can see how one of the text fields is preceded by a label with the text "with."

Figure 9-6: Testing text editing

`java.awt.Label`

- `Label(String s)`

  constructs a label with left-aligned text.

Parameters:	`s`	the text in the label

- `public Label(String s, int align)`

Parameters:	`s`	the text in the label
	`align`	one of `LEFT`, `CENTER`, or `RIGHT`

- `void setText(String label)`

Parameters:	`label`	the text in the label

Selecting Text

The text field and text area classes inherit methods to select (highlight) the text contained in the component. They can also check which text is currently selected.

First, there is the `selectAll()` method, which highlights all the text in the field. You would use this method when presenting users with an input that they either will want to use exactly as provided or that they won't want to use at all. In the latter case, they can just type their own input, and the first keystroke replaces the selection.

The `select` method selects a part of the text. The arguments of `select` are the same as for `substring`: the first index is the start of the substring; the last is one more than the end. For example, `t.select(10, 15)` selects the tenth to fourteenth characters in the text control. End-of-line markers count as one character.

The `getSelectionStart` and `getSelectionEnd` methods return the current selection, and `getSelectedText` returns the highlighted text. How users highlight text is system dependent. In Windows, you can use the mouse or the standard SHIFT + arrow keys.

`java.awt.TextComponent`

- `void selectAll()`

  selects all text in the component.

- `void select(int selStart,int selEnd)`

  selects a range of text in the component.

Parameters:	`selStart`	the first position to select
	`selEnd`	one past the last position to select

- `int getSelectionStart()`

  returns the first position of the selected text.

- `int getSelectionEnd()`

  returns one past the last position of the selected text.

- `String getSelectedText()`

  returns the selected text.

Text Editing

You can write code that modifies the contents of a text area (but not a text field). You can append text at the end, insert text in the middle, and replace text. To delete text, simply replace the text to be deleted with an empty string. Example 9-6 shows how to implement a simple find-and-replace feature. In the program illustrated in Figure 9-6, each time you click on the Replace button, the first match of the text in the first field is replaced by the text in the second field. This is not a very realistic application, but you could use this feature to correct spelling or typing errors in URLs.

Example 9-6: TextEditText.java

```
import java.awt.*;
import java.awt.event.*;
import corejava.*;

public class TextEditTest extends CloseableFrame
{  public TextEditTest()
   {  Panel p = new Panel();

      Button replaceButton = new Button("Replace");
      p.add(replaceButton);
      replaceButton.addActionListener(new ActionListener()
         {  public void actionPerformed(ActionEvent evt)
            {  String f = from.getText();
               int n = ta.getText().indexOf(f);
               if (n >= 0 && f.length() > 0)
                  ta.replaceRange(to.getText(), n,
                     n + f.length());
            }
         });

      from = new TextField(8);
      p.add(from);

      p.add(new Label("with"));
```

```
        to = new TextField(8);
        p.add(to);

        add(p, "South");
        ta = new TextArea(8, 40);
        add(ta, "Center");
    }

    public static void main(String[] args)
    {   Frame f = new TextEditTest();
        f.show();
    }

    private TextArea ta;
    private TextField from, to;
}
```

One point worth noting is the use in the above code of the statement

```
p.add(new Label("with"));
```

This statement uses the controlling flow layout manager to position the label.

API

`java.awt.TextArea`

- `void insert(String str, int pos)`

  inserts a string into the text area.

Parameters:	`str`	the text to insert
	`pos`	the position at which to insert (0 = first position. Newlines count as one character)

- `void append(String str)`

  appends the given text to the end of the text already in the text area.

Parameters:	`str`	the text to insert

- `void replaceRange(String str, int start, int end)`

  replaces a range of text with another string.

Parameters:	`str`	the new text
	`start`	the start position of the text to be replaced
	`end`	one past the end position of the text to be replaced

Making Choices

You now know how to collect text input from users, but there are many occasions where you would rather give users a finite set of choices, rather than have them enter the data in a text component. Using a set of check boxes tells your users what choices they have. (It also saves you from the trouble of error checking.) In this section, you will learn how to program both check boxes and what Java calls choice lists (which are a special type of list box).

Check Boxes

If you just want to collect a "yes" or "no" input, use a check box component. Check boxes automatically come with labels that identify them. The user usually checks the box by clicking inside it and turns off the check mark by clicking inside the box again. (Under Windows, the user can also press the space bar when the focus is at the box.) Figure 9-7 shows a simple program with two check boxes, one to turn on or off the "italic" attributes of a font and the other for boldface. Note that the first check box has focus, as indicated by the dotted rectangle around the label. Each time the user clicks one of the check boxes, we refresh the screen, using the new font attributes.

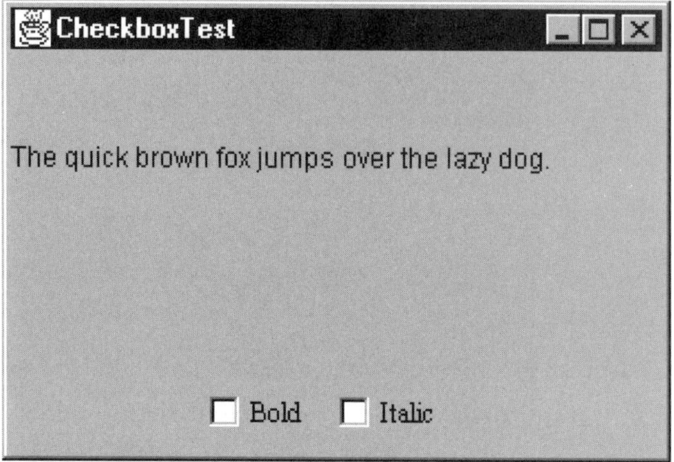

Figure 9-7: Check boxes

Check boxes need a label next to them to identify their purpose. You give the label text in the constructor. (The text will always appear to the right of the check box.) To factor out repetitive code in the constructor, we wrote a small helper procedure that makes the check box, adds it to the panel, and adds the listener.

```
public CheckboxTest()
{  Panel p = new Panel();
   bold = addCheckbox(p, "Bold");
   italic = addCheckbox(p, "Italic");
   add(p, "South");
   . . .
}

Checkbox addCheckbox(Panel p, String name)
{  Checkbox c = new Checkbox(name);
   c.addItemListener(this);
   p.add(c);
   return c;
}
```

When the user clicks on a check box, this action triggers an item event. We trap the event in the `itemStateChanged` method. The `getState` method then retrieves the current state of each check box. It is `false` if unchecked; `true` if checked.

Here is the event handler for the font application. When the state of either check box changes, the code retrieves the current states of both check boxes and then notifies the canvas of the new font attributes to use.

```
public void itemStateChanged(ItemEvent evt)
{  int m = (bold.getState() ? Font.BOLD : 0)
      + (italic.getState() ? Font.ITALIC : 0);
   fox.setFont(m);
}
```

Example 9-7 is the complete program listing for the check box example.

Example 9-7: CheckboxTest.java

```
import java.awt.*;
import java.awt.event.*;
import corejava.*;

public class CheckboxTest extends CloseableFrame
   implements ItemListener
{  public CheckboxTest()
   {  Panel p = new Panel();
      bold = addCheckbox(p, "Bold");
      italic = addCheckbox(p, "Italic");
      add(p, "South");
      fox = new FoxCanvas();
      add(fox, "Center");
   }

   public Checkbox addCheckbox(Panel p, String name)
   {  Checkbox c = new Checkbox(name);
```

```
        c.addItemListener(this);
        p.add(c);
        return c;
    }

    public void itemStateChanged(ItemEvent evt)
    {   int m = (bold.getState() ? Font.BOLD : 0)
            + (italic.getState() ? Font.ITALIC : 0);
        fox.setFont(m);
    }

    public static void main(String[] args)
    {   Frame f = new CheckboxTest();
        f.show();
    }

    private FoxCanvas fox;
    private Checkbox bold;
    private Checkbox italic;
}

class FoxCanvas extends Canvas
{   public FoxCanvas()
    { setFont(Font.PLAIN);
    }

    public void setFont(int m)
    {   setFont(new Font("SansSerif", m, 12));
        repaint();
    }

    public void paint(Graphics g)
    {   g.drawString
            ("The quick brown fox jumps over the lazy dog.", 0, 50);
    }
}
```

java.awt.Checkbox

- `Checkbox(String label)`

Parameters:	`label`	the label on the check box

- `Checkbox(String label, boolean state)`

Parameters:	`label`	the label on the check box
	`state`	the initial state of the check box

- `boolean getState()`

  returns the state of the check box.

- `void setState(boolean state)`

  sets the check box to a new state.

Item events

In the checkbox example, we completely ignored the item event in the `itemStateChanged` method. We simply checked the state of all check boxes to find out how to redraw the canvas.

Often, you want to find out which check box was affected when handling an item event. You can use the `getItem` method to obtain the label of the check box whose state has changed. However, the return value of `getItem` is `Object`, not `String`, so you must use a cast to recover a string object.

```
String label = (String)evt.getItem();
```

Actually, item events can also be generated by check boxes, list and choice components, and by checkbox menu items. For these user interface elements, the value returned by `getItem` is always a string. Presumably, the designers of the AWT anticipated future components that generate item events where the changed item has a different type.

If you are interested in the actual check box whose state was changed, use the `getSource` method of the `ItemEvent` class. Of course, you must then cast the return value to the correct type.

```
if (evt.getSource() instanceof Checkbox)
{   Checkbox source = (Checkbox)evt.getSource();
    . . .
}
```

There is another way that occasionally is more useful. If you use the `getItemSelectable` method of the `ItemEvent` class, you get a reference to the source object *after it has* been cast to an object of `ItemSelectable` type. `ItemSelectable` is an interface that is implemented by `Checkbox`, `CheckboxMenuItem`, `Choice`, and `List`, the four classes that generate item events. It has one useful method, `getSelectedObjects`. That method returns an array of the currently selected objects, or `null` if no objects are selected.

```
Object[] items = evt.getItemSelectable().getSelectedObjects();
if (items != null)
    for (int i = 0; i < items.length; i++)
        do something with (String)items[i];
```

Of course, for a check box, the array returned by `getSelectedObjects` will hold only a single item. But if the event was generated by a list box that had multiple selections, then the array will hold *all* the currently selected strings.

java.awt.event.ItemEvent

- `Object getItem()`

  returns the item that has just been selected or deselected. In the case of a check box, the return value is the *string* labeling the check box.

- `ItemSelectable getItemSelectable()`

  returns the user interface component in which the user changed an item.

java.awt.ItemSelectable

- `Object[] getSelectedObjects()`

  returns an array of the currently selected items in the component that implements the `ItemSelectable` interface, or `null` if no items are currently selected.

Check Box Groups

In the previous example, the user could check either, both, or none of the two check boxes. In many cases, we want to require the user to check only one of several boxes. When another box is checked, the previous box is automatically unchecked. Such a group of boxes is often called a *radio button group* because the buttons work like the station selector buttons on a radio. When you push in one button, the previously depressed button pops out. Figure 9-8 shows a typical example. We allow the user to select a font size among the choices—Small, Medium, Large, and Extra large, but, of course, we will allow the user to select only one size at a time.

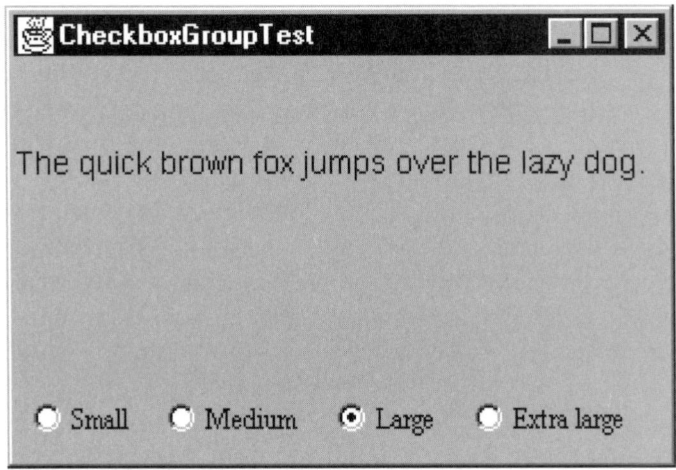

Figure 9-8: A check box group

Implementing radio button groups is easy in AWT. You construct one object of type `CheckboxGroup` for every group of buttons. The object has no data; it simply serves as the common identifier of the group. You pass the group object into the constructors of the individual buttons.

```
CheckboxGroup g = new CheckboxGroup();
small = new Checkbox("Small", g, false);
medium = new Checkbox("Medium", g, true);
large = new Checkbox("Large", g, false);
extraLarge = new Checkbox("Extra large", g, false);
```

The third argument of the constructor is `true` for the box that should be checked initially; `false` for all others.

If you look again at Figures 9-7 and 9-8, you will note that the appearance of the selection indicators is different. Individual check boxes without a group are square and use a check mark. Grouped check boxes are round and use a dot.

The event notification mechanism is simple for a checkbox group. When the user checks a box that is part of a group, Java generates an action event whose source is the checked box. You override `itemStateChanged` to test for these events. (Note that two events are generated, one for the unchecked box and one for the checked box.) You can distinguish between the two by the `getStateChange` method. This method returns `ItemEvent.SELECTED` or `ItemEvent.DESELECTED`. We pay attention to only the events that select an item.

```
public void itemStateChanged(ItemEvent evt)
{  if (evt.getStateChange() == ItemEvent.DESELECTED)
      return;
   if (evt.getItem().equals("Small"))
      fox.setSize(8);
   else if (evt.getItem().equals("Medium"))
      fox.setSize(12);
   else if (evt.getItem().equals("Large"))
      fox.setSize(14);
   else if (evt.getItem().equals("Extra large"))
      fox.setSize(18);
}
```

Example 9-8 is the complete program.

Example 9-8: CheckboxGroupTest.java

```
import java.awt.*;
import java.awt.event.*;
import corejava.*;

public class CheckboxGroupTest extends CloseableFrame
   implements ItemListener
```

```
{  public CheckboxGroupTest()
   {  Panel p = new Panel();
      p.setLayout(new FlowLayout());
      CheckboxGroup g = new CheckboxGroup();
      addCheckbox(p, "Small", g, false);
      addCheckbox(p, "Medium", g, true);
      addCheckbox(p, "Large", g, false);
      addCheckbox(p, "Extra large", g, false);
      add(p, "South");
      fox = new FoxCanvas();
      add(fox, "Center");
   }

   public void addCheckbox(Panel p, String name,
      CheckboxGroup g, boolean v)
   {  Checkbox c = new Checkbox(name, g, v);
      c.addItemListener(this);
      p.add(c);
   }

   public void itemStateChanged(ItemEvent evt)
   {  if (evt.getStateChange() == ItemEvent.DESELECTED)
         return;
      if (evt.getItem().equals("Small"))
         fox.setSize(8);
      else if (evt.getItem().equals("Medium"))
         fox.setSize(12);
      else if (evt.getItem().equals("Large"))
         fox.setSize(14);
      else if (evt.getItem().equals("Extra large"))
         fox.setSize(18);
   }

   public static void main(String[] args)
   {  Frame f = new CheckboxGroupTest();
      f.setSize(400, 200);
      f.show();
   }

   private FoxCanvas fox;
}

class FoxCanvas extends Canvas
{  public FoxCanvas()
   {  setSize(12);
   }

   public void setSize(int p)
```

```
    {   setFont(new Font("SansSerif", Font.PLAIN, p));
        repaint();
    }

    public void paint(Graphics g)
    {   g.drawString
            ("The quick brown fox jumps over the lazy dog.", 0, 50);
    }
}
```

`java.awt.Checkbox`

- `Checkbox(String label, CheckboxGroup group, boolean state)`

Parameters:	`label`	the label on the check box
	`group`	the checkbox group to which this check box belongs
	`state`	the initial state of the check box

`java.awt.CheckboxGroup`

- `setSelectedCheckbox(Checkbox cb)`

  sets the specified check box to be the current choice.

Parameters:	`cb`	the check box to use

`java.awt.event.ItemEvent`

- `int getStateChange()`

  returns `ItemEvent.SELECTED` or `ItemEvent.DESELECTED`.

Choice Boxes (Drop-Down Lists)

If you have more than a handful of alternatives, radio buttons are not a good choice because they take up too much screen space. Instead, you can use a choice box which is a drop-down list box. When the user clicks on the field, a list of choices drops down, and the user can then select one of them (see Figure 9-9).

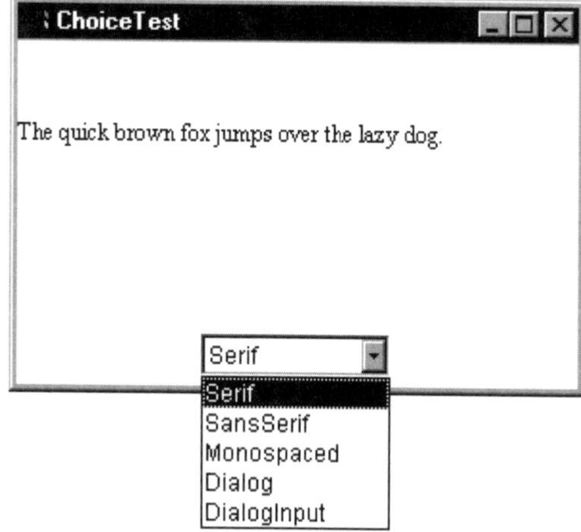

Figure 9-9: A choice box

The `Choice` class implements these lists. In the example program, the user can choose a font style from a list of styles (Serif, SansSerif, Monospaced, etc.). You add the choice items with the `add` method. In our program, `add` is called only in the constructor, but you can call it any time.

```
style = new Choice();
style.add("Serif");
style.add("SansSerif");
. . .
```

This method adds the string at the end of the list. You can add new items anywhere in the list with the `insert` method:

```
style.insert("Monospaced", 0); // add at the beginning
```

If you need to remove items at run time, you have two versions of the `remove` method. You can supply the item to be removed or its position.

```
style.remove("Monospaced");
style.remove(0); // remove first item
```

There is also a `removeAll` method whose name says it all.

When the user selects an item from a choice box, Java generates two item events, one for the deselected item and one for the selected item. As in the previous example, we change only the font that has been selected, and so we ignore deselected items.

```
public void itemStateChanged(ItemEvent evt)
{  if (evt.getStateChange() == ItemEvent.SELECTED)
      fox.setStyle((String)evt.getItem());
}
```

NOTE: The AWT has no "combo box" control. (A combo box is a combination of a text box and a choice list, in which you can pick one of the choices or type in another input.)

`java.awt.Choice`

- `void add(String item)`

  adds an item to this choice component.

Parameters:	`item`	the item to add

- `void insert(String item, int index)`

  inserts the item at the specified position.

Parameters:	`item`	the item to add
	`index`	the position to add (0 is the beginning)

- `void remove(String item)`

  removes the first instance of the item identified by the string.

Parameters:	`item`	the item to remove

- `void remove(int index)`

  removes the item at the specified position.

Parameters:	`index`	the position of the item to remove (0 is the beginning)

- `void removeAll()`

  removes all the items in the choice box.

The `List` Component

The `List` component is similar to the `Choice` component except that the user will always see the items. `List` components take up more screen space but also make it obvious to the user what can be chosen from a list. One other difference is that for a `List` component, but not a `Choice` component, you can allow the user to make multiple selections. If you permit multiple selection for a list box, the user can select any combination of the strings in the box.

Figure 9-10 shows an admittedly silly example. The user can select the attributes for the fox, such as "quick,", "brown," "hungry," "wild," and, because we ran out of attributes, "static,","private," and "final." You can, thus, have the *static, final* fox jump over the lazy dog.

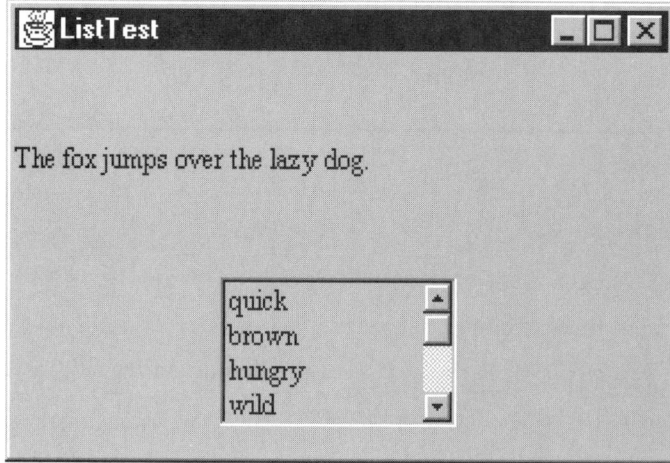

Figure 9-10: A list box

Here is a more realistic application: you are going to design an order-taking system; you will use a list box to give users a choice of items to order. Why a list box rather than a choice box? Well, your employer hopes that customers will order most or all of the items, so you want to make it easy for them to select more than one.

NOTE: List boxes permit the user to select only contiguous items ("simple" multiselection to VB Users). For example, at the present time in Java, you cannot select the first, third, and fifth items in a list.

The most general constructor of a `List` class has

- A parameter that takes the number of rows you want to display at one time
- A flag to indicate whether or not you want to allow multiple selection

If you add more items than the number of available rows, the items scroll. Also note that the number of rows gives only the preferred size—the layout manager could override your settings if it needs to grow or shrink the list box.

You initialize a list box just as you would a choice component (drop-down list): use the `add` method. To activate an initial set of selections, use the `select` method which starts the count at 0.

```
words = new List(4, true); //4 items, allow multiple selections
words.add("quick");
words.add("brown");
```

```
   . . .
   words.add("final");
   words.select(0);
   words.select(1);
```

The method that Java uses to notify a list box of relevant events is not quite as easy as that for the other components. Java triggers an action event *only* when the user double-clicks on an item in the list box. The problem is that this is not very intuitive for most users. Instead, the most user-friendly solution is to track all changes in what the user is selecting (and possibly whether the user presses the ENTER key as well.) Every time the user selects or deselects an item, Java generates an item event. These events can be trapped in the `itemStateChanged` function. (Key events, as usual, can be trapped in the `keyUp`, `keyDown` pair.)

Once you are notified that an event has happened, you will want to find out what items are currently selected. This is phenomenally convenient in Java. The `getSelectedItems` method returns an *array of strings* containing all selected items. (If you have ever done this in C, you probably suffered through a lookup loop, a callback procedure, a memory allocation headache, or all of the above.)

VB NOTE: `getSelectedItems` works the same as the `List` property does in VB.

Here is the event handler for our toy program.

```
public void itemStateChanged(ItemEvent evt)
{  fox.setAttributes(words.getSelectedItems());
}
```

In the item event handler of the choice box in the preceding example, we ignored the `DESELECTED` events because we knew that they would immediately be followed by a `SELECTED` event. In a list box that permits multiple choices, you must process all events.

Example 9-9 is the program listing. Notice how the `setAttributes` function builds up the message string from the selected items.

Example 9-9: ListTest.java

```
import java.awt.*;
import java.awt.event.*;
import corejava.*;

public class ListTest extends CloseableFrame
   implements ItemListener
{  public ListTest()
   {  words = new List(4, true);
      words.add("quick");
```

```
        words.add("brown");
        words.add("hungry");
        words.add("wild");
        words.add("silent");
        words.add("huge");
        words.add("private");
        words.add("abstract");
        words.add("static");
        words.add("final");

        Panel p = new Panel();
        p.add(words);
        words.addItemListener(this);

        add(p, "South");
        fox = new FoxCanvas();
        add(fox, "Center");
    }

    public void itemStateChanged(ItemEvent evt)
    {   fox.setAttributes(words.getSelectedItems());
    }

    public static void main(String[] args)
    {   Frame f = new ListTest();
        f.show();
    }

    private FoxCanvas fox;
    private List words;
}

class FoxCanvas extends Canvas
{   public FoxCanvas()
    {   setAttributes(new String[0]);
    }

    public void setAttributes(String[] w)
    {   text = "The ";
        for (int i = 0; i < w.length; i++)
            text += w[i] + " ";
        text += "fox jumps over the lazy dog.";
        repaint();
    }

    public void paint(Graphics g)
    {   g.drawString(text, 0, 50);
    }

    private String text;
}
```

`java.awt.List`

API

- `List(int rows, boolean multipleSelections)`

  Parameters: `rows` — the number of items to show

  `multipleSelections` — `true` when multiple selections are allowed

- `void add(String item)`

  adds an item to the list box.

  Parameters: `item` — the item to add

- `void add(String item, int index)`

  inserts the item at the specified position (0 is the beginning).

  Parameters: `item` — the item to add

  `int` — the position to add (0 is the beginning)

- `String getItem(int index)`

  gets an item from a list component.

  Parameters: `index` — the position of the item to get

- `void select(int index)`

  selects an item in a list component.

  Parameters: `index` — the position of the item to select

- `String[] getSelectedItems()`

  returns an array containing all selected items.

- `void remove(int index)`

  removes the item at the specified position.

  Parameters: `int` — the position of the item to remove (0 is the beginning)

- `void removeAll()`

  removes all the items in the list box.

- `void makeVisible(int index)`

  forces the item at a specified index to be visible.

  Parameters: `int` — the position of the item to show

Scroll Bars

The two most common uses for scroll bars in a Java application are as follows:

- Using a scroll bar in a control as a slider.
- Placing scroll bars at the right and at the bottom of a window to scroll through its contents. (Actually, the `ScrollPane` class described below is often a more convenient choice for this.)

We will look briefly at both of these uses in this section.

A scroll bar has several important properties:

- *Direction* (`HORIZONTAL` or `VERTICAL`). It is set in the constructor and cannot be changed again.
- *Value*. This is the value corresponding to the current slider position. You can query it with the `getValue` method and set it with the `setValue` method.
- *Range*. The default range is 0–100. You can change it with the `setMinimum` and `setMaximum` methods.
- *Visible area*. If you use scroll bars to scroll through a large region, then the range is the size of the region, and the visible area is the size of the scroll window. A positive visible area value limits scrolling so that the *end* of the scroll window scrolls up to the *end* of the region that is being viewed. It also adjusts the thickness of the slider to reflect the ratio between the visible area and the scroll range. (See Figure 9-11.) If you just use a scroll bar as a slider control to specify a number, set the visible area to zero. You can set this value with the `setVisibleAmount` method.

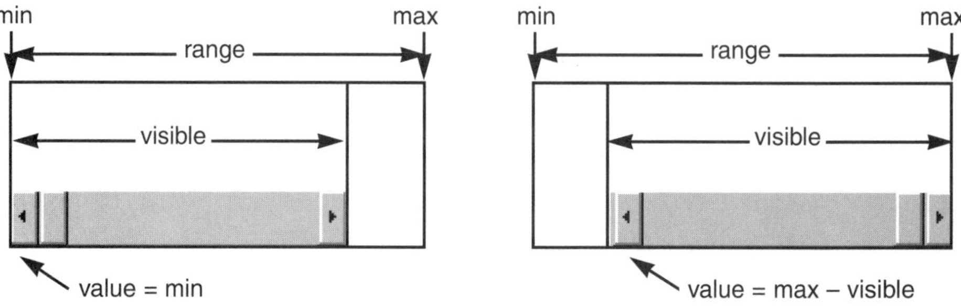

Figure 9-11: The visible area of a scroll bar

- *Unit increment.* When the user clicks on the arrow on either end of the scroll bar, the scroll bar value is changed by this amount. The default is 1. You can change it with the `setUnitIncrement` method.
- *Block increment.* When the user clicks on the area between the arrow and the slider, the value is changed by this amount. The default is 10. You can change it with the `setBlockIncrement` method.

You create a scroll bar by specifying its direction (`HORIZONTAL` or `VERTICAL`) in the constructor. You can set the current value, visible amount, and range simultaneously with the `setValues` method. Instead of using the `setValues` method, you can also use a version of the constructor for the scroll bar class that can accept the initial value, visible amount, and range.

In our first example, we use scroll bars to pick red, green, and blue values to mix and display a color value. (See Figure 9-12.) Here are two ways to initialize a scroll bar.

```
red = new Scrollbar(Scrollbar.HORIZONTAL);
red.setValues(0, 0, 0, 255);
```

or

```
red = new Scrollbar(Scrollbar.HORIZONTAL, 0, 0, 0, 255);
```

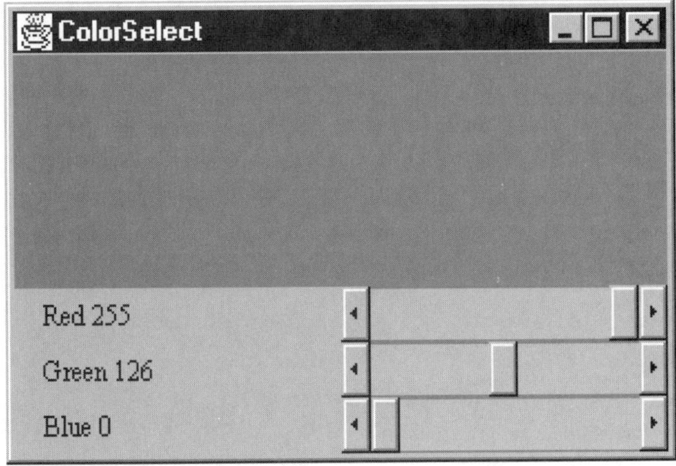

Figure 9-12: Scroll bars at work

When the user clicks on a scroll bar or moves the scroll bar slider to a new position, the scroll bar sends adjustment events to the listener object. Five types of adjustment events are generated by scroll bars—see Table 9-1.

Table 9-1: Adjustment Event Cause

UNIT_INCREMENT UNIT_DECREMENT	Generated when the user clicks on an arrow at either scroll bar end
BLOCK_INCREMENT BLOCK_DECREMENT	Generated when the user clicks between an arrow and the slider
TRACK	Generated when the user drags the slider

If `evt` is an adjustment event, then `evt.getAdjustmentType` returns one of these values.

When processing a scroll bar event, use the `getValue()` method to obtain the current position of the scroll bar. As an example of this, here is the event handler for the color mixer application.

```
public void adjustmentValueChanged(AdjustmentEvent evt)
{  redLabel.setText("Red " + red.getValue());
   greenLabel.setText("Green " + green.getValue());
   blueLabel.setText("Blue " + blue.getValue());
   c.setBackground(new Color(red.getValue(),
      green.getValue(), blue.getValue()));

   c.repaint();
}
```

Example 9-10 is the complete source code for the color selection application.

Example 9-10: ColorSelect.java

```
import java.awt.*;
import java.awt.event.*;
import corejava.*;

public class ColorSelect extends CloseableFrame
   implements AdjustmentListener
{  public ColorSelect()
   {  Panel p = new Panel();
      p.setLayout(new GridLayout(3, 2));

      p.add(redLabel = new Label("Red 0"));
      p.add(red = new Scrollbar(Scrollbar.HORIZONTAL, 0, 0,
         0, 255));
      red.setBlockIncrement(16);
      red.addAdjustmentListener(this);

      p.add(greenLabel = new Label("Green 0"));
      p.add(green = new Scrollbar(Scrollbar.HORIZONTAL, 0,
         0, 0, 255));
```

```
      green.setBlockIncrement(16);
      green.addAdjustmentListener(this);

      p.add(blueLabel = new Label("Blue 0"));
      p.add(blue = new Scrollbar(Scrollbar.HORIZONTAL, 0, 0,
         0, 255));
      blue.setBlockIncrement(16);
      blue.addAdjustmentListener(this);


      add(p, "South");

      c = new Canvas();
      c.setBackground(new Color(0, 0, 0));
      add(c, "Center");
   }

   public void adjustmentValueChanged(AdjustmentEvent evt)
   {  redLabel.setText("Red " + red.getValue());
      greenLabel.setText("Green " + green.getValue());
      blueLabel.setText("Blue " + blue.getValue());
      c.setBackground(new Color(red.getValue(),
         green.getValue(), blue.getValue()));

      c.repaint();
   }

   public static void main(String[] args)
   {  Frame f = new ColorSelect();
      f.show();
   }

   private Label redLabel;
   private Label greenLabel;
   private Label blueLabel;

   private Scrollbar red;
   private Scrollbar green;
   private Scrollbar blue;

   private Canvas c;
}
```

`java.awt.Scrollbar`

- `Scrollbar(int orientation)`

  Parameters: `orientation` either `HORIZONTAL` or `VERTICAL`

- `Scrollbar(int orientation, int value, int visible, int minimum, int maximum`

Parameters:	`orientation`	either `HORIZONTAL` or `VERTICAL`
	`value`	the scroll position
	`visible`	the visible area of the window, or 0 for a slider control
	`minimum`	the minimum position value of the scroll bar
	`maximum`	the maximum position value of the scroll bar

- `void setValue(int value)`

Parameters:	`value`	the new scroll position; set to the current minimum or maximum if it is outside the scroll range

- `void setValues(int value, int visible, int minimum, int maximum)`

Parameters:	`value`	the scroll position
	`visible`	the visible area of the window, or 0 for a slider control
	`minimum`	the minimum position value of the scroll bar
	`maximum`	the maximum position value of the scroll bar

- `void setMinimum(int value)`

Parameters:	`value`	the new minimum value

- `void setMaximum(int value)`

Parameters:	`value`	the new maximum value

- `void setVisibleAmount(int value)`

Parameters:	`value`	the new value for the visible setting

- `void setBlockIncrement(int l)`

  sets the block increment, the amount by which the scroll position changes when the user clicks between the arrows and the slider.

- `void setUnitIncrement(int l)`

  sets the unit increment, the amount by which the scroll position changes when the user clicks on the arrows at the ends of the scroll bar.

- `int getValue()`

  returns the current scroll position.

Scrolling a Window

In this section, we add scroll bars to the drawing application from the section on mouse events in the previous chapter. Suppose we want to allow an area of 600 by 400 pixels to be filled with squares. Our window has an area of only 200 by 200 pixels, so we want the user to be able to scroll over the total area. The basic idea is simple. Whenever we draw the window, we translate the graphics coordinates by the negatives of the scroll values. For example, if the values of the horizontal and vertical scroll bars are 200 and 100, then we want to draw the area starting at (200, 100). We move the origin to (–200, –100) and repaint the entire 600-by-400-pixel image. Much of the image is clipped, but the part of the underlying image that we want to see is then shown in the window (see Figure 9-13).

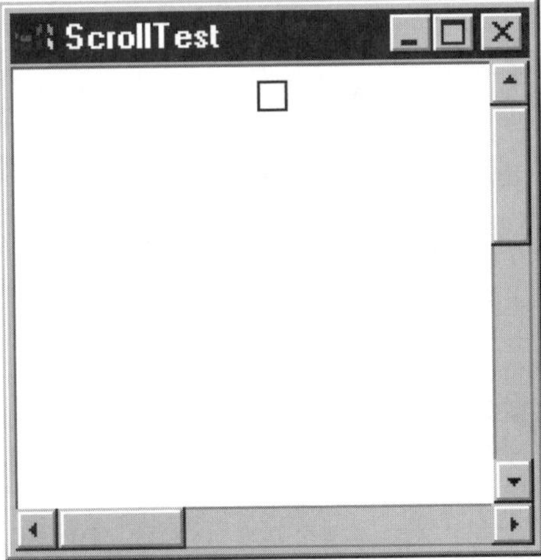

Figure 9-13: A scroll bar test program

Thus, what we need to do is:

- Trap all scroll events.
- Force a redraw of the canvas when an event occurs.

Here's an example of the code to do this:

```
public void adjustmentValueChanged(AdjustmentEvent evt)
{  canvas.translate(horiz.getValue(), vert.getValue());
}
```

The `translate` method of our `canvas` class stores the scroll offset in the fields `dx` and `dy`, then calls `repaint`.

```
public void translate(int x, int y)
  {  dx = x;
     dy = y;
     repaint();
  }
```

The data structure that stores the list of rectangles keeps them in *absolute coordinates,* that is, with x-values ranging from 0 to 600 and y-values ranging from 0 to 400. That is not a problem in the `paint` procedure because we can translate the origin of the graphics context. Rectangles that don't currently fit in the window are clipped and do not get drawn.

```
public void paint(Graphics g)
{  g.translate(-dx, -dy);
   for (int i = 0; i < nsquares; i++) draw(g, i);
}
```

The mouse functions report the mouse locations in *window coordinates.* To test that a mouse click falls inside a square, we must add the scroll offset to all mouse coordinates.

```
public void mouseClicked(MouseEvent evt)
{  int x = evt.getX() + dx;
   int y = evt.getY() + dy;
   current = find(x, y);
   . . .
}
```

When the window is first shown and when it is resized, we have to compute the "visible" values of the scroll bar. Since we measure the coordinates in pixels, the visible amount is the size of the canvas. For example, suppose the current canvas size is 180 by 180 pixels. (The visible area of the window is somewhat less than 200 by 200 because the scroll bars take some amount of space.) Now consider the x-range of the horizontal scroll bar. When it is all the way to the left, then the *left* margin of the canvas must show the absolute x-coordinate 0. When it is all the way to the right, then the *right* margin of the canvas must show the absolute x-coordinate 599, the maximum x-value that we want to show. The *left* margin of the canvas has then x-coordinate 599 – 180 = 419. That means the scroll range is not actually 0 ... 599, but only 0 ... 419. With the visible area set to 180, the scroll range is set correctly and the size of the slider is adjusted to reflect the proportion of the visible area to the total area.

Showing and resizing the window results in a component event. We trap the events and set the visible areas in x- and y-direction.

```
class ScrollTest
{  public ScrollTest()
   {  . . .
      addComponentListener(new ComponentAdapter()
      {  public void componentShown(ComponentEvent evt)
         {  setVisibleAmounts();
         }
         public void componentResized(ComponentEvent evt)
         {  setVisibleAmounts();
         }
      });
   }

   public void setVisibleAmounts()
   {  Dimension d = canvas.getSize();
      horiz.setVisibleAmount(d.width);
      vert.setVisibleAmount(d.height);
   }
   . . .
}
```

To demonstrate that the scroll bars *precisely* sweep out the 600 by 400 area, move them all the way to the right and the bottom. You will just see the red rectangle that delimits the total area. Then resize the window and move the scroll bars all the way to either side. Again, they sweep out precisely the whole area of the canvas. Example 9-11 is the listing of the program.

Example 9-11: ScrollTest.java

```
import java.awt.*;
import java.awt.event.*;
import corejava.*;

public class ScrollTest extends CloseableFrame
   implements AdjustmentListener
{  public ScrollTest()
   {  add(vert = new Scrollbar(Scrollbar.VERTICAL), "East");
      add(horiz = new Scrollbar(Scrollbar.HORIZONTAL),
         "South");
      add(canvas = new SquareCanvas(), "Center");
      vert.addAdjustmentListener(this);
      horiz.addAdjustmentListener(this);
      horiz.setValues(horiz.getValue(), 0, 0,
         SquareCanvas.MAX_XWIDTH);
      vert.setValues(vert.getValue(), 0, 0,
         SquareCanvas.MAX_YHEIGHT);
```

```
        addComponentListener(new ComponentAdapter()
        {   public void componentShown(ComponentEvent evt)
            {   setVisibleAmounts();
            }
            public void componentResized(ComponentEvent evt)
            {   setVisibleAmounts();
            }
        });
    }

    public void setVisibleAmounts()
    {   Dimension d = canvas.getSize();
        horiz.setVisibleAmount(d.width);
        vert.setVisibleAmount(d.height);
    }

    public void adjustmentValueChanged(AdjustmentEvent evt)
    {   canvas.translate(horiz.getValue(), vert.getValue());
    }

    public static void main(String args[])
    {   Frame f = new ScrollTest();
        f.setSize(200, 200);
        f.show();
    }

    private Scrollbar horiz;
    private Scrollbar vert;
    private SquareCanvas canvas;
}


class SquareCanvas extends Canvas
{   public SquareCanvas()
    {   addMouseListener(new MouseAdapter()
            {   public void mouseClicked(MouseEvent evt)
                {   int x = evt.getX() + dx;
                    int y = evt.getY() + dy;
                    current = find(x, y);
                    if (current < 0) // not inside a square
                    {   if (x < MAX_XWIDTH && y < MAX_YHEIGHT)
                            add(x, y);
                    }
                    else if (evt.getClickCount() >= 2)
                    {   remove(current);
                    }
                }
            });
    }
```

```
public void translate(int x, int y)
{  dx = x;
   dy = y;
   repaint();
}

public void paint(Graphics g)
{  g.translate(-dx, -dy);
   g.setColor(Color.red);
   g.drawRect(0, 0, MAX_XWIDTH - 1, MAX_YHEIGHT - 1);
   g.setColor(Color.black);
   for (int i = 0; i < nsquares; i++)
      draw(g, i);
}

public int find(int x, int y)
{  for (int i = 0; i < nsquares; i++)
      if (squares[i].x <= x
            && x <= squares[i].x + SQUARELENGTH
            && squares[i].y <= y
            && y <= squares[i].y + SQUARELENGTH)
         return i;
   return -1;
}

public void draw(Graphics g, int i)
{  g.drawRect(squares[i].x, squares[i].y, SQUARELENGTH,
   SQUARELENGTH);
}

public void add(int x, int y)
{  if (nsquares < MAXNSQUARES)
   {  squares[nsquares] = new Point(x, y);
      nsquares++;
      repaint();
   }
}

public void remove(int n)
{  nsquares--;
   squares[n] = squares[nsquares];
   if (current == n) current = -1;
   repaint();
}

private static final int SQUARELENGTH = 10;

private static final int MAXNSQUARES = 100;
```

```
    private Point[] squares = new Point[MAXNSQUARES];
    private int nsquares = 0;
    private int current = -1;
    private int dx = 0;
    private int dy = 0;

    public static final int MAX_XWIDTH = 600;
    public static final int MAX_YHEIGHT = 400;
}
```

Scroll Panes

Adding scroll bars to an area that is too small to be displayed in a window is an exceedingly common task. Doing this involves adding event handlers for the scroll bars that:

- Track the current scroll offset
- Take the scroll offset into account for mouse events and painting

As you saw in the preceding section, it is a pain to do this by hand. Evidently, the designers of the 1.1 version of the AWT agreed, and so they now supply a class, `ScrollPane`, that does this automatically. A scroll pane is a container that has a scroll bar to the right and the bottom. You simply add the component that you want to be managed by the scroll bars and tell the scroll pane the maximum dimensions of that component. (You can add only one component to a scroll pane. Of course, this could be a panel which could itself contain other components.)

Once you add the component to a scroll pane, you write the code for the component *as if it was displayed at its full size.* The scroll pane takes care of adjusting the coordinates in mouse events and in painting. You never need to worry about scroll offsets. This is clearly a great convenience. Here is what you need to do to take advantage of this new feature in Java.

First:

- Make an object of type `ScrollPane`.

You can specify whether you want the scroll bars to be displayed all the time or only when they are needed. The latter is the default, and it is the more useful setting. The scroll bars simply go away when the window is resized to show the full area of the component that the scroll pane manages. For example:

```
ScrollPane sp = new ScrollPane(); // draw scroll bars as needed
ScrollPane sp = new ScrollPane(ScrollPane.SCROLLBARS_ALWAYS);
```

(There is also a setting `SCROLLBARS_NEVER` that never shows the scroll bars; we are mystified why one would then want to use a scroll pane.)

Next:

- Add the component that you want the scroll pane to scroll. For example,

  `sp.add(new SquareCanvas());`

Then:

- Tell the scroll pane how large that component is. For example,

  `sp.setSize(SquareCanvas.MAX_XWIDTH, SquareCanvas.MAX_YHEIGHT);`

Next:

- Add the scroll pane to the frame. For example,

  `add(sp, "Center");`

Finally, there is one other step that seems essential with the current version of the AWT:

- Call the `pack` method of the `Window` class.

If you don't call `pack()`, the scroll bars will not appear until you resize the window. We don't know why that is necessary. You can't tell from the documentation: the `pack` method "packs the components of the window." The source code for `pack` is also less than illuminating. In our opinion, it should be the job of the framework to automatically do those tasks that the documentation can't explain.

Example 9-12 shows the scroll pane in action. Compare the code for the `SquareCanvas` with that of the preceding example. When the scroll pane is used, the `SquareCanvas` is never aware that it is being scrolled at all!

Example 9-12: ScrollPaneTest.java

```
import java.awt.*;
import java.awt.event.*;
import corejava.*;

public class ScrollPaneTest extends CloseableFrame
{  public ScrollPaneTest()
   {  ScrollPane sp = new ScrollPane();
      sp.add(new SquareCanvas());
      sp.setSize(SquareCanvas.MAX_XWIDTH,
         SquareCanvas.MAX_YHEIGHT);
      add(sp, "Center");
      pack();
   }
```

```
   public static void main(String args[])
   {  Frame f = new ScrollPaneTest();
      f.setSize(200, 200);
      f.show();
   }

   private Scrollbar horiz;
   private Scrollbar vert;
   private SquareCanvas canvas;
}


class SquareCanvas extends Canvas
{  public SquareCanvas()
   {  addMouseListener(new MouseAdapter()
         {  public void mouseClicked(MouseEvent evt)
            {  int x = evt.getX();
               int y = evt.getY();
               current = find(x, y);
               if (current < 0) // not inside a square
               {  if (x < MAX_XWIDTH && y < MAX_YHEIGHT)
                     add(x, y);
               }
               else if (evt.getClickCount() >= 2)
               {  remove(current);
               }
            }
         });
   }

   public void paint(Graphics g)
   {  g.setColor(Color.red);
      g.drawRect(0, 0, MAX_XWIDTH - 1, MAX_YHEIGHT - 1);
      g.setColor(Color.black);
      for (int i = 0; i < nsquares; i++)
         draw(g, i);
   }

   public int find(int x, int y)
   {  for (int i = 0; i < nsquares; i++)
         if (squares[i].x <= x
               && x <= squares[i].x + SQUARELENGTH
               && squares[i].y <= y
               && y <= squares[i].y + SQUARELENGTH)
            return i;
      return -1;
   }
```

```
    public void draw(Graphics g, int i)
    {  g.drawRect(squares[i].x, squares[i].y, SQUARELENGTH,
          SQUARELENGTH);
    }

    public void add(int x, int y)
    {  if (nsquares < MAXNSQUARES)
       {  squares[nsquares] = new Point(x, y);
          nsquares++;
          repaint();
       }
    }

    public void remove(int n)
    {  nsquares--;
       squares[n] = squares[nsquares];
       if (current == n) current = -1;
       repaint();
    }

    public static final int MAX_XWIDTH = 600;
    public static final int MAX_YHEIGHT = 400;

    private static final int SQUARELENGTH = 10;

    private static final int MAXNSQUARES = 100;
    private Point[] squares = new Point[MAXNSQUARES];
    private int nsquares = 0;
    private int current = -1;
}
```

`java.awt.ScrollPane`

- `ScrollPane()`

  creates a new scrollpane with scroll bars only when needed.

- `ScrollPane(int scrollbarType)`

  Parameter: `scrollbarType` one of `SCROLLBARS_ALWAYS`, `SCROLLBARS_AS_NEEDED`, or `SCROLLBARS_NEVER`

Sophisticated Layout Management

We have managed to lay out the user interface components of our sample applications so far by using only panels and canvases. For more complex tasks, this is not going to be enough. In this section, we will give you a detailed discussion of all the layout managers that AWT provides to organize components.

TIP: If none of the layout schemes fit your needs, break the surface of your window into separate panels and lay out each panel separately. Then, use another layout manager to organize the panels.

Using a sophisticated layout manager combined with the appropriate use of multiple panels will give you complete control over how your application will look.

As you know, in the AWT, *components* are laid out inside *containers.* Buttons, text fields, and other user interface elements are components and can be placed inside containers. Therefore, these classes extend the class `Component`. Containers such as panels can themselves be put inside other containers. Therefore, the class `Container` derives from `Component`. Figure 9-14 shows the inheritance hierarchy for `Component`.

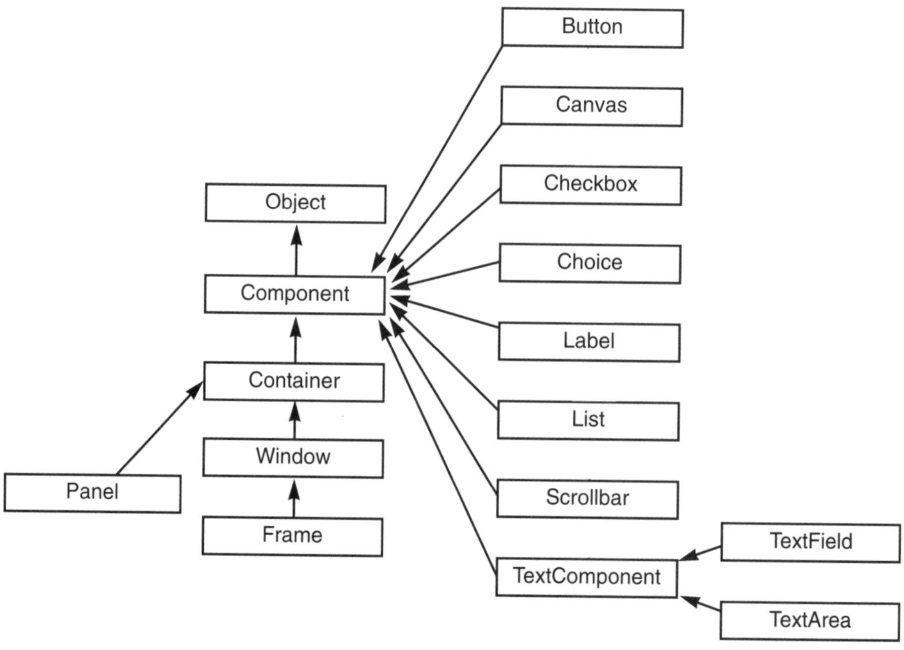

Figure 9-14: Inheritance hierarchy for the Component class and its subclasses

NOTE: Note that some objects belong to classes extending `Component` even though they are not user interface components and cannot be inserted into containers. Top-level windows such as `Frame` and `Applet` cannot be contained inside another window or panel.

As you have seen, to organize the components in a container, you first specify a layout manager. For example, the statement

```
panel.setLayout(new CardLayout());
```

will use the `CardLayout` class to lay out the panels. After you set the layout manager, you add components to the container. The details of doing this depend on the specific layout manager, but in all cases the information will be obtained from the `add` method of the underlying panel. With the flow layout manager that you have already seen, you can insert the components in random order.

```
panel.add(new Button("Ok"), 4);
```

With the border layout manager, you give a string to indicate component placement.

```
panel.add(new TextField(), "South");
```

With the grid layout that you will see shortly, you need to add components sequentially.

```
panel.add(new Checkbox("italic"));
panel.add(new Checkbox("bold"));
```

Traversal Order

The order in which you add the components affects the *traversal order* (the tab index property for VB users). When a window is first displayed, the first component in it has the keyboard focus. Each time the user presses the TAB key, the next component gains focus. (Recall that a component that has the keyboard focus can be manipulated with the keyboard. For example, a button can be "clicked" with the space bar when it has focus.) Currently, the traversal order is fixed—it is the order in which the components were added to the container. Since most layout managers force you to add components in a particular order, you have limited control over the traversal order that the user experiences.

You can transfer the focus explicitly to a particular component, with the `requestFocus` method:

```
okButton.requestFocus();
```

Canvases do not automatically get keyboard focus. If you want to give keyboard focus to a canvas, for example, to allow drawing with the cursor keys, you must use the `requestFocus` method.

java.awt.Component

- `void requestFocus()`

  requests that this component have the input focus.

Flow Layouts Revisited

The simplest layout manager is the one you have already seen: the flow layout. Flow layouts are the default layout for a panel, and so we have used the flow layout for laying out panels in quite a few test programs in this chapter. The flow layout manager lines the components horizontally until there is no more room and then starts a new line of components.

You can choose how you want to arrange the components in each line. The default is to center them in the container. The other choices are to align them to the left or to the right of the container. To use one of these alignments, specify `LEFT` or `RIGHT` in the constructor of the `FlowLayout` object.

```
toolbar.setLayout(new FlowLayout(FlowLayout.LEFT));
```

When the user resizes the container, Java automatically reflows the components to fill the available space.

NOTE: Normally you just let the flow layout manager control the vertical and horizontal gaps between the components. You can, however, force a specific horizontal or vertical gap by using another version of the flow layout constructor. (See the API notes.)

java.awt.FlowLayout

- `FlowLayout(int align)`

  constructs a new `FlowLayout` with the specified alignment.

Parameters:	`align`	one of `LEFT`, `CENTER`, or `RIGHT`

- `FlowLayout(int align, int hgap, int vgap)`

  constructs a new `FlowLayout` with the specified alignment and the specified horizontal and vertical gaps between components.

Parameters:	`align`	one of `LEFT`, `CENTER`, or `RIGHT`
	`hgap`	the horizontal gap to use in pixels (negative values force an overlap)
	`vgap`	the vertical gap to use in pixels (negative values force an overlap)

Border Layout

As was mentioned earlier, the border layout divides the area to be laid out into five areas, called North, South, East, West, and Center (see Figure 9-15).

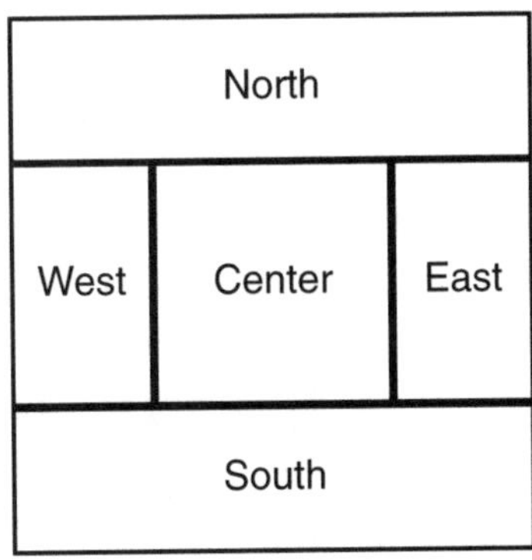

Figure 9-15: Border layouts

The borders are laid out first, and the remaining available space is occupied by the center. When the container is resized, the thickness of the borders is unchanged, but the center area changes its size. You add components by specifying a string that says in what area the object should be placed. You can specify `"North"`, `"South"`, `"East"`, `"West"`, or `"Center"`. (The strings are case sensitive.) Not all of the positions need to be occupied. Here's an example of using a border layout manager:

```
panel.add(new Scrollbar(),"East");
```

As with flow layouts, if you want to specify a gap between the regions, you can do so in the constructor for the `BorderLayout`. Border layout is the default for frames and other windows. You need not specify a layout manager for those containers if the default version of the border layout works for you.

It is not common to use all four border areas simultaneously. Figure 9-16 (whose code is given in Example 9-13) shows a typical case, with scroll bars to the right and bottom and a tool bar on the top. If you look closely, you will notice that the horizontal scroll bar extends below the vertical scroll bar. If you really want to achieve a more symmetrical and pleasant layout of the scroll bars, you should use the grid bag layout that you will see later on in this chapter.

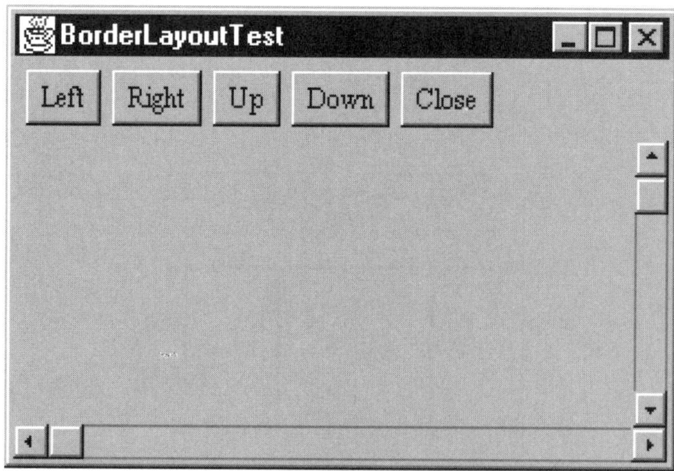

Figure 9-16: Border layout example

Example 9-13: BorderLayoutTest.java

```
import java.awt.*;
import corejava.*;

public class BorderLayoutTest extends CloseableFrame
{  public BorderLayoutTest()
   {  Panel p = new Panel();
      p.setLayout(new FlowLayout(FlowLayout.LEFT));
      p.add(new Button("Left"));
      p.add(new Button("Right"));
      p.add(new Button("Up"));
      p.add(new Button("Down"));
      p.add(new Button("Close"));
      add(p, "North");
      add(new Scrollbar(Scrollbar.VERTICAL), "East");
      add(new Scrollbar(Scrollbar.HORIZONTAL), "South");
   }

   public static void main(String[] args)
   {  Frame f = new BorderLayoutTest();
      f.show();
   }
}
```

`java.awt.BorderLayout`

- `BorderLayout(int hgap, int vgap)`

  constructs a new `BorderLayout` with the specified horizontal and vertical gaps between components.

Parameters:	`hgap`	the horizontal gap to use in pixels (negative values force an overlap)
	`vgap`	the vertical gap to use in pixels (negative values force an overlap)

Card Layout

Windows 95 uses tabbed dialog boxes when there is a lot of related information to set that can still be organized conveniently into panels. The reason is simple: if you need to gather a lot of information from the user, it is not a good idea to cram dozens of fields into one dialog box. As an example of this, consider the "tabbed dialog" in Netscape that organizes a multitude of configuration options (Figure 9-17).

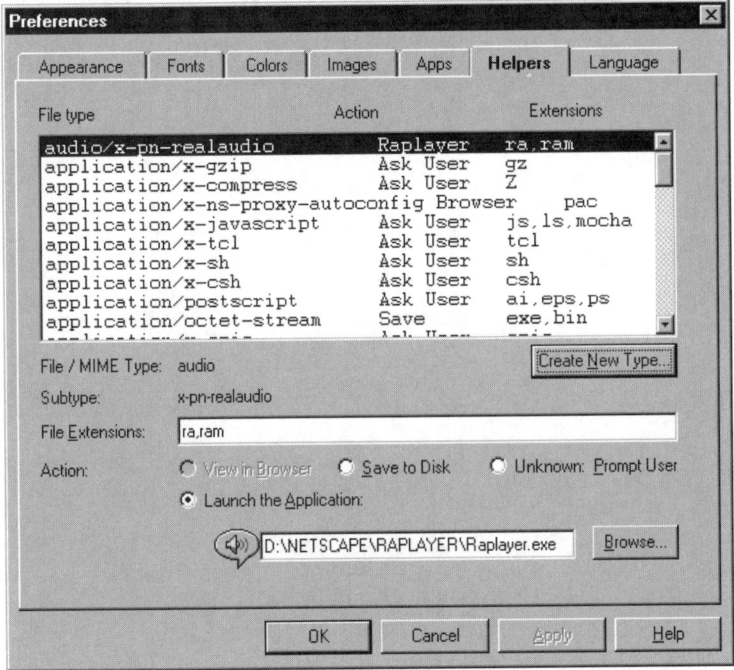

Figure 9-17: A tabbed dialog box

The settings are grouped onto individual "index cards," and you flip through them by clicking on one of the tabs.

Java does not yet have such an elegant-looking dialog layout, but the `CardLayout` manager provides the bare rudiments of this functionality. (It gives you only a bit more functionality than using multiple panels would give—although it is more convenient to use.) Unlike the other layouts, which place the objects to be laid out *next to each other,* the card layout places them *behind each other.*

The Figure 9-18 window consists of two areas. The top area is a panel containing a row of buttons that make the different cards show up in the top area. These are analogous to the "tabs" in the tabbed dialogs. For example, if you click on the Options button, the Options card will show up. Unlike tabbed dialog boxes, we also provided buttons to cycle through the cards and to go to the first and last card in the stack. That probably isn't terribly useful, and we only did it to show how it can be done. The second area holds cards managed by the `CardLayout` manager.

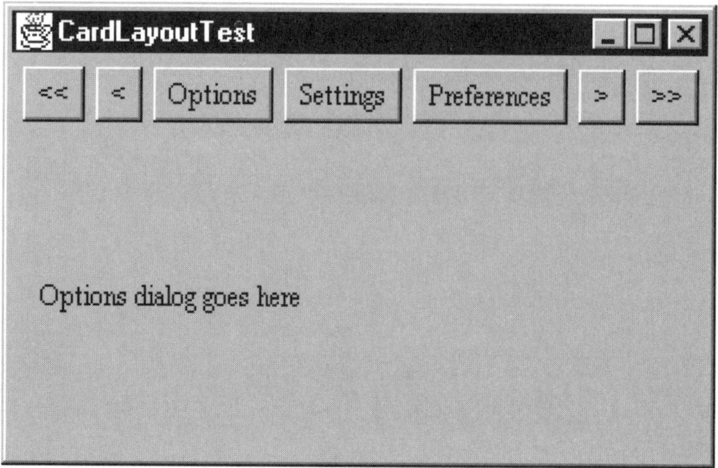

Figure 9-18: Card layout

Here is the procedure to set up a card layout.

1. Make a panel of buttons, one for each card.

```
tabs = new Panel(new FlowLayout());
tabs.add(new Button("Options"));
tabs.add(new Button("Settings"));
```

2. Below it, place another panel. This one will be managed by the `CardLayout` object.

```
cards = new Panel();
layout = new CardLayout();
cards.setLayout(layout);
```

3. Then, add the individual labels that identify the cards with the panel.

```
cards.add(new SimpleDialog("Options"), "Options");
cards.add(new SimpleDialog("Settings"), "Settings");
cards.add(new SimpleDialog("Preferences"), "Preferences");
```

Java internally keeps track of the fact that there are now three "cards," i.e., labels that are filling up the cards. You do not add three different panels when using a card layout manager; instead, you add individual cards via a call to `add`. In our case, the individual cards are identified by the strings `"Options"`, `"Settings"`, and `"Preferences"`. Windows users might want to think of what is going on as analogous to using an MDI interface—with the panel being the parent window and the various cards being child windows. The analogy is, of course, not precise, since one cannot "tile" the cards being managed by a card layout manager.

Finally, write an `actionPerformed` procedure that makes the tab buttons switch the cards. You use the `show` method of the card layout manager in order to show a particular card. The `next` and `previous` methods show another card in the card sequence. The `first` and `last` methods show the first and last cards.

```
public void actionPerformed(ActionEvent evt)
{  String arg = evt.getActionCommand();
   if (arg.equals("<<")) layout.first(cards);
   else if (arg.equals("<")) layout.previous(cards);
   else if (arg.equals(">")) layout.next(cards);
   else if (arg.equals(">>")) layout.last(cards);
   else layout.show(cards, (String)arg);
}
```

Note that we cleverly made the button labels and the card names identical. That way, we can simply pass the button label to the `show` procedure.

To keep this example simple, we didn't actually put any data-entry fields on any of the cards. There's just a label that says, for example, `"Options dialog goes here"`. In an actual program, of course, you would have a full-fledged container that is populated by the necessary components. Example 9-14 is the code listing for the sample program.

Example 9-14: CardLayoutTest.java

```
import java.awt.*;
import java.awt.event.*;
import corejava.*;

public class CardLayoutTest extends CloseableFrame
   implements ActionListener
{  public CardLayoutTest()
   {  tabs = new Panel();

      addButton("<<");
      addButton("<");
      addButton("Options");
      addButton("Settings");
      addButton("Preferences");
      addButton(">");
      addButton(">>");
      add(tabs, "North");

      cards = new Panel();
      layout = new CardLayout();
      cards.setLayout(layout);

      cards.add(new SimpleDialog("Options"), "Options");
      cards.add(new SimpleDialog("Settings"), "Settings");
      cards.add(new SimpleDialog("Preferences"),
         "Preferences");

      add(cards, "Center");
   }

   public void addButton(String name)
   {  Button b = new Button(name);
      b.addActionListener(this);
      tabs.add(b);
   }

   public void actionPerformed(ActionEvent evt)
   {  String arg = evt.getActionCommand();
      if (arg.equals("<<")) layout.first(cards);
      else if (arg.equals("<")) layout.previous(cards);
      else if (arg.equals(">")) layout.next(cards);
      else if (arg.equals(">>")) layout.last(cards);
      else layout.show(cards, (String)arg);
   }
```

```
   public static void main(String[] args)
   {  Frame f = new CardLayoutTest();
      f.setSize(400, 200);
      f.show();
   }

   private Panel cards;
   private Panel tabs;
   private CardLayout layout;
}

class SimpleDialog extends Panel
{  SimpleDialog(String name)
   {  add(new Label(name + " dialog goes here"));
   }
}
```

java.awt.CardLayout

- `CardLayout(int hgap, int vgap)`

  constructs a new `CardLayout` with the specified horizontal and vertical gaps between the edge of the card and the components on the card. This is similar to the `insets` on a `Frame`.

Parameters:	`hgap`	the horizontal gap to use in pixels
	`vgap`	the vertical gap to use in pixels

- `void show(Container parent, String name)`

  flips to a card of the card layout.

Parameters:	`parent`	the container with the card layout
	`name`	the name of the card

- `void first(Container parent)`

  flips to the first card.

  Parameters: `parent` the container with the card layout

- `void next(Container parent)`

  flips to the next card.

  Parameters: `parent` the container with the card layout

- `void previous(Container parent)`

  flips to the previous card.

  Parameters: `parent` the container with the card layout

- `void last(Container parent)`

  flips to the last card.

  Parameters: `parent` the container with the card layout

Grid Layout

The grid layout arranges all components in rows and columns like a spreadsheet. However, for a grid layout, cells are always the same size. The calculator program in Figure 9-19 uses a grid layout to arrange the calculator buttons. When you resize the window, the buttons grow and shrink (but always remain equal in size).

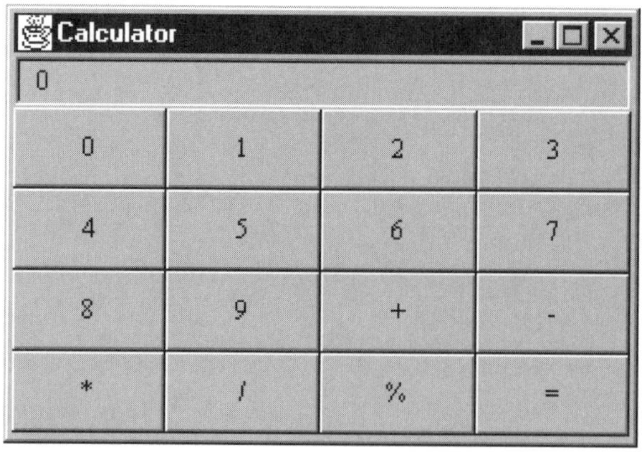

Figure 9-19: A calculator

In the constructor of the grid layout object, you specify how many rows and columns you need.

```
panel.setLayout(new GridLayout(5, 4));
```

As with the other layout managers, you can also specify the vertical and horizontal gaps you want.

You add the components, starting with the first entry in the first row, then the second entry in the first row, and so on.

```
panel.add(new Button("1"));
panel.add(new Button("2"));
```

Example 9-15 is the source listing for the calculator program. This is a regular calculator, not the “reverse Polish” variety that is so oddly popular with Java fans.

Example 9-15: Calculator.java

```
import java.awt.*;
import java.awt.event.*;
import corejava.*;

public class Calculator extends CloseableFrame
   implements ActionListener
{  public Calculator()
   {  display = new TextField("0");
      display.setEditable(false);
      add(display, "North");

      Panel p = new Panel();
      p.setLayout(new GridLayout(4, 4));
      for (int i = 0; i <= 9; i++)
         addButton(p, "" + (char)('0' + i));
      addButton(p, "+");
      addButton(p, "-");
      addButton(p, "*");
      addButton(p, "/");
      addButton(p, "%");
      addButton(p, "=");
      add(p, "Center");
   }

   private void addButton(Container c, String s)
   {  Button b = new Button(s);
      c.add(b);
      b.addActionListener(this);
   }

   public void actionPerformed(ActionEvent evt)
   {  String s = evt.getActionCommand();
      if ('0' <= s.charAt(0) && s.charAt(0) <= '9')
      {  if (start) display.setText(s);
         else display.setText(display.getText() + s);
         start = false;
      }
      else
      {  if (start)
         {  if (s.equals("-"))
            { display.setText(s); start = false; }
            else op = s;
         }
         else
         {  calculate(Integer.parseInt(display.getText()));
            op = s;
```

```
            start = true;
         }
      }
   }

   public void calculate(int n)
   {  if (op.equals("+")) arg += n;
      else if (op.equals("-")) arg -= n;
      else if (op.equals("*")) arg *= n;
      else if (op.equals("/")) arg /= n;
      else if (op.equals("%")) arg %= n;
      else if (op.equals("=")) arg = n;
      display.setText("" + arg);
   }

   public static void main(String[] args)
   {  Frame f = new Calculator();
      f.show();
   }

   private TextField display;
   private int arg = 0;
   private String op = "=";
   private boolean start = true;
}
```

Of course, few applications have as rigid a layout as the face of a calculator. In practice, small grids (usually with just one row or one column) are useful to organize partial areas of a window. When you use a grid layout for that purpose, you will often find it inconvenient that each component in the grid is stretched to fill the entire cell. To avoid that, you can stick the component inside a panel and add the panel inside the grid.

Grid Bag Layout

This is the mother of all layout managers. You can think of a grid bag layout as a piece of graph paper—each component will be told to occupy one or more of the little boxes on the paper. (And, in fact, a stack of graph paper will be one of the most useful high-tech tools you can acquire for working with grid bag layouts.) The idea is that this layout manager lets you align components without requiring that they all be the same size—since you are only concerned with which cells they will occupy. (Many word processors, as well as HTML, have the same capability when editing tables: you start out with a grid, and then can merge adjacent cells if need be.)

Fair warning: using grid bag layouts can be incredibly complex. The payoff is that they have the most flexibility and will work in the widest variety of situations. Keep in mind that the purpose of layout managers is to keep the arrangement of the components reasonable under different font sizes and operating systems, so it is not surprising that you need to work somewhat harder than when you design a layout just for one environment.

Consider the font selection dialog of Figure 9-20. It consists of the following components:

- A list box to specify the font style
- Two check boxes to select bold and italic
- A text field for the font size
- A label for that text box
- A text field at the bottom for the sample string

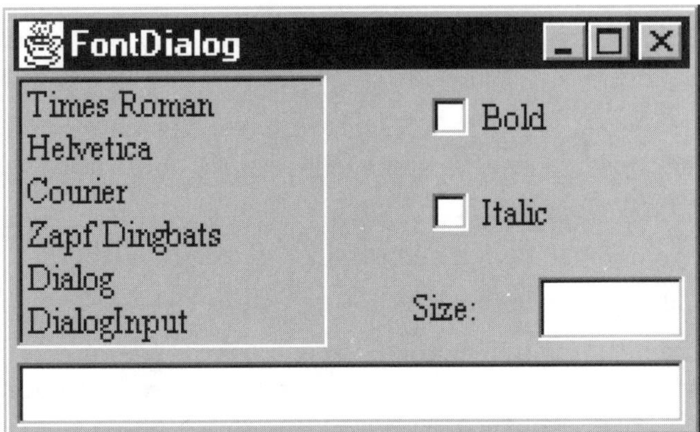

Figure 9-20: Font dialog box

Now, chop up the dialog box into a 4 × 3 grid of cells, as shown in Figure 9-21. As you can see, the list box spans three rows; each check box spans two columns; and the text field at the bottom spans three columns.

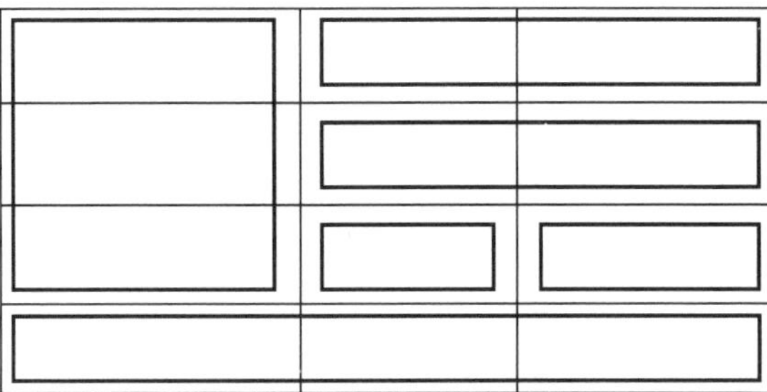

Figure 9-21: Dialog box grid used in design

To describe the layout to the grid bag manager, you must go through the following convoluted procedure.

- Create an object of type `GridBagLayout`. You don't tell it how many rows and columns the underlying grid has. Instead, Java will try to guess it from the information you give it later.
- Set this `GridBagLayout` object to be the layout manager for the component.
- Create an object of type `GridBagConstraints`. The `GridBagConstraints` object will specify how the components are laid out within the grid bag.
- For *each component,* fill in the `GridBagConstraints` object. Then (finally), add the component with the constraints by using the call:

  `add(component, constraints).`

Here's an example of the code needed (we will go over the various constraints in more detail in the sections that follow—so don't worry if you don't know what some of the constraints do).

```
GridBagLayout layout = new GridBagLayout();
panel.setLayout(layout);
GridBagConstraints constraints = new GridBagConstraints();
constraints.weightx = 100;
constraints.weighty = 100;
constraints.gridx = 0;
constraints.gridy = 0;
constraints.gridwidth = 1;
constraints.gridheight = 3;
List style = new List(4);
panel.add(style, constraints);
```

It is obviously best to write a small helper function for this kind of repetitive code—see the listing in Example 9-16 for an example of one.

The trick is knowing how to set the state of the `GridBagConstraints` object; this can be incredibly convoluted. We will go over the most important constraints for using this object in the sections that follow.

The `gridx`, `gridy`, `gridwidth`, *and* `gridheight` *Parameters*

These constraints define where the component is located in the grid. The `gridx` and `gridy` values specify the column and row positions of the upper left corner of the component to be added. The `gridwidth` and `gridheight` values determine how many columns and rows the component occupies.

Weight Fields

You always need to set the *weight* fields (`weightx` and `weighty`) for each area in a grid bag layout. If you set the weight to 0, then the area never grows or shrinks beyond its initial size in that direction. In the grid bag layout for Figure 9-19, we set the `weighty` field of the text field at the bottom to be 0. This allows the bottom field to remain a constant height when you resize the window. On the other hand, if you set the weights for all areas to 0, the container will huddle in the center of its allotted area, rather than stretching to fill it.

Note that the weights don't actually give the relative sizes of the columns. They tell what proportion of the "slack" space Java should allocate to each area. This isn't particularly intuitive. We recommend that you set the weights at 100. Then, run the program and see how the layout looks. If you want to tweak the sizes of the columns or rows, adjust the weights. In our example, we set the weight of the first column to 20, to compress it somewhat relative to the rest of the dialog box.

The `fill` *and* `anchor` *Parameters*

If you don't want a component to stretch out and fill the entire area, you need to set the `fill` field for the layout manager. You have four possibilities for this parameter: the valid values are used in the forms `GridBagConstraints.NONE`, `GridBagConstraints.HORIZONTAL`, `GridBagConstraints.VERTICAL`, and `GridBagConstraints.BOTH`.

If the component does not fill the entire area, you can specify where in the area you want it by setting the `anchor` field. The valid values are `GridBagConstraints.CENTER` (the default), `GridBagConstraints.NORTH`, `GridBagConstraints.NORTHEAST`, `GridBagConstraints.EAST`, and so on.

An Alternative Method to Specify the `gridx`*,* `gridy`*,* `gridwidth`*, and* `gridheight` *Parameters*

The AWT documentation recommends that, instead of setting the `gridx` and `gridy` values to absolute positions, you set them to the constant `GridBagConstraints.RELATIVE`. Then, add the components to the grid bag layout in a standardized order, going from left to right in the first row, then moving along the next row, and so on.

You still specify the number of columns and rows spanned in the `gridwidth` and `gridheight` fields. Except, if the component extends to the *last* row or column, you aren't supposed to specify the actual number, but the constant `GridBagConstraints.REMAINDER`. This tells the layout manager that the component is the last one in its row. And if it is the *next-to-last* component in the current row or column, you are supposed to specify the constant `RELATIVE`.

This scheme does seem to work. But it sounds really goofy to hide the actual placement information from the layout manager and hope that it will rediscover it. Example 9-16 is the complete code to implement the font dialog example.

Example 9-16: FontDialog.java

```
import java.awt.*;
import java.awt.event.*;
import corejava.*;

public class FontDialog extends CloseableFrame
{  public FontDialog()
   {  setTitle("FontDialog");
      GridBagLayout gbl = new GridBagLayout();
      setLayout(gbl);

      style = new List(4, false);
      style.add("Serif");
      style.add("SansSerif");
      style.add("Monospaced");
      style.add("Dialog");
      style.add("DialogInput");
      style.select(0);

      bold = new Checkbox("Bold");
      italic = new Checkbox("Italic");
      Label label = new Label("Size: ");
      size = new IntTextField(10,1);
      sample = new TextField();
```

```
      GridBagConstraints gbc = new GridBagConstraints();
      gbc.fill = GridBagConstraints.BOTH;
      gbc.weightx = 20;
      gbc.weighty = 100;
      add(style, gbc, 0, 0, 1, 3);
      gbc.weightx = 100;
      gbc.fill = GridBagConstraints.NONE;
      gbc.anchor = GridBagConstraints.CENTER;
      add(bold, gbc, 1, 0, 2, 1);
      add(italic, gbc, 1, 1, 2, 1);
      add(label, gbc, 1, 2, 1, 1);
      gbc.fill = GridBagConstraints.HORIZONTAL;
      add(size, gbc, 2, 2, 1, 1);
      gbc.anchor = GridBagConstraints.SOUTH;
      gbc.weighty = 0;
      add(sample, gbc, 0, 3, 4, 1);
      sample.setText("The quick brown fox");

      ItemListener fontChanged = new ItemListener()
         {  public void itemStateChanged(ItemEvent evt)
               { updateFont(); }
         };
      bold.addItemListener(fontChanged);
      italic.addItemListener(fontChanged);
      style.addItemListener(fontChanged);
      size.addActionListener(new ActionListener()
         {  public void actionPerformed(ActionEvent evt)
               { updateFont(); }
         });
   }

   public void add(Component c, GridBagConstraints gbc,
      int x, int y, int w, int h)
   {  gbc.gridx = x;
      gbc.gridy = y;
      gbc.gridwidth = w;
      gbc.gridheight = h;
      add(c, gbc);
   }

   public void updateFont()
   {  sample.setFont(new Font(style.getSelectedItem(),
         (bold.getState() ? Font.BOLD : 0)
            + (italic.getState() ? Font.ITALIC : 0),
         size.getValue()));
      repaint();
   }
```

```
    public static void main(String[] args)
    {  Frame f = new FontDialog();
       f.show();
    }

    private List style;
    private Checkbox bold;
    private Checkbox italic;
    private IntTextField size;
    private TextField sample;
}
```

`java.awt.GridBagConstraints`

- `int gridx, gridy`

  indicates the starting column and row of cell.

- `int gridwidth, gridheight`

  indicates the column and row extent of cell.

- `double weightx, weighty`

  indicates the capacity of cell to grow.

- `int anchor`

  indicates the alignment of the component inside the cell, one of `CENTER`, `NORTH`, `NORTHEAST`, `EAST`, `SOUTHEAST`, `SOUTH`, `SOUTHWEST`, `WEST`, and `NORTHWEST`

- `int fill`

  indicates the fill behavior of the component inside the cell, one of `NONE`, `BOTH`, `HORIZONTAL`, or `VERTICAL`.

- `int ipadx, ipady`

  indicates the "internal" padding around the component.

- `Insets insets`

  indicates the "external" padding along the cell boundaries.

Using No Layout Manager

There will be times when you don't want to bother with layout managers but just want to drop a component at a fixed location. (This is sometimes called *absolute positioning.*) This is not a great idea for platform-independent applications, but there is nothing wrong with it for a quick prototype.

Here is what you do to place a component at a fixed location:

- Don't select a layout manager at all.
- Add the component you want to the container.
- Then specify the position and size that you want.

```
panel.setLayout(null);
Button ok = new Button("Ok");
panel.add(OK);
ok.setBounds(10, 10, 30, 15);
```

java.awt.Component

- `void setBounds(int x, int y, int width, int height)`

  moves and resizes a component.

Parameters:	`x, y`	the new top left corner of the component
	`width, height`	the new size of the component

Custom Layout Managers

In principle, it is possible to design your own `LayoutManager` class that manages components in a special way. For example, you could arrange all components in a container to form a circle (see Figure 9-22). This will almost always be a major effort and a real time sink, but as Figure 9-22 shows, the results can be quite dramatic.

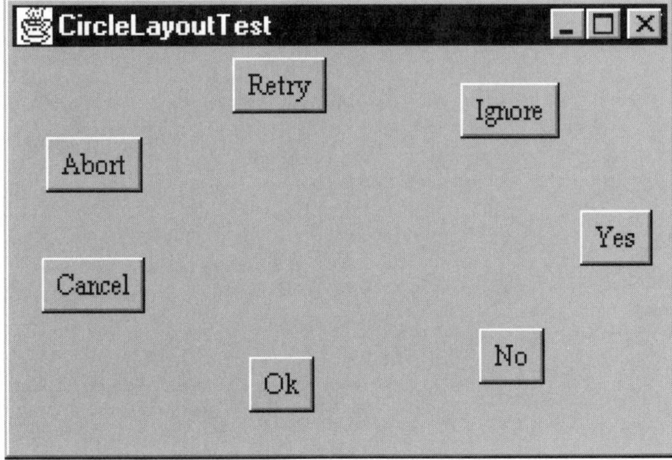

Figure 9-22: Circle layout

If you do feel you can't live without your own layout manager, here is what you do. Your own layout manager must implement the `LayoutManager` interface. You need to override the following five functions.

```
void addLayoutComponent(String s, Component c);
void removeLayoutComponent(Component c);
Dimension preferredLayoutSize(Container parent);
Dimension minimumLayoutSize(Container parent);
void layoutContainer(Container parent);
```

The first two functions are called when a component is added or removed. If you don't keep any additional information about the components, you can make them do nothing. The next two functions compute the space required for the minimum and the preferred layout of the components. These are usually the same quantity. The fifth function does the actual work and invokes `reshape` on all components.

NOTE: The AWT 1.1 has a new interface called `LayoutManager2` with 10 methods to implement rather than 5. The main point of the `LayoutManager2` interface is to allow the user to use the `add` method with constraints. It is unclear whether in the future all layout managers will be required to implement the `LayoutManager2` interface. It is clearly not necessary to do so in Java 1.1.

Example 9-17 is a simple implementation of the `CircleLayout` manager, which, amazingly and uselessly enough, lays out the components along an ellipse inside the parent.

Example 9-17: CircleLayoutTest.java

```
import java.awt.*;
import corejava.*;

public class CircleLayoutTest extends CloseableFrame
{  public CircleLayoutTest()
   {  setLayout(new CircleLayout());
      add(new Button("Yes"));
      add(new Button("No"));
      add(new Button("Ok"));
      add(new Button("Cancel"));
      add(new Button("Abort"));
      add(new Button("Retry"));
      add(new Button("Ignore"));
   }
```

```
   public static void main(String args[])
   {  Frame f = new CircleLayoutTest();
      f.show();
   }

}

class CircleLayout implements LayoutManager
{  public void addLayoutComponent(String name,
      Component comp)
   {}

   public void removeLayoutComponent(Component comp)
   {}

   public void setSizes(Container parent)
   {  if (sizesSet) return;
      int n = parent.getComponentCount();

      preferredWidth = 0;
      preferredHeight = 0;
      minWidth = 0;
      minHeight = 0;
      maxComponentWidth = 0;
      maxComponentHeight = 0;

      for (int i = 0; i < n; i++)
      {  Component c = parent.getComponent(i);
         if (c.isVisible()) {
         Dimension d = c.getPreferredSize();
         maxComponentWidth = Math.max(maxComponentWidth,
            d.width);
         maxComponentHeight = Math.max(maxComponentWidth,
            d.height);
         preferredHeight += d.height;
         }
      }
      preferredHeight += maxComponentHeight;
      preferredWidth = 2 * maxComponentWidth;
      minHeight = preferredHeight;
      minWidth = preferredWidth;
      sizesSet = true;
   }

   public Dimension preferredLayoutSize(Container parent)
   {  Dimension dim = new Dimension(0, 0);
      setSizes(parent);
      Insets insets = parent.getInsets();
```

```
      dim.width = preferredWidth + insets.left
         + insets.right;
      dim.height = preferredHeight + insets.top
         + insets.bottom;
      return dim;
   }

   public Dimension minimumLayoutSize(Container parent)
   {  Dimension dim = new Dimension(0, 0);
      setSizes(parent);
      Insets insets = parent.getInsets();
      dim.width = minWidth + insets.left + insets.right;
      dim.height = minHeight + insets.top + insets.bottom;
      return dim;
   }

   public void layoutContainer(Container parent)
   {  Insets insets = parent.getInsets();
      int containerWidth = parent.getSize().width
         - insets.left - insets.right;
      int containerHeight = parent.getSize().height
         - insets.top - insets.bottom;
      int xradius = (containerWidth - maxComponentWidth)
         / 2;
      int yradius = (containerHeight - maxComponentHeight)
         / 2;

      setSizes(parent);
      int xcenter = insets.left + containerWidth / 2;
      int ycenter = insets.top + containerHeight / 2;

      int n = parent.getComponentCount();
      for (int i = 0 ; i < n ; i++)
      {  Component c = parent.getComponent(i);
         if (c.isVisible())
         {  Dimension d = c.getPreferredSize();
            double angle = 2 * Math.PI * i / n;
            int x = xcenter
               + (int)(Math.cos(angle) * xradius);
            int y = ycenter
               + (int)(Math.sin(angle) * yradius);

            c.setBounds(x - d.width / 2, y - d.width / 2,
               d.width, d.height);
         }
      }

   }
```

```
    private int minWidth = 0;
    private int minHeight = 0;
    private int preferredWidth = 0, preferredHeight = 0;
    private boolean sizesSet = false;
    private int maxComponentWidth = 0;
    private int maxComponentHeight = 0;
}
```

java.awt.LayoutManager

API

- `void addLayoutComponent(String name, Component comp)`

  adds a component to the layout.

Parameters:	`name`	an identifier for the component placement
	`comp`	the component to be added

- `void removeLayoutComponent(Component comp)`

  removes a component from the layout.

Parameters:	`comp`	the component to be removed

- `Dimension preferredLayoutSize(Container parent)`

  returns the preferred size dimensions for the container under this layout.

Parameters:	`parent`	the container whose components are being laid out

- `Dimension minimumLayoutSize(Container parent)`

  returns the minimum size dimensions for the container under this layout.

Parameters:	`parent`	the container whose components are being laid out

- `void layoutContainer(Container parent)`

  lays out the components in a container.

Parameters:	`parent`	the container whose components are being laid out

Printing Components

You have seen in Chapter 7 how to print text and graphics. You request a printer graphics context, and then you use the same drawing commands that draw text and graphics on the screen. The AWT gives you another useful method `printAll` that lets you print out all components in a frame. The printout shows all buttons, text fields, canvases, and so on, just as they appear on the screen.

This feature is very easy to use. Obtain a printer graphics context as described in Chapter 7 and then pass it to the `printAll` method. That method prints an individual component or a container and all of its subcomponents.

```
PrintJob pjob = getToolkit().getPrintJob(this,
   getTitle(), null);

if (pjob != null)
{  Graphics pg = pjob.getGraphics();
   if (pg != null)
   {  printAll(pg);
      pg.dispose(); // flush page
   }
   pjob.end();
}
```

VB NOTE: The `printAll` method corresponds to the `PrintForm` method in VB.

Of course, it is not all that common that you need to print all buttons and text fields in a form, but it is nice to know that it can be done easily. Here is a simple example that shows how you might put this to work in practice. The following application computes the growth of an investment in a savings account compounded monthly. An investment advisor can fill in the numbers and click on Compute to display a graph that represents the growth of the investment (see Figure 9-23).

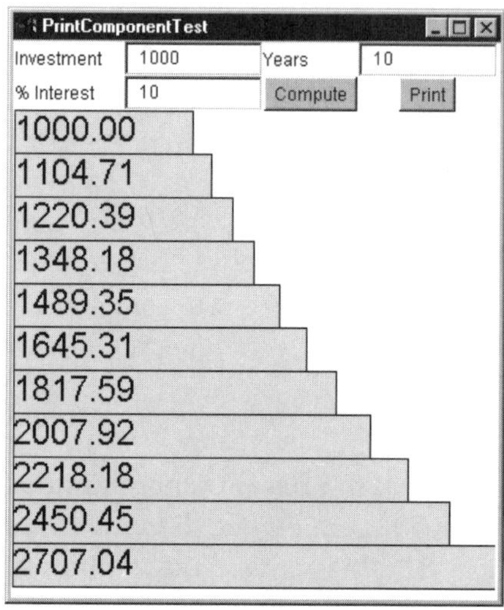

Figure 9-23: Growth of an investment

Clicking on the Print button prints out both the graph and the values of the text fields. The investment advisor can run through various scenarios and leave the printouts with the client. Of course, in practice, the investment would presumably be somewhat more sophisticated than a savings account.

The `printAll` method automatically positions all components on the printout in the same layout as on the screen. It then asks each component to print itself. Controls such as buttons and text fields have a `print` method that renders them on the printout approximately as they look on the screen. To print a canvas, the `printAll` method simply calls the `paint` method of the canvas. That method draws the canvas image onto the printer device context.

TIP: You don't have to print all components of the frame. For example, if you call

```
savingsCanvas.printAll(pg);
```

only the contents of the canvas are printed. However, do *not* call the `print` method for an individual component—it is not intended to be called directly by the programmer.

Example 9-18 shows the code for this program. Most of the code involves the grid bag layout for the fields and the drawing of the graph. Note that there is no special code for printing, except the standard call to `printAll`.

Example 9-18: PrintComponentTest.java

```
import java.awt.*;
import java.awt.event.*;
import corejava.*;

public class PrintComponentTest extends CloseableFrame
   implements ActionListener
{  public PrintComponentTest()
   {  setLayout(new GridBagLayout());

      GridBagConstraints gbc = new GridBagConstraints();
      gbc.fill = GridBagConstraints.HORIZONTAL;
      gbc.weightx = 100;
      gbc.weighty = 0;
      add(new Label("Investment"), gbc, 0, 0, 1, 1);
      add(initialField, gbc, 1, 0, 1, 1);
      add(new Label("Years"), gbc, 2, 0, 1, 1);
      add(yearsField, gbc, 3, 0, 1, 1);
      add(new Label("% Interest"), gbc, 0, 1, 1, 1);
      add(interestField, gbc, 1, 1, 1, 1);
      gbc.fill = GridBagConstraints.NONE;
      Button computeButton = new Button("Compute");
```

```
        computeButton.addActionListener(this);
        add(computeButton, gbc, 2, 1, 1, 1);
        Button printButton = new Button("Print");
        printButton.addActionListener(this);
        add(printButton, gbc, 3, 1, 1, 1);

        gbc.weighty = 100;
        gbc.fill = GridBagConstraints.BOTH;
        add(savingsCanvas, gbc, 0, 2, 4, 1);
    }

    public void add(Component c, GridBagConstraints gbc,
        int x, int y, int w, int h)
    {   gbc.gridx = x;
        gbc.gridy = y;
        gbc.gridwidth = w;
        gbc.gridheight = h;
        add(c, gbc);
    }

    public void actionPerformed(ActionEvent evt)
    {   if (evt.getActionCommand().equals("Compute"))
        {   savingsCanvas.setSavings(initialField.getValue(),
                yearsField.getValue(),
                interestField.getValue());
        }
        else if (evt.getActionCommand().equals("Print"))
        {   PrintJob pjob = getToolkit().getPrintJob(this,
                getTitle(), null);

            if (pjob != null)
            {   Graphics pg = pjob.getGraphics();
                if (pg != null)
                {   printAll(pg);
                    pg.dispose(); // flush page
                 }
                 pjob.end();
            }
        }
    }

    public static void main(String[] args)
    {   Frame f = new PrintComponentTest();
        f.setSize(300,400);
        f.show();
    }

    private IntTextField initialField
        = new IntTextField(10000, 10);
```

```
   private IntTextField yearsField
      = new IntTextField(15, 10);
   private IntTextField interestField
      = new IntTextField(10, 10);
   private SavingsCanvas savingsCanvas = new SavingsCanvas();
}

class SavingsCanvas extends Canvas
{  public void paint(Graphics g)
   {  double maxValue = 0;
      int i;
      for (i = 0; i <= years; i++)
      {  double v = getBalance(i);
         if (maxValue < v) maxValue = v;
      }
      if (maxValue == 0) return;

      Dimension d = getSize();
      int barHeight = (int)(d.height / (years + 1));
      double scale = d.height / maxValue;

      Font f = g.getFont();
      FontMetrics fm = g.getFontMetrics();
      g.setFont(new Font(f.getName(), f.getStyle(),
         f.getSize() * barHeight / fm.getHeight()));
      fm = g.getFontMetrics();

      for (i = 0; i <= years; i++)
      {  double v = getBalance(i);
         int x2 = (int)(d.width * v / maxValue);
         int y1 = i * barHeight;
         g.setColor(Color.yellow);
         g.fillRect(0, y1, x2, barHeight);
         g.setColor(Color.black);
         g.drawRect(0, y1, x2, barHeight);
         g.drawString(new Format("%.2f").form(v),
            0, y1 + fm.getAscent());
      }
   }

   public void setSavings(double init, double y, double p)
   {  initial = init;
      years = y;
      interest = p;
      repaint();
   }
```

```
    public double getBalance(int year)
    {  if (year < 0) return 0;
       return initial * Math.pow(1 + interest / 1200,
          12 * year);
    }

    private double interest;
    private double years;
    private double initial;
}
```

`java.awt.Component`

- `void printAll(Graphics g)`

  prints this component and all subcomponents on the graphics context `g`. When this method is called, the offset and clipping rectangle of `g` are set so that the component is placed into its correct position on the printout.

Dialog Boxes

So far, all of our user interface components have appeared inside a frame window that was created in the application. This is the most common situation if you write *applets* that run inside a Web browser. But if you write applications, you usually want separate dialog boxes to pop up to give or get information from the user.

Just as with most windowing systems, AWT distinguishes between *modal* and *modeless* dialog boxes. A modal dialog box won't let the user interact with the remaining windows of the application until he or she deals with it. You use a modal dialog box when you need information from the user before you can proceed with execution. For example, when the user wants to read a file, a modal file dialog box is the one to pop up. The user must specify a file name before the program can begin the read operation. Only when the user closes the (modal) dialog box can the application proceed.

A modeless dialog box lets the user enter information in both the dialog box and the remainder of the application. One example of a modeless dialog is for a tool bar. The tool bar can stay in place as long as needed, and the user can interact with both the application window and the tool bar as needed.

Figure 9-24 shows a typical modal dialog box, a program information box that is displayed when the user selects the About button.

To implement a dialog box, you derive a class from `Dialog`. This is essentially the same process as deriving the main window for an application from `Frame`.

More precisely:

1. In the constructor of your dialog box, call the constructor of the base class `Dialog`. You will need to tell it the name of the parent frame, the title of the frame, and a Boolean flag to indicate if the dialog box is modal or modeless.
2. Add the controls of the dialog box.
3. Add the event handlers.
4. Set the size for the dialog box.

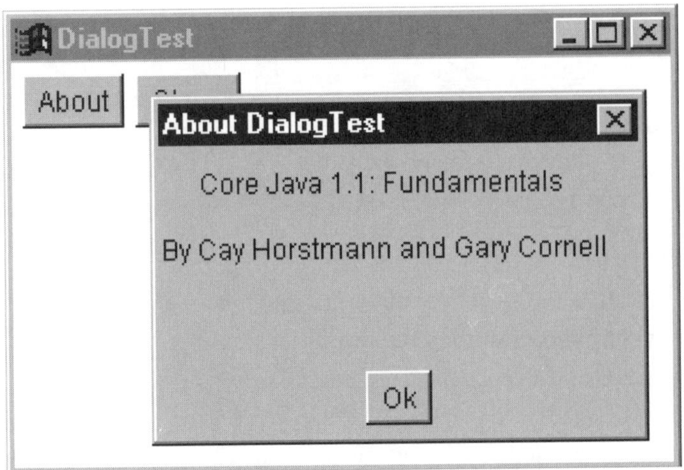

Figure 9-24: An About dialog box

Here's an example of how the code will start:

```
class AboutDialog extends Dialog
{  public AboutDialog(Frame parent)
   {  super(parent, "About DialogTest", true);

      Panel p1 = new Panel();
      p1.add(new Label("CoreJava 1.1: Fundamentals"));
      p1.add(new Label("By Cay Horstmann and Gary Cornell"));
      add(p1, "Center");

      Panel p2 = new Panel();
      Button ok = new Button("Ok");
      p2.add(ok);
      add(p2, "South");
```

```
        ok.addActionListener(new ActionListener() { public void
           actionPerformed(ActionEvent evt) { setVisible(false);
              } } );

        addWindowListener(new WindowAdapter() { public void
              windowClosing(WindowEvent e) { setVisible(false);
                 } } );

        setSize(220, 150);
     }
  }
```

To display the dialog box, you create a new dialog object and invoke the `show` method.

```
Dialog ab = new AboutDialog(this);
ab.show();
```

Actually, in the sample code below, we create the dialog box only once, and so we can reuse it whenever the user clicks the About button.

```
if (ab == null) // first time
   ab = new AboutDialog(this);
ab.show();
```

When the user clicks on the Ok button, the dialog box should close. This is handled in the event handler of the Ok button:

```
ok.addActionListener(new ActionListener() { public void
  actionPerformed(ActionEvent evt) { setVisible(false); } } );
```

If you want your user to be able to cancel a dialog box by closing it (for example, by a click on the close box in Windows 95), you need to provide a handler for the `windowClosing` event.

```
addWindowListener(new WindowAdapter() { public void
   windowClosing(WindowEvent e) { setVisible(false); } } );
```

If you don't supply this handler, the user can close the dialog box only by clicking on the Ok button. Example 9-19 is the code for the About dialog box test program.

Example 9-19: DialogTest.java

```
import java.awt.*;
import java.awt.event.*;
import corejava.*;

public class DialogTest extends CloseableFrame
   implements ActionListener
{  public DialogTest()
   {  Panel p = new Panel();
```

```
      p.setLayout(new FlowLayout(FlowLayout.LEFT));
      addButton(p, "About");
      addButton(p, "Close");
      add(p, "North");

   }

   public void addButton(Container p, String name)
   {  Button b = new Button(name);
      b.addActionListener(this);
      p.add(b);
   }

   public void actionPerformed(ActionEvent evt)
   {  String arg = evt.getActionCommand();
      if(arg.equals("About"))
      {  if (ab == null) // first time
            ab = new AboutDialog(this);
         ab.show();
      }
      else if(arg.equals("Close"))
      {  System.exit(0);
      }
   }

   public static void main(String args[])
   {  Frame f = new DialogTest();
      f.show();
   }

   private AboutDialog ab;
}

class AboutDialog extends Dialog
{  public AboutDialog(Frame parent)
   {  super(parent, "About DialogTest", true);

      Panel p1 = new Panel();
      p1.add(new Label("Core Java 1.1: Fundamentals"));
      p1.add(new Label("By Cay Horstmann and Gary Cornell"));
      add(p1, "Center");

      Panel p2 = new Panel();
      Button ok = new Button("Ok");
      p2.add(ok);
      add(p2, "South");

      ok.addActionListener(new ActionListener() { public void
```

```
            actionPerformed(ActionEvent evt) { setVisible(false); }
               } );

         addWindowListener(new WindowAdapter() { public void
               windowClosing(WindowEvent e) { setVisible(false); }
                  } );

         setSize(220, 150);
      }
   }
```

`java.awt.Dialog`

- `public Dialog(Frame parent, String title, boolean modal)`

  constructs a dialog. The dialog is not visible until it is explicitly shown.

  Parameters:

`parent`	the frame that is the owner of the dialog
`title`	the title of the dialog
`modal`	true for modal dialogs (a modal dialog blocks input to other windows)

Data Exchange

The most common reason to put up a dialog box is to get information from the user. You have already seen how easy it is to make a dialog box object: give it initial data and then call `show()` in order to have Java display the dialog box on the screen. Now let us see how to transfer data in and out of a dialog box.

Consider the dialog box in Figure 9-25 that could be used to obtain a user name and a password to connect to some on-line service.

It is helpful to make a class that contains all data that you want to transfer out of a dialog box. We make a class `ConnectInfo` that holds the name and password. We initialize these data with the defaults that should be shown in the fields when the dialog box starts up. When the user finishes entering the data into the dialog box, the actual user input is put back into the transfer object. However, if the dialog was canceled or closed, we do not transfer back the data. We do all this in a `showDialog` method of our `ConnectDialog` class:

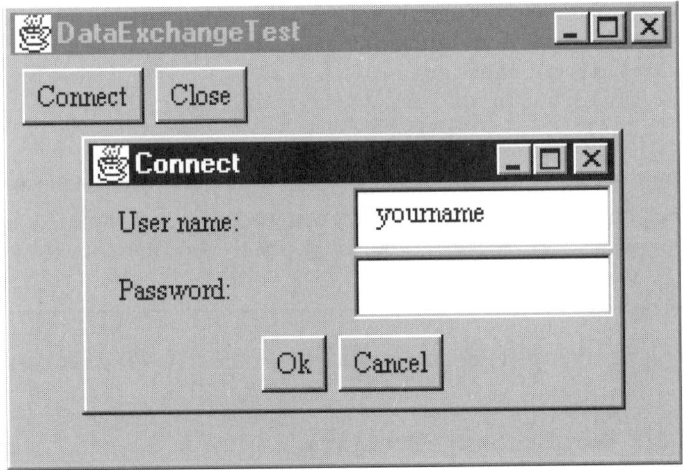

Figure 9-25: Password dialog box

```
public boolean showDialog(ConnectInfo transfer)
{  username.setText(transfer.username);
   password.setText(transfer.password);
   ok = false;
   show();
   if (ok)
   {  transfer.username = username.getText();
      transfer.password = password.getText();
   }
   return ok;
}
```

Note that the call to `show()` does not return until a call to `setVisible(false)` or `dispose` elsewhere in the code . (This is a welcome change in how the AWT works. In the first version of the AWT, the call to `show` returned immediately, *even for modal dialog boxes.* That made it extremely challenging to get the data out of the dialog box.)

There are three ways for the user to close the dialog box: through the Ok button, the Cancel button, and the `windowClosing` event. Each of these three events must call `setVisible(false)`. When the user clicks the Ok button, the `ok` variable must be set to `true` to indicate that the values in the dialog are to be accepted and that they should be moved to the transfer object.

You invoke the dialog box by setting default values in the transfer object and then passing the transfer object to the `showDialog` procedure. If the procedure returned `true`, the user clicked on Ok.

```
ConnectInfo transfer = new ConnectInfo("yourname", "");
if (pd == null) pd = new ConnectDialog(this);
if (pd.showDialog(transfer))
   System.out.println(transfer.username + " "
      + transfer.password);
```

TIP: A realistic password dialog box should probably echo back a character like "*" when the user enters the information. You can do this by using the `setEchoChar` method of the `TextField` class.

Example 9-20 is the complete code that illustrates the data flow into and out of a dialog box.

Example 9-20: DataExchangeTest.java

```
import java.awt.*;

public class DataExchangeTest extends Frame
   implements ResultProcessor
{  public DataExchangeTest()
   {  setTitle("DataExchangeTest");

      Panel p = new Panel();
      p.setLayout(new FlowLayout(FlowLayout.LEFT));
      p.add(new Button("Connect"));
      p.add(new Button("Close"));
      add("North", p);
   }

   public boolean action(Event evt, Object arg)
   {  if (arg.equals("Connect"))
      {   ConnectInfo in = new ConnectInfo("yourname", "");
          ConnectDialog pd = new ConnectDialog(this, in);
          pd.show();
      }
      else if(arg.equals("Close"))
         System.exit(0);
      else return super.action(evt, arg);
      return true;
   }

   public boolean handleEvent(Event evt)
   {  if (evt.id == Event.WINDOW_DESTROY
         && evt.target == this)
         System.exit(0);
      else
```

```
            return super.handleEvent(evt);
        return true;
    }

    public void processResult(Dialog source, Object result)
    {   if (source instanceof ConnectDialog)
        {   ConnectInfo info = (ConnectInfo)result;
            System.out.println(info.username + " "
                + info.password);
        }
    }

    public static void main(String args[])
    {   Frame f = new DataExchangeTest();
        f.resize(300, 200);
        f.show();
    }
}

interface ResultProcessor
{   public void processResult(Dialog source, Object obj);
}

class ConnectInfo
{   String username;
    String password;
    ConnectInfo(String u, String p)
        { username = u; password = p; }
}

class ConnectDialog extends Dialog
{   public ConnectDialog(DataExchangeTest parent,
        ConnectInfo u)
    {   super(parent, "Connect", true);
        Panel p1 = new Panel();
        p1.setLayout(new GridLayout(2, 2));
        p1.add(new Label("User name:"));
        p1.add(username = new TextField(u.username, 8));
        p1.add(new Label("Password:"));
        p1.add(password = new TextField(u.password, 8));
        add("Center", p1);

        Panel p2 = new Panel();
        p2.add(new Button("Ok"));
        p2.add(new Button("Cancel"));
        add("South", p2);
        resize(240, 120);
    }
```

```
   public boolean action(Event evt, Object arg)
   {  if(arg.equals("Ok"))
      {  dispose();
         ((ResultProcessor)getParent()).processResult(this,
            new ConnectInfo(username.getText(),
               password.getText()));
      }
      else if (arg.equals("Cancel"))
         dispose();
      else return super.action(evt, arg);
      return true;
   }

   public boolean handleEvent(Event evt)
   {  if (evt.id == Event.WINDOW_DESTROY)
         dispose();
      else return super.handleEvent(evt);
      return true;
   }

   private TextField username;
   private TextField password;
}
```

`java.awt.TextField`

- `void setEchoChar(char c)`

  sets the character shown to the user regardless of what he or she enters.

Parameters	`char`	the character to show

File Dialogs

When you write an applet, you cannot access files on the remote user's machine, so this topic won't be of great interest to you. However, when you write an application, you usually want to be able to open and save files. A good file dialog box that shows files and directories and lets the user navigate the file system is hard to write, and you definitely don't want to reinvent that wheel. Fortunately, AWT provides a `FileDialog` class that allows you to display the same file dialog box that most native applications use. `FileDialog`s are always modal. Note that the `FileDialog` class is a subclass of `Dialog` so it inherits the methods discussed in the previous section. Figures 9-26 and 9-27 show examples of file dialog boxes under Windows 95 and Solaris.

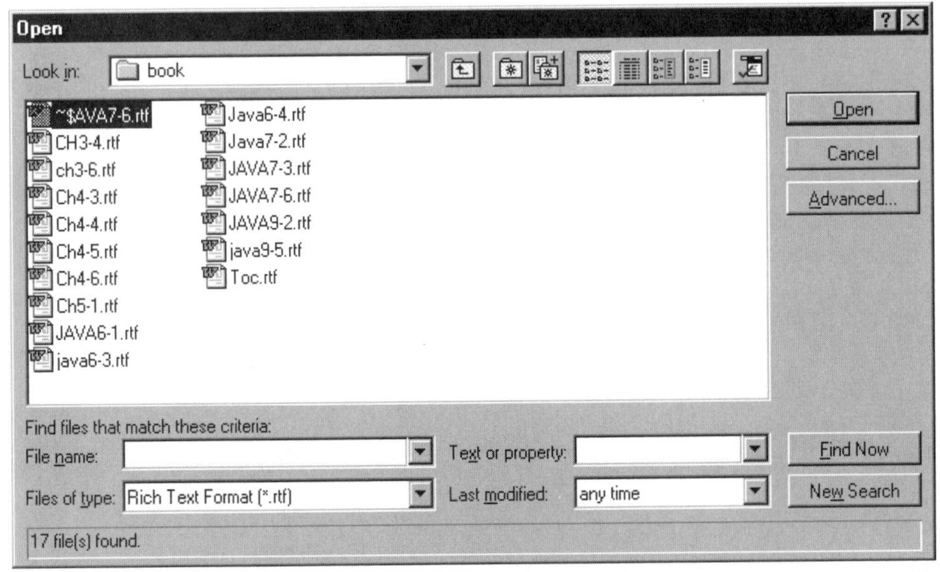

Figure 9-26: File dialog box under Windows 95

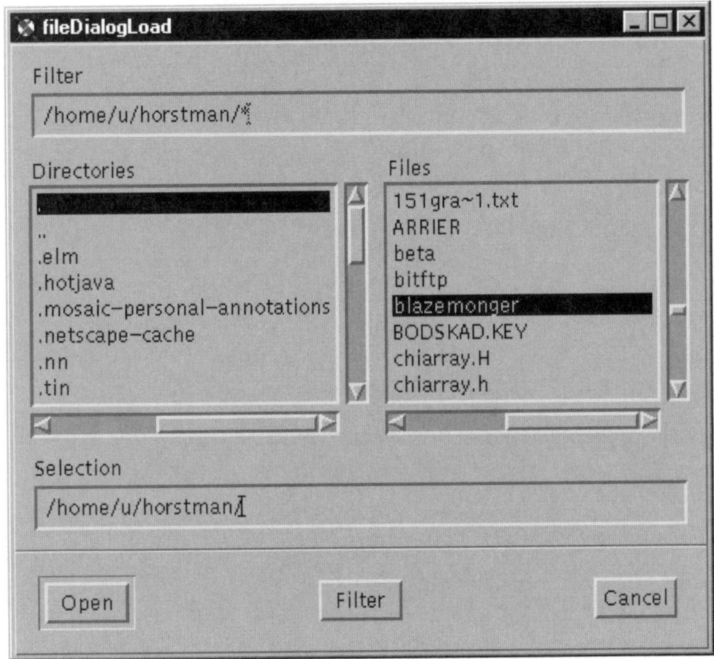

Figure 9-27: File dialog box under Solaris

Here are the steps needed to put up a file dialog box and recover what the user chooses from the box:

1. Make a `FileDialog` object. The usual constructor takes a `Frame` as the parent, a string as the title of the box, and a constant for the type of box.

   For example:

   ```
   FileDialog d = new FileDialog(parentFrame, "Save note
   file", FileDialog.SAVE);
   ```

   The third argument is either the `LOAD` or `SAVE` constant from the `FileDialog` class.

2. Set the directory.

   For example, use:

   ```
   d.setDirectory(".");
   ```

   to use the current directory.

3. If you have a default file name that you expect the user to choose, supply it here.

   ```
   d.setFile(filename);
   ```

4. Show the dialog box.

   ```
   d.show();
   ```

   This call does not return until the user has filled in the file dialog box. You get the selected file back with the `getFile()` method. If the user cancels the dialog box, then `getFile()` returns `null`.

   ```
   filename = d.getFile();
   if (filename != null). . .
   ```

`java.awt.FileDialog`

- `FileDialog(Frame parent, String title, int mode)`

  creates a file dialog box for loading or saving a file.

Parameters:	`parent`	the owner of the dialog box
	`title`	the title of the dialog box
	`mode`	the mode of the dialog box, either `FileDialog.LOAD` or `FileDialog.SAVE`

- `setFilenameFilter(FilenameFilter filter)`

  sets the initial file mask for the file dialog box. This feature has never worked in version 1.0 and does not currently work in the version of 1.1 that we have.

- `setDirectory(String dir)`

  sets the initial directory for the file dialog box.
- `setFile(String file)`

  sets the default file choice for the file dialog box.
- `String getFile()`

  gets the file that the user selected (or returns `null` if the user didn't select any file).

Lightweight User Interface Elements

Before we show you how to build these new kinds of components, let's step back for a moment and see how the Java AWT can work across platforms. The idea is simple: every time you create an AWT component, the AWT automatically creates its counterpart in the native windowing system. For example, an AWT button is mapped to a button on the native operating system. The native equivalent to an AWT component is called a *peer.* Each peer object is managed by a Java interface with the obvious name: `ButttonPeer`, `ChoicePeer`, and so on. The peer interface spells out the methods that you can use with the Java component. The AWT, in turn, is responsible for the native calls that correspond to the peer methods. For example, when you use the `setForeground` method in the `Component` class, the AWT will eventually call a method on the native windowing system that sets the foreground color of the window.

There are some obvious advantages of having a one-to-one correspondence between AWT components and peers on the underlying windows system. For example, peers are why, even under Java 1.0, you could use cut and paste into text components: the peer of the text component knows how to do cut and paste of text. There are, however, both problems and costs to the peer approach:

- Peers require creating a window on the underlying system.

  In certain situations, such as under X, there is a real cost to creating multiple native windows. For example, every time you create a `Panel` to organize components, the AWT creates a peer on the native windowing system. Since panels are for organizational purposes only, why pay for this? (See below for how to build a lightweight panel.)
- You are limited in what components you can have; the AWT *must* use a least common denominator approach.

  For example, Windows 95 has an extremely useful set of "common controls." Since they don't exist on other platforms, JavaSoft cannot use the peer approach to give this functionality to Java. (In fact, one of the main points of the Java Foundation Classes from the JavaSoft/Netscape/IBM alliance is to build a set of common controls in Java using the lightweight UI framework.)

Finally, a related point that JavaSoft makes is:

- Applications look slightly different on each platform since the peers look different.

  We'll leave it to you to decide if this is a benefit or a cost. After, all people get used to the way the widgets look on their platform and often don't like them changed. This is the obvious but also important potential downside in the JavaSoft/Netscape/IBM alliance for including the equivalent of the Windows common controls in their class library.

Building a Lightweight UI

The basic step needed to build a lightweight user interface component is trivial:

- Extend `java.awt.Component` or `java.awt.Container`

For example, here's all the code you need to build a lightweight panel:

```
class LightWeightPanel extends Container {}
```

Not much to it, is there? The point is that a container can collect components just as well as a panel can, but it does not have the overhead of a peer window.

Why do we need to extend the `Container` class? Couldn't we just use `Container` objects instead of `Panel` objects? This does not work—`Container` is an *abstract* class, but it has no abstract methods, which is why we didn't have to redefine any methods when forming the `LightWeightPanel` class. Why make an abstract class with no abstract methods? Because it forces programmers (such as the authors of this book) to clearly separate the concept of a generic container (the `Container` superclass) and a specific container (the `LightWeightPanel`).

You can use the `LightWeightPanel` class exactly as you used the ordinary `Panel` class. For example, you can set a layout manager that the lightweight panel should use to position components inside of it.

Example 9-21 shows a version of the `PanelTest` program that you saw earlier in this chapter. If you compare the code in the two versions, you will see that the only significant changes are:

1. We defined the `LightWeightPanel` class.
2. We replaced the following line of code in the constructor:

   ```
   Panel p = new Panel();
   ```
   by
   ```
   LightWeightPanel p = new LightWeightPanel();
   ```
   (We also only use three buttons this time).

Example 9-21: LightWeightPanelTest.java

```
import java.awt.*;
import java.awt.event.*;
import corejava.*;

public class LightWeightPanelTest extends CloseableFrame
   implements ActionListener
{  public LightWeightPanelTest()
   {  LightWeightPanel p = new LightWeightPanel();
      p.setLayout(new FlowLayout());

      Button yellowButton = new Button("Yellow");
      p.add(yellowButton);
      yellowButton.addActionListener(this);

      Button blueButton = new Button("Blue");
      p.add(blueButton);
      blueButton.addActionListener(this);

      Button redButton = new Button("Red");
      p.add(redButton);
      redButton.addActionListener(this);

      add(p,"North");
   }

   public void actionPerformed(ActionEvent evt)
   {  String arg = evt.getActionCommand();
      Color color = Color.black;
      if (arg.equals("Yellow")) color = Color.yellow;
      else if (arg.equals("Blue")) color = Color.blue;
      else if (arg.equals("Red")) color = Color.red;
      setBackground(color);
      repaint();
   }

   public static void main(String[] args)
   {  Frame f = new LightWeightPanelTest();
      f.show();
   }
}

class LightWeightPanel extends Container {}
```

When you run this program, you will find that it looks *exactly* the same as the `PanelTest` program from the beginning of this chapter. Indeed, the only difference is that the original program puts the three buttons inside a separate window with no decorations, whereas the lightweight version dispenses with that window and places the three buttons directly into the frame window.

To uncover the invisible window (or its absence in the lightweight version), we need to do some sleuthing. We used the Spy utility that is a part of Microsoft Visual C++. One of the many uses of Spy is to peek inside the windows and subwindows of an application. We used the Spy utility to analyze the native windows used in the different versions of the `PanelTest` program. Figures 9-28 and 9-29 show the result.

As you can see by looking at the windows for the two different test programs (highlighted in Figures 9-28 and 9-29), the original panel test program as shown in Figure 9-28 uses an extra window to hold the three buttons. The lightweight panel class does not have a native counterpart, so the components are directly attached to AWTFrame.

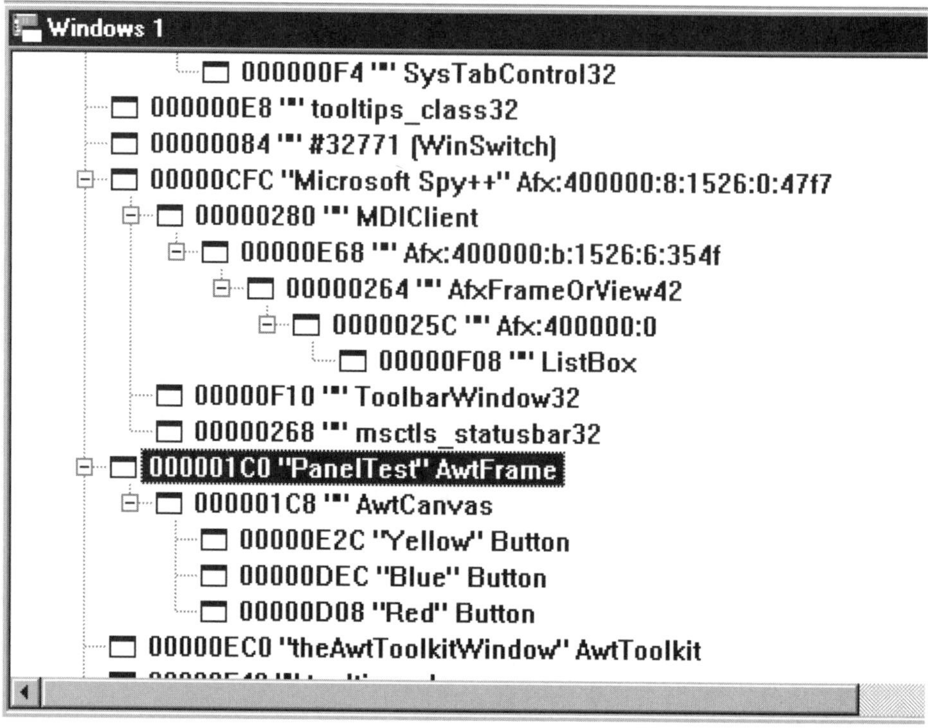

Figure 9-28: Spying on the window layout of the `PanelTest` program

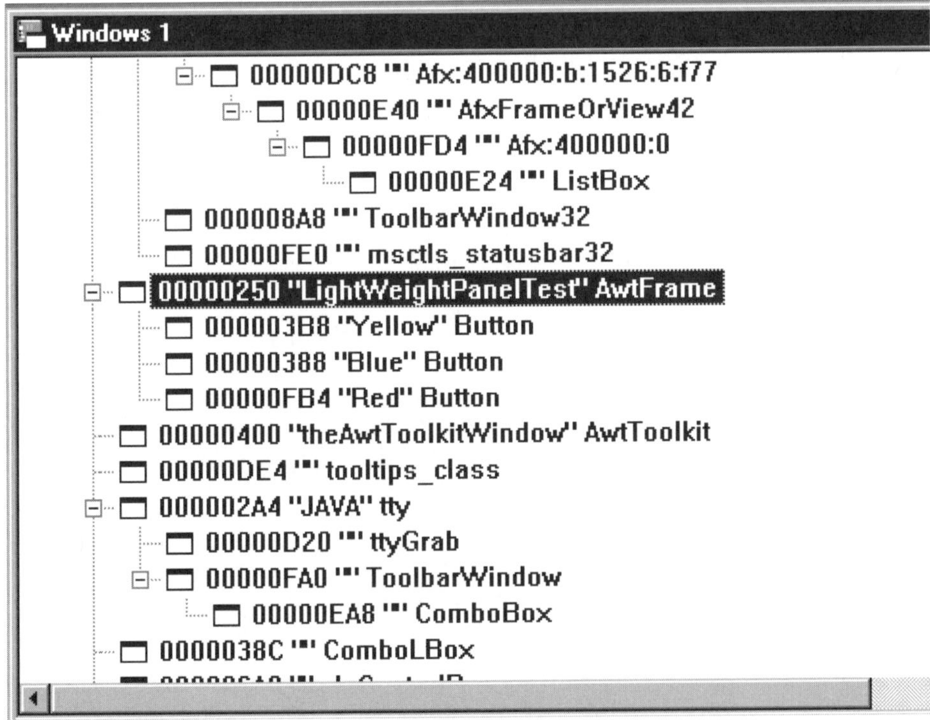

Figure 9-29: The `LightWeightPanelTest` program doesn't use a window to hold the buttons

NOTE: Since lightweight panels have all the advantage of ordinary panels and no disadvantages that we can see, we expect the next version of the AWT to use them exclusively,

More Advanced Lightweight UI Construction

Lightweight components differ from the lightweight panel that you just saw because they extend `Component` (rather than `Container`). You can override the `paint()` method of `Component` in order to draw the lightweight UI. This means that you can have a circular or triangular equivalent of a command button if you want: just don't paint the region you want to be transparent. (See the samples that come with the JDK for a circular command button.)

In this section, we show you how to build an image button. An image button is simply an image that responds to mouse clicks. Image buttons are far more flexible than ordinary buttons, but, of course, you have to write the code to give the user feedback. This can be a pain: you will often need to check where the mouse is and change the image accordingly.

NOTE: JavaSoft has announced that an image button will eventually be a part of Java, but there are no details on it yet.

Most of the code for the constructor of our image button is the kind of boilerplate code you need for managing an image that you saw in Chapter 7. The key new line is set in bold in what follows:

```
{  public ImageButton(String imgSrc)
   {  image = Toolkit.getDefaultToolkit().getImage(imgSrc);
      MediaTracker tracker = new MediaTracker(this);
      tracker.addImage(image, 0);
      try { tracker.waitForID(0); }
      catch (InterruptedException e) {}
      width = image.getWidth(this) + 2 * BORDER_XWIDTH;
      height = image.getHeight(this) + 2 * BORDER_YHEIGHT;
      enableEvents(AWTEvent.MOUSE_EVENT_MASK);
  }
}
```

You saw the `enableEvents` method in Chapter 8: it is how you tell the AWT that your object will be responding to a certain set of events—in this case, mouse events. The next vital step is to write the code that allows the image button to register and remove objects that implement the `mouseListener` interface:

```
public void addActionListener(ActionListener listener)
   {  actionListener =
         AWTEventMulticaster.add(actionListener, listener);
      enableEvents(AWTEvent.MOUSE_EVENT_MASK);
   }

   public void removeActionListener(ActionListener listener)
   {  actionListener =
         AWTEventMulticaster.remove(actionListener, listener);
   }
```

The next bit of code you need is the code to allow the image button to process mouse events and so be able to send them out to listeners. The code looks like this:

```
public void processMouseEvent(MouseEvent e)
   {  if (e.getID() == MouseEvent.MOUSE_PRESSED)
      {  pressed = true;
         repaint();
      }
```

```
        else if (e.getID() == MouseEvent.MOUSE_RELEASED)
        {   if(actionListener != null)
                actionListener.actionPerformed(new ActionEvent(
                    this, ActionEvent.ACTION_PERFORMED, "" + this));
            if (pressed)
            {   pressed = false;
                repaint();
            }
        }
        else if (e.getID() == MouseEvent.MOUSE_EXITED)
        {   if (pressed)
            {   pressed = false;
                repaint();
            }
        }
        super.processMouseEvent(e);
    }
```

The idea of this code is that:

- We need to notify the listeners when the mouse event occurred.
- We need to use a private Boolean instance field called `pressed` that will communicate to the `paint` method whether the user has pressed the button.

Next, note the call to `super.processMouseEvent`. This kind of code is absolutely necessary in your event handling code in order to ensure that the containing component gets a chance to deal with (in this case, mouse) events.

The `paint` method is pretty straightforward (but notice the use of the Boolean flag `pressed` to control the 3D effect):

```
public void paint(Graphics g)
    {   g.drawImage(image, BORDER_XWIDTH, BORDER_YHEIGHT, this);
        g.setColor(Color.gray);
        for (int i = 0; i <= (BORDER_XWIDTH+BORDER_YHEIGHT)/4;
            i++)
            g.draw3DRect(i, i, width - 2 * i - 1,
                height - 2 * i - 1, !pressed);
    }
```

Finally, we also have some boilerplate code to allow the user of our image button to know the minimum and preferred size we want our control to take. Example 9-22 is the complete code for a sample that uses our image button control to change the colors on a frame. Figure 9-30 shows the image button component at work: the images we used are simply GIFs that are little colored balls.

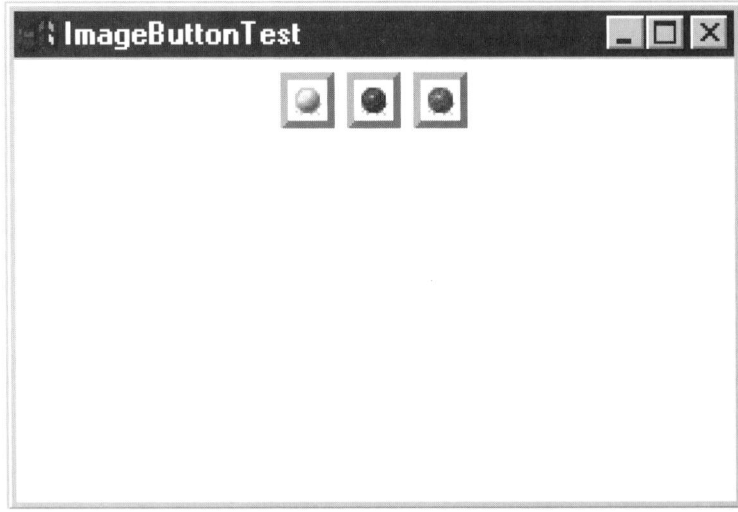

Figure 9-30: Image buttons at work

Example 9-22: ImageButton.java

```
import java.awt.*;
import java.awt.event.*;
import corejava.*;

public class ImageButtonTest extends CloseableFrame
   implements ActionListener
{  public ImageButtonTest()
   {  setLayout(new FlowLayout());

      yellowButton = new ImageButton("yellow-ball.gif");
      add(yellowButton);
      yellowButton.addActionListener(this);

      blueButton = new ImageButton("blue-ball.gif");
      add(blueButton);
      blueButton.addActionListener(this);

      redButton = new ImageButton("red-ball.gif");
      add(redButton);
      redButton.addActionListener(this);
   }
```

```
   public void actionPerformed(ActionEvent evt)
   {  Object src = evt.getSource();
      Color color = Color.black;
      if (src == yellowButton) color = Color.yellow;
      else if (src == blueButton) color = Color.blue;
      else if (src == redButton) color = Color.red;
      setBackground(color);
      repaint();
   }

   public static void main(String[] args)
   {  Frame f = new ImageButtonTest();
      f.show();
   }

   private ImageButton yellowButton;
   private ImageButton blueButton;
   private ImageButton redButton;
}

class ImageButton extends Component
{  public ImageButton(String imgSrc)
   {  image = Toolkit.getDefaultToolkit().getImage(imgSrc);
      MediaTracker tracker = new MediaTracker(this);
      tracker.addImage(image, 0);
      try { tracker.waitForID(0); }
      catch (InterruptedException e) {}
      width = image.getWidth(this) + 2 * BORDER_XWIDTH;
      height = image.getHeight(this) + 2 * BORDER_YHEIGHT;

      enableEvents(AWTEvent.MOUSE_EVENT_MASK);
   }

   public void paint(Graphics g)
   {  g.drawImage(image, BORDER_XWIDTH, BORDER_YHEIGHT, this);
      g.setColor(Color.gray);
      for (int i = 0; i <= (BORDER_XWIDTH+BORDER_YHEIGHT)/4; i++)
         g.draw3DRect(i, i, width - 2 * i - 1,
            height - 2 * i - 1, !pressed);
   }

   public Dimension getPreferredSize()
   {  return getMinimumSize();
   }

   public Dimension getMinimumSize()
   {  return new Dimension(width, height);
   }
```

```
   public void addActionListener(ActionListener listener)
   {  actionListener =
         AWTEventMulticaster.add(actionListener, listener);
      enableEvents(AWTEvent.MOUSE_EVENT_MASK);
   }

   public void removeActionListener(ActionListener listener)
   {  actionListener =
         AWTEventMulticaster.remove(actionListener, listener);
   }

   public void processMouseEvent(MouseEvent e)
   {  if (e.getID() == MouseEvent.MOUSE_PRESSED)
      {  pressed = true;
         repaint();
      }
      else if (e.getID() == MouseEvent.MOUSE_RELEASED)
      {  if(actionListener != null)
            actionListener.actionPerformed(new ActionEvent(
               this, ActionEvent.ACTION_PERFORMED, "" + this));
         if (pressed)
         {  pressed = false;
            repaint();
         }
      }
      else if (e.getID() == MouseEvent.MOUSE_EXITED)
      {  if (pressed)
         {  pressed = false;
            repaint();
         }
      }
      super.processMouseEvent(e);
   }

   public static final int BORDER_XWIDTH = 5;
   public static final int BORDER_YHEIGHT = 5;
   private int width;
   private int height;
   private Image image;
   private boolean pressed = false;
   private ActionListener actionListener;
}
```

Finally, we end this section with three points that you may need to keep in mind when you write a more complex lightweight component.

- If your lightweight component flickers too much, remember that double buffering (see Chapter 7) can eliminate flicker.
- Canvases and panels do not automatically get the focus, which is required for receiving keyboard events. To give a canvas or panel the focus, use the `requestFocus` method. The `mouseClicked` method in the `MouseListener` for a lightweight component that extends `Canvas` or `Panel` should invoke the `requestFocus` method on the component, so that the user can select the component with the mouse and then use keys to change the component state.
- The container of a lightweight component that has a `paint` method must call `super.paint()` or you won't see the lightweight component. All standard Java components do this, but you need to pay attention to this point when you implement your own lightweight containers

In our image button class, we did not pay attention to the first two points, although a well-crafted class would need to implement smooth drawing and a keyboard interface. The third point applies only to lightweight containers.

CHAPTER 10

- Applet Basics
- The Applet HTML Tags
- Passing Information to Applets
- Multimedia
- The Applet Context
- It's an Applet. It's an Application. It's Both!

Applets

At this point, you should be comfortable with using most of the features of Java's *language* as well as most of the features of the AWT graphics library. We hope that you agree with us that Java is a nice (if not perfect), general-purpose OOP language. Of course, the AWT class libraries, despite how much they are improved in 1.1, *still* need a lot more work—but improvements seem to be happening very quickly. Having said all this, a rapidly improving dialect of C++ with a limited set of platform-independent class libraries for graphics development is not why there is so much hype surrounding Java. The unbelievable hype (as was mentioned in Chapters 1 and 2) stems from Java's ability to "activate the Internet." The point is that you can create a special kind of Java program (usually called an *applet*) whose compiled class files a Java-enabled browser can download from the net and then run. This chapter shows you how to write basic applets. Full-featured applets depend on mastering Java's networking abilities along with its ability to handle multiple threads. These advanced topics will be covered in Volume 2.

NOTE: As we write this chapter, Netscape Navigator and Internet Explorer *do not yet support Java 1.1*. This means you probably do not want to deploy applets that use the new features of Java 1.1 (such as the new event model) for general use on the Internet yet. We suggest not doing so until versions of Netscape and Internet Explorer that are Java 1.1-enabled have been available for a few months (to take into account the lag time until people upgrade). The CD that comes with this book has versions of all the code in this chapter that uses Java 1.02. Besides being useful for people moving from Java 1.02 to the new event model in Java 1.1, the code should run in all browsers available now and in the near future.

There was one Java 1.1-enabled browser available to us, the HotJava browser, written by Sun Microsystems. You can get it at `http://www.javasoft.com/products/HotJava/index.html#download`. HotJava is an application (not an applet) written entirely in Java. HotJava is certainly an interesting product: an earlier version was the first application to show off the power of Java applets and, in that sense, inspired the craze that continues unabated today. Versions of it are, therefore, often used as a showpiece for Java. In our opinion, while HotJava 1.0 is certainly flashy, its current performance is disappointing. For example, on Windows we tried the obvious test of trying to read in the file `/java/docs/api/AllNames.html`. HotJava miserably failed this test: we were unable to load this file on any Windows machine we tried, including a 200MHz Pentium computer with 96 Mbytes of memory running Windows 95. We recommend that you use either of the 1.1-enabled versions of Netscape or Internet Explorer when they become available.

Applet Basics

Before Java, HTML was simply a vehicle to indicate elements of a hypertext page. For example, `<TITLE>` indicates the title of the page, and any text that follows this tag becomes the title of the page. You indicate the end of the title with the `</TITLE>` tag. (This is one of the general rules for tags: a slash followed by the name of the element indicates the end of the element.) To use applets via a Web browser, the HTML page must tell the browser which applets to load and where to put each applet on the Web page. It should not come as a surprise that the Java extensions to HTML tell any Java-enabled browser the following:

- The name of the class file
- The location of the class file
- How the applet sits on the Web page (size, location, and so on)

The browser then retrieves the class file from the net (or from a directory on the user's machine) and automatically runs the applet. It then uses its own version of the Java Virtual Machine to interpret the bytecodes. In particular, browser vendors can't simply use the Java Virtual Machine that comes with the JDK. They need to integrate a version of the JVM into the browser—hence, the lag between the availability of the JDK 1.1 and browser support.

In addition to the applet itself, the Web page can contain all the other HTML elements you have seen in use on Web pages: multiple fonts, bulleted lists, graphics, links, and so on. Applets are just one part of the hypertext page. It is always worth keeping in mind that Java is *not* a tool for designing HTML pages; it is a tool for *bringing them to life*. This is not to say that the GUI design elements in a Java applet are not important, but they must work with (and, in fact, are subservient to) the underlying HTML design of the Web page.

NOTE: We do not cover general HTML tags at all; we assume that you know—or are working with someone who knows—the basics of HTML. There are only a few special HTML tags needed for Java applets. We do, of course, cover those later in this chapter. As for learning HTML, there are dozens of HTML books at your local bookstore. One that covers what you need and will not insult your intelligence is *HTML: The Definitive Guide, 2nd edition* by C. Musciano and B. Kennedy from O'Reilly.

A Simple Applet

For tradition's sake, let's modify the `NotHelloWorld` program from Chapter 7 to be an applet. Before we do that, we want to point out that from a programming point of view an applet isn't very strange. An applet is simply a Java class that extends the `Applet` class. The `Applet` class is part of the `java.applet` package. Note that although the `applet` package is not part of the `AWT` package, an applet is an AWT component as the inheritance chain shown in Figure 10-1 illustrates.

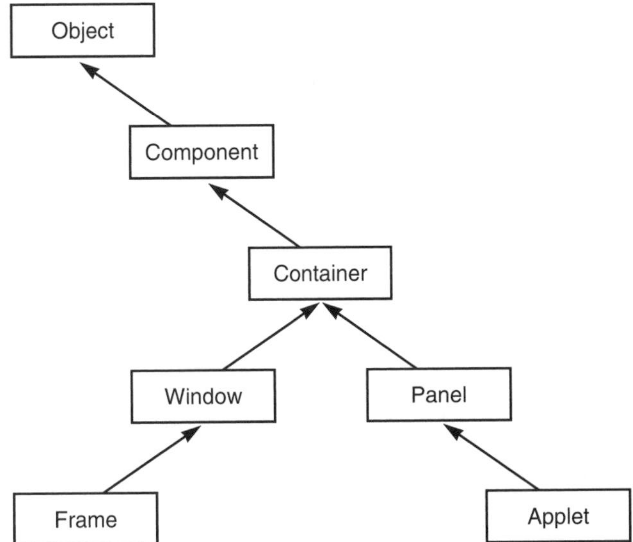

Figure 10-1: Inheritance diagram

This inheritance chain has some obvious but still useful consequences. For example, since applets are AWT components, event handling in applets is done exactly as you saw in Chapter 8, and the basic imaging techniques of Chapter 7 and the advanced image handling techniques from Volume 2 will work with essentially no change as well.

Here's the code for an applet version of "Not Hello World."

```
import java.awt.*;
import java.applet.*;

public class NotHelloAgain extends Applet
{
   public void paint(Graphics g)
   {  Font f = new Font("System", Font.BOLD, 18);
      g.setFont(f);
      g.drawString("We won't use 'hello world.'", 25, 50);
   }
}
```

Notice how similar this is to the corresponding program from Chapter 7. In particular:

- We need a graphics context to draw on.
- We are overriding the `paint` method in order to actually display something.

Next, to make an applet that will work from a Web page that corresponds to this code, you need at a minimum:

- To compile this `.java` file into a class file
- To create an HTML file that tells the browser certain information about the class file

It is customary (but not necessary) to give the HTML file the same name as that of the major applet inside. So, following this tradition, we will call the file: `NotHelloAgain.html`. The minimum information you need in this file looks like this:

```
<APPLET CODE="NotHelloAgain.class" WIDTH=100 HEIGHT=100>
</APPLET>
```

We will explain the options for the `APPLET` tag later in this chapter.

Testing Applets

OK, you have the HTML file and the compiled class file and you want to test your work. First off, the JDK comes with a stand-alone *applet viewer* program that allows you to test your applets in a limited way. For Solaris and Windows 95, this program is simply called `appletviewer`. You will have to check if a version is supplied with the JDK on other platforms and what its name is. You can find it in the `bin` directory below the `java` directory if you use the installation defaults.

To use Sun's applet viewer in our example, enter

```
appletviewer NotHelloAgain.html
```

at the command line. (The command line for the applet viewer program is the name of the HTML file, not the class file.)

TIP: If you are using our customized version of WinEdit or TextPad, then you can get a first glimpse at your applet by compiling and running the source code from within the editor. If you do this, you invoke a (rather weird) batch file that:

1. Tests that the source file contains the string `extends Applet`.
2. Creates a file and puts in the minimum number of HTML tags needed to be able to run your code as an applet (the size of the applet is fixed at 300 by 200 pixels).
3. Saves the file with an HTM extension (so it will not overwrite any of your .html files).
4. Invokes Sun's applet viewer on this file.

Close the applet viewer when you have finished testing your applet. This method gives you a quick and dirty way to test your applets without creating a full-blown HTML page.

The applet viewer is good for the first stage of testing, but at some point you need to run your applets in the ways a user might use them. In particular, the applet viewer program shows you only the applet, not the surrounding HTML text. If an HTML file contains multiple applets, the applet viewer pops up multiple windows.

When it comes to testing your applet in a Java 1.1-enabled browser, then, as mentioned earlier, as we write this, you are restricted to HotJava. This is not a particularly realistic test bed as most of your users will be using either Netscape Navigator or Internet Explorer when their Java 1.1 versions become available. Those browsers will likely have different security settings than does HotJava.

Next, regardless of what Java 1.1-enabled browser you are using, you will want to:

- Try to run the applet locally by loading the HTML file
- Run the applet from across the net by downloading the file. This step is important for performance and for checking security restrictions as well.

NOTE: Netscape 3.0 makes a distinction between opening an HTML file with the File | Open menu and loading it as a local URL (such as `file:///D|/java/docs/api/tree.html`). Applets in files that are loaded with the File | Open menu have no security restrictions. If the same file is loaded through a local URL, the usual applet security restrictions apply. (These restrictions are discussed in the next section.) This feature allows you to check security violations of your applet by opening the HTML file as a file URL instead of as a local file. Please consult the help system on your Java 1.1-enabled browser to see if it also has this useful feature. HotJava doesn't, nor did Internet Explorer 3 and Netscape 4.0.

Security Basics

Because applets are designed to be loaded from a remote site and then executed locally, security becomes vital. In Netscape Navigator and Internet Explorer 3, the viewer of a Web page has only the option of shutting off Java completely. If a user enables Java on the browser, the browser will download all the applet code on the Web page and execute it immediately. For this reason, applets (unlike applications) are restricted in what they can do. The *applet security manager* throws a `SecurityException` whenever an applet attempts to violate one of the access rules. (See Volume 2 for more on security managers.)

What *can* applets do on all platforms? They can show images and play sounds, get keystrokes and mouse clicks from the user, and send user input back to the host from which they were loaded. That is enough functionality to show facts and figures or to get user input for placing an order. But applets playing in the "sandbox" cannot alter the user's system or spy on it. In this chapter, we will look only at applets that run "inside the sand box."

In particular, on most browsers:

- Applets can *never* run any local executable program.
- Applets cannot communicate with any host other than the server from which they were downloaded; that server is called the *originating host*.
- Applets cannot read or write to the local computer's file system.
- Applets cannot find any information about the local computer, except for the Java version used; the name and version of the operating system; and the characters used to separate files (for instance, / or \), paths (such as : or ;), and lines (such as `\n` or `\r\n`). In particular, applets cannot find out the user's name, e-mail address, and so on.
- All windows that an applet pops up carry a warning message.

All this is possible only because applets are *interpreted* by the Java virtual machine and not directly executed by the CPU on the user's computer. Because the interpreter checks all critical instructions and program areas, a hostile (or poorly written) applet will almost certainly not be able to crash the computer, overwrite system memory, or change the privileges granted by the operating system. Table 10-1 shows what we expect most browsers to let Java applets do when they are run in the "sandbox," as well as what stand-alone Java applications can do under the default security manager.

Table 10-1: Java Program Capabilities

	BL	BF	AV	JA
Read local file	no	no	yes	yes
Write local file	no	no	yes	yes
Get file information	no	no	yes	yes
Delete file	no	no	no	yes
Run another program	no	no	yes	yes
Read the `user.name` property	no	yes	yes	yes
Connect to network port on server	yes	yes	yes	yes
Connect to network port on other host	no	yes	yes	yes
Load Java library	no	yes	yes	yes
Call exit	no	no	yes	yes
Create a pop-up window	with warning	yes	yes	yes

BL = Browser loading a URL location, using the default applet security model

BF = Browser loading a local file (however, not all browsers will allow more privileges for local applets)

AV = Applet viewer

JA = Java running an application (not an applet) with no security manager

These restrictions are too strong for some situations. For example, on a corporate Intranet, you can certainly imagine an applet wanting to know on whose machines it is running! To allow for different levels of security under different situations, Java 1.1 introduces *signed applets*. A signed applet carries with it a secure "certificate" that will indicate where the applet came from. With a signed applet then, unless someone breaks the standard encryption systems such as RSA, you can be certain where the applet originates. (We will cover signing in Volume 2.)

The point is that if you trust the signer of the applet, you can tell the browser to give it more privileges. You can, for example, give applets in your corporate Intranet a higher level of trust than those from `www.hacker.com`. Right now, only HotJava and the applet viewer can be configured to recognize security certificates. Netscape has announced that future versions of the Netscape browser will also have customizable security, as almost certainly will Internet Explorer 4. The configurable Java security model allows the continuum of privilege levels you need. You can give completely trusted applets the same privilege levels as local applications. Programs from vendors that are known to be somewhat flaky can be given access to some, but not all, privileges. Unknown applets can be restricted to the "sandbox."

To sum up, Java has three separate mechanisms for enforcing security:

1. Program code is interpreted by the Java virtual machine, not executed directly.
2. A security manager checks all sensitive operations in the Java run-time library.
3. Applets can be signed to identify their origin.

NOTE: In contrast, the security model of the ActiveX technology by Microsoft relies solely on the third option. If you want to run an ActiveX control at all, you must trust it completely. That model works fine when you deal with a small number of trusted suppliers, but it simply does not scale up to the World Wide Web.

Converting Applications to Applets

It is easy to convert a graphical Java application (that is, an application that uses the AWT and that you can start with the `java` command-line interpreter) into an applet that you can embed in a Web page. Essentially, all of the user interface code can stay the same. To understand why this is possible, recall that, as shown in Figure 10-1 on page 465, both the `Applet` and the `Frame` class descend from `Container`. Therefore, you can continue to use the same methods in the `Container` class to add user interface components. For example, you add a button to an applet with a call to

```
add(new Button("Start"));
```

or a canvas with a call to

```
add(new Canvas());
```

On the other hand, there are a few subtle points that can trip you up. Probably the most common is that the default layout managers for frames and applets are

different. Recall that for frames (used in applications), the default layout manager is `BorderLayout`. For panels (and, hence, applets), it is the `FlowLayout` manager. This means that, if you have not set a specific layout manager for your application, you will have implicitly used the `BorderLayout` manager. In that case, you will need to change the layout manager in the applet to `BorderLayout`. Here are the specific steps for converting an application to an applet.

1. Make an HTML page with an `APPLET` tag.
2. Eliminate the `main` method in the application. Usually `main` contains code to make a new frame object. With applets, that task is automatically taken care of by the browser, since it makes an object of the class specified in the `APPLET` tag. Also, `main` or the constructor usually sets the frame size and location. You should remove the reference to `setSize` and `setLocation`; for applets, sizing is done with the `WIDTH` and `HEIGHT` fields of the `APPLET` tag in the actual HTML file, and absolute positioning of an applet on a Web page is currently impossible.
3. Derive the class from `Applet`, not from `Frame`.
4. Replace the constructor with a method called `init`. When the browser creates an object of the applet class, it calls the `init()` method.
5. If the application's frame implicitly uses a border layout, you must set the layout manager for the applet in the `init` function. For example, compare the following code with the constructor for the calculator program in Chapter 7:

```
public class CalculatorApplet extends Applet
{  public void init()
   {  setLayout(new BorderLayout());
         // required in applet, not in frame
      display = new TextField("0");
      display.setEditable(false);
      add(display, "North");
      . . .
   }
}
```

6. If the application calls `setTitle` somewhere, eliminate the call to the method. Applets cannot have title bars. (You can, of course, title the Web page itself, using the `<TITLE>` HTML tag.) If the application uses menus, eliminate them and replace them with buttons or some other user interface component.

As an example of this transformation, we will change the calculator application from Chapter 7 into an applet. In Figure 10-2, you can see how it looks, sitting inside a Web page:

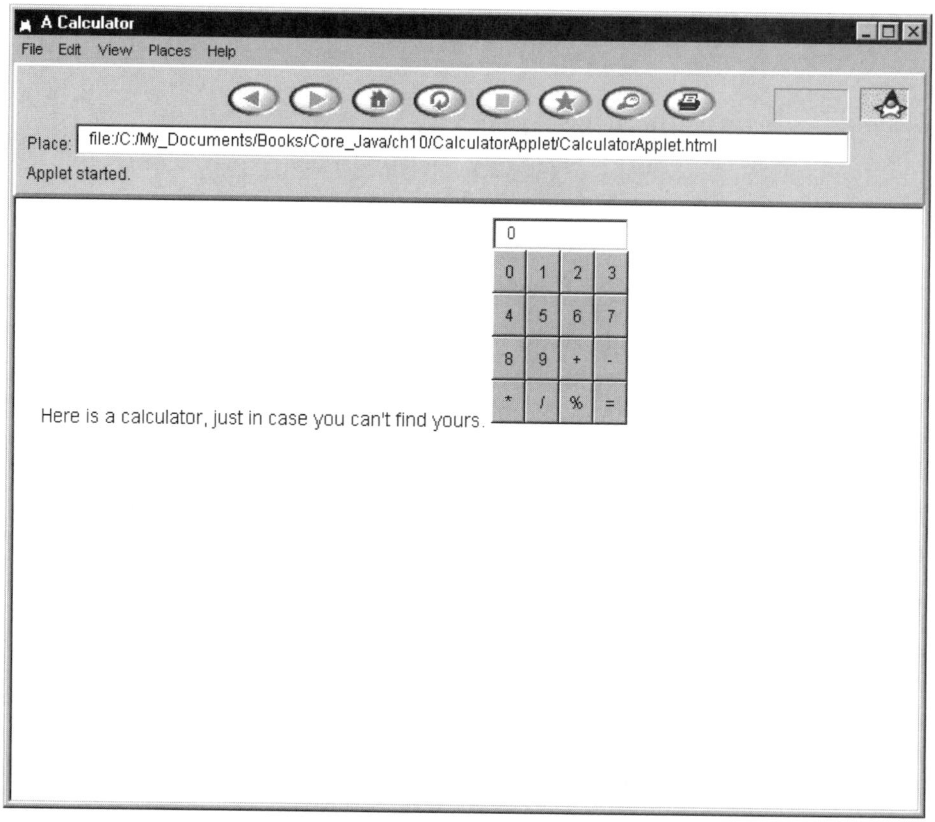

Figure 10-2: A calculator applet

Here is the HTML page:

```
<HTML>
<TITLE>A Calculator</TITLE>
<BODY>
Here is a calculator, just in case you can't find yours.
<APPLET CODE="CalculatorApplet.class" WIDTH=100 HEIGHT=150>
</APPLET>
</BODY>
</HTML>
```

Example 10-1 is the code for the applet.

Example 10-1: CalculatorApplet.java

```
import java.awt.*;
import java.awt.event.*;
import java.applet.*;
import corejava.*;

public class CalculatorApplet extends Applet
   implements ActionListener
{  public void init()
   {  setLayout(new BorderLayout());

      display = new TextField("0");
      display.setEditable(false);
      add(display, "North");

      Panel p = new Panel();
      p.setLayout(new GridLayout(4, 4));
      for (int i = 0; i <= 9; i++)
         addButton(p, "" + (char)('0' + i));
      addButton(p, "+");
      addButton(p, "-");
      addButton(p, "*");
      addButton(p, "/");
      addButton(p, "%");
      addButton(p, "=");
      add(p, "Center");
   }

   public void addButton(Container c, String s)
   {  Button b = new Button(s);
      c.add(b);
      b.addActionListener(this);
   }

   public void actionPerformed(ActionEvent evt)
   {  String s = evt.getActionCommand();
      if ('0' <= s.charAt(0) && s.charAt(0) <= '9')
      {  if (start) display.setText(s);
         else display.setText(display.getText() + s);
         start = false;
      }
      else
      {  if (start)
         {  if (s.equals("-"))
            { display.setText(s); start = false; }
```

```
                else op = s;
            }
            else
            {   calculate(Integer.parseInt(display.getText()));
                op = s;
                start = true;
            }
        }
    }

    public void calculate(int n)
    {   if (op.equals("+")) arg += n;
        else if (op.equals("-")) arg -= n;
        else if (op.equals("*")) arg *= n;
        else if (op.equals("/")) arg /= n;
        else if (op.equals("%")) arg %= n;
        else if (op.equals("=")) arg = n;
        display.setText("" + arg);
    }

    private TextField display;
    private int arg = 0;
    private String op = "=";
    private boolean start = true;
}
```

`java.applet.Applet`

- `void init()`

  is called when the applet is first loaded. Override this method and place all initialization code here.

- `void setSize(int width, int height)`

  requests that the applet be resized. This would be a great method if it worked on Web pages; unfortunately, it does not work in current browsers because it interferes with their page-layout mechanisms. But it does work in the applet viewer, and perhaps future browsers will support it and reflow the page when the applet size changes.

Life Cycle of an Applet

There are four methods in the `Applet` class that give you the framework on which you build any serious applet: `init()`, `start()`, `stop()`, `destroy()`. What follows is a short description of these methods, when these methods are called, and what code you should place into them.

init

This method is used for whatever initializations are needed for your applet. This works much like a constructor—it is automatically called by the system when Java launches the applet for the first time. Common actions in an applet include processing `PARAM` values and adding user interface components.

Applets can have a default constructor, but it is customary to perform all initialization in the `init` method instead of the default constructor.

start

This method is automatically called *after* Java calls the `init` method. It is also called whenever the user returns to the page containing the applet after having gone off to other pages. This means that the `start` method can be called repeatedly, unlike the `init` method. For this reason, put the code that you want executed only once in the `init` method, rather than in the `start` method. The `start` method is where you usually restart a thread for your applet, for example, to resume an animation. If your applet does nothing that needs to be suspended when the user leaves the current Web page, you do not need to implement this method (or the `stop` method).

stop

This method is automatically called when the user moves off the page on which the applet sits. It can, therefore, be called repeatedly in the same applet. Its purpose is to give you a chance to stop a time-consuming activity from slowing down the system when the user is not paying attention to the applet. You should not call this method directly. If your applet does not perform animation, play audio files, or perform calculations in a thread, you do not usually need to use this method.

destroy

Java guarantees to call this method when the browser shuts down normally. Since applets are meant to live on an HTML page, you do not need to worry about destroying the panel. This will happen automatically when the browser shuts down. What you *do* need to put in the `destroy` method is the code for reclaiming any non-memory-dependent resources such as graphics contexts that you may have consumed. Of course, Java calls the `stop` method before calling the `destroy` method if the applet is still active.

`java.applet.Applet`

- `void start()`

  overrides this method for code that needs to be executed *every time* the user visits the browser page containing this applet. A typical action is to reactivate a thread.

- `void stop()`

  overrides this method for code that needs to be executed *every time* the user leaves the browser page containing this applet. A typical action is to suspend a thread.

- `void destroy()`

  overrides this method for code that needs to be executed when the user exits the browser. A typical action is to call `destroy` on system objects.

The Applet HTML Tags

You have already seen the `APPLET` tag in action. In its most basic form, it looks like this:

```
<APPLET CODE="NotHelloAgain.class" WIDTH=100 HEIGHT=100>
```

As you have seen, the `CODE` tag gives the name of the class file and must include the `.class` extension; the `WIDTH` and `HEIGHT` tags size the window that will hold the applet. Both are measured in pixels. You also need a matching `</APPLET>` tag that marks the end of the HTML tagging needed for an applet. These tags are required. If any are missing, the browser cannot load your applet.

All of this information would usually be embedded in an HTML page that, at the very least, might look like this:

```
<HTML>
<HEAD>
<TITLE>NotHelloAgain</TITLE>
</HEAD>
<BODY>
The next line of text is displayed through
the auspices of Java:
<APPLET CODE= "NotHelloAgain.class" WIDTH=100 HEIGHT= 100>
Any text here appears in non-Java enabled browsers only.
</APPLET>
</BODY>
</HTML>
```

NOTE: Whether or not case is relevant in the various applet tags such as <APPLET> depends on your system. Windows 95 and Solaris ignore case in HTML tags. Case is relevant in identifying the name of the applet class. The letter case may be significant in other items enclosed in quotes, such as names of JAR files, if the Web server file system is case sensitive.

What follows are short discussions of the various attributes you can (or must) use following the `<APPLET>` tag in order to position your applet. For those familiar with HTML, these tags are similar to those used with the `<IMG>` tag for image placement on a Web page.

Applet Tags for Positioning

WIDTH, HEIGHT

These attributes are required and give the width and height of the applet, as measured in pixels. In the applet viewer, this is the initial size of the applet. You can resize any window that the applet viewer creates. In Netscape, you *cannot* resize the applet. You will need to make a good guess about how much space your applet requires to show up well for all users.

ALIGN

This attribute specifies the alignment of the applet. There are two basic choices. The applet can be a block with text flowing around it, or the applet can be *inline,* floating inside a line of text as if it were an oversized text character. The first two values (LEFT and RIGHT) make the text flow around the applet. The others make the applet flow with the text.

The choices are described in Table 10-2 and can be seen in Figure 10-3.

Table 10-2: Applet Positioning Tags

Attribute	What It Does
LEFT	Places the applet at the left margin of the page. Text that follows on the page goes in the space to the right of the applet.
RIGHT	Places the applet at the right margin of the page. Text that follows on the page goes in the space to the left of the applet.
BOTTOM	Places the bottom of the applet at the bottom of the text in the current line.
TOP	Places the top of the applet with the top of the current line.
TEXTTOP	Places the top of the applet with the top of the text in the current line.

Attribute	What It Does
MIDDLE	Places the middle of the applet with the baseline of the current line.
ABSMIDDLE	Places the middle of the applet with the middle of the current line.
BASELINE	Places the bottom of the applet with the baseline of the current line.
ABSBOTTOM	Places the bottom of the applet with the bottom of the current line.
VSPACE, HSPACE	These optional attributes specify the number of pixels above and below the applet (VSPACE) and on each side of the applet (HSPACE).

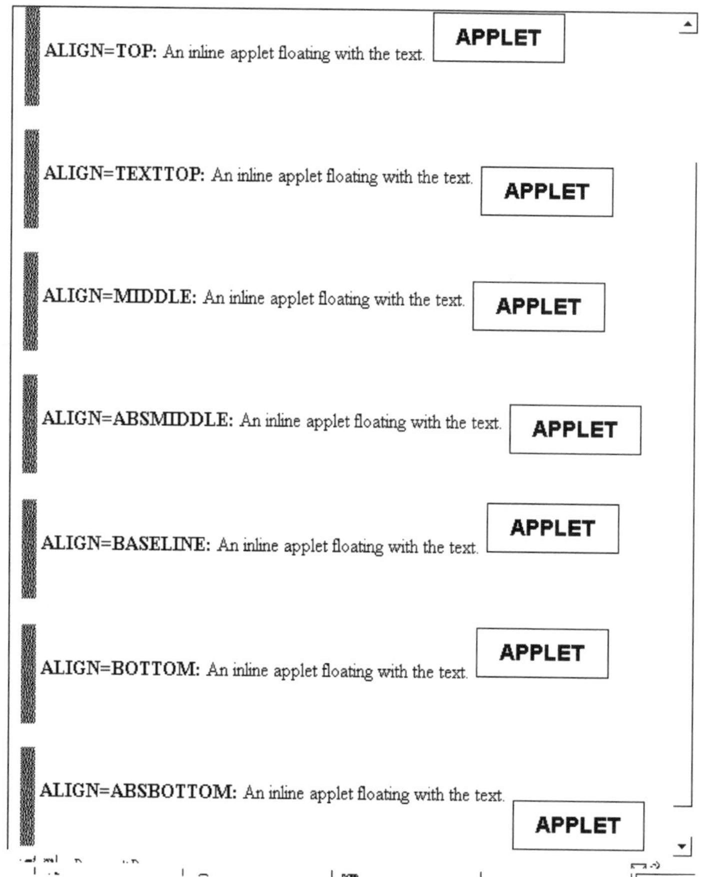

Figure 10-3: Applet alignment

The Applet Tags for Code

Four applet tags work directly with the code you write; here are short descriptions of the first three. The last one is for passing parameters to your applets; we discuss that in the next section.

CODE

This required tag gives the name of the applet's class (or compiled) file. This name is taken relative to where the current page was located. This could be either a local directory or a net URL. You cannot use absolute path names here.

CODEBASE

This optional attribute tells Java that your class files are found below the directory indicated in the CODEBASE tag. For example, if an applet called `FirstApplet.class` is in the directory `MyApplets` and the `MyApplets` directory is *below* the location of the web page, you would use:

```
<APPLET CODE="FirstApplet.class" CODEBASE="MyApplets" WIDTH=100
   HEIGHT=100>
```

ARCHIVE

This optional attribute lists the Java archive file or files that contain classes and other resources for the applet. (See JAR files on page 500 for more on Java archive files.) These files are fetched from the Web server before the applet is loaded. The class loader looks inside these files before fetching files from the server. This technique speeds up the loading process significantly. The files are separated by commas. For example:

```
<APPLET CODE="Retire.class"
   ARCHIVE="RetireClasses.jar,corejava/CoreJavaClasses.jar"
   WIDTH=400 HEIGHT=300
>
```

OBJECT

As another way to specify the applet class file, you can specify the name of a file that contains the serialized applet object. (An object is *serialized* when you write all its data fields to a file. We will discuss serialization in Volume 2.) The object is deserialized from the file in order to return it to its previous state. When you use this tag, the `init` method is *not* called, but the applet's `start` method is called. Before serializing an applet object, its `stop` method should be called. This feature is useful to implement a persistent browser that automatically reloads its applets and has them return to the same state that they were in when the browser was closed. This is a specialized feature, not normally encountered by Web page designers.

Either CODE or OBJECT must be present in every APPLET tag. For example,

```
<APPLET OBJECT="Retire.object" WIDTH=400 HEIGHT=300>
```

NAME

This is a rare tag, but it is essential when you want two applets on the same page to communicate with each other. It specifies a name for the current applet instance. You would pass this string to the getApplet method of the AppletContext class if your browser permits inter-applet communication.

The Applet Tags for Java-Challenged Viewers

If a Web page containing an APPLET tag is viewed by a browser that is not aware of Java applets, then the browser ignores the unknown APPLET and PARAM tags. All text between the <APPLET> and </APPLET> tags is displayed by the browser. Conversely, Java-aware browsers do not display any text between the <APPLET> and </APPLET> tags. You can display messages inside these tags for those poor folks that use a prehistoric browser. For example,

```
<APPLET CODE="Retire.class" WIDTH=400 HEIGHT=300>
If your browser could show Java, you would see
a retirement calculator here
</APPLET>
```

Of course, nowadays most browsers know about Java, but Java may be deactivated, perhaps by the user or by a paranoid system administrator. Use the ALT tag to display a message to these unfortunate souls.

```
<APPLET CODE="Retire.class" WIDTH=400 HEIGHT=300
ALT="If your browser could show Java, you would see
a retirement calculator here"
>
```

Embedding an Applet into a Web Page

Here is a fun and useful applet that calculates whether you are saving enough money for your retirement. You enter your age, how much money you save every month, and so on. Figure 10-4 shows you how it will look in the applet viewer. Note that you must enter integers in the various text fields.

The text box and the graph show the balance of the retirement account for every year. If the numbers turn negative toward the later part of your life and the bars in the graph turn red, you need to do something, for example, save more money, postpone your retirement, or die earlier. As you can see, if you look at the HTML code on the CD, the surrounding Web page tells how to enter the information and how to interpret the outcome.

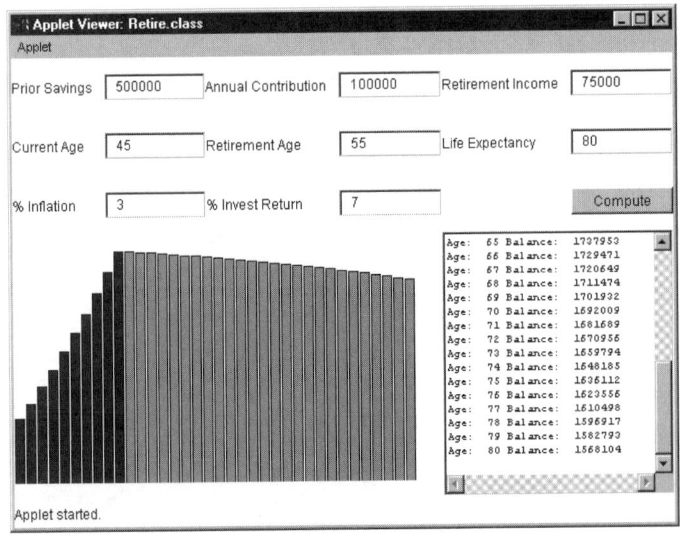

Figure 10-4: A retirement calculator

When you look at the code for the applet in Example 10-2, you will find that it is almost identical to the code for the graphical applications that we discussed in the last two chapters. There are two differences. We derive from `Applet`, not `Frame`, and we move the code from the `main` function and the constructor into the `init` method.

Example 10-2: Retire.java

```
import java.awt.*;
import java.awt.event.*;
import java.applet.*;
import java.io.*;
import corejava.*;

public class Retire extends Applet implements ActionListener
{  public void init()
   {  GridBagLayout gbl = new GridBagLayout();
      setLayout(gbl);

      GridBagConstraints gbc = new GridBagConstraints();
      gbc.fill = GridBagConstraints.HORIZONTAL;
      gbc.weightx = 100;
      gbc.weighty = 100;
      add(new Label("Prior Savings"), gbc, 0, 0, 1, 1);
      add(savingsField, gbc, 1, 0, 1, 1);
      add(new Label("Annual Contribution"),
         gbc, 2, 0, 1, 1);
      add(contribField, gbc, 3, 0, 1, 1);
```

```
      add(new Label("Retirement Income"), gbc, 4, 0, 1, 1);
      add(incomeField, gbc, 5, 0, 1, 1);
      add(new Label("Current Age"), gbc, 0, 1, 1, 1);
      add(currentAgeField, gbc, 1, 1, 1, 1);
      add(new Label("Retirement Age"), gbc, 2, 1, 1, 1);
      add(retireAgeField, gbc, 3, 1, 1, 1);
      add(new Label("Life Expectancy"), gbc, 4, 1, 1, 1);
      add(deathAgeField, gbc, 5, 1, 1, 1);
      add(new Label("% Inflation"), gbc, 0, 2, 1, 1);
      add(inflationPercentField, gbc, 1, 2, 1, 1);
      add(new Label("% Invest Return"), gbc, 2, 2, 1, 1);
      add(investPercentField, gbc, 3, 2, 1, 1);
      Button computeButton = new Button("Compute");
      computeButton.addActionListener(this);
      add(computeButton, gbc, 5, 2, 1, 1);
      add(retireCanvas, gbc, 0, 3, 4, 1);
      gbc.fill = GridBagConstraints.BOTH;
      add(retireText, gbc, 4, 3, 2, 1);
      retireText.setEditable(false);
      retireText.setFont(new Font("Monospaced", Font.PLAIN, 10));
   }

   public void add(Component c, GridBagConstraints gbc,
      int x, int y, int w, int h)
   {  gbc.gridx = x;
      gbc.gridy = y;
      gbc.gridwidth = w;
      gbc.gridheight = h;
      add(c, gbc);
   }

   public void actionPerformed(ActionEvent evt)
   {  if (evt.getActionCommand().equals("Compute"))
      {  if (savingsField.isValid()
            && contribField.isValid()
            && incomeField.isValid()
            && currentAgeField.isValid()
            && retireAgeField.isValid()
            && deathAgeField.isValid()
            && inflationPercentField.isValid()
            && investPercentField.isValid())
         {  RetireInfo info = new RetireInfo();
            info.savings = savingsField.getValue();
            info.contrib = contribField.getValue();
            info.income = incomeField.getValue();
            info.currentAge = currentAgeField.getValue();
            info.retireAge = retireAgeField.getValue();
            info.deathAge = deathAgeField.getValue();
            info.inflationPercent
               = inflationPercentField.getValue();
            info.investPercent
```

```
                  = investPercentField.getValue();
            retireCanvas.redraw(info);
            int i;
            retireText.setText("");
            for (i = info.currentAge; i <= info.deathAge; i++)
            {  retireText.append(
                  new Format("Age: %3d").form(i)
                     + new Format(" Balance: %8d\n")
                     .form(info.getBalance(i)));
            }
         }
      }
   }

   private IntTextField savingsField
      = new IntTextField(0, 10);
   private IntTextField contribField
      = new IntTextField(9000, 10);
   private IntTextField incomeField
      = new IntTextField(0, 10);
   private IntTextField currentAgeField
      = new IntTextField(0, 4);
   private IntTextField retireAgeField
      = new IntTextField(65, 4);
   private IntTextField deathAgeField
      = new IntTextField(85, 4);
   private IntTextField inflationPercentField
      = new IntTextField(5, 4);
   private IntTextField investPercentField
      = new IntTextField(10, 4);
   private RetireCanvas retireCanvas = new RetireCanvas();
   private TextArea retireText = new TextArea(10, 25);
}

class RetireInfo
{  public int getBalance(int year)
   {  if (year < currentAge) return 0;
      else if (year == currentAge)
      {  age = year;
         balance = savings;
         return balance;
      }
      else if (year == age)
         return balance;
      if (year != age + 1)
         getBalance(year - 1);
      age = year;
      if (age < retireAge)
         balance += contrib;
      else
         balance -= income;
```

```
      balance = (int)(balance
         * (1 + (investPercent - inflationPercent) / 100.0));
      return balance;
   }

   int savings;
   int contrib;
   int income;
   int currentAge;
   int retireAge;
   int deathAge;
   int inflationPercent;
   int investPercent;

   private int age;
   private int balance;
}

class RetireCanvas extends Canvas
{  public RetireCanvas()
   {  setSize(400, 200);
   }

   public void redraw(RetireInfo newInfo)
   {  info = newInfo;
      repaint();
   }

   public void paint(Graphics g)
   {  if (info == null) return;

      int minValue = 0;
      int maxValue = 0;
      int i;
      for (i = info.currentAge; i <= info.deathAge; i++)
      {  int v = info.getBalance(i);
         if (minValue > v) minValue = v;
         if (maxValue < v) maxValue = v;
      }
      if (maxValue == minValue) return;

      Dimension d = getSize();
      int barWidth = d.width / (info.deathAge
         - info.currentAge + 1);
      double scale = (double)d.height
         / (maxValue - minValue);

      for (i = info.currentAge; i <= info.deathAge; i++)
      {  int x1 = (i - info.currentAge) * barWidth + 1;
         int y1;
         int v = info.getBalance(i);
```

```
        int height;
        int yOrigin = (int)(maxValue * scale);

        if (v >= 0)
        {  y1 = (int)((maxValue - v) * scale);
           height = yOrigin - y1;
        }
        else
        {  y1 = yOrigin;
           height = (int)(-v * scale);
        }

        if (i < info.retireAge)
           g.setColor(Color.blue);
        else if (v >= 0)
           g.setColor(Color.green);
        else
           g.setColor(Color.red);
        g.fillRect(x1, y1, barWidth - 2, height);
        g.setColor(Color.black);
        g.drawRect(x1, y1, barWidth - 2, height);
     }
  }

  private RetireInfo info = null;
}
```

Passing Information to Applets

Just as applications have the ability to use command-line information, applets have the ability to use parameters that are embedded in the HTML file. This is done via the HTML tag called PARAM. For example, suppose you want to let the Web page determine the size of the font to use in your applet. You could use the following HTML tags:

```
<APPLET CODE="FontTestApplet.class" WIDTH=200, HEIGHT=200>
<PARAM NAME=font VALUE="Helvetica">
</APPLET>
```

You then pick up the value of the parameter, using the `getParameter` method of the `Applet` class, as in the following example of a `paint` procedure:

```
import java.applet.*;
import java.awt.*;

public class FontTestApplet extends Applet
{  public void paint(Graphics g)
   {  String fontName = getParameter("font");
      Font f = new Font(fontName, Font.BOLD, 18);
      g.setFont(f);
      g.drawString("We won't use 'hello world.'", 25, 50);
   }
}
```

Parameters are always returned as strings. You need to convert the string to a numeric type if that is what is called for. You do this in the standard ways: either by using the appropriate method, such as `parseInt` of the `Integer` class, or by using methods such as `atof` in our `Format` class.

For example, if we wanted to add a size parameter for the font, then the HTML code might look like this:

```
<APPLET CODE="FontTestApplet.class" WIDTH=200 HEIGHT=200>
<PARAM NAME=font VALUE="Helvetica">
<PARAM NAME=size VALUE="24">
</APPLET>
```

The following source code shows how to read the integer parameter.

```
import java.awt.*;
import java.applet.*;

public class FontTestApplet extends Applet
{  public void paint(Graphics g)
   {  String fontName = getParameter("font");
      int fontSize = Integer.parseInt(getParameter("size"));
      Font f = new Font(fontName, Font.BOLD, fontSize);
      g.setFont(f);
      g.drawString("We won't use 'hello world.'", 25, 50);
   }
}
```

NOTE: The strings used when you define the parameters via the `PARAM` tag and those used in the `getParameter` method must match exactly. In particular, both are case sensitive.

In addition to ensuring that the parameters match in your code, you should find out whether or not the `size` parameter was left out. You do this with a simple test for `null`. For example:

```
int fontsize;
String sizeString = getParameter("size");
if (sizeString == null) fontSize = 12;
else fontSize = Integer.parseInt(sizeString);
```

Here is a useful applet that uses parameters extensively. The applet draws a bar chart, shown in Figure 10-5.

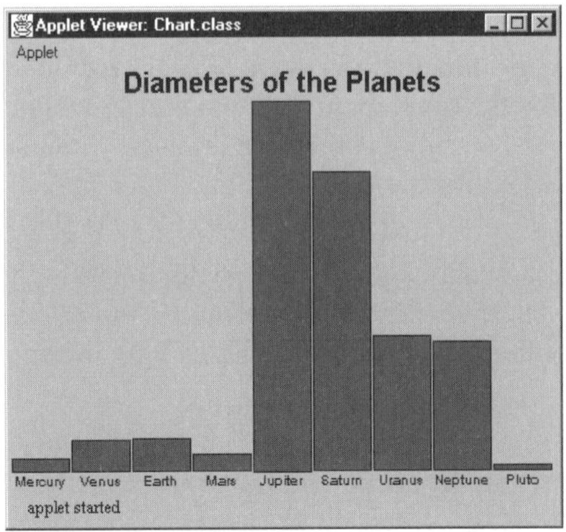

Figure 10-5: A chart applet

The applet takes the labels and the heights of the bars from the PARAM values in the HTML file. Here is what the HTML file for Figure 10-5 looks like:

```
<APPLET CODE="Chart.class" WIDTH=400 HEIGHT=300>
<PARAM NAME="title" VALUE="Diameters of the Planets">
<PARAM NAME="values" VALUE="9">
<PARAM NAME="name_1" VALUE="Mercury">
<PARAM NAME="name_2" VALUE="Venus">
<PARAM NAME="name_3" VALUE="Earth">
<PARAM NAME="name_4" VALUE="Mars">
<PARAM NAME="name_5" VALUE="Jupiter">
<PARAM NAME="name_6" VALUE="Saturn">
<PARAM NAME="name_7" VALUE="Uranus">
<PARAM NAME="name_8" VALUE="Neptune">
<PARAM NAME="name_9" VALUE="Pluto">
<PARAM NAME="value_1" VALUE="3100">
<PARAM NAME="value_2" VALUE="7500">
<PARAM NAME="value_3" VALUE="8000">
<PARAM NAME="value_4" VALUE="4200">
<PARAM NAME="value_5" VALUE="88000">
<PARAM NAME="value_6" VALUE="71000">
<PARAM NAME="value_7" VALUE="32000">
<PARAM NAME="value_8" VALUE="30600">
<PARAM NAME="value_9" VALUE="1430">
</APPLET>
```

You could have set up an array of strings and an array of numbers in the applet. But there are two advantages to using the PARAM mechanism instead. You can have multiple copies of the same applet on your Web page, showing different graphs: just put two APPLET tags with different sets of parameters on the page. And you can change the data that you want to chart. Admittedly, the diameters of the planets will stay the same for quite some time, but suppose your Web page contains a chart of weekly sales data. It is easy to update the Web page because it is plain text. Editing and recompiling a Java file on a weekly basis is more tedious.

In fact, someone has probably figured out how to do fancier graphs than the one in our chart applet. If you find one, you can drop it into your Web page and feed it parameters without ever needing to know how the applet renders the graphs.

Example 10-3 is the source code of our chart applet. Note that the `init` method reads the parameters, and the `paint` method draws the chart.

Example 10-3: Chart.java

```
import java.awt.*;
import java.applet.*;
import java.io.*;
import corejava.*;

public class Chart extends Applet
{  public void init()
   {  String v = getParameter("values");
      if (v == null) return;
      int n = Format.atoi(v);
      values = new double[n];
      names = new String[n];
      title = getParameter("title");
      int i;
      for (i = 0; i < n; i++)
      {  values[i]
            = Format.atof(getParameter("value_" + (i + 1)));
         names[i] = getParameter("name_" + (i + 1));
      }
   }

   public void paint(Graphics g)
   {  if (values == null || values.length == 0) return;
      int i;
      double minValue = 0;
      double maxValue = 0;
      for (i = 0; i < values.length; i++)
      {  if (minValue > values[i]) minValue = values[i];
         if (maxValue < values[i]) maxValue = values[i];
      }

      Dimension d = getSize();
```

```
      int clientWidth = d.width;
      int clientHeight = d.height;
      int barWidth = clientWidth / values.length;

      Font titleFont = new Font("SansSerif", Font.BOLD, 20);
      FontMetrics titleFontMetrics
         = g.getFontMetrics(titleFont);
      Font labelFont = new Font("SansSerif", Font.PLAIN, 10);
      FontMetrics labelFontMetrics
         = g.getFontMetrics(labelFont);

      int titleWidth = titleFontMetrics.stringWidth(title);
      int y = titleFontMetrics.getAscent();
      int x = (clientWidth - titleWidth) / 2;
      g.setFont(titleFont);
      g.drawString(title, x, y);

      int top = titleFontMetrics.getHeight();
      int bottom = labelFontMetrics.getHeight();
      if (maxValue == minValue) return;
      double scale = (clientHeight - top - bottom)
         / (maxValue - minValue);
      y = clientHeight - labelFontMetrics.getDescent();
      g.setFont(labelFont);

      for (i = 0; i < values.length; i++)
      {  int x1 = i * barWidth + 1;
         int y1 = top;
         int height = (int)(values[i] * scale);
         if (values[i] >= 0)
            y1 += (int)((maxValue - values[i]) * scale);
         else
         {  y1 += (int)(maxValue * scale);
            height = -height;
         }

         g.setColor(Color.red);
         g.fillRect(x1, y1, barWidth - 2, height);
         g.setColor(Color.black);
         g.drawRect(x1, y1, barWidth - 2, height);
         int labelWidth
            = labelFontMetrics.stringWidth(names[i]);
         x = i * barWidth + (barWidth - labelWidth) / 2;
         g.drawString(names[i], x, y);
      }
   }

   private double[] values;
   private String[] names;
   private String title;
}
```

java.applet.Applet

- `public String getParameter(String name)`

  gets a parameter defined with a `PARAM` directive in the Web page loading the applet. The string is case sensitive.

- `public String getAppletInfo()`

  is a method that many applet authors override to return a string that contains information about the author, version, and copyright of the current applet. You need to create this information by overriding this method in your applet class.

- `public String[][] getParameterInfo()`

  is a method that many applet authors override to return an array of `PARAM` tag options that this applet supports. Each row contains three entries: the name, the type, and a description of the parameter. Here is an example:

  ```
  "fps", "1-10", "frames per second"
  "repeat", "boolean", "repeat image loop?"
  "images", "url", "directory containing images"
  ```

Dialog Boxes in Applets

An applet sits embedded in a Web page, in a frame of a size that is fixed by the `WIDTH` and `HEIGHT` values in the `APPLET` tag of the HTML page. This can be quite limiting. Many programmers wonder whether they can have a pop-up dialog box or menus to make better use of the available space. It is, indeed, possible to create a pop-up dialog box. Here is a simple applet with a single button labeled Calculator. When you click on the button, a calculator pops up in a separate window.

This is easy to do. We simply use the `Calculator` class from Chapter 7. Recall that it is derived from `Frame`, so we add the necessary code to create a new calculator object as indicated by the bold line of the following code.

```
public class PopupCalculatorApplet extends Applet
   implements ActionListener
{  public void init()
   {  Button calcButton = new Button("Calculator");
      calcButton.addActionListener(this);
      add(calcButton);
   }
   public void actionPerformed(ActionEvent evt)
   {  if (calc.isVisible()) calc.setVisible(false);
      else calc.show();
   }

   private Frame calc = new Calculator();
}
```

When you click on the calculator button, the dialog box pops up and floats over the Web page. When you click on the button again, the calculator goes away.

There is, however, a catch that you need to know about before you put this applet on your Web page. To see how the calculator looks to a potential user, load the Web page from a file URL, for example, by making a bookmark to it, exiting and restarting your browser, and then opening the bookmark. The calculator will be surrounded by a border with an ominous warning message (see Figure 10-6).

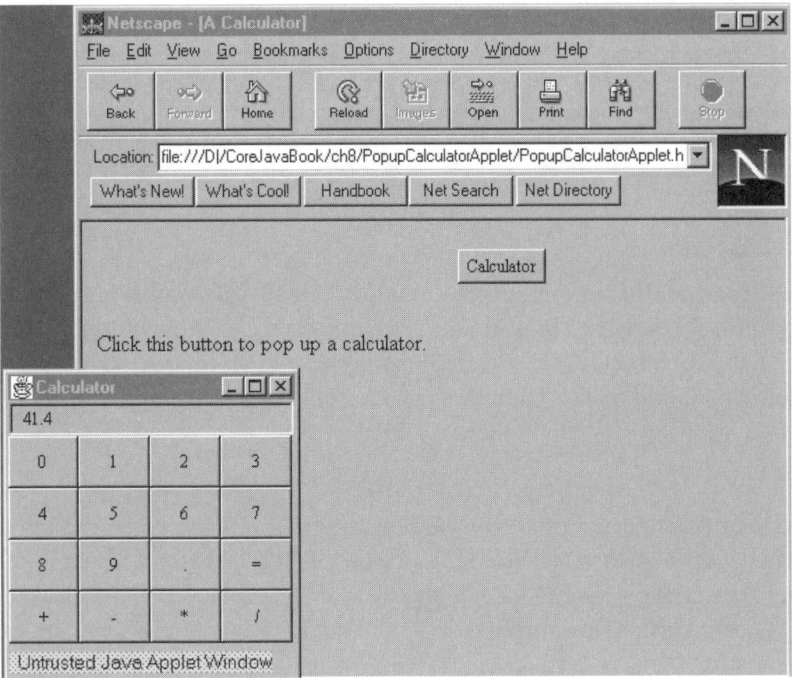

Figure 10-6: A pop-up window inside a browser

This message is a security feature of all Web browsers. The browser wants to make sure that your applet does not launch a window that the user might mistake for a local application. It does this regardless of the fact that it would take a super-human effort to write AWT code that even remotely resembles a professional Windows program. The fear is that if such a feat could be done, an unsuspecting user could visit a Web page, which automatically launches the applets on it, and mistakenly type in a password or credit card number, which the applet would send back to its host.

To avoid any possibility of shenanigans like this, all pop-up windows launched by an applet bear a label such as "Untrusted Java Applet," "Unauthenticated Java Applet," or "Warning: Java Applet." That label is likely to be so scary to most users that you may want to avoid launching any external frames from your applet.

By the way, an applet inside a Web page cannot have menus. But a frame spawned by the Web page can have a menu bar. Of course, such a frame still has a warning border.

NOTE: The Netscape 3.0 browser applied a warning label only if the Web page was loaded through a URL, not if you loaded it through the File | Open File dialog. In Netscape 4.0, the warning border is not displayed if the applet is signed by a trusted entity.

Multimedia

Applets can handle both images and audio. As we write this, images must be in TIF or JPEG form, audio files in Sun's `au` format. You will need to get a program to translate Microsoft's `.wav` files, for example, into `au` format. There are many free ones available on the Web. Usually the files containing this information are specified as URL, so we take them up first.

URLs

A URL is really nothing more than a description of a resource on the Internet. For example, "`http://java.sun.com`" tells the browser to use the hypertext transfer protocol on the file located at `java.sun.com`. Java has the class `URL` that encapsulates URLs. The simplest way to make a URL is to give a string to the URL constructor:

```
URL u = new URL("http://java.sun.com");
```

This is called an *absolute* URL because we specify the entire resource name. Another useful URL constructor is a *relative* URL.

```
URL data = new URL(u, "data/planets.dat");
```

This specifies the file `planets.dat`, located in the `data` subdirectory of the URL `u`.

Both constructors make sure that you have used the correct syntax for a URL. If you haven't, they cause a run-time error, a so-called `MalformedURLException`. Up to now, you have been able to ignore most run-time errors, but this error is one the compiler will not let you ignore. You must tell the compiler that you are prepared for the error condition. The relevant code is as follows:

```
try
{   String s = "http://java.sun.com";
    URL u = new URL(s);
    . . .
}
catch(MalformedURLException e)
{   // deal with error
    System.out.println("Error " + e);
}
```

We will discuss this syntax for dealing with exceptions in detail in Chapter 12. For now, if you see code like this in one of our code samples, just gloss over the `try` and `catch` keywords.

A common way of obtaining a URL is to ask an applet where it came from, in particular,

- What is the URL of the page that is calling it?
- What is the URL of the applet itself?

To find the former, use the `getDocumentBase` method; to find the latter, use `getCodeBase`. You do not need to place these calls in a `try` block.

Obtaining Multimedia Files

You can retrieve images and audio files with the `getImage` and `getAudioClip` methods. For example:

```
Image cat = getImage(getDocumentBase(), "images/cat.gif");
AudioClip meow = getAudioClip(getDocumentBase(),
    "audio/meow.au");
```

Here, we use the `getDocumentBase` method that returns the URL from which your applet is loaded. The second argument to the `URL` constructor specifies where the image or audio clip is located, relative to the base document. (Applets do not need to go through a `Toolkit` object in order to get an image.)

Once you have the images and audio clips, what can you do with them? You saw in Chapter 7 how to display a single image. In the multithreading chapter of Volume 2, you will see how to play an animation sequence composed of multiple images. To play an audio clip, simply invoke its `play` method.

You can also call `play` without first loading the audio clip.

```
play(getDocumentBase(), "audio/meow.au");
```

However, to show an image, you must first load it.

For faster downloading, multimedia objects can be stored in JAR files (see page 500). The `getImage` and `getAudioClip/play` methods automatically search the JAR files of the applet. If the image or audio file is contained in a JAR file, it is loaded immediately. Otherwise, the browser requests it from the Web server.

`java.net.URL`

- `URL(String name)`

  creates a URL object from a string describing an absolute URL.

- `URL(URL base, String name)`

  creates a relative URL object. If the string `name` describes an absolute URL, then the `base` URL is ignored. Otherwise, it is interpreted as a relative directory from the `base` URL.

`java.applet.Applet`

- `public URL getDocumentBase()`

  gets the URL for the page that contains the applet.

- `public URL getCodeBase()`

  gets the URL of the applet code itself.

- `void play(URL url)`
- `void play(URL url, String name)`

  The first form plays an audio file specified by the URL. The second form uses the string to provide a path relative to the URL in the first argument. Nothing happens if the audio clip cannot be found.

- `AudioClip getAudioClip(URL url)`
- `AudioClip getAudioClip(URL url, String name)`

  get an audio clip, given a URL. The second form uses the string to provide a path relative to the URL in the first argument. The function returns `null` if the audio clip cannot be found.

- `Image getImage(URL url)`
- `Image getImage(URL url, String name)`

  get an image, given a URL. These methods always returns an image object immediately, even if the image does not exist. The actual image data are loaded when the image is first displayed. See Chapter 7 for details on image acquisition.

The Applet Context

An applet runs inside a browser such as Netscape or the applet viewer. An applet can ask the browser to do things for it, for example, to fetch an audio clip, show a short message in the status line, or show a different Web page. The

ambient browser can carry out these requests, or it can ignore them. For example, if an applet running inside the applet viewer asks the applet viewer program to show a Web page, nothing happens.

To communicate with the browser, an applet calls the `getAppletContext` method. That method returns an object that implements an interface of type `AppletContext`. You can think of the concrete implementation of the `AppletContext` interface as a communication path between the applet and the ambient browser. In addition to `getAudioClip` and `getImage`, the `AppletContext` interface contains four useful methods, which we discuss in the next few sections.

Inter-Applet Communication

A Web page can contain more than one applet. If a Web page contains multiple applets from the same `CODEBASE`, they can communicate with each other. Naturally, this is an advanced technique that you probably will not need very often. Note that since a security hole was discovered in the implementation of the Java virtual machine when it services multiple applets, some browsers have temporarily deactivated this feature.

If you give `NAME` tags to each applet in the HTML file, you can use the `getApplet(String)` method of the `AppletContext` interface to get a reference to the applet. For example, if your HTML file contains the tag

```
<APPLET CODE="Chart.class" WIDTH=100 HEIGHT=100 NAME="Chart1">
```

then the call

```
Applet chart1 = getAppletContext().getApplet("Chart1");
```

gives you a reference to the applet. What can you do with the reference? Provided you give the `Chart` class a method to accept new data and redraw the chart, you can call this method by making the appropriate cast.

```
((Chart)chart1).setData(3, "Earth", 9000);
```

You can also list all applets on a Web page, whether or not they have a `NAME` tag. The `getApplets` method returns a so-called *enumeration object.* (You will learn more about enumeration objects in Chapter 11.) Here is a loop that prints the class names of all applets on the current page.

```
Enumeration e = getAppletContext().getApplets();
while (e.hasMoreElements())
{  Object a = e.nextElement();
   System.out.println(a.getClass().getName());
}
```

An applet cannot communicate with an applet on a different Web page.

Displaying Items in the Browser

You have access to two areas of the ambient browsers: the status line and the Web page display area. Both use methods of the `AppletContext` class.

You can display a string in the status line at the bottom of the browser with the `showStatus` message, for example,

```
getAppletContext().showStatus("Loading data . . . please wait");
```

TIP: In our experience, `showStatus` is of limited use. The browser is also using the status line, and, more often than not, it will overwrite your precious message with chatter like `"Applet running."` Use the status line for fluff messages like `"loading data . . . please wait,"` but not for something that the user cannot afford to miss.

You can tell the browser to show a different Web page with the `showDocument` method. There are several ways to do this. The simplest is with a call to `showDocument` with one argument, the URL you want to show.

```
URL u = new URL("http://java.sun.com");
getAppletContext().showDocument(u);
```

The problem with this call is that it opens the new Web page in the same window as your current page, thereby displacing your applet. To return to your applet, the user must select Back.

You can tell the browser to show the applet in another window by giving a second parameter in the call to `showDocument`. The second argument is a string. If it is the special string `"_blank"`, the browser opens a new window with the document, instead of displacing the current document. More importantly, if you take advantage of the frame feature in HTML 3.2, you can split a browser window into multiple frames, each of which has a name. You can put your applet into one frame and have it show documents in other frames. We will show you an example of doing this in the next section.

Table 10-3 shows all possible arguments to `showDocument`.

Table 10-3: `ShowDocument` arguments

Second Parameter to `showDocument`	Location
`"_self"` or none	Show the document in the current frame.
`"_parent"`	Show the document in the parent container.
`"_top"`	Show the document in the topmost frame.
`"_blank"`	Show in new, unnamed, top-level window.
any other string	Show in the frame with that name.

`java.applet.Applet`

- `public AppletContext getAppletContext()`

  gives you a handle on the applet's browser environment. On most browsers, you can use this information to control the browser in which the applet is running.

`java.applet.AppletContext`

- `void showStatus(String msg)`

  shows the string specified in the status line of the browser.

- `Enumeration getApplets()`

  returns an enumeration (see Chapter 11) of all the applets in the same context, that is, the same Web page.

- `Applet getApplet(String name)`

  returns the applet in the current context with the given name; returns `null` if none exists. Only the current Web page is searched.

- `void showDocument(URL url)`
- `void showDocument(URL url, String target)`

  show a new Web page in a frame in the browser. In the first form, the new page displaces the current page. The second form uses the string to identify the target frame. The target string can be one of the following: `"_self"` (show in current frame, equivalent to the first form of the method), `"_parent"` (show in parent frame), `"_top"` (show in topmost frame), and `"_blank"` (show in new, unnamed, top-level window). Or, the target string can be the name of a frame.

NOTE: Not every way of seeing an applet will accept these commands. For example, Sun's applet viewer does not show Web pages. The second form of the method requires that the browser support frames.

- `Image getImage(URL url)`

  returns an image object that encapsulates the image specified by the URL. If the image does not exist, this method immediately returns `null`. Otherwise, a separate thread is launched to load the image. See Chapter 7 for details on image acquisition.

- `AudioClip getAudioClip(URL url)`

  returns an `AudioClip` object, which stores the sound file specified by the URL. Use the `play` method to actually play the file.

A Bookmark Applet

This applet takes advantage of the frames feature in HTML 3.2. We divide the screen vertically into two frames. The left frame contains a Java applet that shows a list of bookmarks. When you double-click on any of the bookmarks in the list, the applet then goes to the corresponding Web page and displays it on the right (see Figure 10-7).

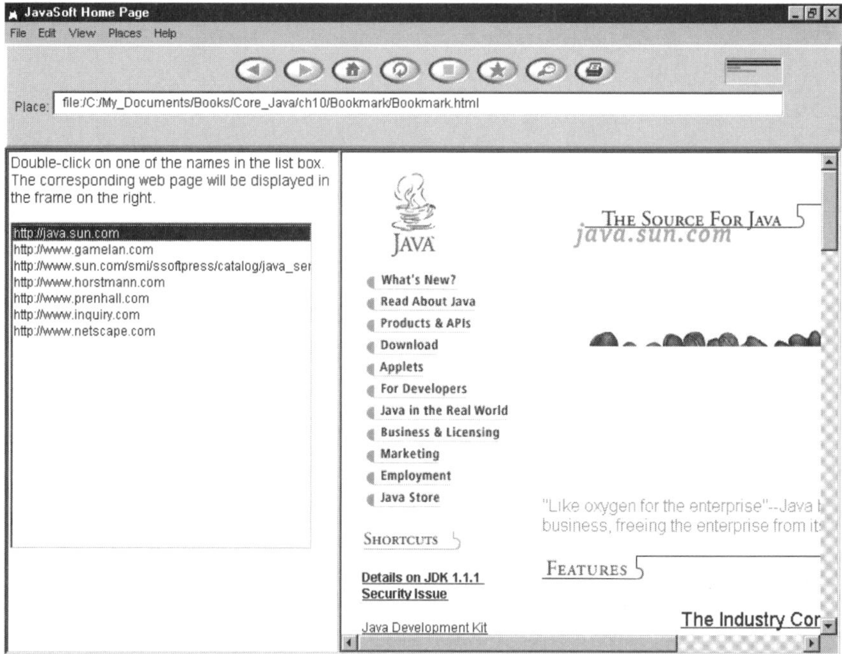

Figure 10-7: A bookmark applet

Frames are a new HTML feature, and you may not have seen the relevant tags. Here is the HTML file (on the CD as well) that defines the frames.

```
<HTML>
<HEAD>
<TITLE>Bookmark Applet</TITLE>
</HEAD>
<FRAMESET COLS="320,*">
<FRAME NAME="left" SRC="Left.html" MARGINHEIGHT=2 MARGINWIDTH=2
   SCROLLING = "no" NORESIZE>
<FRAME NAME="right" SRC="Right.html" MARGINHEIGHT=2 MARGIN-
WIDTH=2
   SCROLLING = "yes" NORESIZE>
</FRAMESET>
</HTML>
```

We will not go over the exact syntax elements. What is important is that each frame has two essential features: a name (given by the `NAME` tag) and a URL (given by the `SRC` tag). We could not think of any good names for the frames, so we simply named them `"left"` and `"right"`.

The left frame loads a file that we called `Left.html`, which loads the applet into the left frame. It simply specifies the applets and the bookmarks. You can customize this file for your own Web page by changing the bookmarks.

```
<HTML>
<TITLE>A Bookmark Applet</TITLE>
<BODY>
Double-click on one of the names in the list box. The corre-
sponding web page will be displayed in the frame on the right.
<P>
<APPLET CODE="Bookmark.class" WIDTH=290 HEIGHT=300>
<PARAM NAME=link_1 VALUE="http://java.sun.com">
<PARAM NAME=link_2 VALUE="http://www.gamelan.com">
<PARAM NAME=link_3 VALUE
="http://www.sun.com/smi/ssoftpress/catalog/java_series.html">
<PARAM NAME=link_4 VALUE="http://www.horstmann.com">
<PARAM NAME=link_5 VALUE="http://www.prenhall.com">
<PARAM NAME=link_6 VALUE="http://www.inquiry.com">
<PARAM NAME=link_7 VALUE="http://www.netscape.com">
</APPLET>
</BODY>
</HTML>
```

The right frame loads a dummy file that we called `Right.html`. (Netscape did not approve when we left the right frame blank, so we gave it a dummy file for starters.)

```
<HTML>
<TITLE>
Web pages will be displayed here.
</TITLE>
<BODY>
Double-click on one of the names in the list box to the left.
The web page will be displayed here.
</BODY>
</HTML>
```

The code for the bookmark applet that is given in Example 10-4 is simple. It reads the values of the parameters `link_1`, `link_2`, and so on, into the list box. When you double-click on one of the items in the list box, the `showDocument` method displays that page in the right frame.

Example 10-4: Bookmark.java

```
import java.awt.*;
import java.awt.event.*;
import java.applet.*;
import java.net.*;
import java.io.*;

public class Bookmark extends Applet implements ActionListener
{  public void init()
   {  setLayout(new BorderLayout());
      add(links, "Center");
      links.addActionListener(this);
      int i = 1;
      String s;
      while ((s = getParameter("link_" + i)) != null)
      {  links.add(s);
         i++;
      }
   }

   public void actionPerformed(ActionEvent evt)
   {  String arg = evt.getActionCommand();
      try
      {  AppletContext context = getAppletContext();
         URL u = new URL((String)arg);
         context.showDocument(u, "right");
      } catch(Exception e)
      {  showStatus("Error " + e);
      }
   }

   private List links = new List(10, false);
}
```

JAR Files

The retirement applet from this chapter uses three classes: `Retire`, `RetireInfo`, and `RetireCanvas`. Furthermore, it uses two classes from the `corejava` package: `IntTextField` and `Format`. You know that the applet tag references the class file that contains the class derived from `Applet`:

```
<APPLET CODE="Retire.class" WIDTH = 400 HEIGHT = 300>
```

When the browser reads this line, it makes a connection to the Web server and fetches the file `Retire.class`. The *class loader* of the Java interpreter that is built into the browser then loads the `Retire` class from that file. During the loading process, the class loader must *resolve* the other classes used in this class. After

doing so, it then knows it needs four more classes to run the applet. The browser, therefore, makes *four* more connections to the Web server, one for each class file. Even for a small applet like the one used in our retirement process, this can be a time-consuming process. Loading an applet that uses dozens of classes can take many minutes.

NOTE: It is important to remember that the reason for this long loading time is not the size of the class files—they are quite small—rather it is because of the *considerable* overhead involved in establishing a connection to the Web server. If you need to make hundreds of separate connections, you will wait a long, long time.

Java 1.1 supports an improved method for loading class files, which allows you to package all the needed class files into a single file. This file can then be downloaded with a *single* http request to the server. Files that archive Java class files are called Java ARchive, or JAR, files. JAR files can contain both class files and other file types such as image and sound files. JAR files can also be compressed, using the familiar ZIP compression format, as defined by PKWARE. Compression further improves download speed, especially for files containing images and sound. You should definitely take advantage of JAR files once your audience has browsers that can deal with them.

You use the `jar` tool to make JAR files. (In the default installation, it's in the `\jdk\bin` directory.) The most common command, to make a new JAR file, uses the following syntax:

```
jar cf JARFileName File1 File2 . . .
```

For example,

```
jar cf RetireClasses.jar *.java icon.gif
```

In general, the `jar` command has the format

```
jar options File1 File2 . . .
```

Here is a list of all the options for the `jar` program. They are similar to the options of the UNIX `tar` command.

Option	Description
`c`	Creates a new or empty archive and adds files to it. If any of the specified file names is a directory, then the `jar` program processes them recursively.
`t`	Displays the table of contents.
`x`	Extracts files. If you supply one or more file names, only those files are extracted. Otherwise, all files are extracted.

Option	Description
`f`	Specifies the JAR file name as the second command-line argument. If this parameter is missing, then `jar` will write the result to standard output (when creating a JAR file) or read it from standard input (when extracting or tabulating a JAR file).
`v`	Generates verbose output.
`m`	Adds a *manifest* to the JAR file. A manifest is a description of the archive contents and origin. Every archive has a default manifest, but you can supply your own if you want to authenticate the contents of the archive. We will discuss this in the security chapter of Volume 2.
`0`	Stores without ZIP compression.
`M`	Does not create a manifest file for the entries.

Once you have a JAR file, you need to reference it in the `APPLET` tag, as in the following example.

```
<APPLET CODE="Retire.class"
   ARCHIVE="RetireClasses.jar"
   WIDTH=400 HEIGHT=300
>
```

Note that the `CODE` attribute must still be present. The `CODE` attribute tells the browser the name of the applet. The `ARCHIVE` is merely another source where the applet class and other files may be located, in addition to the Web server. Whenever a class, image, or sound file is needed, a JAR-aware browser searches the JAR files in the `ARCHIVE` list first. Only if the file is not contained in the archive will it be fetched from the Web server.

Resources

Classes that are used in both applets and applications often use associated data files, such as

- Image and sound files
- Text files with message strings and button labels
- Files with binary data, for example, to describe the layout of a map

In Java, such an associated file is called a *resource.*

NOTE: In Windows, the term "resource" has a more specialized meaning. Windows resources also consist of images, button labels, and so on, but they are attached to the executable file and accessed by a standard programming interface. In contrast, Java resources are stored as separate files, not as part of class files. And it is up to each class to access and interpret the resource data.

For example, consider a class `AboutDialog` that displays a message such as the one in Figure 10-8.

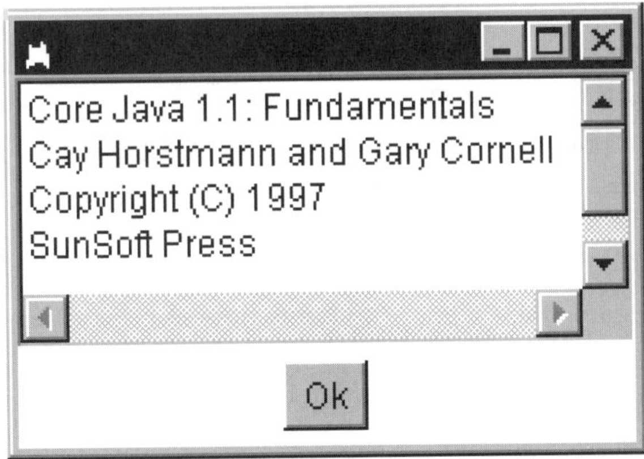

Figure 10-8: An About dialog box

Of course, the book title and copyright year in the dialog box will change for the next edition of the book. To make it easy to track this change, we want to put the text inside a file and not hardcode it as a string in the dialog class.

Suppose we want to place the `AboutDialog.txt` file always in the same location as the class file `AboutDialog.class`. The problem is that a class file can be in one of many locations:

- In the local file system, relative to the class path
- In a JAR file
- On a Web server

The class loader knows how to search all relevant locations until it has located the class file, but we would need to manually repeat this search process to located the associated resource file. The resource loading feature of Java 1.1 automates this task. To load a resource, do the following:

1. Get the `Class` object of the class that has a resource, for example, `AboutDialog.class`
2. Call `getResource(name)` to get the resource file as a URL.
3. If the resource is an image or audio file, read it directly with the `getImage` or `getAudioClip` method.
4. Otherwise, use the `openStream` method on the URL to read in the data in the file. (See Volume 2 for more on streams.)

The point is that the class loader remembers the location where it loaded the class, and then it can search for the associated resource in the same location.

For example, to read in the file `AboutDialog.txt`, you can use the following commands:

```
URL url = AboutDialog.class.getResource("AboutDialog.txt");
InputStream in = url.openStream();
```

Because this combination is so common, there is a convenient shortcut method: `getResourceAsStream` returns an `InputStream`, not a `URL`.

```
InputStream in
   = AboutDialog.class.getResourceAsStream("AboutDialog.txt");
```

To read from this stream, you will need to know how to process input (see the chapter on input and output in Volume 2 for details). In the sample program, we read the stream a line at a time with the following instructions:

```
BufferedReader br = new BufferedReader(new
   InputStreamReader(in));
String line;
while ((line = br.readLine()) != null)
   process line;
```

On the CD-ROM, you will find a JAR file that contains all class files and the resource file. This demonstrates that the applet locates the resource file in the same location as the class file, namely, inside the JAR file.

TIP: As you saw in the preceding section, you can place image and audio files inside a JAR file and simply access them with the `getImage` and `getAudioClip` methods—these methods automatically search JAR files. But to load other files from a JAR file, you need the `getResourceAsStream` method.

Instead of placing a resource file inside the same directory as the class file, you can place it in a subdirectory. You can use a hierarchical resource name such as

```
data/text/AboutDialog.txt
```

This is a relative resource name, and it is interpreted relative to the package of the class that is loading the resource. Note that you must always use the / separator, regardless of the directory separator on the system that actually stores the resource files. For example, on Windows, the resource loader automatically translates / to \ separators.

A resource name starting with a / is called an absolute resource name. It is located by Java in the same way that a class inside a package would be located. For example, a resource

```
/corejava/Title.txt
```

is located in the `corejava` directory (which may be a subdirectory of the class path, inside a JAR file, or on the Web server).

Automating the loading of files is all that the resource loading feature does. There are no standard methods for interpreting the contents of a resource file. Each applet must have its own way of interpreting the contents of its resource files.

Another common application of resources is the internationalization of applets and applications. Language-dependent strings, such as messages and user interface labels, are stored in resource files, with one file for each language. The *internationalization API*, which is discussed in Volume 2, supports a standard method for organizing and accessing these localization files.

Example 10-5: ResourceTest.java

```
import java.io.*;
import java.awt.*;
import java.awt.event.*;
import java.applet.*;
import corejava.*;

public class ResourceTest extends Applet
   implements ActionListener
{  public void init()
   {  Button b = new Button("About");
      b.addActionListener(this);
      add(b);
   }

   public void actionPerformed(ActionEvent evt)
   {  String arg = evt.getActionCommand();
      if(arg.equals("About"))
      {  if (ab == null) // first time
            ab = new AboutDialog();
         ab.show();
      }
   }

   private AboutDialog ab;
}

class AboutDialog extends Frame
{  public AboutDialog()
   {  TextArea ta = new TextArea();
      add(ta, "Center");

      Panel p = new Panel();
```

```
        Button ok = new Button("Ok");
        p.add(ok);
        add(p, "South");

        try
        {  InputStream in = AboutDialog.class.
              getResourceAsStream("AboutDialog.txt");
           BufferedReader br = new BufferedReader(new
              InputStreamReader(in));
           String line;
           while ((line = br.readLine()) != null)
              ta.append(line + "\n");
        } catch(IOException e) {}

        ok.addActionListener(new ActionListener() { public void
           actionPerformed(ActionEvent evt) { setVisible(false); }
              } );

        addWindowListener(new WindowAdapter() { public void
           windowClosing(WindowEvent e) { setVisible(false); }
              } );

        setSize(220, 150);
     }
  }
```

`java.lang.Class`

- `URL getResource(String name)`
- `InputStream getResourceAsStream(String name)`

  find the resource in the same place as the class and then return a URL or input stream you can use for loading the resource. The methods return `null` if the resource isn't found, and so do not throw an exception for an i/o error.

  Parameters: `name` the resource name

It's an Applet. It's an Application. It's Both!

Quite a few years ago, a "Saturday Night Live" skit poking fun at a television commercial showed a couple arguing about a white, gelatinous substance. The husband said, "It's a dessert topping." The wife said, "It's a floor wax." And the announcer concluded triumphantly, "It's both!"

Well, in this section, we will show you how to write a Java program that is *both* an applet and an application. That is, you can load the program with the applet viewer or a browser, or you can start it from the command line with the `java` interpreter. We are not sure how often this comes up—we found it interesting that this could be done at all and thought you would, too.

The screen shots in Figure 10-9 show the *same* program, launched from the command line as an application and viewed inside the applet viewer as an applet.

Figure 10-9: The calculator as an applet and an application

Let us see how this can be done. Every class file has exactly one public class. In order for the applet viewer to launch it, that class must derive from `Applet`. In order for Java to start the application, it must have a static `main` method. So far, we have

```
class AppletApplication extends Applet
{  public void init() { . . . }
   . . .
   static public void main(String[] args) { . . . }
}
```

What can we put into `main`? Normally, we make an object of the class and invoke `show` on it. But this case is not so simple. You cannot show a naked applet. The applet must be placed inside a frame. And once it is inside the frame, its `init` method needs to be called.

To provide a frame, we create the class `AppletFrame`, like this:

```
public class AppletFrame extends CloseableFrame
{  AppletFrame(Applet a, int x, int y)
   {  setTitle(a.getClass().getName());
      setSize(x, y);
      add("Center", a);
      a.init();
      show();
      a.start();
   }
   . . .
}
```

The constructor of the frame puts the applet (which derives from `Panel`) inside the frame, calls the `init` function, calls `show` (to show the frame) and then starts the applet. The frame also supplies a handler to close the program when the user closes the window.

In the `main` method of the applet/application, we make a new frame of this kind. In this example, we just reuse the calculator.

```
class AppletApplication extends Applet
{  . . .
   public static void main(String args[])
   {  new AppletFrame(new AppletApplication(), 620, 400);
   }
}
```

There is one catch. If the program is started with the `java` interpreter and not the applet viewer, and it calls `getAppletContext`, it gets a `null` pointer because it has not been launched inside a browser. This causes a run-time crash whenever we have code like

```
getAppletContext().showStatus(message);
```

While we do not want to write a full-fledged browser, we do need to supply the bare minimum to make calls like this work. The call displays no message, but at least it will not crash the program. It turns out that all we need to do is implement two interfaces, `AppletStub` and `AppletContext`.

You have already seen applet contexts in action. They are responsible for fetching images and audio files and for displaying Web pages. They can, however, politely refuse, and this is what our applet context will do. The major purpose of the `AppletStub` interface is to locate the applet context. Every applet has an applet stub (set with the `setStub` method of the `Applet` class).

In our case, `AppletFrame` implements both `AppletStub` and `AppletContext`. We supply the bare minimum functionality that is necessary to implement these two interfaces.

```
public class AppletFrame extends Frame
   implements AppletStub, AppletContext
{  . . .

   // AppletStub methods
   public boolean isActive() { return true; }
   public URL getDocumentBase() { return null; }
   public URL getCodeBase() { return null; }
   public String getParameter(String name) { return ""; }
   public AppletContext getAppletContext() { return this; }
   public void appletResize(int width, int height) {}
```

```
    // AppletContext methods
    public AudioClip getAudioClip(URL url) { return null; }
    public Image getImage(URL url) { return null; }
    public Applet getApplet(String name) { return null; }
    public Enumeration getApplets() { return null; }
    public void showDocument(URL url) {}
    public void showDocument(URL url, String target) {}
    public void showStatus(String status) {}
}
```

Next, the constructor of the frame class calls `setStub` on the applet to make itself its stub.

```
public class AppletFrame extends CloseableFrame
implements AppletStub, AppletContext
{  AppletFrame(Applet a, int x, int y)
   {  setTitle(a.getClass().getName());
      setSize(x, y);
      add("Center", a);
      a.setStub(this);
      a.init();
      show();
      a.start();
   }
   . . .
}
```

One final twist is possible. Suppose we want to use the calculator as an applet and application simultaneously. Rather than moving the methods of the `CalculatorApplet` class into the `AppletApplication` class, we will just use inheritance. Here is the code for the class that does this.

```
public class CalculatorAppletApplication extends
CalculatorApplet
{  public static void main(String args[])
   {  new AppletFrame(new CalculatorApplet(), 150, 100);
   }
}
```

You can do this with any applet. For example, if you like, you can make a `RetireAppletApplication` in exactly the same way as we made a `CalculatorAppletApplication`. All you need to do is pass a `new Retire()` object to the `AppletFrame`.

CHAPTER 11

- Vectors
- Bit Sets
- Hash Tables
- Linked Lists
- Queues
- Stacks
- Multi-Dimensional Arrays

Data Structures

OOP encapsulates the data inside classes, but this doesn't make how you organize the data inside the classes any less important than in traditional programming languages. Of course, how you choose to structure the data depends on the problem you are trying to solve. Does your class need a way to easily search through thousands (or even millions) of items quickly? Does it need an ordered sequence of elements *and* the ability to rapidly insert and remove elements in the middle of the sequence? Does it need an arraylike structure with random-access ability that can grow at run time? The way you structure your data inside your classes can make these problems easy—or almost impossible—to solve.

This chapter shows how Java can help you accomplish the traditional data structuring needed for serious programming. Equally traditionally, there is a course called *Data Structures* that takes at least a semester to complete at most schools, so there are many, many books devoted to this important topic. Exhaustively covering all the data structures that may be useful is not our goal in this chapter; instead, we cover the fundamental ones such as dynamic, arraylike objects (vectors), hash tables, and linked lists. We hope that, after you finish this chapter, you will find it easy to translate any of your data structures to your Java programming.

Vectors

In many programming languages—in particular, C and C++—you have to fix the sizes of all arrays at compile time. Programmers hate this because it forces them into uncomfortable trade-offs. How many items will the customer order? Surely no more than 10. What if one customer needs 15 items? Do we want to waste 14 entries if the majority of customers want only one item?

In Java, the situation is much better. You can set the size of an array at run time.

```
int n;
. . .
Item[] itemsOrdered = new Item[n + 1];
```

Of course, this code does not completely solve the problem of dynamically modifying arrays at run time. Once you set the array size, you cannot change it without using the new reflection mechanism of Java 1.1 that was described in Chapter 5. It's overkill to use reflection and the kind of code that was given in Chapter 5 for the routine situation where you don't know how many items the customer will order before taking the order information. Instead, the easiest way to deal with this situation in Java is to use another Java object that can shrink and grow automatically. This object is called a *vector:* vectors are array-like objects that can grow and shrink automatically without you needing to write any code to make it happen.

NOTE: The name "vector" is a bit of a misnomer. Vectors in Java have nothing to do with the vectors used in mathematics and physics. (There, vectors are arrays of floating-point numbers, but their dimensions are fixed.)

You make a new vector by specifying its initial *capacity* in the `Vector` constructor.

```
Vector itemsOrdered = new Vector(3);
    // start out with space for one order item,
    // plus two items for tax and shipping charges
```

There is an important distinction between the capacity of a vector and the size of an array. If you allocate an array with three entries, then the array has three slots, ready for use. A vector with a capacity of three elements has the potential of holding three elements (and, in fact, more than three), but at the beginning, even after its initial construction, a vector holds no elements at all.

You use the `addElement` method to add new elements. For example, suppose you have a class called `Item` and use the following code to create three item objects.

```
Item nextItem = new Item();
Item stateTax = new Item();
Item shipping = new Item();
```

Then, you use the following code to add these items to a vector called `itemsOrdered` (that started out with a capacity of three objects, as indicated in the above code):

```
itemsOrdered.addElement(nextItem);
itemsOrdered.addElement(stateTax);
itemsOrdered.addElement(shipping);
```

CAUTION: There is one important difference to keep in mind between Java vectors and Java arrays:

- Arrays in Java hold any type, including number types and all class types.
- Vectors in Java must hold instances of `Object`.

For example, for a vector of integers, you will need to cast the integers to the `Integer` object wrapper.

Let's suppose you created the vector so that it had an original capacity of three items. If you insert another item, then you have exceeded the capacity of the vector in our example. This is where vectors work their magic: the vector *relocates and resizes itself* automatically. The vector finds a bigger home and automatically copies all the objects it is currently storing to its new home.

How much more space is allocated? By default, the space allocated doubles each time the vector relocates. Because of the problem of exponential growth, you *will not* want to rely on this for potentially massive memory reallocation for enormous vectors. Instead, specify a *capacity increment* as the second constructor argument when you create the vector. For example:

```
Vector itemsOrdered = new Vector(3, 10);
```

Now the vector grows in increments of 10 at each relocation.

On the other hand, if Java has to reallocate the space for the vector often, it slows down your program, so it pays to set reasonable estimates for the initial capacity and the capacity increment—so 10 may turn out to be too small an increment.

NOTE: For simple programs, you may not want to worry about the capacity and capacity increment for your vectors at all. If you use the default constructor

```
Vector itemsOrdered = new Vector();
```

the vector has an initial capacity of 10 and doubles in size every time the capacity is exceeded. This works fine for situations in which the items to be handled are few, and it frees you from micromanaging the vector allocations.

C++ NOTE: The Java `Vector` class differs in a number of important ways from the C++ `vector` template. Most noticeably, since `vector` is a template, only elements of the correct type can be inserted, and no casting is required to retrieve elements from the vector. For example, the compiler will simply refuse to insert a `Rectangle` object into a `vector<Employee>`.

The C++ `vector` template overloads the `[]` operator for convenient element access. Since Java does not have operator overloading, it must use explicit method calls instead.

C++ vectors are copied by value. If `a` and `b` are two vectors, then the assignment `a = b;` makes `a` into a new vector with the same length as `b`, and all elements are copied from `b` to `a`. The same assignment in Java makes both `a` and `b` refer to the same vector.

VB NOTE: If you don't mind the extra syntax and occasionally casting a basic type to its wrapper class (and casting the retrieved objects), vectors in Java give you all the convenience of Redim Preserve (and quite a bit more).

Working with an Existing Vector

The `size` method returns the current number of elements in the vector. Thus,

```
v.size()
```

is the vector equivalent of

```
a.length
```

for an array `a`. Of course, the size of a vector is always less than or equal to its capacity.

Once you are reasonably sure that the vector is at its permanent size, you can call the `trimToSize` method. This method adjusts the size of the memory block to use exactly as much storage space as is required to hold the current number of elements. The garbage collector will reclaim any excess memory.

NOTE: Once you trim a vector's size, adding new elements will move the block again, which takes time. You should only use `trimToSize` when you are sure you won't add any more elements to the vector.

Example 11-1, illustrated in Figure 11-1, lets the user add new order entries to a purchase order. A vector holds the entries. When the user clicks on Done, the tax and shipping charge are added, and the vector is trimmed to size.

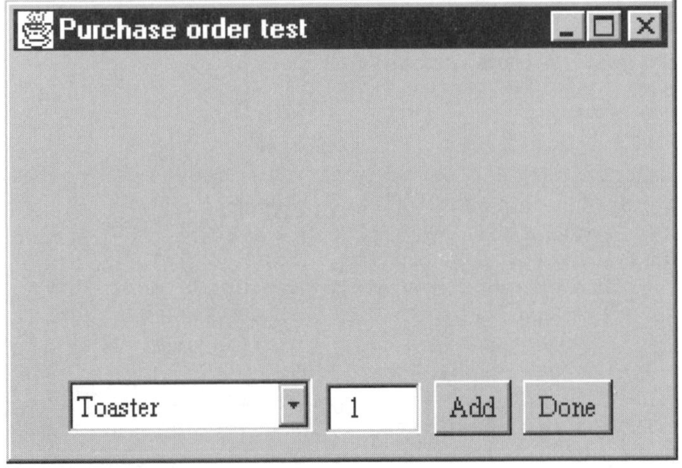

Figure 11-1: Purchase order test application

Example 11-1: PurchaseOrderTest.java

```
import java.awt.*;
import java.awt.event.*;
import java.util.*;
import corejava.*;

public class PurchaseOrderTest extends CloseableFrame
   implements ActionListener
{  public PurchaseOrderTest()
   {  Panel p = new Panel();
      p.setLayout(new FlowLayout());
      name = new Choice();
      name.add("Toaster");
      name.add("Blender");
      name.add("Microwave oven");
      name.add("Citrus press");
      name.add("Espresso maker");
      name.add("Rice cooker");
      name.add("Waffle iron");
      name.add("Bread machine");
      quantity = new IntTextField(1, 4);
      p.add(name);
      p.add(quantity);
      addButton(p, "Add");
      addButton(p, "Done");
      add(p, "South");
      add(canvas = new PurchaseOrderCanvas(), "Center");
      canvas.redraw(a);
   }
```

```
    public void addButton(Container c, String name)
    {  Button b = new Button(name);
       b.addActionListener(this);
       c.add(b);
    }

    public void actionPerformed(ActionEvent evt)
    {  String arg = evt.getActionCommand();
       if (arg.equals("Add"))
       {  if (quantity.isValid())
             a.addElement(new Item(name.getSelectedItem(),
                quantity.getValue(), 0.00));
       }
       else if (arg.equals("Done"))
       {  a.addElement(new Item("State Tax", 1, 0.00));
          a.addElement(new Item("Shipping", 1, 5.00));
          a.trimToSize();
       }
       canvas.redraw(a);
    }

    public static void main(String args[])
    {  Frame f = new PurchaseOrderTest();
       f.show();
    }

    private Vector a = new Vector();
    private Choice name;
    private IntTextField quantity;
    private PurchaseOrderCanvas canvas;
    private int m = 1;
}

class Item
{  public Item(String n, int q, double u)
    {  name = n;
       quantity = q;
       unitPrice = u;
    }

    public String toString()
    {  return new Format("%-20s").form(name)
          + new Format("%6d").form(quantity)
          + new Format("%8.2f").form(unitPrice);
    }

    private String name;
    private int quantity;
    private double unitPrice;
}
```

```
class PurchaseOrderCanvas extends Canvas
{  public void redraw(Vector new_a)
   {  a = new_a;
      repaint();
   }

   public void paint(Graphics g)
   {  Font f = new Font("Monospaced", Font.PLAIN, 12);
      g.setFont(f);
      FontMetrics fm = g.getFontMetrics(f);
      int height = fm.getHeight();
      int x = 0;
      int y = 0;
      int i = 0;
      for (i = 0; i < a.size(); i++)
      {  y += height;
         g.drawString(a.elementAt(i).toString(), x, y);
      }
   }

   private Vector a;
}
```

`java.util.Vector`

- `Vector()`

  constructs an empty vector (initial capacity is 10, and the capacity doubles whenever current capacity is exceeded).

- `Vector(int initialCapacity)`

  constructs an empty vector with the specified capacity.

  Parameters: `initialCapacity` the initial storage capacity of the vector

- `Vector(int initialCapacity, int capacityIncrement)`

  constructs an empty vector with the specified capacity and the specified increment.

  Parameters:

`initialCapacity`	the initial storage capacity of the vector
`capacityIncrement`	the amount by which the capacity is increased when the vector outgrows its current capacity

- `void addElement(Object obj)`

  appends an element at the end of the vector so that it becomes the last element of the vector.

Parameters:	`obj`	the element to be added

- `int size()`

  returns the number of elements currently stored in the vector. (This is different from, and, of course, never larger than, the vector's capacity.)

- `void setSize(int n)`

  sets the size of the vector to exactly `n` elements. If `n` is larger than the current size, null elements are added to the end of the vector. If `n` is less than the current size, all elements from index `n` on are removed.

Parameters:	`n`	the new size of the vector

- `void trimToSize()`

  reduces the capacity of the vector to its current size.

Accessing Vector Element

Unfortunately, nothing comes for free; the extra convenience that vectors give requires a more complicated syntax for accessing the elements of the vector. Also, the `Vector` class is not a part of the Java language; it is just a utility class programmed by someone and supplied in the standard library.

NOTE: Vectors, like arrays, are zero-based.

The two most important differences in working with vectors, as opposed to arrays, are as follows:

1. Instead of using the pleasant `[]` syntax to access or change the element of an array, you must use the `elementAt` and `setElementAt` methods.

Array	**Vector**
`x = a[i];`	`x = v.elementAt(i);`
`a[i] = x;`	`v.setElementAt(x, i);`

   This is not so wonderful. It would have been nice if the author of the vector class could have called these methods `get` and `set`.

TIP: You can sometimes get the best of both worlds—flexible growth and convenient element access—with the following trick. First, make a vector and add all the elements.

```
Vector v = new Vector();
while (. . .)
{   String s = . . .
    v.addElement(s);
}
```

When you are done, make an array and copy the elements into it. There is even a special method ,`copyInto`, for this purpose.

```
String[] a = new String[v.size()];
v.copyInto(a);
```

PITFALL: Do not call `v.setElementAt(x, i)` until the *size* of the vector is larger than `i`. For example, the following code is wrong:

```
Vector v = new Vector(10); // capacity 10, size 0
v.setElementAt(0, x); // no element 0 yet
```

There are two remedies. You can use `addElement` instead of `setElementAt`. Or, you can call `setSize` after the vector is created.

```
Vector v = new Vector(10);
v.setSize(10);
```

---

2. There is a single `Vector` class that holds elements of any type: a vector stores a sequence of *objects.*
   That is not a problem when inserting an element into a vector—all classes implicitly inherit from `Object`. (Actually, there is a problem if you want to build a vector of numbers. Then you must use a wrapper class like `Integer` or `Double`.) But it can be a problem when retrieving data from a vector.

For example, consider

```
Item nextItem = new Item();
itemsOrdered.setElementAt(nextItem, n);
```

The variable `nextItem` is automatically cast from the type `Item` to the type `Object` and then inserted into the vector. *But* when you read an item from the vector, you get an `Object` and you must cast it back to the type that will work with it.

```
Item currentItem = (Item)itemsOrdered.elementAt(n);
```

If you forget the (`Item`) cast, the compiler generates an error message.

Vectors are inherently somewhat *unsafe.* It is possible to accidentally add an element of the wrong type to a vector.

```
Rectangle r = new Rectangle();
itemsOrdered.setElementAt(r, n);
```

The compiler won't complain. It is perfectly willing to convert a `Rectangle` to an `Object`, but when the accidental rectangle is later retrieved out of the vector container, it will probably be cast into an `Item`. This is an invalid cast that causes the program to abort. That *is* a problem! And it is unique to vectors. Had `itemsOrdered` been an array of `Item` values, then the compiler would not have allowed a rectangle inside it.

```
Rectangle r = new Rectangle();
itemsOrdered[n] = r; // ERROR
```

How serious is this problem? It depends. In practice, you can often guarantee that the elements inserted into a vector are of the correct type, simply because there are only one or two locations in the code where the insertion into the vector takes place. You can then write code that checks the type before you store it in the vector.

Consider the example of a `PurchaseOrder` class.

```
class PurchaseOrder
{   . . .
   public void add(Item i)
   {  itemsOrdered.addElement(i);
   }
   . . .
   private Vector itemsOrdered;
}
```

The `itemsOrdered` vector is a private field of the `PurchaseOrder` class.

The only function that adds objects into that vector is `add`. Plainly, since the argument of `add` is an `Item`, only items can be added into the vector. The compiler can check the type at that level—a call to `order.add(new Rectangle())` will give an error message. Thus, we can safely remove elements from that vector and cast them as `Item` objects.

There is another way to achieve the same effect. Create the class `ItemVector` (derive it from `Vector`), in which you check that the inserted items are of the correct type. (As an added convenience, we also provide a retrieval function that casts the objects into items.)

```
class ItemVector extends Vector
{  public void set(Item i, int n)
   {  setElementAt(i, n);
   }
   public void append(Item i)
   {  addElement(i);
   }
   public Item get(int n)
   {  return (Item)elementAt(n);
   }
}
```

This gives the user completely safe `set`, `append`, and `get` vector access methods. Unfortunately, there is no way to hide the unsafe `setElementAt` in the derived class. All we can do is hope that the programmer will be seduced into using the safer functions `set` and `get` because they are easier to type. After all, we are not concerned about stopping malicious programmers, only about enlisting the compiler's help to prevent accidental errors!

On very rare occasions, vectors are useful for *heterogeneous collections.* Objects of completely unrelated classes are inserted into the vector on purpose. When retrieving a vector entry, the type of every retrieved object must be tested, as in the following code:

```
Vector purchaseOrder;
purchaseOrder.addElement(new Name(. . .));
purchaseOrder.addElement(new Address(. . .));
purchaseOrder.addElement(new Item(. . .));
. . .
Object obj = purchaseOrder.elementAt(n);
if (obj instanceof Item)
{  Item i = (Item)obj;
   sum += i.price();
}
```

Actually, this is a crummy way to write code. It is not a good idea to throw away type information and laboriously try to retrieve it later. Of course, there are exceptions. One exception will occur if Java can eventually handle OLE. OLE automation information is difficult to type ahead of time.

VB NOTE: You may be wondering about arrays of variants. Well, we think using variants, except for OLE automation or where their special properties are really needed, is also a crummy way to write code. For example, copying arrays is faster if you turn them into variants, so they are great for that. Using them for numbers, on the other hand, is a sure way to slow down your program.

Finally, this is a good time to explain the use of the *wrapper classes,* like `Integer` and `Double` for vectors.

Suppose we want a vector of `Double`. As mentioned previously, simply adding numbers won't work.

```
Vector v = new Vector();
v.addElement(3.14); // ERROR
```

The floating-point number 3.14 is not an `Object`. Here, the `Double` wrapper class comes in. An instance of `Double` is an object that wraps the `double` type.

```
v.addElement(new Double(3.14));
```

Of course, to retrieve a number from a vector of `Double` objects, we need to extract the actual value from the wrapper.

```
double x = ((Double)v.elementAt(n)).doubleValue();
```

Ugh. Here it really pays off to derive the class `DoubleVector`, with methods `get` and `set` that hide all this ugliness.

`java.util.Vector`

- `void setElementAt(Object obj, int index)`

  puts a value in the vector at the specified index, overwriting the previous contents.

Parameters:	`obj`	the new value
	`index`	the position (must be between `0` and `size() - 1`)

- `Object elementAt(int index)`

  gets the value stored at a specified index.

Parameters:	`index`	the index of the element to get (must be between `0` and `size() - 1`)

Inserting and Removing Elements in the Middle of a Vector

Instead of appending elements at the end of a vector, you can also insert them in the middle.

```
int n = itemsOrdered.size() - 2;
itemsOrdered.insertElementAt(nextItem, n);
```

The elements at locations `n` and above are shifted up to make room for the new entry. After the insertion, if the new size of the vector after the insertion exceeds the vector's current capacity, then Java reallocates its storage.

Similarly, you can remove an element from the middle of a vector.

```
Item i = (Item)itemsOrdered.removeElementAt(n);
```

The elements located above it are copied down, and the size of the array is reduced by one.

Inserting and removing elements is not terribly efficient. It is probably not worth worrying about for small vectors. But if you store many elements and frequently insert and remove in the middle of the sequence, consider using a linked list instead. We talk about linked lists later in this chapter.

`java.util.Vector`

- `void insertElementAt(Object obj, int index)`

  shifts up elements in order to insert an element.

Parameters:	`obj`	the new element
	`index`	the insertion position (must be between `0` and `size()`)

- `void removeElementAt(int index)`

  removes an element and shifts down all elements above it.

Parameters:	`index`	the position of the element to be removed (must be between `0` and `size() - 1`)

Running a Vector Benchmark

The dynamic growth of vectors makes them more convenient to use than arrays in many circumstances. It is reasonable to ask what price, if any, one pays in terms of efficiency. To answer this question, we ran two benchmark tests to measure the cost of relocating arrays and vectors, and the cost of accessing array and vector elements. When running the benchmark program (see Example 11-2) on a 200-MHz Pentium with 96 MBytes of memory and the Windows 95 operating system, we obtained the following data.

```
Allocating vector elements: 17910 milliseconds
Allocating array elements:   4220 milliseconds
Accessing vector elements:  18130 milliseconds
Accessing array elements:   10110 milliseconds
```

As you can see, vectors are significantly slower than raw arrays. There are two reasons. It takes longer to call a method than it takes to access an array directly. And the vector methods are *synchronized.* When two threads access the same vector, the method calls are queued so that only one thread updates the vector at one time. Synchronization is a performance bottleneck. (We will discuss threads and synchronized methods in the multithreading chapter in Volume 2.)

Vectors are undeniably convenient. They grow dynamically and they manage the distinction between size and capacity for you, but element access is both cumbersome and slow. We prefer vectors over arrays to collect small data sets of variable size. They are also useful in multithreaded programs. Otherwise, it makes sense to use raw arrays and use the reflection mechanism described in Chapter 5 if you need to make them grow.

Example 11-2: VectorBenchmark.java

```
import java.util.*;

class VectorBenchmark
{  public static void main(String[] args)
   {  Vector v = new Vector();

      long start = new Date().getTime();
      for (int i = 0; i < MAXSIZE; i++)
         v.addElement(new Integer(i));
      long end = new Date().getTime();
      System.out.println("Allocating vector elements: "
         + (end - start) + " milliseconds");

      Integer[] a = new Integer[1];
      start = new Date().getTime();
      for (int i = 0; i < MAXSIZE; i++)
      {  if (i >= a.length)
         {  Integer[] b = new Integer[i * 2];
            System.arraycopy(a, 0, b, 0, a.length);
            a = b;
         }
         a[i] = new Integer(i);
      }
      end = new Date().getTime();
      System.out.println("Allocating array elements:  "
         + (end - start) + " milliseconds");

      start = new Date().getTime();
      for (int j = 0; j < NTRIES; j++)
         for (int i = 0; i < MAXSIZE; i++)
         {  Integer r = (Integer)v.elementAt(i);
            v.setElementAt(new Integer(r.intValue() + 1), i);
         }
      end = new Date().getTime();
      System.out.println("Accessing vector elements:  "
         + (end - start) + " milliseconds");
```

```
      start = new Date().getTime();
      for (int j = 0; j < NTRIES; j++)
         for (int i = 0; i < MAXSIZE; i++)
         {  Integer r = a[i];
            a[i] = new Integer(r.intValue() + 1);
         }
      end = new Date().getTime();
      System.out.println("Accessing array elements:    "
         + (end - start) + " milliseconds");
   }

   public static final int MAXSIZE = 100000;
   public static final int NTRIES = 10;
}
```

Bit Sets

The Java `BitSet` class stores a sequence of bits. (It is not a *set* in the mathematical sense—bit *vector* or bit *array* would have been more appropriate terms.) Use a bit set if you need to store a sequence of bits (for example, flags) efficiently. Because a bit set packs the bits into bytes, it is far more efficient than using a vector of Boolean objects. The `BitSet` class gives you a convenient interface for reading, setting, or resetting individual bits. This avoids the masking and other bit-fiddling operations that might otherwise be necessary.

For example, for a `BitSet` named `bucketOfBits`,

```
bucketOfBits.get(i)
```

returns `true` if the `i`'th bit is on, and `false` otherwise. Similarly,

```
bucketOfBits.set(i)
```

turns the `i`'th bit on. Finally,

```
bucketOfBits.clear(i)
```

turns the `i`'th bit off.

C++ NOTE: The C++ `bitset` template has the same functionality as the Java `BitSet`.

`java.util.BitSet`

- `BitSet(int nbits)`

  Parameters: `nbits` the initial number of bits

- `boolean get(int bit)`

  gets a bit.

  Parameters: `bit` the position of the requested bit

- `void set(int bit)`

  sets a bit.

  Parameters: `bit` the position of the bit to be set

- `void clear(int bit)`

  clears a bit.

  Parameters: `bit` the position of the bit to be cleared

- `void and(BitSet set)`

  logically ANDs this bit set with another.

  Parameters: `set` the bit set to be combined with this bit set

- `void or(BitSet set)`

  logically ORs this bit set with another.

  Parameters: `set` the bit set to be combined with this bit set

- `void xor(BitSet set)`

  logically XORs this bit set with another.

  Parameters: `set` the bit set to be combined with this bit set

The Sieve of Eratosthenes Benchmark

As an example of using bit sets, we want to show you an implementation of the "sieve of Eratosthenes" algorithm for finding prime numbers. (A prime number is a number like 2, 3, or 5 that is divisible only by itself and 1, and the sieve of Eratosthenes was one of the first methods discovered to enumerate these fundamental building blocks.) This isn't a terribly good algorithm for finding the number of primes, but for some reason it has become a popular benchmark for compiler performance. (It isn't a good benchmark either, since it mainly tests bit operations.)

Oh well, we bow to tradition and include an implementation. This program counts all prime numbers between 2 and 1,000,000. (There are 78,498 primes, so you probably don't want to print them all out.) You will find that the program takes a little while to get going, but eventually it picks up speed.

Without going into too many details of this program, the key is to march through a bit set with one million bits. We first turn on all the bits. After that, we turn off the bits that are multiples of numbers known to be prime. The positions of the bits that remain after this process are, themselves, the prime numbers. Example 11-3 illustrates this program in Java, and Example 11-4 is the C++ code. (The CD has the VB Code.)

Example 11-3: Sieve.java

```
import java.util.*;

public class Sieve
{  public static final boolean PRINT = false;

   public static void main(String[] s)
   {  int n = 1000000;
      long start = new Date().getTime();
      BitSet b = new BitSet(n);
      int count = 0;
      int i;
      for (i = 2; i <= n; i++)
         b.set(i);
      i = 2;
      while (i * i <= n)
      {  if (b.get(i))
         {  if (PRINT) System.out.println(i);
            count++;
            int k = 2 * i;
            while (k <= n)
            {  b.clear(k);
               k += i;
            }
         }
         i++;
      }
      while (i <= n)
      {  if (b.get(i))
         {  if (PRINT) System.out.println(i);
            count++;
         }
         i++;
      }
      long end = new Date().getTime();
      System.out.println(count + " primes");
      System.out.println((end - start) + " milliseconds");
   }
}
```

NOTE: Even though the sieve isn't a good benchmark, we couldn't resist timing the process as implemented in different languages. The CD contains implementations in C++ and one for Visual Basic. We used C++ and VB implementations that are as close as possible to the one used in Java. In VB, we used class modules and tried to imitate the functionality of the bitset class as closely as we could. We also used an array of bytes rather than an array of Boolean values in both cases. In the VB version, we also wrote the appropriate property procedures for manipulating bits in order to make the code as similar as possible to that used in the C++ and Java versions. (Which is a little unfair to VB since VB should work with an array of bits, not an array of bytes, for maximum efficiency.)

Here are the timing results on a Pentium-166 with 80 megabytes of RAM, running Windows 95.

C++	1.43 seconds
Java 1.02 (JDK, no JIT)	25.92 seconds
Java 1.02 (Café, JIT)	2.21 seconds
Java 1.1 (no JIT yet available)	27.60 seconds
VB4	35.92 seconds
VB5 (compiled code)	6.92 seconds

The results are instructive. C++ Is by far the fastest, but a JIT clearly makes Java competitive, so JITs for Java 1.1 are desperately needed.

TIP: The easiest way to do timings in Java is with the `CurrentTimeMillis` method in `java.lang`.System.

Example 11-4: Sieve.cpp

```
#include <iostream.h>
//C++
class BitSet
{
public:
   BitSet(int n) : bits(new char[(n - 1) / 8 + 1]), size(n) {}
   bool get(int n)
   {  if (0 <= n && n < size)
         return (bits[n >> 3] & (1 << (n & 7))) != 0;
      else return false;
   }
   void set(int n)
   {  if (0 <= n && n < size)
         bits[n >> 3] |= 1 << (n & 7);
   }
   void clear(int n)
   {  if (0 <= n && n < size)
         bits[n >> 3] &= ~(1 << (n & 7));
   }
```

```
private:
   char* bits;
   int size;
};

void main()
{  int n = 1000000;
   BitSet b(n);
   int count = 0;
   int i;
   for (i = 2; i <= n; i++)
      b.set(i);
   i = 2;
   while (i * i <= n)
   {  if (b.get(i))
      {  count++;
         int k = 2 * i;
         while (k <= n)
         {  b.clear(k);
            k += i;
         }
      }
      i++;
   }
   while (i <= n)
   {  if (b.get(i))
         count++;
      i++;
   }
   cout << count << " primes\n";
}
```

Hash Tables

Suppose you want to keep a list of employees. All employees have an ID number (possibly their social security number). You want to be able to find the records of an individual employee quickly, *given* the employee ID number. If the ID number is a small integer, that is, if your employee numbers are 1, 2, 3, and so forth, you can use a vector. But if you use social security numbers, they will be too long for an array index.

The `Hashtable` class in Java offers a solution to this kind of problem. Data items that are Java objects (like employee records) are identified by a *key* (like the ID number). The hash table then computes a small integer out of the key, called a *hash code*. The computation does not matter much, provided it is quick and the resulting integers are evenly distributed. Then the hash table stores the key and the data item in an array, at the location given by the hash code. All this is invisible to the user of Java's `Hashtable` class.

Here is how we set up a hash table for storing employees.

```
Hashtable staff = new Hashtable();
Employee harry = new Employee("Harry Hacker");
staff.put("987-98-9996", harry);
. . .
```

NOTE: The name of the class is `Hashtable`, with a lowercase `t`. Under Windows, you'll get strange error messages if you use `HashTable`, because the Windows file system is not case sensitive, but the Java compiler is.

Whenever you add an object to a hash table, you must supply a key as well. In our case, the key is a string, and the corresponding value is an `employee` object. Neither the key nor the value stored in a hash table can be `null`.

To retrieve an object, you must use (and, therefore, remember) the key.

```
String s = "1411-16-2536";
e = staff.get(s); // gets harry
```

If no information is stored in the hash table with the particular key specified, then `get` returns `null`.

NOTE: As with vectors, hash tables store everything as an object. This means you *must* cast the return value of `get` to the correct type, as was done in the example code above.

Keys must be unique. You cannot store two values with the same key. If you call the `put` method twice with the same key, then the second value replaces the first one. In fact, `put` returns the previous value stored with the key parameter. (This feature is useful; if `put` returns a non-`null` value, then you know you replaced a previous entry.)

The `remove()` method removes an element from the hash table. The `size()` method returns the number of entries in the hash table. In the section on enumerations on page 537, we will see how to iterate through all entries in a hash table.

You can think of a hash table as implementing a number of "buckets." Ideally, every bucket contains, at most, one object, but so-called *collisions* (keys with the same hash value) are inevitable. These are then placed in the same bucket by the hash table implementation. Thus, some buckets will contain lists with multiple

values. The `Hashtable` class then has to implement special code in order to take care of buckets with more than one item in them. Again, you don't need to worry about what is going on under the hood to resolve these collisions.

If you want more control over the performance of the hash table, you can specify the initial bucket count. The bucket count gives the number of buckets that are used to collect objects with identical hash values. If too many elements are inserted into a hash table, the number of collisions increases, and retrieval performance suffers. Then, the hash table should be reallocated with a larger number of buckets.

If you know approximately how many elements will eventually be in the table, then you should set the initial bucket size to about 150 percent of the expected element count. It is actually a good idea to make the size of the hash table a prime number because this prevents a clustering of keys. For example, if you need to store about 100 entries, set the initial bucket size to 151.

```
Hashtable staff = new Hashtable(151);
```

You can also set the *load factor* in the constructor. The load factor gives a percentage threshold before Java moves the hash table to a new location. For example, if the load factor is 0.75 (which is the default) and the hash table becomes more than 75 percent full, then Java automatically allocates a larger table with twice as many entries. Java reorganizes all the entries into the bigger table. This is a good strategy because hash tables that are nearly full perform poorly. For most applications, it is reasonable to leave the load factor at 0.75. (In the current implementation, the size of the larger table is not automatically a prime number as it should be for maximum efficiency.)

Example 11-5 illustrates the hash table interface at work. We use a hash table to store prices for products.

Example 11-5: HashTable.java

```
import java.awt.*;
import java.awt.event.*;
import java.util.*;
import corejava.*;

public class HashtableTest extends CloseableFrame
   implements ActionListener
{  public HashtableTest()
   {  Panel p = new Panel();
      p.setLayout(new FlowLayout());
      name = new Choice();
      add("Toaster", 19.95);
      add("Blender", 59.95);
```

```
        add("Microwave oven", 179.95);
        add("Citrus press", 19.95);
        add("Espresso maker", 199.95);
        add("Rice cooker", 29.95);
        add("Waffle iron", 39.95);
        add("Bread machine", 119.95);
        quantity = new IntTextField(1, 4);
        p.add(name);
        p.add(quantity);
        Button addButton = new Button("Add");
        p.add(addButton);
        addButton.addActionListener(this);

        add(p, "South");
        add(canvas = new PurchaseOrderCanvas(), "Center");
        canvas.redraw(a);
    }

    public void add(String n, double price)
    {   name.add(n); // add to choice field
        prices.put(n, new Double(price));
    }

    public void actionPerformed(ActionEvent evt)
    {   if (evt.getActionCommand().equals("Add"))
        {   if (quantity.isValid())
            {   String n = name.getSelectedItem();
                double price =
                    ((Double)prices.get(n)).doubleValue();
                a.addElement(new Item(n, quantity.getValue(),
                    price));
            }
            canvas.redraw(a);
        }
    }


    public static void main(String args[])
    {   Frame f = new HashtableTest();
        f.show();
    }

    private Vector a = new Vector();
    private Choice name;
    private IntTextField quantity;
    private PurchaseOrderCanvas canvas;
    private Hashtable prices = new Hashtable();
    private int m = 1;

}
```

```
class Item
{  public Item(String n, int q, double u)
   {  name = n;
      quantity = q;
      unitPrice = u;
   }

   public String toString()
   {  return new Format("%-20s").form(name)
         + new Format("%6d").form(quantity)
         + new Format("%8.2f").form(unitPrice);
   }

   private String name;
   private int quantity;
   private double unitPrice;
}

class PurchaseOrderCanvas extends Canvas
{  public void redraw(Vector new_a)
   {  a = new_a;
      repaint();
   }

   public void paint(Graphics g)
   {  Font f = new Font("Monospaced", Font.PLAIN, 12);
      g.setFont(f);
      FontMetrics fm = g.getFontMetrics(f);
      int height = fm.getHeight();
      int x = 0;
      int y = 0;
      int i = 0;
      for (i = 0; i < a.size(); i++)
      {  y += height;
         g.drawString(a.elementAt(i).toString(), x, y);
      }
   }

   private Vector a;
}
```

`java.util.Hashtable`

- `Hashtable()`

  constructs an empty hash table.

- `Hashtable(int initialCapacity)`

  constructs an empty hash table with the specified capacity.

Parameters:	`initialCapacity`	the initial number of buckets

- `Hashtable(int initialCapacity, float loadFactor)`

  constructs an empty hash table with the specified capacity and load factor.

Parameters:	`initialCapacity`	the initial number of buckets
	`loadFactor`	a number between 0.0 and 1.0 that determines at what percentage of fullness the hash table will be rehashed into a larger one

- `Object get(Object key)`

  gets the object associated with the key; returns the object associated with the key, or `null` if the key is not found in the hash table.

- `Object put(Object key, Object value)`

  puts the association of a key and an object into the hash table. If the key is already present, the new object replaces the old one previously associated with the key. This method returns the old value of the key, or `null` if the key was not previously present.

Parameters:	`key`	the key to use for retrieval (may not be `null`)
	`value`	the associated object (may not be `null`)

- `Object remove(Object key)`

  removes the key and the element associated with it. Does nothing if the key is not present. This method returns the value of the key, or `null` if the key was not found.

Parameters:	`key`	the key whose association you want to remove

- `int size()`

  returns the number of elements contained in the hash table.

Keys and Hash Functions

We were able to use strings as keys because the `String` class has a `hashCode` method that computes a *hash code* for a string. A hash code is an integer that is somehow derived from the characters in the string. Table 11-1 lists a few examples of hash codes that result from the `hashCode` function.

Table 11-1: Hash Codes Resulting from the `hashCode` Function

String	Hash code
`Hello`	`140207504`
`Harry`	`140013338`
`Hacker`	`884756206`

In fact, every object has a default hash code that is derived from the object's memory address. In general, this is not a good hash code to use because objects with identical contents may yield different hash codes. Consider this example.

```
String s = "Ok";
Button bs = new Button(s);
System.out.println(s.hashCode() + "  " + bs.hashCode());
String t = "Ok";
Button bt = new Button(t);
System.out.println(t.hashCode() + "  " + bt.hashCode());
```

Table 11-2 shows the result:

Table 11-2: Hash Codes of Objects with Identical Contents

`"Ok"`	`"Ok"`
`String`	`Button`
hash code	**hash code**
`3030`	`20526976`
`3030`	`20527144`

Note that the strings `s` and `t` have the same hash value because, for strings, the hash values are derived from their *contents.* The buttons `bs` and `bt` have different hash values because no special hash function has been defined for the `Button` class, and the default hash code function in the `Object` class derives the hash code from the object's memory address.

Hashable Classes Creation

In the Java library, all classes that define their own `hashCode` method form the hash code according to the contents of their objects. If your hash table keys are objects of a class that you defined yourself, you should define the `hashValue` method of the key class. This method should return an integer (which can be negative). The hash table code will later reduce the integer by dividing by the bucket count and taking the remainder. Just scramble up the hash codes of the data fields in some way that will give the hash codes for different objects a good chance of being widely scattered.

For example, suppose we have the class `PartNumber` for inventory part numbers. A part number consists of a description string and a release number.

```
pn = new PartNumber("WDGT", 4);
```

If we want to use part numbers as keys in a hash table, we need to define a hash code.

```
class PartNumber
{  . . .
   public int hashCode()
   {  return 13 * description.hashCode() + 17 * version;
   }
   . . .
   private String description;
   private int version;
}
```

There is another important function that we need to define for user-defined key classes, namely `equals`. The `Object` class defines `equals`, but the function only tests whether or not two objects are *identical*. We need to redefine `equals` to check for equal contents.

```
class PartNumber()
{  . . .
   public boolean equals(Object b)
   {  if (b instanceof PartNumber)
      {  PartNumber p = (PartNumber)b;
         return description.equals(p.description)
            && version == p.version;
      }
      else
         return false;
   }
   . . .
   private String description;
   private int version;
}
```

If we don't redefine `equals`, then a lookup like the one below will always fail—a new part number is never identical to one in the hash table.

```
Hashtable parts;
. . .
PartNumber pn = new PartNumber("WDGT", 4);
p = (Part)parts.get(pn);
```

`java.lang.Object`

- `boolean equals (Object obj)`

  compares two objects for equality; returns `true` if both objects are equal; `false` otherwise.

  Parameters: `obj` the object to compare with the first object

- `int hashCode()`

  returns a hash code for this object. A hash code can be any integer, positive or negative. Equal objects need to return identical hash codes.

Enumerations

Suppose we want to print all employees in a `staff` hash table. If we have a separate list of all ID numbers, then, of course, we can call `get` for every ID number and retrieve the employee records, one by one. But suppose we don't actually have the ID numbers handy. We can't very well try all keys in turn—if we use social security numbers as keys, then there are a billion possible keys.

Instead, we call the `elements()` method of the `Hashtable` class. It returns an object of a type that implements the `Enumeration` interface.

```
Enumeration e = staff.elements();
```

The `Enumeration` interface has two methods, `hasMoreElements` and `nextElement`. The following loop uses these methods to iterate through all values in the hash table.

```
while (e.hasMoreElements())
{   String id = (String)e.nextElement();
    . . .
}
```

Why does the hash table return an object of a new type instead of just having methods called `getFirstElement` and `getNextElement`? There are a number of advantages, and this is why many Java classes return objects that implement the `Enumeration` interface. (These are often called enumeration objects.) For example, if you have a vector `v` of items, then `v.elements()` returns an enumeration object that can be used to traverse all elements of the vector. Once you have an enumeration object, you can pass it to a method that retrieves the data. The big advantage is that this method does not need to know to which data structure the enumeration is attached.

For example, here is code that adds a sequence of items to a purchase order. It does not matter from where the items came. Their source might have been a vector, a hash table, or another container that reveals an enumeration of its elements.

```
class PurchaseOrder
{   . . .
    void addItems(Enumeration e)
    {   while (e.hasMoreElements())
        {   Object i = e.nextElement();
            if (i instanceof Item)
                itemsOrdered.addElement(i);
        }
    }
    . . .
}
```

NOTE: If you want to enumerate just the keys of a hash table, not the elements, use the `keys` method to get an enumeration object for the keys.

C++NOTE: The Java enumeration roughly corresponds to the iterators in the C++ standard template library, or, more precisely, to a `forward_iterator`. The `elements` method is the same as the call `p = a.begin()`, which yields an iterator pointing to the beginning of the container. The `nextElement` method is the same as the `*p++` operation on an iterator. The `hasMoreElements` test is the same as the test `p != a.end()`.

`java.util.Enumeration`

- `boolean hasMoreElements()`

  returns `true` if there are more elements yet to be inspected.

- `Object nextElement()`

  returns the next element to be inspected. Do not call this method if `hasMoreElements()` returned `false`.

`java.util.Hashtable`

- `Enumeration keys()`

  returns an enumeration object that traverses the keys of the hash table.

- `Enumeration elements()`

  returns an enumeration object that traverses the elements of the hash table.

java.util.Vector

API

- `Enumeration elements()`

  returns an enumeration object that traverses the elements of the vector.

Property Sets

A *property set* is a tabular structure that is essentially a hash table of a very special type. It has three particular characteristics.

- The keys and values are strings.
- The table can be saved to a file and loaded from a file.
- There is a secondary table for defaults.

The Java class that implements a property set is called `Properties`.

Property sets are useful in specifying configuration options for programs. The environment variables in UNIX and DOS are good examples. On a PC, your `AUTOEXEC.BAT` file might contain the settings:

```
SET PROMPT=$p$g
SET TEMP=C:\Windows\Temp
SET CLASSPATH=c:\jdk\lib;c:\CoreJavaBook;.
```

Here is how you would model those settings as a property set in Java.

```
Properties settings = new Properties();
settings.put("PROMPT", "$p$g");
settings.put("TEMP", "C:\\Windows\\Temp");
settings.put("CLASSPATH", "c:\\jdk\\lib;c:\\CoreJavaBook;.");
```

Use the `save` method to save this list of properties to a file. Here, we just print the property set to the standard output. The second argument is a comment that is included in the file.

```
settings.save(System.out, "Environment settings");
```

The sample table gives the following output.

```
#Environment settings
#Sun Jan 21 07:22:52  1996
CLASSPATH=.;c:\\jdk\\lib
TEMP=C:\\Windows\\Temp
PROMPT=$p$g
```

System Information

Here's another example of the ubiquity of the `Properties` set: Java stores information about your system in a `Properties` object that is returned by a method of the `System` class. Applications have complete access to this information, but applets that are loaded from a Web page do not—a security exception is thrown if they try to access it. The following code prints out the key value pair in the `Properties` object that stores the system properties. In this program, keep in mind that the `nextElement` method in the `Enumeration` interface returns an `Object`, so we need to do an explicit cast to a string in order to retrieve the key value via a call to `getProperty`.

```
import java.util.*;

public class SystemInfo
{  public static void main(String args[])
   {   Properties systemStuff = System.getProperties();
       Enumeration enum = systemStuff.propertyNames();
       while (enum.hasMoreElements())
       {   String key = (String)enum.nextElement();
           // nextElement gives objects, keys must
           // be strings, so cast
           System.out.println(key + " value is " +
              systemStuff.getProperty(key));
       }
   }
}
```

Here is an example of what you would see when you run the program. You can see all the values stored in this `Properties` object. (What you would get will, of course, reflect your machine's settings):

```
user.language value is en
java.home value is D:\JAVA\BIN\..
awt.toolkit value is sun.awt.windows.WToolkit
file.encoding.pkg value is sun.io
java.version value is 1.1.1
file.separator value is \
line.separator value is

user.region value is US
file.encoding value is 8859_1
java.vendor value is Sun Microsystems Inc.
user.timezone value is PST
user.name value is Cay
os.arch value is x86
os.name value is Windows 95
java.vendor.url value is http://www.sun.com/
user.dir value is D:\cay\books\cj3\CoreJavaBook\ch11\SystemInfo
java.class.path value is
.;d:\java\lib;d:\CoreJavaBook;D:\JAVA\BIN\..\classes;D:\JAVA\BIN\.
.\lib\classes.zip
java.class.version value is 45.3
os.version value is 4.0
path.separator value is ;
user.home value is D:\JAVA\BIN\..
```

When Netscape 3.0 executes a locally loaded applet, it permits access to a subset of all the system properties. Figure 11-2 shows an example of what you will see if you modify this program to be an applet running under Netscape 3.0 loaded as a local file.

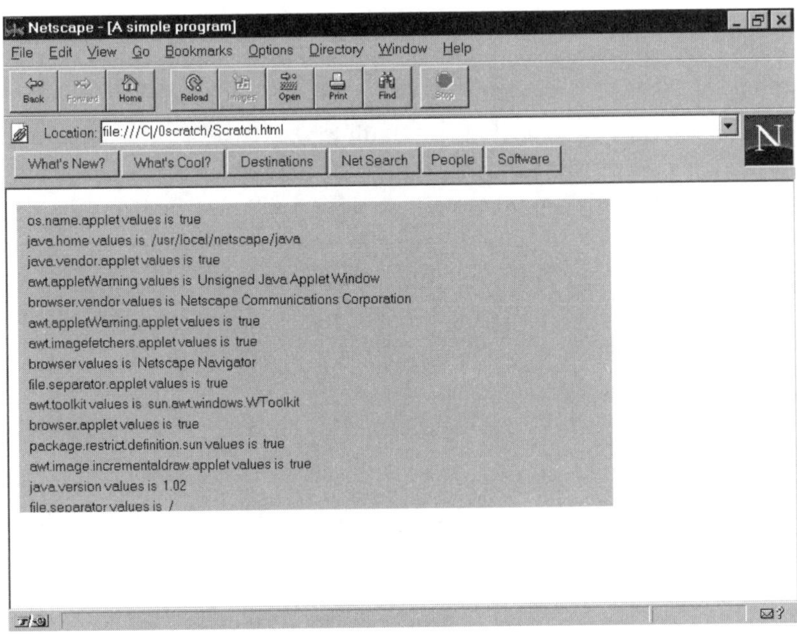

Figure 11-2: The output of the System Info program in Netscape 3.0

NOTE: You may be wondering why we don't show you this applet loaded from a URL. The answer is that Netscape doesn't let an applet running this way get at the system properties object as a whole because of security concerns.

Property Defaults

A property set is also a useful gadget whenever you want to allow the user to customize an application. Here is how your users can customize the `NotHelloWorld` program to their hearts' content. We'll allow them to specify the following in the configuration file `CustomWorld.ini`:

- window size
- font
- point size
- background color
- message string

If the user doesn't specify some of the settings, we will provide defaults.

The `Properties` class has two mechanisms for providing defaults. First, whenever you look up the value of a string, you can specify a default that should be used automatically when the key is not present.

```
String font = settings.getProperty("FONT", "Courier");
```

If there is a `"FONT"` property in the property table, then `font` is set to that string. Otherwise, `font` is set to `"Courier"`.

If you find it too tedious to specify the default in every call to `getProperty`, then you can pack all the defaults into a secondary property set and supply that in the constructor of your lookup table.

```
Properties defaultSettings = new Properties();
defaultSettings.put("FONT", "Courier");
defaultSettings.put("SIZE", "10");
defaultSettings.put("MESSAGE", "Hello, World");
. . .
Properties settings = new Properties(defaultSettings);
FileInputStream sf = new FileInputStream("CustomWorld.ini");
settings.load(sf);
. . .
```

Yes, you can even specify defaults to defaults if you give another property set parameter to the `defaultSettings` constructor, but it is not something one would normally do.

Example 11-6 is the customizable `"Hello, World"` program. Just edit the `.ini` file to change the program's appearance to the way *you* want.

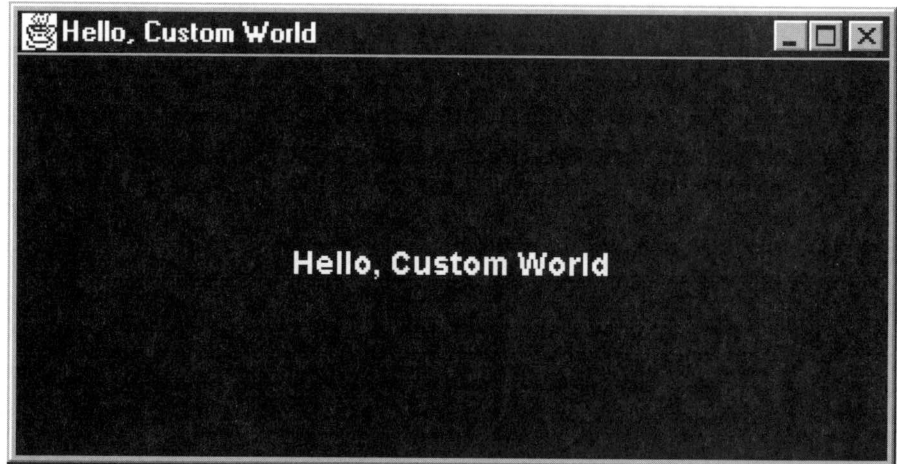

Figure 11-3: The customized Hello World program

Example 11-6: CustomWorld.java

```
import java.awt.*;
import java.util.*;
import java.io.*;
import corejava.*;

public class CustomWorld extends CloseableFrame
{  public CustomWorld()
   {  Properties defaultSettings = new Properties();
      defaultSettings.put("FONT", "Monospaced");
      defaultSettings.put("SIZE", "300 200");
      defaultSettings.put("MESSAGE", "Hello, World");
      defaultSettings.put("COLOR", "0 50 50");
      defaultSettings.put("PTSIZE", "12");

      Properties settings = new Properties(defaultSettings);
      try
      {  FileInputStream sf = new FileInputStream
            ("CustomWorld.ini");
         settings.load(sf);
      }
      catch (FileNotFoundException e) {}
      catch (IOException e) {}

      StringTokenizer st = new StringTokenizer
         (settings.getProperty("COLOR"));
      int red = Format.atoi(st.nextToken());
      int green = Format.atoi(st.nextToken());
      int blue = Format.atoi(st.nextToken());

      setBackground(new Color(red, green, blue));
      foreground = new Color(255 - red, 255 - green,
         255 - blue);

      String name = settings.getProperty("FONT");
      int size = Format.atoi(settings.getProperty("PTSIZE"));
      f = new Font(name, Font.BOLD, size);

      st = new StringTokenizer
         (settings.getProperty("SIZE"));
      int hsize = Format.atoi(st.nextToken());
      int vsize = Format.atoi(st.nextToken());
      setSize(hsize, vsize);
      setTitle(settings.getProperty("MESSAGE"));
   }
```

```
   public void paint(Graphics g)
   {  g.setColor(foreground);
      g.setFont(f);

      String s = getTitle();
      FontMetrics fm = g.getFontMetrics(f);
      int w = fm.stringWidth(s);

      Dimension d = getSize();
      Insets in = getInsets();
      int clientWidth = d.width - in.right - in.left;
      int clientHeight = d.height - in.bottom - in.top;
      int cx = in.left + (clientWidth - w) / 2;
      int cy = in.top + (clientHeight + fm.getHeight()) / 2;

      g.drawString(s, cx, cy);
   }

   public static void main(String args[])
   {  Frame f = new CustomWorld();
      f.show();
   }

   private Color foreground;
   private Font f;
}
```

Here are the current property settings.

```
#Environment settings
#Sun Jan 21 07:22:52  1996
FONT=Times New Roman
SIZE=400 200
MESSAGE=Hello, Custom World
COLOR=0 25 50
PTSIZE=14
```

NOTE: The `Properties` class *extends* the `Hashtable` class. That means, all methods of `Hashtable` are available to `Properties` objects. Some functions are useful. For example, `size` returns the number of possible properties (well, it isn't *that* nice—it doesn't count the defaults). Similarly, `keys` returns an enumeration of all keys, except for the defaults. There is also a second function, called `propertyNames`, that returns all keys. The `put` function is downright dangerous. It doesn't check that you put strings into the table.

Does the *is-a* rule for using inheritance apply here? Is every property set a hash table? Not really. That these are true is really just an implementation detail. Maybe it is better to think of a property set as having a hash table. But then the hash table should be a private data field. Actually, in this case, a property set has two hash tables, one for the defaults and one for the non-default values.

We think a better design would be the following:

```
class Properties
{  public String getProperty(String) { . . . }
   public void put(String, String) { . . . }
   . . .
   private Hashtable nonDefaults;
   private Hashtable defaults;
}
```

We don't want to tell you to avoid the `Properties` class in the Java library. Provided you are careful to put nothing but strings in it, it works just fine. But think twice before using "quick and dirty" inheritance in your own programs.

---

java.util.Properties

- `Properties()`

  creates an empty property list.

- `Properties(Properties defaults)`

  creates an empty property list with a set of defaults.

Parameters:	`defaults`	the defaults to use for lookups

- `String getProperty(String key)`

  gets a property association; returns the string associated with the key, or the string associated with the key in the default table if it wasn't present in the table.

Parameters:	`key`	the key whose associated string to get

- `String getProperty(String key, String defaultValue)`

  gets a property with a default value if the key is not found; returns the string associated with the key, or the default string if it wasn't present in the table.

Parameters:	`key`	the key whose associated string to get
	`defaultValue`	the string to return if the key is not present

- `void load(InputStream in) throws IOException`

  loads a property set from an `InputStream`.

Parameters:	`in`	the input stream

- `void save(OutputStream out, String header)`

  saves properties to an `OutputStream`.

Parameters:	`out`	the output stream
	`header`	the header comment string

Hash Sets

Sometimes, you just want to collect a bunch of objects, but no obvious key comes to mind. Suppose you need a collection of fonts. What can you use as a key? The face name? No, keys must be unique. Helvetica 10-point and Helvetica 14-point bold both have the same face name, "Helvetica," but they are not the same font. If you need to use the face name, point size, and style of a font, then you might as well use the font object itself as the key.

We just want to collect the fonts, test whether or not a particular font is in our set, and, perhaps, iterate through the ones we collected. A data structure that supports these operations is called a *set.* Of course, we can implement a set as a vector, but it isn't very efficient. Testing whether or not a particular object is already in the set (so we don't insert it twice) requires that we test all elements. A hash table is a much more attractive solution since it tests only elements with the same hash code.

We will use the standard `Hashtable` class in Java as the basis for our set implementation. Because we are interested only in the keys, we could use any non-`null` object for the value field. The simplest method is to use the same entry for the key and the value.

Here is a `HashSet` class that implements this idea:

```
class HashSet extends Hashtable
{  public void put(Object o) { super.put(o, o); }
   public boolean contains(Object o)
   {  return super.containsKey(o);
   }
   public Enumeration elements()
   {  return super.keys();
   }
}
```

In this case, we don't mind inheriting from `Hashtable` because it turns out that none of the base class methods do anything dangerous.

Example 11-7 shows how to put a hash set to work.

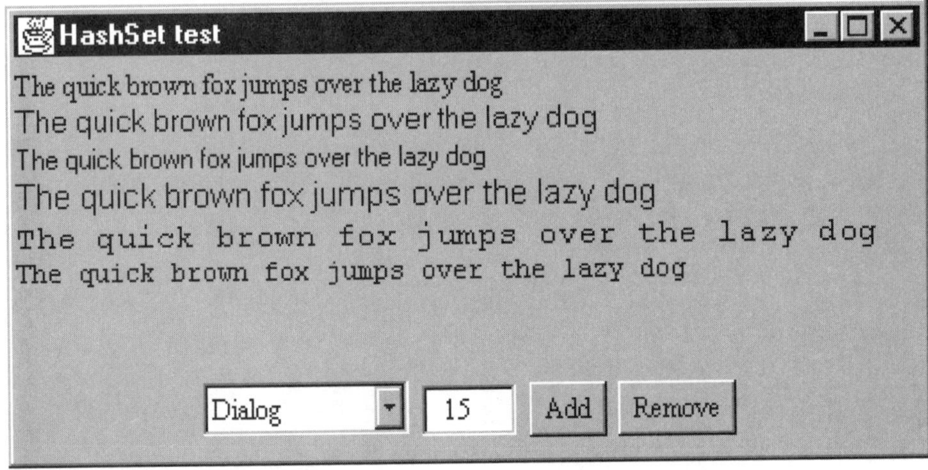

Figure 11-4: Hash set demo

Example 11-7: HashSetTest.java

```
import java.awt.*;
import java.awt.event.*;
import java.util.*;
import corejava.*;

public class HashSetTest extends CloseableFrame
   implements ActionListener
{  public HashSetTest()
   {  Panel p = new Panel();
      p.setLayout(new FlowLayout());
      name = new Choice();
      String[] f = Toolkit.getDefaultToolkit().getFontList();
      int i;
      for (i = 0; i < f.length; i++)
         name.add(f[i]);
      ptsize = new IntTextField(12, 4);
      p.add(name);
      p.add(ptsize);
      addButton(p, "Add");
      addButton(p, "Remove");
      add(p, "South");
      add(canvas = new FontCanvas(), "Center");
      canvas.redraw(fonts);
   }
```

```
    public void addButton(Container c, String name)
    {  Button b = new Button(name);
       b.addActionListener(this);
       c.add(b);
    }

    public void actionPerformed(ActionEvent evt)
    {  String arg = evt.getActionCommand();
       if (arg.equals("Add"))
       {  if (ptsize.isValid())
          {  String n = name.getSelectedItem();
             fonts.put(new Font(n, Font.PLAIN,
                ptsize.getValue()));
          }
       }
       else if (arg.equals("Remove"))
       {  if (ptsize.isValid())
          {  String n = name.getSelectedItem();
             fonts.remove(new Font(n, Font.PLAIN,
                ptsize.getValue()));
          }
       }
       canvas.redraw(fonts);
    }

    public static void main(String args[])
    {  Frame f = new HashSetTest();
       f.show();
    }

    private Choice name;
    private IntTextField ptsize;
    private FontCanvas canvas;
    private HashSet fonts = new HashSet();

}

class HashSet extends Hashtable
{  public void put(Object o) { super.put(o, o); }
   public boolean contains(Object o)
   {  return super.containsKey(o);
   }
   public Enumeration elements()
   {  return super.keys();
   }
}
```

```
class FontCanvas extends Canvas
{  public void redraw(HashSet new_a)
   {  a = new_a;
      repaint();
   }

   public void paint(Graphics g)
   {  Enumeration e = a.elements();
      int x = 0;
      int y = 0;
      while (e.hasMoreElements())
      {  Font f = (Font)e.nextElement();
         g.setFont(f);
         FontMetrics fm = g.getFontMetrics(f);
         y += fm.getHeight();
         g.drawString(
        "The quick brown fox jumps over the lazy dog", x, y);
      }
   }

   private HashSet a;
}
```

Linked Lists

So far, we have seen two data structures for collecting elements: vectors and hash sets. Hash sets perform well when all that you are interested in doing is adding and removing elements from the structure. The drawback is that the elements are scattered all over the hash table. In particular, the order in which the elements were inserted is completely lost when we enumerate the elements.

If you want an ordered sequence of elements *and* the ability to rapidly insert and remove elements in the middle of the sequence, then you need a linked list. Figure 11-5 shows a diagram for a linked list data structure. The *list header* contains a pointer to the first *link*, which stores a data item and a pointer to the next link. That link, likewise, stores a data item and a pointer to the next link, and so on. The last link has a `null` pointer to denote the end of the list.

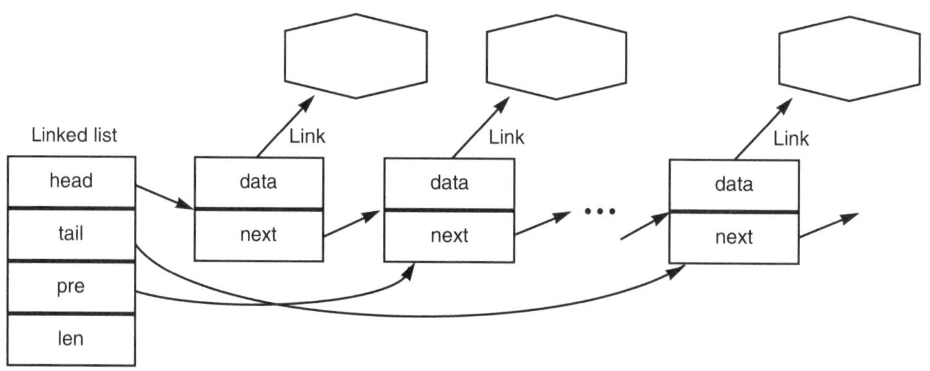

Figure 11-5: Linked lists

Some people think that you cannot program a linked list in Java because linked lists need pointers and Java doesn't have them. Nothing could be further from the truth. Lists are actually easier to program in Java than in just about any other programming language. Every object reference in Java is already a pointer. This makes a basic `Link` class particularly simple.

```
class Link
{  Object data;
   Link next; //pointer to another object of the class
}
```

In addition, we need a `List` class. It holds a pointer to the head link, and, in order to make rapid insertion at the tail end of the list easier, we include a pointer to the tail as well. We also keep a field for the list size, so we don't need to traverse the entire list every time the caller wants to have an element count.

Furthermore, there must be some way of inserting in the middle of the list. We do this by storing a *cursor* with the list object. The cursor marks a specific element in the linked list. The `reset` method resets the cursor to the beginning of the list. The `nextElement` method advances it to the next element. This permits positioning of the cursor anywhere in the linked list. The `remove` method removes the element under the cursor, and the `put` method inserts a new object before the cursor. (The cursor functions just like the cursor on a terminal. Characters are inserted before the cursor and deleted from under the cursor.)

The advantage of using a cursor is that the individual links are completely hidden from the list user, so the list user can't mess them up.

There is a technical difficulty with storing the cursor position. When implementing the `remove` operation, we must relink the *predecessor* of the cursor link. But

in a singly linked list, we cannot easily locate a link's predecessor. For that reason, we actually save the cursor's predecessor—not the actual cursor position—in the `List` data structure.

Before we look at the implementation code, here is an example of how you use the list. We first insert all employees in a list and then remove those whose salary is less than $50,000.

```
LinkedList a = new LinkedList();
for (i = 0; i < staff.length; i++) a.append(staff[i]);
a.reset();
while (a.hasMoreElements())
{  Employee e = (Employee)a.currentElement();
   if (e.salary() < 50000) a.remove();
   else a.nextElement();
}
```

The Code for Our Linked List Class

Unless you are a list enthusiast, you probably don't want to look at the details of the linking and unlinking. Note, however, that there is one significant difference between the Java code and its equivalent C++ code: because of garbage collection, you *never* need to worry about recycling links. Example 11-8 gives you the code for the `LinkedList` class. It can be found in the `corejava` directory.

Example 11-8: LinkedList.java

```
package corejava;


public class LinkedList
{  /**
   * resets the cursor
   */

   public void reset()

   {  pre = null;
   }



   /**
    * @return true iff the cursor is not at the end of the
    * list
    */
    public boolean hasMoreElements()

   {  return cursor() != null;
   }
```

```
/**
 * move the cursor to the next position
 * @return the current element (before advancing the
 * position)
 * @exception java.util.NoSuchElementException if already at
 * the end of the list
 */
public Object nextElement()
{  if (pre == null) pre = head; else pre = pre.next;
   if (pre == null)
      throw new java.util.NoSuchElementException();
   return pre.data;
}


/**
 * @return the current element under the cursor
 * @exception java.util.NoSuchElementException if already at
 * the end of the list
 */

public Object currentElement()
{  Link cur = cursor();
   if (cur == null)
      throw new java.util.NoSuchElementException();
   return cur.data;
}


/**
 * insert before the iterator position
 * @param n the object to insert
 */

 public void insert(Object n)
{  Link p = new Link(n, cursor());

   if (pre != null)
   {  pre.next = p;
      if (pre == tail) tail = p;
   }
   else
   {  if (head == null) tail = p;
      head = p;
   }
```

```
      pre = p;
      len++;
   }

   /**
    * insert after the tail of the list
    * @param n - the value to insert
    */

   public void append(Object n)
   {  Link p = new Link(n, null);
      if (head == null) head = tail = p;
      else
      {  tail.next = p;
         tail = p;
      }
      len++;
   }


   /**
    * remove the element under the cursor
    * @return the removed element
    * @exception java.util.NoSuchElementException if already at
    * the end of the list
    */

   public Object remove()
   {  Link cur = cursor();
      if (cur == null)
         throw new java.util.NoSuchElementException();
      if (tail == cur) tail = pre;
      if (pre != null)
         pre.next = cur.next;
      else
         head = cur.next;
      len--;
      return cur.data;
   }

   /**
    * @return the number of elements in the list
    */

   public int size()
   {  return len;
   }
```

```
    /**
     * @return an enumeration to iterate through all elements
     * in the list
     */

     public java.util.Enumeration elements()
    {  return new ListEnumeration(head);
    }


    public static void main(String[] args)
    {  LinkedList a = new LinkedList();
       for (int i = 1; i <= 10; i++)
          a.insert(new Integer(i));
       java.util.Enumeration e = a.elements();
       while (e.hasMoreElements())
          System.out.println(e.nextElement());

       a.reset();
       while (a.hasMoreElements())
       {  a.remove();
          a.nextElement();
       }
       a.reset();
       while (a.hasMoreElements())
          System.out.println(a.nextElement());
    }

    private Link cursor()
    {  if (pre == null) return head; else return pre.next;
    }

    private Link head;
    private Link tail;
    private Link pre; // predecessor of cursor
    private int len;
}

class Link
{  Object data;
   Link next;
   Link(Object d, Link n) { data = d; next = n; }
}
     /**
     * A class for enumerating a linked list
     * implements the Enumeration interface
     */
```

```
class ListEnumeration implements java.util.Enumeration
{  public ListEnumeration( Link l)
   {  cursor = l;
   }

   /**
    * @return true iff the iterator is not at the end of the
    * list
    */
    public boolean hasMoreElements()
   {  return cursor != null;
   }

   /**
    * move the iterator to the next position
    * @return the current element (before advancing the
    * position)
    * @exception NoSuchElementException if already at the
    * end of the list
    */

    public Object nextElement()
   {  if (cursor == null)
      throw new java.util.NoSuchElementException();
      Object r = cursor.data;
      cursor = cursor.next;
      return r;
   }

   private Link cursor;
}
```

A Linked List Demonstration

Example 11-9 is a graphical program that shows how the lists really work (shown in Figure 11-6). Click on the buttons to simulate the list operations, and see the list change before your very eyes!

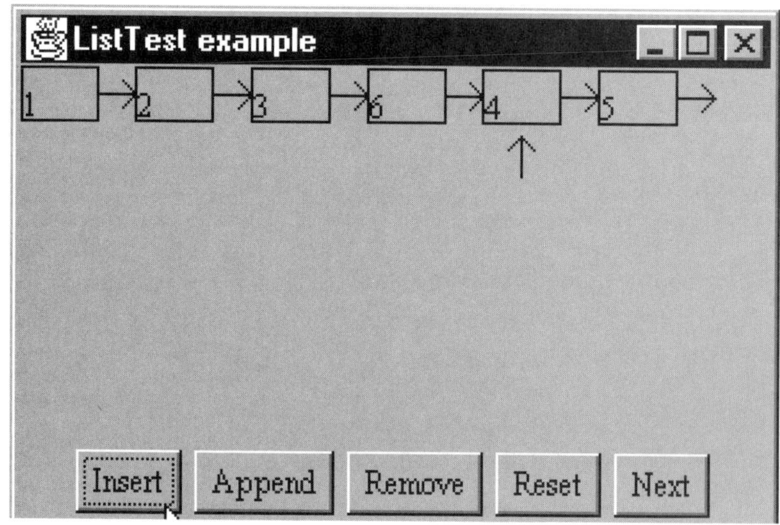

Figure 11-6: Linked list demo at work

Example 11-9: ListTest.java

```
import java.awt.*;
import java.awt.event.*;
import java.util.*;
import corejava.*;

public class ListTest extends CloseableFrame
   implements ActionListener
{  public ListTest()
   {  Panel p = new Panel();
      p.setLayout(new FlowLayout());
      addButton(p, "Insert");
      addButton(p, "Append");
      addButton(p, "Remove");
      addButton(p, "Reset");
      addButton(p, "Next");
      add(p, "South");
      add(canvas = new ListCanvas(), "Center");
      canvas.redraw(a);
   }

   public void addButton(Container c, String name)
   {  Button b = new Button(name);
      b.addActionListener(this);
      c.add(b);
   }
```

```
   public void actionPerformed(ActionEvent evt)
   {  String arg = evt.getActionCommand();
      if (arg.equals("Insert"))
      {  a.insert(new Integer(m));
         m++;
      }
      else if (arg.equals("Append"))
      {  a.append(new Integer(m));
         m++;
      }
      else if (arg.equals("Remove"))
         a.remove();
      else if (arg.equals("Next"))
         a.nextElement();
      else if (arg.equals("Reset"))
         a.reset();
      canvas.redraw(a);
   }

   public static void main(String args[])
   {  Frame f = new ListTest();
      f.show();
   }

   private LinkedList a = new LinkedList();
   private ListCanvas canvas;
   private int m = 1;
}

class ListCanvas extends Canvas
{  public void redraw(LinkedList new_a)
   {  a = new_a;
      repaint();
   }

   public void paint(Graphics g)
   {  Enumeration e = a.elements();
      int x = 0;
      int y = 0;
      int cx = 0;
      while (e.hasMoreElements())
      {  g.drawRect(x, y, 30, 20);
         Integer i = (Integer)e.nextElement();
         if (a.hasMoreElements()
            && i.equals(a.currentElement()))
            cx = x;

         g.drawString(i.toString(), x + 1, y + 19);
```

```
            g.drawLine(x + 30, y + 10, x + 45, y + 10);
            g.drawLine(x + 45, y + 10, x + 40, y + 5);
            g.drawLine(x + 45, y + 10, x + 40, y + 15);
            x += 45;
        }
        if (!a.hasMoreElements()) cx = x;
        g.drawLine(cx + 15, 25, cx + 15, 40);
        g.drawLine(cx + 15, 25, cx + 10, 30);
        g.drawLine(cx + 15, 25, cx + 20, 30);
    }

    private LinkedList a;
}
```

Linked List Enumeration

If you need to inspect all elements in a list, you can use the following traversal code:

```
a.reset();
while (a.hasMoreElements())
{  Object o = a.nextElement();
   do something with o;
}
```

However, that procedure messes up the list cursor. This can be a problem: maybe the cursor was at an important position before the traversal, but after the traversal the old cursor position is lost—it is now at the end of the list. For that reason, and as a general token of support for the `Enumeration` interface, we also supply an `elements` method that returns an `Enumeration` object. You can use it just like you use any other object that implements the enumeration interface.

```
Enumeration e = a.elements();
while (e.hasMoreElements())
{  Object o = e.nextElement();
   do something with o;
}
```

So far, we have been consumers of enumeration objects, and the `List` class is the producer of such an object. This is a good place to learn how to create such an entity. `Enumeration` is an interface, not a class, so we cannot simply call `new Enumeration()` to get a new enumeration object.

Even if `Enumeration` were a class, it couldn't possibly know about the structure of our `List` class, since it is not a part of standard Java. Instead, we need to design a new class that implements the `Enumeration` interface.

```
class ListEnumeration implements Enumeration
{   public boolean hasMoreElements()
    {   return current != null;
    }
    public Object nextElement()
    {  Object r = current.data;
       current = current.next;
       return r;
    }
    ListEnumeration(Link first) { current = first; }
    private Link current;
}
```

The `elements` method of the `LinkedList` class generates a new enumeration object.

```
class LinkedList
{   . . .
    Enumeration elements()
    {   return new ListEnumeration(head);
    }
}
```

Access to Links

Note that the data fields of the `Link` structure are defined without either `public` or `private` access specified in the list module. Of course, we didn't want them to be public, but we couldn't make them private either. The `LinkedList` class needs access to the data fields of the links. Making the data items private and supplying public access methods wouldn't have done us any good. We don't want any class but the `LinkedList` class to call those methods.

The Java protection mechanism is not exact enough to express this concept. In Java, you can set the protection to the class (`private`), the world (`public`), the package and all subclasses (`protected`), or the package (the default). The first three options are not appropriate in this case, so we settled for the last one—the package. That does mean that any other code in the same package has the potential to mess with the links. If we put the `LinkedList` class in a separate package, like `corejava`, then it is unlikely that other programmers will smuggle their code to the package just to invade the links. But if the `List` class is part of the default package, then Java offers no good method for protecting the linked data.

Can we use *inner classes* to get better protection? We can easily define `Link` to be an inner class of `List`:

```
class List
{  private class Link
   {  Object data;
      Link next;
      Link(Object d, Link n) { data = d; next = n; }
   }
   . . .
}
```

However, there are two drawbacks to using inner classes. The `ListEnumeration` class also needs to be able to access the links. If we make `Link` a private inner class of `List`, then that access is not allowed. And, more importantly, if `Link` is an inner class, then every `Link` object carries a reference to the list object that generated it! Since we have no need for these outer references, this process is wasteful.

C++ NOTE: In C++, you can use the `friend` mechanism to build more complex relationships of trust than are possible with the simple `public`/`private` access control. Java has no analog to this mechanism.

Queues

In many programs, data are generated faster than can be processed. Then, you want to put the incoming data into a queue and remove it later, so that the first item inserted also becomes the first one removed. This is often called FIFO (first in, first out). Linked lists are ideally suited for this purpose. We simply append elements at the end of the list and remove them from the head. Here is a queue class that implements this idea.

```
class Queue
{  public void append(Object o) { data.append(o); }
   public Object remove() { return data.remove(); }
   public int size() { data.size(); }
   public Enumeration elements() { data.elements(); }
   private LinkedList data;
}
```

The following example program uses a queue to produce a *breadth-first* listing of a directory tree. We start at the root directory. Whenever we visit a new directory, we get all subdirectories and add them to the tail of the queue. Then we remove the head of the queue and repeat the process. Because the first directories in the queue are the children of the root directory, we first visit all subdirectories in level 1. Then, their subdirectories are added to the queue, and we visit the level 2 subdirectories. The process is repeated until all subdirectories have been visited. Try it out—you will find the order of the subdirectories somewhat

unconventional. It is just the opposite of the *depth-first* listing that you get from the DOS DIR/S or TREE commands. Here's an example of what you might see:

```
\.
\.\CoreJavaBook
\.\CoreJavaBook\ch8
\.\CoreJavaBook\WinEdit
\.\CoreJavaBook\corejava
\.\CoreJavaBook\ch2
\.\CoreJavaBook\ch3
\.\CoreJavaBook\ch4
\.\CoreJavaBook\ch5
\.\CoreJavaBook\ch6
\.\CoreJavaBook\ch7
\.\CoreJavaBook\ch9
\.\CoreJavaBook\ch12
\.\CoreJavaBook\ch10
\.\CoreJavaBook\ch11
\.\CoreJavaBook\ch13
\.\CoreJavaBook\ch10\Chart
\.\CoreJavaBook\ch10\Retire
\.\CoreJavaBook\ch10\AppletApplication
```

Example 11-10 shows the program.

Example 11-10: DirQueue.java

```
import java.io.*;
import java.util.*;
import corejava.*;

public class DirQueue
{  public static void main(String[] args)
   {  Queue dirs = new Queue();
      dirs.append(new File(File.separator + "."));
      while (dirs.size() > 0)
      {  File f = (File)dirs.remove();
         System.out.println(f);

         String[] s = f.list();
         if (s != null)
         {  for (int i = 0; i < s.length; i++)
            {  File d = new File(f.getAbsolutePath()
               + File.separator + s[i]);
               if (d.isDirectory())
                  dirs.append(d);
            }
         }
      }
   }
}
```

```
class Queue
{  public void append(Object o) { data.append(o); }
   public Object remove() { return data.remove(); }
   public int size() { return data.size(); }
   public Enumeration elements() { return data.elements(); }
   private LinkedList data = new LinkedList();
}
```

Stacks

In the last section, you saw how to implement a FIFO data structure. Occasionally, a "last in, first out" structure is required. The Java library supplies such a data structure, called `Stack`. The `push` method in the `Stack` class adds an element to the top of the stack; the `pop` method removes the top element from the stack.

The `Stack` class derives from `Vector`. Conceptually, this is dubious because you can use the `Vector` methods to change the stack contents in the middle. On the other hand, you can also use the `elements` method to inspect the elements of the vector, which is occasionally useful.

We traverse all directories on a disk, pushing newly found directories onto the top of the stack. Since we always pop the most recently found directory for further investigation, we get a *depth-first* traversal of the directory tree. Here's what you will see:

```
\.\CoreJavaBook\ch11
\.\CoreJavaBook\ch11\CompoundInterest
\.\CoreJavaBook\ch11\PropertiesTest
\.\CoreJavaBook\ch11\DirStack
\.\CoreJavaBook\ch11\HashSetTest
\.\CoreJavaBook\ch11\HashtableTest
\.\CoreJavaBook\ch11\PurchaseOrderTest
\.\CoreJavaBook\ch11\CustomWorld
\.\CoreJavaBook\ch11\ListTest
\.\CoreJavaBook\ch11\Pascal
\.\CoreJavaBook\ch11\DirQueue
\.\CoreJavaBook\ch11\Sieve
\.\CoreJavaBook\ch11\Sieve\Release
\.\CoreJavaBook\ch11\Sieve\Debug
\.\CoreJavaBook\ch11\Sieve\sieve
\.\CoreJavaBook\ch11\Sieve\sieve\Debug
\.\CoreJavaBook\ch5
\.\CoreJavaBook\ch5\MailboxTest
\.\CoreJavaBook\ch5\EmployeeSortTest
\.\CoreJavaBook\ch5\ManagerTest
```

Example 11-11 shows the program.

Example 11-11: DirStack.java

```
import java.io.*;
import java.util.*;

public class DirStack
{  public static void main(String[] args)
   {  Stack dirs = new Stack();
      dirs.push(new File(File.separator + "."));
      while (dirs.size() > 0)
      {  File f = (File)dirs.pop();
         System.out.println(f);
         String[] s = f.list();
         if (s != null)
         {  for (int i = 0; i < s.length; i++)
            {  File d = new File(f.getAbsolutePath()
                  + File.separator + s[i]);
               if (d.isDirectory())
                  dirs.push(d);
            }
         }
      }
   }
}
```

`java.util.Stack` API

- `void push(Object item)`

  pushes an item onto the stack.

  Parameters: `item` the item to be added

- `Object pop()`

  pops and returns the top item of the stack. Don't call this method if the stack is empty.

- `Object peek()`

  returns the top of the stack without popping it. Don't call this method if the stack is empty.

Multi-Dimensional Arrays

Suppose you want to make a table of numbers that shows how much an investment of $10,000 will grow after a number of years under different interest rate scenarios in which interest is paid monthly and reinvested. Table 11-3 illustrates this scenario.

Table 11-3: Interest Rates for Different Investment Time Periods

	Interest rate					
Years	**5.00%**	**5.50%**	**6.00%**	**6.50%**	**7.00%**	**7.50%**
10	16453.09	17293.07	18175.94	19103.88	20079.20	21104.31
20	26959.70	29770.53	32874.42	36301.92	40086.77	44266.24
30	43997.90	51024.07	59172.28	68621.70	79580.14	92288.56
40	71519.81	87070.09	106001.40	129048.88	157107.49	191266.77
50	115804.66	147944.43	189004.10	241459.24	308472.48	394084.20

The obvious way to store this information is in a two-dimensional array (or matrix), which we will call `balance`.

The definition of a matrix in Java is simple enough. For example:

```
double[][] balance;
```

As always in Java, you cannot use an array until you initialize it with a call to `new`. In this case, the initialization is as follows:

```
balance = new double[5][6];
```

Once the array is initialized, you can access individual elements:

```
balance[i][j] = futureValue(10000, 10 + 10 * i, 5 + 0.5 * j);
```

Example 11-12 shows the full program that computes the table.

Example 11-12: CompoundInterest.java

```
import corejava.*;

public class CompoundInterest
{  public static double futureValue(double initialBalance,
   double p, double nyear)
   {  return initialBalance * Math.pow(1 + p / 12 / 100,
      12 * nyear);
   }
```

```
   public static void main(String[] args)
   {  double[][] balance;
      balance = new double[5][6];
      int i;
      int j;
      for (i = 0; i < 5; i++)
         for (j = 0; j < 6; j++)
            balance[i][j] = futureValue(10000, 10 + 10 * i,
               5 + 0.5 * j);
      System.out.print("    ");
      for (j = 0; j < 6; j++)
         Format.print(System.out, "%9.2f%", 5 + 0.5 * j);
      System.out.println("");
      for (i = 0; i < 5; i++)
      {  Format.print(System.out, "%3d", 10 + 10 * i);
         for (j = 0; j < 6; j++)
            Format.print(System.out, "%10.2f",
               balance[i][j]);
         System.out.println("");
      }

   }
}
```

So far, what you have seen is not too different from other programming languages. But there is actually something subtle going on behind the scenes that you can sometimes turn to your advantage: Java has *no* multi-dimensional arrays at all, only one-dimensional arrays. Multi-dimensional arrays are faked as "arrays of arrays."

For example, the `balance` array in the preceding example is actually an array that contains five elements, each of which is an array of six floating-point numbers.

The expression `balance[i]` refers to the `i`'th subarray, that is, the `i`'th row of the table. It is, itself, an array, and `balance[i][j]` refers to the `j`'th entry of that array.

Because rows of arrays are individually accessible, you can actually swap them!

```
double[] temp = balance[i];
balance[i] = balance[i + 1];
balance[i + 1] = temp;
```

It is easy to make "ragged" arrays, that is, arrays in which different rows have different lengths. Here is the standard example. Let us make an array to store "Pascal's triangle." Pascal's triangle is the following arrangement:

```
              1
           1     1
        1     2     1
     1     3     3     1
  1     4     6     4     1
1    5    10    10    5    1
1    6    15    20    15    6    1
```

You put a 1 at the corners of the triangle and then fill each element with the sum of the two numbers above it diagonally. To store the triangle as a matrix, simply visualize the rows pushed to the left, like this:

```
1
1    1
1    2    1
1    3    3    1
1    4    6    4    1
1    5    10   10   5    1
1    6    15   20   15   6    1
```

Actually, there is no need to store the right half of a row because it is identical to the left half read backwards. So we will simply store the following:

```
1
1
1    2
1    3
1    4    6
1    5    10
1    6    15   20
```

That is, the `i`'th row has `(i / 2) + 1` elements. (Recall that the top row corresponds to `i = 0`.) To build this ragged array, first allocate the array holding the rows.

```
int[][] binom = new int[n + 1][];
```

Next, allocate the rows.

```
for (i = 0; i <= n; i++)
   binom[i] = new int[i / 2 + 1];
```

Now that the array is allocated, we can access the elements in the normal way, provided we do not overstep the bounds.

```
for (i = 0; i <= n; i++)
    for (j = 0; j <= i / 2; j++)
        if (j == 0)
            binom[i][j] = 1;
        else if (2 * j < i)
            binom[i][j] = binom[i - 1][j - 1] + binom[i - 1][j];
        else
            binom[i][j] = 2 * binom[i - 1][j - 1];
```

C++ NOTE: Recall that a one-dimensional array in Java really corresponds to a C++ pointer to a heap array. That is,

```
int[] numbers = new int[50]; // Java
```

is not the same as

```
int numbers[50]; // C++
```

but rather

```
int* numbers = new int[50]; // C++
```

Similarly,

```
double[][] balance = new double[5][6]; // Java
```

is not the same as

```
double balance[5][6]; // C++
```

or even

```
double (*balance)[6] = new double[5][6]; // C++
```

Instead, an array of five pointers is allocated:

```
double** balance = new double*[5];
```

Then, each element in the pointer array is filled with an array of 6 numbers:

```
for (i = 0; i < 5; i++) balance[i] = new double[6];
```

Mercifully, this loop is automatic when you ask for a `new double[5][6]`. When you want ragged arrays, you allocate the row arrays separately.

Just for fun, we give a nice application of the Pascal triangle. We compute the remainders of the numbers in the triangle and color them with different colors. For example, if you choose the quotient 5 in the text field, all values in the Pascal triangle that are divisible by 5 show up as one color, all that leave a remainder of 1 as another color, and so on, as shown in Figure 11-7 and Example 11-13.

Figure 11-7: Pascal's triangle

Example 11-13: Pascal.java

```
import java.awt.*;
import java.awt.event.*;
import corejava.*;

public class Pascal extends CloseableFrame
   implements ActionListener
{  public Pascal()
   {  Panel p = new Panel();
      p.setLayout(new FlowLayout());
      addButton(p, "-");
      addButton(p, "+");
      label = new Label("2     ");
      p.add(label);
      add(p, "South");
      canvas = new PascalCanvas();
      add(canvas, "Center");
   }

   public void addButton(Container c, String name)
   {  Button b = new Button(name);
      b.addActionListener(this);
      c.add(b);
   }
```

```
   public void actionPerformed(ActionEvent evt)
   {  String arg = evt.getActionCommand();
      if (arg.equals("-"))
      {  if (m > 2) m--;
         label.setText(m + "    ");
         canvas.redraw(m);
      }
      if (arg.equals("+"))
      {  m++;
         label.setText(m + "    ");
         canvas.redraw(m);
      }
   }

   public static void main(String args[])
   {  Frame f = new Pascal();
      f.setSize(400, 400);
      f.show();
   }

   private Label label;
   private PascalCanvas canvas;
   private int m = 2;
}

class PascalCanvas extends Canvas
{  public int[][] pascal(int n, int m)
   {  int[][] binom = new int[n + 1][];
      int i;
      int j;
      for (i = 0; i <= n; i++)
         binom[i] = new int[i / 2 + 1];
      for (i = 0; i <= n; i++)
         for (j = 0; j <= i / 2; j++)
            if (j == 0)
               binom[i][j] = 1;
            else if (2 * j < i)
               binom[i][j] = (binom[i - 1][j - 1]
                  + binom[i - 1][j]) % m;
            else
               binom[i][j] = (2 * binom[i - 1][j - 1]) % m;
      return binom;
   }

   public void redraw(int new_m)
   {  m = new_m;
      repaint();
   }
```

```
    public void paint(Graphics g)
    {   int i;
        int j;

        int nmax = 1 + getSize().height / 10;
        if (nmax > MAX) nmax = MAX;
        int[][] binom = pascal(nmax, m);

        for (i = 0; i <= nmax; i++)
        {   for (j = 0; j <= i; j++)
            {   int k = 2 * j <= i ? j : i - j;
                int b = binom[i][k] % m;
                g.setColor(new Color((255 * b) / (m - 1), 0, 0));
                g.fillRect(5 * (nmax + 1 - i + 2 * j), 10 * i,
                    10, 10);
            }
        }
    }

    private int m = 7;
    private final int MAX = 100;
}
```

CHAPTER 12

- Dealing with Errors
- Catching Exceptions
- Some Tips on Using Exceptions
- Debugging Techniques
- Using the JDB Debugger

Exceptions and Debugging

In a perfect world, users would never enter data in the wrong form, files they choose to open would always exist, and code would never have bugs. So far, we have mostly presented code as though we lived in this kind of perfect world. It is now time to turn to the mechanisms Java has for dealing with the real world of bad data and buggy code.

Encountering errors is unpleasant. If a user loses all the work he or she did during a program session due to a programming mistake or some external circumstance, that user may forever turn away from your program. At the very least, you must:

- Notify the user of an error
- Save all work
- Allow users to gracefully exit the program

For exceptional situations, such as bad input data with the potential to bomb the program, Java uses a form of error-trapping called, naturally enough, *exception-handling*. Exception-handling in Java is similar to that in C++ or Delphi. It is far more flexible than the `On Error GoTo` syntax used in VB. The first part of this chapter covers Java's exceptions.

The second part of this chapter concerns finding bugs in your code before they cause exceptions at run time. Unfortunately, if you just use the JDK, then bug detection is just as it was back in the dark ages. We give you some tips and a few tools to ease the pain. Then, we explain how to use the command-line debugger as a tool of last resort. For the serious Java developer, products such as Sun's Java WorkShop, Symantec's Café and Microsoft's Visual J++ have quite useful debuggers that alone can make the products well worth their cost.

Dealing with Errors

Suppose an error occurs while a Java program is running. The error might be caused by a file containing wrong information, a flaky network connection, or (we hate to mention it) an invalid array index or trying to reference an object that is pointing to `null` in your code. Users expect that programs will act sensibly when errors happen. If an operation cannot be completed because of an error, the program ought to either:

- Return to a safe state and enable the user to execute other commands

or

- Allow the user to save all his or her work and terminate the program gracefully

This may not be easy to do: the code that detects (or even causes) the error condition is usually far removed from the code that can roll back the data to a safe state, or the code that can save the user's work and exit cheerfully. The mission of error-handling is to transfer control from where the error occurred to an error-handler that can deal with the situation. To handle exceptional situations in your program, you must take into account the errors and problems that may occur. What sorts of problems do you need to consider?

User input errors. In addition to the inevitable typos, some users like to blaze their own trail instead of following directions. Suppose, for example, that a user asks to connect to a URL that is syntactically wrong. Your code should check the syntax, but suppose it does not. Then the network package will complain. Similarly, a user may enter a syntactically correct URL to a Web page that no longer exists or is too busy.

Device errors. Hardware does not always do what you want it to. The printer may be off. Serial ports may be unavailable. Devices will often fail in the middle of a task. For example, a printer may run out of paper in the middle of a printout.

Physical limitations. Disks can fill up; you run out of available memory.

Code errors. A method may not perform correctly. For example, it could deliver wrong answers or use other methods incorrectly. Computing an invalid array index, trying to find a nonexistent entry in a hash table, and trying to pop an empty stack are all examples of a method's responding to code errors.

The traditional reaction to an error in a method is to return a special error code that the calling method analyzes. For example, methods that read information back from files return a –1 end-of-file value marker rather than a standard character. This is still an efficient method for dealing with many exceptional conditions, and for certain i/o operations, Java does return `null` if the operation

wasn't successful. (You saw an example of this with the resource streams in Chapter 10.) Unfortunately, it is not always possible to return an error code. There may be no obvious way of distinguishing valid and invalid data. A method returning an integer cannot simply return –1 to denote the error—the value –1 might be a perfectly valid result.

Instead, as we mentioned back in Chapter 5, Java allows every method an alternate exit path if it is unable to complete its task in the normal way. In that case, the method does not return a value. Instead, it *throws* an object that encapsulates the error information. The method exits immediately; it does not return a value. Java doesn't activate the code that called the method; instead, the exception-handling mechanism begins its search for a *handler* that can deal with that particular error condition.

Exceptions have their own syntax and are part of a special inheritance hierarchy. We take up the syntax first and then give a few hints on how to use this language feature effectively.

The Classification of Error Types

In Java, an exception is always an instance of a class derived from `Throwable`. In particular, as you will soon see, you can create your own exception classes by inheritance if the ones built into Java do not suit your needs.

Figure 12-1 is a simplified diagram of the exception hierarchy in Java.

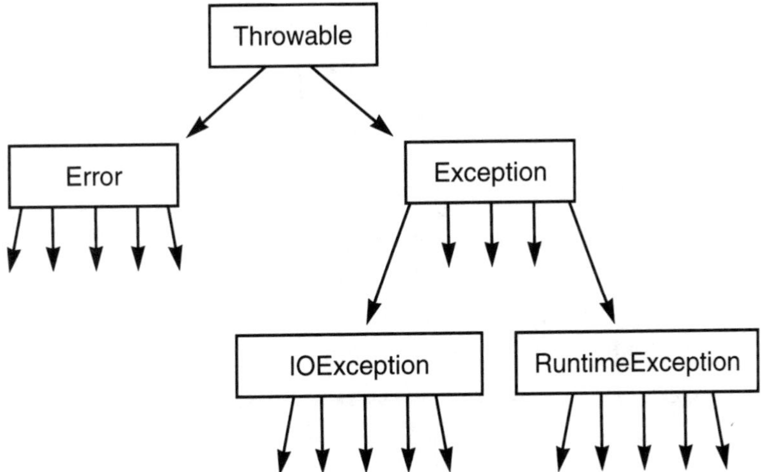

Figure 12-1: Exception hierarchy in Java

Notice that all exceptions descend from `Throwable`, but the chain immediately split into two branches: `Error` and `Exception`.

The `Error` hierarchy describes internal errors and resource exhaustion inside the Java run-time system. You should not throw an object of this type. There is little you can do if such an internal error occurs, beyond notifying the user and trying to terminate the program gracefully. These error conditions are quite rare.

In Java programming, you will focus on the `Exception` hierarchy. The `Exception` hierarchy also splits into two branches: exceptions that derive from `RuntimeException` and those that do not. The general rule is this:

- A `RuntimeException` happens because you made a programming error. Any other exception occurs because a bad thing, such as an I/O error, happened to your otherwise good program.

Exceptions that inherit from `RuntimeException` include such problems as:

- A bad cast
- An out-of-bounds array access
- A null pointer access

Exceptions that do not inherit from `RuntimeException` include:

- Trying to read past the end of a file
- Trying to open a malformed URL
- Trying to find a `Class` object for a string that does not denote an existing class

The rule "If it is a `RuntimeException`, it was your fault" works pretty well. You could have avoided that `ArrayIndexOutOfBoundsException` by testing the array index against the array bounds. The `NullPointerException` would not have happened had you checked whether or not the variable was `null` before using it.

How about a malformed URL? Isn't it also possible to find out whether or not it is "malformed" before using it? Well, different browsers can handle different kinds of URLs. For example, Netscape can deal with a `mailto:` URL, whereas the applet viewer cannot. Thus, the notion of "malformed" depends on the environment, not just on your code.

NOTE: The name `RuntimeException` is somewhat confusing. Of course, all of the errors we are discussing occur at run time.

C++ NOTE: If you are familiar with the (much more limited) exception hierarchy of the ANSI C++ library, you will be really confused at this point. C++ has two fundamental exception classes, `runtime_error` and `logic_error`. The `logic_error` class is the equivalent of Java's `RuntimeException` and also denotes logical errors in the program. The `runtime_error` class is the base class for exceptions caused by unpredictable problems. It is equivalent to exceptions in Java that are *not* of type `RuntimeException`.

Advertising the Exceptions That a Method Throws

A Java method can throw an exception if it encounters a situation it cannot handle. The idea is simple: a method will not only tell the Java compiler what values it can return, *it is also going to tell the compiler what can go wrong*. For example, code that attempts to read from a file knows the file might not exist or might be empty. The code should be able to throw some sort of `IOException`.

The place you advertise that your method can throw an exception is in the header of the method. The header changes to reflect the exceptions the method can throw. For example, here is the header for a method in Java's `BufferedReader` class that is supposed to read a line of text from a stream, such as a file or network connection. (See Volume 2 for more on streams.)

```
public String readLine() throws IOException
```

This method returns a string, but it also has the capacity to go wrong, in which case the method will not return a string but instead will throw a special object of the `IOException` class. If it does, then Java will begin to search for a handler that can deal with `IOException` objects.

Java throws an exception in any of the following four scenarios:

- You call a method that throws an exception, for example, the `readLine` method of the `BufferedReader` class.
- You detect an error and throw an exception with the `throw` statement (we cover the `throw` statement in the next section).
- You make a programming error, such as `a[-1] = 0`.
- An internal error occurs in Java.

When either of the first two scenarios occurs, you must tell the people who will use your method that using your method may force Java to throw an exception. Why? Any method that throws an exception is a potential death trap. If no handler catches the exception, the program terminates.

As with built-in Java methods, you declare that your method may throw an exception with an *exception specification* in the method header.

```
class Animation
{  . . .
   public Image loadImage(String s) throws IOException
   {  . . .
   }
}
```

If a method must deal with more than one exception, you must indicate all exceptions in the header:

```
class Animation
{  . . .
   public Image loadImage(String s)
      throws EOFException, MalformedURLException
   {  . . .
   }
}
```

However, you do not need to advertise internal Java errors, that is, exceptions inheriting from `Error`. Any code could potentially throw those exceptions, and they are entirely beyond your control.

Similarly, you should not advertise exceptions inheriting from `RuntimeException`.

```
class Animation
{  . . .
   void drawImage(int i)
      throws ArrayIndexOutOfBoundsException // NO!!!
   {  . . .
   }
}
```

These run-time errors are completely under your control. If you are so concerned about array index errors, you should spend the time needed to fix them instead of advertising the possibility that they can happen.

The Java Language Specification calls any exception that derives from the class `Error` or the class `RuntimeException` an *unchecked* exception. All other exceptions are called *checked* exceptions. This is useful terminology that we will adopt. The checked exceptions are the ones you should deal with. Unchecked exceptions are either beyond your control (`Error`) or result from conditions that you should not have allowed in the first place (`RuntimeException`).

The Java rule for exception specifications is simple:

A method must declare all the checked exceptions it throws.

When a class declares that it throws an exception of a particular class, then it may throw an exception of that class or its child classes. For example, the `readLine` method of the `BufferedReader` class says that it throws an

IOException. We do not know what kind of IOException. It could be a plain IOException or an object of one of the various child classes, such as EOFException.

If you override a method from a parent class, the child class method cannot throw more checked exceptions than the parent class method. (It can throw fewer, if it likes.) In particular, if the parent class method throws no checked exception at all, neither can the child class.

C++ NOTE: The throws specifier is the same as the throw specifier in C++, with one important difference. In C++, throw specifiers are enforced at *run time*, not at compile time. That is, the C++ compiler pays no attention to exception specifications. But if an exception is thrown in a function that is not part of the throw list, then the unexpected function is called, and, by default, the program terminates.

Also, in C++, a function may throw any exception if no throw specification is given. In Java, a method without a throws specifier may not throw any checked exception at all.

How to Throw an Exception

Let us suppose something terrible has happened in your code. You are reading in a file whose header promised

```
Content-length: 1024
```

But you get an end of file after 733 characters. You decide this situation is so abnormal that you want to throw an exception.

You need to decide what exception type to throw. Some kind of IOException would be a good choice. Perusing the tree.html file in the Java API documentation, you find an EOFException with the description "Signals that an EOF has been reached unexpectedly during input." Perfect. Here is how you throw it:

```
throw new EOFException();
```

or, if you prefer,

```
EOFException e = new EOFException();
throw e;
```

The EOFException has a second constructor that takes a string argument. You can put this to good use by describing the exceptional condition more carefully.

```
String gripe = "Content-length: " + len + " Received: " + n;
throw new EOFException(gripe);
```

Here is how it all fits together:

```
String readData(BufferedReader in) throws EOFException
{  . . .
   while (. . .)
   {  if (ch == -1) // EOF encountered
      {  if (n < len)
            throw new EOFException();
      }
      . . .
   }
   return s;
}
```

As you can see, throwing an exception is easy:

1. Find an appropriate exception class.
2. Make an object of that class.
3. Throw it.

Once Java throws an exception, the method does not return to its caller. This means that you do not have to worry about cooking up a default return value or an error code.

C++ NOTE: Throwing an exception is the same in C++ and in Java, with one small exception. In Java, you can throw only objects of child classes of `Throwable`. In C++, you can throw values of any type.

Creating Exception Classes

Your code may run into a problem that is not adequately described by any of the standard exception classes. In this event, you can create your own exception class. Just derive it from `Exception` or from a child class such as `IOException`. It is customary to give both a default constructor and a constructor that contains a detailed message. (The `toString` method of the `Throwable` base class prints out that detailed message, which is handy for debugging.)

```
class FileFormatException extends IOException
{  public FileFormatException() {}
   public FileFormatException(String gripe)
   {  super(gripe);
   }
}
```

Now you are ready to throw your very own exception type.

```
String readData(BufferedReader in) throws FileFormatException
{  . . .
   while (. . .)
   {  if (ch == -1) // EOF encountered
      {  if (n < len)
            throw new FileFormatException();
      }
      . . .
   }
   return s;
}
```

java.lang.Throwable

- `Throwable()`

  constructs a new `Throwable` object with no detailed message.

- `Throwable(String message)`

  constructs a new `Throwable` object with the specified detailed message. By convention, all derived exception classes support both a default constructor and a constructor with a detailed message.

- `String getMessage()`

  gets the detailed message of the `Throwable` object.

Catching Exceptions

You now know how to throw an exception. It is pretty easy. You throw it and you forget it. Of course, some code has to catch the exception. Catching exceptions requires more planning.

If an exception occurs that is not caught anywhere in a nongraphical application, Java will terminate the program and print a message to the console giving the type of the exception and a stack trace. In a graphics program (both an applet and an application), Java prints the same error message, but the program goes back to its user interface processing loop.

To catch an exception, you set up a `try/catch` block. The simplest form of the `try` block is as follows:

```
try
{  code
   more code
   more code
}
catch(ExceptionType e)
{  handler for this type
}
```

If any of the code inside the `try` block throws an exception of the class given in the `catch` clause, then,

1. Java skips the remainder of the code in the `try` block.
2. Java executes the handler code inside the `catch` clause.

If none of the code inside the `try` block throws an exception, then Java skips the `catch` clause.

If any of the code in a method throws an exception of a type other than the one named in the `catch` clause, Java exits this method immediately. (Hopefully, one of its callers has already coded a `catch` clause for that type.)

Here is some code in our `Console` class from our `corejava` package.

```
public static String readString()
{  int ch;
   String r = "";
   boolean done = false;
   while (!done)
   {  try
      {  ch = System.in.read();
         if (ch < 0 || (char)ch == '\n')
            done = true;
         else
            r = r + (char) ch;
      }
      catch(IOException e)
      {  done = true;
      }
   }
   return r;
}
```

Notice that most of the code in the `try` clause is straightforward: it accumulates characters until we encounter the end of the line or the end of the file. As you can see by looking at the Java API, there is the possibility that the `read` method will throw an `IOException`. In that case, the `if` statement is skipped and we set `done` to `true`. We figure that if there is a problem with the input, the caller does not want to know about it and wants to use only the characters that we have accumulated so far. For the `Console` class, that seems like a reasonable way to deal with this exception. What other choice do we have?

Often, the best choice is to do nothing at all. If an error occurs in the `read` method, let the caller of the `readString` method worry about it! If we take that approach, then we have to advertise the fact that the method may throw an `IOException`.

```
public static String readString()
    throws IOException
{   int ch;
    String r = "";
    boolean done = false;
    while (!done)
    {   ch = System.in.read();
        if (ch < 0 || (char)ch == '\n')
            done = true;
        else
            r = r + (char) ch;
    }
    return r;
}
```

The compiler strictly enforces the `throws` specifiers. If you call a method that throws a checked exception, you must either handle it or propagate it.

Which of the two is better? As a general rule, you should catch those exceptions that you know how to handle and propagate those that you do not know how to handle. When you propagate an exception, you must add a `throws` modifier to alert the caller that an exception may be thrown.

Look at the Java API documentation to see what methods throw which exceptions. Then, decide whether you should handle them or add them to the `throws` list. There is nothing embarrassing about the latter. It is better to direct an exception to a competent handler than to squelch it.

There is one exception to this rule. If you are writing a method that overrides a parent class method that throws no exceptions (such as `start` in `Applet`), then you *must* catch each checked exception in the method's code. You are not allowed to add more `throws` specifiers to a child class method than are present in the parent class method.

TIP: Your fellow programmers will hate you if you write methods that throw exceptions left and right, and that they must handle or propagate. If you can do something intelligent about an exception, then you should catch it.

C++ NOTE: Catching exceptions is almost the same in Java and in C++. Strictly speaking, the analog of

```
catch(Exception e) // Java
```

is

```
catch(Exception& e) // C++
```

There is no analog to the C++ `catch(...)`. This is not needed in Java because all exceptions derive from a common base class.

Catching Multiple Exceptions

You can catch multiple exception types in a `try` block and handle each type differently.

```
try
{   code that might
    throw exceptions
}
catch(MalformedURLException e1)
{   // emergency action for malformed URLs
}
catch(UnknownHostException e2)
{   // emergency action for unknown hosts
}
catch(IOException e3)
{   // emergency action for all other I/O problems
}
```

The exception object (`e1`, `e2`, `e3`) may contain information about the nature of the exception. To find out more about the object, try

```
e3.getMessage()
```

to get the detailed error message (if there is one), or

```
e3.getClass().getName()
```

to get the actual type of the exception object.

Rethrowing Exceptions

Occasionally, you need to catch an exception without addressing the root cause of it in order to do some local cleanup. In this case, you want to take your emergency action and again call `throw` to send the exception back up the calling chain.

```
Graphics g = image.getGraphics();
try
{   code that might
    throw exceptions
}   catch(MalformedURLException e)
{   g.dispose();
    throw e;
}
```

The above code shows one of the most common reasons for having to rethrow an exception that you have caught. If you do not dispose of the graphics context object in the `catch` clause, it will never be disposed of since it is a local object of this method. (Of course, its `finalize` method might dispose of it, but that can take a long time.)

On the other hand, the underlying cause, the malformed URL exception, *has not disappeared.* You still want to report it to the authorities, who presumably know how to deal with such an exception. (See the next section for a more elegant way to achieve the same result.)

You can also throw a different exception than the one you catch.

```
try
{   acme.util.Widget a = new acme.util.Widget();
    a.load(s);
    a.paint(g);
}
catch(RuntimeException e)
{   // sheesh—another ACME error
    throw new Exception("ACME error");
}
```

The `finally` Clause

When Java throws an exception, it stops processing the remaining code in your method. This is a problem if the local method has acquired some resource that only it knows about and if that resource must be cleaned up. One solution is to catch and rethrow all exceptions. But this solution is tedious because you need to clean up the resource allocation in two places, in the normal code and in the exception code.

Java has a better solution, the `finally` clause:

```
Graphics g = image.getGraphics();
try
{   code that might
    throw exceptions
}
catch(IOException e)
{   done = true;
}
finally
{   g.dispose();
}
```

Java executes the code in the `finally` clause whether or not an exception was caught. This means in the example code above, Java will dispose of the graphics context *under all circumstances.*

Let us look at the three possible situations where Java will execute the `finally` clause.

1. The code throws no exceptions. In this event, Java first executes all the code in the `try` block. Then, it executes the code in the `finally` clause and then executes the first line after the `try` block.

2. The code throws an exception that is caught in a `catch` clause, in our case, an `IOException`. For this, Java executes all code in the `try` block, up to the point at which the exception was thrown. The remaining code in the `try` block is skipped. Then, Java executes the code in the matching `catch` clause, and then the code in the `finally` clause.

   If the `catch` clause does not throw an exception, then Java executes the first line after the `try` block. If it does, then the exception is thrown back to the caller of this method.

3. The code throws an exception that is not caught in any `catch` clause. For this, Java executes all code in the `try` block until the exception is thrown. The remaining code in the `try` block is skipped. Then, Java executes the code in the `finally` clause, and the exception is thrown back to the caller of this method.

C++ NOTE: There is one fundamental difference between C++ and Java with regard to exception-handling. Java has no destructors; thus, there is no stack unwinding as in C++. This means that the Java programmer must manually place code to reclaim resources in `finally` blocks. Of course, since Java does garbage collection, there are far fewer resources that require manual deallocation.

A Final Look at Java Error- and Exception-Handling

Example 12-1 deliberately generates a number of different errors and catches various exceptions (see Figure 12-2).

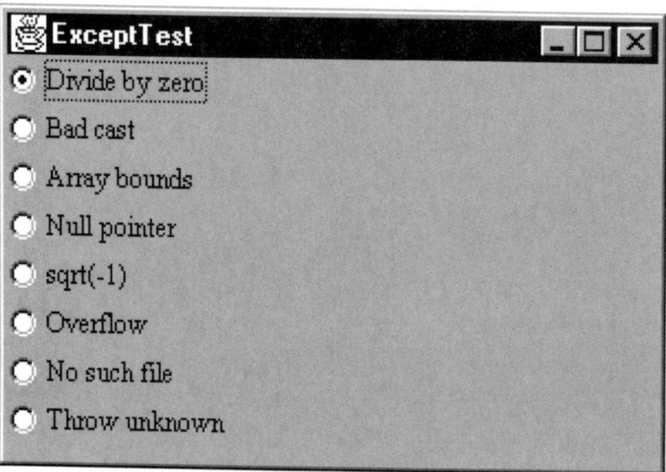

Figure 12-2: A program that generates exceptions

Try it out. Click on the buttons and see what exceptions are thrown.

As you know, a programmer error such as a bad array index throws a `RuntimeException`. An attempt to open a nonexistent file triggers an `IOException`. The program catches `RuntimeException` objects, then general `Exception` objects.

```
try
{  // various bad things
}
catch(RuntimeException e)
{  System.out.println("Caught RuntimeException: " + e);
}
catch(Exception e)
{  System.out.println("Caught Exception: " + e);
}
```

You can see which exception you caused in the Console window. If you click on the Throw Unknown button, an `UnknownError` object is thrown. This is not a child class of `Exception`, so our program does not catch it. Instead, the user interface code prints an error message and a stack trace to the console.

NOTE: As you can see from this program in Example 12-1, not all the bad things you can do in Java throw exceptions. Divides by zero, overflows, and math errors do not throw any exceptions at all.

Example 12-1: ExceptTest.java

```
import java.awt.*;
import java.awt.event.*;
import java.io.*;
import corejava.*;

public class ExceptTest extends CloseableFrame
   implements ItemListener
{  public ExceptTest()
   {  setLayout(new GridLayout(8, 1));
      CheckboxGroup g = new CheckboxGroup();
      addCheckbox("Divide by zero", g);
      addCheckbox("Bad cast", g);
      addCheckbox("Array bounds", g);
      addCheckbox("Null pointer", g);
      addCheckbox("sqrt(-1)", g);
      addCheckbox("Overflow", g);
      addCheckbox("No such file", g);
      addCheckbox("Throw unknown", g);
   }
```

```
   private void addCheckbox(String s, CheckboxGroup g)
   {  Checkbox cb = new Checkbox(s, g, false);
      cb.addItemListener(this);
      add(cb);
   }

   public void itemStateChanged(ItemEvent evt)
   {  try
      {  String name = (String)evt.getItem();
         if (name.equals("Divide by zero"))
         {  a[1] = a[2] / (a[3] - a[3]);
         }
         else if (name.equals("Bad cast"))
         {  f = (Frame)evt.getItem();
         }
         else if (name.equals("Array bounds"))
         {  a[1] = a[10];
         }
         else if (name.equals("Null pointer"))
         {  f = null;
            f.setSize(200, 200);
         }
         else if (name.equals("sqrt(-1)"))
         {  a[1] = Math.sqrt(-1);
         }
         else if (name.equals("Overflow"))
         {  a[1] = 1000 * 1000 * 1000 * 1000;
            int n = (int)a[1];
         }
         else if (name.equals("No such file"))
         {  FileInputStream is = new FileInputStream(name);
         }
         else if (name.equals("Throw unknown"))
         {  throw new UnknownError();
         }
      }
      catch(RuntimeException e)
      {  System.out.println("Caught RuntimeException: " + e);
      }
      catch(Exception e)
      {  System.out.println("Caught Exception: " + e);
      }
   }

   public static void main(String[] args)
   {  Frame f = new ExceptTest();
      f.show();
   }

   private double[] a = new double[10];
   private Frame f = null;
}
```

Some Tips on Using Exceptions

There is a tendency to overuse exceptions. After all, who wants to go to the trouble to write methods that parse input before using it when exception-handling makes it so easy? Instead of parsing a URL when the user enters it, just send it off to a method that catches a `MalformedURLException`. Saves time, saves trouble. Wrong! Exception-handling will almost always cost time. Misusing exceptions can slow your code down dramatically. Here are three tips on using exceptions.

1. *Exception-handling is not supposed to replace a simple test.*

As an example of this, we wrote some code that uses the built-in `Stack` class (see Chapter 9). The following code tries 1,000,000 times to pop an empty stack. It first does this by finding out whether or not the stack is empty.

```
if (!s.empty()) s.pop();
```

Next, we tell it to pop the stack no matter what. Then we catch the `EmptyStackException` that tells us that we should not have done that.

```
try()
{  s.pop();
}
catch(EmptyStackException e)
{
}
```

On our test machine, we got the timing data in Table 12-2.

Table 12-2: Timing Data

Test	Throw/Catch
990 milliseconds	18020 milliseconds

As you can see, it took roughly 18 times longer to catch an exception than it does to perform a simple test. The moral is: Use exceptions for exceptional circumstances only.

2. *Do not micromanage exceptions.*

Many people wrap every statement in a separate `try` block.

```
istream is;
Stack s;

for (i = 0; i < 100; i++)
{  try
   {     n = s.pop();
   }
   catch (EmptyStackException s)
   {     // stack was empty
   }
   try
   {     out.writeInt(n);
   }
   catch (IOException e)
   {     // problem reading file
   }
}
```

This blows up your code dramatically. Think about the task that you want the code to accomplish. Here we want to pop 100 numbers off a stack and save them to a file. (Never mind why—it is just a toy example.) There is nothing we can do if a problem rears its ugly head. If the stack is empty, it will not become occupied. If there is an error in the file, this will not magically go away. It therefore makes sense to wrap the *entire task* in a `try` block. If any one operation fails, you can then abandon the task.

```
try
{  for (i = 0; i < 100; i++)
   {  n = s.pop();
      out.writeInt(n);
   }
}
catch (IOException e)
{ // problem reading file
}
catch (EmptyStackException s)
{ // stack was empty
}
```

This looks much cleaner. It fulfills one of the promises of exception-handling, to *separate* normal processing from error-handling.

3. *Do not squelch exceptions.*

In Java, there is the tremendous temptation to shut up exceptions. You write a method that calls a method that might throw an exception once a century. The compiler whines because you have not declared the exception in the `throws` list of your method. You do not want to put it in the `throws` list because then the

compiler will whine about all the methods that call your method. So you just shut it up:

```
Image loadImage(String s)
{  try
   {  lots of code
   }
   catch(Exception e)
   {} // so there
}
```

Now your code will compile without a hitch. It will run fine, except when an exception occurs. Then, the exception will be silently ignored. If you believe that exceptions are at all important, you need to make some effort to handle them right.

4. *Propagating exceptions is not a sign of shame.*

Many programmers feel compelled to catch all exceptions that are thrown. If they call a method that throws an exception, such as the `FileInputStream` constructor or the `readLine` method, they instinctively catch the exception that may be generated. Often, it is actually better to *propagate* the exception instead of catching it:

```
void readStuff(String name) throws IOException
{  FileInputStream in = new FileInputStream(name);
   . . .
}
```

Higher-level methods are often better equipped to inform the user of errors or to abandon unsuccessful commands.

Debugging Techniques

Suppose you wrote your program and made it bulletproof by catching and properly handling all exceptions. Then you run it, and it does not work right. Now what? (If you never have this problem, you can skip the remainder of this chapter.)

Of course, it is best if you have a convenient and powerful debugger. These will be available for Java 1.1 on most platforms, but none were available to us except in very early beta form as we write this. Until they are available (or if you are on a budget or work on an unusual platform), you will need to do a great deal of debugging by the time-honored method of inserting print statements into your code.

Useful Tricks for Debugging

Here are some tips for efficient debugging if you have to do it all yourself.

1. You can print the value of any variable with code like this:

   ```
   System.out.println("x = " + x);
   ```

   If `x` is a number, it is converted to its string equivalent. If `x` is an object, then Java calls its `toString` method. Most of the classes in the Java library are very conscientious about overriding the `toString` method to give you useful information about the class. This is a real boon for debugging. You should make the same effort in your classes.

2. To get the state of the current object, print the state of the `this` object.

   ```
   System.out.println("Entering loadImage. this = " + this);
   ```

   This calls the `toString` method of the current class, and you get a printout of all instance fields. Of course, this works best when the `toString` method in this class does a conscientious job and reports the values of all data fields.

3. Recall that we gave you the code for a generic `toString` method in Chapter 5—we used the reflection feature to enumerate and print all data fields. Here is an even shorter version of that code.

   ```
   public String toString()
   {  java.util.Hashtable h = new java.util.Hashtable();
      Class cls = getClass();
      Field[] f = cls.getDeclaredFields();
      for (int i = 0; i < f.length; i++)
      { try { h.put(f[i].getName(), f[i].get(this)); }
        catch (IllegalAccessException e) {}
      }
      if (cls.getSuperclass().getSuperclass() != null)
         h.put("super", super.toString());
      return cls.getName() + h;
   }
   ```

   The code uses the reflection feature of Java 1.1 to enumerate all fields. It puts the pairs (field name, field value) into a hash table. It then uses the `toString` method of the `Hashtable` class to print out the names and values. Here is a typical printout:

```
Employee{hireDay=Day[1996,12,1], salary=35000.0, name=Harry Hacker}
```

   Unfortunately, you must paste the code into each class—only the class itself can peek inside its private data.

4. You can get a stack trace from any exception object with the `printStackTrace` method in the `Throwable` class. The following code catches any exception, prints the exception object and the stack trace, and rethrows the exception so it can find its intended handler.

```
try
{  . . .
}
catch(Throwable t)
{  t.printStackTrace();
   throw t;
}
```

5. One seemingly little-known but very useful trick is that you can put a separate `main` method in each public class. Inside it, you can put a unit test stub that lets you test the class in isolation. Make a few objects, call all methods, and check that each of them does the right thing. You can leave all these `main` methods in place and call the Java interpreter separately on each of the files to run the tests. When you run an applet, none of these `main` methods are ever called. When you run an application, Java calls only the `main` method of the start-up class. All others are ignored. (For example, look at our `Format.java` file in the `corejava` directory. It has a `main` method that tests the formatting extensively.)

`java.lang.Throwable`

- `void printStackTrace()`

  prints the `Throwable` and the stack trace.

Trapping AWT Events

When you write a fancy user interface in Java, you need to know what events AWT sends to what components. Unfortunately, the AWT documentation is somewhat sketchy in this regard. For example, suppose you want to show hints in the status line when the user moves the mouse over different parts of the screen. AWT does generate mouse and focus events that you may be able to trap.

We give you a useful `MessageCracker` class to spy on these events. It prints out a text description of the event, cracking the event codes and printing only those fields of the `Event` structure that are relevant to a particular event. See Figure 12-3 for a display of the cracked messages. (Look in the terminal window.)

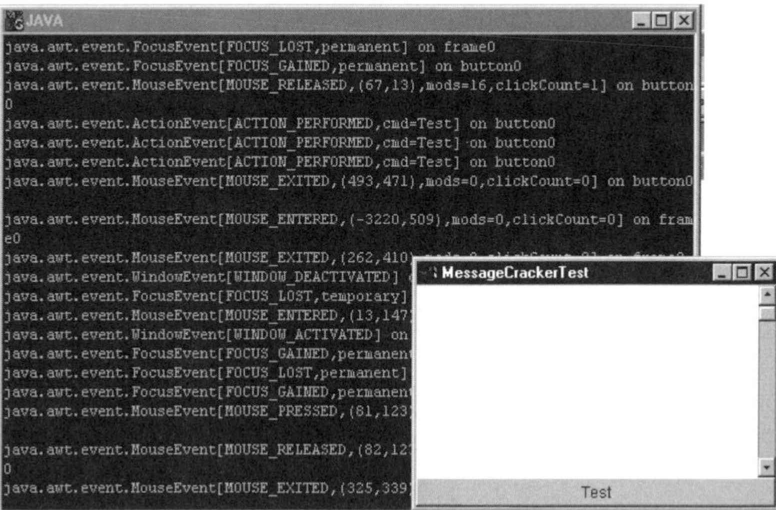

Figure 12-3 : The `MessageCracker` class at work

To spy on messages, you need only import the `corejava` package and add one line of code to your frame class constructor or the `init` method of your applet.

```
public class MyFrame extends CloseableFrame
{  public MyFrame()
   {  // add components
      new MessageCracker().add(this);
   }
   . . .
}
```

This prints out a textual description of all events, except for mouse motion events. (You would not want to see a flood of events every time you move the mouse.) Example 12-2 shows you how a class might use the `MessageCracker` class; the key line is set in bold.

Example 12-2: MessageCrackerTest.java

```
public class MessageCrackerTest extends CloseableFrame
{  MessageCrackerTest()
   {  add(new Button("Test"), "South");
      add(new Scrollbar(), "East");
      new MessageCracker().add(this);
   }

   public static void main(String[] args)
   {  Frame f = new MessageCrackerTest();
      f.show();
   }
}
```

Example 12-3 is the actual `MessageCracker` class. The idea behind the class is easy even if the implementation is a bit tedious.

1. The class finds out the type of each component that is in the class that is using it (through the `this` reference set in bold in the preceding code).
2. The class directly implements every possible listener interface by implementing each of the required event handlers to simply print out the event.

Example 12-3: MessageCracker.java

```
class MessageCracker
    implements MouseListener, ComponentListener,
    FocusListener, KeyListener, ContainerListener,
    WindowListener, TextListener, AdjustmentListener,
    ActionListener, ItemListener
{   public void add(Component c)
    {   c.addMouseListener(this);
        c.addComponentListener(this);
        c.addFocusListener(this);
        c.addKeyListener(this);
        if (c instanceof Container)
        {   ((Container)c).addContainerListener(this);
            Component[] a = ((Container)c).getComponents();
            for (int i = 0; i < a.length; i++)
                add(a[i]);
        }
        if (c instanceof Window)
            ((Window)c).addWindowListener(this);
        if (c instanceof TextComponent)
            ((TextComponent)c).addTextListener(this);
        if (c instanceof Scrollbar)
            ((Scrollbar)c).addAdjustmentListener(this);
        if (c instanceof Button)
            ((Button)c).addActionListener(this);
        if (c instanceof Button)
            ((Button)c).addActionListener(this);
        if (c instanceof Button)
            ((Button)c).addActionListener(this);
        if (c instanceof List)
        {   ((List)c).addActionListener(this);
            ((List)c).addItemListener(this);
        }
        if (c instanceof TextField)
            ((TextField)c).addActionListener(this);
        if (c instanceof Checkbox)
            ((Checkbox)c).addItemListener(this);
        if (c instanceof Choice)
```

```
        ((Choice)c).addItemListener(this);
  }
  public void mouseClicked(MouseEvent e)
  {  System.out.println(e);
  }
  public void mouseEntered(MouseEvent e)
  {  System.out.println(e);
  }
  public void mouseExited(MouseEvent e)
  {  System.out.println(e);
  }
  public void mousePressed(MouseEvent e)
  {  System.out.println(e);
  }
  public void mouseReleased(MouseEvent e)
  {  System.out.println(e);
  }

  public void componentHidden(ComponentEvent e)
  {  System.out.println(e);
  }
  public void componentMoved(ComponentEvent e)
  {  System.out.println(e);
  }
  public void componentResized(ComponentEvent e)
  {  System.out.println(e);
  }
  public void componentShown(ComponentEvent e)
  {  System.out.println(e);
  }

  public void focusGained(FocusEvent e)
  {  System.out.println(e);
  }
  public void focusLost(FocusEvent e)
  {  System.out.println(e);
  }

  public void keyPressed(KeyEvent e)
  {  System.out.println(e);
  }
  public void keyReleased(KeyEvent e)
  {  System.out.println(e);
  }
  public void keyTyped(KeyEvent e)
  {  System.out.println(e);
  }
```

```
    public void windowActivated(WindowEvent e)
    {  System.out.println(e);
    }
    public void windowClosed(WindowEvent e)
    {  System.out.println(e);
    }
    public void windowClosing(WindowEvent e)
    {  System.out.println(e);
    }
    public void windowDeactivated(WindowEvent e)
    {  System.out.println(e);
    }
    public void windowDeiconified(WindowEvent e)
    {  System.out.println(e);
    }
    public void windowIconified(WindowEvent e)
    {  System.out.println(e);
    }
    public void windowOpened(WindowEvent e)
    {  System.out.println(e);
    }

    public void componentAdded(ContainerEvent e)
    {  System.out.println(e);
    }
    public void componentRemoved(ContainerEvent e)
    {  System.out.println(e);
    }

    public void textValueChanged(TextEvent e)
    {  System.out.println(e);
    }

    public void adjustmentValueChanged(AdjustmentEvent e)
    {  System.out.println(e);
    }

    public void actionPerformed(ActionEvent e)
    {  System.out.println(e);
    }

    public void itemStateChanged(ItemEvent e)
    {  System.out.println(e);
    }
}
```

Displaying Debug Messages in Graphics Programs

If you run an applet inside a browser, you may not be able to see any messages that are sent to `System.out`. We expect that most browsers will have some sort of Java Console Window. (Check the help system for your browser.) For example, Netscape 3.0 had one. You can see an example of this for Netscape 3.0 in Figure 12-4. This window displays all the strings sent to `System.out`. In Netscape 3.0, the Java console window has a set of scroll bars, so you can retrieve messages that have scrolled off the window, a definite advantage over the DOS shell window in which the `System.out` output normally appears.

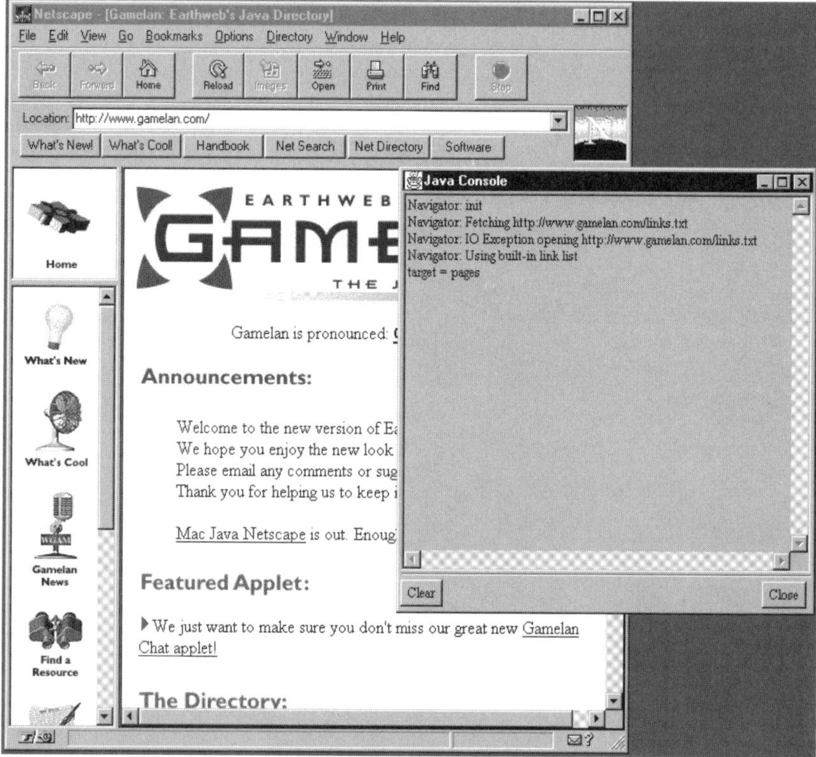

Figure 12-4: Netscape's "Java Console"

This is a nice feature, and we give you a similar window class so you can enjoy the same benefit of seeing your debugging messages in a window when not running a browser that has a Java console. Figure 12-5 shows our `DebugWinTest` class in action.

The class is easy to use. You make a variable of type `DebugWin` in your `Frame` or `Applet` class and use the `print` method to print an object in the window. Here is an example of debugging code to spy on an action event.

```
class MyFrame extends CloseableFrame
      implements ActionListener
{  . . .
   public void actionPerformed(ActionEvent evt)
   {  dw.print("Event = " + evt);
      . . .
   }
   . . .
   private DebugWin dw = new DebugWin();
}
```

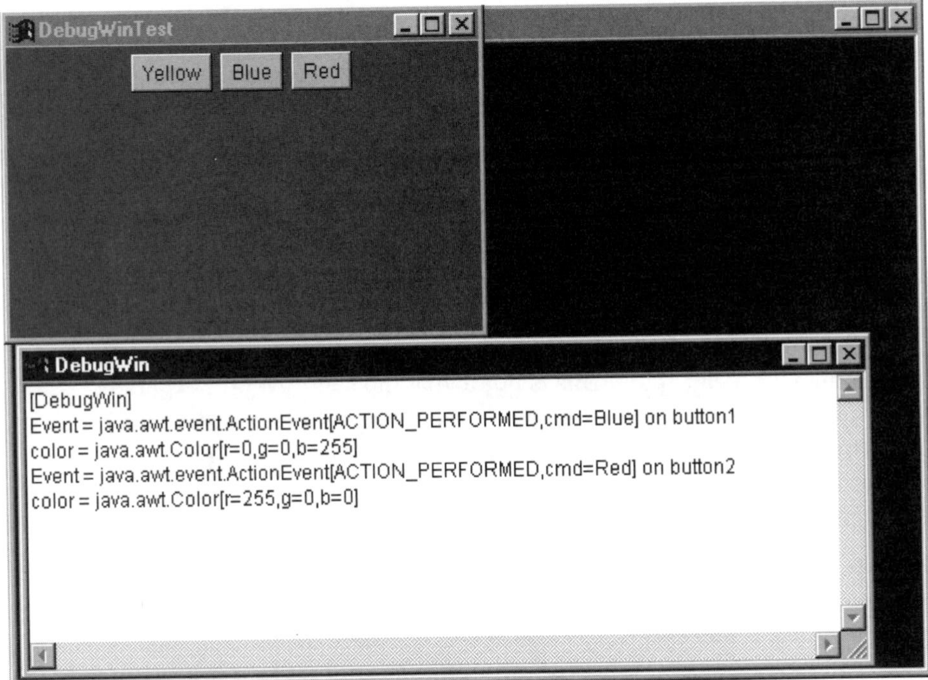

Figure 12-5: The debug window

Example 12-4 lists the code for the `DebugWin` class.

Example 12-4: DebugWin.java

```
import java.awt.*;
import java.awt.event.*;

class DebugWin extends Frame
{  public void print(Object ob)
   {  output.append("\n" + ob);
   }

   public DebugWin()
   {  setTitle("DebugWin");
      output.setEditable(false);
      output.setText("[DebugWin]");
      add(output, "Center");
      setSize(300, 200);
      setLocation(200, 200);
      addWindowListener(new WindowAdapter() { public void
         windowClosing(WindowEvent e)
         { setVisible(false); } } );
      show();
   }

   private TextArea output = new TextArea();
}
```

Using the JDB Debugger

Debugging with print statements is not one of life's more joyful experiences. You constantly find yourself adding and removing the statements, then recompiling the program. Using a debugger is better because a debugger runs your program in full motion until it reaches a breakpoint, and then you can look at everything that interests you.

The JDK includes JDB, an extremely rudimentary command-line debugger. Its user interface is so minimal that you will not want to use it except as a last resort. It really is more a proof of concept than a useable tool. We, nevertheless, give a brief introduction because there are situations in which it is better than no debugger at all. Of course, by the time you read this, many Java programming environments will be available for Java 1.1. Those environments will have far more convenient debuggers. The main principles of all debuggers are the same, and you may want to use the example in this section to learn to use the debugger in your environment instead of JDB.

Have a look at a deliberately corrupted version of the `ButtonTest` (Figure 12-6) program from Chapter 7.

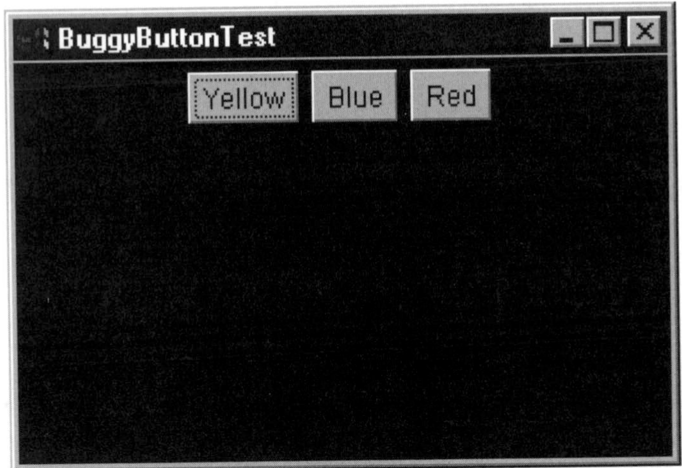

Figure 12-6: The buggy button application

When you click on any of the buttons, the background changes to black. Look at the source code—it is supposed to set the background color to the color specified by the button name.

Example 12-5: BuggyButtonTest.java

```
import java.awt.*;
import java.awt.event.*;
import corejava.*;

public class BuggyButtonTest extends CloseableFrame
   implements ActionListener
{  public BuggyButtonTest()
   {  setLayout(new FlowLayout());

      Button yellowButton = new Button("Yellow");
      add(yellowButton);
      yellowButton.addActionListener(this);
         // who is gonna listen? this frame

      Button blueButton = new Button("Blue");
      add(blueButton);
      blueButton.addActionListener(this);

      Button redButton = new Button("Red");
      add(redButton);
      redButton.addActionListener(this);
   }

   public void actionPerformed(ActionEvent evt)
   {  String arg = evt.getActionCommand();
```

```
      Color color = Color.black;
      if (arg.equals("yellow")) color = Color.yellow;
      else if (arg.equals("blue")) color = Color.blue;
      else if (arg.equals("red")) color = Color.red;
      setBackground(color);
      repaint();
   }

   public static void main(String[] args)
   {  Frame f = new BuggyButtonTest();
      f.show();
   }
}
```

In a program this short, you may be able to find the bug just by reading the source code. Let us pretend that this was so complicated a program that reading the source code is not practical. Here is how you can run the debugger to locate the error.

To use JDB, you must first compile your program with the `-g` option, for example:

```
javac -g BuggyButtonTest.java
```

Then you launch the debugger:

```
jdb BuggyButtonTest
```

Once you launch the debugger, you will see a display that looks something like this:

```
Initializing jdb...
0x139f3c8:class(BuggyButtonTest)
>
```

The > prompt indicates the debugger is waiting for a command. Table 12-3 shows all the debugger commands. Items enclosed in [...] are optional, and the suffix (es) means that you can supply more than one argument.

Table 12-3: Debugging Commands

`threads [`*threadgroup*`]`	lists threads
`thread` *thread_id*	sets default thread
`suspend [`*thread_id(s)*`]`	suspends threads (default: all)
`resume [`*thread_id(s)*`]`	resumes threads (default: all)
`where [`*thread_id*`] or all`	dumps a thread's stack
`threadgroups`	lists threadgroups
`threadgroup name`	sets current threadgroup

Table 12-3: Debugging Commands *(continued)*

`print` *name(s)*	prints object or field
`dump` *name(s)*	prints all object information
`locals`	prints all current local variables
`classes`	lists currently known classes
`methods` *class*	lists a class's methods
`stop in` *class.method*	sets a breakpoint in a method
`stop at` *class:line*	sets a breakpoint at a line
`up [`*n*`]`	moves up a thread's stack
`down [`*n*`]`	moves down a thread's stack
`clear` *class:line*	clears a breakpoint
`step`	executes the current line
`cont`	continues execution from breakpoint
`catch` *class*	breaks for the specified exception
`ignore` *class*	ignores the specified exception
`list [`*line*`]`	prints source code
`use [`*path*`]`	displays or changes the source path
`memory`	reports memory usage
`gc`	frees unused objects
`load` *class*	loads Java class to be debugged
`run [`*class* `[`*args*`]]`	starts execution of a loaded Java class
`!!`	repeats last command
`help (or ?)`	lists commands
`exit (or quit)`	exits debugger

We will cover only the most useful JDB commands in this section. The basic idea, though, is simple: you set one or more breakpoints, then run the program. When the program reaches one of the breakpoints you set, it stops. Then, you can inspect the values of the local variables to see if they are what they are supposed to be.

To set a breakpoint, use the

```
stop in class.method
```

or

```
stop at class:line
```

command.

For example, let us set a breakpoint in the `actionPerformed` method of `BuggyButtonTest`. To do this, enter:

```
stop in BuggyButtonTest.actionPerformed
```

Now we want to run the program up to the breakpoint, so enter.

```
run
```

The program will run, but the breakpoint won't be hit until Java starts processing code in the `actionPerformed` method. For this, click on the Yellow button. The debugger breaks at the *start* of the `actionPerformed` method. You'll see:

```
Breakpoint hit: BuggyButtonTest.actionPerformed (ButtonTest:52)
```

Because the debugger does not give you a window with the current source line showing, it is easy to lose track of where you are; the `list` command lets you find this out. While the program is stopped after you enter `list`, the debugger will show you the current line and a couple of the lines above and below it. You also see the line numbers. For example:

```
48                  redButton.addActionListener(this);
49              }
50
51              public void actionPerformed(ActionEvent evt)
52      =>      {  String arg = evt.getActionCommand();
53                  Color color = Color.black;
54                  if (arg.equals("yellow")) color = Color.yellow;
55                  else if (arg.equals("blue")) color = Color.blue;
56                  else if (arg.equals("red")) color = Color.red;
```

Type `locals` to see all local variables. For example:

```
Method arguments:
  this = BuggyButtonTest[frame0,0,0,300x200,
    layout=java.awt.FlowLayout,resizable
    ,title=BuggyButtonTest]
  evt = java.awt.event.ActionEvent[ACTION_PERFORMED,
    cmd=Yellow] on button0
Local variables:
  color is not in scope.
  arg is not in scope.
```

For more detail, use:

```
dump variable
```

For example,

```
dump evt
```

displays all instance fields of the `evt` variable.

```
evt = (java.awt.event.ActionEvent)0xe84360 {
    protected transient Object source = (java.awt.Button)0xe819b0
    private transient int data = 0
    protected int id = 1001
```

```
protected boolean consumed = true
String actionCommand = Yellow
int modifiers = 0
```

Unfortunately, there is no good way to single-step through the program. The `step` command steps into every method call and easily becomes confused between threads. (Volume 2 covers threads.)

Now let us set a breakpoint in the next line and one at the end of the `if` statement.

```
stop at BuggyButtonTest:55
stop at BuggyButtonTest:57
```

To continue the program until it encounters the next breakpoint, type:

```
cont
```

The program stops in line 55. Type `list` one more time to see where you are.

```
51              public void actionPerformed(ActionEvent evt)
52              {  String arg = evt.getActionCommand();
53                 Color color = Color.black;
54                 if (arg.equals("yellow")) color = Color.yellow;
55      =>         else if (arg.equals("blue")) color = Color.blue;
56                 else if (arg.equals("red")) color = Color.red;
57                 setBackground(color);
58                 repaint();
59              }
```

That is not what should have happened. It was supposed to set the `color` variable to yellow and then go to the `setBackground` command.

Now we can see what happened. The value of `arg` was `"Yellow"`, with an uppercase Y, but the comparison tested

```
if (arg.equals("yellow"))
```

with a lowercase y. Mystery solved.

To quit the debugger, type:

```
quit
```

As you can see from this example, the debugger can be used to find an error, but only with a lot of work. Setting breakpoints in an `actionPerformed` method or another event-handler works pretty well to find out why an event-handler wasn't triggered, for example. Remember to use `list` and `locals` whenever you are confused about where you are. Get a better debugger as soon as one is available.

Appendix I
Java Keywords

Keyword	Meaning	See Chapter
`abstract`	an abstract class or method	5
`boolean`	the Boolean type	3
`break`	breaks out of a `switch` or loop	3
`byte`	the 8-bit integer type	3
`case`	a case of a `switch`	3
`catch`	the clause of a `try` block catching an exception	12
`char`	the Unicode character type	3
`class`	defines a class type	4
`const`	not used	
`continue`	continues at the end of a loop	3
`default`	the default clause of a `switch`	3
`do`	the top of a `do/while` loop	3
`double`	the double-precision floating-number type	3
`else`	the `else` clause of an `if` statement	3
`extends`	defines the parent class of a class	4
`final`	a constant, or a class or method that cannot be overridden	5
`finally`	the part of a `try` block that is always executed	12
`float`	the single-precision floating-point type	3
`for`	a loop type	3
`future`	not used	
`generic`	not used	
`goto`	not used	
`if`	a conditional statmement	3
`implements`	defines the interface(s) that a class implements	6
`import`	imports a package	4
`inner`	not used (but see Chapter 6)	
`instanceof`	tests if an object is an instance of a class	5
`int`	the 32-bit integer type	3

`interface`	an abstract type with methods that a class can implement	6
`long`	the 64-bit long integer type	3
`native`	a method implemented by the host system (see Volume 2)	
`new`	allocates a new object or array	3
`null`	a null reference	3
`operator`	not used	
`outer`	not used (but see Chapter 6)	
`package`	a package of classes	4
`private`	a feature that is accessible only by methods of this class	4
`protected`	a feature that is accessible only by methods of this class, its children, and other classes in the same package	5
`public`	a feature that is accessible by methods of all classes	4
`rest`	not used	
`return`	returns from a method	3
`short`	the 16-bit integer type	3
`static`	a feature that is unique to its class, not to objects of its class	3
`super`	the superclass object or constructor	4
`switch`	a selection statement	3
`synchronized`	a method that is atomic to a thread (see Volume 2)	
`this`	the implicit argument of a method, or a constructor of this class	4
`throw`	throws an exception	12
`throws`	the exceptions that a method can throw	12
`transient`	marks data that should not be persistent (see Volume 2)	
`try`	a block of code that traps exceptions	12
`var`	not used	
`void`	denotes a method that returns no value	3
`volatile`	not used	
`while`	a loop	3

Appendix II
The javadoc Utility

The javadoc utility parses source files for classes, methods, and /** . . . */ comments. It produces an HTML file in the same format as the API documentation. In fact, they are basically the javadoc output of the Java source files.

If you add comments that start with the special delimiter /** to your source code, you too can produce professional looking documentation easily. This is a very nice scheme because it lets you keep your code and documentation in one place. Traditional documentation efforts suffered from the problem that the code and comments diverged over time. But since the comments are in the same file as the source code, it is an easy matter to update both and run javadoc again.

We used the /** comments and javadoc on the files in our corejava package. Point your Web browser to \CoreJavaBook\corejava\api\tree.html, and you will see the corejava documentation in a format that looks startlingly familiar.

How to Insert Comments

The javadoc utility extracts information for every

package

public class

public interface

public or protected method

public or protected instance variable

public or protected constant

You can (and should) supply a comment for each of these features.

Each comment is placed immediately *above* the feature it describes. A comment starts with a /** and ends with a */. Each separate line of the comment must start with an *. Like all comments, they are ignored by the Java compiler.

A comment is free-form text with optional HTML markups, followed by *tags*. A tag starts with an @ and extends to the end of the line. In the free-form text, you can use HTML modifiers such as <i>...</i> for italics, <tt>...</tt> for a monospaced "typewriter" font, <b>...</b> bold for bold, and even <img ...> to include an image. You should, however, stay away from heading <h1> or rules <hr> since they interfere with the formatting of the document.

The following tags are supported.

```
@see class
@see class#method
```

These tags add a hyperlink to the class or method.

```
@version text
```

This tag makes a "version" entry. Can be used only with classes and interfaces.

```
@author name
```

This tag makes an "author" entry. There may be multiple author tags, but they must all be together. Can be used only with classes and interfaces.

```
@param variable description
```

This tag adds an entry to the Parameters section of the current method. The description can span multiple lines and can use HTML tags. All `@param` tags for one method must be kept together. Can be used only with methods.

```
@return description
```

This tag adds a Returns section to the current method. The description can span multiple lines and can use HTML tags. Can be used only with methods.

```
@throws class description
```

This tag adds an entry to the Throws section of the current method. A hyperlink is automatically created. The description can span multiple lines and can use HTML tags. All `@throws` tags for one method must be kept together. Can be used only with methods.

Here is an example of a class comment:

```
/**
 * A class for formatting numbers that follows <tt>printf</tt>
 * conventions. Also implements C-like <tt>atoi</tt> and
 * <tt>atof</tt> functions
 * @version 1.01 15 Feb 1996
 * @author Cay Horstmann
 */
```

Here is an example of a method comment:

```
/**
* Formats a double into a string (like <tt>sprintf</tt> in
C)
* @param x the number to format
* @return the formatted string
* @throws IllegalArgumentException if bad argument
*/
```

How to Extract Comments

Here, `docDirectory` is the name of the directory you want the HTML files to go to. Follow these steps:

1. Move to the directory that contains the source files you want to document. If you have nested packages to document, such as `COM.horstmann.corejava`, you must be in the directory that contains the subdirectory `COM`.

2. Run the command

   ```
   javadoc -d docDirectory nameOfPackage
   ```

   for a single package. Or run

   ```
   javadoc -d docDirectory nameOfPackage1 nameOfPackage2...
   ```

   to document multiple packages.

Note that the HTML files expect GIF files in a subdirectory named `images`. You can just copy the GIF files from `\java\api\images`.

Index

613

615

E

617

H

I

621

M

N

O

P

Q

R

S

T

627

X

Java™ Development Kit
Version 1.1.x
Binary Code License

This binary code license ("License") contains rights and restrictions associated with use of the accompanying software and documentation ("Software"). Read the License carefully before installing the Software. By installing the Software you agree to the terms and conditions of this License.

1. Limited License Grant. Sun grants to you ("Licensee") a non-exclusive, non-transferable limited license to use the Software without fee for evaluation of the Software and for development of Java™ compatible applets and applications. Licensee may make one archival copy of the Software. Licensee may not re-distribute the Software in whole or in part, either separately or included with a product. Refer to the Java Runtime Environment Version 1.1 binary code license (http://www.javasoft.com/products/JDK/1.1/index.html) for the availability of runtime code which may be distributed with Java compatible applets and applications.

2. Java Platform Interface. Licensee may not modify the Java Platform Interface ("JPI", identified as classes contained within the "java" package or any subpackages of the "java" package), by creating additional classes within the JPI or otherwise causing the addition to or modification of the classes in the JPI. In the event that Licensee creates any Java-related API and distributes such API to others for applet or application development, Licensee must promptly publish an accurate specification for such API for free use by all developers of Java-based software.

3. Restrictions. Software is confidential copyrighted information of Sun and title to all copies is retained by Sun and/or its licensors. Licensee shall not modify, decompile, disassemble, decrypt, extract, or otherwise reverse engineer Software. Software may not be leased, assigned, or sublicensed, in whole or in part. **Software is not designed or intended for use in on-line control of aircraft, air traffic, aircraft navigation or aircraft communications; or in the design, construction, operation or maintenance of any nuclear facility. Licensee warrants that it will not use or redistribute the Software for such purposes.**

4. Trademarks and Logos. This License does not authorize Licensee to use any Sun name, trademark or logo. Licensee acknowledges that Sun owns the Java trademark and all Java-related trademarks, logos and icons including the Coffee Cup and Duke ("Java Marks") and agrees to: (i) to comply with the Java Trademark Guidelines at http://java.com/trademarks.html; (ii) not do anything harmful to or inconsistent with Sun's rights in the Java Marks; and (iii) assist Sun in protecting those rights, including assigning to Sun any rights acquired by Licensee in any Java Mark.

5. Disclaimer of Warranty. Software is provided "AS IS," without a warranty of any kind. ALL EXPRESS OR IMPLIED REPRESENTATIONS AND WARRANTIES,

INCLUDING ANY IMPLIED WARRANTY OF MERCHANTABILITY, FITNESS FOR A PARTICULAR PURPOSE OR NON-INFRINGEMENT, ARE HEREBY EXCLUDED.

6. Limitation of Liability. SUN AND ITS LICENSORS SHALL NOT BE LIABLE FOR ANY DAMAGES SUFFERED BY LICENSEE OR ANY THIRD PARTY AS A RESULT OF USING OR DISTRIBUTING SOFTWARE. IN NO EVENT WILL SUN OR ITS LICENSORS BE LIABLE FOR ANY LOST REVENUE, PROFIT OR DATA, OR FOR DIRECT, INDIRECT, SPECIAL, CONSEQUENTIAL, INCIDENTAL OR PUNITIVE DAMAGES, HOWEVER CAUSED AND REGARDLESS OF THE THEORY OF LIABILITY, ARISING OUT OF THE USE OF OR INABILITY TO USE SOFTWARE, EVEN IF SUN HAS BEEN ADVISED OF THE POSSIBILITY OF SUCH DAMAGES.

7. Termination. Licensee may terminate this License at any time by destroying all copies of Software. This License will terminate immediately without notice from Sun if Licensee fails to comply with any provision of this License. Upon such termination, Licensee must destroy all copies of Software.

8. Export Regulations. Software, including technical data, is subject to U.S. export control laws, including the U.S. Export Administration Act and its associated regulations, and may be subject to export or import regulations in other countries. Licensee agrees to comply strictly with all such regulations and acknowledges that it has the responsibility to obtain licenses to export, re-export, or import Software. Software may not be downloaded, or otherwise exported or re-exported (i) into, or to a national or resident of, Cuba, Iraq, Iran, North Korea, Libya, Sudan, Syria or any country to which the U.S. has embargoed goods; or (ii) to anyone on the U.S. Treasury Department's list of Specially Designated Nations or the U.S. Commerce Department's Table of Denial Orders.

9. Restricted Rights. Use, duplication or disclosure by the United States government is subject to the restrictions as set forth in the Rights in Technical Data and Computer Software Clauses in DFARS 252.227-7013(c) (1) (ii) and FAR 52.227-19(c) (2) as applicable.

10. Governing Law. Any action related to this License will be governed by California law and controlling U.S. federal law. No choice of law rules of any jurisdiction will apply.

11. Severability. If any of the above provisions are held to be in violation of applicable law, void, or unenforceable in any jurisdiction, then such provisions are herewith waived to the extent necessary for the License to be otherwise enforceable in such jurisdiction. However, if in Sun's opinion deletion of any provisions of the License by operation of this paragraph unreasonably compromises the rights or increase the liabilities of Sun or its licensors, Sun reserves the right to terminate the License and refund the fee paid by Licensee, if any, as Licensee's sole and exclusive remedy.

...Also available from Sun Microsystems

JAVA BY EXAMPLE, Second Edition

JERRY R. JACKSON and ALAN L. McCLELLAN

380 pages; (includes CD-ROM)
ISBN 0-13-272295-X

There's no better way to learn Java than by example. If you're an experienced programmer, JAVA BY EXAMPLE is the quickest way to learn Java. By reviewing example code written by experts, you'll learn the right way to develop Java applets and applications that are elegant, readable, and easy to maintain.

Step-by-step, working from examples, you'll learn valuable techniques for working with the Java language. The Second Edition provides even more extensive coverage.

TOPICS INCLUDE:

- Memory and constructors
- Input/output
- Multithreading
- Exception handling
- Animation
- Remote methods invocation (RMI)
- Networking
- Java Database Connectivity (JDBC) API

The CD-ROM includes all source code for examples presented in the book along with Java WorkShop 1.0 30-Day Free Trial from Sun Microsystems and the latest JDK for Solaris, Windows 95, Windows NT, and Macintosh.

INSTANT JAVA, Second Edition

JOHN A. PEW

398 pages; (includes CD-ROM)
ISBN 0-13-272287-9

INSTANT JAVA™ applets—no programming necessary! Now anyone can use Java to add animation, sound, and interactivity to their Web pages! Instant Java is your guide to using more than 75 easy-to-customize Java applets. The Second Edition contains even more applets and examples—plus updated, foolproof instructions for plugging them into your Web pages.

APPLETS INCLUDE:

- Text applets
- Image applets
- Animation applets
- Slide shows
- Tickers

You'll find all the applets on the cross-platform CD-ROM—along with sample HTML pages and valuable tools including Java™ WorkShop™ 1.0 30-Day Free Trial from Sun Microsystems and the latest JDK for Solaris,™ Microsoft Windows 95, Microsoft Windows NT, and Macintosh. This is an invaluable tool for adding Java special effects to your HTML documents!

NOT JUST JAVA

PETER van der LINDEN

313 pages; ISBN 0-13-864638-4

NOT JUST JAVA is the book for everybody who needs to understand why Java and other Internet technologies are taking the software industry by storm. Peter van der Linden, author of the best-selling JUST JAVA, carefully explains each of the key technologies driving the Internet revolution and provides a much-needed perspective on critical topics including:

- Java and its libraries—present and future
- Security on intranets and the Internet
- Thin clients, network computers, and webtops
- Multi-tier client/server system
- Software components, objects and CORBA
- The evolution and role of intranets
- JavaBeans™ versus ActiveX

Also included are case studies of leading-edge companies that show how to avoid the pitfalls and how to leverage Java and related technologies for maximum payoff.

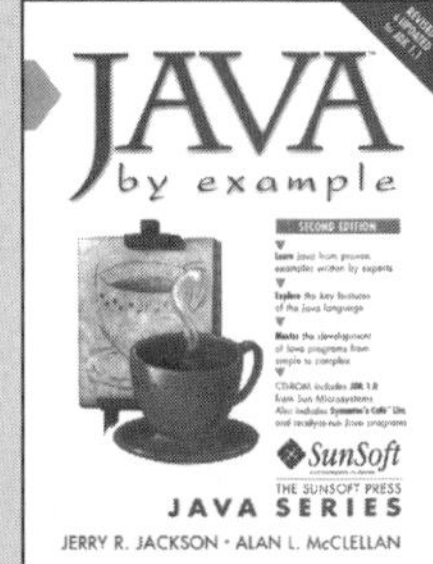

"...the most complete and effective treatment of a programming topic since Charles Petzold's classic Programming Windows."

— COMPUTER SHOPPER

"Fantastic book/CD package for HTML authors...practical, hands-on instructions get you off to a fast start."

— COMPUTER BOOK REVIEW

...Also available from Sun Microsystems

"Of the current spate of books about the World Wide Web, this is definitely among the best."

— MILES O'NEAL, *UNIX Review*, January 1996

INSIDE JAVA WORKSHOP
LYNN WEAVER and BOB JERVIS

ISBN 0-13-858234-3 (includes CD-ROM)

INSIDE JAVA™ WORKSHOP™ takes you on a working tour of the Java development environment from Sun Microsystems. You'll learn everything you need to create, test, debug, and publish portable Java applications. Starting with an insider's view of how to think about your development problem before you begin, the book gives you an understanding of and experience with every tool in Java WorkShop, plus developer tips and tricks from the team who created Java WorkShop. CD-ROM contains Java WorkShop 30-day free trial, plus all the examples from the book. Second Edition coming Fall 1997.

JUMPING JAVASCRIPT
JANICE WINSOR and BRIAN FREEMAN

1200 pages; (includes CD-ROM)
ISBN 0-13-841941-8

JUMPING JAVASCRIPT™ is a hands-on tutorial with loads of examples that will show both programmers and non-programmers how to use JavaScript to easily incorporate the interactivity of Java into their Web sites. It covers both basics such as scripting concepts, embedded Java applets, image maps, and buttons as well as advanced topics such as creating JavaScript objects and the cookies property. CD-ROM contains all the scripts discussed in the book.

WEB PAGE DESIGN
A Different Multimedia

MARY E. S. MORRIS and RANDY J. HINRICHS

200 pages; ISBN 0-13-239880-X

Everything you always wanted to know about practical Web page design! Anyone can design a web page, but it takes more than basic HTML skill to build a world-class Web site. Written for Web page authors, this hands-on guide covers the key aspects of designing a successful Web site and shows how to integrate traditional design techniques into Web sites. Contains sixteen full color examples of successful Web pages, and techniques for:

- Cognitive and content design
- Audience consideration
- Interactivity, organization, and navigational pathways
- Designing with VRML and Java
- Working with templates, style sheets, and Netscape™ Frames
- Evolving your design

HTML FOR FUN AND PROFIT
Gold Signature Edition

MARY E. S. MORRIS

306 pages; (includes CD-ROM)
ISBN 0-13-242488-6

A special edition of the best-seller, with a new chapter and HTML examples specifically about working with the Netscape browser. If you are interested in writing HTML pages for the World Wide Web, HTML FOR FUN AND PROFIT is for you. Step-by-step instructions present all the information you need to get started with Web page authoring. Although the examples are based on working with the UNIX® system, authoring on PC and Macintosh platforms is also discussed.

...Also available from Sun Microsystems

CONFIGURATION AND CAPACITY PLANNING FOR SOLARIS SERVERS

BRIAN L. WONG

448 pages; ISBN 0-13-349952-9

A complete reference for planning and configuring Solaris servers for NFS, DBMS, and timesharing environments, featuring coverage of SPARC station 10, SPARC center 2000, SPARC server 1000, and Solaris 2.3.

"...This book could be a lifesaver."

— MILES O'NEAL, *UNIX Review*, January 1996

PANIC!
UNIX System Crash Dump Analysis

CHRIS DRAKE and KIMBERLEY BROWN

480 pages; (includes CD-ROM)
ISBN 0-13-149386-8

UNIX systems crash—it's a fact of life. Until now, little information has been available regarding system crashes. PANIC! is the first book to concentrate solely on system crashes and hangs, explaining what triggers them and what to do when they occur. PANIC! guides you through system crash dump postmortem analysis towards problem resolution. PANIC! presents this highly technical and intricate subject in a friendly, easy style that even the novice UNIX system administrator will find readable, educational, and enjoyable.

TOPICS COVERED INCLUDE:

- What is a panic? What is a hang?
- Header files, symbols, and symbol tables
- A comprehensive tutorial on adb, the absolute debugger
- Introduction to assembly language
- Actual case studies of postmortem analysis

A CD-ROM containing several useful analysis tools—such as adb macros and C tags output from the source trees of two different UNIX systems—is included.

SUN PERFORMANCE AND TUNING:
SPARC and Solaris

ADRIAN COCKCROFT

254 pages; ISBN 0-13-149642-5

This book is an indispensable reference for anyone working with Sun workstations running the Solaris environment. Written for system administrators and software developers, it includes techniques for maximizing system performance through application design, configuration tuning, and system monitoring tools. The book provides detailed performance and configuration information on all SPARC™ machines and peripherals and all operating system releases from SunOS™ 4.1 through Solaris 2.4.

HIGHLIGHTS INCLUDE:

- Performance measurement and analysis techniques
- Uni- and multiprocessor SPARC system architectures and performance
- Hardware components: CPUs, caches, and memory management unit designs
- Kernel algorithms and tuning rules

Second Edition coming early 1998!

WABI 2:
Opening Windows

SCOTT FORDIN and SUSAN NOLIN

383 pages; ISBN 0-13-461617-0

WABI™ 2: OPENING WINDOWS explains the ins and outs of using Wabi software from Sun Microsystems to install, run, and manage Microsoft Windows applications on UNIX systems. Easy step-by-step instructions, illustrations, and charts guide you through each phase of using Wabi—from getting started to managing printers, drives, and COM ports to getting the most from your specific Windows applications.

...Also available from Sun Microsystems

AUTOMATING SOLARIS INSTALLATIONS
A Custom Jumpstart Guide

PAUL ANTHONY KASPER and ALAN L. McCLELLAN

282 pages; (includes a diskette)
ISBN 0-13-312505-X

AUTOMATING SOLARIS INSTALLATIONS describes how to set up "hands-off" Solaris installations for hundreds of SPARC™ and x86 systems. It explains in detail how to configure your site so that when you install Solaris, you simply boot a system and walk away—the software installs automatically! The book also includes a diskette with working shell scripts to automate pre- and post-installation tasks, such as:

- Updating systems with patch releases
- Installing third-party or unbundled software on users' systems
- Saving and restoring system data
- Setting up access to local and remote printers
- Transitioning a system from SunOS™ 4.x to Solaris 2

SOLARIS IMPLEMENTATION
A Guide for System Administrators

GEORGE BECKER, MARY E. S. MORRIS, and KATHY SLATTERY

345 pages; ISBN 0-13-353350-6

Written by expert Sun™ system administrators, this book discusses real world, day-to-day Solaris 2 system administration for both new installations and for migration from an installed Solaris 1 base. It presents tested procedures to help system administrators improve and customize their networks and includes advice on managing heterogeneous Solaris environments. Provides actual sample auto install scripts and disk partitioning schemes used at Sun.

TOPICS COVERED INCLUDE:

- Local and network methods for installing Solaris 2 systems
- Configuring with admintool versus command-line processes
- Building and managing the network, including setting up security
- Managing software packages and patches
- Handling disk utilities and archiving procedures

SOLARIS PORTING GUIDE, Second Edition

SUNSOFT DEVELOPER ENGINEERING

695 pages; ISBN 0-13-443672-5

Ideal for application programmers and software developers, the SOLARIS PORTING GUIDE provides a comprehensive technical overview of the Solaris 2 operating environment and its related migration strategy.

The Second Edition is current through Solaris 2.4 (for both SPARC and x86 platforms) and provides all the information necessary to migrate from Solaris 1 (SunOS 4.x) to Solaris 2 (SunOS 5.x). Other additions include a discussion of emerging technologies such as the Common Desktop Environment from Sun, hints for application performance tuning, and extensive pointers to further information, including Internet sources.

TOPICS COVERED INCLUDE:

- SPARC and x86 architectural differences
- Migrating from common C to ANSI C
- Building device drivers for SPARC and x86 using DDI/DKI
- Multithreading, real-time processing, and the Sun Common Desktop Environment

"This book is a must for all Solaris 2 system administrators."
— TOM JOLLANDS, Sun Enterprise Network Systems

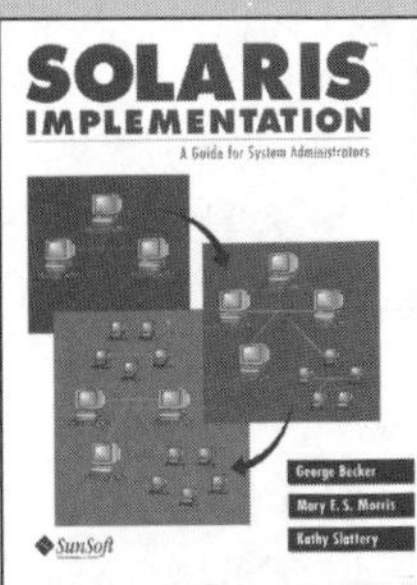

"[This book] deals with daily tasks and should be beneficial to anyone administering Solaris 2.x, whether a veteran or new Solaris user."
— *SYS ADMIN*, May/June 1995

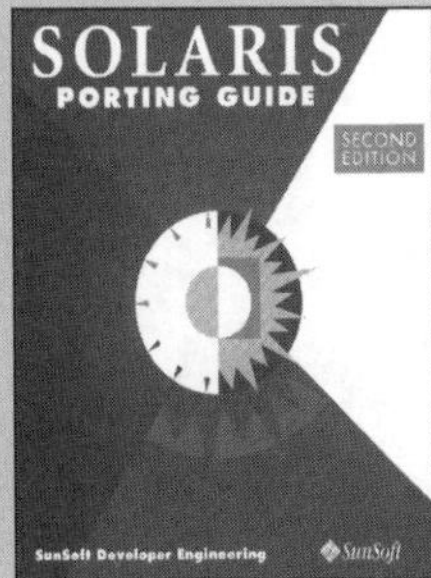

...Also available from Sun Microsystems

DESIGNING VISUAL INTERFACES

Communication Oriented Techniques

KEVIN MULLET and DARRELL K. SANO

262 pages; ISBN 0-13-303389-9

DESIGNING VISUAL INTERFACES applies the fundamentals of graphic, industrial, and interior design to solve human/ computer interface problems. It describes basic design principles (the what and why), common errors, and practical techniques. Readers will gain a new perspective on product development as well as an appreciation for the contribution visual design can offer to their products and users.

DEVELOPING VISUAL APPLICATIONS XIL:

An Imaging Foundation Library

WILLIAM K. PRATT

368 pages; ISBN 0-13-461948-X

A practical introduction to using imaging in new, innovative applications for desktop computing. DEVELOPING VISUAL APPLICATIONS breaks down the barriers that prevent developers from easily integrating imaging into their applications. It covers the basics of image processing, compression, and algorithm implementation and provides clear, real-world examples for developing applications using XIL™ a cross-platform imaging foundation library. More experienced imaging developers can also use this book as a reference to the architectural features and capabilities of XIL.

READ ME FIRST!

A Style Guide for the Computer Industry

SUN TECHNICAL PUBLICATIONS

256 pages; (includes CD-ROM)
ISBN 0-13-455347-0

User documentation should be an asset, not an afterthought. The READ ME FIRST! style guide can help technical publications groups outline, organize, and prepare high quality documentation for any type of computer product. Based on the award-winning Sun Microsystems documentation style guide, READ ME FIRST! includes complete guidelines—from style pointers to legal considerations, from writing for an international audience to forming a documentation department.

TOPICS INCLUDE:

- Grammar and punctuation guidelines
- Technical abbreviations, acronyms, and units of measurement
- How to set up your own documentation department

The CD-ROM includes ready-to-use FrameMaker templates for instant page design and the entire book in searchable FrameViewer and HTML format for easy reference.

"All GUI designers should have this book on their bookshelves."
— MILES O'NEAL, *UNIX Review*, January 1996

...Also available from Sun Microsystems

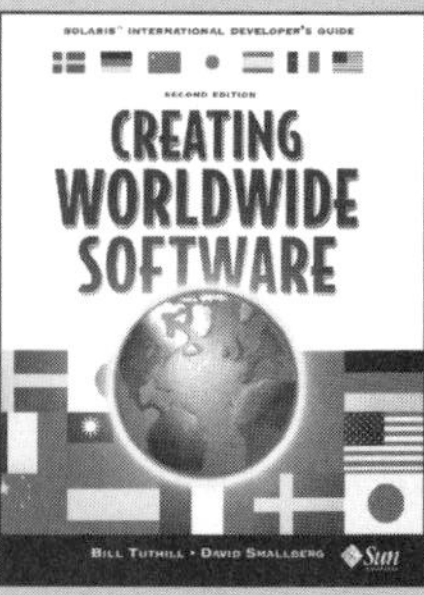

INTRANET SECURITY:
Stories From the Trenches

LINDA McCARTHY

300 pages; ISBN 0-13-894759-7

Do you have response procedures for systems break-ins? Is your e-mail encrypted? Is your firewall protecting your company? Is your security staff properly trained? These are just a few of the security issues that are covered in INTRANET SECURITY: STORIES FROM THE TRENCHES. Author Linda McCarthy, who in her job as a worldwide security team leader at Sun has broken into thousands of corporate intranets, presents detailed case studies of real-life break-ins that will help you make your systems safer. She explains how each breach occurred, describes what steps were taken to fix it, and then provides a practical and systematic solution for preventing similar problems from occurring on your network!

CREATING WORLDWIDE SOFTWARE
Solaris International Developer's Guide, Second Edition

BILL TUTHILL and DAVID SMALLBERG

ISBN 0-13-494493-3

A new edition of the essential reference text for creating global applications, with updated information on international markets, standards organizations, and writing international documents. This expanded edition of the Solaris International Developer's Guide includes new chapters on CDE/Motif, NEO/OpenStep, Universal codesets, global internet applications, code examples, and studies of successfully internationalized software.

INTRANETS:
What's the Bottom Line?

RANDY J. HINRICHS

420 pages; ISBN 0-13-841198-0

INTRANETS: WHAT'S THE BOTTOM LINE? is for decisions makers, who want bottom line information in order to figure out what an Intranet is and how it will help their organizations. It's a compelling case for the corporate Intranet. This book will give you a high-level perspective on Intranets and will answer your questions: What is an Intranet? What is it made of? What does it buy me? How much does it cost? How do I make it work? How do I know it's working?

...Also available from Sun Microsystems

HANDS-ON INTRANETS

VASANTHAN S. DASAN and LUIS R. ORDORICA

ISBN 0-13-857608-4

This hands-on guide will show you how to implement a corporate Intranet, or a private network comprised of the open, standards-based protocols and services of the Internet. IS professionals and others interested in implementing an Intranet will learn the key Intranet protocols, services, and applications.The book also describes the technical issues such as security, privacy, and other problems areas encountered in Intranet implementation and integration, while providing practical solutions for each of these areas. You will learn how to realize the Intranet's potential.

RIGHTSIZING THE NEW ENTERPRISE:
The Proof, Not the Hype

HARRIS KERN and Randy JOHNSON

326 pages; ISBN 0-13-490384-6

The "how-to's" of rightsizing are defined in this detailed account based on the experiences of Sun Microsystems as it re-engineered its business to run on client/server systems. This book covers rightsizing strategies and benefits, management and system administration processes and tools, and the issues involved in transitioning personnel from mainframe to UNIX support. RIGHTSIZING THE NEW ENTERPRISE presents you with proof that rightsizing can be done...and has been done.

MANAGING THE NEW ENTERPRISE:
The Proof, Not the Hype

HARRIS KERN, RANDY JOHNSON, MICHAEL HAWKINS, and ANDREW LAW, with WILLIAM KENNEDY

212 pages; ISBN 0-13-231184-4

MANAGING THE NEW ENTERPRISE describes how to build a solid technology foundation for the advanced networking and systems of the enterprise. Learn to re-engineer your traditional information technology (IT) systems while reducing costs! As the follow-up to RIGHTSIZING THE NEW ENTERPRISE, this volume is about relevant, critical solutions to issues challenging corporate computing in the 1990s and beyond. Topics include:

- Creating reliable UNIX distributed systems
- Building a production-quality enterprise network
- Managing a decentralized system with centralized controls
- Selecting the right systems management tools and standards

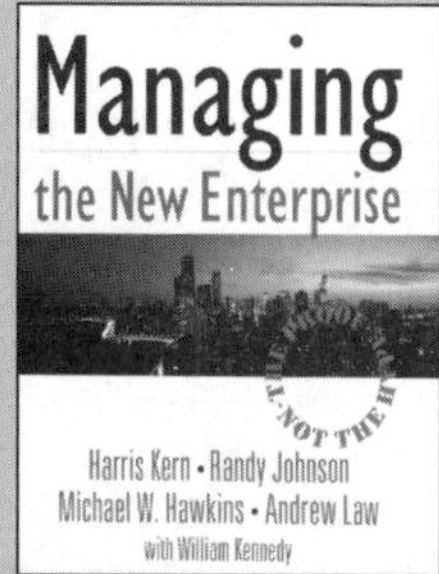

"This book has helped me clarify the essence of UNIX systems management in Client/Server technologies. It's a most valuable addition to our reference library."

— KEVIN W. KRYZDA, Director, Information Services Department Martin County, Florida

The Core Java 1.1 CD-ROM is a standard ISO-9660 disc. Software on this CD-ROM requires Windows 95, Windows NT, or Solaris 2.

Windows 3.1 IS NOT SUPPORTED